THE ESSENTIAL HISTORY OF WEST HAM UNITED

KIRK BLOWS AND TONY HOGG

FOREWORD BY BILLY BONDS MBE

HEADLINE

First published in 2000
by HEADLINE BOOK PUBLISHING
for WHSmith, Greenbridge Road, Swindon SN3 3LD

1 3 5 7 9 10 8 6 4 2

ISBN 0 7472 7036 8

Design by designsection, Frome, Somerset.
All photographs supplied by Colorsport.
Memorabilia supplied by the authors.
The authors would like to thank Terry Connelly, Rob Bolle, John Bolle, Claire Dunsford, the late George Kerr, Alice Kerr, John Helliar, the late Jack Helliar, Peter Stewart, Tony McDonald, Geoff Thompson, Cliff Wood, Chris Raistrick, Marney Whyte, Mitchell Sutton, Christopher Hogg, Gordon Sharrock of the *Bolton Evening News*, the late Albert York, Jenny Cooper

Printed and bound in Great Britain by Clays Ltd, St Ives PLC, Bungay, Suffolk

HEADLINE BOOK PUBLISHING
A division of Hodder Headline
338 Euston Road
London NW1 3BH

www.headline.co.uk
www.hodderheadline.com

Contents

Foreword
By Billy Bonds MBE

Billy Bonds

I spent 27 years at West Ham as a player, coach and manager and have to admit it's sad that I'm not able to get to Upton Park on a regular basis nowadays because the club was a huge part of my life. I had the privilege of playing with so many different characters, from the 1966 World Cup-winning lads such as Bobby Moore, Geoff Hurst and Martin Peters, great players such as Trevor Brooking and Alan Devonshire and, later on, the likes of Tony Cottee, Frank McAvennie and Paul Ince, to name just a few. I can still recall arriving as a youngster from Charlton in 1967 and feeling totally overawed, but I soon got used to it and just fell in love with the club.

I enjoyed a very special relationship with the fans from day one. I can remember my debut, against Sheffield Wednesday, which we lost 3-2 after being 2-1 up. It was a disaster but the crowd took to me straight away because I was just a big raw full-back who had bags of energy and strength, would run all day and could tackle. West Ham fans have always wanted to see the game played with passion and somebody who personifies that nowadays is Paolo Di Canio.

The managers I played under – Ron Greenwood and John Lyall – brought up the youths at West Ham to have certain standards. Ron referred to them as 'good habits' and they helped us – on and off the field. He was a very intelligent person, a deep thinker, a good tactician and loved his teams to get the ball down and pass it. We didn't work on defensive issues that much because it was all about how we were going to score goals, although that changed a little under John.

But Ron never compromised how he wanted the game played. I can remember us throwing away a three-goal lead to lose 4-3 against Stoke in one of my first games and that was typical of West Ham – we could lose to the bottom club and then beat the best team in the country. Maybe that's the special appeal of the club.

West Ham have always appealed to a certain type of supporter and, even though different people are being attracted to the game nowadays, I think the majority of fans at Upton Park are still working class people. They're capable of generating a special atmosphere and some of the European nights at Upton Park were the best.

I really loved having the extra responsibility of being captain, although I'd still have been doing the same things – bawling people out, egging them on and clenching my fist. I felt that added to my game and just loved to roll up my sleeves and get out there.

People often mention the two FA Cup wins to me but I can't say I really enjoyed the 1975 final as a match because I was only 70 per cent fit and everything just flew by. We'd been expected to beat Fulham, who were a Second Division side, but when we returned to Wembley five years later it was our turn to be underdogs and beating Arsenal was very special.

The 1980-81 team is often referred to as one of West Ham's best, but the irony is that it was playing in Division Two. If a side containing the likes of Brooking, Devonshire and Alvin Martin got relegated nowadays there'd probably be a wholesale exodus, but we had tremendous loyalty and there was never any thought of us leaving.

People might laugh but on reflection I think I retired too early. I honestly think I could have continued for another three or four years, not necessarily in the top flight but certainly in a lower division. I worked hard at keeping fit and also consider myself fortunate to have avoided major injury with the way I played and the many tackles I made during my career. But I'm glad I didn't move elsewhere to continue playing because I wouldn't have got to manage West Ham and I'm so pleased I did that.

When I took over in 1990 the team was halfway down the Second Division and gates were low. But everybody started pulling in the same direction and we got things back on track. There were some great lads at the club, including Liam Brady, and we shared a mutual respect which helped make my job easier. We won promotion the following year and it's my view that we only got relegated in 1992 because of the impact of the Bond Scheme. But you couldn't blame fans for feeling the way they did. We got promoted the next season and only had around £250,000 to spend on striker Lee Chapman so it's a measure of how much the club has progressed in seven years that the likes of Frederic Kanoute are now arriving for £4 million.

I wish I could have left West Ham in different circumstances but I'm proud to say I managed the club and like to think my record was good. I wouldn't want to complain too much about what happened in 1994 because it's water under the bridge and life goes on, although my trust was certainly misplaced. The board wanted Harry Redknapp to take over and for me to move upstairs but my pride would not have allowed me to do that. Whatever has happened between myself and Harry does not alter my feelings for the club – I'm still a West Ham man and always will be.

The club have done well in recent years, although the performances in the cups have been disappointing. Good young players such as Rio Ferdinand, Frank Lampard, Joe Cole and Michael Carrick provide a nucleus that West Ham haven't had for some time but to hold on to those youngsters the club needs to start winning things again. If they can keep their best players then the future looks really bright and that's good to see because I still have great affection for the club.

BILLY BONDS MBE

Prologue
The Triumph and Tragedy

As the fog of sleep enveloped the mind, the sense of anxiety became greater... 'It mustn't happen... got to get across to the touchline and tell Harry – he mustn't play!' I'm desperately trying to force my way through the army of bodies, but all motion has been lost as I'm slowly sucked back into the crowd. I'm yelling for them to change their minds, but nobody can hear me, they don't realise... 'Stop!!!' And then the nightmare turned into reality...

It seemed an event of such insignificance that it merited no mention whatsoever in the following day's newspaper reports. But little did any of the 23,974 supporters present at Upton Park on 15 December 1999 appreciate the impact that Manny Omoyinmi's surprise appearance would have on West Ham United's season.

From the moment the 21-year-old Nigerian forward tripped across the touchline, as a 112th-minute substitute for Hammers striker Paulo Wanchope, the Hammers fell headlong into trouble, with the subsequent events of an already tense and titanic Worthington Cup quarter-final tie against Aston Villa ultimately being rendered null and void.

No matter that Omoyinmi had no direct influence on the remaining eight minutes of extra-time played with the score standing at 2-2. Or that he stood only as a witness and cheerleader while his team-mates won a dramatic penalty shoot-out by five spot-kicks to four, thanks ultimately to goalkeeper Shaka Hislop's thwarting of Villain Gareth Southgate. For the damage had already been done, with the youngster having made two appearances in the competition earlier in the season while on loan at Gillingham and thus being ineligible to play any further part.

With this fact yet to come to light, however, West Ham's officials, players and supporters rejoiced in the belief that the club had qualified for its first domestic cup semi-final appearance since 1991. But the celebrations and buoyancy of mood were cut painfully short when the Football League announced within 48 hours of the end of the match that, following an official complaint from Aston Villa, an investigation would be held and a verdict – which could, in theory, result in disqualification – would soon be made.

With the East End supporters expecting the worst, it was almost with a sense of relief that it was swiftly confirmed that a replay would take place the following month. But West Ham's officials were understandably aggrieved, feeling that no advantage had been gained through making a genuine administrative error.

'The club acted in good faith and we're very disappointed to have this decision imposed upon us,' said company secretary Graham Mackrell, while team boss Harry Redknapp complained, 'Why should 26,000 people who love this football club have to suffer for a slight oversight by somebody? It's very harsh.'

As the internal inquest got underway, the accusations from frustrated fans began to fly. Some, perhaps unfairly, blamed the manager for not remembering that he'd granted Omoyinmi permission to play for the Gills in an earlier round. 'There's a difference between giving permission and actually *knowing* he's played,' argued Redknapp, while also – publicly at least – shielding the player concerned. 'I'm not going to blame the kid. I asked him why he didn't say anything and he said he didn't think.'

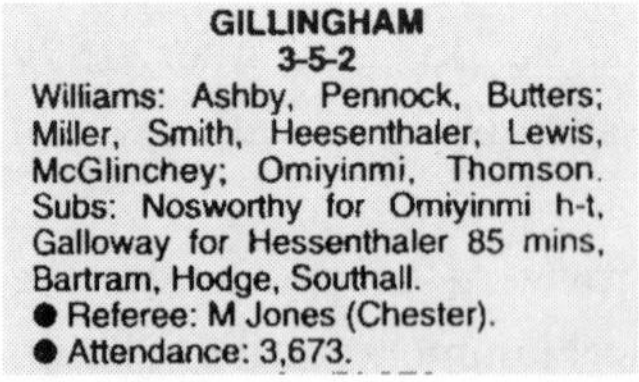
GILLINGHAM
3-5-2
Williams: Ashby, Pennock, Butters; Miller, Smith, Heesenthaler, Lewis, McGlinchey; Omiyinmi, Thomson. Subs: Nosworthy for Omiyinmi h-t, Galloway for Hessenthaler 85 mins, Bartram, Hodge, Southall.
● Referee: M Jones (Chester).
● Attendance: 3,673.

Omoyinmi's name clearly appears in the Gills' team line-up while out on loan to them.

While most would have expected Manny to have volunteered the fact that he was already cup-tied, whatever his enthusiasm for making his first appearance of the season, ultimate responsibility for advising team management of player eligibility existed with the secretaries' office. Hence, Mackrell and football secretary Alison O'Dowd – both at the club a mere six months – tendered their resignations.

Graham pledged to remain in office until a replacement was found, leaving him to experience the anguish of seeing the Hammers dumped out of the competition in the re-match.

And as if the supporters hadn't gone through enough heartache, they had to watch their side lose a one-goal lead with just nine minutes of normal play remaining, fall 2-1 behind in extra-time and then see maverick striker Paolo Di Canio waste a penalty-kick. A third goal for Villa simply banged the lid on West Ham's coffin and a grieving Redknapp was left to confess, 'Tonight will haunt me for ever'.

Fortune's always hiding, indeed.

For many lifelong Hammers fans, this distasteful episode typified – in the most extreme form – the conflict of emotions experienced after discovering one has claret and blue blood. A mixture of pain and pleasure. Agony and ecstasy. Tragedy and triumph. (But not necessarily in that order.)

West Ham legend Billy Bonds once shrugged in reference to the League Cup (as the tournament was traditionally known), 'No, we never had a lot of luck in that competition.' In stark contrast to his tenacious tackles of yore, it was a classic case of understatement.

Five semi-finals (1964, 1967, 1972, 1989 and 1990) and two finals (1966 and 1981) had been reached since the tournament's inception in 1960 but a combination of injured goalkeepers, missed penalties, plastic pitches and dubious refereeing decisions, among other things, has resulted in the trophy always heading in the wrong direction.

Supporters can turn towards the FA Cup for greater memories, of course, with the thrilling victories of the 1964, 1975 and 1980 finals paving the way for the club's most successful European adventures (winning the European Cup Winners' Cup in 1965 and reaching the final in 1976). But younger fans will more instantly recall the shock of seeing Tony Gale sent off in the 1991 semi-final against Nottingham Forest, as referee Keith Hackett etched his name indelibly into Hammers history.

The cup competitions have always offered West Ham United the best opportunities in its pursuit of glory, because the club's attractive footballing philosophies, of playing with style and guile, have never proved conducive to consistency. On their day, whatever the team's league position, they've proved they can beat the best if the gods are smiling. Manchester United's championship hopes were dashed on the rock of the Boleyn Ground's steps twice in the 1990s, in seasons when relegation was the key concern down Green Street way. But when fate is frowning against the Hammers, however, anything can happen, as numerous embarrassing cup upsets confirm.

For some, it's that very unpredictability which has proved almost as irresistible as the club's finely carved traditions for producing football with flair. It's also generated a strength of loyalty among the support that's mirrored only by the club's faith in its homegrown personnel, holding the record for the fewest number of team managers in league history (eight).

It's all made for an undulating voyage across the years, full of surprise peaks and troughs, but the rewards have proved twice as satisfying. The journey begins here...

Thames Iron workers, whose football club started the West Ham United story.

Chapter One: 1895-1909
Formation and Early Years

Young Charlie Dove left his family's two-up, two-down terraced house in West Ham in more of a rush than usual on a sultry late June morning in 1895.

It was not his haste to start work early that had put an extra spring into his step on this particular day. Chas, as his pals preferred to call him, had heard a rumour that there was to be an announcement in the firm's newspaper, The *Thames Iron Works Gazette*, regarding the foundation of a works football club.

The Thames Iron Works occupied 5 acres at the mouth of the River Lea at Blackwall and 30 acres at West Ham on the Essex side of Bow Creek where herons dared not fish and otters never swam. The firm built the first British ironclad battleship there, HMS *Warrior* in 1860, which was then the biggest warship in the world. The company later held the ultimately more doubtful distinction of building two battleships for the Imperial Japanese Navy.

But these feats, dubious or otherwise, were probably far from the thoughts of Charlie Dove as he signed on for his day's shift as an apprentice to the riveters at Orchard Yard, exactly opposite where the Millennium Dome now stands. Before embarking on his first task of the day, which

The first ever Thames Iron Works FC team, 1895.

would have been to collect the rivets from the store and take them to the riveters, it's likely that Charlie grabbed the first copy of the *Gazette* that he could lay his hands on.

There, in the edition dated 29 June 1895, was the immortal statement, 'Mr Taylor, who is working in the shipbuilding department, has undertaken to get up a football club for next winter and I learn that quoits and bowls will also be added to the attractions of the Hermit Road ground.'

The news of a football club was what really mattered in an area that had been described by one contemporary scribe as being 'football mad', with 'hundreds of urchins kicking paper balls in the streets'.

Association Football, or 'Tartan Footy' as the Scots called it, was well established in the British Isles before the turn of the nineteenth century. The earliest administrators of the Football Association, formed in London in 1863, were largely from a public school background, but, unlike cricket and rugby, the game quickly became the almost exclusive preserve of the working classes.

In 1888, three years after the legislation of professionalism, the Football League was formed by the collaboration of 12 clubs from the midlands and the north and included teams that were to become famous, such as Aston Villa, Preston North End and Blackburn Rovers.

Thames Iron Works FC

By 1895, two London clubs had been formed by factory workers – Woolwich Arsenal and Millwall – and were about to be joined by the forebears of another club who would become a force in the land and their fierce rivals into the new millennium, Thames Iron Works FC.

A schoolboy player of great repute, Charlie Dove had been a member of the renowned Park School of West Ham team, playing at full back and having won two medals with them. On leaving school he joined his local side Forest Swifts as a centre forward and later captained Plaistow Melville. As a member of two other prominent local teams, Upton Park and South West Ham, Charlie was regarded as a prodigious talent in the area and was considered well qualified to play for the new works team.

The Founder of Thames Iron Works FC: Arnold Hills.

Part of the Thames Iron Works factory

Although he would have been considered no more than a boy by the older, more experienced men in the yard – who were as hard as the steel and iron with which they plied their vital trade – Charles, who was almost 6 feet (1.8 m) tall and weighed a healthy 12 stone (76 kg), had an advantage – he was super-fit due to his years playing football.

It was just as well because the riveting gangs were regarded as the front line troops of the yard – the élite – even though it needed 20 or more different tradesmen to construct the ships which sailed the seven seas.

The rivets – 200 panheads to the hundredweight (50.8 kg) bag – might have to be hauled to men working 100 feet (30.5 m) from the ground, on gravity-defying narrow scaffolding attached to the skeletal framework of a giant ironclad warship under construction in all weathers. The men worked in teams of five. The apprentice would start a chain reaction by delivering the sacks of rivets to the rivet heater, who was known as the rivet boy – no matter what his age.

They would then transport them to the site where they were working and heat them over coals in shallow pans using bellows to fan the flames until white hot. Then they were tonged to the catch boy who would pick them up with a smaller pair of tongs and ram them into the appropriate holes in the steel plate, for which reason he was also known as the 'putter-in'.

The holder-on (or 'older-on in cockney-speak) would complete the next stage of the process by aiming a 16 pound (7.2 kg) sledgehammer at the centre of the still red-hot rivet. When driven home as hard as it would go, the holder-on would then press on the head of the rivet with his hammerhead in preparation for the next part of the operation.

The catch boys and the holders-on worked on the inside of the ship while on the exterior, exposed to all elements, worked the riveters, one left-handed, the other right-handed, a pair assigned to each holder-on. They used smaller mallet-type hammers, with long thin heads, which they wielded with unerring accuracy to complete the process. The same hammers would later symbolise the origins of the new football team on the club's crest.

With as many as 25-man teams working in close proximity, holders-on with bass hammers, riveters with baritones, backed up by the incessant, dull thud-thud chorus of half a dozen giant steamhammers, they would beat out a cacophonous heavy metal symphony which echoed across Old Father Thames. This, as night fell, would be accompanied by a Victorian-age light show featuring a thousand cascading sparks from a hundred molten metal meteors flying across decks, ricocheting along platforms, bouncing off bulkheads like so many shooting stars. Reflected all, mirror image on the glassy black water.

In the distance, as if in answer to the Thames men's metallic orchestral renditions, sifting through the other myriad sounds of the rivers, could be heard the low rumble from the Millwall Iron Works as they rolled their steel and plotted to undercut the Thames men at any opportunity as the two yards chased the same contracts. Millwall Iron Works smelted their steel from iron ore and rolled it; Thames reconstituted scrap and hammered it. But the men from the two yards had one thing in common – they were rivals before a football had been kicked between them.

Recreation for the Workers

When the men broke for lunch on that red letter day of 29 June 1895, it's likely their talk consisted of little other than the founding of the new Thames Iron Works Football Club. Arnold Hills, the company's paternalistic owner, had given his blessing and monetary support to fund the new venture which was to be run in its inaugural year by Dave Taylor who, in addition to being a foreman at the works, was also a local referee.

Thames Iron Works employees were invited to apply for membership at the cost of half a crown (12½p) a year which entitled them to take part in practise matches and training on Tuesday and Thursday nights. As he supped on his strong tea that was brewed on the rivet fire, Charlie Dove could have been excused for worrying about that half-a-crown enrolment fee – representing as it did a third of his weekly wage. But perhaps he also thought that once they realised how good he was they'd soon be paying him to play – like other clubs were paying the new professionals. In any case, he duly signed and was in the team for its first season.

Although Hills, who had the privilege of being educated at Harrow and Oxford and was an English mile champion, had genuinely instigated the football club to provide recreation for his workers, he was also anxious to end the bad feeling caused by a recent strike at the works and must have seen the new club as a way of wiping away the bitterness left behind.

As a man of great social conscience and a crusader for good causes, Hills had been a top class footballer himself, representing Oxford against Cambridge in the varsity match and England in the team that defeated Scotland 5-4 at Kennington Oval in 1879, while playing for the Old Harrovians FC.

As if to underline his empathy with his workers, he chose to live among them in a small house in the East India Dock Road from where in the evenings he organised and visited recreation centres for his employees. He steadfastly refused to bow to pressure to move his operation away from the cramped confines of West Ham and Blackwall to Dagenham or Tilbury, where it may have been able to function more efficiently and profitably, for fear of harming the fragile economy and spirit of the neighbourhood he'd come to love.

Hills may have been a God-fearing, teetotal philanthropist but he still exercised the dubious right to employ 'black' labour when his workers went on strike over poor pay and conditions. It was a practise which led to unimaginable bitterness and resentment among the workforce and, bearing in mind his generally benevolent and compassionate nature, must have caused him much soul-searching and personal heartache.

Below the Poverty Line

A survey published in the late 1880s had indicated that 60 per cent of the population existed below the poverty line in the Limehouse and Canning Town areas. Sickness, poverty, overcrowding, pollution, unemployment... this was the prevailing social, economic and political climate of the day. But just like the ironclad battleships, which slid down the slipways at Bow Creek, at first slowly and then gaining momentum, Thames Iron Works Football Club were well and truly launched. Nothing now could stop them.

The birth of the new Thames Iron Works Football Club coincided with the death and demise of another established club, Old Castle Swifts. When the Swifts – who like TIW were a company club sponsored by the Castle Shipping Line and held the distinction of being the first professional football club in Essex – folded conveniently in 1895, Thames simply took over the tenancy of the stricken club's ground at Hermit Road, Canning Town. In addition, they signed four first-team players from the defunct organisation and another well known local club, parish side Old St Luke's

FC, who also took on the remnants of the Swift's playing personnel in a loose kind of amalgamation. Variously described at the time as being a 'barren waste' and a 'cinder heap', the Hermit Road ground was surrounded by a moat and canvas sheeting was used as fencing.

The First Season

It was against this distinctly unglamorous setting that the Iron Works kicked off their first ever fixture, a friendly match against Royal Ordnance reserves on Saturday, 7 September 1895. No record remains as to the identity of the Irons XI who lined up for this historic game, but the match ended in a 1-1 draw. It is likely that the pioneering Irons who did battle against the Ordnance men, recognised as an unofficial sort of nursery team for Woolwich Arsenal FC, would have had a fair sprinkling of Thames Iron Works employees among their ranks and quite possibly included our young hero, Charlie Dove. A likelihood confirmed by later Hammers manager Syd King as he explained the early formation and policies of the club in the *Book of Football*, published in 1906:

'In the summer of 1895, when the clanging of "hammers" was heard on the banks of Father Thames and the great warships were rearing their heads above the Victoria Dock Road, a few enthusiasts, with the love of football within them, were talking about the grand old game and the formation of a club for the workers of the Thames Iron Works Limited.

The West Stand of West Ham's Boleyn Ground circa 1906.

'There were platers and riveters in the Limited who had chased the big ball in the north country. There were men among them who had learned to give the subtle pass and to urge the leather goalwards.

'No thought of professionalism, I may say, was ever contemplated by the founders. They meant to run their club on amateur lines and their first principal was to choose their team from men in the works.'

Among those who played in the first match would probably have been J. Lindsay, who played at inside or centre forward and was previously with Castle Swifts, and winger G. Sage who was later to play in the club's first FA Cup tie at Chatham the following month. He was also an ex-member of the defunct Swifts.

Another likely starter would have been John Wood, who is the second player from the right in the back row of the first ever team group photograph taken in 1895 and reproduced on page 11. John Thomas Archer Wood, to give him his full name, also played cricket for Essex and was a cousin of the champion jockey, Fred Archer.

Yet another former Castle Swifts man was Scot Robert Stevenson, who could fill any of the three half back positions with equal effectiveness and was recognised as being the first player of any note to wear a TIWFC shirt having previously been with Woolwich Arsenal and captain of that club. Born at Barrhead, Glasgow in 1869, Bob joined the Castle Swifts from the Gunners in March 1895 but returned to Scotland following the break up of the club.

He was recalled to Hermit Road for the Irons' initial campaign, however, and was promptly installed as club captain, playing at full back and centre forward as well as his normal half back role.

Such was the confidence and optimism sweeping through the club, the Thames 'upstarts' even had the audacity to enter for the FA Cup competition proper, the momentous step later recorded in the *Thames Iron Works Gazette*, 'Having some good men in the club, we somewhat presumptuously considered it would be wise to enter for the English Association Cup.'

Having followed up the opening 1-1 draw with resounding victories over Dartford (4-0), Manor Park (8-0) and Streatham (3-0) in friendly fixtures, the 'good men' of Thames duly took on the men of Kent at Chatham after reluctantly relinquishing home advantage at their opponent's request due to the 'unsuitability' of the Hermit Road enclosure.

In what was effectively the club's first real competitive match – all other fixtures, with the exception of the West Ham Charity Cup, were friendlies in that first season – Thames were left to rue their decision to give up home advantage to the Medway men, as Chatham ran out 5-0 winners. Despite this setback, Irons were still destined to achieve the commendable feat of lifting some silverware in their first year of existence via the West Ham Charity Cup.

Having defeated Park Grove 1-0 in the semi-final at Plaistow, Irons were set to meet Barking in the final, but in a Victorian-style version of more recent events, Irons were forced to replay the tie after their opponents protested over a technicality. Unlike their present day counterparts, however, Irons won the replayed tie even more convincingly, 3-0 at Beckton Road, to claim their rightful place in the final.

The battle with Barking turned into an epic confrontation that needed three meetings to decide the winner. After a stirring 2-2 draw at the Old Spotted Dog ground at Upton Lane, the replay at the same venue also ended in stalemate, 0-0.

But it was the Irons who drank their fill from the handsome trophy as they triumphed 2-1 in the second replay to put their name on the cup at the first time of asking, to conclude a successful first season during which they won 30 of 47 matches played, drew five and lost 12 with a goals total of 136 for, with 68 against.

Bolstered by their impressive first season performances the *TIWG* was able to announce:

'With reference to the forthcoming season [1896-97], it has been decided to enter for the English Cup, London Senior Cup, West Ham Charity Cup, South Essex League senior and junior and if possible, one or two others. There will be very few dates left open for "friendly" matches, so it ought to be a good thing for the club financially.'

In addition to the competitions listed in the Gazette, more importantly the club also entered the London League (although West Ham was officially part of Essex at the time). And the Irons fancied their chances in the competition of which Arnold Hills was president and had TIWFC's committee chairman Francis Payne helping to draft its rules.

In their first ever competitive league fixture, Irons met a team named Vampires at Hermit Road, but drew first blood, going on to win 3-0.

In cup competitions, visits across the Thames to Kent again proved to be the Irons' 'hopping pot' when they went down 8-0 to Sheppey United and 2-0 at Bromley, after a second replay in the FA Cup and London Senior Cup respectively. The team against Sheppey was: Southwood, Stevenson, Holstock, Bird, Dandridge, Davie, Nicholls, Rossiter, Hutton, Gresham and Morrison.

Charlie Dove, Irons' first star.

With the exception of Bob Stevenson, inside forward George Gresham was probably the best known of the Irons on duty that day, being the first of many players to join TIW/WHU from Lincolnshire club Gainsborough Trinity. In addition to appearing at least 15 times in the first season, he also turned out in three FA Cup ties in 1897-88 and scored twice against Woolwich Arsenal in the 'floodlight friendly' of 3 March 1896.

Moving Home

Shortly after their exit from the FA Cup, Thames were hit by another disaster, when they were served with an eviction notice from the Hermit Road ground allegedly for violating their terms of tenancy, by building a pavilion and perimeter fence and charging the public admission fees.

Now effectively 'homeless', the team were forced to play their next four fixtures on opponents' territory until a new ground could be found, the first of which ended in a 4-1 reverse at eventual champions 3rd Grenadier Guards, on 22 October 1896.

It took Arnold Hills several months to secure a new home for the club, but when he eventually leased a piece of land in East Ham it did not spell the end of the team's problems, as Syd King explained in his 1906 history, 'For some reason, not altogether explained, the local public at this place did not take kindly to them and the records show that Browning Road was a wilderness both in the matter of luck and support.' But despite all their problems and nomadic existence, the Irons still managed to finish second in the London League table as worthy runners-up to the 3rd Grenadier Guards. No mean feat given their uncertain circumstances.

As early as January 1897, however, Hills had earmarked a large piece of land at Canning Town to develop as 'an athletic ground' with facilities 'for cycling, tennis and football'. Commissioned by Hills and built at a cost of £20,000 in less than six months, the Memorial Grounds were opened to coincide with the sixteenth anniversary of the accession to the throne of Queen Victoria on Jubilee Day, June 1897.

Situated close to West Ham station (which opened in 1901) the Memorial Grounds were equidistant from the Thames Iron Works factory and Charlie

Dove's Old Park School at one and a half miles (2.4 km) and the site still retains a sporting connection to this day as the home of the East London Rugby Club.

In their heyday, the grounds were reckoned 'good enough to stage the English Cup final'. Encircling the football pitch was a cycle track of a third of a mile (0.35 km) inside which was a cinder running track. The site also boasted an outdoor swimming pool, which was over 100 feet (30.4 m) in length and reputed to be the biggest in the country.

A New Start

As the club kicked off their second season in the London League with a 1-0 victory over Brentford on 11 September 1897 amid their salubrious new surroundings, the Thames players had the comforting knowledge that the club committee had insured them against loss of wages that might result from football related injuries. It was a benefit unlikely to have been bestowed on the unfortunate Bob Stevenson back in his native Scotland and an indication of how seriously sport was being taken in the south.

50 Greatest Players

ROBERT STEVENSON Full back

Born: Scotland

Joined TIW: 1898 **From:** Woolwich Arsenal

Debut: Not available

Appearances: Not available

Goals: Not available

Left TIW: 1898 **For:** Arthurlie

Bob Stevenson's decision to return home to Scotland for the second time was an event recorded in the book *Association Football And The Men Who Made It* by Dickford and Gibson, published in 1905: 'Robert Stevenson, a full back of merit, who captained the Arsenal team in their early Second Division struggles, was among those who helped to build warships when the suggestion of a football club was made at the Thames Iron Works, and he was the first captain of the team.

'There was not much of him in the way of physique, but he was a wonderfully good player and invaluable as an advisor to the fathers of the club.

'He remained with TIW until the second season, when they were located at Browning Road, East Ham. About halfway through their campaign at this enclosure, Stevenson returned home to Scotland and played for Arthurlie.'

The Irons won their first six league matches, the second of which was a 4-0 thrashing of Leyton at the Memorial Grounds. Under the heading, 'Leyton took a weak team to Canning Town and lost by four goals to nil', contemporary football reporter TAM wrote in the *Morning Leader* of Wednesday, 6 October 1897:

'Nearly 2,000 spectators saw the match, which was commenced by the Ironworks in real earnest. Twenty-five minutes after the start the Ironworks, who so far had the best of matters, obtained their first point in the following manner: Hatton secured about fifty yards from goal and after dodging and wriggling through the whole of the Leyton defence, tested Sterling with a stinger that was only partially cleared and Hatton, pouncing on the ball again, promptly rushed it through.

'Three minutes later, Gresham scored a second, so enabling the Thames to cross over with a deserved lead of two goals. For the best part of the game it was Thames forwards v Leyton's defence and although beaten twice before the finish by Reid and Edwards, they were in no way disgraced.

'Hatton was the most conspicuous of the Ironworks forwards, while Dove, Neill, Dandridge and Chisholm all played well in defence with goalkeeper Furnell having a very easy task.'

Although they went out of the FA Cup in the third qualifying round 2-0 at St Albans and lost 3-1 at home to local rivals Ilford in the third round of the London Senior Cup, Irons were almost unbeatable in the London League.

In fact, they lost just one game all season, the penultimate fixture against runners-up Brentford at Shotters Field, where they went down 1-0. A 3-1 victory at Grenadier Guards ensured that they pipped their West London rivals – who lost to Barking Woodville in their last match – to the title by a single point.

Charlie Dove (Thames Ironworks)

By this stage of the club's development, our own Charlie Dove was an almost permanent fixture in the side and considered important enough to be made the subject of a feature in the *East Ham Echo* prior to the vital match with Brentford of 23 April 1898.

Under the title 'Football Sketches – 1. Charlie Dove (Thames Ironworks)', the unnamed writer was effusive in his praise of the young star as he waxed lyrical over his attributes in the typically quaint and flowery writing style of the period: 'If not absolutely the finest right half back in Essex, the subject of our sketch is undoubtedly one of the most brilliant men in the county in that position.

'Born just over 19 years ago, Charles Dove first began his football career with Park School – a team that has always been classed as one of the finest schoolboy combinations. There he figured at full back and just by way of encouragement won two medals when playing in this position.

'Leaving school life he migrated to Forest Swift Juniors as a centre forward and subsequently captained the old Plaistow Melville.

'He also figured in the lines of Upton Park and South West Ham and three seasons ago joined the ranks of Thames Ironworks and has played with them ever since.

'Even when joining them his true position was not apparent. He played centre forward and full back and it was not until he had occupied nearly every place – with the exception of goal – that his worth as a right half was demonstrated.

'In this berth he plays a brilliant game, full of resource and the Thames Limited combination sadly missed him in their opening matches. However, he is expected to be fit and able to turn out on Saturday against Brentford, when he will considerably strengthen the team.'

Such was the progress made by this time, the club successfully applied for entry to the Second Division (London Section) of the Southern League where they would be pitting their skills against such prominent opposition as Fulham, Watford and Brentford again.

The Arrival of Professionalism

But off-field events almost overshadowed the excitement engendered by the prospect of Irons' first season as a Southern League team when it was revealed that the club had decided to take a massive step and embrace professionalism.

Arnold Hills, imbued with the Corinthian spirit, was definitely not amused, but even he, as an extremely educated man, must have known that a move towards the paid ranks was inevitable when he hinted, 'It may be necessary to introduce a little ferment of professional experience to leaven the heavy lump'. One wonders, with the benefit of hindsight, if in his wildest dreams he realised where it all might lead to a century later.

A 3-0 away win over Shepherd's Bush got the new professionals off to a good start on the 1898-99 season's opening day and was followed by a 3-1 Memorial Ground revenge victory against Brentford on 24 September, when Sam Hay (2) and Dove got the goals. After a 2-1 defeat at Uxbridge in the following match, Irons travelled to Wycombe on 29 October and were thrashed 4-1. There was a story behind the surprise win for the Buckinghamshire side who'd lost their previous five matches. Thames arrived at Loakes Park an hour late after missing their train. This obviously unsettled them and Wycombe dominated most of the game, which was played in torrential rain.

Jim Aldridge put the Blues two up in the first 15 minutes and completed his hat-trick just before half-time. The home side made it 4-0 before inside forward James Reid, formerly of Port Vale and Hibernian, pulled one back for the visitors two minutes from time in the gathering darkness.

For the Irons it was the last defeat of the season and the next time the two teams met, at the Memorial Grounds on 14 January 1899, they were well on their way to take the championship. The scoreline was completely reversed with Wycombe having trouble with the trains this time.

Goalkeeper Ernie Wheeler missed his connection and didn't arrive until late in the game. The visitors started with only 10 men and had full back Henry Turner between the sticks. He was soon picking the ball out of the net as a defender headed an own goal past him.

A spectator, who often filled in when Wycombe were short, then took over in goal. He too quickly conceded a goal when centre half McEwan scored with a low shot. David Lloyd then wasted two good chances before scoring twice to put the Irons 4-0 ahead at half-time. The same player lost the chance of a hat-trick when he fired a penalty wide, unlike Fred Keen, who converted his to earn the Blues a consolation.

In between the two matches with Wycombe, Charlie Dove achieved the unique distinction of playing in every position for the team when he deputised for regular goalkeeper Tommy Moore and kept a clean sheet in a 4-0 win at Maidenhead on 31 December 1898 – a victory which kept the Irons on course for their second championship victory in consecutive seasons.

The First Test

Despite the fact that they finished the campaign nine points ahead of their nearest rivals, Irons were still required to play a series of Test Matches to gain promotion to the First Division of the Southern League.

The first, against Cowes from the Isle of Wight who had won all their 10 matches in a six-club section of the Southern League representing the South West, was staged at the supposedly 'neutral' venue of Millwall's East Ferry Road. The 10,000 crowd made it better than a home match for Thames who won 3-1 with goals from Lloyd, Henderson and Patrick Leonard.

Then Thames were ordered to take on Sheppey United, who had finished 12th out of the 13 strong Southern League First Division. The match, staged at Chatham, ended 1-1 with Lloyd again getting on the scoresheet. But in the end it was all academic. Before a replay could be staged it was decided to enlarge the top division to 19 clubs, enabling all four Test Match contestants, and also QPR and Bristol Rovers, to join the higher section.

Money Strengthens the Team

Anxious to ensure that the team's promotion would be a success, Arnold Hills made £1,000 available to football club secretary Francis Payne to strengthen the team which had already been bolstered by the arrival of Tom Bradshaw, Bill Joyce and Kenny McKay from Tottenham and future manager Syd King from New Brompton.

Payne engaged an agent to approach a player in Birmingham on the club's behalf but he was adjudged to be poaching and hauled before the Football Association. The agent was suspended for two years and the club two weeks, in addition to being fined £25. Payne was suspended in his absence and subsequently resigned over the unsavoury affair which left a stain on the club's character and must have realised Hills' worst nightmare.

It was against this besmirched background that the team lost its first fixture of the 1899-1900 season, 1-0 at Reading. And although they

50 Greatest Players

TOM BRADSHAW Winger

Born: Lancashire

Joined West Ham: 1899 **From:** Tottenham Hotspur

Debut: v Reading, 16 September 1899

Appearances: 12 **Goals:** 2

Left West Ham: 1900 (died)

Courageous former England international left winger Tom Bradshaw had actually played and scored in a 2-1 Memorial Ground FA Cup defeat by Millwall just 16 days before he died, in front of a then-record 13,000 crowd at the venue. Syd King commented on the situation of that time in his brief 1906 history:

'The record of 1899-1900, however, would not be complete without some reference to poor Tom Bradshaw, who came from the Spurs with Joyce. How well I remember that match with Queens Park Rangers during the Christmas holidays, when Joyce brought over the sad message to the Memorial Grounds that our comrade had passed away. Poor Tom was one of the cleverest wing forwards I have ever known and he was immensely popular with everybody. He joined the club with me and with us in the team were MacEachrane, Craig – my partner at full back – Carnelly and Joyce.'

50 Greatest Players

RODDY MacEACHRANE Half back

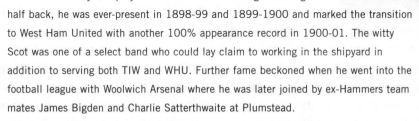

Born: Inverness, Scotland, 1878

Joined TIW: 1898 **From:** Inverness Thistle

Debut: v Shepherd's Bush, 10 September 1898

Appearances: TIW 53 **Goals:** 1

WHU 60 **Goals:** 5

Left West Ham: 1901 **For:** Woolwich Arsenal

Roddy made the long haul from Inverness to Canning Town to work at the TIW factory and play for the works side. A tough tackling half back, he was ever-present in 1898-99 and 1899-1900 and marked the transition to West Ham United with another 100% appearance record in 1900-01. The witty Scot was one of a select band who could lay claim to working in the shipyard in addition to serving both TIW and WHU. Further fame beckoned when he went into the football league with Woolwich Arsenal where he was later joined by ex-Hammers team mates James Bigden and Charlie Satterthwaite at Plumstead.

chalked up a 4-0 Memorial Ground victory over Chatham two days later, when McKay and a new inside forward from Bristol City, Albert Carnelly, scored two goals apiece, a 7-0 drubbing at White Hart Lane confirmed that this was going to be a long hard season for the Irons.

It was a sad one, too, with the announcement that skipper Tom Bradshaw had died on Christmas Day. His death was attributed to an injury sustained in a 1-0 win over Bedminster in the season's second match. A disastrous mid-season run of seven successive defeats left Thames needing to defeat West London rivals Fulham in a Test Match at Tottenham to preserve their First Division status.

Fulham, who were Second Division runners-up and had former Iron David Lloyd in their side, were dispatched 5-1 although only 600 fans turned up to see Joyce bag a hat-trick on his old stamping ground.

Described as a footballer with 'few fancy frills', Joyce had previously been with Greenock Morton and Bolton as well as Spurs and had provided another of the few highlights that season, when he scored a previous hat-trick in a 4-1 win against FA Cup finalists Southampton, at Canning Town.

The Formation of West Ham United

The events of the campaign were quickly to be overshadowed by off-field developments concerning the future direction of the football club and indeed, the Thames Iron Works company itself. In June 1900 the company had acquired another engineering firm and, in order to raise new capital to finance the takeover, was to become a public company. An appeal was launched and four thousand 10 shilling (50p) shares were issued and offered initially to TIW staff and then to the general public. Still showing commendable generosity, Hills offered to match the sale of any shares one-to-one.

In a premeditated move at the end of June 1900, Thames Iron Works FC resigned from the Southern League and was officially wound up. A week later, however, on 5 July 1900 the club was reformed under the new title of West Ham United FC and accepted an offer of the Southern League place left vacant by their forebears.

A new secretary was appointed, Welshman Lew Bowen, who was a clerk at the Iron Works and had reported on the club's early progress in the *TIWG*.

In addition to old favourites like Syd King, Charlie Dove, Roddie MacEachrane and goalkeeper Tommy Moore, the new club had no less than seven new signings to start their first season as West Ham United FC. The new men were goalkeeper Hugh Mounteith (ex-Bristol City), full back Walter Tranter (Chatham), right winger Fergus Hunt (Arsenal), left winger Freddie Fenton (Gainsborough), centre forward James Reid (Burslem Port Vale), inside left Albert Kaye (Chatham) and inside right Billy Grassam

The first ever West Ham United team, 1900.

(Burslem Port Vale). All were present as the Memorial Ground crowd bade farewell to the old Irons and welcomed the new Hammers who could hardly have wished for a better start as they thrashed Gravesend 7-0 in their first fixture on 1 September 1900. Grassam, a Scot, scored four on his debut – a feat that remains a Hammers record to this day.

Despite the new regime, Hammers didn't sever all links with their past and Tom Robinson, whose connections in local sporting circles went right back to the old Castle Swifts in the 1880s, was still trainer. His involvement with the Hammers made him a well-known figure whose services extended to training local cyclists and boxers participating in events at the Memorial Grounds (which nowadays would be recognised as a multi-function sports centre, such was its innovation and novelty at the time). Sporting a fashionable drooping moustache, Tom could often be spotted in his typical trainer's 'uniform' of cloth-cap and roll-neck sweater of those days, conducting 'training spins' along the Turnpike Road, now Beckton Road. Before supervising training in a schoolroom at the old Trinity Church School in the Barking Road, Tom would often invite the players to breakfast with him at his house in Benledi Street, Poplar, where he dispensed hospitality to many of the Hammers team including Bob Allan, Hughie Montieth, Billy Grassam and Rod MacEachrane (who went on to make a record number of appearances for Woolwich Arsenal).

Despite their promising start and the fact that they had a fair sprinkling of Scots in the side, Hammers hardly set the leather alight in that first season, finishing sixth. They did put up a good show against First Division Football League opponents Liverpool in the first round proper of the FA Cup, going down to a solitary goal at the Memorial Ground. But the club shot themselves in the foot financially by doubling admission charges and suffered the consequences when only 6,000 turned up for the game.

Charlie Dove, meanwhile, had done the unthinkable and joined bitter rivals Millwall where he sustained a bad injury in 1902 and was forced to retire. Such is football... and life.

Winning six out of seven of their 1901-02 opening matches, Hammers would have been championship contenders had they not suffered a mid-season slump.

They still managed to finish fourth and drew the biggest ever crowd to a football match at the Memorial Grounds when 17,000 attended the 1-0 defeat to FA Cup holders Spurs on 2 November 1901. A figure no doubt helped by the opening of West Ham railway station at Manor Road the previous January.

The First 'Giant-Killing'

However, in the FA Cup, some worrying trends were emerging. Due to an official's oversight, the fact that Hammers were also scheduled to meet Leyton in an FA Cup third qualifying tie at the Memorial Grounds on 2 November was overlooked. Reluctant to relinquish the lucrative gate receipts from the Tottenham clash, the club decided to surrender their home advantage in the cup tie and send their reserve team to Leyton. Against the odds, the second string secured a 1-0 victory at Leyton.

When the Hammers were drawn at home to little Essex village side Grays in the next round and able to call on their first-team, the result was considered to be a foregone conclusion. But Grays had other ideas.

Former Hammers goalkeeper Tommy Moore had been unable to oust Hughie Montieth from the first-team and had moved to the Essex team. Nicknamed the 'Dancing Dervish' because of his unorthodox methods in evading opposing forwards, Tommy, who had been a regular first choice in the TIW days, played a 'blinder' and saved everything the West Ham forwards could throw at him, with the exception of a solitary reply to Grays' two goals from left winger Billy Linward at a fog-bound Memorial Grounds as Hammers succumbed to their first ever 'giant-killing'.

The season was not a success as Hammers finished 10th in the Southern League table and went out of the FA Cup following a 2-0 defeat in the first round against Football League Lincoln City at Sincil Bank.

Hammers were watched by an amazing 18,000 crowd when they went down 2-0 to Portsmouth at Fratton Park on Boxing Day, but home attendances were poor and, what was worse, the three-year rent-free tenure of the Memorial Grounds, so generously granted by Arnold Hills, was coming to an end.

The 1903-04 season opened to an uncertain background and a 4-2 defeat at North Greenwich against Millwall – with whom a recognised rivalry was literally really beginning to kick-in. Charlie Satterthwaite, the replacement for Billy Grassam who'd gone to Glasgow Celtic, scored against the Lions on his debut and was one of the few success stories of a season in which Hammers finished a poor 12th out of 18 teams in the Southern League First Division. Formerly with Liverpool and New Brompton, he finished the season as Hammers' top scorer with 13 goals in the league and five in the FA Cup. His haul included a four and three in 5-0 wins over Brighton and Chatham respectively.

By the close season of 1903-04 the club were in dire financial straits. The directors, who had known from the start of the year that their occupancy of the Memorial Grounds had to be re-negotiated in the summer, failed to reach a satisfactory agreement with Arnold Hills for a continuance of the leasehold for seven, 14 or 21 years at a rent the club could afford while still exercising sole control.

At this time the club were homeless and penniless and in grave danger of being wound up. They made the acquaintance of a good fairy in the form of a local brewery, however, which advanced them a loan to assist in the purchase of a new ground, but still their troubles were not over.

A piece of wasteland was offered by West Ham corporation but was deemed unsuitable and, with the 1904-05 season approaching, the club had to satisfy the Southern League authorities that it could fulfil fixtures.

Tommy Allison, West Ham's senior player in the early 1900s.

The Boleyn Castle Field

The future was looking bleak when a match was being played between boys of two Home Office Schools. One of the Catholic Brothers, who attended the Boleyn Castle Roman Catholic Reformatory School, happened to be watching the game alongside officials from West Ham. In conversation, the Irons' problems came to light and out of the blue an arrangement was made for the club's representative to view the Boleyn Castle field, just off Green Street, East Ham. The club's delegation, led by secretary Syd King, immediately agreed to rent the ground (which was described by some as a 'vegetable patch') from the Catholic Ecclesiastical Authorities, but were thrown into despair when they learned that the Home Office disapproved of the Brother's action. But Syd King was not to be denied, explaining, 'A deputation of directors waited upon MP Sir Ernest Gray and, through his good offices, subject to certain conditions, we were finally allowed to take possession of Boleyn Castle.'

Further light may be shed on the nature of the 'certain conditions' and the identity of the Brother who was West Ham's mystery saviour in the following extract from Colm Kerrigan's biography, *Gatling Gun George Hilsdon*:

'George made his first recorded appearance in local club football early in 1904. The club he played for was Boleyn Castle FC, near to his home in East Ham and getting its name from a castle alongside the ground that was supposed to have associations with Anne Boleyn.

'The ground was owned by the Catholic diocese of Westminster and was also used by Boleyn Castle Reformatory. The boys in this institution had a very strong team and in 1903 beat all the local Board Schools in an open competition.

'Brother Norbert of the Reformatory, when interviewed by the East Ham and Barking Free Press, was found to have been a football enthusiast on principle. And here is the reason he gave, "A few years ago, before the introduction of football – and cricket – into the school, it required 10 masters to control the boys, where only one master suffices now."

'The move made provision for Boleyn Castle FC to join up with West Ham United, with their best players getting the chance to play in West Ham's reserve team. Hurried improvements were undertaken during the summer to have the ground ready for the new season. While they were not finished on time, the ground was able to accommodate the 12,000 who came to see West Ham beat Millwall 3-0 on the opening day of the 1904-05 season.

Great Managers – 1902-1932

SYD KING

The story of E.S. 'Syd' King is synonymous with the early history of West Ham United as he was connected with the Hammers and before them the Irons for over 33 years. He began his playing career with Northfleet as a full back and claimed to have conceded a hat-trick of own goals for that club in a match against Charlie Paynter's home town club, Swindon. Transferring to New Brompton in 1897, he spent two seasons with the Kent club before joining TIW in the summer of 1899.

At the time King was considered to be the best full back in the Southern League and as soon as they signed him, Irons had to turn down an offer from Derby County for his services. Had the Rams bid succeeded, things may have been very different for West Ham United, as he was a major influence during the club's promotion to Football League status as well as appearing in the first FA Cup final to be staged at Wembley in 1923.

'It is not known how many of Boleyn Castle's 'best players' were invited to join West Ham's playing staff at the Boleyn Ground, but at least two, Vettini and Rayment, appeared during the 1904-1905 season for West Ham's reserves.

'Neither ever made it into the first eleven. Perhaps it rankled George that he was not among those invited to stay at the Boleyn Ground, as his reminiscences make no mention of ever playing for Boleyn Castle FC.

'He does say that he spent half a season with South West Ham. This club was based in Canning Town and was previously known as Victoria Swifts, the name probably having something to do with the nearby Victoria Docks.'

The Syd King Era Begins

Although unanimously considered to be Hammers' first ever manager, Syd King was still officially club secretary on the eve of the 1904-05 season. Indeed, he is listed as such on the reverse of a postcard-sized team photograph issued at that time to promote Oxo, which bears his endorsement, 'When training, Oxo is the only beverage used by our team and all speak of the supreme strength and power of endurance which they have derived from its use' – E.S. King, Secretary, West Ham United FC.

Thus fortified, the 'beefed-up' Hammers took on the Lions of Millwall and triumphed in their first ever appearance at Upton Park on Thursday 1 September 1904. Confusion reigns as to whether centre forward Billy Bridgeman scored a hat-trick on that historic day or just two goals, as some reports credited Jack Flynn with getting on the scoresheet. Most importantly, though, Hammers had got off to a winning start and at the same time recorded their first victory over their great rivals in almost four years.

Only half-a-dozen players escaped the clear-out of the summer of 1904 and only half back Tommy Allison was paid during the break. Among the unpaid heroes were Billy Bridgeman, Charles Cotton, Aubrey Fair and Len Jarvis. Trainer Bill Johnson was also a victim of the purge, his job going to returnee Tom Robinson, who had a certain Charles Paynter as his assistant.

Several new faces were brought in, however, including goalkeeper Matt Kingsley and full back Tommy Bamlett both from Newcastle, two Scottish internationals – Dave Gardner, a full back from Grimsby and forward Bill McCartney from Manchester United – centre back Frank Piercey and winger Chris Carrick from Middlesbrough, Jack Flynn and Joe Fletcher – both forwards from Reading – and, most famously, inside forward 'Chippy' Simmons from West Bromwich Albion.

The Hammers finished 11th in the Southern League First Division that season in what was a time of consolidation for the club. They went out of the FA Cup at the first attempt following a disappointing 2-1 Upton Park defeat to Brighton.

Most significantly, the club made a profit for the first time in its history.

The season's performance set a trend that continued up to the outbreak of World War 1 – only on rare occasions did they pose a threat of winning the Southern League Championship, nor were they often in danger of relegation.

In 1905-06 Hammers again finished in 11th position; in 1906-07, 5th;1907-08, 10th; 1908-09, 17th; 1909-10, 9th; 1910-11, 5th; 1911-12, 13th; 1912-13, 3rd; 1913-14, 6th; 1914-15, 4th.

Nicknamed 'Tiddler', Herbert Ashton was a popular winger.

Many memorable matches were staged and a host of great players pulled on the claret and blue shirt, however, as the club served its apprenticeship to join football's élite during those 10 years.

An Early Cup Reputation

FA Cup ties in particular brought a taste of future fame and fortune the competition would bring to the club as the Edwardian-age Hammers staked their claim as redoubtable cup fighters.

Receiving byes until the first round proper for the first time in their short history, Hammers drew 1-1 with Woolwich Arsenal at Plumstead thanks to a penalty converted by new keeper George Kitchen! This was not an unusual phenomenon for George – who was one of the game's great characters and later became a golf pro – was well known for taking penalties. It was the duty of a team-mate to place the ball on the spot as George ran from his own area to toe-punt it past his opposite number.

With the assistance of three former West Ham men, Bigden, Satterthwaite and MacEachrane, the Gunners won a muddy replay at Boleyn Castle 3-2. Hammers' goals were scored by Lionel Watson and Billy Bridgeman, a Marner Street School pal of another prodigious local goalscorer, who had played a handful of games for Irons but had inexplicably been allowed to slip away on a free transfer to Chelsea where Bridgeman would soon join him.

In January 1907 West Ham claimed their first ever Football League scalp, when they defeated Second Division Blackpool 2-1 at Upton Park before a crowd of 13,000. Hammers' marksmen were outside left Arthur Winterhalder and centre forward Harry Stapley. The latter was a slightly built centre forward who won the first of 10 amateur caps for England the following year. A schoolmaster by profession, Harry was the club's top scorer in the three seasons he was with the Hammers and when he left to join Glossop he topped the Football League club's goalscoring lists for a further seven consecutive seasons.

In another home tie, Hammers lost by the same scoreline as they'd defeated Blackpool, 2-1, to First Division Everton who noted the fine form of Winterhalder and signed him at the season's end.

Billy Glassam, meanwhile, had returned to the fold after spells with Glasgow Celtic, Manchester United and Leyton and soon proved he hadn't lost his scoring touch to the relief of the Upton Park fans. Grassam once again pulled off his early season party-trick by scoring in his first game, but it wasn't enough to prevent Hammers going down 2-1 at home to Swindon. He managed to score in four of the five opening matches, helped by the improved service provided by England international left winger Fred Blackburn, who was born in the Lancashire town and naturally played for Rovers.

By the time the cup ties had come round in January, Fred was joined in the forward line by a scheming inside forward his home town club would smash the British transfer record to obtain the services of – but not before he'd become a legend in East London – Danny Shea.

Disposing of Rotherham County 1-0 in the FA Cup first round on New Year's Day 1908, with the compliments of a Fred Blackburn goal at Boleyn Castle, Hammers were drawn at mighty Newcastle in the next round, where they would face ex-colleague Dick Pudan.

Dickie, as he was affectionately known by early century patrons of the Memorial Grounds, was one of West Ham's first young local discoveries having been born in Canning Town. He formed a notable, although short-lived, partnership with Charlie Craig during Irons' initial Southern League season in 1900-1901.

Pudan's progress encapsulates the description, although somewhat fanciful in the form of its prose, given the book *Association Football* in 1905 on the ability of West Ham to unearth new talent:

'It is the proud boast of the West Ham club that they turn out more local players than any other team in the South. The district has been described as a hot-bed of football and it is so. The raw material is found on the marshlands and open spaces round about; and after a season or so, the finished player leaves the East End workshop to better himself, as most ambitious young men will do. In the ranks of other organisations many old West Ham boys have distinguished themselves.

William Barnes, who scored the winning goal for Sheffield United in a Cup final; Bill Yenson, who played centre forward for Bolton Wanderers against Manchester United in another Cup final; James Bigden, who has done good work in Woolwich Arsenal's half back line and Dick Pudan, who operated at full back for Bristol Rovers when they won the Championship of the Southern League, are among those who learned to kick a ball, to give the subtle pass, and to score a goal with West Ham.'

Playing in front of by far the biggest crowd that would watch them until their appearance in the 1923 FA Cup final – 47,000 baying Geordies in the cup tie at Gallowgate – West Ham were dealt a cruel blow when they lost goalkeeper Kitchen five minutes after half-time with a serious leg injury.

With only 10 men and centre half Frank Piercey deputising in goal, Hammers succumbed to two goals from the Magpies centre forward, Bill 'Cockles' Appleyard who had a reputation for putting the opposing keeper in the net – as well as the ball.

The Boleyn Castle crowd were pleased to see George Kitchen recovered from injury and back in goal as the Hammers kicked off the 1908-09 season with a 2-0 victory over West London rivals QPR, courtesy of goals from Blackburn and new centre forward Jack Foster.

By coincidence, the two teams were drawn together in the first round of the FA Cup and 17,000 spectators crammed into Rangers' Park Royal Ground to witness a 0-0 stalemate. But with Shea now an automatic choice at inside right and Blackburn's orthodox approach complemented on the opposite wing by the more intricate skill of the new crowd favourite, Herbert 'Tiddler' Ashton, West Ham fancied their chances in the replay.

Sure enough, it was Shea, with his inquisitive, constant prompting who scored the game's solitary goal to set up a second round clash with Leeds City at Elland Road. Twenty-three-year-old centre forward Walter Miller, who Hammers had signed from Leeds' Yorkshire rivals Sheffield Wednesday, scored the goal that earned a 1-1 draw and an Upton Park replay against their Football League opponents.

The Yorkshiremen looked like hanging on to an early goal until Shea equalised with just a few minutes left of normal time and then scored the winner in the last minute of extra-time to give notice of his own and West Ham United's aspirations in what was already recognised as the most famous football competition in the world.

Destiny decided that once again Hammers' burgeoning reputation as feared cup fighters would be pitched against opponents whose traditions in that department could not be questioned... the Magpies from St James' Park. But this time, West Ham had the home advantage. Newcastle offered West Ham £1,000 in cash to have the game switched to St James' Park but Hammers would have none of it and the match ended in a 0-0 deadlock in front of a 17,000 crowd at Upton Park.

Undaunted, Hammers travelled to St James' Park still optimistic of the outcome. After all, hadn't the Magpies had their black and white feathers severely ruffled when they lost by a staggering 9-1 to deadly rivals Sunderland in a First Division match on the same ground just two months earlier?

Hammers' high hopes seemed well founded when the weasel-like Shea equalised a first-half goal by the Geordies' centre forward Albert Shepherd in the second period. In a gallant display, Hammers only succumbed to winger Andrew Anderson's goal eight minutes from time and were given a standing ovation by the 36,000 crowd.

Newcastle reached the semi-final stage where they met Manchester United at Bramall Lane and were beaten by a goal from United's England international forward Howard Halse, which thwarted them of the 'double'.

Halse, who was born in Stratford, succeeded Charlie Dove as a pupil at Park Road School, West Ham and was also a playing contemporary of George Hilsdon. He somehow managed to avoid the attentions of West Ham and was signed instead by new Southern League Division Two club Southend United with whom he scored 200 goals in the two seasons preceding his move to Manchester United's Bank Street headquarters. Hammers' 'one that got away' won a League Championship and FA Cup winners medal at United, adding another cup winner's medal with Chelsea in 1915.

Just three days after the Newcastle replay, with understudy David Clarke deputising for Kitchen, who had been injured at St James' for the second successive season, Hammers slumped to a disastrous 6-0 defeat at Southern League champions elect Northampton Town.

But although they were struggling in the First Division of the Southern League and allowing distinctly provincial clubs like Reading, Swindon, Southampton and Northampton to outperform them in the table, the shrewd grammar school-educated Syd King realised that to impress the administrators of the Football League the club had to prove themselves against those already a part of the élite, which could only be achieved through extended runs in the FA Cup.

An inside forward converted to left half on the instructions of Charlie Paynter, Tommy Randall survived his debut in the No. 6 shirt against the Cobblers and went on with his mentor to achieve an Edwardian-age reverse of Ron Greenwood's famous conversion of Geoff Hurst 54 years later.

50 Greatest Players

GEORGE WEBB Striker

Born: Poplar, London, 1888

Joined West Ham: 1909 **From:** Amateur

Debut: v Leyton, 9 April 1909

Appearances: 62 **Goals:** 32

Left West Ham: 1912 **For:** Manchester City

Famously the first West Ham player to win an England cap against Wales and Scotland in 1911, George was staunchly corinthian and jealously guarded his amateur status throughout his short but illustrious career. Described as 'fast, had a great shot while a hefty physique made him even more redoubtable', he was also capped by his country seven times at amateur level. Scored on his debut and maintained a goal every other game scoring ratio while a West Hammer and was selected for the Southern League v Irish League along with team-mates George Kitchen and Danny Shea in 1911. After a short spell in the Football League with Manchester City, George dropped out of the limelight and it was a great shock to all at Upton Park when the born and bred East Ender died of consumption at just 28 years of age in 1915.

Beginning his Upton Park career as an amateur inside forward, although he scored on his debut against Fulham in 1906, the fans took an immediate dislike to his thoughtful, slow approach to the game, calling him 'Old Mother Randall' and almost drove him out of football with their barracking. Charlie remembered that Tom had played at No. 6 as a favour to him in his testimonial match against Woolwich Arsenal and had performed well. Tom went on to skipper the side and was an almost ever-present up to World War I. Another great name to emerge during the 1908-09 season was centre forward George Webb.

From 1910 up to the outbreak of the World War I, Hammers' reputation as feared FA Cup fighters became even more pronounced and every January and February the sports pages were full of their exploits. Syd King, his straw boater making him look for all the world like an official at the Royal Regatta than a football manager, could not have been more pleased, for he knew the power of the press and how to manipulate it for the needs of his club.

You can almost imagine him waxing his moustache with glee as his beloved Hammers took yet another Football League club scalp. The year 1910 was no exception. After disposing of little Carlisle at Boleyn Castle 5-0, with goals from Blackburn (2), Shea, Webb and Randall, it was the turn of the mighty Wolves.

Chapter Two: 1909-19 Consolidation

Twice winners of the trophy in 1893 and 1908, Second Division Wolves would hardly have been trembling in their boots at the prospect of a visit from a mere Southern League team, even though Spurs had been the first team from outside the Football League to win the cup in 1901 while flying the Southern League banner.

With 10 of the men who had won the cup two years earlier on duty at Molineux, the wearers of the famous old gold and black were considered 'racing certainties' to brush the East End contenders aside but, in a dazzling display, two goals from Webb (who topped the Southern League goalscorers list that season with 28) and a hat-trick from Shea blew the form-book away as Hammers romped home 5-1 victors.

In the next round, Hammers were again paired with league and London rivals QPR and, in a repeat of the previous season, a 1-1 draw at Park Royal necessitated an Upton Park replay. Still smarting over a controversial referee's decision to allow a distinctly offside-looking goal from Rangers' amateur W. Steer to equalise an earlier strike by his Hammers counterpart Webb in the first match, the Irons were also out of luck in the return meeting. Deadlocked 0-0 at the end of 90 minutes, the tie looked destined to go to a second replay when Steer scored the winner just three minutes from the end of extra time to earn a quarter-final place.

The Hammers were back with a vengeance the following 1910-1911 season, however, when they served notice of their ambitions with three victories in succession over previous winners of the trophy, Nottingham Forest, Preston North End and Manchester United.

First to fall were Forest who went down 2-1 in a fog shrouded first round encounter at Boleyn Castle to two goals from the prolific Shea.

The next visitors to Upton Park, in the second round on 4 February 1911, were Preston North End, dubbed the 'Invincibles' after winning the first championship of the Football League without losing a match and the FA Cup without conceding a goal in 1888-1889. Hammers paid scant respect to 'Proud Preston''s reputation and a celebrated hat-trick from 'big occasion' player Webb sealed a famous 3-0 victory.

Drawn at home to First Division leaders and champions-elect Manchester United in the third round, most contemporary reporters and neutral observers were of the opinion that Hammers' cup run – that had sent ripples through the game – would end here. In the event, even though admission prices were controversially doubled, a record 27,000 crowd attended the tie. Many scaled the roof of the stand and clambered up advertising hoardings to catch a glimpse of the famous United players like Billy Meredith, Charlie Roberts and Enoch 'Knocker' West, as well as their own favourites who included inside-left George Butcher and Tommy Caldwell who'd taken over Blackburn's No. 11 shirt the previous season.

The record Upton Park assembly witnessed one of the biggest shocks so far in English football, when with the teams level at 1-1 with two minutes left, Caldwell added to Shea's obligatory goal to win the tie for the underdogs from London's East End.

As Caldwell was shouldered off the pitch by the ecstatic home fans, the ripples had turned to shockwaves that could be felt all the way to the Football League headquarters in, ironically enough, Preston.

East London Goes Cup Crazy

A 2-1 defeat against Northampton was Hammers' only home defeat of 1910-11, not that anyone was too bothered in cup crazy East London, especially as the quarter-final draw had pitted the Irons against an out-of-sorts Blackburn Rovers at Upton Park.

Blackburn, however – destined to win the First Division of the Football League in both 1912 and 1913 and, with legendary England captain Bob Crompton at full back – proved formidable opponents. Twice they went ahead but, roared on by the majority of the 20,000 crowd, with almost Herculean effort, twice Hammers equalised through Butcher. But the Lancastrians' Welsh international Davies ended West Ham's hopes when he scored the winner in a goalmouth scramble minutes from time.

Albert Denyer, signed from Ilford in 1912.

After losing the opening fixture of the 1911-12 season 1-0 at Crystal Palace, goals from inside left Fred Harrison – signed from Fulham the previous season – and Webb's deputy Bill Kennedy, opened Hammers' account in the 2-2 home draw with Southampton.

The first round of the FA Cup paired Irons at home to a club with which they enjoyed close ties right from the Thames Iron Works days up to the outbreak of World War II, Gainsborough Trinity. A hard fought 2-1 victory over the Lincolnshire side was secured by goals from Webb and Harrison, the latter of whom scored West Ham's counter in the 1-1 draw at Middlesbrough in the second round and was on target again in the replay with 'Tiddler' Ashton as Hammers again triumphed 2-1 to get through to the third round for the fourth successive year. It proved to be a costly victory for Kennedy, though, as he injured a knee against the Teessiders and never played again.

Home advantage was not enough to get Hammers through the tough third round tie with Southern League champions Swindon Town, even though 20,000 turned up to see Butcher give them an early lead.

The Railwaymen, who had not finished lower than fourth in the Southern League First Division in five seasons, equalised through their England international forward Harold Fleming before the interval to set up a replay at the County Ground.

Swindon, as the Southern League's top scorers for the previous four seasons and destined to be so this campaign, didn't really need any help in the goalscoring department, but accepted two own-goals from hapless Hammers full back Vic Glover anyway. Swindon ran out 4-0 winners to put the breaks on the Hammers' FA Cup train for another year as it hit the buffers in the railway town.

Jack Geggus, who was sharing the goalkeeping responsibilities with local discovery Joe Hughes following Kitchen's transfer to Southampton, had a traumatic experience in a 3-1 league defeat at Leyton on 9 April 1912.

After conceding a couple of 'soft' goals he was subjected to a torrent of abuse from Hammers fans in the 3,000 crowd and walked off the field in disgust. Although he was persuaded to return, Hammers went down 3-1 in an embarrassing defeat to the bottom club.

Formerly with Docklands club Custom House, it's a wonder he was so sensitive to the crowd's reaction as the fans of West Ham's near-neighbours had a fearsome reputation for barracking as Peter Mason, in his history of Southend United published in 1993, noted: 'Some of the grounds had a gritty atmosphere too. Custom House, for instance – where according to a local reporter "even the most foul-mouthed linguist could scarcely have visited the enclosure without adding some new words to his vocabulary" – was renowned for its hostile crowd.'

Once again, the FA Cup brought the name of West Ham United to national prominence in the 1912-13 season, when they were drawn against the previous year's finalists, West Bromwich Albion, in the first round and the

The Founder

ARNOLD HILLS

Four days before West Ham United sensationally sank Preston North End 3-0 in the second round of the FA Cup on 4 February 1911 at Upton Park, the world's largest battleship, HMS *Thunderer*, was launched at the club's ancestral home, the Thames Iron Works factory at Canning Town for the Royal Navy. Despite the euphoria surrounding the event, all was not well on the banks of the Lea.

For years Arnold Hills, now riddled with arthritis, had been complaining about undercutting and monopolies exercised by the northern shipyards of the Tyne and Clyde which won most of the Admiralty orders and now TIW were in deep waters financially. Hills was convinced that there was collusion afoot and made pointed observations about Naval Dockyards' northern 'rings' and the fact that from 1904 to 1910 TIW received a paltry £1 million of a total of £67 million of Admiralty orders dispensed over that period. In 1912 a great campaign was launched to save the company. A deputation waited on Winston Churchill, the new first lord, but to no avail.

On New Year's Day, 1912, a massive meeting was held in Trafalgar Square, attended by Hills. Lying prone on a stretcher, his drawn features visible between the blankets and the rim of his trilby, he was lifted bodily by his men onto the plinth of Nelson's Column and addressed the vast crowd. But his spirited oratory could not disguise the fact that Thames Iron Works was in its death throes and on 21 December 1912, the closure notice was placed on the main gate at Blackwall. Later in the day, a further notice appeared which due to its naive and pathetic nature could only serve to have compounded the general bitterness and despair of the workforce: 'Do not let such a notice spoil your Christmas. This fight is not yet finished and no battle is lost until it is. I will not desert you in the darkest hour before the dawn. I bid you be of good cheer. Our extremity is God's opportunity and I do not doubt there is still in store for us a Happy New Year.' These were the watersheds and the death knell was sounding for the last great shipbuilders of the Thames. Banks refused further loans and the works shut down in the autumn of 1912. The *Daily Mail* called Arnold Hills 'The invalid builder of Dreadnoughts', a fitting epitaph for a crippled David fighting two Goliaths, who made the armour and slings.

In later years Hills was completely paralysed and was 'unable to lift a pen', a sad end for a man who was a great patriot and without whom West Ham United Football Club would not exist today. Arnold Hills died at his home in Penshurst in 1927 at the house named, appropriately enough, 'Hammerfield'.

eventual winners Aston Villa in the second. They also finished the season occupying their highest ever position in the First Division of the Southern League – third.

Denyer, Hilsdon and Puddefoot

The season was also notable for the return to Upton Park, like a 'prodigal son' of George Hilsdon who still had some goals left in him after a tremendously successful six-year sojourn at Chelsea, during which he'd represented the Football League and England at full international level on eight occasions, scoring a phenomenal 13 times.

Corresponding with the arrival of a young amateur centre forward from Ilford, Albert Denyer, it was a timely return as the pair were able to compensate for the sensational departure for a record £2,000 fee of Shea to Blackburn Rovers in January 1913, together with the later emergence of another famous centre forward who would also go on to distinguish himself with Blackburn and England – Sydney Puddefoot.

Although sometimes barracked by the Boleyn Castle crowd for his lack of pace, upon his return Hilsdon could always be relied upon for a goal or two and his vast experience was an asset to those around him as the reporter of the *East Ham Echo* emphasised following the 3-1 defeat of eventual champions Plymouth Argyle in October 1912, 'Good as Shea has always been, he is 20 per cent better since the introduction of Hilsdon.'

Following a 1-1 draw at the Hawthorns where Harrison levelled for Hammers, Albion were twice ahead in the replay when 'Gatling Gun' pulled them back on each occasion to set up a second replay at his old Stamford Bridge stamping ground. A correspondent of the *Players' Union Magazine* at the 2-2 draw noted that while George had lost some pace, 'in the fine art of ball manipulation, keenness of perception and judgement, he is as good as ever.' So the scene was set for little West Ham of the Southern League to take on the mighty men from the midlands, who had twice won the famous trophy and four times been finalists, for the right to meet the team who were the Throstles' biggest rivals and the team who Hammers copied the colours of – Aston Villa.

Captained by England's regular left-back Jesse Pennington, who was renowned for his great sportsmanship, Albion were still favourites. The Blackcountrymen's odds lengthened after a disputed seventh-minute goal from Hilsdon and it was 'all bets off' when the latter and young Denyer scored either side of the interval with no reply from Albion, to secure another sensational result for 'that fella King's team' from London's Docklands.

Almost inevitably, Hammers succumbed to Villa in Birmingham, going down 5-0 to a club who had already won the cup four times and would do so again by defeating First Division Champions Sunderland 1-0 at Crystal Palace that year. But once again, Hammers had sent out a clear message to the country's leading Football League clubs that one day they would be joining their ranks and wouldn't rest until their ambitions were realised.

With Hilsdon marshalling the team so well, Hammers were enjoying their best ever run in the Southern League too and would remain undefeated during a 16-match sequence between January and September 1913.

Towards the end of 1912-13 Hammers recorded a 3-1 win over Millwall at Cold Blow Lane before a 24,000 crowd and were still in contention for the Southern League title with four games to play.

Hammers were back at The Den for the opening match of 1913-14 watched by just half the attendance figure of the previous April. 'Gatling Gun' fired the Irons goal in the 1-1 draw from the penalty spot after he was felled.

His miss from the 12-yard spot five days later in the first home match proved costly, however. A record 25,000 crowd turned up to witness the opening of the new West Stand and the debut of centre-forward Dick Leafe, signed from Sheffield United. Again the *East Ham Echo* reflected, 'The

50 Greatest Players

DANNY SHEA Inside forward

Born: Wapping, London, November 1887

Joined West Ham: 1907 **From:** Amateur

Debut: v Norwich City, 7 December, 1907

Appearances: 217 **Goals:** 134

Left West Ham: 1913 **For:** Blackburn Rovers

Shea, who was once described by a northern football writer of having the 'uncanny ability to pass to himself', had been discovered playing for the Builders Arms pub team one Sunday morning, by Charlie Paynter in Stratford, almost on the club's doorstep. He became a regular in the side and became a prolific scorer. During the FA Cup competition of the 1910-11 season Nottingham Forest went down 2-1 to the Hammers in a fog-shrouded first round encounter at Boleyn Castle to two goals from Shea, who much later admitted to punching them in, unseen by the referee in the 'pea-souper'. All was fair in love and war – and winning FA Cup ties it seems. He left in 1913 for a record transfer fee of £2,000 to Blackburn Rovers.

magnificent new stand came in for much favourable comment.' Leafe, too, was a success with two goals, but Swindon – the team who had edged the Hammers out of second place on goal difference the previous season and who would win the Southern League title by the same manner in 1913-14 – were again superior in that department as they took three points back to Wiltshire with a 3-2 victory.

Jack Tresadern – a wing half from Barking – and, later in the season, centre forward Arthur Stallard from Chatham, were two significant signings but the player who really hit the headlines was last season's debutant, Syd Puddefoot. By the time the first round of the FA Cup had come round, 'Our Syd' or 'Puddy' as the fans liked to call him, was already a fixture in the side at centre forward having forced Leafe – who would top the scoring list with 21 goals – to move to inside left to accommodate him. Puddefoot's five goals, including a hat-trick in seven minutes in the 8-1 win against Chesterfield in the FA Cup first round tie at Upton Park in January 1913, remains an individual scoring record for a West Ham player in the competition and the score represents West Ham's best ever win in the tournament.

Two goals by another promising youngster – Dan Bailey, who had been signed from Custom House the previous year to fill the No. 8 shirt left vacant by Shea's departure – against Crystal Palace secured a 2-0 second round win at Boleyn Castle and set up a third round clash with twice First Division Champions, Liverpool. After a 1-1 draw in the first meeting at Upton Park it was Hammers' turn to take a drubbing as they went down 5-1 in front of 45,000 at Anfield. But Puddefoot proved he could compete with the best by scoring both West Ham's goals over the two matches. Had Puddefoot's progress not been put on hold by a bad ankle injury, it is likely that he would have finished as the club's top goalscorer for 1913-14. As it was he scored 16 times in 20 Southern League and cup matches as Hammers finished sixth. Better still, the club made a trading profit on the season of a handsome £2,200 and the new stand had been paid for entirely from gate revenue.

Syd Puddefoot's five goals against Chesterfield in the FA Cup in January 1913 remains an individual scoring record for West Ham United.

The Great War is Declared

On 28 June 1914 an event took place in Yugoslavia, however, that would put football – and indeed almost everything else – to the back of people's minds for the next four years. Archduke Ferdinand of Austria and his consort were assassinated at Sarajevo. It proved to be the spark that ignited the powder-keg of Europe and would transplant the young men of Great Britain from the football fields of home to the killing fields of France.

As the players reported back for training in August 1914 the 'war to end all wars' had been declared and by the time the season kicked off, the British Expeditionary Force was in France helping the French to stem the German invasion into the country through Belgium.

Despite opposition from some quarters, it was decided to allow the 1914-15 season to continue on the grounds that some form of normality at home would help morale at the front and also because the large crowds attracted by matches were seen as an ideal opportunity to stage recruitment drives by the authorities.

Yet again, Hammers met Newcastle in the cup, this time in the first round and they made a spirited comeback to draw 2-2, thanks to goals from Leafe after being two down at half-time. Another goal from Leafe, who was now playing at outside right, and one from his opposite flankman Jack Casey was not enough to overcome the Magpies in the St James' Park replay which was lost 3-2 before a 28,000 crowd.

Puddefoot was the Hammers' top scorer with 18 goals as the side finished in fourth place, seven points behind champions Watford against whom they were the only team to achieve the 'double'. The great 'Puddy' was forced to move from the centre forward position to inside right to make way for the highly rated Arthur Stallard for the last 11 matches, a switch more than vindicated by the latter's seven goals in that period.

Last Rites

Although no one realised it at the time, West Ham's 1-1 draw at home to Norwich City on April 24, 1915, was destined to be their last ever match in the Southern League.

To Stallard goes the honour of scoring the club's last goal in the competition they graced for 15 years, but it could so easily have been Hilsdon, who missed a penalty and the chance to make it 2-1. He may have found consolation in the knowledge that even if his spot-kick had not been saved by the keeper, a win would not have placed his team any higher in the final table behind Watford, Reading and Cardiff City. Stallard's rich promise was further underlined by 17 goals in 24 wartime appearances in the London Combination. Sadly, Arthur Stallard was destined to die for his

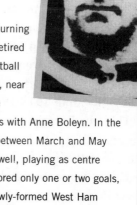

50 Greatest Players

GEORGE HILSDON Forward

Born: Bromley-by-Bow, London, August 1885

Joined West Ham: 1904 **From:** Boleyn Castle

Debut: v New Brompton, 11 February 1905

Appearances: 92 **Goals:** 35

Left West Ham: 1905, 1915 **For:** Chelsea (returning in 1912), retired

George made his first recorded appearance in local club football early in 1904. The club he played for was Boleyn Castle FC, near to his home in East Ham and getting its name from a castle alongside the ground that was supposed to have associations with Anne Boleyn. In the handful of games George Hilsdon played for Boleyn Castle between March and May 1904, he was thought by the *East Ham Echo* to have done well, playing as centre forward or inside forward and although he seems to have scored only one or two goals, he had a part in many others. He went on to play for the newly-formed West Ham before being transferred to Chelsea. He returned to West Ham for the 1912-13 season and proved that he still had some goals left in him after a tremendously successful six-year sojourn at Chelsea, during which he'd represented the Football League and England at full international level on eight occasions, scoring a phenomenal 13 times.

country during the conflict – falling on the battlefield in France on 30 November 1917. The ill-fated Bill Kennedy, who had his West Ham career cut short by injury, also perished in battle while serving the London Scottish Regiment in France. So too did Frank Costello, an inside forward with the club in 1908-09 – killed in action early in the war – and Frank Cannon, a centre forward in 1909-10, who fell in February 1916. George Hilson did not escape unscathed either, suffering the effects of mustard gas poisoning while serving the East Surrey Regiment.

Although Southern League football was suspended for the duration of the war, the game still continued at home, albeit in the somewhat ersatz form of the London Combination. Made up of Southern League and Southern-based Football League clubs, team selection often relied on the availability of 'guest' players who could be from any team in the country, but billeted from the south.

West Ham, in particular, made full use of the system and some famous names appeared in claret and blue to supplement their often depleted ranks. Danny Shea was a welcome returnee and was joined by the other star performers such as later Hammers legend Ted Hufton and Bill Masterman of Sheffield United, Andy Cunningham from Glasgow Rangers and George Harrison, John Macconachie, W. Kirsopp and Sam Chedgzoy, all members of Everton's 1914-1915 Championship-winning team. Chedgzoy, who was a winger, was credited for being responsible for forcing a change in the laws of the game. On one occasion Everton were awarded a corner-kick, he dribbled the ball into the opposing penalty area, rightly claiming that there was nothing in the rule book at that time outlawing such an act.

With such radical reformers on board, it was hardly surprising that the Hammers had an impressive record in the London Combination which read: 1915-16 – 4th; Supplementary tournament – 2nd; 1916-17 – 1st; 1917-18 – 2nd; 1918-19 – 3rd.

This good track record helped considerably when West Ham United successfully applied to join the enlarged Second Division of the Football League following the Armistice of November 1918, to open a new and exciting chapter in the club's history.

At the acceptance meeting held in Manchester, March 1919, Hammers polled 32 votes behind Coventry's 35 following a vigorous campaign to gain the support of the Football League club chairmen. Finally they were in the élite. The Southern League authorities were none too pleased with West Ham, however, fining their former members the colossal sum of £500 for failing to serve them proper notice.

Castle Street in 1905, with the uncovered South Bank on the left.

Chapter Three: 1919-23
Into the Leagues... and the Cup

For the first historic Football League match against Lincoln City at Upton Park on 30 August 1919, Hammers fans had to fork out double the amount they'd paid before the war. But the new 1/- (5p) admission price didn't deter 20,000 die-hards from turning up to watch their heroes in their elevated status. In the event it was all a bit of an anti-climax as the teams fought out a 1-1 draw. To inside right James Moyes goes the honour of scoring the club's first ever League goal, equalising the Imps' earlier penalty goal in the 65th minute.

A crushing 7-0 defeat at Barnsley set alarm bells ringing a couple of days later but King's six changes for the return fixture against Lincoln steadied the ship as Hammers ran out 4-1 winners at Sincil Bank in the shadow of the great cathedral.

Although the fourth match of the season saw Barnsley complete a quick double on 8 September, with a 2-0 victory at Upton Park, Hammers actually finished the season six places above the Yorkshiremen in seventh position as Syd King drew upon the experience of the biggest ever peacetime playing staff at his disposal which numbered 39.

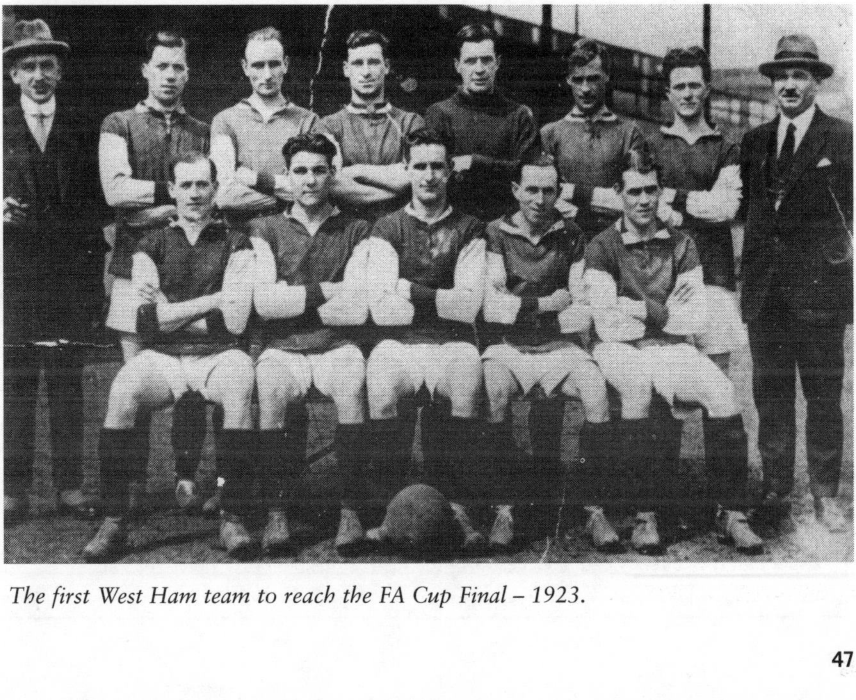

The first West Ham team to reach the FA Cup Final – 1923.

Among the survivors from the pre-war days was the tough tackling full back Billy Cope who was signed from Oldham Athletic in 1914 and was reckoned to be a better exponent of the offside trap than Newcastle's famous Bill McCracken; his regular partner Frank 'Bronco' Burton who was born in Mexico and recovered from shrapnel wounds received while serving the Royal Fusiliers in World War I; wing half Alf Fenwick who was signed from Hull City; fellow half back 'Dapper Dan' Woodards who later became groundsman; left or right half Jack Tresadern who would play in the 1923 Cup final and later manage Spurs; winger Dick Leafe, who later joined the backroom staff; veteran inside forward and later half back, Jack Macksey; inside forwards Dan Bailey and George Butcher and, of course, the great Syd Puddefoot.

The new recruits were legendary goalie Ted 'Tiger' Hufton, who was sometimes tagged the 'penalty king' due to his propensity for saving spot-kicks and who went on to play over 400 times for the first team, winger turned full back Jack Young, who came from Southend United and played in the 1923 FA Cup final alongside Hufton, and Percy Allen who was commissioned during World War I and was an ever-present during the 1921-22 season at right half.

50 Greatest Players

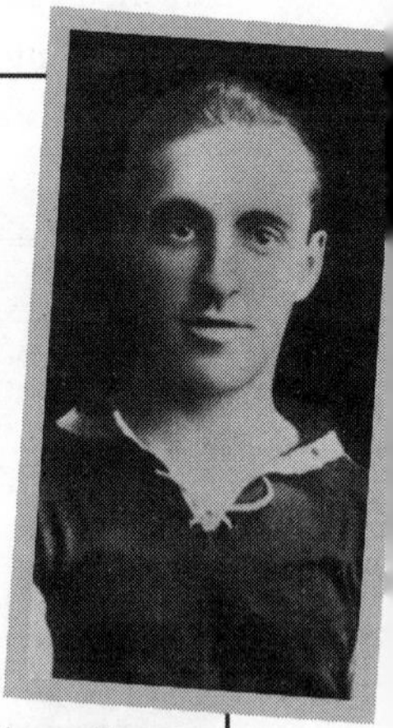

SYD PUDDEFOOT Forward

Born: Bow, London, 17 October, 1894

Joined West Ham: 1912 **From:**

Debut: v Norwich City (h), 1 March 1913

Appearances: 194 **Goals:** 107

Left West Ham: 1922, 1933 **For:** Falkirk (returning in 1932), retired

The transfer of Syd Puddefoot in February 1922 for a record £5,000 to Scottish Division 1 club Falkirk, for whom he had guested during World War I, was sensational. His departure, which nearly caused a riot among Hammers fans, was explained in the programme for the fixture with Hull City on 11 February, 1922, 'The departure of Syd Puddefoot came as no surprise to those intimately connected with him. It is an old saying that everyone has one chance in life to improve themselves and Syd Puddefoot is doing the right thing for himself in studying his future. We understand that he will be branching out in commercial circles in Falkirk and when his football days are over he will be assured of a nice little competency.' It is likely that the calm tone of the notes were influenced by the fact that the club were richer and aware that they already had a successor in the team at inside left... Victor Watson.

A team group of the renowned Park School, featuring Jim Barrett (middle row) and the boy who inspired the 'Bubbles' theme song, Bill Murray (bottom left)

Steady, if unspectacular progress was made during the team's first three seasons in the Second Division leading up to the halcyon days of 1922-1923 as Hammers finished 7th in 1919-20, 5th in 1920-21 and 4th in 1921-22.

In the same seasons, Hammers bowed out if the FA Cup 3-0 at Spurs in the third round (then the equivalent of today's fifth round as First and Second Division clubs entered in round one), 1-0 in the first round at Sheffield Wednesday and 1-0 to Swansea Town at Ashton Gate after 0-0 and 1-1 draws with the Swans in the first round.

The 'Bubbles' Story

Incidentally, a history of Swansea City published in 1982 threw up a connection with the South Wales club and the theme song that Hammers have long regarded solely as their own, 'I'm Forever Blowing Bubbles'.

Commenting on a game from the 1920-21 season, the history states, 'In January, Bury, were drawn to play at the Vetch in the first round of the FA Cup and 21,300 people thronged the ground to create a new attendance record, having paid £1,470 for the privilege. One feature of the game which was to be repeated for many years was the singing of "Bubbles", with the crowd on the main bank swaying back and forth in unison as they sang.' No doubt the song was in evidence again as the Swans won 1-0 in that second replay at Bristol City's ground in the 1921-22 season.

Team Changes

The events of the latter season were destined to be overshadowed in any case by the sensational transfer of Syd Puddefoot in February 1922 for a record £5,000 to Scottish First Division club Falkirk, who he had guested for during World War I.The calm manner with which West Ham announced the news was probably dictated by the fact that the club were now £5,000 richer and aware of the fact that they already had Puddey's successor in the number 9 shirt in the team at inside left... Victor Watson. Signed for the princely sum of £50 from Wellingborough the previous summer, Cambridgeshire-born Watson was destined to set every goalscoring record in the club's history and play centre forward for England.

Several other components of West Ham's great side of 1922-23 were also in place, including full back William Henderson who had joined Hammers from Aberdare in January 1922 to replace the injured Jack Hebden; Cup final captain and centre half George Kay who was formerly with Bolton Wanderers and went on to manage Southampton and Liverpool whom he led to the First Division Championship in 1946-47; his wing half partner Syd 'Sticks' Bishop who later joined Leicester where he was capped for England; play-anywhere utility man Billy Brown, who also won an England cap, and the immortal Jimmy Ruffell who became Hammers' highest ever scoring winger and held the club's appearance record until his 548 total was overhauled by Bobby Moore in 1973. Jim played six times for England.

Further fortified by the signings of inside forward Billy Moore from Sunderland and Charlie Crossley from Everton, in addition to wingers Billy Charlton and Dick Richards from South Shields and Wolves respectively, Hammers kicked off the 1922-23 season with high hopes of achieving their long-held ambition – promotion to the First Division.

Yet in a disastrous start during which Hammers won just three of their opening 14 fixtures, losing seven and drawing the remaining four, the season seemed to hold little in store with the possible exception of relegation to the Third Division South. Then an amazing spell of 32 league and FA Cup matches, during which they suffered just one defeat, saw them not only challenging for promotion but through to the first ever FA Cup final to be staged at Wembley against First Division Bolton Wanderers.

Far from impeding their progress in the league, Irons' marathon cup run seemed to help the momentum of the push for promotion as the Eastenders accounted for Hull City, Brighton, after a replay, Plymouth and Southampton, following two replays, to set up a semi-final clash with fellow Second Division side Derby County. Although they trailed West Ham by some 12 places in the Second Division table, Derby had disposed of Blackpool, Bristol City, Sheffield Wednesday and Spurs to reach the last four without conceding a goal and were regarded as favourites by most critics to go through.

One member of the 50,795 that assembled at Stamford Bridge was life-long Hammers fan the late George Kerr who used to live in Boleyn Road. George told the story in his own words, before he died in 1997, how the Hammers took the lead against Derby,

'I arrived at the Bridge in good time and took up a position to the right of an area known as the Shed. According to the critics Derby were favourites to win this one, largely based on what they had done to Tottenham Hotspur in the previous round at White Hart Lane.

'West Ham lined up: Hufton, Henderson, Young, Bishop, Kay, Tresadern, Richards, Brown, Watson, Moore, Ruffell.

'For the first few minutes the ball hardly left the Hammers' half. Then Hufton took a goal-kick straight down the middle. Watson trapped the ball then swung around hitting it out to the left about 10 yards ahead of Ruffell who took it in his stride and carried it about another 20 yards before he swung over a slightly lofted centre which Brown volleyed into the top left-hand corner of the net.'

It was the spark which lit the powder keg as a few minutes later a free-kick from the halfway line by Tresadern was pounced on by the Geordie Brown who unleashed a terrific shot at goal. Olney, the Derby goalkeeper could only push it out to where Moore was waiting, to put the unfancied Irons two up with just 10 minutes gone.

A minute into the second half a fine passing movement between Ruffell and Moore ended up with the latter holding the ball, beating two defenders before shooting a third past the hapless Olney. Then, after a fine solo run, Watson laid on a fourth for Brown to put the unfashionable former works team within touching distance of the first Wembley Cup final. Hammers' hearts fluttered briefly when Derby hit a double riposte to pull the score back to 4-2 but a fierce cross-shot from Ruffell sealed a famous victory. West Ham had reached the FA Cup final.

Cup final captain George Kay.

Great Matches

FA CUP FINAL **Wembley, London, 28 April 1923**

Bolton Wanderers 2 West Ham United 0 **Attendance: 126,047**
Jack
J.R. Smith

Exhilarated by the Hammers' great semi-final victory over the Rams, 17-year-old George Kerr was up bright and early on the morning of Saturday, 28 April 1923 – Cup final day!

'Having witnessed the thrilling victory at Stamford Bridge, I was thrilled to bits and I booked my seat on a London General Omnibus, open-topped, "top heavy" bus with solid tyres to go to Wembley. It was scheduled to leave Barking at 11 a.m. but actually left at 11.30 a.m. But who cared? With a 3 p.m. kick-off there was no worry, or so we thought.

'In those days there was no North Circular Road, so we had to go straight up through Aldgate. From there I could no more tell of the route than fly. We made continual diversions and nearly all the traffic seemed to be going in one direction. It should be borne in mind that normally, in those days, there was only a fraction of the traffic that we have today. But, in spite of this, after leaving Aldgate we were making diversions about every half a mile. But there was a carnival atmosphere in the air heightened by the fantastic embellishing of some of the vehicles, many trade vehicles carrying the colours. One that stands out in my mind was a brewer's lorry. It carried a gigantic hammer made out of a very large beer barrel serving as the head, with a large tree trunk serving as the handle about 10 ft (3 m) long, inserted into the barrel and it looked about 15 ins (38 cm) in diameter at the thick end. It was brilliantly decorated with the claret and blue and there were two smaller hammers made in the same fashion placed either side of the big one. They also carried about five or six supporters at times rendering "Bubbles" or chanting "one, two three, four, five... ", as were many others we met up with en route.

'All along the route the roads were lined with onlookers, many giving us vocal support. I remember going through the Harrow Road and the Harlesden area. When we were about two or three miles away from the stadium we suffered a shock. We were told by some coming away from the stadium that it was no good going on because the gates were closed, but we pressed on. The buses finally stopped about three-quarters of a mile away from the stadium which was about as close as they could get. I ran the last three-quarters of a mile. I saw that the turnstiles had been built into wooden structures that were about 8 ft (2.5 m) high, the turnstiles themselves were locked and deserted but bodies were climbing over them like monkeys and I quickly followed suit. These structures formed an outside perimeter with about 50 yards (45 m) to go to the steps leading to the entrance gates. These, as we had rightly been told, were all shut. However, I noticed that there was a large bulge of bodies at one spot. Here the iron gates had been smashed down, unbelievably so because they looked strong enough to withstand anything that might be used on them.

'I got behind the crowd and soon was being pushed forward by others who got behind me. I was literally pushed into the ground. I reached the top of the steps of the terrace and had to keep going straight forward because of the pressure behind, then there was another surprise. I could not see the pitch. The position was at one end of the ground close to the goal area. I progressed from there to my right until I was adjacent to one of the main stands, the one opposite the royal box. I should point out that the thought in most everybody's mind was that there would be no game. At that point I had a large slice of good fortune. I happened to glance behind me at the stand and saw that there were large open spaces and, for no particular reason, I climbed over the barrier into the stand. Minutes after this the mounted police made their entrance including the famous Grey. When they started charging at the crowd, there was a stampede for safety.

'The stand where I was quickly filled as did all the other available spaces in the

PC George Scorey and Billie the famous white horse.

stands. When a space had been made in the centre of the pitch the teams came on. The pitch was finally cleared but only just. The half circles behind each goal were completely covered by the crowd sitting on the grass. Likewise, the spaces all around the ground beside the touchlines were all filled. In front of them and all seated was a line of policemen with their arms linked to hold the crowd behind them. Play got underway but two or three times in the first few minutes play had to be stopped because in some places on the touchline the police could not bear the strain of the pressure behind them and their blockade broke with bodies falling over the line. But after a few minutes this was sorted out and play proceeded.

Happy Hammers fans await the start of the match – it was not to be their day.

'It must be said that the conditions did not suit West Ham. They relied heavily upon speed and the long ball, usually using Jimmy Ruffell plied by the other speed merchant Victor Watson. But it was clearly inhibiting to Ruffell with the danger of tripping over spectators' legs and the general feeling of being jammed in. Bolton, on the other hand, had Ted Vizard at outside left, a full Welsh international, sturdily built and a great tactician.

'The first goal came after about six minutes play and it emanated from these two. The ball was held between them – Vizard was close to the touchline about level with the edge of the West Ham penalty area with Smith about 12 yards to the right and towards the centre of the field. Each were static and were banging the ball backwards and forwards first time to each other. Sid Bishop stood off about midway between the two nearer to his own goal and his head was going backwards and forwards like a spectator on the centre court of Wimbledon, only the movement was faster. After Smith received the ball for about the fourth time he allowed it to pass him on the left and swung around to hit it with his right foot back towards the centre circle where David Jack was laying in wait unmarked. He took the ball in his stride and, with a dribble between Tresadern and Young, hit a beautiful shot into the top left-hand corner of the net. Hufton went for it but was unable to reach. It was a great goal and I got the impression that it was a well rehearsed ploy. Smith's pass to Jack was delivered with pinpoint accuracy although he had not once looked in that direction until he turned and hit it. To me it seemed clear that he knew where to find Jack before he turned. The rest of the half was fairly even, neither side creating anything of any significance. The second half saw Hammers create the only real scoring chance that I can recall. It was a hard low cross from Richards on the right wing arriving about chest-high outside the six-yard box. Watson went for it and had he contacted he must have scored but Pym, the goalie, managed to get his hand to it, knocking it down and collecting it. The Bolton second goal came about ten minutes into the second half. It was through a breakaway on the right, the centre came in and George Kay at the centre half went for it but was beaten by J.R. Smith who hit a fast ground shot inside the right post and that was it.

'The conditions certainly did not suit the Hammers' style of play and I believe that a different result might have been possible if conditions had been normal. But it has to be said that Bolton were the more experienced side. I left the ground somewhat disappointed for West Ham.

'I then began to think about my return journey and worry about finding my bus. I had made no special note of its position when I left it. I hurried back and without a lot of trouble, found it. But of the six buses that left Barking together, only one remained. The equivalent of five bus-loads did not reach the stadium or if they did they were unable to gain entrance. As I left the stadium a bunch of Bolton supporters began taking the mickey, chanting: "Five, four, three, two, one, nought" – with the emphasis on the nought. This, I should add, was all in good fun. Hostility between rival supporters in those days was unheard of. Along the road our contingent were a little disheartened but some of them decided to liven themselves up by chanting: "Five, four, three, two, one, nought" – greeted by other onlooking supporters with cries of, "But you're going the wrong way!" I got off the bus when it reached the Boleyn public house at the top of Green Street which was close to my home address, tired and hungry but happy that I had witnessed and experienced something quite out of the ordinary.'

Bolton Wanderers: Pym, Haworth, Finney, Nuttall, Seddon, Jennings, Butler, Jack, Smith JR, Smith J, Vizard.

West Ham United: Hufton, Henderson, Young, Bishop, Kay, Tresadern, Richards, Brown, Watson, Moore, Ruffell.

Referee: D.H. Asson

From Cup Agony to Promotion Glory

Hammers didn't have time to feel sorry for themselves for long in the aftermath of the emotionally draining 2-0 defeat by Bolton. Although two successive away defeats at Barnsley (2-0) on 16 April and at Notts County by the same deficit two day's later had dented their promotion hopes, a 1-0 victory against Fulham, thanks to a vital strike from Vic Watson at Upton Park on 21 April, had kept Hammers in contention.

Just two days after the chaotic scenes and fiasco of Wembley, King's leg weary troops pulled off a tremendous 2-0 victory at Sheffield Wednesday to go to the top of the Second Division ahead of Leicester on goal average and ensure that the promotion issue would go right to the last day of the season on Saturday, 5 May 1923.

West Ham, Leicester and Notts County went into the final fixture level at the top with 51 points each. As if anything was needed to heighten the excitement of the final day, Notts County were the visitors to Upton Park. Leicester were playing at Bury that same afternoon, but kicking off earlier (were Sky involved in the schedule?). For Hammers the equation was simple – if they won, the Championship was theirs. If City and County both won they went up, if it was a draw and City won, Leicester would be Champions and West Ham would be promoted with a better goal average than County. If Leicester lost, County and Hammers would win promotion regardless of the result at Upton Park.

With the expectations and tensions running at an almost unbearably high level, the teams lined up as follows: West Ham United: Hampson, Henderson, Young, Bishop, Kay, Tresadern, Richards, Moore, Watson, Brown, Ruffell. Notts County: Iremonger, Ashurst, Cope, Flint, Dinsdale, Wren, Platts, Cooper, Cock, Hill, Price.

In an almost carnival atmosphere, the majority of the 'full-house' crowd of 26,000 had come to pay homage to West Ham's gallant cup finalists and urge them to make the last effort needed to join football's elite.

Reporting on the match for the *Daily Graphic*, 'Corinthian' timed the first goal as coming seven minutes before half-time, but unfortunately for Hammers and the wildly partisan crowd it was scored by Hill of County.

Hammers toiled tirelessly in the second half for what they believed might be a vital equaliser but they needn't have worried as 'Corinthian' explained so eloquently, 'The news of Leicester's loss was signalled from the veranda of the director's pavilion whilst a fierce struggle was going on around the Notts goal. Immediately there was a cheer, which swelled into a mighty roar as it was taken up by the crowd all around the ground.

50 Greatest Players

BILLY MOORE Winger

Born: Newcastle-upon-Tyne, 6 October 1894

Joined West Ham: 1922 **From:** Sunderland

Debut: v Bradford City, 26 August 1922

Appearances: 202 **Goals:** 48

Left West Ham: 1929 (retired)

An interesting sidelight to the West Ham v Derby game was revealed in an auction of football memorabilia at Christies in Glasgow which took place on 14 October 1992. Lot 201 was 'A leather football used in the FA Cup semi-final between West Ham and Derby County on 24 March 1923, autographed by the West Ham team who won 5-2, belonging to Billy Moore.'

Also the property of the canny Geordie was lot 202 – 'A leather football autographed by both Bolton and West Ham teams who took part in the 1923 Cup final.' Bill played in all 51 of Hammers' first-team fixtures in his first season, following his arrival from Sunderland. His playing career ended in 1928-29, by which time he'd made 202 appearances and scored 48 goals in addition to winning an England cap against Sweden in 1923 when he scored two goals in the England victory. On his retirement he was appointed assistant trainer under Charlie Paynter for three seasons before becoming head of the training staff. He held this position for a further 28 years until he retired in May 1960. He sadly passed away in 1968, at the age of 73.

'For the moment the players were confounded and the play seemed to hang in suspense, but immediately the loss of enthusiasm became apparent – it was a thrilling scene. An interesting touch was added when Donald Cock, the Notts County centre, found the opportunity on the field to shake hands with George Kay, the West Ham captain.'

George Kerr saw things from a slightly different angle: 'The second half began much as before, with the Hammers striving hard but creating little in the way of scoring chances.

'As time began to run out the crowd became more and more subdued, there was high drama, but not on the pitch. The half-time scoreboard was situated in an elevated position at the rear of the North Bank. At the extreme right as we looked at it was a cubby-hole with a telephone and in which the operator was housed. We noticed that he was walking along the gang-plank to the opposite end and having reached it adjacent to the sign which would indicate the score of the Leicester City v Bury match, he marked the full-time result – 0-1 to Bury. Immediately the mood of the crowd was transformed from one of utter dejection to complete ecstasy.

'We were in the First Division!'

Having pipped Leicester on goal average, the importance of Hammers' 6-0 win at Filbert Street back in February now took on a new significance and the goals scored by Moore (3), Richards, Ruffell and Tresadern were worth their weight in gold.

Ivan Sharpe, talking about goalkeepers in his book, *40 Years in Football* published in the 1950s, told an amusing tale regarding the West Ham v Notts County match, 'Fatty Foulke was big and beefy, really fat. Noticeably tall – fully 6 ft 4 ins (1.95m), lean as a lamp-post and still more colourful as a character was Albert Iremonger, who stayed for 20 years beneath the crossbar of Notts County and was one of the most difficult goalkeepers to defeat in the whole history of the game.

'He was an exasperating opponent because a ball which would beat nine goalkeepers out of 10 would be tipped out of danger by this man with the telescopic touch.

'A woman at West Ham ran onto the field in 1923 and assaulted him with her umbrella because he was threatening to stand between United and promotion to the First Division of the League.'

Some things never change!

50 Greatest Players

GEORGE KAY Centre half

Born: Manchester, 21 September 1891

Joined West Ham: 1919 **From:** Bolton Wanderers

Debut: v Barnsley, 8 September 1919

Appearances: 259 **Goals:** 17

Left West Ham: 1926 **For:** Stockport County

George was the first West Ham player to chalk up 200 Football League appearances in claret and blue and had the honour of skippering the side which won promotion to the First Division and reached the first FA Cup final to be staged at Wembley in 1923. Formerly with Bolton Wanderers, George recorded another first when he became the only Englishman ever to captain an Irish League team during his spell with Belfast Celtic. Along with team-mate Jack Tresadern, George was one of the first ex-Hammers to make a mark in management as boss of Southampton and Liverpool whom he steered to the First Division Championship in 1946-47 and also the 1950 FA Cup final v Arsenal.

Chapter Four: 1923-32
Into the Top Flight

As a reward for their prodigious efforts in reaching the FA Cup final and the exalted heights of the First Division, the players were taken on tour to Hungary and Austria during the summer of 1923. The trip continued a trend that had begun in 1921 when West Ham won all four of their tour matches in Spain without conceding a goal to forge their first links on the continent. Again Hammers returned home undefeated despite being without Moore and Tresadern who were on duty for England on tour in Sweden.

Three of the five new faces who signed up at the start of that historic first season in Division One, centre half 'Big Jim' Barrett, wing half Jimmy 'Lottie' Collins and winger Tommy Yews, would go on to amass 1,164 league and cup appearances between them and become household names in the East End.

Goalkeeper Bill Kaine – who like Barrett and Collins was a product of local football – and inside forward Norman Proctor from Rotherham County, made just seven first-team appearances each in comparison.

Two days after drawing 0-0 with Sunderland before a 35,000 crowd at Roker Park in their first ever Division One match on 25 August 1923, Hammers were hosts to Arsenal. Playing without Vic Watson who was injured at Roker Park and sidelined for most of the season, his replacement Albert Fletcher got himself into the history books with the only goal of the game against the Gunners, but like James Moyes who had scored Hammers' first league goal in 1919, it was destined to be the only goal that he scored in the claret and blue.

Dominance of the North

It was the beginning of a nine-year association with the First Division for Hammers during which they were never able to seriously challenge the dominance of the northern clubs like Huddersfield Town, Newcastle United and Sheffield Wednesday in the league, only once finishing as high as sixth in 1926-27 and seventh in 1929-30 when Vic Watson set the club goalscoring record with 50 goals in 44 league and cup games.

On two occasions Hammers progressed to the sixth round of the FA Cup to revive memories of their earlier triumphs, reaching that stage in 1928-29 when they lost unluckily 3-2 at Portsmouth, when Jim Barrett scored twice playing at inside left, and again the following season when losing 3-0 at home to Arsenal having defeated arch rivals Millwall 4-1 in the previous round at Upton Park. Typically, West Ham gained revenge the next Saturday when the same 22 men took the field at the same venue for a First Division fixture by winning 3-1.

West Ham finished seven places above Arsenal in the First Division table in that 1929-30 season in seventh position but Arsenal went on to win the cup by beating Huddersfield Town 2-0 at Wembley.

Huddersfield, who'd won the First Division Championship in 1924 and 1925 under the management of visionary Herbert Chapman were also successful in 1926 when they finished five points ahead of Arsenal to become the first club to win a hat-trick of titles, even though Chapman had left them to join the Highbury club. With four matches left to play of the 1925-26 season, West Ham were the visitors to Town's Leeds Road ground on 10 April 1926, when the Yorkshiremen hoped to clinch their unique 'treble'. Among the 25,000 crowd that day hoping to cheer Town on to victory was Huddersfield-born future Labour Prime Minister Harold Wilson.

'The game against West Ham was to be the most crucial of the season,' recalled Lord Wilson in Fred Eyre's book, *Star Games*, published in 1984, 'and it provided me with my proudest moment in football.'

'There was an extra air of excitement about the town on the morning of the match,' he remembered. 'I could feel the expectancy as the tram clanged

By 1925 West Ham had established themselves as a First Division outfit.

Full back Alf Earl was a regular fixture on the team bus in the late 1920s.

its way to Leeds Road. Most Yorkshiremen knew we were just a few hours away from a unique record in Association Football, a hat-trick of league titles. This was the dawn of a memorable day.'

'Young Harold Wilson arrived at the ground around 11 o'clock as usual,' Eyre continued, 'only to find that his normal position, just to the right-hand side of the goal, had been taken, so he moved down towards the corner flag.

'Loud cheers greeted the home side as skipper Clem Stephenson led them onto the field... but they were aghast at the audacity of West Ham who showed scant respect for Town's reputation and set about spoiling the proposed celebration by taking the lead after only six minutes through Stan Earle.

'A change of tactics by Huddersfield after half-time brought an immediate and sensational impact. Town started to feed the ball to Alec Jackson much more and the little winger responded with two goals in a five-minute spell.

'The first came by courtesy of the good old-fashioned shoulder-charge as goalkeeper Hufton caught a tame shot from Cook and proceeded to pirouette around his penalty area, casually wasting time before the statuary boot up-field.

'This was fatal with a man like George Brown rampaging about,' laughed Lord Wilson, 'and the Huddersfield centre forward simply charged him over, gained possession of the ball as it squirmed from the keeper's grasp and knocked it square to Jackson who gratefully sidefooted into the empty net.

50 Greatest Players

TED HUFTON Goalkeeper

Born: Southwell, Notts, 25 November 1892

Joined West Ham: 1919 **From:** Sheffield United

Debut: v Lincoln City, 30 August 1919

Appearances: 402

Left West Ham: 1933 **For:** Watford

Ted 'Tiger' Hufton holds the unique distinction of being the only West Ham goalkeeper to have been capped at full international level by England. Injured in action with the Coldstream Guards during World War I, it was after he had been on sick leave recovering from shrapnel wounds that he made the first of 64 war-time guest appearances for Hammers. Also nicknamed the 'Penalty King' for saving 11 out of 18 spot-kicks against him in two seasons, he won the first of six caps v Belgium in 1924. Ted was an ever-present in Hammers' nine-match 1922-23 FA Cup run which led to the first historic final v Bolton Wanderers at Wembley.

'Two minutes later Jackson scored again – but this goal was a much more clinical affair, started in midfield by Cook who hit a lovely pass into Jackson's path.'

'I met Alec Jackson years later,' recalled Lord Wilson, 'and I spoke to him about that historic game and asked him of his memories of the great occasion.

'He obviously immediately remembered his two goals – and I then reminded him that in the dying seconds West Ham were still pressing and Ruffell had the ball on the left wing confronted by Roy Goodall.

'The West Ham winger jinked past Goodall and was about to centre when a flurry of blue and white appeared from nowhere and booted the ball off his toe and into the crowd behind the goal for a corner.

'Jackson laughed and recalled the incident vividly because he didn't often come back to help in defensive situations – but with only seconds to go in this crucial affair he thought it wise.'

Alec then confided that because tackling wasn't really one of his strong points in his game he was happy simply to boot the ball into the crowd... but was horrified to see it smack a little boy in the face.

'I know,' said Harold Wilson triumphantly to his hero. 'That little boy was me. And it was the proudest moment of my football life... being knocked over by a shot from the immortal Alec Jackson!'

Stanley Earle, who scored the Hammers goal at Leeds Road which almost forced Town to put their Championship celebrations on hold, was a leading light at inside right in the Hammers' attack of the 1920s and early 30s. He had bagged two goals playing for Arsenal against Hammers when the Gunners won 4-1 in a First Division clash at Highbury in 1923. As he was still an amateur at the time, Hammers were able to sign him the following year and he went on to sign pro and appear in 273 league and cup games in the claret and blue in which he scored 58 goals and made countless others for his colleagues. A superbly creative player who stood at six-foot plus, he was capped for England versus Northern Ireland in 1928 when he helped his country to a 2-1 victory at Goodison Park with West Ham team-mate Hufton.

Alf Earl, a tall constructive full back who played almost 200 times during the same era as his near namesake Stan, became famous for scoffing four hot-cross buns one Good Friday morning before a match and collapsing with indigestion on the field. Alf, who naturally enough was born in Earlsfield, later played for a French team, Seucaux, in Paris where he no doubt further cultivated his gastronomic tendencies.

Another great amateur who starred for Hammers over virtually the same 10-year or so period between 1923 and 1932, was centre forward Vivian Gibbins, who like Stan Earle began his career with local amateurs Clapton and won the first of his two full England caps along with Stan, scoring in a 3-1 win against France in Paris in May, 1924.

West Ham tour party circa late 1920s.

50 Greatest Players

JACK TRESADERN Wing half

Born: Leytonstone, London, 1893

Joined West Ham: 1913 **From:** Barking

Debut: v Watford (Southern League), 1 April 1914

Appearances: 166 **Goals:** 5

Left West Ham: 1924 **For:** Burnley

A tenacious, tough tackling wing half, Jack was yet another of the 1923 FA Cup final side to be picked for England, against Scotland and Sweden in 1923. A prominent amateur before joining the paid ranks, 'Tres' served in the Royal Garrison Artillery in World War I along with George Kat and the pair became the forerunners of the famed West Ham managerial 'Academy' when they took up management after hanging up their boots, Jack with Northampton Town, Crystal Palace, Spurs (who he guided into the First Division) and Plymouth Argyle. He took up the reins of three non-league clubs after the war, Chelmsford City, Hastings United and Tonbridge.

Decline and Fall

As the 'roaring twenties' gave way to the threat-filled thirties, the Upton Park crowds could have been excused for thinking that their team's First Division status would be preserved during the new decade, given the top class players at manager Syd King's disposal.

Hufton, Barrett, Earle, Watson, Gibbins, Ruffell and later a briefly returning Puddefoot – England internationals whose names tripped off the tongue like a fine vintage claret.

Vic Watson, in particular, ended the decade on a high-note and had it not been for a certain Dixie Dean, he would surely have been England's automatic choice at centre forward. His record-breaking season of 1929-30, when he scored nine goals in three matches against Leeds United alone to revive memories of his six-goal haul in an 8-2 win over the hapless Yorkshiremen the previous season, saw him picked ahead of Dean, however, whose Everton side had finished rock-bottom of Division One and been relegated. Vic was wearing the number nine shirt against Scotland at Wembley in April 1930 and scored two of the goals as England almost exacted complete revenge for the 'Wembley Wizards' 5-1 win there two years previously when Ted Hufton was in goal, by winning 5-2.

Hammers began the 1930-31 season the same way as they'd ended the previous campaign – brimful of goals and gusto. Following a 2-1 opening day win over Huddersfield at Upton Park, courtesy of two more goals from Cambridgeshire-born Watson, the rampant router of opposing defenders doubled that tally two days later when he plundered four more in a 7-0 slaughter of Liverpool as Hammers again fully capitalised on their home advantage.

A sign of things to come surfaced in the first away game, however, when Aston Villa gained ample revenge for a 3-2 defeat inflicted by the Hammers when Watson hit a hat-trick at Villa Park the previous April, by winning 6-1 before a 40,000 crowd in Birmingham when 'Pongo' Waring hit four of Villa's goals and Watson almost inevitably scored the East Londoners' solitary reply. By the time the Hammers met Villa in the return fixture of that 1930-31 season on 3 January 1931 alarm bells were ringing at Upton Park. Still reeling from a 6-1 defeat sustained five days before Christmas at Sunderland and languishing in the lower reaches of the First Division, Hammers must have faced the visit of high-scoring Villa with some apprehension. But Irons could have won by the odd goal in 11 had they been awarded a certain penalty.

The week after the 5-5 thriller with Villa, Chelsea ended East London's FA Cup hopes with a 3-1 third round victory at the Boleyn and, in a sad decline, the team could finish no higher than 18th in the First Division table to give a fore-warning of what was to come in 1931-32.

50 Greatest Players

VICTOR WATSON Striker

Born: Girton, Cambridgeshire, 10 November 1897

Joined West Ham: 1920 **From:** Wellingborough

Debut: v Port Vale, 3 September 1921

Appearances: 505 **Goals:** 326

Left West Ham: 1935 **For:** Southampton

Vic Watson scored on his debut for West Ham and forgot to stop! The holder of all the club's scoring records, the broad shouldered number nine remains West Ham's most prolific goalscorer of all time. Another member of the 1923 FA Cup final side, he contributed five goals on the run up to Wembley and was awarded the first of his five England caps the same year. Scored six against Leeds at Upton Park (9 February 1929) and the following season hit a bullseye of goals with 42 First Division tallies and eight in the FA Cup. The six goal blast v Leeds apart, Vic scored four goals in a match on three separate occasions and an amazing 13 hat-tricks during his Hammers career.

Fresh from a three-match unbeaten mini tour of Switzerland, there was no hint of the trials and tribulations to come as Hammers opened the season with a 1-0 first-ever victory over Bolton Wanderers at Burnden Park which, according to contemporary reports, was far more convincing than the scoreline suggested.

Two days later, Watson, who'd lost no time in opening his account at Bolton, was again on the scoresheet with Tony Weldon, who'd been signed from Hull City and ex-Villa utility man Fred Norris, in a 3-1 win over London rivals Chelsea at Boleyn Castle.

However, even disastrous defeats in succession put an entirely different complexion on the season. Two goals from Watson in a 2-1 FA Cup third round victory over Charlton at the Valley in early January raised hopes that the competition might provide some relief from Hammers' plight in the First Division, but in the next round Chelsea knocked out their East London rivals for the second successive season by the same 3-1 scoreline, this time at Stamford Bridge.

Following successive away defeats at Sheffield Wednesday 6-1, Blackpool 7-2 and a 3-1 home reverse to Blackburn Rovers, another 6-1 defeat at Everton – who Hammers had helped consign to the Second Division just two seasons earlier but were now heading for the First Division Championship – drove another nail into the West Ham relegation coffin.

A subsequent match report in the Everton programme of that period exonerated our goalkeeper Ted Hufton of the blame for the reverse: 'The display against the Londoners was brimful of interest and though there was but a narrow margin at the interval, there could be no mistaking our superiority during the second portion. Dunn was the star artist in the forward line, but not among the scorers because of the brilliance of the West Ham goalkeeper Hufton, but for whom a double figure score might have been established.'

The position at the wrong end of the table prior to the last match of the season on 7 May, 1932, had West Ham one place off the bottom with a meagre 31 points, just one ahead of Grimsby Town. To survive Hammers needed a point more than Blackpool and Grimsby not to win at home to third-placed Sheffield Wednesday. In the event they did – and so did Blackpool against Sheffield United at Bramall Lane. But it was all irrelevant because Hammers went down to yet another away defeat, this time by 3-2 to Chelsea in West London after leading 1-0 at half-time West Ham's and manager Syd King's nine-year love affair with the First Division was over. So, almost, was his very life.

Chapter Five: 1932-40
The Depression

Two days after West Ham lost their ninth match of the season at Bradford Park Avenue 3-0 on Guy Fawkes day, 1932, the West Ham board enacted their own version of the 'gunpowder plot'. An abrupt statement in the minutes of the board meeting held at Upton Park on 7 November signalled Syd King's demise: 'It was unanimously decided that until further notice C. Paynter be given sole control of players and that E.S. King be notified accordingly.' The terse announcement which stunned football blew King's world apart and was in direct contrast to one which appeared in the *East Ham Echo* in its FA Cup final edition 10 years earlier which trumpeted, 'West Ham is Syd King'.

King, whose fondness for alcohol was no secret at Upton Park, had allegedly walked into a board meeting in an intoxicated state and 'during the discussion on the team, was drunk and insubordinate'. At an emergency meeting called the following night, King was suspended for three months without pay and banned from the ground for the same period. The board also cast doubts over King's honesty while running the club's affairs and authorised Alan Searles, who had been appointed temporary secretary as a result of the crisis, to collect 'all keys, documents and property' from him.

Ironically, Searles, the trusted bookkeeper, was later sacked because of his 'defalcations' while cheating his employer by 'cooking the books'. Following a turbulent board meeting on 3 January 1933, the secretary (Searles) was instructed to advise King that the board had passed a resolution not to re-employ him in any capacity and he was effectively dismissed, albeit with an ex-gratia payment of £3 a week.

King, who earned £10 a week in 1920 and was presented with a cheque for £1,500 tax free to commemorate his 20 years' service to the club that year, was rich beyond the wildest dreams of 99 per cent of the crowds that flocked to pay to see his teams at the Boleyn Ground. He was also given a bonus of £300 for negotiating the controversial transfer of Syd Puddefoot to Falkirk in 1922 and received a bonus of £100 per annum. In addition to these riches he was also appointed a shareholder in 1931. Not that he had much time to muse on the matter because less than a month after his sacking King committed suicide by consuming an alcoholic beverage laced with a corrosive liquid.

The inquest into his death decided he had killed himself 'while of unsound mind' and noted he had suffered from persecution delusions for some time. His son told the inquest that his father had become very depressed when the team were relegated from the First Division and that his paranoia had begun at that time.

Ted Fenton, who 30 years on would be sacked from his position as West Ham manager by a board of West Ham directors which included descendants of the directorate that dismissed King, recalled his time under King as a young player at Upton Park in the early 1930's in his book *At Home with the Hammers*, published in 1960,

'The boss at West Ham was Syd King, an outsize, larger-than-life character with close-cropped grey hair and a flowing moustache. He was a personality plus man, a man with flair. Awe struck, I would tip-toe past his office but invariably he would spot me. "Boy," he would shout. "Get two dozen bottles of Bass." Down to the Boleyn pub on the corner I would go on my errand and when I got back to the office Syd King would flip me a two-shilling piece for my trouble.'

Last Links with the Iron Works

With Charlie Paynter now at the helm and providing one of the last links of the shipbuilding days at old Thames Iron Works, Hammers suffered just one loss in 10 games up to the turn of the year following that fateful defeat at Valley Parade on 5 November 1932 and were poised to embark on another great cup run destined to take them within a whisker of Wembley.

In the third round Hammers were drawn away to famous amateur side Corinthian and won through to the next round following a comfortable 2-0 victory at the Crystal Palace with goals from Watson and Wally Pollard. First Division West Bromwich Albion fell at Upton Park in the fourth round and this time Watson had a different scoring partner in another 2-0 win – inside forward Arthur Wilson who was signed from Southampton for £500 and would repay that fee 10 times over before the season's end. A Geordie who was equally at home at inside left or right, Arthur liked to get his goals in pairs and did so in four vital Second Division victories at Boleyn Castle that season. The omens looked good for a return to Wembley when Hammers were drawn away at Brighton & Hove Albion in the fifth round, since they'd also met the Seagulls on their way to the first ever final at the twin towers in 1923.

There were even more feelings of *déjà vu* when a record Goldstone Ground crowd of 35,000 witnessed Irons come back from two goals down to force a replay. Watson pulled one back and right half Joe Musgrave struck a memorable equaliser in a repeat of events 10 years previously.

They were even happier four days later when a goal from young left winger Jackie Morton gave their team a 1-0 extra-time win before 36,742 at Upton Park in the replay and a plum home draw against First Division Birmingham in the quarter-finals. Hammers were not overawed at the prospect of meeting the Blues until an off-field incident lengthened the odds against them. Returning from a postponed Second Division fixture at Oldham Athletic on 25 February 1933 in foul weather, Jim Barrett and goalkeeper George Watson were involved in a car accident. 'Big' Jim got away with shock and bruising, but George sustained serious head injuries which would rule him out of the forthcoming cup tie.

Paynter was forced to draft in an untried rookie Pat McMahon who'd been signed from Glasgow junior side St Anthony's. After soaking up half an hour of Birmingham pressure and looking distinctly second best, Hammers had two strokes of luck.

First full back Syd Barkas put an own goal past his England international goalkeeper Harry Hibbs, then the latter was injured trying to prevent Morton scoring a second direct from a corner at the South Bank end just two minutes later.

Further goals from Wilson and Pollard – picked ahead of Puddefoot in a gamble by Paynter – compounded Birmingham's blues and sealed a sensational result setting up the club's biggest match since the 1923 final; a semi-final meeting with Everton – Dixie Dean et al – at Molineux.

Although Barrett made his intention to keep Dixie Dean quiet perfectly clear, it was Everton who took the initiative and scored after only six minutes through their Scottish international inside-forward Jimmy Dunn.

Hammers' hopes were raised just before half-time when Watson equalised with a header after Wilson drew the defence and passed to Morton who centred for the No. 9 to score, but the East Ender's Wembley dreams were dashed when right-winger Ted Critchley, who had been playing in the reserves, scored a 'soft' winner seven minutes from time.

Vic Watson, Hammers' pre-war goal machine.

There was little time to dwell on the exit as the team found themselves embroiled in a dog-eat-dog relegation fight and successive defeats to a Stanley Matthews inspired Stoke City, London rivals Charlton and Chesterfield on a not-so-Good Friday, left Irons propping up the Second Division table and looking favourites for relegation to the Third Division South.

Priceless Goals

The following day saw the start of a remarkable transformation, however, when, with new boys Joe Cockcroft and Len Goulden beginning to exert their influence down the left side, Hammers overcame Forest 4-3 in an exciting clash at Upton Park with goals from Barrett, Gouldon, Morton and Wood. Three more goals from Morton, Pollard and Watson continued the revival and secured a 3-1 win in the return fixture with Chesterfield on Easter Monday to give Hammers hope for their next two vital matches away to Manchester United and at home to Spurs, which would decide their fate. There was no getting away from it. West Ham were in deep water and, despite their nautical heritage, didn't like it one bit.

But 'cometh the hour, cometh the man' as they say and the hero of the hour was undoubtedly inside forward Arthur Wilson who'd taken over the role of the ageing Syd Puddefoot in the side. 'I can still remember my winner when we beat United 2-1 at Old Trafford,' Arthur recalled with relish when interviewed recently. Arthur, who is the club's oldest surviving former player at the grand old age of 91, also remembered, 'It was a real belter from 30 yards. The ball hit the underside of the bar and struck the goalkeeper on the back of the neck before crossing the line. The force of the shot knocked him to the floor.'

Even more crucial was Arthur's next goal for the claret and blue cause the following week. It was the only goal of the vital penultimate game of the season before a packed 35,000 Boleyn crowd against London rivals Spurs, who needed to win to take the Second Division Championship.

In the event, they missed out by one point and had to be content with the runners-up spot behind Stoke while, at the other end of the table, Chesterfield and Charlton were relegated with Hammers escaping the drop by one precious point thanks to Wilson's priceless goal. 'The club promised us a Continental tour as a reward for our efforts,' laments Arthur, whose crucial contribution to the club's history has been overlooked until now. 'But we had to make do with an extra day in Devon when we lost 1-0 at Plymouth in the last match of the season, travelling down on the Thursday instead of the Friday as we normally would.'

It was during a pre-war trip to the naval town that 'Big' Jim Barrett came out with his famous quip while visiting a fish and chip shop with several of his team-mates. Pulling his fashionable trilby down over his eyes, he barked at the startled counter-hand: 'A pennorf of chips for little Jimmy'. Barrett was a great practical joker with a larger-than-life personality as his old team-mate Arthur Wilson confirms, '"Big" Jim was a great character who I used to go to the races with while at West Ham. He was the only bloke I knew who could back the first five winners and still come out losing!'

Another joker of the 1930s was winger Jackie Wood who like Ron Cater, Billy Lewis, Billy West and Ernie Gregory played for Leytonstone who served as an unofficial 'nursery' side for West Ham in those days before the advent of organised youth schemes at the club.

His capers were particularly remembered by Eddie Chapman who joined Hammers in 1937 as a 16-year-old and went on to serve the club for 49 years as a player and secretary and was awarded the Football League long-service award in 1978.

'A famous Jackie Wood prank came at Southend where we used to train one day a week,' recounts Eddie. 'The lads used to have lunch at Garon's Restaurant and one day as we got on the coach to come back to London there was an almighty clatter.

Len Goulden – a prince among inside forwards.

'As everyone sat down in the coach it was discovered that a lot of us had knives and forks stuffed into our coat pockets bearing the name of Garon's – but they were all returned the following week. Needless to say, the mischievous "Woody" was the culprit yet again.'

Ernie Gregory – another recipient of the Football League long-service award in recognition of his 21 years as West Ham's last line of defence, during which time he amassed 406 league and cup appearances – also remembers 'Woody' fondly.

Ernie's all-time West Ham favourite remains that prince among inside forwards, England international Len Goulden, who, as we've heard, was just breaking into the team at the end of the eventful 1932-33 season.

'We've had some great forwards over the years at West Ham but Len was the greatest – the daddy of them all,' our old goalkeeper enthuses. 'He was the one I paid my money to see before the war and I'd signed on the groundstaff myself in 1936.

'Len formed the left-sided triangle with winger Jackie Morton and wing half Joe Cockroft in the great West Ham team of 1939-40, which would have won promotion if it hadn't been for the war. Morton joined Len in the England team and Joe was unlucky not to have been capped with them. I can still see Len now – controlling the ball, he killed it instantly. And that was the heavy old Thomson 'T' ball with the lace. But don't just take my word for it, ask any of the old-timers – they'll tell you the same, Len was the tops.'

Eddie Chapman served West Ham for 49 years, while Ernie Gregory, as a player and then coach, put in 51 years service – a century between them.

A Lack of Ambition?

West Ham never finished as low as the 20th position they occupied in the Second Division table at the end of the 1932-33 season again, managing seventh in 1933-34, third in 1934-35, fourth in 1935-36, sixth in 1936-37, ninth in 1937-38 and eleventh in 1938-39. Over the same period early cup exits were the order of the day with the exception of 1938-39 when they went out at eventual cup winners Portsmouth in the fifth round after an epic three-match encounter with Spurs in round four. Near misses in the promotion stakes in 1934-35 and 1935-36, when they finished third and fourth, led to unfounded allegations that the club lacked ambition and were secretly quite happy to 'poodle along' in the Second Division.

50 Greatest Players

JIM BARRETT Centre half

Born: West Ham, London, 1907

Joined West Ham: 1923 **From:** Fairbairn House Boys Club

Debut: v Spurs, 28 March 1925

Appearances: 467 **Goals:** 53

Left West Ham: 1945 (retired)

'Big' Jim Barrett's name looms large in the history of West Ham. One of the great characters of the inter-war period, anecdotes about his exploits are legion but, most importantly, he formed the solid bedrock of Hammers' defence throughout the 1920s and 30s. He filled every defensive position in his 20 years as a player including one wartime match in goal and was even drafted into attack on occasions with some success. Perversely, he made only one appearance for England. His four minutes on the field against Ireland in 1928, before injury ended his aspirations, remains the shortest recorded international career. He was succeeded by his son, Jim Barrett junior, at Upton Park after the war.

In the penultimate match of the 1934-35 campaign, Hammers had suffered a 3-1 defeat at their old adversaries Bolton Wanderers and, despite winning the last match at home to Oldham Athletic 2-0, subsequently missed out on promotion to second-placed Wanderers on goal average.

The following season Hammers were again in the final shake up with much hinging on the outcome of the final game of the season against fellow promotion candidates Charlton Athletic.

With the gates shut an hour before kick-off on an attendance that some newspapers put in excess of 43,000 the match with Jimmy Seed's men was literally a four-pointer. Although centre forward Peter Simpson cancelled out Prior's goal for the South Londoners before the interval, two second-half goals from Robinson and Hobbis clinched promotion.

Certainly, West Ham director A.C. 'Bert' Davis seemed to have already thrown in the towel when he unwisely stated in the *London Evening News* two days after the Charlton defeat, 'From a monetary point of view it might be better for the club to stay in the Second Division.' In the same article, the blundering Davis was also quoted as saying he preferred to have West Ham near the top of the Second Division rather than in the First Division 'because it is a better paying proposition'.

Although the board passed a resolution distancing themselves from their colleague's 'purported' statement, the damage was done and Bert Davis' comments helped to perpetuate a myth that persisted until well after World War II that West Ham didn't really want First Division football.

Ted Fenton recalled late, 'We got together a fine side and we were always there or thereabouts at the top of the Second Division without quite making promotion. One year Charlton pipped us by winning 3-1 at Upton Park at the end of the season. That Charlton game brought abusive letters from so-called "supporters" of West Ham, some of whom accused us of "selling the game". I wish they could have seen us in the dressing room. We took it hard – yet still the accusations and sneers continued. One fellow stopped me in the street and tried to make the point about us being in the hands of the bookies and big business. I ended that conversation with a sharp punch on the nose – my boxing background came in handy!'

Against an ever-increasing background of uncertainty in Europe, West Ham manager Charlie Paynter and coach Bob John were imperviously attempting to strengthen the club's playing staff with a combination of shrewd acquisitions and bringing in local talent. Fiery red-headed Scot Archie Macaulay had arrived from Glasgow Rangers, full-backs Charlie Bicknell and Charlie Walker came from Bradford City and Arsenal

50 Greatest Players

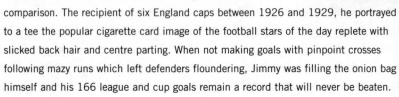

JIMMY RUFFELL Winger

Born: Doncaster, Yorkshire, 8 August 1900

Joined West Ham: 1921 **From:** Wall End United

Debut: v Port Vale, 10 September 1921

Appearances: 548 **Goals:** 166

Left West Ham: 1937 **For:** Aldershot

Jimmy Ruffell is rated the finest winger ever to don the claret and blue. His record of appearances and goals bear no comparison. The recipient of six England caps between 1926 and 1929, he portrayed to a tee the popular cigarette card image of the football stars of the day replete with slicked back hair and centre parting. When not making goals with pinpoint crosses following mazy runs which left defenders floundering, Jimmy was filling the onion bag himself and his 166 league and cup goals remain a record that will never be beaten.

respectively, Dick Walker had taken over Barrett's role at centre half and would become almost as legendary as his predecessor and young Benny Fenton had joined big brother Ted in the West Ham side at inside forward.

War Clouds Gather Again

Making the biggest impact as war clouds gathered was yet another import from that rich source of talent Gainsborough Trinity, winger Stan Foxall. Spurs, who knocked Hammers out in the fourth round 4-1 at White Hart Lane in 1934, really felt the full force of the Lincolnshire born sharp-shooter at the same stage of the 1938-39 competition. Foxall, who'd already scored in a 2-1 Second Division defeat at Spurs back in October, was on the right wing in the West Ham team printed in the match programme of 21 January 1939 for the fourth round FA Cup tie before a 42,716 crowd at Upton Park. He would switch position with centre forward Sam Small during the match to devastating effect.

The Times reported on the tie which had caught the imagination of the public, 'On a pitch that was so generously covered in sand as to suggest spades and donkey rides rather then football, not only did Foxall score two brilliant goals but his mere presence in the centre – after a somewhat unprofitable time on the right wing until West Ham were two down – seemed to revitalise the team. Almost immediately he scored a magnificent goal after a long dribble and, when he did very much the same thing again 10 minutes from the end, West Ham drew level.'

In the replay at White Hart Lane, this time before a crowd of 50,798, Foxall and Small again swapped roles. After Archie Macaulay had missed a spot-kick, Spurs went in front after 29 minutes through Sargent but four minutes later Foxall equalised for the third time in three matches against Spurs when he got on to the end of a Charlie Walker free-kick.

Now the saga moved to neutral Highbury where Spurs again led through Morrison after 15 minutes and Small missed a 'sitter'. The North Londoners held their advantage until the last quarter of an hour's play when Foxall, again in the centre, beat three Spurs players to the ball to equalise and pave the way for Macaulay's winner before another 50,000-plus crowd. But Hammers lost 2-0 to Portsmouth at Fratton Park in the next round.

Despite the fact that Neville Chamberlain's 'peace in our time' pledge from Adolf Hitler at Munich in 1938 was now looking as secure as a Robert Maxwell pension fund and two thirds of the playing staff had joined up with the Essex Regiment Territorials, the writer of the foreword in the club's annual handbook still looked forward optimistically to the coming season, 'It is with more than ordinary optimism that we Hammers face 1939-40 season's prospects,' adding, 'our players are our greatest asset and we expect more from them than any previous staff.'

Only after making note of the fact that the club chairman W.J. 'Jimmy' Cearns had been elected to the committee of the Football League, Len Goulden had been the recipient of further FA honours and Ted Fenton had captained the England XI against South Africa in the last test, did the writer hint of the true uncertainties of the period with the ominous mention that 'preparatory training will assume a rather unusual aspect this year, as only about a third will present themselves at Upton Park on 31 July, the rest being in camp with the Territorials.'

The Football League programme for 1939-40 kicked off on 26 August in as normal fashion as possible against the unreal background of the Phoney War. West Ham travelled to Plymouth to face the Argyle who were managed by former Hammer Jack Tresadern and returned from the west country two points and three goals to the good by courtesy of two tallies from new signing from Hull, Cliff Hubbard, and another from Jackie Wood to a solitary reply from the Pilgrims. Two days later another goal from Woody and one from Ted Fenton secured a 2-1 home win over Fulham which seemed to justify the optimism of fans, players and neutral observers alike that this really could be Hammers' year. True to form, the same XI who had started so brightly went down 2-0 to Leicester City at Upton Park on 2 September 1939 to cast doubts over the high hopes held.

50 Greatest Players

LEN GOULDEN Inside forward

Born: Hackney, London, 16 September 1912

Joined West Ham: 1932 **From:** School

Debut: v Charlton Athletic, 8 April 1932

Appearances: 253 **Goals:** 55

Left West Ham: 1945 **For:** Chelsea

Yet another member of Second Division West Ham's remarkable 'England International Club' of the 1930s, inside left Len Goulden was truly the jewel in the crown of that select band which included such luminaries as Ted Hufton, Jim Barrett, Jackie Morton, Jimmy Ruffell and Vic Watson. Len's star shone as brightly as any as he became a permanent fixture in England's forward line before the war. His total of 16 England caps were not under threat until the emergence of Bobby Moore but the most improbable aspect of Len's career remains the fact that the only honour he won at club level was a Football League war medal in 1940.

War is Declared

With many of the watching crowd of 13,400 already in uniform, it was all irrelevant anyway, for with German Panzers already in Poland the 'Blitzkrieg' had begun and the following day Great Britain declared war on Germany.

Fearing mass air raids the government introduced swingeing measures to restrict large gatherings at cricket matches, theatres, racetracks and, inevitably, football stadiums. The Football League programme was abandoned forthwith and the three matches played by most clubs deleted from the records.

On the Monday following the declaration of war, Upton Park was commandeered by the military and young Eddie Chapman had an experience he wouldn't forget in a hurry, 'I was welcomed in the forecourt with a bayonet at my throat. It happened on 4 September 1939 and being only 16 years of age I wasn't fully aware of everything that was going on.'

War or no war, West Ham were destined to taste one more slice of glory and return to Wembley for what became known as the 'Forgotten Final' of 1940. In fact, the Football League War Cup competition which was staged in the spring of 1940 was the only bona fide national knock-out competition played during the conflict, as all future tournaments were limited to a regional basis with a separate cup for north and south.

The 'Forgotten' FA Cup Run

Only the first two rounds were regionalised in the 1940 competition and staged over two legs. In the first round, Hammers overcame Chelsea 5-2 on aggregate then Leicester 4-1; 16-year-old Eddie Chapman appeared in the 3-0 second-leg victory at Upton Park and the 30/- (£1.50) match fee must have seemed like a fortune to him then. Hammers drew Huddersfield Town in the third round as the tournament reached the 'sudden death' stage but still needed two attempts to dispose of Town with a 3-1 victory at the Boleyn after a thrilling 3-3 draw at Leeds Road necessitated a replay.

Next came a 4-2 Upton Park victory over Birmingham in the quarter-finals with Foreman, Goulden, Macaulay and Small hitting the decisive goals.

The choice of Stamford Bridge as the venue for the semi-final clash with Fulham must have appeared to neutral observers to favour the West Londoners, just a brisk walk from Putney Bridge away, while Fulham Broadway was a fair few stops on the District Line for most West Ham fans.

But Hammers regarded Stamford Bridge as a happy hunting ground. After all, hadn't they defeated First Division West Bromwich Albion there 3-0 in an FA Cup second replay as a Southern League side in 1913 with the help of two goals from George 'Gatling Gun' Hilsdon... and favourites Derby County 5-2 in an FA Cup semi-final in 1923... in addition to beating Chelsea 2-0 in their present run?

Two up at half-time against Fulham through an own goal and one from the peerless Goulden, it appeared that Hammers wouldn't need any lucky omens to overcome the Cottagers as they increased their lead to 4-0 with further goals from Foxall and Small in front of the biggest crowd to watch a war-time match so far – 32,799. But they reckoned without the exceptional goalscoring prowess of Fulham's Ronnie Rooke and Vivian Woodward who scored three in 17 minutes to set up a nerve-tingling finale. But Hammers held on... just.

Thirty five years later the Bridge would again reverberate to the melancholy strains of 'Bubbles' and play host and good fairy to a team of happy Hammers and a new generation of their claret and blue bedecked army of fans on their way to the famous Twin Towers, but now was a time for their forefathers to rejoice and briefly forget the perils of war.

Quiet Glory

The final on Saturday, 8 June 1940 was set to kick-off at 6.30 p.m., so as not to impede the war effort. The proceedings lacked some of the sense of occasion and pomp and ceremony usually associated with a normal FA Cup final, but the authorities did their best to make it a day to remember and most of the traditional ceremonies were still performed, although there was still a feeling of going through the motions. The National Anthem was played by the band of His Majesty's Irish Guards and also that of our French allies and the 42,000 crowd did their best to sing along.

Foxall and on two occasions Foreman both forced spectacular saves from Rovers' munitions worker goalkeeper Jim Barron before the Irons scored the game's only goal in the 34th minute. A pass from Foxall to Goulden enabled the inside left to baffle the Rovers' rearguard before putting Foreman in with a chance on goal.

Foreman, who went on to score exactly 200 goals in war-time for Irons, fired in a fierce shot that Barron could only fist out to the waiting Sam Small who scored easily from close-range. For an hour, with Goulden and Macaulay running the midfield and Fenton and Cockroft providing support from defence, West Ham dictated the match and were comfortable with it. But during the second half with full back and captain Charlie Bicknell and key man Goulden both carrying injuries, the pace and lush Wembley turf began to take its toll. For a while Hammers, as Dick Walker put it, 'struggled a bit'. But despite the best efforts of Rovers' ex-Hammers outside left Billy Guest (sometimes confused as a wartime guest!), West Ham held out and it was Bicknell who lifted the handsome cup, which, as the only permanent trophy awarded during hostilities, remains in the club trophy room to this day.

With the evacuation of Dunkirk rightly taking up the front page news, West Ham's win meant little outside of East London and even there the celebrations were decidedly low-key. As Dick Walker recalled in the *West Ham United Football Book* by Dennis Signy, published in 1968, 'Most of the lads had an informal cup winning reception in the Boleyn pub near the ground. We got back there in time to get in a few pints before closing time. I remember my medal going round and round the public bar.'

Ted Fenton, however, remembered things differently, 'Austerity was the watchword everywhere. The Wembley crowd was restricted in numbers by the police and after the game the players quietly split up and went straight back to our service units.'

Army duty stopped Ernie Gregory – and a good many club-mates – from even being at that 1940 first Wartime Cup final. 'We'd all joined the TA before the war – they thought that it would encourage other lads to do the same if we did. So we were called up straight away when it started. Archie Macaulay got away to play in the final and the rest of us didn't even know what the score was until he got back to the unit again.'

Chapter Six: 1940-57
After the War

After winning the Football League Wartime Cup outright, the rest of the regionalised makeshift wartime competitions represented something of an anti-climax to the Hammers. Nevertheless, they more than held their own in the restricted league they competed in for the duration of the conflict, finishing second five times, as well as third, sixth and seventh.

In 1944-45 Irons battled to the semi-finals of the Football League South Cup but lost 2-1 to Chelsea at White Hart Lane. If the Wembley win over Blackburn represents the forgotten final of West Ham's history, the wartime playing career of full back Bill Lewis must earn him the title of the forgotten player of West Ham. When the book, *Who's Who of West Ham* came out, a few old timers enquired why Canning Town-born Billy wasn't in it. The fact is, Bill never played a first-team game in peace time for Hammers – all of his 115 appearances in the claret and blue were made between 1940 and '45 when he transferred to Blackpool.

An old pal of Hammers' record-breaking goalkeeper Ernie Gregory, Bill never signed professional forms at Upton Park and was a team-mate of Gregory, Jackie Wood, Ron Cater and Billy West at amateurs Leytonstone in the late 1930s. Bill made a further 41 wartime appearances for Blackpool in 1945-46 and then played 30 times for the Tangerines in the First Division between 1946-49 when he would have been a team-mate of George Dick who joined Hammers from the 'Pool in 1948.

Joining Norwich City in 1949, the former England schoolboy international turned out on 332 occasions for the Canaries' Third Division south side and was a member of the Norfolk club side which narrowly missed out on promotion to the Second Division in three successive seasons in the early 50s. He later worked for Eastern Counties Newspapers in Norwich. Ron Cater transferred to Os in 1951, as did Jackie Wood two years earlier.

Unlike World War 1, no players with West Ham connections lost their lives in the Hitler war but the conflict took its toll in other ways. As the players began arriving back at Upton Park following demobilisation from all points of the compass in the summer of 1945, it became clear that many of them had lost their best years to the war.

Pre-war wing stars Stan Foxall and Jackie Morton would never again pull on the famous claret and blue shirts they'd worn with such distinction due to injuries and that prince among inside forwards, Len Goulden, transferred to Chelsea for whom he'd guested during the conflict.

Some sense of normality returned in the 1945-46 season with the resumption of the FA Cup, although the first two rounds were regionalised and played over two legs on a home and away basis. Drawn at home to North London rivals Arsenal in the first leg of the third round, Hammers were four up at half-time and won 6-0 with goals from Almer Hall (2), Jackie Wood (2), Ken Bainbridge and George Foreman. The shock result stunned the post-war football public. But Hammers went out 2-1 on aggregate to Chelsea in the next round.

In the improvised League South campaign of 1945-46, the prolific George Foreman scored his last goal for the club in a 2-1 win at Plymouth Argyle on 9 February 1946 before transferring to Spurs, but Hammers had a ready-made replacement in Manchester-born centre forward Don 'Sailor' Travis, who'd already given notice of his intentions by scoring four times on his reserve team debut and was installed in the side in time for the Upton Park return match against the Argyle a week later.

Once again he hit a double brace to emulate Billy Grassam's feat of 1900 in a 7-0 rout of the Pilgrims which also saw right winger Terry Woodgate score a seven-minute hat-trick to equal Syd Puddefoot's three in the same time span in that record 8-1 FA Cup victory over Chesterfield in 1913.

West Ham finished 7th in that last makeshift 1945-46 season which saw them defeat champions Birmingham. With most players now back from active service, including flying officer Ken Wright who was awarded the distinguished Flying Cross in recognition of his heroic deeds as a Lancaster bomber pilot in the RAF, things were back to normal – including the prospect of another 10 years of largely uneventful Second Division fare and a distinct lack of FA Cup success, with the exception of 1955-56.

The old guard of pre-war days was all but disbanded. Long-serving Ted Fenton had left to take up the player-manager post at Colchester United but would return. Charlie Walker had taken up a similar position at Kent League Margate, goalkeeper Harry Medhurst had joined Goulden at Chelsea, wing half Reg Attwell changed his club (but not his colours) by joining Burnley who would win promotion and reach the FA Cup final, Archie Macaulay transferred to First Division Brentford and War Cup final captain Charlie Bicknell left at the end of the season to become boss of Bedford Town.

Twelfth position in the Second Division table and a 2-1 FA Cup home defeat to Leicester City in the third round began a depressingly familiar trend of underachievement at the back end of the 1940s.

Prospects But Little Progress

Despite heralding the beginning in earnest of goalkeeper Ernie Gregory's magnificent West Ham career and also the emergence of some exciting young forward prospects in Eric Parsons, Terry Woodgate and Ken Tucker, 1947-48 saw Hammers finish in a better sixth place in Division Two but again exit the FA Cup at the first hurdle.

Seventh spot in 1948-49 and another early cup exit was followed by a disastrous 1949-50 season when five out of the last six league games were lost and almost cost the team their place in the Second Division. Had it not been for the goalscoring prowess of forward Bill Robinson, relegation to the Third Division South would have been a foregone conclusion.

Signed from Charlton Athletic for £7,000 the previous season, when he scored on his debut against West Bromwich Albion and totalled 10 goals in 17 appearances that campaign, Bill had been a member of Charlton's victorious FA Cup winning side of 1947 and a team-mate there of ex-Hammer Benny Fenton.

The 1950-51 season was another disappointing one for Hammers who finished 13th in the table and went out of the cup in the fourth round 1-0 at Stoke, but the campaign represented a high-water mark for Whitburn-born Robinson who hit 26 goals in 40 Second Division outings – a figure which remained a post-war record until John Dick surpassed it with 27 in 41 appearances on the club's return to the First Division in 1958-59.

50 Greatest Players

DICK WALKER Centre half

Born: Hackney, London, 22 July 1913

Joined West Ham: 1934 **From:** Park Royal

Debut: v Burnley August 1934

Appearances: 311 **Goals:** 2

Left West Ham: 1957 (retired)

As Jim Barrett gradually made fewer and fewer first-team appearances from the mid-30s onwards, his ready-made replacement Dick Walker made progressively more. Like his predecessor, Walker was also a dominant figure at the heart of Hammers defence, but the similarities between the two legends didn't end there, for Walker too was a larger than life character who played his game with a swagger and played hard both on and off the field. His famous quote, 'I couldn't play but I could stop those who could,' provides an accurate summary and as he faded from the limelight he devoted endless hours helping the club's younger players – most notably his successor Ken Brown.

Bill is also revered at Upton Park for his part in setting up Hammers vaunted youth section when he hung up his boots at the end of 1952-53 with assistance from pre-war defenders Albert Walker and 'star finder' Wally St Pier. He played a major role in unearthing local talent like Bobby Moore, Geoff Hurst and Martin Peters.

Big Ambitions

One event overshadowed everything else at Upton Park in the dawn of what would eventually be a tumultuous new decade for East London – the retirement of long-serving manager Charlie Paynter and the appointment of Ted Fenton, who had been brought back to the club two years earlier with the express purpose in mind, as his successor.

Ted Fenton had big ambitions for West Ham. He'd cut his teeth in management at Southern League Colchester United and put the little Essex club on the map by masterminding an amazing FA Cup run that enthralled the nation during the ration-book winter of 1948. Born at Forest Gate, on West Ham's doorstep in 1914, Ted had been recruited from local soccer by Hammers' assistant manager Dick Leafe in 1932 and made 176 appearances, scoring 27 goals before the war. During the conflict he attained the rank of physical training sergeant major in the army and saw action in North Africa. In short, he was a tough nut. And like Syd King before him, Fenton knew how to cultivate the press. If they wanted a story he gave them one.

Although their cup run came to an end with a 5-0 defeat inflicted by the eventual finalists Blackpool, little Colchester were front page news, whereas before these exploits they'd found it almost impossible to reach the back pages of the nationals. Within two years, the team from Garrison Town were elected to the Football League (Third Division South) and it was all down to the power of the press and the intoxicating magic of the FA Cup – drawing direct parallels to the Hammers' own election to the league in 1919.

Despite the promise engendered by Fenton's new regime, results were still disappointing in league and cup in the early to mid-fifties. In 1951-52 the side finished a dismal twelfth in the Second Division table, then fourteenth in 1952-53, thirteenth in 1953-54 and eighth in 1954-55. Nor did they progress any further than the fourth round of the FA Cup in any of those four years. A poor return.

Ted Fenton would have been the first to admit that he was never a great tactician, his great strength laying in his shrewd manipulation of the transfer market with the most limited cash resources at his disposal.

He revelled in the cloak and dagger world of signing players – often from under the noses of rival clubs – and by the mid-fifties many of the components of the 1957-58 promotion-winning side were already installed at Upton Park thanks to Fenton's wheeling and dealing.

Eric Parsons, Hammers' top scorer in season 1947-48.

A classic example of Fenton's formula was the signing of Scottish international inside-left Johnny Dick who was billeted at Colchester on National Service duty with R.E.M.E. and playing for Crittal Athletic in the Eastern Counties League at the time in 1953. Dick was on demob leave and Fenton spent hours tramping the streets of his native Glasgow before eventually locating his target at his parents' home in the Cardonald district of the city. An hour after he'd persuaded 'Rangers daft' Dick to sign for Hammers, Arthur Rowe – the manager of Spurs' famous 'push and run' team – arrived on the much sought-after Scot's doorstep to sign him for First Division Tottenham.

Another coup was the signing of winger Malcolm Musgrove. A Geordie by birth, 'Mussy' was playing for his village side Lynemouth Colliery in 1953 but was wanted by Sunderland. Unbeknown to the Rokerites, however, Lynemouth had been unofficially adopted by West Ham as a nursery club – one of their leading officials was an East Ham man – and once again, Fenton made a long journey north to get his man.

But the signing which was to have most impact on the future of the club was made two years earlier in 1951 and a lot nearer to home – that of centre half and budding football visionary Malcolm Allison for £6,500 in a deal which was financed by the sale of winger Eric Parsons for a then staggering fee of £22,500 to Chelsea a year previously. Badly disillusioned by life at the Valley due to manager Jimmy Seed's lack of communication skills and the fact that he'd made just two First Division appearances in seven years with the loosely run South East London club, it is impossible to exaggerate the influence he would wield on training, tactics and coaching techniques at Upton Park during a decade in which English football was still living in the dark ages in comparison to what was happening on the continent.

In his autobiography, *Colours Of My Life*, published by Everest in 1975, Malcolm explains his feelings at the time, 'When I was transferred from Charlton Athletic to West Ham I led myself to believe that the futility and bitterness was over. For a while I was happier but it was merely a change of environment which had broken the monotony. Within six months I was more disillusioned than ever. Not only did West Ham know less about training than Charlton, a feat which I would have believed impossible, but they asked for less effort. The only difference in training sessions were that West Ham's were shorter. The facilities were disgraceful. We used to train on a pock-marked, scruffy little track at the back of the ground.

'We used to have to run in and out of a copse of trees. It was impossible for the trainer to keep his eyes on all of the players. If he was alert he might spot blue cigarette smoke filtering through the trees.

'My relationship with Fenton was much closer than the one I had with Jimmy Seed but it was scarcely satisfactory. I did give him some problems but they arose chiefly out of my frustration with the way the club was run. And eventually I began to run the team, with his tacit agreement. He could see that I was getting results. Player power is a phrase which has become fashionable in modern football. But it was being practised in the West Ham dressing room 20 years ago. I began to draw up my own training schedules and people like Noel Cantwell, John Bond and Frank O'Farrell came in with me.'

A Rude Awakening

English football had suffered a rude awakening and two debilitating defeats at the hands of the Hungarians in 1953 and 1954, 6-3 at Wembley and 7-1 in Budapest when on both occasions Ferenc Puskas, Sandor Kocsis and Nandor Hidegkuti ran amok to expose the deficiencies of our game. Malcolm Allison was at Wembley that fateful day in November 1953, with his West Ham team-mate, Scottish winger Jimmy Andrews, and the pair watched transfixed as they absorbed the lessons of the 'magnificent Magyars' playing a fluid 4-2-4 formation against England's outmoded 2-3-5 pattern.

John Dick hit 26 league goals in his second season.

Andrews was another disciple of the Allison doctrine who, along with Bond, Cantwell, O'Farrell, Dave Sexton and Malcolm Musgrove, sat with him for hours in Cassetteri's cafe just around the corner from the ground on the Barking Road, endlessly discussing soccer tactics and ways of improving their game. Many times the pepper

Great Managers – 1932-50

CHARLIE PAYNTER

Although Charlie Paynter was born in Swindon in 1879, he was regarded as an adopted Cockney after moving to East London at an early age, living at Blanche Street, Plaistow with his parents. He made a name playing for the Victoria Swifts, a well-known local club in the 1890s with connections with the Victoria Docks. His interest in physiotherapy started very early in his sporting career – while he was still in his teens and playing football – and led to him assisting as trainer, masseur and coach at the West Ham Memorial Grounds, the centre of athletics and cycling that later became the home of West Ham's predecessors, Thames Iron Works FC.

At the start of the 1900-1901 season, Charlie was playing on the wing for South West Ham – as Victoria Swifts had become by this time – and on 5 November 1900 he was invited by Lou Bowen (then secretary of WHUFC) to visit the Memorial Grounds where a trial game was being staged after which he signed forms for the club in the South Essex League, later recalling that there was even a firework display to mark the occasion.

At this time Charlie was also playing Sunday football and was approached more than once by Harry Sims to join the Hammers. The following August he made the acquaintance of Syd King, the club's first manager, and signed amateur forms at his instigation. His first wage packet contained the princely sum of half-a-crown after a match against Luton Town.

In a match against Woolwich Arsenal at Plumstead in 1902, Paynter sustained a knee injury which effectively ended his playing career but opened the way for another when, after assisting first-team trainer Tom Robinson, the club directors appointed him reserve-team trainer on the club's move to Boleyn Castle. On 15 November 1906, the highly regarded Paynter was the recipient of the first benefit match ever awarded to any servant by West Ham United, and Woolwich Arsenal manager Phil Kelso sent out a strong team from Plumstead to provide the opposition for the match at Upton Park.

Forty-four years later the Gunners were again West Ham's opponents for the testimonial match for Charles W. Paynter staged at Upton Park on Monday 18 September, 1950 to celebrate his 50 years with the club as a player, trainer, trainer–manager, secretary–manager and finally manager to complete a unique golden jubilee.

The post-match reception was attended by several famous former Hammers who considered Charlie Paynter their mentor and a father figure they took their problems to as players, among them Jackie Morton, Vic Watson, Joe Cockroft, Jim 'Lottie' Collins, Tommy Hodgson, Dick Leafe, Herman Conway, Dave Mangnall, Ted Hufton, Len Young, Stan Foxall, Len Goulden and not least Ted Fenton, who had the task of following in his footsteps.

pot became Puskas and the salt cellar Hidegkuti as 'Big Mal' analysed another Hungarian move as the first seeds of the Academy were sown.

A little over a month after the Hungarians' appearance at Wembley, West Ham entertained some very special visitors of their own at Upton Park in a floodlight friendly – AC Milan. Boasting five internationals of different nationalities in their forward line, the Italian giants handed out the academy scholars an abject lesson in the finer points of the game that chilly December night as they won 6-0.

A young Ken Brown was Hammers' centre half and when his No. 9 opponent, the Swede Gunnar Nordal, appeared in the centre circle he exclaimed: 'Oh God, what a bloody giant!' His fears were well founded as the 15 stone (92 kg) 6 ft 3 ins (1.9 m) superman ran amok with his Argentine team-mate Schiaffano to make it a night the Boleyn patrons wouldn't forget in a hurry.

The next day there was a special meeting in the West Ham players' unofficial headquarters and in a heated inquest, sauce bottles, cups and saucers, knives, forks, spoons and anything else that could be moved supplemented the salt and pepper pots as makeshift subbuteo players in an attempt to unravel the events of the debacle.

Learning Fast

But the Hammers were learning fast and by the mid-50s were a half decent side and strongly fancied to win promotion in the not too distant future. John Bond recalls, 'We used to come out of that cafe smelling of egg and chips and all sorts, but you wouldn't get players today showing that enthusiasm.'

Still Hammers finished a disappointing sixteenth in the Second Division table of 1955-56 but served notice of their intentions by knocking three First Division teams out of the FA Cup – Preston North End (5-2), Cardiff City (2-1) and Blackburn Rovers (3-2) after a 0-0 draw at Upton Park.

The win at Ewood Park set up the club's most important match since pre-war days – a sixth round clash with old rivals Spurs at White Hart Lane. Although Spurs progressed to the semi-finals after an epic 3-3 draw and a 2-1 replay win at Upton Park, Hammers were becoming a side to be reckoned with.

Winger Harry Hooper, who patrolled the right touchline displaying sublime skills and an inventiveness which hadn't been seen since the pre-war days of Tommy Yews at Upton Park, became the first Hammer to represent England at Under-23 level when he played versus Italy, against whom he scored twice in a 5-2 win at Stamford Bridge, and Scotland in 1955. Harry was brought to Upton Park as a 17-year-old in 1950 by his father Harry Hooper snr, when the latter was appointed reserve-team coach. His £25,000 transfer to Wolves in March 1956 – a record for a winger then – caused as much uproar among the fans as Puddefoot's move to Falkirk 34 years earlier and refuelled arguments that West Ham lacked ambition.

Fans favourite Harry, who later had successful spells with Birmingham City and Sunderland before going into non-league football with Kettering where he still lives, reveals, 'The truth is I never wanted to leave West Ham. I explained to Ted (Fenton) that I didn't want to go but he said there was nothing he could do – the club needed the money because the school in Castle Street wanted their land back, which was then serving as the main entrance to the ground on Green Street.

'The money received from Wolves paid for the current main entrance which was completed in time for the club's promotion in 1958.'

Another major player in that epic confrontation with Spurs, Eire international wing half Frank O'Farrell, was on his way before the 1956-57 season was eight matches old – to First Division Preston North End in a straight swap for their former Manchester United centre forward Eddie Lewis.

50 Greatest Players

MALCOLM ALLISON Centre half

Born: Dartford, Kent, September 5 1927

Joined West Ham: 1951 **From:** Charlton Athletic

Debut: v Chesterfield, 17 March 1951

Appearances: 255 **Goals:** 10

Left West Ham: 1958 (retired)

Just as Dickie Walker superceded Jim Barrett, by the early 50s it was time for Dick too to be replaced in the number 5 shirt by a younger man. But rather than promote from within, Ted Fenton decided to bring in an outsider – Malcolm Allison. 'Big Mal', as he would later become known, was signed for £7,000 from Charlton, but in football terms he might as well have been from another planet because, although he didn't realise it at the time, Fenton had signed much more than a centre half – he'd found a footballing visionary who in six short years would revolutionise the club's archaic regime and transform training, coaching techniques and tactics to secure promotion to the first division in 1958. Sadly, Mal couldn't join the party as TB cut short his career. But as we all now know, he was destined for greater fame in another sphere.

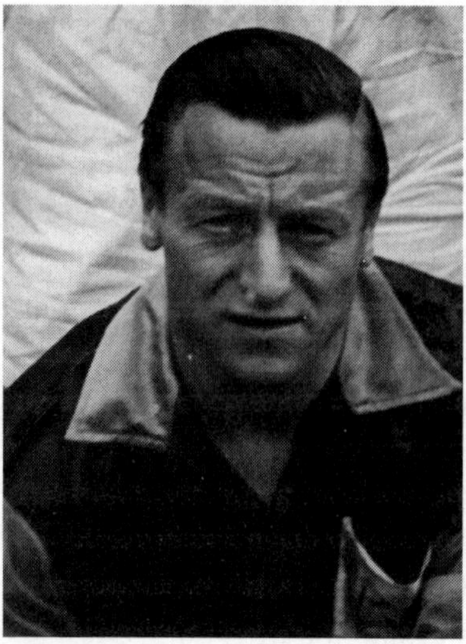

Billy Dare's transfer from Brentford to West Ham was live on BBC TV.

In spite of these departures the team finished eighth in the Second Division table with Lewis and Billy Dare tying on nine goals apiece as leading scorers and former ground-staff lad Johnny Smith earning rave reviews at inside right. The diminutive Dare, a live-wire who could play anywhere in attack, was the perfect foil for the rangy Dick and was signed in a typical piece of publicity seeking by Fenton, his £5,000 move from Brentford being televised live on BBC's *Sportsview*.

With right winger Mike Grice already in place and facing the unenviable task of following in Hooper's footsteps after his £8,500 move from Fenton's former club Colchester United as his replacement on the same day Hooper left in March 1956, there was just one piece of the promotion jigsaw waiting to be filled. But the eventful 1957-58 season would be well under way before Hammers got their man.

50 Greatest Players

ERNIE GREGORY Goalkeeper

Born: Stratford, London, November 10 1921

Joined West Ham: 1936 **From:** Leytonstone

Debut: v Plymouth Argyle, 28 December 1946

Appearances: 406

Left West Ham: 1960 (retired)

Ernie the elder joined the West Ham groundstaff way back in 1936, but had to wait 10 years to make his League debut! Once in the side he became a permanent fixture and although he could only rival Ted Hufton's achievements on the international front with an England 'B' cap v France in 1952, he would surely have emulated his feats had he accepted an offer to join Arsenal. West Ham rewarded his loyalty with a testimonial match v The LDA Club of Costa Rica in 1960 and the Football League followed suit by awarding Ernie a long service statuette when he retired the same year. He then started a second career as coach at Upton Park until 1987 when he received a special award for 50 years service after which he continued on a part-time basis! Still a regular spectator at matches.

Chapter Seven: 1957-61
Back to the Top

West Ham began the 1957-58 season in an unremarkable fashion. Only a Malcolm Allison penalty gave Hammers a 2-2 opening day home draw with Lincoln City followed by an unlucky 2-1 defeat at Blackburn. Despite three London derby victories over Fulham (3-2), Leyton Orient (3-2) and Charlton (3-0) at the Valley, Hammers had secured only 12 points from the same amount of matches by mid-October – a poor return for a side widely tipped to win promotion. Indeed, had it not been for 10 goals from Dare in the absence of any from the curiously out-of-touch Dick, things could have been a good deal worse. But a saviour was at hand who would transform both the out-of-sorts Scotsman and West Ham's season.

Ted Fenton first signed centre forward Vic Keeble for the then Southern League Colchester United in July 1947 from King George Youth Club and had a gentleman's agreement on the first option to sign him if he left the 'U's. Instead he joined Newcastle United for £15,000 in 1952 and played for the Magpies in their victorious 1955 FA Cup final against Manchester City.

Having failed to sign former Everton centre forward Dave Hickson from Huddersfield, who returned to Goodison, Fenton was determined to renew acquaintance with his former discovery and, after much bargaining and indecision on behalf of the Newcastle management, duly did so for £10,000 – a hefty fee for West Ham in those days. After scoring on his debut in a disappointing 1-1 home draw with bottom club Doncaster Rovers, Keeble's presence then rejuvenated the Hammers attack as four straight wins were recorded over Rotherham United (2-1), Huddersfield (5-2), Grimsby (2-1) and Stoke (5-0), with Keeble claiming a hat-trick and the match ball against the Potters who were above West Ham in the table.

Two 6-1 victories before and after Christmas against Lincoln City and Bristol Rovers put Hammers third in the table and, although goalscorers Smith (3), Keeble (2) and Dick grabbed the headlines, right winger Mike Grice – who was on the transfer list at his own request along with full back George Wright – had his best game since joining the club, prompting Fenton to comment, 'I'm still hoping that Mike will change his mind... if only the crowd would give him a better deal.'

Wright apparently retorted, 'I want regular first-team football and my request still stands.'

The blond haired Wright, who had joined Irons from non-league Margate in 1951 and was deputising for the injured Eire international and West Ham skipper Noel Cantwell, would have the perfect chance to prove his worth to any potential buyers as Hammers had drawn First Division Blackpool at home in the third round of the FA Cup and he would have the task of marking the Tangerines' most famous player – Stanley Matthews.

Sea Air and Brine Treatment

As had become standard procedure before important cup ties, Hammers went down to Brighton for a week's training to prepare for the tie and enjoy sea air and brine treatment. Resplendent in two-tone tracksuits (claret and blue, of course!) complete with club badge, the players worked out at Hove greyhound stadium, which must have been manna from heaven for Messrs Cantwell, Keeble and Dick, the latter of whom particularly enjoyed more than the occasional 'flutter'. As club captain Noel Cantwell recalled in his autobiography, *United We Stand*, 'Johnny Dick was a livewire both on and off the field. He came up to me one day and asked me, as skipper, to see the boss and request a few days' leave for him as his mother had had a "shock".

'A shock sounded odd to me and I asked him if he meant that she had had a stroke. "Aye, that'll be right. Anyway, all I want is a few days to go and visit her in Glasgow," he said. I saw the manager and he readily agreed, but while Johnny was away it was found his passport needed renewing for the summer tour the club was making.

'Mr Fenton, being in the vicinity of Johnny's home one morning soon afterwards, called round to get the out-of-date passport from Johnny's wife. He knocked at the door and while waiting for an answer a woman neighbour leaned over the fence and said to the boss, "If you're waiting to see Johnny Dick, you've missed him. He's just gone out."

'Manager Fenton did not wait any longer. He came back to the ground in a towering rage and when we heard what had happened we guessed exactly where Johnny had gone. It was the Cesarewitch meeting at Newmarket and, knowing Johnny's keenness for horse-racing, we knew he would be there. The boss knew it too and was back at the house waiting for the horse-race-loving forward when he got back that night.

'Jovial Johnny had an uncomfortable interview, but he is one of those people you just cannot stay angry with and he got away with it, without any serious punishment.'

Unlike First Division Blackpool and Stanley Matthews, as Hammers paid scant respect to reputations and tore into their illustrious

John Bond spent 15 years as a player at Upton Park.

opponents even after going one down after just two minutes play through Scottish international Hugh Kelly's penalty.

George Farm, another Scottish cap, was twice beaten by headers from Dick to relay his own message to the Scottish selectors and three times by his partner in crime, Vic Keeble, who added another match ball to his rapidly expanding collection as Hammers ran out 5-1 winners to provide one of the biggest shocks of the day.

Reserve full back Wright played Matthews superbly, drawing this comment from the reporter of the *London Evening News*' Saturday night special edition, 'Matthews was moving all over the field to escape from Wright'.

The *Ilford Recorder* added, 'On Saturday, football's Peter Pan, Peerless Stan Matthews added his tribute. Sitting dejected in the churchyard-like silence of Blackpool's dressing room, he said, "West Ham played some great football. They would do well in the top grade".'

Cup Crash Prompts Good League Form

Now on fire, Hammers showed no sign of letting up as they resumed their league programme with a 3-2 win at Derby and the following week thrashed Swansea – who included Cliff Jones and Mel Charles – 6-2 with goals from Keeble (2), Dick, Bond, Cantwell and Billy Lansdowne at Upton Park.

In the FA Cup fourth round Hammers were almost on the receiving end of a 'giant killing' at home to Third Division Stockport County, but scraped through 3-2.

After a couple of draws in the league, promotion rivals Fulham were Irons' next FA Cup visitors for an encounter of high expectation and drama. Watched by a crowd of 37,500, the Eastenders took the lead after just 90 seconds through Grice but 10 minutes later Reg Dwight equalised as he lobbed Gregory. With Fulham's Gibraltar-born goalkeeper Tony Macedo playing his customary 'blinder' at Upton Park, the Cottagers gained in confidence and, in an atmosphere of almost unbearable tension, took the lead after 56 minutes when Dwight crossed for Jimmy Hill to volley home on the far post at the north bank end.

Although Bond equalised with a twice-taken penalty after Lewis had encroached into the penalty area, the West Londoners were not to be denied and Johnny Haynes scored what proved to be the decisive goal 15 minutes from time to leave West Ham a bitterly disappointed team. But it may have been a blessing in disguise as Fulham eventually fell between the twin stools of league and cup, finishing fifth in the final Second Division table and losing 5-3 to Manchester United in a replayed FA Cup semi-final at Highbury.

Five days later, playing in their 'lucky' away strip of white shirts with distinctive claret and blue chest bands, Hammers surged back to the top of the table thanks to a 4-1 thrashing of near neighbours Leyton Orient (who included Phil Woosnam) in front of the biggest crowd of the season at Brisbane Road of 25,284. The win put Hammers above second-placed Charlton on goal average with 12 matches still to play, Smith, Dare, Keeble and Dick getting the goals.

It was the start of a charge which saw the Cockneys win their next three matches to keep top spot and culminated in an 8-0 record-breaking win over Rotherham United at the Boleyn.

Club captain Malcolm Allison, who hadn't played since mid-September when he was given the shocking news that he had tuberculosis and had been in a convalescent home in Sussex following an operation to remove a lung, was at the match which must have provided him with a much-needed tonic as he watched his academy boys tear the Millers apart from the directors box. Commenting with some understatement in the *Ilford Recorder*, Big Mal observed, 'Our forward line today was just great.'

John Dick's four goals against the hapless Yorkshiremen made him the first Hammer to hit a double brace since Vic Watson in the 7-0 mauling of Liverpool back in September 1930 and he obviously hogged most of the headlines along with Smith and Keeble who cracked two apiece to set a club record winning margin that wouldn't be equalled for 10 more years. But buried away in that same edition of the paper's sports pages was another item that at first glance seemed of little consequence. Under the heading 'Smillie Stars in Debut' ran the scoreline: Brentford Reserves 1 West Ham Reserves 1. Billy Dare, unable to get into the first team at this stage, was playing against his old team and amateur inside left Micky Newman, who had scored a vital promotion goal in a 1-1 Christmas Day Upton Park draw with Ipswich Town, scored the second-string's equaliser. The report also noted that there were four 16-year-olds in the side – Derek Woodley, Andy Smillie, Tony Scott and a certain Robert Moore.

Bobby Moore, along with Trevor Brooking, would add to Geoff Hurst's six goals against Sunderland to equal that 8-0 scoreline in the First Division 10 years later.

Close Finish

True to style, Hammers kept their long-suffering fans on tenterhooks right to the end but, in one of the closest and most exciting finishes to a season the Second Division had ever staged, they held on grimly to a priceless one point lead to return to the top flight after 26 years in the wilderness.

In the penultimate match against promotion rivals Liverpool, the Upton Park roar was born as a 37,750 crowd spurred their favourites on with

Great Matches

FOOTBALL LEAGUE DIVISION TWO — **Ayresome Park, 26 April 1958**

Middlesbrough 1 — **West Ham United 3** — **Attendance 30,526**

Middlesbrough 1	West Ham United 3
Fitzsimons	Dick
	Keeble
	Musgrove

Middlesbrough were swept aside in the Championship-clinching last match of the season at Ayresome Park. Centre half Ken Brown kept England star Brian Clough quiet while Dick had a fine match. In the 14th minute John 'Muffin' Bond drove a low ball into the goalmouth and Dick back-heeled it past an astonished Peter Taylor. After Boro drew level on 24 minutes Dick provided the pass for Keeble to restore Irons' advantage five minutes before the interval and, literally on the stroke of half-time, the irrepressible Scot centred for Mal Musgrove to make it 3-1 with a rare headed goal. That was also the final score.

Greeted by thousands of ecstatic supporters when they arrived back at King's Cross that unforgettable April night, manager Ted Fenton, with emotion in his voice and tears of happiness in his eyes, put the success down to team spirit, fitness and strength in depth, adding above the din as skipper Noel Cantwell was hoisted onto the shoulders of his fans, 'I'm glad we played it out in real style. We've made it on our reserve strength, which never once failed us, and on the success of Vic Keeble's transfer from Newcastle. I feel confident we can do well in the First Division.' The reserves Fenton referred to were: Brian Rhodes, George Wright, Malcolm Pyke, Bill Lansdowne, Fred Cooper, Andy Nelson, Eddie Lewis, Bill Neville, Fred Blackburn, Dick Wragg and Micky Newman.

Middlesbrough: Taylor P., Stonehouse, Robinson, Harris, Dicks, Birbeck, Taylor C., Fitzsimons, Clough, Peacock, Holliday.

West Ham United: Gregory, Bond, Cantwell, Malcolm, Brown, Nelson, Grice, Smith, Keeble, Dick, Musgrove.

what those present described as a 'constant wall of sound' to equalise an early Billy Liddell goal for the 'Pool. John Bond obliged with a 20-yard free-kick as the Reds unwisely decided to put just three men in the wall.

Muffin's long-range rocket set up the prospect of a nail-biting final match at Middlesbrough's Ayresome Park, where Hammers held their nerve to clinch top spot with a thrilling 3-1 victory.

First Division Fever

So through Vic Keeble, Fenton had bought goals from Newcastle, but could he deliver in the First Division? It took the Hammers' marksman just 37 minutes of the opening game of the 1958-59 season to answer that question when he scored West Ham's first goal in the top flight for over a quarter of a century to put his side one up against Portsmouth and send the large contingent of East Londoners among the 40,470 crowd into raptures. Dick, not to be outdone by his sharp-shooting compardre duly added a second five minutes after the break to give Hammers a confidence-boosting first win back among the top people with the same side that clinched the title, with the exception of Lansdowne who replaced Nelson.

The sides had lined up as follows: Portsmouth: Uprichard, McGhee, Hayward, Phillips, Dickinson, Casey, Harris (P), Gordon, Dougan, Harris H., Newman. West Ham: Gregory, Bond, Cantwell, Malcolm, Brown, Lansdowne, Grice, Smith, Keeble, Dick, Musgrove.

Two days later, in front of a capacity crowd of 37,485 under the Upton Park lights, Dick became the first West Ham player to score a First Division goal in front of the home fans since Tony Weldon against Birmingham in April 1932. A second from Smith clinched an unforgettable 2-0 victory over the First Division champions and put the happy Hammers on cloud nine – which was the number of goals that the Boleyn Ground patrons got for their admission fee the following Saturday as the newcomers played host to those other midland giants, Aston Villa.

Happily, SEVEN were scored by the homesters through Dick (2), Keeble (2), Musgrove (2) and Lansdowne to give the team its best start to a season that anyone could remember and put the fans in seventh heaven. An unchanged team took a hard-earned point off Wolves in a 1-1 draw at Molineux to continue the unbeaten run but the bubble had to burst – and it did typically enough at unfashionable Luton Town.

Kenilworth Road had long been a bogey ground for West Ham who hadn't won there since 1949 when a Bill Robinson goal gave Irons a rare 1-0 win. On this occasion the Hatters hit four to but a solitary reply from

Vic Keeble to prove that the indian sign was still working – as it would continue to be for the next four decades – prompting author Robert Banks to entitle his West Ham fan book *An Irrational Hatred of Luton.*

Hammers were much more comfortable tackling one of the most famous teams in the country – Manchester United – which they did in their next match at the Boleyn and triumphed 3-2 against the Red Devils in a never-to-be forgotten contest by goals from Dick, Smith and Musgrove and the help of debutante Bobby Moore who'd been picked ahead of his mentor and founder of the Academy, Malcolm Allison.

Inevitably, Hammers couldn't keep up the blistering pace of their opening matches and results began to form a more familiar pattern. Even so, the new boys still managed to achieve league 'doubles' over Aston Villa, Blackburn Rovers, Bolton Wanderers, Portsmouth and Tottenham Hotspur over Christmas, although Spurs gained swift revenge by winning the third round FA Cup tie 2-0 before a crowd of 56,000 at White Hart Lane.

Headed for the 'Big Time'

For some reason, not altogether explained, the West Ham management had harboured doubts about the inside right position even though its occupant, young Jimmy Smith, had won many plaudits for his fine play and was particularly well thought of because he'd come up through the ranks and was a shining example of West Ham's much vaunted youth policy.

Smith could perform equally as well at right half, however, and with this in mind Ted Fenton swooped to sign Leyton Orient's brilliant Welsh international inside right Phil Woosnam in a £30,000 deal in November 1958 which killed at a stroke any lingering doubts that West Ham lacked ambition and didn't really care about being in the 'big time'. Woosnam had a BA, was a schoolmaster at Leyton County High School, an academic and intellectual and would also become the first truly world-class player West Ham ever bought. He took time to settle in the West Ham side which finished 6th in their first season back in Division One but once he did he went on to play 15 times for the principality, represent the Football League versus the Italian League in 1960 and attracted a bid from Inter Milan.

In 1958-59 Fenton used just 20 players, of whom full backs Bond and Cantwell and half backs Andy Malcolm and Ken Brown were ever-presents and forwards Dick and Musgrove missed just one and two games respectively. After beating Arsenal 2-1 on aggregate in the two-legged semi-final, the youth team reached the final of the FA Youth Cup for the second time in three years only to lose the two-leg final by the same score to

Blackburn Rovers following a 1-1 draw at Upton Park. The West Ham team featured eight players who would go on to appear for the first team with varying degrees of success and three played in the 1964 FA Cup final. That team was: Caskey, Cripps, Burkett, Bovington, Moore, Brooks, Woodley, Cartwright, Beesley, Smillie, Scott.

Two years earlier the first signs that the hard work put in by people like youth team organiser Bill Robinson, chief scout Wally St Pier and player coaches Malcolm Allison, John Bond, Noel Cantwell and Mal Musgrove was coming to fruition, came when the youth team reached the first final against Manchester United's 'Busby Babes', but lost 8-2 on aggregate. The line up that day was: Goymer, Kirkup, Howe, Lewis, Walker, Lyall, Rowlands, Smith, Fenn, Cartwright, McDonald.

Joe Kirkup took part in West Ham's greatest ever triumph, the European Cup Winners' Cup final victory over TSV Munich 1860 at Wembley in 1965, Lyall became synonymous with the history of the club as a player, coach and manager and Cartwright progressed to the first team, although the latter only fleetingly.

50 Greatest Players

NOEL CANTWELL Defender

Born: Cork, 28 February 1932

Joined West Ham: 1952 **From:** Cork United

Appearances: 263 **Goals:** 11

Debut: v Fulham, 6 April 1953

Left West Ham: 1960 **For:** Manchester United

A buccaneering, adventurous left back, Cantwell was captain of West Ham United's 1958 Second Division promotion side and the Republic of Ireland. His partnership with right back John Bond was one of the most enduring an productive seen at Upton Park as the casual duo switched from defence to attack at will, often causing manager Fenton palpitations with their ultra laid-back approach. An ever-present during Hammers' first season back in the top flight in 1958-59, Canters even filled in at centre forward when needed. Manchester United broke the British record for a full back when they splashed out £30,000 to take him to Old Trafford on 1960 where he won an FA Cup winners medal as captain in 1963. An Academy graduate, Noel succeeded ex-Hammers team-mate Mal Musgrove as chairman of the PFA in 1966 and managed Coventry City, Peterborough United, the New England Tea Men and the Republic of Ireland with whom he was capped on 17 occasions while with West Ham.

Terry McDonald, a fast, tricky, flaxen-haired winger moved on to Leyton Orient to secure regular first-team football and was a member of the legendary O's side which won promotion to the First Division in 1962 along with fellow former Hammers Eddie Lewis and Dave Dunmore. McDonald remembers playing in long-serving centre half Dick Walker's testimonial match against Sparta Rotterdam in October 1957 when Vic Keeble made his first appearance for Hammers 36 hours after signing from Newcastle in front of a 19,375 crowd at Upton Park. West Ham won 5-0 with Jackie Dick getting a hat-trick. Then 16 years of age, Terry was told he would be twelfth man for a match against Huddersfield but when the team sheet went up he wasn't on it.

'I complained to Malcolm Allison,' recalls Terry 'and he ripped the sheet off the dressing room wall and went to see Ted. The next thing I know is I'm in the party – Allison ran the team then, there is no doubt about it. But don't just take my word for it, ask any of the players who were there at the time. He made West Ham.'

It is interesting to note that McDonald, who won an England youth cap against Hungary in 1956, was just one of nine players who appeared in those two FA Youth Cup finals to represent England at that level, including John Lyall, Johnny Cartwright, Johnny Smith, Roy Walker, Andy Smillie, Tony Scott, Derek Woodley and Bobby Moore.

Although it is easy to go along with the pre-Allison lobby – and he obviously wielded great influence – it is also worth remembering that it was the late Ted Fenton who instigated the club's successful youth policy, gave 'Big' Mal carte blanche and, most importantly, signed the players who got the club back into the First Division on the most stringent of budgets. In short, West Ham owe a great deal to Ted Fenton.

Dodgy Keeper?

Finishing a credible sixth in their first season back in the top flight, it was a happy bunch of Hammers who kicked off a deserved European tour in that summer of 1959 with a 0-0 draw against Charleroi in Belgium, but a more thoughtful party returned home after the tour yielded just one victory over Dutch side Fortuna Geelen and five defeats against crack European opposition the calibre of Rot Weiss Essen (3-2), Borussia Dortmund (3-1), Aachen (5-2), Moscow Spartak (5-1) and Red Star Bratislava (3-2).

Nevertheless, the Hammers won three and drew the other of their four opening games of the 1959-60 season and by mid-November, following a 3-1 win over Arsenal at Highbury sporting the famous light blue shirts with

50 Greatest Players

PHIL WOOSNAM Inside forward

Born: Caersws, Wales, 22 December 1932

Joined West Ham: 1958 **From:** Leyton Orient

Appearances: 153 **Goals:** 29

Debut: v Arsenal, 8 November 1958

Left West Ham: 1963 **For:** Aston Villa

A sublimely gifted inside forward, Phil Woosnam was capped by Wales on 14 occasions while with West Ham. A member of the Os team which won the Division Three Championship in 1956, Hammers broke their existing transfer record when they signed the brainy Welshman two years later for £30,000. Phil virtually ran the team's attacking options in his four years at Upton Park when transfer speculation was never far away. Hammers managed to keep their star until 1962 when he joined Aston Villa for £25,000. When he retired in 1966 he emigrated to the USA to become player coach of Atlanta Chiefs and later did more to put soccer on the map stateside than any other single individual.

claret chest bands for the first time, the unlikely lads from London's East End looked down on all the other 91 league clubs as table-toppers with 23 points from 17 games on goal average from Preston North End and Wolves.

Harry Obeney (deputising for the injured Keeble), Dick and Musgrove got the goals that gave Hammers their second win in successive seasons over the Gunners in north London. When the famous Wolves succumbed to a hat-trick from Dick as the Champions lost 3-2 at the Boleyn the following Saturday, Irons consolidated their position at the top of the table.

But not for long. 'Reaper' of the *Sunday Express* began his report of the following week's visit to Sheffield Wednesday with, 'The Big Flop... The Saturday after the Lord Mayor's Show... Hammers were bewitched, bewildered and bothered... they can have no complaints.'

The Owls were tethered for the first five minutes then the floodgates opened with three goals in eight minutes through Johnny Fantham (2) and Howard Wilkinson with Alan Finney making it 4-0 at half-time. Bobby Craig made it five in the 67th minute and, despite being reduced to 10 men when Tony Kay was injured, Wednesday added insult to injury with further goals from Keith Ellis and Finney again to complete a 7-0 record-equalling rout. The West Ham defence had a nightmare afternoon and individual reporters blamed various players for the debacle, but one contemporary match report put the blame squarely on the shoulders of Hammers' brilliant but erratic Eire international goalkeeper Noel Dwyer, who'd been replaced by reserve Brian Rhodes the previous week, 'The man who took the biggest sucker punch of all was goalkeeper Noel Dwyer. He just couldn't take or punch the ball clear as it came across from the wing. He was beaten through rank bad judgement.'

This would not be the last time the Irishman's performance would be called into question. Conceding 19 goals in eight games following the defeat at Hillsborough, things came to a head after a 5-3 home defeat by Newcastle on 20 February 1960. Bookmakers had reported unusually large amounts of money being wagered on the fixed-odds betting – all of it backing Newcastle to win. Three down after 27 minutes against the Magpies, Hammers staged a heroic fight-back to level the scores by half-time with goals from Dick and Woosnam (2), but two soft goals by the Geordies in the 60th and 64th minutes justified the punters' confidence in an away win.

One West Ham director was so incensed by the result that he left the ground in disgust and Woosnam was said to be apoplectic with rage. Dwyer never played for West Ham again and was sold to Swansea Town for £3,000. Although rumours that the match was 'fixed' persisted, nothing was ever proved and the scandal blew over.

Vic Keeble scored 49 goals in 80 games.

Irons were knocked out of the FA Cup in a third round Upton Park replay by a Denis Law-inspired Second Division Huddersfield Town, who adapted better to the frozen conditions with the help of rubber boots. Seventeen-year-old Law didn't score but scampered around as sure-footed as a mountain goat as five goals flew past Dwyer to but a solitary reply from Musgrove who would be the club's highest goalscorer with 16 league and cup goals and repeat the feat in 1960-61 by top-scoring with 18. With

John Smith transferring to Spurs in a straight exchange deal for centre forward Dave Dunmore on deadline day in March 1960, the burly Yorkshireman managed just two goals as Hammers slumped to a disappointing 14th position in the final table.

'They Don't Sack Managers'

Winning seven of their first eight home matches of 1960-61 and drawing the other, the seventh success was a 6-0 Guy Fawkes Day demolition of Arsenal when Dunmore hit a hat-trick, wing half Andy Malcolm scored his only First Division goal and Scottish and Welsh internationals Dick and Woosnam also scored to make it a 5 November the Gunners wouldn't forget in a hurry.

The following week's trip to Manchester City saw Hammers inflict the Mancunians first home defeat of the season at Maine Road as Dunmore and Grice got the goals that saw the East Londoners through 2-1. The victory put Hammers in a comfortable mid-table position with 20 points from 18 games, but told a tale of its own. It was the Cockneys' first away win in two days short of a year and was destined to be the last for another 10 months as the team slid down the table accordingly.

The paucity of points away from home was compounded by two early round cup defeats on opponents' territory; the first a second round exit in the newly formed Football League Cup competition at Fourth Division Darlington and then FA Cup defeat in a third round replay at Second Division Stoke City. By March 1961 the team's previously excellent home form began to falter and after losing at home to WBA on 4 March and 4-0 to Preston a week later, manager Ted Fenton was granted sick leave in mysterious circumstances.

On the 13 March 1961, two days after the defeat at Deepdale, chairman Reg Pratt issued the following statement, 'For some time Mr Fenton had been working under quite a strain and it was agreed he should go on sick leave. For the time being we shall carry on by making certain adjustments in our internal administration,' adding that the decision to take over the team 'was made after a great deal of thought'. The *Recorder* reminded its readers that 'the Upton Park club are proud of their tradition of never having sacked a manager. The present position gives a distinct impression that a compromise has been attempted to preserve that tradition.'

In his book *At home With The Hammers*, Ted Fenton tactfully perpetuated this most prevalent of all myths surrounding West Ham United – that they don't sack managers – when the truth is (with the exception of Charlie Paynter and Ron Greenwood) they'd sacked and would continue to sack every manager they'd ever employed. In his book, written just months earlier, Fenton said, 'Some clubs seem to treat their managers as a species of faith healer. The club has a bad spell, the fans and the shareholders start howling – and out goes the manager. A new man takes his place and if he's lucky things will improve, simply because a long-term policy set in motion some two or three managers back starts to pay off.' Unwittingly or otherwise, Ted Fenton had written the script for his own dismissal.

Under the distinctly ungrammatical headline, 'They gave me no money and sacked me – Fenton', West Ham's promotion manager gave his first public interview on the events surrounding his sacking to Jason Tomas in the *Evening Standard* London Football series of Saturday, 17 October 1970, saying he 'couldn't get tuppence' out of the directors for new players.

Great Managers – 1950-61

TED FENTON

A member of a famous East End sporting family, one of Ted Fenton's earliest memories was of seeing an illuminated tram bedecked in claret and blue as part of the celebrations following Hammers' appearances in the 1923 FA Cup final. As a useful footballer it was perhaps only natural that he would find his way to Upton Park, first as a pre-war player (176 apps., 27 goals) and as manager after cutting his teeth with Southern League Colchester United. It was Ted's shrewd wheeling and dealing in the transfer market which was largely responsible for delivering the team back to the First Division after an absence of 25 years in 1958. No less than seven of the 1964 FA Cup-winning side were also Fenton signings. But by that time Ted was three years 'down the road' following his shock dismissal in March 1961. Ted's brother Benny Fenton also played for Hammers before the war, but sadly passed away in early August 2000.

'I have always wondered why capital became available to Ron Greenwood but not me. For example, I wanted Leslie six months before and could have got him for only £6,000. Had I been able to sign some experienced players to back up youngsters coming through from the reserves at the time like Bobby Moore, Martin Peters and Geoff Hurst, I might still have been manager today. I was amazed when I got the sack. After all West Ham had finished sixth in their first season in the First Division and 14th the following season. This wasn't bad considering the initial results of other newly-promoted clubs in the past. Unfortunately, the directors panicked. It was a hell of a strain getting into the First Division and some of our older players were over the hill. Unfortunately the West Ham directors opposed my idea of promoting Bobby Moore and co from the reserves and they also said that there wasn't any money available to buy from other clubs. I was in an impossible situation.

'Still, it's all over now. I no longer have any animosity towards the West Ham board – indeed, I often sit in the directors box when West Ham are at home. My affection for the club is as strong as ever. My biggest kick was seeing West Ham win the FA Cup in 1964 – eight members of that side were lads I had signed for nothing.'

Despite the fact that chairman Reg Pratt had intimated a week after the sacking of Fenton that 'the board had no plans to name a new manager' and that the team 'would be managed by the board with advice from their trainer Albert Walker and Phil Woosnam', less than a month after Fenton's dismissal, on 13 April 1961, Ron Greenwood was appointed the new manager of West Ham United.

Greenwood, who was assistant manager of Arsenal prior to his new appointment and also boss of the England Under-23s, had actually been 'sounded out' about the West Ham job by his great mentor Walter Winterbottom who'd taken his full England team to Upton Park for a 'behind closed doors' practise match on the very day that Fenton was given his marching orders. But Greenwood declined Hammers' initial overtures, telling Winterbottom, 'I'm happy at Arsenal. In any case, if they're going to sack people like they did last night, it's obviously not a happy club'. Any lingering doubts Greenwood may have harboured were dispelled within a few short weeks of joining the West Ham family, when he realised the goldmine of talent he'd inherited and told his new charges, 'You're a bit like your theme song – what you've got to do is stop the bubbles from bursting.'

Chapter Eight: 1961-63
The New Order

Although a 3-0 defeat at Second Division Plymouth in the third round of the FA Cup was a major disappointment, Greenwood's first full season in charge saw a marked improvement on the performance of the previous year as the team made up eight places to finish a creditable eighth position in the First Division table of 1961-62, when they were rarely out of the top half with a high water-mark of second place in a season which saw unfashionable Ipswich Town take the title.

Argyle's FA Cup win at Home Park avenged the Pilgrim's 3-2 first round League Cup defeat at Upton Park as Hammers again failed to get past the second stage of the new competition when they went down 3-1 at home to holders Aston Villa. As a reward for their efforts, the team were taken on a close-season tour of Africa and everything went well until the final Ghana leg of the trip, as Greenwood recalled in his autobiography, *Yours Sincerely*, in 1984, 'Nobody met us at the airport at Accra – the excuse given later was they thought we were on another plane. By this time, though, we knew there was only one flight a day from Johannesburg to Accra. We then found ourselves being shown into a hotel that was nothing more than a doss-house. The blankets almost crawled. Nobody slept, except Johnny Dick, who could sleep anywhere. The tour had a hidden bonus for us, however. Through all its adversity our team spirit grew stronger. The problems we

WEST HAM UNITED
THIS WAS THE PLATE REMOVED FROM ENGINE 61672
NAMED WEST HAM UNITED SCRAPPED MARCH 1960
THE LOCOMOTIVE WAS OF THE B.17. PART 4 CLASS
DESIGNED BY SIR NIGEL GRESLEY FOR L.N.E.R. JULY 1937

Memories of a Fan

'We lived our lives through them. Scruffy kids, everything they were we wanted to be. But could never aspire to...

'We used to get the train from Gidea Park to Forest Gate where we'd get on the number 40 or 58 bus to the ground. Moving down Green Street you could see the floodlights in the distance and you'd get a funny feeling in the pit of your stomach. It was Manchester United at home on the first day of the season and we'd got a new manager, Ron Greenwood, a new goalkeeper, Lawrie Leslie, a new winger, Ian Crawford, new floodlights and a new roof over our spiritual home, the North Bank. The shouts of the crowd mingled in with the cries of the street vendors and programme sellers and pervading everywhere the irresistible aroma of hot dogs and onions.

'We drew 1-1 with United, Dick equalising an early goal from Nobby Stiles. But it was the prospect of the first away match which really fired the imagination... a visit to "double winning" Spurs. They too had brand new floodlights but in the very split second they turned them on five minutes before half-time, Phil Woosnam christened them by crashing a 30-yard piledriver past Bill Brown in the Spurs goal to equalise a Terry Dyson opener and stun the Spurs fans in the 50,000 crowd. Ten minutes after the break, Mal Musgrove, not to be outdone, hammered home from a similar range to put our side ahead, but Dyson levelled to add to the anticipation of the return fixture at Upton Park the following Monday night. It seemed as though the whole of the East End wanted to see their heroes take on the "double" champions in a match that posed a big test for Greenwood's mixture of new and old talent.

'For big matches it was advisable to get to the ground early to be sure of getting right down the front behind the goal. Under-14s got in for nine pence but sometimes the turnstile operators would turn a "blind eye" as youngsters were lifted over the turnstile. Officially 36,348 saw Tony Scott give West Ham the lead five minutes before half-time in a match that those present on that hot, humid night of 28 August 1961 will never forget. Many fainted in the heat of the jam-packed terraces and untold children were transported over the heads of the crowd on a conveyor belt of human hands towards the waiting arms of the St John's Ambulance men. Others, like the six-foot-plus giant who was hit full in the face by a piledriver from Spurs' 15-stone dreadnought of a centre forward Bobby Smith, were not so lucky. Knocked unconscious, he remained on his feet within the densely packed crowd until a flurry of hankies alerted the intrepid St John's men to his plight.

On the field, Les Allen equalised for Spurs but Alan Sealey atoned for missing two earlier "sitters" with a 77th-minute "wonder goal" to set the East End crowd alight as they began celebrating victory over the "double" winners by chanting, "We want six!"'

shared welded us together. It also taught me a lot about the character of my players. I noted all those who had a good sense of humour, those I could count on, those who looked for problems and those who were idle. And on my first tour as manager I discovered much about myself.'

Johnny Byrne Arrives

The most important event of Greenwood's first season at West Ham occurred some months earlier, however – the signing of centre forward Johnny Byrne from Crystal Palace for a record-breaking £65,000 in March 1962. Greenwood had long been an admirer of the multi-talented individual who was nicknamed 'Budgie' because of his non-stop chatter and had seen at first hand his daunting array of skills when he picked him for the England Under-23 team as a Fourth Division player in 1961. Already a full England international, West Ham paid £62,500 cash for Byrne plus Ronnie Brett, a skilful centre forward who had started his career at Selhurst Park.

After a shaky start, Byrne went on to become one of the central figures of West Ham's success in the mid-sixties while fate dealt Brett, who had the distinction of scoring against Manchester United both at home and away in September 1960, a tragic hand when he was killed in a car crash just five months after his transfer. His former team-mate and friend, goalkeeper Brian Rhodes, escaped unscathed.

The opening of the 1962-63 season coincided with West Ham's most disastrous start to a campaign for many a year. A 3-1 defeat at Villa Park was followed by a 4-1 beating under the Boleyn bulbs by Wolves and the following Saturday Spurs triumphed 6-1 to record their biggest ever victory at Upton Park. John Lyall, who'd taken over the No. 3 shirt following Noel Cantwell's £30,000 move to Manchester United two years earlier, inadvertently started the rout by conceding an own-goal. A 0-0 draw at Molineux gained some relief but then Leyton Orient, fielding three former Hammers in Lewis, McDonald and Dunmore, inflicted further humiliation on their close neighbours with a 2-0 victory in heatwave conditions at Brisbane Road. Dunmore, who joined Os in a straight swap for Alan Sealey scored the first goal to rub it in.

A 1-0 home win over Liverpool and two spectacular away successes at Manchester City 6-1 and Blackburn 4-0 helped stop the rot but Hammers never really recovered from that nightmare start and were destined to finish in mid-table. Once again, Irons were drawn at home to Plymouth in the first round of the League Cup and halted the Pilgrims' progress with a 6-0 win that punished the Argyle for their temerity of the previous January. But for

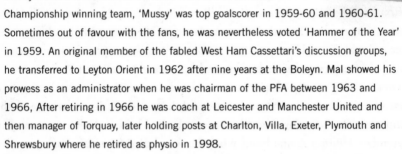

Great Players

MALCOLM MUSGROVE Outside left

Born: Newcastle-Upon-Tyne, 8 July 1933

Joined West Ham: 1954 **From:** Lynemouth Colliery

Debut: v Brentford, 27 February 1954

Appearances: 301 **Goals:** 89

Left West Ham: 1962 **For:** Leyton Orient

Mal Musgrove holds the distinction of being the second highest goalscoring winger in West Ham's history behind the legendary Jimmy Ruffell. A member of the 1957-58 Second Division Championship winning team, 'Mussy' was top goalscorer in 1959-60 and 1960-61. Sometimes out of favour with the fans, he was nevertheless voted 'Hammer of the Year' in 1959. An original member of the fabled West Ham Cassettari's discussion groups, he transferred to Leyton Orient in 1962 after nine years at the Boleyn. Mal showed his prowess as an administrator when he was chairman of the PFA between 1963 and 1966, After retiring in 1966 he was coach at Leicester and Manchester United and then manager of Torquay, later holding posts at Charlton, Villa, Exeter, Plymouth and Shrewsbury where he retired as physio in 1998.

the third season running the Boleyn boys went out in the second round, this time 3-1 at Second Division Rotherham United.

Cup Drama

By the time the FA Cup got under way – most third round ties weren't started until February due to the 'big freeze' – many of the old favourites from Fenton's regime had departed. Tough-as-teak wing half Andy Malcolm had gone to Chelsea the previous season for £23,000 after nine seasons of sterling service, winger Mal Musgrove went to Orient for £11,000 following a 10-season tour of duty in which he'd become the second highest goalscoring winger in the history of the club behind Jim Ruffell, 'Welsh Wizard' Phil Woosnam had left for Villa for £25,000 still hankering after a manager's job and that loveable character Jackie Dick had joined Brentford for £17,500 where his 23 goals would fire the Bees to the Fourth Division Championship.

When the much-postponed home third round tie with Fulham finally went ahead on a snowbound pitch on 2 February 1963 under the Upton Park lights, temperatures were still below zero and the match would never have got the go-ahead today. It finished 0-0 but in the replay at Craven

Cottage 18 days later, which was played in a snowstorm, Hammers twice managed to get the orange ball past Macedo in the Fulham goal, through Ronnie Boyce and a Byrne penalty after the former had been brought down, to get through to the next round to meet Swansea and former keeper Noel Dwyer at Upton Park. Dwyer, who left Hammers under a cloud, naturally enough had a 'blinder' but even his heroics couldn't prevent Boyce scoring on a 'mud-heap' to put his team through to face champions-elect Everton, again at the Boleyn, in round five.

The Merseysiders were altogether a different proposition to Hammers' earlier opponents and very much the product of Littlewoods Pools millionaire chairman John Moore's cheque book. The team included full internationals of all the home countries as well as the Republic of Ireland and would provide the toughest test yet for Greenwood's talented young advocates. Thousands of vociferous Everton fans had arrived early and colonised a large part of the North Bank, traditionally inhabited by home supporters. All seemed to be wearing blue and white paper hats with 'Follow Everton with the Daily Express' emblazoned on them and carrying bottles of beer. The atmosphere was tense and there was trouble in the air.

Everton, who dominated the first half, were niggly and nasty and Tony Kay (who would later be jailed for match-fixing) in particular never missed an opportunity to

Great Players

JOHN DICK Inside left

Born: Goran, Glasgow, 19 March 1930

Joined West Ham: 1953 **From:** Crittal Athletic

Appearances: 351 **Goals:** 166

Debut: v Lincoln City, 19 August 1953

Left West Ham: 1962 **For:** Brentford

After a shaky opening spell, during which he failed to score in his first 12 games, Jackie Dick developed into the third highest goalscorer in the club's history behind Vic Watson and Geoff Hurst. He became Hammers' first ever Scottish international when he was selected for the annual England v Scotland fixture at Wembley in 1959, which was to remain his sole cap. After top scoring with 25 league and cup goals in 1961-62, John was transferred to Fourth Division Brentford for £17,500 in September 1962 where his 23 goals shot the Bees to the Championship to more than justify his price tag. John is still involved in grass roots football in Essex by his involvement with his beloved Santos Boys team.

intimidate West Ham's young players at set-pieces. The threatened trouble finally erupted when Dennis Stevens was adjudged by referee Jim Finney to have fouled Bobby Moore and he awarded West Ham a debatable penalty. Against a background of total mayhem at the North Bank end, Johnny Byrne calmly slotted the ball past Everton's Gordon West to put Hammers ahead. The incensed Everton fans threw dozens of bottles onto the pitch and a policeman was injured by a piece of flying concrete.

It was the worst display of football hooliganism seen in post-war football in England and was the catalyst for the cancer of football violence as we know it today. West Ham held on to their slender lead against an increasingly hostile background to go through to the quarter-finals, the 'Academy' triumphing over the 'School of Science', but really there was only one winner on what was a fateful day for football – the football hooligan – and nothing would ever quite be the same again.

Drawn at Liverpool on Grand National Day in the sixth round, 'Pool had the support of both the red and blue halves of Merseyside as the Hammers fell at the final hurdle to a solitary Roger Hunt goal nine minutes from time at Anfield after silencing the Kop for long periods with an adventurous brand of 4-2-4 which deserved at least a replay. But Hammers were not down for long and spirits were lifted a few days after the Liverpool defeat following a 2-0 midweek win over Sheffield Wednesday when it was announced that West Ham had been invited to compete in the prestigious International Soccer League to be staged in the USA in the summer of 1963.

Lawrie Leslie, a £14,000 signing from Airdrie.

Strength in Depth

Although his charges had finished in an undistinguished twelfth place in the final First Division table of 1962-63, Greenwood was 'over the moon' when his youngsters finally won the coveted FA Youth Cup with an exciting 6-5 aggregate victory in the final over Liverpool. After losing the first leg 3-1 at Anfield, the young Hammers stunned their Liverpudlian counterparts with an exhilarating 5-2 second-leg victory at Upton Park when centre forward

Martin Britt scored four goals – all with his head – to add to the one he'd scored at Anfield to ensure the cup came to the East End for the first time. Ten of that victorious team would go on to appear in the first team, including Johnny Sissons and a red-headed winger by the name of Harry Redknapp.

The addition of right-winger Peter Brabrook to the squad earlier in the season following a protracted £35,000 transfer from Chelsea had provided the final component of Greenwood's team-building plan and the signing of the East Ham-born wing wizard effectively brought him 'home'.

In the States Hammers were pitted against a truly international mixture of top class opposition and after a shaky start went onto win their group which included Kilmarnock, Mantova (Italy), Oro (Mexico), Munster (West Germany) and Recife (Brazil) who West Ham played in that order in New York, Chicago and Detroit. After drawing 3-3 with 'Killie' in the opening game, in which goalkeeper Lawrie Leslie was Hammers' hero and losing the second match 4-2 to Mantova, the turning point came when Moore and Byrne, oozing confidence after playing in England's 8-1 victory over Switzerland in Basle, where 'Budgie' scored twice, rejoined the team for the match against Oro at New York's Randalls Island stadium. Arriving just 24 hours before the game, Moore said perceptively, 'If you turn the league table upside-down you might see the final winners.'

Hammers never looked back as they defeated Oro 3-1 then beat Valenciennes 3-1 and Munster 2-0 in the Motor City before drawing 1-1 with Recife back in New York to top the table as Moore had so confidently

Peters blocks Hunt of Liverpool in the 2-1 win at Anfield in September 1963.

predicted. The match was marred by the bad sportsmanship of the South Americans, however, and there was fighting among the fans as well as trouble on the pitch as Recife's star forward, Guimares, was sent off along with – harshly – Alan Sealey.

Bobby Moore – England's most famous footballer.

The conduct of the Brazilians was only a precursor for worse trouble when Hammers returned to the States to play the winners of the other group, Gornik Zabrze, over two legs at Randalls Island for the right to meet the previous year's winners, Dukla Prague of Czechoslovakia in the final of the American Challenge Cup. 'Budgie' Byrne hit the goal that earned his team a 1-1 draw in the first match before beer cans were thrown onto the pitch by disgruntled East European fans when the English referee refused their side a penalty. But worse was to follow in the second leg when the Poles had two goals disallowed by Scottish referee Jim McLean and hundreds of exiled Polish fans invaded the pitch and attacked the officials.

With the score at 0-0 West Ham used the enforced stoppage time until order was restored to work out where they'd been going wrong and Hurst got the decisive goal after good work in midfield by Byrne. The final against Dukla was again a two-legged affair with the first match staged at the 110,000-capacity Soldier Field arena in Chicago where the Czechs won 1-0. Tony Scott put the Hammers level in the second game back in New York, but the famous wing half and captain Josef Masopust got the decisive goal of a match in which the Czech keeper Pavel Kouba saved his side time and time again. Masopust predicted that 'West Ham would win a major European tournament within two years' and manager Greenwood claimed, 'We learned more that summer than we would have done in five European campaigns about how the game was evolving around the world.'

Geoff Hurst returned home as the tournament's top scorer with nine goals following his inspired conversion from wing half to striker by Greenwood earlier in the season and Moore proudly clutching the Eisenhower Trophy as the Player of the Series. But more importantly, the team had grown up Stateside and those that had left England as boys had returned as men with a burning ambition for more success.

Chapter Nine: 1963-70
The Halcyon Years

Following a good start to the 1963-64 season, it seemed the lessons learned during the summer of success had been temporarily forgotten as the team once again slumped into an infuriating pattern of inconsistency in the league. Yet Liverpool were defeated 2-1 at Anfield in September when young Dave Bickles, who'd played his first game in the U.S. against Kilmarnock, made his full league debut and kept the Reds' volatile centre forward Ian St John quiet in a match which saw Hammers' Worcestershire cricketer-cum-goalkeeper Jim Standen save a Ronnie Moran penalty to clinch the points. Hammers also defeated the 'Pool 1-0 at Upton Park to complete a double over the eventual champions.

At Old Trafford in late October, a Martin Britt goal gave Irons a surprise win, but the turning point of the season came in the guise of a record-breaking 8-2 home defeat by Blackburn Rovers on Boxing Day. Greenwood, who had to take his shell-shocked side for a return at Rovers 48 hours later, due to the enormity of the defeat at first considered making wholesale changes but instead settled for just one – Eddie Bovington to replace the gifted Martin Peters at right half. The inclusion of 'Bov', who possessed a granite-hard tackle and was almost an exact replica in style of the former occupant of the No. 4 shirt, Andy Malcolm, enabled Hammers to pull in the full backs and force play out wide, nullifying the threat of Rovers' playmaker England international Brian Douglas, who was man-marked by Bovington.

Hurst shoots in the 1964 FA Cup final against Preston North End.

The Simple Solution

The solution was so effective that West Ham won 3-1 at Ewood Park and found the formation that would take them all the way to Wembley: Standen, Bond, Burkett, Bovington, Brown, Moore, Brabrook, Boyce, Byrne, Hurst, Sissons. Six days after winning at Blackburn, Hammers – playing with a new-found conviction – easily overcame Charlton 3-0 in the FA Cup third round with goals from Hurst, Brabrook and Sissons before 34,155 at Upton Park. Next came a tricky tie at Leyton Orient who had unluckily gone down by two goals to one in the League Cup earlier in the season and, as then, would field left winger Mal Musgrove against his old team-mates in addition to Lewis and Dunmore. The crowd of 34,345 which assembled at Brisbane Road remains an Orient record to this day and witnessed Os take the lead from a second-minute header by diminutive Norman Deeley, but Brabrook equalised from close range just before the break to take the tie back to Upton Park where an extra thousand fans saw the second stage of a very East London affair. Any late-comers would have missed all the key action as West Ham had the game sewn up with goals in the first 15 minutes from Byrne and Hurst who was thwarted of a hat-trick by amateur Mike Pinner who saved his second-half penalty to ensure the score stayed at 3-0.

The Second Division again provided the opposition when Hammers were drawn away to Swindon in the fifth round and whom West Ham had also eliminated from the League Cup in an Upton Park replay earlier in the campaign. No replay was necessary on this occasion, however, as the same scoring sequence from Byrne and Hurst saw Irons through 3-1 for a sixth round showdown at Upton Park with those other famous wearers of the claret and blue – Burnley.

The headline above Denis Compton's match report of the West Ham-Burnley clash pretty well summed things up, proclaiming, 'Magnificent is the word for brilliant Byrne.' Under the 3-2 scoreline in favour of the home side it went on, 'Bravo, Johnny Byrne – the man who sent West Ham zooming into the FA Cup semi-finals with one of the most brilliant centre forward displays I have ever seen. Make no mistake, this was Byrne's match. His speed of movement and superb ball control on a greasy, treacherous surface bordered at times on the fantastic.'

Trailing to an early individual goal from winger John Connolly at the interval, Sissons equalised from an impossible angle at the South Bank end in the 57th minute before 'Budgie's double act. First he volleyed an unstoppable shot from Brabrook's cross past Adam Blacklaw and then dribbled round the Scottish international keeper after pouncing on a defensive error by Brian Miller to make the score 3-1 in the 68th minute of a pulsating cup tie played against a deafening background of sound provided by a capacity crowd of 36,651. Burnley pulled one back through Ray Pointer, but West Ham went through 3-2 to their first FA Cup semi-final for 30 years.

The Cup Tradition Continues

Also through to the semi-finals was former Hammers 'black sheep' goalkeeper Noel Dwyer who'd played a 'blinder' for Swansea as they defeated Liverpool 2-1 at Anfield to set up an all-Second Division clash with Preston at Villa Park while Hammers drew the 'short straw' – Manchester United at Hillsborough! When United comprehensively defeated the East End's Cockney cup hopes by 2-0 on their own ground just a week before the semi-final meeting, the Mancunians became red hot favourites to reach Wembley.

But the bookies and pundits had overlooked an important factor – the great cup fighting traditions of West Ham United which went right back to the earliest days of the century and which were never more evident than when the Hammers were cast in the role of the 'underdog'. Privately seething about being written off in the media, which even extended to Wally Barnes' BBC radio commentary of the match, London's last cup hopes went into the clash against Law, Best and Charlton et al with an iron resolve in keeping with their proud heritage and were still holding their illustrious opponents 0-0 at half-time in a downpour that became a deluge to turn the pitch into a rain-sodden morass.

Kicking into the Leppings Lane end in the second period, Hammers knew of United keeper Gaskell's tendency to wander off his line and the unsung workhorse of the West Ham team, inside-right Ronnie Boyce, exploited just that weakness when he lobbed him from 30 yards out to put unfancied, unfashionable Irons ahead in the 57th minute to the massed delight of their thousands of rain-drenched supporters. Five minutes later, with the 'Bubbles' anthem beginning to swirl around the ground, Hammers won a corner on the left. Sissons, seeing Jackie Burkett making a run towards him, went to play it short to the full back, but Crerand came across to cover. Sissons made as if to take an orthodox corner, but then with Crerand retreating back into the middle, Burkett ran back to crack the 18-year-old's short ball onto the head of Boyce on the six-yard line plumb centre of goal who glanced it just inside the far post to make it 2-0.

For one brief, heart-stopping moment, after Law had lunged two-footed at Standen in goal, there was the threat of a famed United fightback when Law outjumped a still-dazed Standen to score with a header. But then centre half Bill Foulkes was pulled wide to the touchline by Hurst, as Moore – playing like a trojan – swept nonchalantly past three United men on the halfway line before releasing a perfect through-ball for Hurst to run onto and drill low past Gaskell for the 'killer' goal from the edge of the box. United were finished and West Ham were through to the their first Wembley final since 1923 and once again there were bubbles in the air.

In his moment of triumph Greenwood was still cautious, however, saying, 'Remember, we've still to win the cup. We have only reached Wembley. We haven't won there yet.' But West Ham did, 3-2, after twice being behind to proud Preston who overcame Swansea in the other semi-final. First Sissons became the youngest player to score in a cup final when he equalised Doug Holden's shock early goal for North End, then Hurst levelled Alex Dawson's header that put the Lancastrians 2-1 up at half-time with one of his own in the 52nd minute before that man Boyce struck again with a dramatic winning header in injury time from Brabrook's cross to write himself into East End folklore and gain his team a passport to Europe.

Great Matches

FA CUP FINAL — **Wembley, 2 May 1964**

West Ham United 3	Preston North End 2	Attendance 100,000
Sissons	Holden	
Hurst	Dawson	
Boyce		

Ron Greenwood averted a major disaster with a half-time team talk as inspired as it was timely. Preston, with Spavin, Lawton and Kendall running the midfield, had dominated the first half and looked anything but Second Division underdogs. Ken Brown was struggling to combat the twin aerial threat of Dawson and Ashworth so Greenwood moved Moore into the centre of defence to support him, enabling Bovington to push forward more. The result was a more flexible formation and Boyce won it for Hammers with an injury-time header from Brabrook's cross.

West Ham United: Standen, Bond, Burkett, Bovington, Brown, Moore, Brabrook, Boyce, Byrne, Hurst, Sissons.

Preston North End: Kelly, Ross, Smith, Lawton, Singleton, Kendall, Wilson, Ashworth, Dawson, Spavin, Holden.

Referee: A. Holland.

London's new cup kings came close to becoming the first English team to win two domestic cups in one season, but went down 6-3 on aggregate to a strong Leicester City side in an enthralling two-legged semi-final who went on to defeat Lawrie Leslie's new team, Stoke City, in the final.

For the second successive season West Ham finished their league programme with 40 points from 42 matches, but it was only enough to secure fourteenth position in the final First Division table of 1963-64 as against twelfth place the year before.

Moore lifts the FA Cup aloft after the Wembley victory of 1964 over Preston North End.

New Campaign

The cup holders prepared for the new campaign with a three-match tour of Austria and Germany in which they defeated FK Austria 3-0 and GAK Graz 1-0 before losing 1-0 to FC Nuremberg. In the official 'curtain raiser' Hammers took on League Champions Liverpool – who they'd defeated home and away the previous campaign – in the annual Charity Shield match at Anfield and drew 2-2. Johnny Byrne wasted no time in getting off the mark with the first equaliser. Hurst's second leveller came in the 84th minute and exorcised Roger Hunt's same-time tally which consigned Hammers to that heart-breaking 1-0 defeat at the same venue in the FA Cup sixth round the year before.

After defeating Fulham 2-1 at Craven Cottage on the season's opening day, the first home game against semi-final opponents Manchester United was staged in carnival-like atmosphere as, in a nice touch, Hammers detailed three of their apprentice professionals to parade the FA Cup and Charity Shield before the start. Watched by England manager Alf Ramsey and 37,069 others in fiesta mood, the new Cockney cup heroes responded with an enthralling display of attacking soccer which produced a replica of

West Ham United with the FA Cup and Charity Shield in 1964.

the Hillsborough result as Sissons, Byrne and Hurst reaffirmed their mastery over the Mancunians for whom Law again scored a consolation.

The European Adventure Begins

Drawn against the unfashionable and largely unknown Belgian part-timers of La Gantoise in the first round of the European Cup Winners' Cup, Hammers typically struggled to get past the stubborn Ghent team who were nicknamed the 'Buffaloes'. Only another priceless goal from the head of midfield dynamo Ronnie Boyce gave the European new boys a slender 1-0 lead to take back to East London. In the second leg, Byrne, Hurst, Boyce and Moore all missed 'sitters' and paid the price when Peters hit an intended back-pass past deputy goalkeeper Alan Dickie to give the Belgians a shock lead.

An inspired run and cross from Sissons allowed Byrne to convert the equaliser to save Hammers' blushes just before the interval, but the 1-1 final scoreline was a moral victory for their unfancied opponents who were cheered off the field by the sporting Upton Park fans who reserved only boos and jeers for their own inept favourites. At this stage Josef Masopust's bold prediction was looking optimistic, to say the least, and there would need to be a distinct upturn in performance if Greenwood's young team were to overcome their next European hurdle – crack Czechs Spartak

Prague Sokolovo – especially as Bobby Moore would be out of action for three months after undergoing a 'groin operation', although it is now clear that his absence was caused by his first brush with the deadly cancer that would so tragically take him from us three decades later.

The Czechs were a typically dour, well-drilled 'Iron Curtain' side and the same soubriquet could be used to describe their defence, as Hammers were to discover in the first leg at Upton Park. The East Europeans packed their defence with nine men – sometimes 10 – and did not stand on ceremony, inflicting a catalogue of gruesome fouls on Byrne, Sissons, Peters and Hurst before they finally cracked in the 59th minute. From yet another free-kick, the ball was cleared to full back Bond, the West Ham special agent with a licence to score, who hit a first-time left-foot volley from 25 yards to at last pierce the Czech defence.

In a match of almost relentless West Ham pressure, Spartak's goalkeeper, Kramerius, saved them time and time again, but was finally beaten for the second occasion eight minutes from the end when Sealey, who had his first shot blocked, slammed in the rebound from close range. But would two goals be enough?

The answer came soon enough when Sissons put West Ham 3-0 up on aggregate after just 14 minutes of the return leg at the National Stadium in Prague to stifle the chant of 'Spartak, Spartak' as 45,000 Czech fans were silenced by the discipline, determination and, above all, the bravery of Hammers' all-English team as they triumphed over some savage tackling and indifferent decisions by the Bulgarian referee to reach the quarter-finals. To get there, despite defeat on the day as Spartak scored twice in the second half, Hammers had to fight like they'd never fought before. They had to survive a relentless pounding from opponents who threw themselves like a suicide squad at the barrier of blue that was always before them. Relief only came at the final whistle when their bruised bodies and torn legs bore testimony to the battering they had taken. Sissons – manhandled off the field by the ref – and Sealey, who needed seven stitches in a shin gash, were the injured heroes but the real saviour was goalkeeper Standen who saved Spartak skipper Masek's penalty.

Detailed Dossiers

Safely ensconced in the top half of the table at the turn of the year, the holders had a fight on their hands when they found themselves 2-1 down at half-time to Birmingham City in their first defence of the trophy in the FA Cup third round at Upton Park. But Hammers remembered who they were after the interval and went through 4-2 with two goals from Hurst and another from Sissons to add to the one by Byrne just before the interval. The crowd were in sombre mood for the visit of Chelsea in the fourth round three weeks later as they and the players observed a minute's silence in memory of Sir Winston Churchill and stayed that way as a 10th-minute strike from Bobby Tambling ended Irons' hold on the trophy. Of the goal, Ken Brown claimed, 'If my boots had been a size bigger I'd have got to it.' Meanwhile, Joe Kirkup and Peter Brabrook – who couldn't get into the side – both asked to be transfer-listed but were refused with Greenwood probably mindful that he'd need all his players while still in Europe, where Swiss cup holders Lausanne Sports were barring the way to the semi-finals.

A typical piece of opportunism by Brian Dear and a wonderful solo goal from Byrne in the first leg of the quarter-final tie in Switzerland seemed to make Hammers' progress to the last four of the Cup Winners' Cup a formality as they brought a 2-1 lead back to London. But the Lausanne lambs turned out to be lions at the Boleyn as they played their part in a match which had as many twists and turns as an Agatha Christie thriller before going down 4-3 to earn a standing ovation from the sporting home crowd.

Throughout their European campaign, Hammers benefited tremendously from detailed dossiers on their continental opponents – compiled by Ron Greenwood and his assistant Albert Walker – but they could have been excused for passing on Hammers' semi-final opponents Real Zaragoza as it would have made daunting reading, although Greenwood's opposite numbers at Dundee and Cardiff City could have provided him with first-hand information on the Spaniards who'd eliminated both clubs from that season's competition – the Welshmen in the quarter-finals.

For the first 30 minutes of their first-leg Upton Park meeting, West Ham paid scant regard to their visitors' reputation and were 2-0 up through Dear and Byrne in that time and seemingly only had to book their coach for a return to Wembley. But then the forward line known as the 'magnificent five' in Spain began to assert themselves as did former Real Madrid centre half and captain Santamaria at the back, who had played in a final or two with his old club. After much pressure, Canario pulled one back and by the end Hammers were glad to hang on to a slender 2-1 lead on a night that began with cheers and finished with jeers and the slow hand-clap from their own fans.

A return now to the famous twin towers – and with it the chance of emulating the great Spurs side who became the first team from these isles to win a major European trophy in this very same competition two years earlier – seemed less likely. But those who doubted West Ham's chances of gaining further glory chose to discount the unique team spirit which was first forged on that calamitous tour out of Africa in the summer of 1961 and further galvanised on the sun-baked fields of New York, Detroit and Chicago in 1963, when boys became men and a good team became a great team almost overnight.

West Ham went into battle against the Spaniards – unbeaten at La Ramereda Stadium – without their trump forward ace Byrne who'd been injured playing for England against Scotland two weeks earlier but Brian 'Stag' Dear was in the mood, having hit a record-breaking five goals in 20 minutes versus WBA on Good Friday. This time he turned provider,

Great Matches

EUROPEAN CUP WINNERS' CUP FINAL **Wembley, 19 May 1965**

West Ham United 2 TSV Munich 1860 0 **Attendance 100,000**

Sealey 2

West Ham's opponents in their second Wembley final in just over a year would be TSV Munich 1860, a tough side who had rarely been out of the Bundesliga top five all season and had eliminated Oporto, Legia Warsaw and Torino to get to Wembley. With what amounted to be better than home advantage – the support of 90,000 Hammers fans at Wembley – West Ham knew they'd never stand a better chance, although Geoff Hurst sparked a note of caution when he admitted, 'They will not be an easy side to beat.'

After pummelling the Munich defence for over an hour to no avail that night, Hurst's prediction seemed like the understatement of the year as the West Ham forwards were thwarted time and again. But something had to give and after suffering some scares of their own at the other end to which Standen responded brilliantly, West Ham struck twice in three minutes to win the match – and the cup! Both goals were scored by outside right Alan 'Sammy' Sealey. Boyce made the first when he pushed a pass between two defenders for the winger to move on to and unleash an unstoppable shot into the top of the net to send the massed ranks of Hammers fans into exaltation. Then the obviously rattled Radenkovic ran out of his goal to pull down Dear outside the area. Following the free-kick, skipper Moore centred high and Sealey pounced on the bounce off Peters to ram home from close in. West Ham could have had more but settled for 2-0 in what was and still is the finest match seen at Wembley.

West Ham United: Standen, Kirkup, Birkett, Peters, Brown, Moore, Sealey, Boyce, Hurst, Dear, Sissons.

TSV Munich 1860: Radenkovic, Wagner, Kohlars, Bena, Reich, Luttrop, Heiss, Kuppers, Brunnenmeier, Grosser, Rabele.

Referee: I. Zsolt.

50 Greatest Players

ALAN SEALEY Winger

Born: Hampton, Middlesex, 22 April 1942

Joined West Ham: 1961 **From:** Leyton Orient

Debut: v Leicester City, 3 April 1961

Appearances: 128 **Goals:** 26

Left West Ham: 1967 **For:** Plymouth Argyle

Guaranteed a place in any 'Hammers Hall of Fame' by virtue of his two historic goals against TSV Munich 1860 at Wembley in 1965 which brought the European Cup Winners' Cup to Upton Park. 'Sammy,' as he was affectionately known, was originally a centre forward, but enjoyed more success when switched to the right wing. A freak training ground injury sustained while playing an impromptu game of cricket virtually ended his career. Alan sadly passed away in 1996 and was honoured with an emotive minute's silence before the home FA Cup tie v Grimsby Town.

threading a finely judged through pass down the middle into the path of Sissons who hit a right-foot shot past Yarza to equalise Lapetra's first-half strike in the 54th minute and put his team of brave battlers ahead 3-2 on aggregate. Thousands of fans at home, tuning into the BBC's radio commentary, joined the tiny band of Hammers fans in Spain to celebrate as their heroes held on for an historic victory... West Ham, the little team from the Iron Works factory in Canning Town, had reached a European cup final – and at Wembley, to boot.

Sipping tea in the dressing room after the famous victory against Munich, Greenwood said, 'This was our greatest game... a tremendous advertisement for football.' And Sealey, 'I've got to thank Ronnie Boyce for the first one. I just had to beat their goalkeeper who was so fantastic. The second was the result of a planned free-kick.' 'Kaiser' Moore added, 'We felt we let the fans down last year against Preston and we didn't do ourselves justice. Now we have come back and achieved all we set out to do. That makes two Wembley cup wins for me. Now I want to lead England to victory in the World Cup next year.'

Three weeks later the proud new holders of the European Cup Winners' Cup defeated Munich again in the International Soccer League in New York, 2-1, with Sealey again netting the winner. But Hammers flopped badly in the rest of the tournament to finish bottom of their group. The American dream was over. The youth team enjoyed better fortunes in the International Youth Tournament, however, winning the competition in

Moore leads his victorious troops down Wembley's steps in 1965.

Augsberg, Germany for the third year running and the right to keep the cup indefinitely. Harry Redknapp won a portable radio as the best player of the tournament. Roger Cross and Frank Lampard were also in the team which beat Bologna in the final.

The Cup Conscious Cockneys

West Ham warmed up for the 1965-66 season with a three-match mini-tour of Germany where they lost 1-0 to FVB Stuttgart, beat Eintracht Frankfurt 2-1 and drew 1-1 with by now familiar opponents TSV Munich 1860. With four key men injured at the start of the season, Byrne, Brown, Dear and Sealey, who had badly broken a leg in a freak training ground accident playing cricket and would never be the same player again, Hammers slumped to a 3-0 defeat at West Bromwich Albion on the opening day. Four successive defeats during the first 11 days of September when the defence haemorrhaged 17 goals at Sunderland (2-1), Sheffield United (5-3) and at home to Leicester (5-2) and Liverpool (5-1), quickly put paid to any notions of winning the First Division championship and it became apparent that any success would once again have to come via cup competitions.

Indeed, Hammers were destined to play almost the equivalent of half a league programme in cup ties as they reached the League Cup final, the semi-final of the ECWC and the FA Cup fourth round including two replays – 20 games in all. Combined with league games, the 62-match total remains the most ever contested by West Ham in a single season.

Receiving a bye as holders from the first round of the ECWC, Hammers were paired with Greek cup winners Olympiakos Piraeus in the second round. As if by magic, West Ham suddenly rediscovered much of their old flair and inventiveness that had led to their success in winning the trophy the previous year but had so far deserted them in the bread and butter quest for league points. In the first leg at Upton Park, Moore's men were 2-0 ahead at half time through typical strikes from Geoff Hurst and only the brilliance of the Greeks' goalkeeper Fronimidis and a host of missed chances kept the score down to 4-0 as Byrne and the recalled Brabrook added further goals for what looked like an unassailable lead to take to Piraeus. When Martin Peters scored his and Hammers' second goal in the 53rd minute of the return leg to silence the 40,000 partisan Greek fans, the holders' lead was impregnable as they were not only 6-0 ahead on aggregate but had the advantage of two away goals which would count double in the unlikely event of the Greeks drawing level. Only an own-goal by Bovington and a scandalous penalty awarded by Russian referee Bakhramov allowed the home side to save face before their fanatical support. Bakhramov would make amends six months later when he adjudged Geoff Hurst's crucial third goal in the 1966 World Cup final against West Germany legitimate when consulted by the referee in his capacity of linesman on that historic occasion.

Brian Dear declares his allegiance after the Cup Winners' Cup victory.

By the time Irons were due to face Aufbau Magdeburg of East Germany in the quarter-finals of the Cup Winners' Cup in early March, they had already secured a place in the two legged final of the Football League Cup against WBA having disposed of Bristol Rovers 3-2 (after a 3-3 draw at Eastville), Mansfield Town 4-0, Rotherham United 2-1 at Millmoor, Grimsby Town 1-0 (after a 2-2 draw at Blundell Park) and Cardiff City who they defeated 5-1 in both legs of the semi-final. In addition the club had played four FA Cup ties, having defeated Oldham Athletic 2-1 (following a 2-2 draw at Boundary Park) before crashing 4-1 in a fourth round replay at Blackburn after a 3-3 draw at Upton Park when new £6,500 signing Jimmy Bloomfield from Brentford scored the first goal for Hammers.

Playing two games a week at this stage, leg-weary Irons managed only a slender 1-0 lead to take behind the Iron Curtain following Byrne's vital first leg strike against Magdeburg at the Boleyn. Before playing the second leg in East Germany the cup conscious Cockneys also secured a narrow 2-1 lead in the first leg of the League Cup final at Upton Park over West Brom, when Moore equalised Geoff Astle's opener for Albion and Byrne cracked the winner seconds from time.

With the 16 March transfer deadline approaching, Greenwood sold Joe Kirkup to Chelsea for £35,000 and Martin Britt to Blackburn for £25,000. Nice business. Meanwhile, Martin Peters was claiming, 'I haven't a hope of getting in the World Cup team now. I lost my chance when I was moved to inside-forward. If I ever play for England I'm convinced it will be at wing half. Still, I'm not bitter about it, the needs of my club come first and they needed me at inside forward.'

Despite being forced to defend almost from start to finish, West Ham drew 1-1 with Magdeburg before 35,000 spectators at the Ernst Grube Stadium to qualify for the semi-finals of the ECWC and continue their European adventure against all the odds. There was no denying the spirit of the Londoners. When, after yet another spell of heavy pressure, they eventually broke through to score in the 77th minute through Walter, West Ham sprang into life to shatter the Germans. Less than 60 seconds later Hammers were level, a brilliant move involving Hurst, Brabrook and Peters ending with Sissons scoring another precious away goal from close range. It was a killer blow because even if Magdeburg had scored a second time, West Ham would still have gone through on the away-goal rule. It meant the Germans had to score twice in the last 12 minutes which was an impossible task against a well-organised West Ham side who, with skipper Moore as sweeper and inside-forwards Boyce and Peters coming back to form an eight-man defence at the slightest danger, threw up an impregnable barrier.

The second leg of the Football League Cup final against WBA before a crowd of 31,925 at the Hawthorns was a different story, however. It was all over in the first 35 minutes as Albion hit Hammers with a four-goal blitz to turn a 2-1 deficit into a 5-2 lead with goals from Kaye, Brown, Clark and Williams. As Albion lifted the cup in the last final to be played over two legs in favour of a single Wembley showpiece, it had proved a game too far for Hammers who had their dreams of winning a major cup competition for the third successive season destroyed by the Throstles' whirlwind start.

But the defeat was swiftly forgotten with the bombshell news that Bobby Moore wanted to quit West Ham and wouldn't be renewing his contract. The timing of his announcement – on the eve of the club's vital semi-final with Borussia Dortmund at Upton Park – was particularly unfortunate and

Greenwood promptly stripped his former right hand man of the captaincy in favour of Johnny Byrne but still played Moore against the Germans who, in Tilkowski, Held and Emmerich, had three members of West Germany's World Cup squad in their side. Greenwood was quoted as saying, 'Let's face it, we shall probably be murdered.'

Will He, Won't He?

West Ham started the match as if their lives depended on it and, putting their off-field problems out of their minds, played some of their best football of the season to put the Borussia defence under immense pressure to the delight of their fans who created a constant barrage of sound in support of their claret and blue clad heroes. Deposed captain Moore was superb in defence while Byrne was a revelation under his new responsibilities in attack, but somehow Borussia managed to go in at half-time without conceding a goal. But seven minutes after the interval, Peters got the goal his team deserved when, taking a pass from Bloomfield, he ran at the heart of the Germans' defence before hammering a low shot past Tilkowski's left hand at the North Bank end which erupted into a crescendo of deafening celebration.

With four minutes left and the West Ham fans wondering if one goal was enough to take to Germany, they suddenly realised that it wasn't even enough for the night as Emmerich plundered a shock equaliser. Two minutes later the same player got onto the end of a cross from Held and prodded home the winner before crashing into a goalpost. Emmerich was hurt but not as much as West Ham on the night when they tried to play football and win – but succeeded only in playing football.

Two days later, on Good Friday 1966, West Ham went to White Hart Lane and raised hopes of their second-leg chances by thrashing Spurs 4-1 with goals from Redknapp, Hurst, Byrne and Boyce with Moore watching from the stand. The following day they went to Chelsea with Moore reinstated and lost 6-2. Moore was quoted in the *London Evening News* as saying, 'Only two people, Mr Greenwood and myself, knew I was not going to renew my contract at the end of the season. We agreed that it would be kept secret until the end of the heavy Easter programme. I kept my end of the bargain.' And Greenwood countered, 'If the picture has been presented wrongly, I am to blame. After a talk with the board I decided it was time the public knew what was happening – they have a right to know.'

Having made five changes from the team that was so heavily defeated at Stamford Bridge, West Ham embarked on their eighth European adventure

Fans in the Chicken Run at Upton Park saw many tremendous matches during the halcyon years of the 1960s.

in 18 months comforted by the knowledge that they'd never failed to score away from home in the competition.

The man who barred their to the final was once again that lanky, lethal left winger Lothar Emmerich who increased Dortmund's aggregate lead to 4-1 with his second goal of the match to delight the flag-waving, klaxon-hooting 35,000 crowd at Westfalenstadion. Just before half-time Johnny Byrne gave the small band of irrepressible Cockney fans who'd made the trip a small glimmer of hope when he headed past the black garbed Tilkowski to give London's sole representatives in Europe just 45 minutes to turn a 2-1 deficit into a 3-2 win on the night to go through on away goals. But for once the task was beyond a team that had previously risen above every challenge as they cut a claret and blue swathe across two continents, beginning suddenly that summer in New York. Full back Cyliax's goal five minutes from time tied it up for the Germans but at least Greenwood's gallant team of Englishmen had the consolation of knowing they'd been defeated by the best side in the competition, as was proved when they went on to defeat Liverpool 2-1 in the final.

West Ham and stand-in skipper Byrne, in particular, quickly bounced back by winning three consecutive home matches against Arsenal 2-1, Spurs 2-0 and Manchester United 3-2. Byrne, who converted two penalties against Tottenham and was also on target from the spot against both United and the Gunners, had his spirits lifted when Alf Ramsey announced that he was included in the 28-strong squad for England's final 1966 World Cup preparation at Lilleshall in June, along with Moore, Hurst and Peters.

West Ham Win the World Cup

The selection of the 'West Ham four' gives a fair indication of the club's standing in world football at that time. 'Budgie', who'd been badly injured filling in at full back for England against Scotland at Wembley in 1965, didn't make the final shake-up for the finals staged in England for the first time, but Moore, Peters and Hurst did. Hurst got the 'nod' over Jimmy Greaves to play against Argentina in the Wembley quarter-final and used it to head the only goal of the game from Peters' cross.

Hurst turned provider for Bobby Charlton in the 2-1 win over Portugal in the semi-final, but got back on the goal standard to devastating effect against West Germany at Wembley as he wrote himself indelibly into the record books as the only man to score a hat-trick in a World Cup final. Peters got England's other goal as the host nation triumphed 4-2 after 30 heart-stopping minutes of extra-time with a little help from that Russian linesman with whom the Hammers had made acquaintance six months earlier in Greece. Some people even went as far as to suggest that West Ham won the World Cup just because the Hammers triumvirate of Moore, Peters and Hurst scored the goals and were behind most of the moves behind England's greatest ever triumph. The blond colossus Moore, who was voted the outstanding player of the series and provided the passes for Hurst's first and last goals, also achieved his burning ambition to become the first captain to lead cup-winning teams at the grand old stadium three years in succession. A unique hat-trick that will never be equalled.

As Hammers prepared to embark on yet another tour of Germany on the eve of the 1966-67 season there was some good news... some very good news. Bobby Moore, the man we called the 'Colonel' in our house and who'd made our lives less ordinary, was staying at West Ham. It was in the papers – he'd signed a new contract that would keep him at Upton Park until 1972 – phew! The healing of a breach that opened at the end of the previous season saw a now happy Moore sign for three years, with West Ham having the option on his services for a further three years. The 'golden boy' had been on a monthly agreement since the start of the World Cup and was at the end of a one-year contract.

Despite the 'feelgood' factor generated by the World Cup win, Hammers still lost their first three matches of the season, even though Moore, Hurst and Peters were in the side. But the team embarked on another extended run in the Football League Cup that would take them past Spurs 1-0, Arsenal 3-1 (at Highbury), Leeds 7-0 and Blackpool 3-1 at Bloomfield Road before the bubble eventually burst with a 4-0 defeat in the first leg of the semi-final at 'bogey side' West Brom after which Irons could only manage a 2-1 return-leg win. The rout of Leeds caused such disbelief that when the result was phoned through to the offices of the *Yorkshire Post* they asked for confirmation three times!

In September West Ham provided no less than four of the players who represented the Football League against the Irish League at a packed Home Park, Plymouth – Moore, Hurst, Peters and Byrne. Budgie hit four and Hurstie two of the League's 12-0 winning margin over the Irish part-timers.

A purple patch in which Hammers scored 32 goals in just nine league games in November and December, and included a 6-1 home win against Fulham, a 4-3 win at Spurs and a 5-5 draw at Chelsea, was soon forgotten as Hammers added fuel to the countless comedian jibes about West Ham 'coming down with the Christmas decorations', with a shock exit from the FA Cup in the third round replay at Third Division Swindon Town and an appalling run of seven straight First Division defeats including a 6-1 mauling by Manchester United who clinched the title at Upton Park as Irons finally ended a disappointing sixteenth in the table. But there was hope for the future as Billy Bonds was signed from Charlton for £49,500.

50 Greatest Players

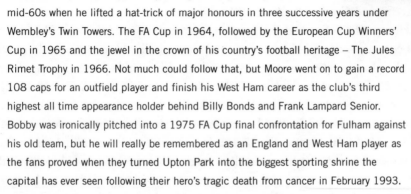

BOBBY MOORE OBE Defender

Born: Barking, Essex, 12 April 1941

Joined West Ham: 1958 **From:** Groundstaff

Debut: v Manchester United, 8 September 1958

Appearances: 642 **Goals:** 28

Left West Ham: 1974 **For:** Fulham

All the superlatives in the English dictionary would hardly do justice to this blonde colossus who bestrode the world's playing fields on behalf of England and West Ham United for 15 seasons in the sun. Majestic, magnificent Moore was the motivating force behind the successes of his club and country during the halycon days of the mid-60s when he lifted a hat-trick of major honours in three successive years under Wembley's Twin Towers. The FA Cup in 1964, followed by the European Cup Winners' Cup in 1965 and the jewel in the crown of his country's football heritage – The Jules Rimet Trophy in 1966. Not much could follow that, but Moore went on to gain a record 108 caps for an outfield player and finish his West Ham career as the club's third highest all time appearance holder behind Billy Bonds and Frank Lampard Senior. Bobby was ironically pitched into a 1975 FA Cup final confrontation for Fulham against his old team, but he will really be remembered as an England and West Ham player as the fans proved when they turned Upton Park into the biggest sporting shrine the capital has ever seen following their hero's tragic death from cancer in February 1993.

50 Greatest Players

MARTIN PETERS Midfielder/striker

Born: Plaistow, London, 8 November 1943

Joined West Ham: 1961 **From:** Groundstaff

Debut: v Cardiff City, 20 April 1962

Appearances: 364 **Goals:** 100

Left West Ham: 1970 **For:** Tottenham Hotspur

Martin Peters was, quite simply, a manager's dream. In nine seasons at Upton Park he played in every position including goal and was by far the most versatile player on the staff. The complete footballer in the eyes of three of the all-time great managers, Ron Greenwood, Alf Ramsey and Billy Nicholson, it was his adaptability and ability to ghost in on the blind side of defences to score 'goals from nowhere' that set him apart. Martin won a European Cup Winners' Cup medal with Hammers in 1965 and was awarded 33 England caps as a West Hammer until Spurs broke the existing British transfer record to take him to North London in a deal which saw Jimmy Greaves make the opposite journey as a makeweight in the transaction. Peters' greatest achievement was, of course, winning a World Cup winners' medal in 1966 along with Moore and Hurst when he contributed the vital second goal.

Building for the Future

By the start of the 1967-68 season Bonds was joined by world record goalkeeper signing, Scottish international Bobby Ferguson from Kilmarnock for £65,000 and Celtic reserve centre half John Cushley, but Hammers still lost 3-2 on the opening day at home to Sheffield Wednesday. Bonds' battling displays at right back were to endear him to the Upton Park faithful but the jury was out on Ferguson – especially as Greenwood could have signed Gordon Banks for £15,000 less.

Hurst, who'd finished the previous season as top scorer with 41 goals in all competitions and Hammer of the Year had, like Moore, pledged himself to the club for the next six years and would again top the scoring charts with a more modest total of 25. A promising run in the FA Cup looked to be under way, after two good away wins in the third and fourth rounds at Burnley and Stoke, Sheffield United ended Hammers' hopes with a shock 2-1 win in front of a massive 38,440 crowd at the Boleyn. In the League Cup Irons went out 2-0 at the equivalent stage at Second Division Huddersfield.

There was nothing to get excited about in the league either as the team occupied a mediocre twelfth place in the final table. As usual there was a silver lining, however. This year his name was Trevor Brooking, who scored nine goals in 25 league games and looked like he might be quite useful...

Following yet another pre-season trip to Germany, the West Ham players must have been almost as fluent in the native language as they were in their own Cockney rhyming slang – what's double pie and mash in German? Hammers at last got off to a good start in the First Division as they lost just one of their opening 12 league matches and sandwiched in a 7-2 Upton Park League Cup win over Bolton for good measure before going out in a thrilling replay at Coventry in the next round to the odd goal in five.

In the league, excitement continued unabated when Harry Redknapp became the first West Ham player to be sent off in seven years, following a bust-up with his red-headed counterpart Billy Bremner at Elland Road. And then, on 19 October 1968, Geoff Hurst again wrote his name large in the record books when he scored six against Sunderland at Upton Park to equal Vic Watson's feat against Leeds in 1929.

Once again Hammers fought through to the fifth round of the FA Cup but, in a famous 'giant killing', Third Division Mansfield Town triumphed 3-0 at Field Mill. Flying high in the First Division at the end of March, Hammers fluffed their chance of Fairs Cup qualification by failing to win even one of their last nine matches, finishing eighth in what was another season of under-achievement. Hurst was yet again top scorer with 31 goals and Hammer of the Year. He rounded off his season with two goals for England in the 4-1 win over Scotland at Wembley, while Peters got the other two.

After the obligatory pre-season tour to – you've guessed it – Germany, where Hammers faced opponents of the calibre of Franz Beckenbauer, Gerd Muller, Sepp Maier (Bayern Munich) and Wolfgang Overath (Cologne), Irons won their first two matches of 1969-70 at home to Newcastle and Chelsea, 1-0 and 2-0 respectively, before deciding to give up on the rest of the season. That's the way it seemed anyway, as the team finished in its lowest position since Greenwood's appointment as manager (17th) and crashed out of the League Cup in the third round at Nottingham Forest and the FA Cup at Second Division Middlesbrough at the same stage.

Alan Stephenson, signed from Crystal Palace for £80,000 in March 1968, didn't seem to fit the bill as a long-term replacement for the departed Ken Brown at centre half and neither did Peter Eustace, a £90,000 acquisition from Sheffield Wednesday, look to be in the same class as Martin Peters in midfield, who had been sold to Spurs for £200,000 plus Jimmy Greaves in a record-breaking deal completed five hours before the midnight transfer deadline in March 1969. After the euphoria of Greaves' two debut goals in

50 Greatest Players

GEOFF HURST Striker

Born: Ashton-Under-Lyne, Lancs, 8 December 1941

Joined West Ham: 1958 **From:** Groundstaff

Debut: v Nottingham Forest, 21 February 1960

Appearances: 499 **Goals:** 252

Left West Ham: 1972 **For:** Stoke City

Arguably the most famous post-war Hammer with the exception of Bobby Moore, Sir Geoff Hurst wrote his name indelibly into football folklore with his hat trick against West Germany in the 1966 World Cup final at Wembley. His goalscoring exploits for West Ham and England became legendary following his inspired conversion from wing half to striker by his manager and mentor Ron Greenwood. Equalled Vic Watson's six goals in a match record in First Division clash with Sunderland at Upton Park in October 1968 and remains Hammers' second highest scorer of all time behind Vic. Ended his league career at WBA before becoming player boss of Telford United. A successful businessman, Geoff currently hosts the '66 Club on matchdays at Upton Park and recently put his unique collection of caps, shirts and medals up for auction at Christies.

a 5-1 win over Manchester City at Maine Road had subsided, West Ham looked to have got the thin end of the wedge in the transaction.

West Ham had lost one of their treasured trinity, but they were still united in their resolve to retain the World Cup for England that summer in Mexico. They travelled to Columbia with the rest of the party and starred in two warm-up victories over Columbia and Ecuador. But Moore had to call on all his reserves of inner strength as he was caught up in a Latin-American plot to undermine England's confidence before they defended their world title.

Held in Bogota on a trumped-up charge of stealing a gold bracelet, he was released without charge just three days before the start of the tournament after being forced to stay behind in the Colombian capital as the rest of the party flew on to Mexico. His performance in England's opening 1-0 win of the tournament over Columbia, when Hurst got the vital goal, gave little hint of his ordeal as he put in his usual immaculate display. Although England's brave quest for further glory faltered in the heat, humidity and altitude of the heart-breaking quarter-final defeat to their old rivals West Germany, the enduring memory for many of the 1970 World Cup remains the poignant picture of Pele swapping shirts with Moore as they congratulate each other after their epic confrontation at Guadalajara.

Chapter Ten: 1970-74
Into the Seventies

As Simon & Garfunkel topped the charts in the summer of 1970, the Hammers found themselves facing their own somewhat shaky 'Bridge Over Troubled Water'. The new league season commenced with not a single win in 10 outings and just a paltry four victories from the first 28 games – the Hammers worst start to a league campaign in nearly 40 years.

Jimmy Greaves opened his season's account in the thrilling 2-2 draw at his old club Tottenham on the first day, but he had to wait a further two months before finding the net again for his 350th career goal. In September, however, it was announced that John Lyall – described as a 'quiet, deep thinking tactician' – was to be promoted from his post as Metropolitan League team boss to become Ron Greenwood's assistant.

A Geoff Hurst hat-trick against Burnley on 3 October brought a huge sigh of relief as the Hammers finally secured their first league win while the following home game saw another 2-2 draw with Spurs. The match was notable for Hurst displacing Jimmy Ruffell as the club's second-highest scorer (behind Vic Watson) and centre half Tommy Taylor making his debut following an £80,000 switch from Orient.

Jimmy Greaves scored on his debut but struggled to find his scoring form thereafter.

West Ham's other goal had been scored by record signing Peter Eustace who, frustrated with his lack of opportunities, was already in the news for allegedly calling the East End 'a dump' compared to his former home of Sheffield. But those headlines paled into insignificance compared to those created by Billy Bonds, who found himself facing an FA disciplinary committee after being sent off in a League Cup victory over Hull City. With a 21-day suspended sentence already hanging over his head, Bonds incurred a further two-week ban and was fined £120.

His absence from the right back berth allowed John McDowell to make his debut in the 2-1 home win against Blackpool on 31 October, which saw the team climb to 16th in the table. But it was the FA Cup game against the same club two months later that made the biggest impact.

Off-the-Pitch Shenanigans

As if being trounced 4-0 by the team who would ultimately finish bottom of the First Division wasn't embarrassing enough, further shame was brought upon the club with the revelation that four West Ham players – Bobby Moore, Jimmy Greaves, Clyde Best and Brian Dear – had spent the early hours of matchday refreshing themselves in a nightclub.

'That whole thing was blown out of all proportion', insists Dear. 'We had a meal and a couple of beers in our hotel, then went on to a club for a short while, but we were all in bed by one o'clock. We were staying in the hotel that the Blackpool squad were having their pre-match meal in and we got grassed up. I wouldn't mind but I didn't even play!'

In fact the striker would never play for the Hammers again, being released at the season's end. All four men, who admitted breaching club rules, were fined a week's wages and, with the exception of Best (who hadn't drunk alcohol), were excluded from the team desperately trying to dig itself out of trouble. It was the first time that Moore – who'd just collected a cheque for £15,000 following his testimonial match against Celtic in November – had been dropped in over 10 years and it's open to debate as to whether more damage was done to the skipper's public image or to his relationship with Ron Greenwood.

The players' enforced omission was the last thing the team needed with its top-flight status in serious jeopardy and a humiliating 4-1 home loss to Derby County in February – with Moore's position as substitute prompting a banner in the crowd to proclaim it as 'the final sick joke' – completing a run of five successive league defeats.

With Moore returning to the starting line-up three days later for the match at Coventry, the Hammers gained a vital 1-0 win with the similarly reinstated Greaves scoring the all-important goal. The next point gained came a week and a half later, at home to Manchester City, with John Lyall taking control of the team for the very first time as Greenwood travelled to Newcastle to watch another game. His target was Bryan 'Pop' Robson and by the time the Hammers faced Nottingham Forest four days later, the little striker was wearing a claret and blue shirt, a club record £120,000 having secured his services. The new signing promptly scored in a 2-0 home win and his presence had strike-partner Geoff Hurst exclaiming, 'Hallelujah!'

A sequence of three successive victories (including one against Manchester United at home), amid a run of 15 games in which just four were lost, helped ensure the team's survival, finishing just one place but seven points clear of relegated Burnley who sat second from bottom.

Robson may have only scored a further two goals during the run-in, less than both Hurst and Greaves, but his glory days were still to come. That clearly wasn't the case with Greaves, however, and the 31-year-old swiftly announced his retirement, complaining, 'The game has gone a bit sick.'

With the club deciding to drop its Metropolitan League team for the following season, a pruning of the professional staff was required and Ron Greenwood duly granted seven players (including Dear plus 26-year-old John Charles) free transfers while also listing Jimmy Lindsay, David Llewelyn, Peter Eustace and... Trevor Brooking as up for sale! Having been dropped after the Derby disaster and making just one further appearance as substitute, the 22-year-old was frustrated both with the prospect of reserve-team football and a lack of funds through loss of first-team bonuses. 'I had to think seriously about whether I should continue in football,' admitted Trevor years later.

Fortunately, no moves materialised and, while the others listed all soon departed (Eustace eventually returning to Sheffield Wednesday), Brooking reclaimed his midfield position once Tommy Taylor moved back into defence alongside Bobby Moore at the expense of Alan Stephenson.

Greater Stability

When the Hammers kicked off the 1971-72 season with not a goal or point in sight after three games, fans were entitled to expect another nine months of struggle. However, a run of 12 league and cup outings with just one loss between late August and October hoisted the side to a respectable ninth place. A nightmare run of four successive league defeats in November somewhat spoilt things a little, but generally the team was benefiting from greater stability.

Goalkeeper Bobby Ferguson, having reclaimed his position from Peter Grotier during the previous season, had kept seven clean sheets in the first 15 league games, John McDowell had now made the right back position his own, Frank Lampard was fully established at left back, Bobby Moore

Bobby Ferguson collects as Frank Lampard keeps an eye on him.

and Tommy Taylor were cemented into the centre half positions and Billy Bonds was ever-present having been pushed into midfield. Trevor Brooking's playing future and financial position were looking much improved as he amassed a total of 54 appearances on the way to becoming Hammer of the Year, while Clyde Best, Geoff Hurst and Pop Robson accumulated 53 goals between them in all competitions.

Indeed, after watching his team eclipse the Hammers by two goals to one at Goodison Park, Everton chairman George Watt described West Ham as 'the best side I have seen in years' (in stark contrast to Jack Charlton's quote the previous year that Leeds had just beaten 'the worst West Ham team I've ever seen').

The mid-table league position hardly supported such a generous claim, but in the League Cup the Hammers were far more convincing. After making hard work of getting past Second Division strugglers Cardiff in round two, Ron Greenwood's men then had a formidable hurdle to overcome in Don Revie's championship-chasing Leeds United. After a 0-0 draw at Upton Park, Revie conceded that West Ham were unlucky to have two seemingly good goals ruled out by referee Bob Matthewson – who, for his sins, was pelted with drink cans by the home crowd but sportingly refused to report the incident, insisting that 'it was nothing very important'.

Another goalless 90 minutes ensued in the Elland Road replay before Best decided the match with a header in extra-time to set up a home clash with

50 Greatest Players

CLYDE BEST Striker

Born: Somerset, Bermuda, 24 February 1951

Joined West Ham: April, 1969 **From:** Amateur

Debut: v Arsenal, 25 August 1969

Appearances: 218 **Goals:** 58

Left West Ham: February, 1976 **For:** Tampa Bay Rowdies

A powerful forward, big Clyde possessed a lethal shot and smashed 23 goals during 1971-72, to top score in his most productive campaign. A Bermudan international, he was only the second black player to represent the Hammers (after John Charles) and one of the very few outfielders to find himself in goal, against Leeds in April, 1973. He shared the top scorers' position with Billy Bonds in 1973-74 but after falling out of contention Best went on loan to help Tampa Bay Rowdies win the North American Soccer League. After a brief period back in London, he returned to the US on a permanent basis and now coaches the Bermuda team.

Liverpool, also pushing for the championship. Harry Redknapp, enjoying a fruitful run on the right flank at the expense of the injured John Ayris, once again created the winning goal, crossing for Robson to seal a 2-1 victory.

Mid-table Sheffield United were then sent packing 5-0, with Robson hitting his first hat-trick for the club to catapult the Hammers into a semi-final battle with Stoke City. And when Hurst and Best struck to claim a 2-1 win in the first leg at the Victoria Ground on 8 December, Wembley was firmly in sight.

Not so. A Paul Ritchie goal for Stoke in the second leg at Upton Park levelled the aggregate score to take the game into extra-time, but the home crowd exploded with anticipation when Redknapp was pulled down by Gordon Banks with just three minutes remaining. With an England legend in goal the penalty could hardly be considered a formality and Banks duly defied the laws of gravity to fist Hurst's powerful kick over the bar.

Yet another two hours of football were played in a third match at Hillsborough (drawn 0-0) as the battle between the two sides started to reach epic proportions, but the drama was far from over. In the second replay, at Old Trafford on 26 January, Bobby Moore found himself replacing Bobby Ferguson in goal for a 20-minute period after the West Ham keeper was concussed in a clash with Stoke's Terry Conroy. The captain even managed to block Mike Bernard's 33rd-minute spot-kick, but the Stoke man drove the rebound into the net. Incredibly, despite their temporary 10-man handicap, the Hammers turned deficit into advantage with strikes from Bonds and Brooking, but a dazed Ferguson returned to the action only to be beaten twice in the second half.

It wasn't the only sickening result for West Ham fans that season. A three-goal lead had been surrendered in a 3-3 draw at Southampton the previous month, while in February the Hammers were beaten 4-2 in the fifth round of the FA Cup by bottom-of-the-table Huddersfield Town. On a more positive note, Manchester United were thrashed 3-0 in the league and a brilliant Brooking goal in the 2-0 home win over Tottenham in April helped the team to a welcome double over their London rivals on their way to a final position of 14th.

Tommy Taylor formed a rock-like partnership with Bobby Moore.

While the league placing was an improvement on the previous two seasons' efforts, there was little to suggest that the momentum would be maintained to the extent of the team finishing the 1972-73 season in an equal best-ever position of sixth.

More Departures and Arrivals

Ron Greenwood had bemoaned the lack of goals – the figure of 47 for the previous league season had been the second lowest in the club's Division One history – and Geoff Hurst, having requested a transfer, had decided to join Stoke City in an £80,000 deal. The 30-year-old striker's eight league goals had been by far his lowest tally in 10 years (although he matched the figure in the cups) and, with his England career winding down, he admitted that he fancied 'a new challenge'. Other departures included Harry Redknapp, who'd agreed to join John Bond's Bournemouth in a £31,000 deal, while defender Alan Stephenson switched to Portsmouth for a similar fee. Hereford winger Dudley Tyler, meanwhile, arrived as Redknapp's replacement.

With no new strikers on board it was somewhat surprising that West Ham should enjoy such a successful season. Much credit must go to the predatory instincts of eventual Hammer of the Year Pop Robson, who scored 28 times in 44 league games (just one short of Hurst's post-war record). The search for a new partner for Robson continued throughout the campaign, with Bournemouth ace Ted MacDougall repeatedly being linked. 'Super Mac' eventually arrived at Upton Park in February 1973 – after an unhappy five months at Manchester United – for a club record fee of £170,000 and scored four times in 10 games.

At the other end of the pitch, meanwhile, 'the improvement in defence has been the most notable advance,' claimed the *Evening Standard* early in the campaign, with Moore earning the paper's Footballer of the Month trophy for the third time (shortly before breaking Jimmy Ruffell's club record of 505 league appearances) and Frank Lampard winning his first England cap against Yugoslavia. Moore was in the twilight of his England career but could have found himself seeing it out as a Derby County player, had Brian Clough's combined £400,000 offer for him and Trevor Brooking that season been successful.

For all the improvement in league performances, however, the same couldn't be said for the cups. The League Cup third round saw the Hammers fall 2-1 at Stockport County – the club's first ever defeat by Fourth Division opposition – while Second Division Hull City secured a 1-0 win in a fourth round tie. Even more disappointing was the fact that the club's sixth position was not sufficient to land them UEFA Cup qualification, missing out by just one point to fifth-placed Wolves.

The new season, 1973-74, saw one win in 20 games. Needless to say, the Hammers' dressing room wasn't the happiest of environments at that time. Bobby Ferguson was dropped for remarking that 'there are too many

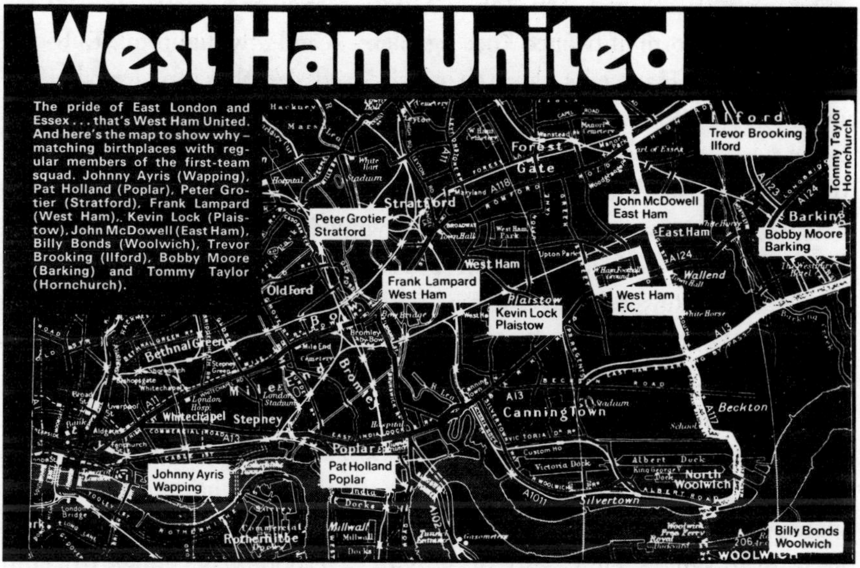
West Ham United
The pride of East London and Essex... that's West Ham United. And here's the map to show why – matching birthplaces with regular members of the first-team squad. Johnny Ayris (Wapping), Pat Holland (Poplar), Peter Grotier (Stratford), Frank Lampard (West Ham), Kevin Lock (Plaistow), John McDowell (East Ham), Billy Bonds (Woolwich), Trevor Brooking (Ilford), Bobby Moore (Barking) and Tommy Taylor (Hornchurch).
Trevor Brooking Ilford
Tommy Taylor Hornchurch
John McDowell East Ham
Bobby Moore Barking
Peter Grotier Stratford
Frank Lampard West Ham
West Ham F.C.
Kevin Lock Plaistow
Johnny Ayris Wapping
Pat Holland Poplar
Billy Bonds Woolwich

Always strongly associated with the East End of London, this map shows how many of the West Ham team of the early 1970s were born within the area.

gutless, spineless men in the team' and Bobby Moore – frustrated at not being allowed to join Derby and understandably feeling that he was part of the club's past rather than its future – expressed his desire to move on. In response Greenwood promised him a free transfer at the end of the season.

Harmony was difficult to find, with a number of people playing out of position at times. Goalscoring was also a problem with MacDougall netting just twice in 15 games. And as soon as Greenwood made definite strides in November to resolve the problem, recruiting Bobby Gould from Bristol City and allowing MacDougall to move to Norwich City in part-exchange for midfielder Graham Paddon, he then lost Pop Robson to injury for nearly four months. Christmas saw the Hammers at the bottom of the table.

The corner was slowly turned, however, with Paddon scoring twice against his old Norwich side in a 4-2 win in which MacDougall also hit a double against his former team-mates. A 10-match unbeaten run in the league between January and March saw the Hammers claw their way out of the relegation zone (newly expanded to three places), but the improved form wasn't reflected in two FA Cup third round games against Third Division Hereford United. Pat Holland had saved West Ham's blushes with an 88th-minute equaliser at Upton Park but Hereford – with Dudley Tyler back in their side – enjoyed a night of glory with a 2-1 win in the replay.

The initial match had seen Bobby Moore sustain the worst injury of his career – in the form of twisted knee ligaments – and it would prove to be the last time West Ham fans saw the much-loved defender perform in their colours. Two months later, on 14 March (transfer deadline day), Moore signed for Second Division Fulham, with £25,000 being paid for his services. Although released a few months earlier than anticipated, Bobby was still annoyed to discover a fee had been demanded. 'West Ham had years of service from me and now they were using me to balance the books,' he complained, feeling that Greenwood's earlier pledge had been broken.

Moore's famous No. 6 shirt was assumed for the closing part of the season by Mick McGiven, a £20,000 buy from Sunderland following a spell on loan, with the West Ham captaincy transferring to Billy Bonds, still operating in midfield. 'Bonzo' could certainly be deemed the club's saviour that term, earning the Hammer of the Year award as he scored 13 goals (including a hat-trick against Chelsea) to equal Clyde Best's total and shoot the team to safety. A final-day draw with Liverpool was enough to claim 18th place, just a point above the relegation trap door.

Great Managers – 1961-1974

RON GREENWOOD

So strong has Ron Greenwood's association with West Ham become that it's long been forgotten by many that, as a player, he represented Bradford, Brentford, Chelsea and Fulham, before managing Eastbourne United, coaching the England youth and Under-23 teams and holding the position of chief coach at Arsenal prior to taking control at Upton Park in April, 1961. West Ham finished eighth in Ron's first season and although he invested heavily in the likes of Byrne, Brabrook, Stephenson and Eustace during the 1960s, it was the emergence of Moore, Hurst and Peters that helped enable the manager to impose his progressive footballing philosophies.

The team may have fluctuated around the mid-table positions for much of the era but Greenwood enjoyed considerable success in the cup competitions, winning the FA Cup in 1964, the European Cup Winners' Cup in 1965, reaching the final of the League Cup in 1966 and the semi-final of the same tournament in 1967 and 1972. The team finished in sixth place in 1972-73 to mark the club's best ever league position at that point but after a season of struggle Ron handed first-team responsibilities to John Lyall in 1974. He remained at the club for the next three years, in the role of general manager, before replacing Don Revie as England boss. He guided the nation to the 1980 European Championships and World Cup finals two years later, before retiring in 1982.

Chapter Eleven: 1974-78
Cup Highs, League Lows

Changes were afoot during the close season of 1974 and the Upton Park faithful were entitled to ponder exactly what impact the two key ones would make. With some having called for Greenwood's head at various times over the years, there would have been mixed feelings when it was announced that John Lyall would assume responsibility for first-team affairs, including training and selecting the team. Ron, meanwhile, aged 52 and with a home in Brighton, would become 'general manager' and oversee both the scouting and financial side of things.

Lyall later admitted to being surprised when offered the post, even though some had anticipated it for some time. Admitting to the board of directors that he was happy with his present terms – £80 a week – John accepted the new challenge and, in the short term at least, remained on the same contract.

Over time the senior players would recognise the difference in approaches between the two coaches. Remembers Billy Bonds, 'Ron was more, "This is how we're going to win today," while John tended to take a more balanced overview of situations – maybe pointing out that we were losing too many goals at set-pieces and putting that right before exploring our own attacking options.'

The first task for Lyall was that of replacing the departed Pop Robson, who'd charitably been allowed to return to his Sunderland home for a fee of £145,000.

A 4-0 opening day defeat at Manchester City was a painful way for Lyall to commence his management tenure and by match five, with another two defeats and just one win in the bag, the only Hammers who'd hit the back of the net were Billy Bonds, Frank Lampard and John McDowell. Thankfully, two new strikers arrived in September in the shape of Billy Jennings (from Watford for £110,000) and Keith Robson (from Newcastle for £45,000).

Both men made an immediate impact, with Jennings scoring five times in his first five games and Robson going even better with five in his first four league outings. With Bobby Gould joining them in a three-man forward line, the Hammers bounced off the foot of the table with an emphatic 6-2 home win against Leicester, a 3-0 victory over Birmingham and a 5-3 win at Burnley – all in the space of a week. Add in the 6-0 mauling of Tranmere Rovers in the second round of the League Cup and it's no wonder that John Lyall picked up the September Manager of the Month award.

Flying High

By December, with a run of just one defeat in 17 league games, the team had scaled to the heights of fifth and all three strikers were well on their way to double figures for the season. Ironically, the trio would muster just one each in the FA Cup, the competition that would ultimately bring most reward.

Perhaps it was no coincidence that, as West Ham's 1974-75 cup prospects grew, the league form deteriorated. As the old joke about the Christmas decorations goes, down came the Hammers in the New Year with just two league wins in 20 games as they slumped to 16th place by April. No matter, because by that time the East End was looking forward to a visit to the twin towers of Wembley to face Fulham in the FA Cup final.

Second Division Southampton (2-1 at the Dell), Third Division Swindon (also 2-1 away, in a replay) and First Division QPR (with yet another 2-1 scoreline) had all been dispatched to see West Ham through to the last eight of the competition without the name of Alan Taylor so much as appearing on a single team-sheet. The striker had been picked up from Fourth Division Rochdale for a mere £40,000 back in November, with Ron Greenwood acknowledging the raw 21-year-old's pace.

Despite the lack of immediate appearances, Lyall decided to gamble by playing Taylor in the club's sixth round tie at Arsenal at the expense of

Great Players

BRYAN 'POP' ROBSON Striker

Born: Sunderland, 11 November 1945

Joined West Ham: 1971 **From:** Newcastle United

Debut: v Nottingham Forest, 24 February 1971

Appearances: 254 **Goals:** 104

Left West Ham: 1974, 1979 **For:** Sunderland (returning in 1976), twice

When Ron Greenwood returned from watching 'Pop' Robson in action for Newcastle in February 1971, he told John Lyall, 'I've seen an outstanding player. He does everything I would have liked to have coached into a player – but he does it naturally.' A club record £120,000 subsequently secured the striker's services and he responded by scoring 53 goals in 139 games before returning to his native Sunderland in 1974 for a fee of £145,000. Two years later he was back at Upton Park, at a cost of £80,000, grabbing 51 goals in 115 outings and claiming the 1979 Adidas Golden Shoe award. For the second time, however, Pop returned to his homeland just a year ahead of the Hammers tasting FA Cup glory.

Alan Taylor scores against Fulham in the 1975 FA Cup final.

Bobby Gould. Needless to say, the rookie striker's two goals against the Gunners, in the 15th and 46th minutes, secured his place in the team for the rest of the season and, despite scoring just twice in the league, he delivered when it mattered most.

The semi-final against Bobby Robson's Ipswich Town at Villa Park on 5 April finished goalless, but Taylor's two goals in the Stamford Bridge replay four days later were enough to sweep the Hammers into the final, despite Billy Jennings' own goal.

Somewhat ironically, Bobby Moore – West Ham's finest son – would stand in opposition in Second Division Fulham's colours (just as he had done – successfully – in a League Cup game earlier in the season), but 3 May 1975 was not to be his day. In true Roy of the Rovers style, Taylor hit yet another brace – twice capitalising on loose balls after goalkeeper Peter Mellor failed to hold efforts from Jennings and Paddon within the space of three second-half minutes – and the fairytale was complete. Credit also went to Pat Holland – in the team because of injury to Keith Robson – for his invaluable contribution towards the victory. The attacking midfielder may have been 24 years of age but, having spent a number of years trying to establish himself, he was described as being part of 'the next generation' as West Ham celebrated their victory.

'I was soon to learn that days like that are few in the life of a football manager,' reflected Lyall in his 1989 autobiography, admitting that his second league campaign was 'less than successful'. It got off to a bright

Great Matches

FA CUP FINAL **Wembley, London, 3 May, 1975**
West Ham United 2 **Fulham 0** **Attendance 100,000**
Taylor 2

FA Cup finals have a habit of throwing up heroes and villains and this match was a classic example, providing Alan Taylor with the opportunity to complete a hat-trick of cup braces in successive rounds at the expense of Fulham's Peter Mellor. Taylor took advantage of the goalkeeper spilling shots in the 61st and 64th minutes to ensure the trophy would be heading to East London.

Incredibly, the hero of the day left Wembley complaining of having missed two chances to gain a hat-trick. 'I want to kick this habit of only scoring twice,' he quipped, despite clutching the match ball regardless.

Skipper Billy Bonds, meanwhile, admits he could so easily have missed out on West Ham's moment of glory. 'I'd had a groin problem that I thought might even finish my career and was needing cortizone injections and painkillers before being wheeled out for the cup games. So it was just a case of getting through the match against Fulham before having an operation that was thankfully successful. Before I knew where I was, though, the day was over.'

Despite the Hammers being favourites against Second Division opposition, Alec Stock's Fulham (with veterans Bobby Moore and Alan Mullery in the side) proved an equal match for the first hour, with Mervyn Day needing to save twice from John Mitchell before Taylor struck.

Remembers Pat Holland, 'I still look at the medal I won that day and wonder how I managed to hang on to it. Straight after the presentation, some of us started off on a lap of honour but suddenly we got cut off from the rest of the lads as delirious fans got onto the pitch. I tried to get towards the Royal Box but a policeman wouldn't let me return. I'm standing there in a West Ham kit – clutching an FA Cup winners' medal – and he thinks I'm a punter!'

West Ham United: Day, McDowell, Lampard, Bonds, Taylor T, Lock, Jennings, Paddon, Taylor A, Brooking, Holland.

Fulham: Mellor, Cutbush, Lacy, Moore, Frazer, Mullery, Conway, Slough, Mitchell, Busby, Barrett.

Referee: P. Partridge.

Pat Holland (left) and Billy Jennings experience cup joy.

enough start, however, with Alan Taylor scoring four times in the first three games (excluding the 2-0 defeat to League Champions Derby County in the Charity Shield) and the Hammers remaining unbeaten in 11 outings, including two European Cup Winners' Cup first round ties against Finnish part-timers Lahden Reipas.

European Heartbreak

Brooking and Bonds scored the goals in a 2-2 draw in Helsinki's Olympic Stadium, while Keith Robson, Holland and Jennings did the damage in a 3-0 second-leg home win. By the time the Hammers headed out to the USSR to take on Ararat Erevan in the latter part of October, they'd returned to the top of Division One for a week, having amassed 22 points from a possible 30. Striker Billy Jennings missed both second round games against the Soviets but Alan Taylor scored away from home in the 1-1 draw – with German referee Hans Weyland bizarrely allowing Sambel Petrosian to head the ball out of keeper Mervyn Day's hands to equalise – before Paddon, Robson and Taylor (again) netted in the return leg. With Taylor, Robson, Gould, Best and even Brooking filling the attacking slots, Jennings returned to fitness towards the end of November only to discover that his place in the starting line-up was by no means assured. A hat-trick against Stoke on 20 December soon put the smile back on his face but there was not much else in the

Hammers fans on the march.

league to look pleased about during the next few months. The following week saw Keith Robson sent off for punching Ipswich Town's George Burley in a 2-1 home defeat and he subsequently picked up a four-match ban.

It was the absence of Billy Bonds that perhaps hit the Hammers most, though. The skipper was ruled out for three months after damaging his groin in November and by the time he returned on 28 February – for the 4-0 defeat at Manchester United – the Hammers' slide down the First Division table was well under way. Liverpool had also ripped the Eastenders' grip off the FA Cup, with Kevin Keegan and John Toshack scoring the goals in a 2-0 win at Upton Park.

The collapse at Old Trafford – the team's sixth match without a win – was hardly the best way to prepare for the Cup Winners' Cup quarter-final first leg against Den Haag on 3 March. And had Ron Greenwood – standing in for flu casualty John Lyall – been able to foresee what lay in store in Holland, he just might have told his players to leave their passports at home.

For the second European round running the Hammers found themselves victims of a German official's incompetence. With the Dutch side already one goal ahead, referee Rudi Glockner erroneously deemed Mick McGiven to have handled in the penalty area. Captain Aad Mansveld duly scored from the spot to claim his second of a game that was barely 15 minutes old. Glockner then decided to award another penalty after defender Kevin Lock clearly fouled Simon van Vliet *outside* the box (Mansveld completing his hat-trick) before curiously awarding a drop ball to the Dutchmen, who netted a fourth goal through Lex Schoenmaker just before half-time as the Hammers stood around in confusion. Consider the fact that the German also booked Robson and Lock for minor dissent and repeatedly stopped play to order West Ham's players to roll up their socks and it's not surprising that one national newspaper described Glockner's performance as 'one of the poorest refereeing displays ever seen in Europe'. With a mountain to climb in the second half, the Hammers somehow hit back with two goals from Billy Jennings to offer some hope for the return leg. And it was those two goals in Holland that ultimately made the difference as a 3-1 win at Upton Park on 17 March – thanks to a machine-gun burst of three strikes in eight first-half minutes from Taylor, Lampard and Bonds – saw the East Londoners through 5-5 on the away goal rule.

With Lyall spying on semi-final opponents Eintracht Frankfurt, his side capitulated just three days later to a 6-1 defeat by Arsenal. The contrast in spirit shown between the two games accurately reflected the fortunes of the team in the respective competitions. The last league win had been against QPR back on 24 January and not another domestic victory would be claimed that season as the club slumped to 18th, mirroring the previous campaign's neglect of Division One duties for the sake of cup glory.

Wrote the *Sun* after the Hammers' narrow 2-1 semi-final first-leg defeat in Frankfurt, 'West Ham tamed the shrew of West German football with a performance of steely dedication and gritty purpose.' Graham Paddon had hit a 30-yard screamer past goalkeeper Kunter to score a vital away goal and give the Hammers an early lead, but the Germans then hit back through Neuberger and Kraus. And urged on by a season-best crowd of 39,202 in the second leg, West Ham scored three second-half goals, through Brooking (twice) and Robson, to Frankfurt's one to win 4-3 on aggregate.

Pat Holland (far right) scores after 29 minutes against the Belgian side Anderlecht in the 1976 European Cup Winners' Cup final.

John McDowell (left) congratulates Keith Robson on the equaliser.

Reflects Tommy Taylor, a virtual ever-present that season, 'West Ham fans have always been the best. During our run to that final in 1976 they were quite unbelievable and more than once roared us home against the odds.' That support proved not to be enough to win the trophy, however, with the 4-2 defeat by Anderlecht in Brussels on 5 May leaving Taylor in a flood of tears, such was the emotion and drama of a match described by one reporter as 'as brilliant a cup final as I have ever seen'.

Pat Holland's 29th-minute goal had been a fitting reward for his side's enterprising play at the Heysel Stadium and it seemed that one hand had been placed on the trophy. But tragedy was to occur just three minutes before half-time, when Frank Lampard's attempted back-pass to Mervyn Day was intercepted by Peter Ressel, who squared for Robbie Rensenbrink to equalise. 'I felt a twinge in my stomach as I turned to pass, with the result that I only half-hit the ball,' explained Lampard afterwards, having failed to appear for the second half because of the injury which would ultimately require surgery.

That moment proved to be the turning point and, with the Hammers still adjusting after bringing on Alan Taylor as substitute and moving John McDowell into the left back position, Francois Van der Elst sped into the penalty box to put Anderlecht into the lead. Even though Keith Robson levelled with just over 20 minutes remaining, heading a Brooking curler in off a post, West Ham succumbed as Holland fouled Rensenbrink to concede a penalty (taken by the man himself) and the brilliant Belgian then set up Van der Elst for his second to seal the victory at the death.

'There is no way it was a penalty,' insisted Holland after the match, but it no longer mattered. The European dream was over. But many friends had been won through the club's exploits and the challenge for John Lyall was to build on the positive aspects of the 1975-76 campaign.

'Europe has been a marvellous experience but perhaps we have allowed those games to distract us from the domestic programme,' said Lyall in the aftermath of defeat.

No Excuses

There was no such excuse the following season, of course, but the Hammers spent most of 1976-77 entrenched in the bottom two. The team got off to a dreadful start, winning just one of the opening 12 league games and losing six matches in succession (including the League Cup) in the month of October to establish the club's worst run since 1958.

Just nine goals had been scored in those dozen league outings and there lay the team's illness. Billy Jennings missed several early games through injury and then struggled to find his form. Keith Robson barely figured at all after requiring fluid to be drained from a damaged thigh. Bobby Gould, having lost his first-team place, had been allowed to rejoin Wolves the previous season for a fee of just £30,000. And Clyde Best had moved to the United States, still reeling from the disappointment of not being included in West Ham's FA Cup final squad the previous summer.

Such was Lyall's desperation for goals that he was forced to deploy Tommy Taylor in a centre forward's position, alongside Alan Taylor, at the beginning of the season as the search for a new face commenced. Burnley's Ray Hankin rejected a move south despite West Ham's bid of £200,000 being accepted, while Walsall's Alan Buckley was also linked. Meanwhile, the injuries continued to mount up. Midfielder Pat Holland fractured a shin bone in September, ruling him out for rest of the season, while defender John McDowell would miss the entire campaign with a serious knee problem. And with Tommy Taylor moved up-field, Bill Green (an £80,000 summer signing from Carlisle) endured a baptism of fire in defence as the team dragged its knuckles across the division's basement.

Cue the return of old favourite Pop Robson. The 30-year-old had spent two seasons in the Second Division with Sunderland but, despite recently winning promotion to the top flight, was delighted to return to Upton Park in October for a second period.

The £80,000 deal wasn't to be the last of the club's spending, with Ron Greenwood having secured first option on the signing of Plymouth Argyle's prolific marksman Paul Mariner. A fee of £200,000 was agreed, only for the Second Division club to suddenly enter into discussions with Ipswich Town. 'It's not possible to do business with people like that,' stormed Greenwood after learning of the future England international's preference for a move to East Anglia.

With Alan Taylor picking up an ankle injury in October, a second new striker was imperative but still the struggle continued. Charlton Athletic refused to listen to offers for Derek Hales, Bristol Rovers' Alan Warboys

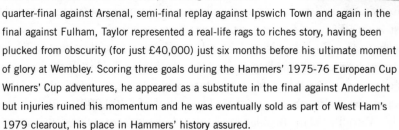

50 Greatest Players

ALAN TAYLOR Striker

Born: Lancaster, Lancashire, 14 November 1953

Joined West Ham: 1974 **From:** Rochdale

Debut: v Leeds United, 7 December 1974

Appearances: 123 **Goals:** 36

Left West Ham: 1979 **For:** Norwich City

Nicknamed 'Sparrow' (because of his spindly legs) but often described as a whippet because of his pace, Alan will forever be remembered for single-handedly scoring the goals that enabled West Ham to win the 1975 FA Cup. Netting twice in the quarter-final against Arsenal, semi-final replay against Ipswich Town and again in the final against Fulham, Taylor represented a real-life rags to riches story, having been plucked from obscurity (for just £40,000) just six months before his ultimate moment of glory at Wembley. Scoring three goals during the Hammers' 1975-76 European Cup Winners' Cup adventures, he appeared as a substitute in the final against Anderlecht but injuries ruined his momentum and he was eventually sold as part of West Ham's 1979 clearout, his place in Hammers' history assured.

didn't fancy becoming 'a stop-gap' and Coventry City's David Cross turned down a £140,000 move because he preferred to stay in the midlands.

When John Radford arrived from Arsenal for £80,000 in December, fans were entitled to feel that the Hammers had been forced to settle for second best. The 29-year-old survivor from the Gunners' 1970-71 double-winning side was clearly past his peak and while Pop Robson top-scored with 14 goals in 30 league games, Radford failed to find the net once in 19 attempts.

As Lyall tried to find the answers to the team's problems in attack, he also made changes in midfield. Graham Paddon, a self-confessed 'roamer', returned to Norwich City for £110,000 in November 1976, with Anton Otulakowski arriving from Barnsley in a £60,000 deal. The Yorkshireman (of Polish extraction) made considerably less impact than Alan Devonshire, another new face recruited from non-league Southall for a mere £5,000. The 20-year-old may have been discarded by Crystal Palace as a teenager, but his skill for deceiving opponents on the left flank and his developing understanding with Trevor Brooking would quickly establish him as a star in the making. Meanwhile, Alan Curbishley and Geoff Pike – two local lads who'd progressed through the club's youth ranks – provided further competition for places.

Turning the Corner

Slowly but surely, West Ham started to turn the corner. A 2-0 win at Manchester United in November had been the club's first away from home in the league for over a year, while champions Liverpool succumbed by the same scoreline at Upton Park on 18 December.

Three wins in succession – at Arsenal and at home to Stoke and Bristol City – during February proved crucial, although the wheels fell off in spectacular fashion with a 6-0 hammering at fellow-strugglers Sunderland on 5 March. But with (a half-fit) Pop Robson hitting 11 goals in the remaining 15 games, during which they lost just twice, the Hammers did just enough to keep their necks above water before going into their final couple of matches – against the year's two FA Cup finalists. A 0-0 draw at Liverpool, who'd just clinched the League Championship for the second successive season, meant that West Ham's fate was at least in their own hands. All they needed to do was beat Manchester United!

Typically, it was to be a match of high drama. Gordon Hill swept the visitors into a 30-second lead, but Frank Lampard restored parity just before the half-hour mark. When Brooking was then tripped in the box by Lou Macari, Geoff Pike had the opportunity to give his side a much-needed half-time lead. The ball ended up in the arms of the crowd and the despair grew, until Pike duly made amends by driving home shortly after the break. When Robson scored a third it should have been all over but, no, Stuart Pearson volleyed a second for United in the 67th minute to raise the heat again. But that man Robson was to have the final say, wrapping things up with a header to secure a 4-2 win, a rare double over United and, most importantly, First Division survival.

The season's climax had seen five players – Billy Jennings, Tommy Taylor, Kevin Lock, Keith Coleman and Keith Robson – officially transfer-listed by the club, but only Coleman (a full back who'd played second fiddle to Lampard and McDowell but had chalked up over 117 appearances in four years) and bad boy Robson were to leave during the summer of 1977.

Far more significant in terms of West Ham's history, of course, was the departure of Greenwood himself after a total of 16 years service with the club. England manager Don Revie had defected to the United Arab Emirates and Ron was the Football Association's choice – ahead of people's favourite Brian Clough – to take over, initially as caretaker and, from December 1977, on a permanent basis.

John Lyall, meanwhile, having spent three years in charge of training and team selection under the controlling umbrella of Greenwood, now found himself absorbing responsibility for scouting, transfers, contract negotiations and all the rest of the management demands. 'I suddenly felt very lonely,' admitted Lyall, who once asked Ron what it was really like to be manager. Replied Greenwood, 'You'll never know until you're on your own.'

Injury Jinx

John later described the 1977-78 season as a disaster, which was an appropriate summary given that West Ham would be relegated. The injury jinx struck after just five games, with Billy Jennings rupturing an Achilles tendon and subsequently missing the rest of the campaign. Indeed, the striker would make just four more appearances for the club (in 1978-79) and then join Orient. With Pat Holland and John McDowell still not back in action yet and Billy Bonds and Trevor Brooking, among others, missing early games, Reg Pratt could point to obvious causes for the team's woeful start (which included a 5-0 hammering at Nottingham Forest in the League Cup) in a special 'Message from the Chairman' in the club programme, 'Transfers cost money... and because of our fairly small ground we have never been a wealthy club, and are never likely to be. The Safety of Sports Grounds Act recently came into force and we are being engulfed with the legislation imposed by the GLC. This is likely to cost us £200,000 and that will leave us with very little in hand.'

It wouldn't be the last time the club found itself trying to juggle its resources in terms of improving the Boleyn Ground while preserving the team's status in the top flight. Ironically, despite the investment of nearly £300,000 between September and December 1977 on strikers Derek Hales and David Cross, it was to prove in vain (in the short term, at least).

Both men had been pursued a year earlier but left Charlton and Coventry to join Derby County and West Bromwich Albion respectively. Hales had endured a miserable time at County and was now available for a third of his original £300,000 fee. Cross, meanwhile, had scored 18 goals in 40 games for Albion and therefore his value had increased by £40,000.

By the time Cross made his debut, ironically against his former club at the Hawthorns (a 1-0 defeat), the Hammers were languishing in 21st place with just 12 points from 20 games. An attacking line-up of Hales, Pop Robson and John Radford had failed to spark, especially with the latter failing to find the net in 11 appearances that season. It was no surprise when he was sold to Blackburn Rovers shortly after Christmas (typically scoring on his debut!).

Hales and Cross did indeed score goals, totalling 19 between them in 47 appearances, while Robson, surprisingly, had a poor year with just nine in

37 league outings. The major problems, however, were at the back. The loss of Bonds – now in the centre of defence – in the early months had not helped, but it was the form of Mervyn Day which caused most concern. With just three clean sheets to the goalkeeper's name in the first 22 games of 1977-78, John Lyall was forced to take the 22-year-old out of the firing line after two blunders at Chelsea on 27 December saw the Hammers go down 2-1. Bobby Ferguson, 10 years Day's senior, was reinstated for just his second game since 1973 but in his seventh appearance he found himself beaten on six occasions as QPR ran riot in an FA Cup fourth round replay.

Relegation Looms

In retrospect, it seems inconceivable that a side containing the firepower of Cross, Hales and Robson, supported by the likes of Brooking and Devonshire in midfield and warriors such as Bonds and Lampard in defence, should get relegated. But too many enforced changes over the course of the season – with the likes of Pike, Curbishley and Holland coming into midfield at different periods, plus young defenders Paul Brush and Alvin Martin getting their first games – made it difficult to build momentum. After 33 league games, they'd won just six.

Alan Devonshire of England and Holland's Rudi Kroll in 1977.

50 Greatest Players

MERVYN DAY Goalkeeper

Born: Chelmsford, Essex, 26 June 1955

Joined West Ham: 1971 (as apprentice)

Debut: v Ipswich Town, 27 August 1973

Appearances: 233

Left West Ham: 1979 **For:** Orient

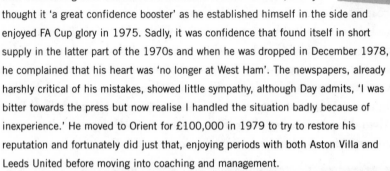

When Ron Greenwood famously declared in 1973 that Day would be West Ham's No. 1 'for the next 10 years', the fact that he'd still only be 28 at that time was not lost on the goalkeeper. Nevertheless, rather than considering such acclaim as a millstone around his neck, Mervyn thought it 'a great confidence booster' as he established himself in the side and enjoyed FA Cup glory in 1975. Sadly, it was confidence that found itself in short supply in the latter part of the 1970s and when he was dropped in December 1978, he complained that his heart was 'no longer at West Ham'. The newspapers, already harshly critical of his mistakes, showed little sympathy, although Day admits, 'I was bitter towards the press but now realise I handled the situation badly because of inexperience.' He moved to Orient for £100,000 in 1979 to try to restore his reputation and fortunately did just that, enjoying periods with both Aston Villa and Leeds United before moving into coaching and management.

A Cross hat-trick against Ipswich in March kick-started a run of five wins in six games (including a 3-1 home success against Chelsea and a 2-1 victory at Leeds), but a 3-0 loss at Manchester United on 22 April left Hammers clinging on by their fingertips. A hot Cross double in the penultimate game at Middlesbrough had Lyall declaring that a miracle escape was still on. But it wasn't to be, with European Champions Liverpool effectively sealing the Hammers' fate with a 2-0 win at Upton Park. Wolves needed to lose both their games in hand to go down instead, but a win against Aston Villa three days later confirmed what everyone had already anticipated. The 20-year stay in Division One was over.

As he surveyed the West Ham wreckage, local reporter Trevor Smith was deeply critical of the club's lethargy in the transfer market. In an article titled 'I accuse Ron Greenwood', in which he suggests that the 'downward path began the day the team won the 1975 FA Cup final', he wrote, 'His (Greenwood's) failure since 1975 to sign the right players at the right time must surely be regarded as the biggest single factor in the circumstances which combined to result in relegation.'

Chapter Twelve: 1978-81
Time to Rebuild

The major fear for supporters following relegation was whether the club would lose its greatest playing asset, Trevor Brooking. The cultured performer had just won the Hammer of the Year award for the third year running, established himself as the most creative force in the England team and enjoyed a successful testimonial match (versus an England XI) the previous autumn. Over 23,000 fans had shown their appreciation of the midfield maestro's talents and Trevor was eager to show loyalty in return. 'I want to end all speculation and help the club bounce back,' he announced.

Having been being assured by Ron Greenwood that his England career would not be seriously threatened as long as he continued to perform well, Brooking pledged his commitment. Frank Lampard, meanwhile, was transfer-listed after failing to agree terms with the club. Admits Frank, 'I got a bit low when we got relegated and thought a move might be best for me. But it was a natural depression and it soon passed.'

Indeed, there was surprisingly little transfer activity following the drop. Kevin Lock ended his nine-year association with the Hammers by making a £50,000 switch to Fulham, while Bill Green moved on to Peterborough for £90,000. But it was the sale of striker Derek Hales to former club Charlton for £85,000 that was perhaps most surprising. The 26-year-old was accused of never really settling in and missing too many scoring opportunities, but his record of 10 goals in 24 league games for the Hammers was far from embarrassing. Manager Lyall clearly considered the hairy hitman as being surplus to requirements, planning on a strike-pairing of Cross and Robson (with Alan Taylor and Billy Jennings waiting in the wings along with the emerging Nicky Morgan and Billy Lansdowne Jnr). The Hammers were installed as 5/1 favourites for promotion and a Cross hat-trick in the 5-2 win against Notts County on the opening day of the 1978-79 season looked to support such confidence. But even though the team tasted defeat on just four occasions in the first 18 league games, they never hit the summit of the division and spent the second half of the season just outside the top three.

Cross and Robson had little trouble racking up goals – scoring 43 times between them that term – but keeping clean sheets was still proving something of a problem. Bobby Ferguson remained between the posts until the end of October, when a damaged shoulder demanded the return of

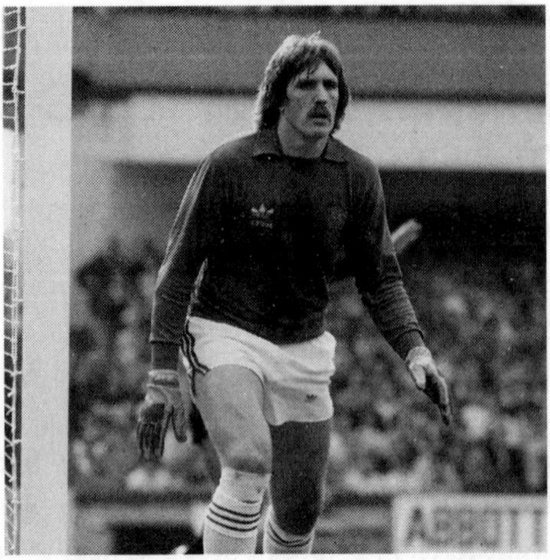

Phil Parkes, bought from QPR, was the most expensive goalkeeper in the world at the time.

Mervyn Day. The goalkeeper won great praise for his comeback performance in a 2-1 win at Brighton but sadly he couldn't maintain his form. 'Sad Day puts Palace top' was the *Daily Express* headline after the Hammers had allowed their south London rivals to leave Upton Park with a 1-1 draw on 18 November, while the same paper blamed him for costing Hammers victory in the 3-3 home draw with Sunderland on 10 February. 'Too many performances such as Day's would cripple West Ham's promotion prospects,' wrote David Miller, without realising that he was effectively writing an obituary for the 23-year-old's Boleyn career. Day would never play for the Hammers again.

Stepping Down to Step Back Up

On 22 February, 1979, the Hammers shocked football by spending £565,000 to make QPR's Phil Parkes the most expensive goalkeeper in the world. 'I believe I am stepping down a division to step back up,' said the 28-year-old midlander. The purchase of Parkes was a huge statement of intent on behalf of the club, with manager Lyall insisting that he was looking very much towards the long-term. Which was just as well because, despite three-goal victories against Oldham and Luton in the keeper's first two matches, the Hammers subsequently slipped to fifth as a result of firing blanks in five out of seven games during March and April. Ironically, the period saw a five-goal thrashing of Newcastle but any joy was offset against the disappointment of seeing Trevor Brooking limp off with a twisted ankle, an injury that would sideline him for 11 games and effectively end any lingering hopes of promotion that season.

Those dreams virtually died with a disastrous 1-1 home draw with struggling Wrexham on 28 April. In a comical game, Welsh goalkeeper Dai Davies was sent off for manhandling referee Ken Baker, who allowed Billy Bonds' 28th-minute goal to stand despite Pop Robson clearly handling the ball. Yet despite gaining the lead in fraudulent circumstances and having a one-man advantage against a team who had to place an outfield player in goal, the Hammers still blew victory with just two minutes remaining. 'I told the boys we had let our supporters down,' fumed John Lyall afterwards (just as he'd done earlier in the season when embarrassingly slipping out of the League and FA Cups to Third Division Swindon and Fourth Division Newport respectively).

Lyall's Clearout

The summer of 1979 was to witness a huge clearout by Lyall. Defender Tommy Taylor joined Mervyn Day and Billy Jennings for the short journey to Orient, John McDowell and Alan Taylor moved to Norwich City and Mick McGiven was given a free transfer. None of these departures were particularly surprising, certainly when compared with that of midfielder Alan Curbishley, who complained that his career had not progressed sufficiently under the club's supervision. 'Trevor Brooking is a great player but everything seems to revolve around getting the ball to him,' moaned the 21-year-old who'd made 28 appearances in his final season before joining Birmingham City for a fee of £225,000. He may have had a point but such a ploy hadn't stopped fellow midfielder Alan Devonshire impressing enough to win the Hammer of the Year award for the first time.

A friendlier farewell was bid by 33-year-old striker Pop Robson, who joined Sunderland for a second time for a fee of £40,000 to pursue his business interests in the north east. 'I'll be leaving a team who play my kind of football, a manager who has always treated me well, a club full of close friends and an area I enjoy living in,' said the winner of the *Daily Express*/Adidas Golden Shoe, having finished the season as the Second Division's top scorer (with 26 league and cup goals).

West Ham played 'my kind of football' said Bryan Robson.

In the boardroom, Len Cairns was elected as the club's new chairman following the retirement of 74-year-old Reg Pratt after an incredible 29 years. Eddie Chapman, meanwhile, was named as the club's first chief executive. In his final season,

Pratt had committed £250,000 to the modernisation of the club's Chadwell Heath training facilities (including the installation of an all-weather astroturf surface). 'We are spending a lot of money on rebuilding the kind of youth policy that produced seven or eight players in the first-team in the mid-1960s,' he said, while also expressing his view that John Lyall was 'doing a first-class job' as he looked to turn West Ham's fortunes around.

The biggest headache for Lyall that summer was replacing his leading goalscorer. After unsuccessfully enquiring about Aston Villa's Brian Little and AZ Alkmaar's Kees Kist, the Hammers boss decided to invest £220,000 on 30-year-old Manchester United's Stuart Pearson. The former England international had only played twice during the previous campaign because of cartilage problems, so the question was not so much the number of goals he would score but the number of appearances he would make.

With Pearson limping off twice during the season's opening four league games – three of which were lost to see the team slump to 21st position – fans had cause for concern, but spirits were lifted by two further new signings as the rebuilding continued. First Lyall paid Dundee United £430,000 to make defender Ray Stewart the most expensive teenager in British history, then he completed his search for a winger by

50 Greatest Players

PAT HOLLAND Midfielder

Born: Poplar, London, 13 September 1950

Joined West Ham: April, 1969 **From:** Amateur

Debut: v Arsenal, 21 April 1969

Appearances: 296 **Goals:** 32

Left West Ham: 1984 **For:** Orient

Certainly one of the unluckiest West Ham players of modern times, 'Patsy' missed out on the 1980 FA Cup final due to injury, while the knee ligaments he damaged when scoring in a league match at Notts County in January 1981 not only cost him the opportunity of playing in the 1981 League Cup final but his Upton Park career. He failed to play another first-team game for the Hammers and, after remaining on the staff in a coaching capacity, had similar roles at Orient, QPR and Spurs before returning to Orient as manager. Back in the mid-seventies, however, Pat was one of the unsung heroes of the teams that won the FA Cup and reached the final of the European Cup Winners' Cup (indeed he opened the scoring in the 4-2 defeat by Anderlecht), operating mostly on the right wing.

spending £140,000 on Norwich City's Jimmy Neighbour. With Paul Brush and Frank Lampard established in the full back positions, Stewart would spend some of his first season playing as a centre half alongside eventual Hammer of the Year Alvin Martin.

The new boys certainly played their part in improving the team's fortunes as they embarked on a run of 15 wins from 22 league games. By 1 March the Hammers were sitting in fifth place, just two points behind leaders Chelsea and with two games in hand. Sadly, the momentum couldn't be sustained and successive defeats by Fulham, Swansea City and Cambridge United – amid a run of six league games without a win during March – heavily undermined the efforts of the previous months.

Continuing Appeal of the Cup

The mood was far from gloomy, however, with an exciting FA Cup run in progress. Cup fever had already started to spread via the League Cup with a nine-game run to the quarter-finals, which saw European Champions Nottingham Forest finally win a City Ground replay with three extra-time goals. Less than a month later, goals from Geoff Pike and Trevor Brooking ensured an FA Cup third round replay win against West Bromwich Albion, after Stuart Pearson had scored in the 1-1 draw at the Hawthorns.

Two goals from Ray Stewart (one a penalty), plus an own-goal, secured a 3-2 fourth round win at Orient (skippered by Tommy Taylor), while strikes from 17-year-old Paul Allen and David Cross in the final five minutes of the Upton Park clash with Swansea saw the Hammers through to the quarter-finals – the first time the club had reached that stage in both cups during the same season.

Over 36,000 fans packed into the Boleyn Ground to witness the game against Aston Villa, who came under siege for most of the 90 minutes. Just when it seemed as if the First Division side had held out for a replay, defender Ken McKnaught handled a Brooking corner to concede an 89th-minute penalty. With chaos breaking out all around him, Ray Stewart calmly placed the ball on the spot before blasting it into the back of the net to send West Ham into the last four. The drama continued in the semi-final tie against Everton at Villa Park and Stewart was again a key figure, getting involved in a second-half scuffle with Brian Kidd who was sent off as a result. 'This was not so much a semi-final as a 90-minute explosion, having never seen a cup game to match it for drama and excitement,' wrote Alan Hoby of the *Daily Express* after the 1-1 draw. First referee Colin Seel inexplicably awarded Everton a first-half penalty, adjudging Alan

Paul Allen, became the youngest player to appear in an FA Cup final in 1980.

Devonshire to have pushed Andy King. Kidd scored from the spot but Everton's lead was wiped out when Stuart Pearson side-footed Brooking's cross home. As West Ham turned the screw in the closing stages, Paul Allen seemed to have won the match, only for his 'goal' to be disallowed with Brooking harshly being ruled offside.

'The FA should relieve Colin Seel of duty for the replay,' wrote one journalist, while the official himself admitted, 'I picked up the papers after the first game and thought, "God, what a mess I've made of this!"'

The midweek replay, just four days after the original clash, was surprisingly designated to take place at Leeds United's Elland Road ground. Geography alone meant that the majority of the 40,000 crowd were Evertonians and, with the Merseysiders a division above the Hammers, the odds were stacked against the Londoners. 'Never has there been such an unforgettable match in West Ham's history than this one,' declared the *Express* after the topsy-turvey epic.

The game remained goalless for 90 minutes but in extra-time Alan Devonshire traded passes with Stuart Pearson and waltzed into the penalty box to give his side the lead. Hammers fans were euphoric but delight turned to despair when Bob Latchford headed home from close range with just seven minutes remaining to make it 1-1, the striker leaping onto the fencing to embrace his supporters. It seemed as if destiny was against the Irons, but little did anybody realise that a fairytale story was unfolding. With just 120 seconds remaining, a curling Brooking cross found its way via David Cross on to the head of a diving Frank Lampard to score an unbelievable winner and catapult the travelling Londoners into fits of ecstasy.

Lampard, playing his 505th first-team game and at 31 the club's longest-serving player, had missed the first semi-final and had only been drafted into the side when Alvin Martin fell victim to tonsillitis. 'People still ask me what the hell I was doing that far up the field,' says Frank. 'It's certainly left a lasting impression on the fans. Even now they sing, "The ball came over, and Frank fell over… "'

Great Matches

FA CUP FINAL **Wembley, London, 10 May 1980**

West Ham United 1 **Arsenal 0** **Attendance: 100,000**

Brooking

How fitting that Trevor Brooking – making his 500th first-team appearance for Second Division West Ham – should score the goal against the holders that took the FA Cup back to Upton Park for the second time in five years.

The Hammers' 13th-minute lead, following a great cross from Alan Devonshire on the left and efforts on goal from David Cross and Stuart Pearson before Brooking headed home, proved surprisingly comfortable for the rest of the match, as Arsenal's centre halves – Willie Young and David O'Leary – wondered exactly who each should be marking.

The game represented a tactical triumph for John Lyall, who withdrew Pearson into a deeper role to leave Cross up front on his own. Explained the Hammers boss, 'I felt we needed to come up with something that would confuse Arsenal and perhaps disturb their defensive organisation.'

At first glance it could be assumed that Pearson was making the major sacrifice, but on reflection it was Cross. 'I only wish I'd had a different role,' says the striker. 'John Lyall took a big gamble but it paid off. Arsenal couldn't do anything to remedy the situation until the second half and by that time the game was as good as won. But I couldn't help lamenting afterwards that I might have scored a couple like Alan Taylor did in 1975 if I'd been allowed to play my normal game.'

Another key talking point of the game was the opportunity denied 17-year-old Paul Allen, who could have claimed a further piece of history by becoming the youngest player to ever score in a Cup final had he not been professionally fouled by Young when closing in on goal in the closing minutes. Reflects Young, 'There would have been no way back if Paul had scored, so I did what I had to do. As I helped him up, Paul said, "No hard feelings, I would've done the same to you". ' However, it's not a version of events that Allen acknowledges. 'I said nothing of the sort! I don't hold a grudge about what he did, but nothing was said between us.' The tears running down Allen's face as he collected his winners' medal said more than a thousand words.

West Ham United: Parkes, Stewart, Lampard, Bonds, Martin, Devonshire, Allen, Pearson, Cross, Brooking, Pike.

Arsenal: Jennings, Rice, Devine (Nelson), Talbot, O'Leary, Young, Brady, Sunderland, Stapleton, Price, Rix.

Referee: G. Courtney.

John Lyall with the FA Cup, 1980.

Yet it was Devonshire who won the Man-of-the-Match awards. 'That was the best game of football I ever played,' says Alan. 'It was as near to perfection as I ever got.'

The same might also be said of John Lyall's tactical approach to the final against existing FA Cup holders Arsenal, on 10 May, with the West Ham manager electing to play David Cross as a lone striker and dropping Stuart Pearson into a deeper role. Although effectively marked out of the match, Cross could console himself with the knowledge that he played a part in the game's only goal, shooting goalwards from Devonshire's cross and the ball rebounding to Pearson who fired across the six-yard box for Brooking to stoop and head home in the 13th minute. Pearson could also take pride from his contribution, proving he was far from finished by making 36 appearances that season.

In fact, had Paul Allen – making history for becoming the youngest ever player to appear in an FA Cup final, at 17 years and 256 days – not been deliberately tripped by Young when clean through on goal late on, then the winning margin would probably have been greater.

Every Hammer played their part in the victory, including Billy Bonds who had been forced to sweat over a possible suspension for the final after being sent off for fighting with Birmingham's Colin Todd on 22 April. Not only did the 2-1 home defeat kill any faint hopes of promotion, but it seemed possible that the West Ham skipper would miss out on a Wembley appearance for exceeding disciplinary 20 points until the FA deemed a warning was sufficient.

With First Division Arsenal contesting the European Cup Winners' Cup final against Valencia a few days later, victory was a remarkable achievement by the East End underdogs and John Lyall was offered an extended contract as his reward for taking the team to two FA Cup wins within five years.

50 Greatest Players

DAVID CROSS Striker

Born: Heywood, Lancashire, 8 December 1950

Joined West Ham: 1977 **From:** West Bromwich Albion

Debut: v West Bromwich Albion 17 December 1977

Appearances: 223 **Goals:** 97

Left West Ham: 1982 **For:** Manchester City

Nicknamed 'Psycho' by the Upton Park crowd following his £180,000 club record signing, Cross had the perfect combination of ability, audacity and aggression. 'The fan who first dubbed me Psycho was right on the ball because I could be the nicest man off the field but a horrible, nasty bloke on a Saturday afternoon,' admits David. The general victims of that nastiness were opposing defences, as Cross bagged nearly a hundred goals in his four and a half years in London, including four at Tottenham in 1981. He scored his 97th and final goal in claret and blue on the final day of the 1981-82 season and, having refused to sign a new contract because of a desire to return north, he was allowed to join Manchester City.

As the champagne bubbles floated up into the East End sky, an air of expectation grew for the forthcoming Second Division campaign. The 1-0 Charity Shield defeat by mighty Liverpool was disappointing but, by the time the two clubs met again at Wembley the following March, in the League Cup final, the Londoners were as good as promoted.

The First Division Beckons

Just a few days after the season's curtain-raiser, West Ham signed a QPR player for a club record fee for the second time in 18 months, with 20-year-old striker Paul Goddard following Phil Parkes east as an £800,000 replacement for the injury-hit Stuart Pearson.

The Hammers machine may have coughed and spluttered initially, losing 2-1 at home to Luton Town and drawing at Bristol City and Preston, but when the engine slipped into gear the team rampaged through the division on full throttle. A 4-0 home win against Notts County at the end of August, with Goddard striking twice, effectively commenced the race and by the time the chequered flag was waved the following May West Ham had left the rest of the pack trailing distantly in their wake.

An incredible 16 home league games were won in succession between August and March, a sequence only halted when the exhausted Hammers returned from European Cup Winners' Cup action in Tbilisi and performed against Oldham Athletic as if carrying sacks of spuds on their backs. Even then they earned a 1-1 draw, before winning their remaining home matches to make it 19 victories in 21 league fixtures at Upton Park – a phenomenal statistic.

The Hammers were almost as convincing on their travels, winning more away games than any other Second Division side and losing on just three occasions. David Cross was unstoppable, scoring four times in the championship-clinching 5-1 triumph at Grimsby Town on 11 April as he stockpiled an exceptional 33 goals in total for the season.

The league programme was wrapped up with a 1-0 win at Sheffield Wednesday, Nicky Morgan's goal enabling the Hammers to set a post-war Second Division points record of 66 for the season. It was an incredible feat, given the fact that the team could so easily have been distracted by their 19-game run in the cups.

The FA Cup win had taken West Ham back into Europe and their Cup Winners' Cup campaign kicked off against Real Madrid's nursery side Castilla amid the most unsavoury of headlines. 'Night of havoc!' screamed one paper as stories emerged of English fans fighting with Spanish police during the match at the Bernabeu Stadium and around the city. And in a separate incident outside the ground, a fan was killed after being run over by a coach. The press generated predictable headlines, the fans complained of police brutality and an angry John Lyall called for jail sentences of 'at least three years' for the hooligans.

As the dust settled, it was confirmed that around 20 fans had been injured and a handful arrested, as well as the likelihood that West Ham would be punished for the behaviour of their travelling support. At first UEFA decided that the Hammers would have to play their second leg – in which they had to try and overturn a two-goal deficit, having lost 3-1 – at least 187 miles away from Upton Park. After a four-man delegation had attended an appeal hearing in Zurich, however, it was subsequently announced that the game could indeed take place at the Boleyn Ground... behind closed doors.

And so West Ham's lowest ever crowd – just 253, made up purely of officials – witnessed a match played in the most bizarre of environments. First-half goals from Geoff Pike, Cross and Goddard seemed to have seen Castilla off, but a 25-yard goal from the Spanish brought the aggregate back to 4-4 and the game into extra-time, before Cross scored twice to grab professional football's most quietly-celebrated hat-trick.

The Sound of Silence: West Ham v Castilla.

A 4-0 home victory in the second round against Poli Timisoara – with three goals being scored in an amazing three minutes in front of 27,257 fans grateful for the sight of some European action – rendered the second leg in Romania a formality (losing 1-0), before the Hammers came up against Dynamo Tbilisi in the third round.

The Georgians produced a devastating display at Upton Park to cruise to an emphatic 4-1 win that earned them a standing ovation from bewildered Hammers fans. A late Stuart Pearson goal to win the away leg, following a 27-hour journey, salvaged some pride but the tie was already over and Tbilisi went on to win the competition. European elimination took place just a few days after West Ham had returned to Wembley for the third time in 10 months to face Liverpool again. By the time the Hammers had relinquished their hold on the FA Cup in January, following three tight games with Second Division Wrexham, they'd fought their way through to the semi-finals of the League Cup. Burnley (with a 6-0 aggregate score), Charlton (2-1 away) and Barnsley (2-1 at home) had all been disposed of before the East Enders were thrown into a quarter-final confrontation with Tottenham Hotspur. The First Division side contained the likes of Glenn Hoddle, Ossie Ardiles and Ricky Villa, but David Cross decided matters with just nine minutes remaining with 'a strange goal' but one that 'made sure that justice was done' according to the *Daily Telegraph*.

In the semi-finals the Hammers found themselves facing one of Cross's former clubs, Coventry, over two legs. Future West Ham goalkeeper and coach Les Sealey – nephew of West Ham's 1965 Cup Winners' Cup hero Alan – experienced a nightmare in the first match at Highfield Road, allowing a Billy Bonds header and a back-pass from team-mate Garry Thompson to elude him to give the Londoners a 2-0 half-time lead. But Hammers buckled under second-half pressure to concede three goals (two by Thompson) and return down the M1 motorway with their tails between their legs.

Fortunately, come the hour (and a half) of need, West Ham delivered their very best to win the second leg 2-0 (with goals from Paul Goddard and, with seconds to spare, Jimmy Neighbour). 'The first 45 minutes was the best football I have seen in my time at the club,' purred John Lyall afterwards.

And so to the final on March 14 against the red machine that would lift the European Cup for the third time in five seasons just a couple of months later. The Hammers had done well to keep the game goalless during 90 minutes and most of the subsequent half-hour of extra-time, but with just a few minutes remaining the match exploded when Alan Kennedy's goal was controversially allowed. And so commenced the most sensationally dramatic two minutes of play seen in West Ham's history. With the red half of Wembley delirious at seemingly witnessing victory in the dying seconds, the Hammers pressed forward one final, desperate time. When Alan Devonshire was cynically tripped on the edge of the box it seemed all over. When Ray Stewart's fierce drive was brilliantly tipped over the bar by Ray Clemence it seemed all over. When Trevor Brooking's corner floated into the box it seemed all over. But Alvin Martin headed forcefully towards goal and, with Clemence beaten, Terry McDermott leapt to fist the ball away. PENALTY!

Liverpool's controversial goal, Wembley, 1981.

Stewart duly thumped the ball past Clemence with his usual conviction and the sound of the final whistle was drowned out by ecstatic cheers from jubilant Hammers fans behind the goal.

Sadly, Liverpool won the replay, at Villa Park, by two goals to one. Paul Goddard headed West Ham into a 10th-minute lead, but the Merseysiders turned up the heat to reply through Kenny Dalglish and an effort from Alan Hansen that hit Bonds and found its way into the net.

Stewart celebrates his last-gasp penalty equaliser at Wembley.

Great Matches

LEAGUE CUP FINAL **Wembley, 14 March 1981**

West Ham United 1 **Liverpool 1*** **Attendance 100,000**

Stewart (pen) **Kennedy A.**

***After extra time**

'Through all the chronicles of sporting drama, there can be little to match the bewildering climax to a match that ended with two sensational goals and a bonfire of controversy that was still raging long afterwards,' enthused James Mossop of the *Sunday Express* as the dust began to settle the following day.

Returning to Wembley again as a Second Division side less than a year after the FA Cup success against Arsenal, West Ham had survived a relatively uneventful 118 minutes against reigning league champions Liverpool until events took a sudden turn. An Alan Kennedy shot beat Phil Parkes to hit the back of the net but with the ball passing over the head of grounded Liverpool midfielder Sammy Lee, who was several yards offside, the effort seemed surely to be disallowed, with the linesman having raised his flag. Incredibly, Welsh referee Clive Thomas awarded the goal and then refused to consult his linesman, who'd by that point dropped his flag. 'Lee was on the ground so I felt there was no way he could be interfering with play,' insisted Thomas, but Parkes was adamant that he'd been unsighted by the player.

A major injustice seemed to have given the Merseysiders certain victory, until midfielder Terry McDermott punched the ball over his own bar to deny Alvin Martin a last-gasp equaliser and a penalty was awarded. Remembers Ray Stewart, given the responsibility for rescuing the match, 'Billy Bonds told me that it didn't matter if I missed, because no one else wanted to take it.'

The final whistle sounded as the ball hit the back of the net and a war of words immediately erupted, with referee Thomas publicly accusing John Lyall of calling him a cheat. 'I simply told Clive I didn't want to talk to him because I felt we'd been cheated,' clarified the West Ham boss, although he did somewhat ambiguously state on *The Big Match*, 'I'm entitled to an opinion... and I'm sticking to it!'

The Red Machine overpowered the Hammers in the replay two weeks later, but nobody present at Wembley for this first match will ever forget the sensational contrast of emotions in those final few minutes.

West Ham United: Parkes, Stewart, Lampard, Bonds, Martin, Devonshire, Neighbour, Goddard (Pearson), Cross, Brooking, Pike.

Liverpool: Clemence, Neal, Kennedy A, Irwin, Kennedy R, Hansen, Dalglish, Lee, Heighway (Case), McDermott, Souness.Referee: C. Thomas

Referee: C. Thomas.

Consolation in Promotion

Genuine consolation soon came in the form of promotion to the top flight after an absence of three years. In being fortunate enough to draw on no more than 17 players during the entire 1980-81 campaign – the smallest figure in the club's history – the team was able to develop into a finely-tuned and highly-efficient unit. But it was ability as much as stability that really counted and this was reflected in the amount of international recognition bestowed upon West Ham's players around this time. Trevor Brooking was the established England man in the camp and nobody could forget his stunning goal in the crucial World Cup qualifier in Hungary in 1981. Indeed, he scored twice in that 3-1 victory.

Midfield partner Alan Devonshire had already seen his club form rewarded with his first full caps in 1980 (he went on to make 8 appearances for England in all) while Frank Lampard received a surprise call-up for the match against Australia for his second and final England outing. Fellow full-back Ray Stewart won the first of his 10 Scotland caps in 1981, while central defender Alvin Martin followed up several appearances in youth internationals and an England 'B' outing with the first of his 17 full caps against Brazil that summer.

At just 22, Martin had a potentially long international career ahead of him, but if fate had not intervened he'd have had his 34-year-old West Ham defensive partner alongside him in the 1-0 defeat by the South Americans. England boss Ron Greenwood had called up Billy Bonds for the friendly but the Hammer was cruelly ruled out of the Wembley date after injuring a rib in his club's final league game of the season away at Sheffield Wednesday.

Paul Goddard had forged a 56-goal partnership with David Cross in 1980-81 and would win his one and only England cap as a substitute against Iceland in 1982. Young Paul Allen, meanwhile, broke Bobby Moore's appearance record for the England youth team during the promotion season, despite missing most of the campaign with a succession of injuries. The 18-year-old was still able to help the West Ham youngsters to an excellent 'double', winning both the FA Youth Cup (over a two-legged final against Spurs) and the South East Counties League (with a team containing future first-teamers Alan Dickens and Bobby Barnes).

With two Wembley finals in 10 months, a return to Europe and promotion to Division One in the most convincing fashion possible, it was certainly a special time to be at Upton Park. As Paul Goddard remembers, 'It was a wonderful team and some of the football we played was out of this world.'

Chapter Thirteen: 1981-86
Great Expectations

It was little wonder that John Lyall saw few reasons to meddle with the side for the sake of it following promotion. The only departure of note was that of goalkeeper Bobby Ferguson who decided to set off for a new life in Australia. Tom McAlister – a free transfer from Swindon Town – arrived to provide cover for Parkes.

Although the club was linked with various names, no other new faces would arrive until January 1982, by which time the Hammers had consolidated their place back among football's élite. Despite Trevor Brooking missing the first seven games with a damaged calf muscle, the momentum of the previous season inspired the team to a run of 10 unbeaten games, the most thrilling of which was a 4-0 win at Tottenham Hotspur.

Following an opening day draw with Brighton at Upton Park (sporting the newly-seated West Stand lower tier), the Hammers headed to White Hart Lane on 2 September and promptly ran riot, with David Cross indulging in a four-goal frenzy. 'King Cross leaves Spurs in a shambles!' boomed the *Daily Express*, after the striker had embarrassed England keeper Ray Clemence, making his home debut after leaving Liverpool.

Billy Bonds broke Bobby Moore's club appearance record in 1982-83.

Cross hit the net again in a 2-0 win at Sunderland in the next game but allowed Paul Goddard to steal some of the limelight with two goals in the 3-2 victory against Stoke which took the Hammers to the top of the table with 10 points from four games (with three points for a win having just been introduced). 'West Ham are championing the kind of football everyone wants to see,' wrote James Mossop and Goddard followed up with 3 goals in a 4-2 win against Southampton.

Almost inevitably, the Hammers couldn't sustain their form, drawing six of their next eight league games before embarking on an awful run of five successive defeats (including League Cup elimination by West Brom) around the turn of the year. By January 30, when West Brom returned to Upton Park, the team had slipped to 12th, but met fire with fire to secure a 3-1 win. WBA manager Ronnie Allen accused the Hammers of strong-arm tactics. 'They might win a few points but they'll lose some friends,' he moaned.

The match was also featured the home league debuts of new signings Francois Van der Elst and Neil Orr. Belgian Van der Elst had starred in Anderlecht's 1976 Cup Winners' Cup final victory over the Hammers and the 26-year-old arrived in a £400,000 deal with New York Cosmos, with Lyall showing the kind of progressive thinking – in terms of exploiting continental talent – that would become commonplace 15 years later. Defender Orr, a Scottish U-21 international, commanded the same fee when transferring from Morton and both men played their part in helping West Ham to a respectable 9th place.

Trevor Brooking was one of West Ham finest ever players.

Three Scots Make a Better Team

When David Cross refused to sign a new contract with the club, Lyall moved quickly in recruiting Sandy Clark, whose 18 goals as a part-timer with Airdrie had won him much attention in Scotland. 'I always felt that any team in England is all the better for having three Scots,' said the Hammers boss after spending £200,000 to introduce the 25-year-old striker to first-team compatriots Ray Stewart and Neil Orr. Cross eventually joined Manchester City and how the team would cope with the loss of its top scorer for the second time in three years remained to be seen.

The immediate interest was how England would fare in that summer's World Cup finals in Spain, although West Ham's involvement was limited to that of Brooking and Van der Elst, representing England and Belgium respectively. Each nation won its first round group, but both failed to progress beyond the second round stage, with England being eliminated without actually losing a match. Ron Greenwood's men needed to beat Spain in their final game and Brooking – along with fellow injury-victim Kevin Keegan – only appeared for the last 27 minutes, having missed the rest of the tournament with groin problems. Sadly, the goal didn't come and

Greenwood retired from his post a disappointed man, although he has continued to defend his decision not to play Brooking and Keegan for the full 90 minutes. 'Both had been injured and could have suffered permanent damage if I had played them for the entire match,' he said.

Such caution was justified when Brooking's problems continued into the 1982-83 season and after an operation the midfielder made just one first-team appearance that campaign.

The Hammers finished their second season back in the top flight in eighth place, which, given the absence of their main creative force, was certainly a satisfactory sign of consolidation. A run of five victories in succession during September and October, including a 3-2 success at Arsenal and a 3-1 home against league-leaders Liverpool, elevated the team to second in the table. But for the second year running John Lyall's side lost its momentum and, although still sitting in a top five position at Christmas, a sequence of six successive defeats in the early part of 1983 wrecked any hopes of tangible reward. That run included a 2-0 FA Cup defeat at Manchester United, as well as a hard-to-stomach Milk Cup fifth round loss at Liverpool (Graeme Souness scoring an 86th-minute winner).

Goals were being scored but the team was becoming increasingly reliant on the likes of Van der Elst (joint top marksman with Goddard on 12 goals), three of which came in a thrilling 3-3 Milk Cup draw at Notts County) and Ray Stewart (11 goals, including 10 penalties). It was always going to be difficult for new striker Sandy Clark to make the transition from part-time Scottish football to the English First Division and so it proved, despite a promising run of five goals in five league games early on. With just two strikes in the next 17 league games, Clark's relationship with the West Ham support had reached an untenable situation by the time he was substituted in the 1-1 draw with Southampton on 26 February, with the Boleyn crowd singing 'bye bye, Sandy' as he left the field.

Francois Van der Elst scored all the goals in a 3-3 draw with Notts County.

Within weeks Clark was back in Scotland, having joined Glasgow Rangers

50 Greatest Players

TREVOR BROOKING CBE Midfielder

Born: Barking, Essex, 2 October 1948

Joined: West Ham: 1965 (as apprentice)

Debut: v Burnley, 29 August 1967

Appearances: 635 **Goals:** 102

Left West Ham: 1984 (retired)

Considered one of modern football's ultimate gentlemen, Trevor personified skill, intelligence and elegance on the ball. A one-club man, he remained loyal to the Hammers during relegation in 1978 and scored the goal against Arsenal to win the FA Cup in 1980. Hammer of the Year a record five times (1972, 1976, 1977, 1978 and 1984), it's incredible to think that Brooking almost left Upton Park on two occasions in the early 1970s, particularly when included in a £400,000 deal that nearly took Bobby Moore to Derby County. 'I can't say I'd have relished the idea of working for Brian Clough,' admitted Trevor many years later, no doubt remembering the manager's mystifying comment in 1980 that Brooking 'floated like a butterfly... and stung like one.' He 'stung' in goalscoring terms on 102 occasions, sitting eighth in Hammers all-time charts, while his 635 appearances places him fourth in the club's list. His 47 England caps were amassed between 1974 and 1982 and when he played his final game for West Ham in 1984 he found himself virtually carried on his lap of honour by the adoring East End faithful.

for £160,000, while Dave Swindlehurst was recruited from Derby County for a fee of £200,000. The 27-year-old former Crystal Palace striker made his mark with the winning goal against Watford on 2 April, in just his second match. But 'Swindles' wasn't the only new forward to make an impact. Stuart Pearson had been granted a free transfer before the season started and when Paul Goddard was sidelined before the New Year's Day clash with Tottenham Hotspur at Upton Park, 17-year-old Tony Cottee was thrust into action. He duly marked his debut by heading West Ham ahead in a match they would win 3-0, before hitting another goal in the 3-2 defeat by Luton Town three days later. With Cottee and fellow youth product Alan Dickens both scoring in the 2-1 home win over Brighton on March 3, and midfielder Paul Allen now an established part of the side, the local press quite rightly acknowledged the club's work in developing its own talent, under the control of chief scout Eddie Baily.

Injury Agony

Alvin Martin had bounced back from missing the World Cup finals the previous summer to earn the Hammer of the Year award for the second year running and return to the England squad, but there was to be despair for fellow hopeful Alan Devonshire. Midway through the 1983-84 campaign, in an FA Cup third round tie against Third Division Wigan Athletic, the majestic midfielder tore medial ligaments in his right knee and was stretchered off, ultimately being sidelined for the next year and a half.

Another major casualty that season was Paul Goddard, who was restricted to just five league appearances after finding himself in plaster. Paul Allen lost the first half of the campaign to ankle problems, while Billy Bonds – who'd broken Bobby Moore's record of making 544 league appearances for the Hammers the previous season – was out for three months with eye and calf injuries.

Far more distressing, however, was the news in January 1984 that two West Ham players had been hospitalised following a serious car crash. Alvin Martin suffered six broken ribs when being thrown from his vehicle after hitting a lamp-post on the way home from a match at Birmingham, while team-mate Steve Whitton – signed from Coventry for £175,000 the previous summer – incurred a dislocated shoulder and damage to his collar bone at the same time.

The absence of Bonds and then Martin required much defensive reshuffling on Lyall's part, with Steve Walford – another pre-season signing (from Norwich for £165,000) – Ray Stewart, Frank Lampard, Paul Brush and Neil Orr operating in various positions to plug the gaps. With the club's worst-ever injury crisis (as it was reported) taking its toll, it's not surprising that the team's form deteriorated as the season progressed, for the third year in succession. Francois van der Elst had returned to Belgium the previous summer, joining Lokeren, but with Whitton in the No. 7 shirt the Hammers had set a scorching pace at the beginning of campaign. They trounced Birmingham 4-0 at home on the opening day, won 1-0 at Everton, won 2-0 at Tottenham and then beat Leicester 3-1 and Coventry 5-2 at Upton Park.

Paul Goddard's Hammers career was dogged by injury.

Great Players

FRANK LAMPARD Defender

Born: East Ham, London, 20 September 1948

Joined West Ham: 1964 (as apprentice)

Debut: v Manchester City, 18 November 1967

Appearances: 663 **Goals:** 21

Left West Ham: 1985 **For:** Southend United

A tremendous servant across three decades and the club's second-highest appearance maker, Frank was a full back who took few prisoners. Tenacious in the tackle, it's ironic that he's now best remembered for the diving header against Everton that took the Hammers through to the 1980 FA Cup final. Nearly 20 years later, his son Frank repeated his merry jig around the Elland Road corner flag after scoring at the same ground. Lampard senior enjoyed a number of successes, playing in the 1975 and 1980 FA Cup final victories, as well as playing 38 times in the Hammers' 1980-81 Second Division championship-winning programme. An amazing eight years divides his two full England caps (also making four Under-23 appearances) and, following his departure in 1985, he was brought back to Upton Park as assistant manager when brother-in-law Harry Redknapp assumed control in 1994.

The scintillating form was taken into the Milk Cup and poor Third Division Bury suffered in the most painful manner, being thrashed 10-0 in their second-round second-leg visit to the Boleyn Ground on October 25. Tony Cottee feasted himself on four goals, while Brooking and Devonshire grabbed two apiece. 'West Ham hot-shots just Bury 'em alive!' screamed one paper after the massacre which set records for both the Milk Cup and the club's own statistics. It was just the second match in which the Hammers' shirts featured the name of club sponsors Avco Trust, although it's doubtful that any Bury player had time to read the branding, such was the speed and thought of movement from the Londoners. Of course, fans were much amused when John Lyall later bought Bury centre half Paul Hilton in a bid to resolve his defensive injury problems.

With there being so many enforced changes to the side, however, all momentum was soon lost and, although the team still sat fourth in the table at the end of March, just one victory in the final 12 games (which included a humiliating 6-0 thrashing at Liverpool on April 7) saw them slide out of UEFA Cup contention down to a season-low of ninth.

Changing Personnel

It was a particularly disappointing conclusion to a campaign which had initially promised so much, especially for Hammer of the Year Trevor Brooking who'd announced his decision to retire at the end of the season. The 35-year-old's career ended in anti-climax as West Ham lost their final two games – both at home – to Nottingham Forest and Everton, but with European qualification gone by the last match the only thing that mattered to the fans was having the opportunity to say farewell to a player who'd given them so much pleasure.

Replacing the midfielder was an impossibility, but that didn't stop the media hyping the emerging Alan Dickens as 'the new Brooking'. Surprisingly, the youngster was initially happy to accept such an accolade. 'Trevor was one of the greatest West Ham players ever so there could be no bigger compliment than being compared to him,' says Dickens. 'But it did get to me after a few years and became too much to handle.'

Billy Bonds (37) and Frank Lampard (35) also felt the time was right to withdraw from first-team contention in 1984, although they would remain contracted to the club for the following season. Bonds was particularly vocal about his decision to step down. 'I haven't been enjoying the game lately and the first team needs some new faces,' he said.

Perhaps with club president Reg Pratt – known as 'Mr West Ham' – passing away in March that year, after a long battle with cancer, the feeling was that the end of an era had been reached. Mr Pratt, 79, had done much as chairman to support the judgement of John Lyall and the manager honoured his former colleague by declaring, 'He gave far more to the game than he took from it.'

Lyall may well have felt that some kind of watershed had been reached in the summer of 1984, especially when approached by QPR (who'd just finished fifth) about their management vacancy. John initially decided to accept their lucrative offer, hoping to recruit coach Mick McGiven and scout Eddie Baily to the Rangers cause while leaving coaches Ronnie Boyce and Tony Carr at Upton Park 'to maintain the club's traditional continuity'. However, when West Ham chairman Len Cairns demanded that compensation be paid because the manager was still under contract (albeit for just one more year), Lyall nobly withdrew his acceptance, reluctant to be at the centre of a tug of war. John, who was also been linked with Spurs, eventually signed a new contract that tied him to the Hammers until June 1989.

With Brooking retired, Bonds and Lampard preparing to offer only cameo roles when required, Devonshire needing another year to recover from knee

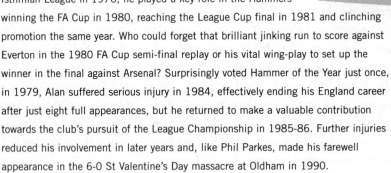

Great Players

ALAN DEVONSHIRE Midfielder

Born: Park Royal, London, 13 April 1956

Joined West Ham: 1976 **From:** Southall

Debut: v QPR, 27 October 1976

Appearances: 446 **Goals:** 32

Left West Ham: 1990 **For:** Watford

A player of immense flair, the sight of 'Dev' in full flight was a joy to all fans. Costing a mere £5,000 when recruited from the Isthmian League in 1976, he played a key role in the Hammers winning the FA Cup in 1980, reaching the League Cup final in 1981 and clinching promotion the same year. Who could forget that brilliant jinking run to score against Everton in the 1980 FA Cup semi-final replay or his vital wing-play to set up the winner in the final against Arsenal? Surprisingly voted Hammer of the Year just once, in 1979, Alan suffered serious injury in 1984, effectively ending his England career after just eight full appearances, but he returned to make a valuable contribution towards the club's pursuit of the League Championship in 1985-86. Further injuries reduced his involvement in later years and, like Phil Parkes, made his farewell appearance in the 6-0 St Valentine's Day massacre at Oldham in 1990.

surgery and goalkeeper Phil Parkes also requiring a knee operation that would rule him out of action for half the campaign (Tom McAlister filling in), perhaps it was no surprise that the 1984-85 season should witness the worst league placing since the Hammers returned to the First Division in 1981.

Yet for the fourth year running, fans were swayed into false optimism by a promising start. Tony Gale, the Fulham centre half who'd had to fill Bobby Moore's boots in the mid-seventies as a youngster, was now asked to fill the vacuum created by the retreating Bonds after making the opposite journey to the former England captain in a tribunal-set £200,000 deal. The 24-year-old went straight into the side (alongside Alvin Martin) and three successive victories during the first week of September lifted the team to second place. But fortunes quickly deteriorated.

Striker Dave Swindlehurst was unavailable with a knee injury for some time and, although Tony Cottee (24 goals across all competitions) and a fit again Paul Goddard (17 goals) hit the target on a regular basis, a failure to keep a clean sheet in 24 of 28 league matches between September and April resulted in the team dropping perilously close to the relegation zone. Five goals were conceded in visits to Manchester United and Watford, leaving the Hammers in 19th place after just three wins in a run of 21 league games.

Billy Bonds, despite his close-season declaration, had found himself thrown into midfield duty for half the campaign due to another injury crisis that deprived the team of, among others, Alan Dickens for several months.

Tony Cottee averaged around 20 goals a season for the claret and blues.

The only real joy came in the shape of an FA Cup run that saw victories against Port Vale (4-1), Norwich (2-1) and Wimbledon (5-1, thanks mainly to a Cottee hat-trick), although a Norman Whiteside hat-trick ensured Manchester United a quarter-final success (4-2).

Goalkeeper Parkes finally returned to first-team action in April after McAlister had broken two ribs in the 4-2 defeat at Loftus Road and a run of three unbeaten games helped ease the side's nerves, although the a 5-1 defeat at West Brom instantly increased them. An 86th-minute winner against Norwich City from substitute winger Bobby Barnes, however, provided a ray of hope (the team's first victory at home in 11 attempts) and wins against Stoke City (5-1, watched by just 13,362 in dreadful conditions) and Ipswich (1-0 at Portman Road) ensured that the final-day 3-0 defeat by Liverpool mattered little.

Further Departures

'I was glad to get the 1984-85 season behind me,' admitted John Lyall after watching his side finish 16th (just two points above relegated Norwich) and having felt unsettled during his lengthy contract negotiations.

The manager would have further discussions to undertake as a number of players headed out of the Boleyn Ground's gates during the summer of 1985. Veteran Frank Lampard had made the last of his 665 appearances for the Hammers in the match against Liverpool and joined Southend United on a free transfer to see out his final playing days. Fellow full back Paul Brush would also soon depart to Crystal Palace, for a small fee. And striker Dave Swindlehurst, no longer first choice with Cottee and Goddard impressing, moved on to Sunderland for a nominal amount.

By far the most worrying of departures, however, was that of Paul Allen. Still only 22, he'd had enjoyed a fantastic season on the right side of midfield, but with his contract expiring several big clubs were joining the chase. Much to the fans' annoyance, the Hammer of the Year agreed to join fierce rivals Spurs, with a league tribunal setting a £400,000 transfer fee. Some felt that Allen had engineered the move, but it's a suggestion he's anxious to deny. 'I was happy at West Ham and would have stayed had I been offered a new contract,' he insisted.

The £340,000 arrival of Frank McAvennie from St Mirren in the summer of 1985 had some reports suggesting he would be Allen's direct replacement and, although bought as a midfielder, the 25-year-old Scot was intended to support the attack in a more central role. Eventually Allen's successor arrived in the diminutive shape of Oldham winger Mark Ward, for a fee of £250,000. And with Alan Devonshire returning from his 18-month absence, the Hammers were entitled to feel as if they'd made another new signing.

The 1985-86 season arrived with the knowledge that both Billy Bonds (nearly 39) and the industrious Geoff Pike would be unavailable through toe and groin injuries respectively and Hammers' resources were further depleted when Goddard injured his left shoulder in the first half of the opening day defeat at Birmingham City. Alan Dickens came into midfield and McAvennie was pushed up into attack alongside Cottee. And hence was born the club's most productive striking partnership since Geoff Hurst and Martin Peters in the late sixties. Frank scored twice in the 3-1 win over QPR three days later on his home debut and bagged another two at Upton Park in a 2-2 draw against Liverpool three games later. But while there was joy for the Scot, for Cottee there was not, the little hitman failing to score in the first five matches and finding himself dropped to the bench for the 1-1 draw at Southampton on 3 September. Anxious to prove a point upon his recall, Tony scored 10 times in his next 10 appearances as the Hammers put a disappointing start of one win in the first seven Division One outings behind them to embark on a run of 18 unbeaten league games (to equal the club record). An incredible nine league games were won in succession between October and December and by Christmas the team were sitting third in the table with 45 points from 22 games. The only disappointment during this period was a controversial Milk Cup exit at Manchester United, in which Mark Ward had a perfectly good late equaliser disallowed after the referee deemed his indirect free-kick to have gone straight into the net, despite United keeper Gary Bailey clearly palming the ball into the goal.

But it was mainly McAvennie making the headlines, scoring both on and off the pitch as his playboy image quickly developed. 'On current form West Ham are the best team in the land,' wrote Joe Melling, while conceding, 'the feeling remains that their title challenge will fade once again.' And so it appeared when three games out of four (at Liverpool, Arsenal and Aston Villa, in which Ray Stewart and Alvin Martin were sent off) were lost in the new year to dump the Hammers down to seventh. The team's momentum had been totally destroyed by bad weather with only one league game – the 2-1 home victory over Manchester United – between 19 January and 14 March. That period did witness a number of FA Cup games, however, with West Ham beating Ipswich Town in a fourth round second replay and Manchester United in a fifth round replay at Old Trafford (Pike and Stewart scoring the goals in a 2-0 win) before bowing out of the competition at Sheffield Wednesday in the quarter-finals.

A Brilliant Run

Revenge against Wednesday was gained in a 1-0 home win on 22 March as the team set off on another brilliant run. A 4-0 blitzing of Chelsea at Stamford Bridge a week later confirmed that the Hammers were back in their championship-chasing stride again, with Cottee (two), McAvennie and Devonshire on the scoresheet. The latter was playing arguably the best football of his career, having established a great relationship with fellow midfielders Dickens, Pike and the impressive Ward. Behind them Martin and Gale were proving huge obstacles in the middle of defence, while George Parris quickly impressed as an emergency replacement for injured left back Steve Walford in the closing months.

The severe weather had caused havoc with the fixture list, however, with West Ham having to play their final 11 matches in just five weeks. An astonishing 8-1 savaging of Newcastle United on 21 April – in which Martin etched himself into the history books by becoming the first player to score against three different keepers in one match – gave West Ham the taste for blood and it continued to flow with taut 1-0 victories against Coventry and Manchester City. By the time strugglers Ipswich arrived at Upton Park on 30 April, the tension was unbelievable with the Hammers needing victory to close the gap on Liverpool to four points with a game in hand (and just two more to play). When Kevin Wilson put the visitors ahead in the 63rd minute it seemed as if the title dream was over, but a majestic curling shot from Dickens levelled matters shortly afterwards and the home crowd exploded into euphoria as Stewart converted a furiously-contested 87th-minute penalty. West Ham therefore travelled to long-relegated West Bromwich on the final Saturday needing victory while hoping that Liverpool would fail to win at Chelsea on the same afternoon.

Great Players

PHIL PARKES Goalkeeper

Born: Sedgley, West Midlands, 8 August 1950

Joined West Ham: 1979 **From:** Queens Park Rangers

Debut: v Oldham, 24 February 1979

Appearances: 436

Left West Ham: 1990 (released)

Purchased for £565,000, a world record fee for a goalkeeper in 1979, Phil Parkes proved to be worth every penny over the course of the next decade. Considered the safest pairs of gloves to ever defend the club's honour, proper international recognition (he received just one England cap) was only denied him by the presence of the legendary Peter Shilton and Ray Clemence. In fact it was Shilton who declared upon Parkes' arrival at Upton Park, 'West Ham have not gambled in paying that kind of money, they have invested'. Phil kept a club-record 22 clean sheets during 1980-81 and was rewarded with that season's Hammer of the Year trophy as West Ham celebrated promotion and League Cup final place. A key member of the successful 1985-86 side, he made his final appearances in 1990 at the age of 39.

That would then leave the Hammers with a potential title-decider at current champions Everton just two days later.

Ultimately, their efforts were in vain. The Hammers squeezed a 3-2 win at the Hawthorns (McAvennie scoring his 28th goal of the season) while all sorts of rumours circulated the ground as to what was happening at Stamford Bridge. But as the players headed for the dressing room an official made the announcement, 'Sorry, lads, Liverpool have won.'

'West Ham have proved that attractive football can also be effective football,' wrote Patrick Collins amid the disappointment, adding, 'They have grown into the most appealing side in England.' Said Lyall as tears began to flow, 'Don't cry for the team. Instead, be proud of what has been achieved.'

Drained by the emotion of the final few months, his exhausted side slid to a 3-1 defeat to Everton in the battle for second place. But even though the Hammers would receive little reward for finishing third – the highest in the club's history – as English clubs were banned from European competition following the Heysel disaster the previous year, Lyall remained typically philosophical and upbeat.'Think of what we can achieve with these players over the next two or three years,' he said. 'The future looks marvellous.'

Chapter Fourteen: 1986-89
Lyall's Lament

The old cliche about not fixing what isn't broken may ring true, but in football it's vital that clubs build on any success by exploiting their appeal to the game's top players. It's something that West Ham criminally ignored during the summer of 1986, negligently sitting dormant while others improved their squads. 'There is no point in buying players of similar calibre to the ones we already have,' insisted John Lyall.

The team's start to the 1986-87 season would certainly have given the Hammers boss a false sense of security. Maximum points from the first two games – including a fabulous 3-2 win at Old Trafford – and just one defeat in 11 league games between mid-September and mid-November suggested that it was going to be another reasonably successful year. But then the milk turned sour...

John Lyall, a loyal servant to West Ham on and off the pitch for 34 years.

Lyall had persuaded Paul Goddard to sign a new three-year contract in the summer by agreeing to let the frustrated striker move on should another club make an acceptable bid – a pledge the boss had to honour when Newcastle United offered £425,000 in November. To receive a club record fee for a player with limited first-team opportunities may have seemed good business but, with Goddard only recently being recalled for three games to deputise for the injured McAvennie, fans were entitled to worry about the effect on the squad's strength in depth.

Frank had scored five times in 10 league games but his form then deteriorated dramatically, the Scot netting just twice in 26 further appearances as his hedonistic lifestyle started to take effect. Fortunately, Cottee had lost none of his potency in front of goal (scoring 28 times, including three hat-tricks) but a combination of injuries and a lack of quality reinforcements resulted in an alarming slide down the table.

Billy Bonds and 'Chippy' Brady clowning around for the cameras.

A Legend Arrives

Just two league games were won between December and March and the club said goodbye to the Littlewoods and FA Cups with depressing defeats by Tottenham (5-0 away) and Sheffield Wednesday (2-0 at home) respectively. To try and arrest the slump Lyall splashed £700,000 on Arsenal's former England U-21 midfielder Stewart Robson in January and the Highbury connection was increased when the Hammers boss swooped for the legendary Liam Brady, ending his seven-year sojourn in Italy.

The 31-year-old Republic of Ireland international signed from Ascoli for a bargain £100,000 in March, declaring his admiration for the way the Hammers played the game, while other new recruits arrived in the shape of Lincoln City centre half Gary Strodder (£100,000) and Aberdeen left back Tommy McQueen (£150,000). The latter pair would typify the type of signings the club would generally make over the next few years.

With the team sitting in 15th position with 10 games remaining, Alvin Martin declared that 'teams have sussed us out', but the biggest problem was fielding consistent line-ups with Lyall having to draw on 25 players for the season (as opposed to just 18 the year before). Defender Steve Potts had his first run of games in the side (having made his debut in January 1985) while young midfielders Paul Ince and Kevin Keen both made seven appearances in a side badly lacking in confidence. Even Billy Bonds was drafted into action (for the first time since May 1985) to lend hands to the pumps and his 24 performances won him not just the Hammer of the Year award (for the fourth time) but a new 12-month contract.

Four home wins – including a 3-1 victory over Arsenal in which Brady appropriately scored his first West Ham goal – in the final months of the season ensured survival by a clear 10 points, but a long-term malaise had set in – and Tony Cottee knew it. As well as feeling frustrated that John Lyall hadn't reinforced much earlier, TC's ambitions had grown considerably as a result of having mixed with more successful players when selected for England – as had started to occur from the autumn of 1986. With the desire to win trophies also burning bright, the striker submitted a written transfer request to secretary Tom Finn, but Lyall succeeded in persuading the player to withdraw his request.

Having purchased four players in early 1987 and the youth system producing the likes of Ince, Keen and Potts, Lyall no doubt felt comfortable in allowing players such as Geoff Pike, Neil Orr and Steve Walford to move on during the following close season. In fact he described the first-team squad as being 'the strongest I can recall' but such an assessment was extremely ill-judged as the team scraped just one win from the opening 12 games of the 1987-88 season. Alan Devonshire had injured

50 Greatest Players

TONY COTTEE Striker

Born: West Ham, London, 11 July 1965

Joined West Ham: 1982 (as apprentice)

Debut: v Tottenham Hotspur, 1 January 1983

Appearances: 335 **Goals:** 145

Left West Ham: 1988, 1996 **For:** Everton (returning in 1994), Selangor

A born goalscorer, 'TC' never looked back after netting on his debut as a 17-year-old. The pocket-sized striker bagged five league goals in just eight league appearances in that first season (1983-84) and hit another 112, including 26 during 1985-86 when West Ham finished a best-ever third (winning the Hammer of the Year award), before a combination of frustration and ambition encouraged him to accept a British record £2.2m move to Everton in 1988. After six seasons on Merseyside, Tony returned to the club he supported as a boy, as West Ham sought Premiership consolidation.

Surprisingly sent-off on his second debut (at Liverpool), it was business as usual as he scored against Aston Villa in his first home outing, finishing the season with 15 goals to his name. Seemingly a veteran but just 31 years of age, he was lured to Selangor of Malaysia in 1996 after Hammers accepted a fee of £800,000 but later returned to England with Leicester. Currently sitting fifth in West Ham's all-time scoring lists, it's incredible to realise he won just seven full England caps during his career.

an Achilles tendon in the 3-0 home defeat by QPR on the opening day and would miss the entire campaign, while Tony Gale missed half the season with a similar injury. Goalkeeper Phil Parkes, meanwhile, had incurred an elbow injury at the end of March and would make just one appearance towards the end of the term.

A 'Crisis' Looms

Amid newspaper speculation of Cottee making a move to Everton, Hammers fans were shocked to see Frank McAvennie allowed to join his boyhood idols Celtic for a record £750,000 at the end of September. 'I didn't feel I could deny him the chance to fulfil an ambition,' explained John Lyall, displaying a compassion that some may have felt wasn't necessarily in West Ham's best interests (despite the striker's poor form). A 5-2 home defeat by Second Division Barnsley in the second round of the Littlewoods Cup a week later had papers talking of an Upton Park 'crisis' and speculating that Lyall's position could be in jeopardy.

A replacement for McAvennie was paramount but with interest in Chelsea's Kerry Dixon, Southampton's Colin Clarke, Luton Town's Mick Harford and Manchester United's Peter Davenport coming to nothing, poor Cottee had to operate as the long genuine striker with midfielder Alan Dickens pushed into an emergency attacking role. The loss of just two of a dozen league games prior to Christmas lifted the side to 10th position, but just two wins in the next 18 games saw a slide down to the 18th place that would ultimately involve a club in a play-off to avoid relegation (with the division being reduced to 20 clubs).

Goalkeeper Allen McKnight arrived from Celtic for £250,000 in 1988.

Lyall finally landed a striker in March when he paid £275,000 for Fulham's Leroy Rosenior. The 23-year-old instantly ingratiated himself with the Boleyn faithful by scoring in his first three games and striking twice (before being sent off) in the crucial 4-1 home win over Chelsea on May 2 that ultimately condemned the visitors to relegation.

Knowing a loss of six goals or more at Newcastle in the final game could still endanger the club's status, Lyall created history by naming a goalkeeper as substitute for the very first time. Julian Dicks – a £300,000 deadline-day arrival from Birmingham to solve the problem left back slot after George Parris had broken his ankle – duly scored his first goal in claret and blue – for the opposition – but the 2-1 defeat was narrow enough to see the Hammers finish in 16th, above Chelsea on goal difference.

The season ended with Lyall knowing he would lose two players who'd enjoyed fabulous careers with West Ham. Billy Bonds – recently awarded an MBE – had made his club record 795th and final appearance at Southampton on April 30 and, at the age of 41 and after 21 years of service, was finally calling it a day.

Keen to keep Bonds within the Upton Park framework, Lyall appointed him as youth team boss, but one face that definitely wouldn't be seen for a while was that of Tony Cottee. His frustration with having to shoulder the team's scoring responsibilities had long been eroding his appetite, his form had suffered (scoring only 15 times in 40 games) and, to compound his misery, he failed to make it into Bobby Robson's England squad for the 1988 European Championship finals.*

Lyall insisted to the club's board that West Ham must receive a net figure of £2 million for the 23-year-old but, although Everton eventually paid that British record fee, it was little surprise to dispirited fans that the manager spent less than half that amount before the 1988-89 season kicked off. Walsall striker David Kelly may have supposedly had Bayern Munich and Paris Saint-Germain tracking his progress and snubbed Tottenham to make a £600,000 move to West Ham, but the frightening thought was that the club was now pinning its hopes on two forwards (Kelly and Rosenior) who'd spent most of the previous season playing Third Division football.

David Kelly, a £600,000 signing from Walsall.

As Frank McAvennie raised a glass in memory of his 1987-88 Scottish League and Cup double success with Celtic and Cottee kicked his Everton career off with a debut hat-trick, the Hammers were getting thrashed 4-0 at Southampton on the opening day of the 1988-89 season. Another three goals were conceded by goalkeeper Tom McAlister at home to Charlton a week later and Lyall decided to hand a debut to Allen McKnight – a £250,000 signing from Celtic in the summer – for the following 1-0 win at Wimbledon.

A 2-2 draw at home to Aston Villa saw Kelly score his first for the club but four successive league defeats dumped the Hammers onto the bottom of the table. While the team continued to struggle in the league, the Littlewoods Cup inspired much better form, with Second Division Sunderland being pushed aside 5-1 on aggregate and First Division Derby County demolished 5-0. With the team having lost 2-0 at home to Liverpool in a league match at the end of October, though, few gave West Ham much chance when the reigning league champions were drawn to make a return visit to Upton Park on 30 November in the fourth round.

Great Matches

LEAGUE CUP FOURTH ROUND — **Upton Park, 30 November 1988**

West Ham United 4 Liverpool 1 — **Attendance 26,971**

West Ham United 4	Liverpool 1
Ince 2	Aldridge (pen)
Staunton o.g.	
Gale	

With the Hammers sitting 19th in Division One and Liverpool the reigning league champions, many thought the outcome a formality. Yet, as the *Daily Express* wrote, 'Liverpool were humbled beneath an avalanche of attacking football.' The match signalled the true arrival of Paul Ince, who opened the scoring with a fine volley in the 20th minute and followed up with a header just three minutes later, prompting Liam Brady to predict a long England future for the 21-year old. A 34th-minute penalty from John Aldridge, after Alvin Martin had climbed over the striker's back, narrowed the lead, but when Steve Staunton turned David Kelly's 56th-minute cross into his own goal the Reds began to crumble. The icing on the cake was provided when Tony Gale curled home a brilliant free-kick with 14 minutes remaining, confirming Liverpool's biggest cup defeat since 1939. 'That was one of the great East End nights,' reflects Gale, while boss John Lyall described the performance as 'magnificent'. And so it was.

West Ham United: McKnight, Potts, Dicks, Gale, Martin, Devonshire, Brady, Kelly, Rosenior, Dickens, Ince.

Liverpool: Hooper, Ablett, Venison, Nicol (Watson), Whelan, Spackman, Beardsley, Aldridge, Saunders, Houghton, McMahon (Durnin).

Referee: J. Ashworth.

Young midfielder Paul Ince received all the plaudits for helping to inflict Liverpool's heaviest cup defeat since the war, but it was also significant that Lyall had been able to start with Brady and Devonshire for the very first time. Ince scored the winner at Millwall the following weekend but by Christmas the Hammers had sunk to the bottom again.

The Bell Starts to Toll

'It's time John Lyall stepped aside,' declared former Hammer John Bond, reflecting on his own management experiences at Norwich, Manchester City and Birmingham. 'There are too many old faces at the place and changes need to be made.'

Two changes the fans wanted made were the in selections of Kelly and McKnight. Kelly had scored just five league goals in 17 appearances by the turn of the year and, with Rosenior only hitting the back of the net once in 14 league games up to that point, it wasn't surprising that Lyall had admitted to being keen on bringing Frank McAvennie back to Upton Park as early as December. The Scot would eventually return to London at the end of March (Kelly being withdrawn from the firing line), by which time West Ham's cause looked hopeless.

But the chief scapegoat was goalkeeper McKnight, who made a series of blunders to attract a number of 'McKnightmare!' headlines. 'Goalkeeping is 30 per cent ability, 70 per cent confidence and mine was in tatters,' admits the Irishman on reflection. 'I was also taking the rap for other people's blunders and found that difficult to handle.'

He also found a football 'difficult to handle' on occasions, one of which was the 2-2 draw with Arsenal on 8 January in the third round of the FA Cup. The Hammers had actually led the league-leaders by two goals and when Paul Merson struck twice to take the tie back to Highbury the team's interest in the tournament seemed to

Alvin Martin – a towering defender whose career followed West Ham's rise in the early 1980s.

Great Players

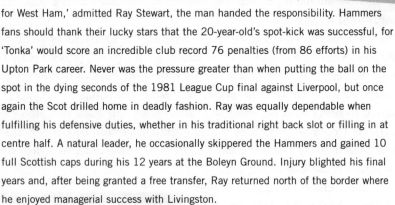

RAY STEWART Defender

Born: Stanley, Scotland, 7 September 1959

Joined West Ham: August, 1979 **From:** Dundee United

Debut: v Barnsley, 4 September 1979

Appearances: 430 **Goals:** 84

Left West Ham: 1991 (released)

The date was 8 March, 1980 and the Hammers had been awarded an 89th-minute penalty in their FA Cup quarter-final tie against Aston Villa. 'I knew that if I missed I'd never take another penalty for West Ham,' admitted Ray Stewart, the man handed the responsibility. Hammers fans should thank their lucky stars that the 20-year-old's spot-kick was successful, for 'Tonka' would score an incredible club record 76 penalties (from 86 efforts) in his Upton Park career. Never was the pressure greater than when putting the ball on the spot in the dying seconds of the 1981 League Cup final against Liverpool, but once again the Scot drilled home in deadly fashion. Ray was equally dependable when fulfilling his defensive duties, whether in his traditional right back slot or filling in at centre half. A natural leader, he occasionally skippered the Hammers and gained 10 full Scottish caps during his 12 years at the Boleyn Ground. Injury blighted his final years and, after being granted a free transfer, Ray returned north of the border where he enjoyed managerial success with Livingston.

have ended. A late header from Rosenior in the replay, however, provided one of the shocks of the season and further cup joy was experienced the next week when goals from Ince and Kelly helped secure a 2-1 victory against Aston Villa to take the club into the semi-finals of the Littlewoods Cup.

With Wembley just 180 minutes away, West Ham were full of hope as they took on holders Luton Town in the first leg at Upton Park on 12 February, but their dreams lay in tatters after a disastrous 3-0 defeat, with McKnight once again attracting heavy criticism. (The second leg was a formality, with Luton winning 2-0 on their plastic pitch.) 'I don't know if I want to play at Upton Park again,' declared the keeper and Lyall duly put the him out of his misery by recalling 38-year-old Phil Parkes. The veteran returned for the FA Cup fifth round tie at Charlton and a goal from youth product Stuart Slater was enough to take the Hammers into the sixth round, where they fell to Norwich in a replay.

Within a few days of that 3-1 defeat, Frank McAvennie was making his second debut for West Ham, having ignored champions-elect Arsenal to make a club record £1.25 million return to the East End. Sadly, the gamble failed to pay off...

McAvennie failed to score in any of his eight starts – although three of those games ended in victory – and his season was virtually ended when he pulled a hamstring at Newcastle on May 3. The 2-1 win at St James' Park was the second win in succession, following the 3-0 home triumph against Millwall and further victories against fellow strugglers Luton (at home) and Sheffield Wednesday (away) suddenly gave birth to the belief that the Hammers could produce a Houdini act. With 10 fixtures remaining the team had been 10 points adrift from safety (albeit with two matches in hand) but suddenly, with three games left, they sat just three points behind fourth-from-bottom Luton (who had just one more to play).

The odds were still stacked firmly against survival, however, with all three games being played away from home – two of them on Merseyside. A 3-1 defeat at Everton meant that Hammers needed to win both their remaining fixtures. A Rosenior double at Nottingham Forest at least left West Ham's fate in their own hands – all they had to do was win at championship-chasing Liverpool.

Paul Ince impressed in his early career with some spectacular goals.

John Aldridge put the Reds ahead after 20 minutes but Rosenior quickly levelled. With just half an hour remaining the score remained at 1-1 but, aware that a point was not enough, the Hammers became more adventurous. With gaps being left at the back, Liverpool ultimately cruised to a 5-1 win, two of the goals being scored by Ray Houghton who'd left West Ham four years earlier on a free transfer.

There'd already been much speculation about the impact of relegation on the manager's position, especially with his contract expiring at the end of the season, but Lyall had faith that a certain amount of loyalty would be shown, without making any assumptions. Chairman Len Cearns had earlier insisted, 'Whether we stay up or not will not alter our consideration about

Great Managers – 1974-89

JOHN LYALL

John Lyall had already spent 19 years at Upton Park prior to assuming control of first-team affairs from Ron Greenwood in 1974. Born in Ilford in 1940, the youngster initially took an office position at the club while undergoing his playing apprenticeship. He made his league debut against Chelsea on 6 February, 1960 but made just 34 appearances as a full back during three years in which he struggled with injury. He ultimately bowed to the inevitable and was the beneficiary of testimonial game in 1964, before moving up the club's coaching ladder.

John enjoyed instant success as first-team boss, taking the side to FA Cup glory in his first full season while bringing his own ideas into practise. Says Trevor Brooking, 'Rather than going to some grounds and impressing with our attacking ability as we lost, we would later battle for a 0-0 draw.' Trevor is also of the view that, in terms of man-management, John displayed 'a harder edge' than his predecessor.

Lyall also took the club to the final of the European Cup Winners' Cup in 1976 but was unable to prevent relegation in 1978. A three-year stay in Division Two was compensated by further FA Cup glory in 1980 and an appearance in the 1981 League Cup final. Promotion was gained in spectacular fashion the same season and after finishing in the top half of the table three years running, the team bounced back from a disappointing year to finish third in the First Division during 1985-86.

Sadly, Lyall was unable to build on that platform and when the club was relegated again in 1989, his 34-year tenure was brought to an abrupt end. Controversy engulfed the club, with Paul Ince later justifying his decision to move on because of what had happened. 'It was a disgrace,' he said. 'I thought that if the club could treat somebody as loyal as John like that, then what was the point in me being loyal to the club?'

'John was without doubt the best manager I ever played under,' states Phil Parkes, who renewed his association with his boss as a coach at Ipswich Town, with whom John won the Second Division championship in 1992.

John's contract.' But with Lyall being told on 5 June that his services were no longer required, the logical conclusion was that the board had made up its mind at least a month before the club's fate was sealed.

Despite seeing his 34-year association with the club terminated in clinical fashion, John accepted the decision with dignity, even sending a letter of gratitude to the players for their efforts. Says Ray Stewart, 'John was a great manager and I learned a lot from him. A lot of people who left West Ham to join other clubs made them more professional in their outlook because of what they learned from John. It was all about keeping good habits.'

Chapter Fifteen: 1989-93
Turbulent Times

Whatever those 'good habits' were under John Lyall, his successor Lou Macari – a controversial choice as manager given his lack of association with the club during his player and managerial career with Manchester United, Celtic and Swindon Town – was more concerned with ridding the club of habits he considered detrimental to the team's potential. One of his chief targets was Julian Dicks, who'd established himself as a tough and tenacious tackler with a cultured left foot since his arrival 15 months earlier. The new boss disapproved of Julian's pre-match preparations – such as drinking cans of coke – and immediately tried to impose his personal philosophies in terms of diet, to much resistance. 'Had Julian played in the days of Billy Bonds and Trevor Brooking then maybe he wouldn't have been so misguided,' says Lou, 'but if you're in an environment where everyone's a little bit sloppy, you've got a job on your hands to change their attitude.'

Lou had arrived at West Ham with a number of problems to try and solve, not least placating those players looking to make a swift exit following the

50 Greatest Players

TONY GALE Defender

Born: Westminster, London, 19 December 1959

Joined West Ham: 1984 **From:** Fulham

Debut: v Ipswich Town, 25 August, 1984

Appearances: 360 **Goals:** 7

Left West Ham: 1994 **For:** Blackburn Rovers

A stylish central defender who always looked comfortable on the ball, Tony provided 10 years of excellent service following his tribunal-set £200,000 move from Fulham in 1984. Forming a rock solid partnership with Alvin Martin as the Hammers enjoyed their best ever league campaign in 1985-86, Tony can consider himself unlucky never to have won England recognition. Will always be remembered for being the victim of referee Keith Hackett's extraordinary decision to brandish a red card during West Ham's 1991 FA Cup semi-final against Nottingham Forest and admitted that it 'hurt like hell' when inappropriately being told of his release from the club on the morning of his testimonial match in 1994. Less than a year later, however, he enjoyed League Championship success after being picked up by Blackburn Rovers.

dismissal of John Lyall. These included midfielders Paul Ince, Alan Dickens, Mark Ward and Kevin Keen, plus defender Alvin Martin, among others.

Only two of these players were sold during the summer of 1989, with newly-promoted Chelsea snapping up Dickens for £600,000 as the 24-year-old's contract was about to expire. Alan's career took a distinct nosedive away from Upton Park, but the same could not be said of a far more controversial departure as the new season kicked off. Paul Ince had emerged as one of the country's finest midfield prospects and the fans' Hammer of the Year wasted little time in expressing his desire to join Manchester United, to the extent of actually being photographed in one of their shirts prior to any move being finalised. Such action was unprecedented and when the picture appeared in the *Daily Express* there was understandable outrage.

Ince has since explained that he'd acted under the instructions of his agent, believing the photograph would only be published in the event of a transfer being agreed while he was away on holiday. This misguided act not only caused embarrassment but created an untenable situation between Ince and West Ham's supporters, with the club having little option but to sell the England U-21 international. United eventually got their man, for a bargain fee of £800,000 plus £5,000 per appearance up to a total of £1.7m (after fears over a pelvic injury threatened to scupper the deal) and the player subsequently became Public Enemy No. 1 in the eyes of unforgiving Hammers fans.

Ince did make one last appearance in a Hammers shirt, in the 1-1 draw at Stoke City on the opening day of the 1989-90 season – a match that will also be remembered for the tackle by Stoke's Chris Kamara that resulted in Frank McAvennie breaking a leg and missing most of the rest of the season.

Lou Macari's tenure as manager was short-lived but memorable.

More Ins and Outs

Macari's short tenure as manager may be viewed as ill-fated, but he did at least instigate major changes in terms of playing personnel. Midfielder Martin Allen (£660,000) and defender Colin Foster (£750,000) arrived from QPR and Nottingham Forest respectively, before the dispirited Mark Ward was despatched to Manchester City in exchange for stylish midfielder Ian Bishop and busy forward Trevor Morley just before Christmas. Another striker arrived in the shape of Bradford City's Jimmy Quinn for £320,000 and slightly less was later invested in Czechoslovakian international goalkeeper Ludek Miklosko. Most of these new signings would go on to establish themselves as popular Hammers, but Macari was less successful in trying to impose a more direct style of play than the club was traditionally accustomed to. Says Julian Dicks, 'You couldn't do that with the likes of Liam Brady in your team. Lou's teams were predictable and the lads had no respect for him.'

Despite a good start which saw only one defeat in the first eight league games, a run of 10 matches that produced just one win saw the Hammers slip into a miserable mid-table position by the turn of the year. Progress had been made in the Littlewoods Cup, with victories over Birmingham City, Aston Villa and Wimbledon, but the latter game had been marred by the sending off of Dicks and a 17-man brawl that resulted in the club being fined £20,000.

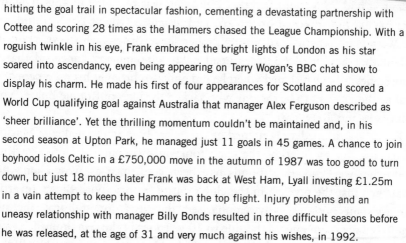

50 Greatest Players

FRANK McAVENNIE Striker

Born: Glasgow, Scotland, 22 November 1960

Joined West Ham: August, 1985 **From:** St. Mirren

Debut: v Birmingham City, 17 August 1985

Appearances: 186 **Goals:** 57

Left West Ham: 1987, 1992 **For:** Celtic (returning in 1989), released

Seeking to take pressure off his strikeforce of Tony Cottee and Paul Goddard in 1985, John Lyall paid £340,000 to secure the services of McAvennie as an attacking midfielder. Pushed forward when Goddard was injured, McAvennie responded by hitting the goal trail in spectacular fashion, cementing a devastating partnership with Cottee and scoring 28 times as the Hammers chased the League Championship. With a roguish twinkle in his eye, Frank embraced the bright lights of London as his star soared into ascendancy, even being appearing on Terry Wogan's BBC chat show to display his charm. He made his first of four appearances for Scotland and scored a World Cup qualifying goal against Australia that manager Alex Ferguson described as 'sheer brilliance'. Yet the thrilling momentum couldn't be maintained and, in his second season at Upton Park, he managed just 11 goals in 45 games. A chance to join boyhood idols Celtic in a £750,000 move in the autumn of 1987 was too good to turn down, but just 18 months later Frank was back at West Ham, Lyall investing £1.25m in a vain attempt to keep the Hammers in the top flight. Injury problems and an uneasy relationship with manager Billy Bonds resulted in three difficult seasons before he was released, at the age of 31 and very much against his wishes, in 1992.

But there was worse to come. Disillusioned assistant manager Mick McGiven severed his 16-year association with the club as player and coach when quitting on the eve of the FA Cup third round tie at Torquay United. And by the time the players trudged off the Plainmoor pitch after a humiliating 1-0 defeat by the Fourth Division outfit, the club was engulfed in controversy as a skeleton fell out of Macari's cupboard and smashed its bones all over the back pages.

When the FA charged the Hammers boss for making illegal bets during his time at Swindon, his days at Upton Park were numbered, especially when further newspaper stories alleged that he'd been involved in his former club making irregular payments to players. It was in this turbulent environment that West Ham somehow forced themselves into the Littlewoods Cup semi-finals, with a patched-up side gaining a 0-0 draw at First Division Derby County before winning the replay 2-1 (Stewart Robson making his first appearance after 16 months of injury).

For the second season in succession the Hammers found themselves playing a semi-final tie on a plastic surface, with Second Division Oldham Athletic the opponents this time. And yet again their Wembley dreams were shattered after a heavy first-leg defeat, being hit for six at wet and windy Boundary Park on 14 February.

Macari Out, Bonds In

When the team's bus pulled in at Macari's former club Swindon just four days later, the Hammers boss was nowhere to be seen. Within hours of the 2-2 draw at the County Ground, in which goalkeeper Miklosko made his debut, it had been confirmed that Lou (who was planning to appeal against the £1,000 fine imposed by the FA) had resigned. One of Lou's confidantes at West Ham was official photographer Steve Bacon, who says, 'Lou did admit that he felt like a real outsider. He subsequently conceded that he should never have resigned when he did and also brought his own people in. But he didn't want to be the one who sacked the likes of Ronnie Boyce, Mick McGiven and Tony Carr.'

Boyce was immediately named as caretaker boss in the wake of Macari's departure but by the time the team took on Blackburn at Upton Park the following weekend, Billy Bonds had been confirmed as West Ham's new manager, just the seventh in the club's entire history. With Boyce reverting to assistant boss as Billy emphasised the need for stability, the new management team guided the side to 10 victories in the remaining 17 league games. It wasn't enough, however, with the Hammers finishing the 1989-90 campaign in seventh position, just one place and two points below the play-off zone. Once again Oldham had an influence, reversing their 3-0 Littlewoods Cup semi-final second leg defeat (which saw the Latics through to Wembley 6-3 on aggregate) to wreck West Ham's hopes of promotion. But the season ended on a positive – and fitting – note, when Liam Brady scored the fourth and final goal against Wolves just two minutes from the end of his final match before retiring.

Some 29 players had been used during a transitional season for the club (in the boardroom as well, with Martin Cearns replacing his father Len as chairman), but the hope was that the momentum of recent months could be carried into the 1990-91 campaign. And so it did, with the Hammers justifying their position as promotion favourites by embarking on a club record run of 21 unbeaten league games. These included a 2-1 win against a Leicester side spearheaded by former Hammer David Kelly (following his

50 Greatest Players

BILLY BONDS MBE Defender

Born: Woolwich, London, 17 September 1946

Joined West Ham: May, 1967 **From:** Charlton Athletic

Debut: v Sheffield Wednesday, 19 August 1967

Appearances: 795 **Goals:** 59

Left West Ham: 1988 (retired); became manager 1990, left 1994

Much loved for his commitment on the pitch and composure off it during an incredible 21 years of service as a West Ham player (following his £49,500 switch from Charlton), for which he was rewarded with two testimonials, 'Bonzo' captained the team to two FA Cup final victories (1975 and 1980) and led the club to the Second Division championship in 1981. An outstanding professional, it's beyond comprehension that he failed to win a single full England cap, the closest being when named as an unused substitute for a match against Italy in 1977 (although he holds two U-23 caps). Remembers former team-mate Pat Holland: 'Billy was my role model because everything he achieved was through sheer hard work.' The club's record appearance holder and a Hammer of the Year on four occasions (1971, 1974, 1975 and 1987), he was the people's favourite to assume the manager's chair in 1990 and guided the club to two promotions to the top flight, in 1991 and 1993. After leaving Upton Park in controversial circumstances in 1994, Bonds took a coaching position at QPR before taking hold of the management reins at Millwall. Currently providing analysis for radio's Capital Gold Sport.

50 Greatest Players

ALVIN MARTIN Defender

Born: Walton, Liverpool, 29 July 1958

Joined West Ham: 1974 **From:** School

Debut: v Aston Villa, 19 March 1978

Appearances: 580 **Goals:** 33

Left West Ham: May, 1996 **For:** Leyton Orient

Arriving at Upton Park as a schoolboy and making his debut four years later as West Ham slid into the Second Division, Alvin emerged to become one of the country's outstanding defenders, surely deserving more than the 17 full caps he eventually earned. Recognised for his courage in the air and composure on the ground, as he established successful partnerships with first Billy Bonds and then Tony Gale, he won the Hammer of the Year award in 1980, 1982 and 1983. There was heartbreak for 'Stretch' when he missed out on a place in Ron Greenwood's 1982 World Cup squad after twice breaking a collarbone, but he inherited the West Ham captaincy from Bonds in 1984 and led the side to a best ever third place in 1986. Indeed, he scored three of his 33 goals in an 8-1 victory against Newcastle that season, beating three different goalkeepers in the process! After enjoying a second testimonial during the 1995-96 season, Alvin ended his 22-year association with the club to take a playing/coaching role at Leyton Orient before briefly managing Southend United.

£300,000 move earlier in the year) and future Hammer Paul Kitson, a 3-1 home victory against Ipswich Town (newly managed by John Lyall), plus a spectacular 7-1 demolition of Hull City – in which defender Steve Potts scored his first (and only) West Ham goal.

Jimmy Quinn, the previous term's top scorer, and Frank McAvennie, fully recovered from his broken leg, both did well as partners for in-form Trevor Morley up front, while Ian Bishop quickly established himself as a typical West Ham player with his midfield flair. Stuart Slater was helping to provide ammunition, along with midfielder Kevin Keen, while in defence Colin Foster formed solid relationships with both Alvin Martin and Tony Gale.

Sadly, the Hammers lost the services of skipper Julian Dicks early in the campaign, when the left back damaged his left knee in a 1-1 draw at Bristol City. Incredibly, Dicks started the following two games, before it was realised that ligaments had been torn and major surgery would be required. Bonds moved fast to recruit a replacement, signing Tottenham's Irish international Chris Hughton – initially on loan and then on a free transfer – while Tim

Breacker was bought from Luton Town for £600,000 to fill the other full back position. A 2-0 Boxing Day victory over top-of-the-table rivals Oldham gave the Hammers the advantage in the pursuit of the Second Division championship, but a period of seven league games and one win during February and March saw top spot surrendered. In the FA Cup meanwhile, Aldershot and Luton had been thumped in replays (6-1 and 5-0 respectively), while a Quinn goal against Crewe was enough to take West Ham into the quarter-finals, where they were drawn to play Everton at Upton Park.

Hammers' chances were not helped, however, by the unexpected loss of top scorer Morley, who found himself in hospital after a bizarre – and still unexplained – stabbing incident at his home.

McAvennie and Quinn formed the striking partnership against Everton in the absence of the team's 16-goal hitman, but it was Colin Foster and Stuart Slater who got on the scoresheet as the Hammers produced a thrilling performance to win 2-1. If ever a match catapulted one player to stardom it was this one for Slater, who almost single-handedly destroyed the Merseysiders and hit a superb winner.

But difficult times were ahead. Slater was dropped to the bench for the trip to Oxford in mid-March and the 2-1 defeat pushed Hammers down to

50 Greatest Players

IAN BISHOP Midfielder

Born: Liverpool, 29 May, 1965

Joined West Ham: December, 1989 **From:** Manchester City

Debut: v Leicester City (a), 30 December, 1989

Appearances: 293 **Goals:** 16

Left West Ham: March, 1998 **For:** Manchester City

A stylish midfielder who arrived with striker Trevor Morley in an exchange deal involving winger Mark Ward, 'Bish' experienced numerous highs and lows during his eight and a half years at Upton Park, playing under three managers. With his long flowing hair becoming as much of a trademark as his footballing flair, the likeable Scouser won friends with his stylish play, even gaining the captaincy in 1991. His creativity played a key role in the early nineties, during which the club won two promotions, and even earned himself an England B cap (v Switzerland in 1991). Remained loyal to the cause, even when out of favour, but eventually returned to Maine Road in 1998 in the pursuit of first-team football.

second. Three days later third-placed Sheffield Wednesday inflicted a first home defeat on Bonds (after 31 Upton Park games) and in the following match, against Bristol City, McAvennie was sent off for appearing to elbow an opponent in the face. With Morley still nursing the worst kind of tummy trouble imaginable, Bonds invested £480,000 in Luton striker Iain Dowie and the Northern Ireland international immediately won friends by scoring in the 3-2 win against Barnsley on his home debut. A 1-0 win at Port Vale on 6 April returned the Hammers to the top of the table but most thoughts were on the forthcoming FA Cup semi-final against Nottingham Forest.

That particular match, at Villa Park on April 14 – by which time Morley had returned as a replacement for the suspended McAvennie – will forever be remembered for the controversial sending off of defender Tony Gale by referee Keith Hackett. With 26 minutes played, Gale clashed with Forest's Gary Crosby heading towards goal and was astonished when his challenge was deemed a professional foul. Reduced to 10 men, the Irons fought valiantly, even hitting the woodwork twice, but their resolve faltered after Crosby scored shortly into the second half. Future Hammers Stuart Pearce and Gary Charles added to Roy Keane's 58th-minute goal, but the 4-0 scoreline did little justice to the West Ham team urged on by one of the most extraordinary displays of crowd support the game has ever seen.

Coming Up

A huge hangover was expected, but successive wins at John Lyall's Ipswich and at home to Swindon Town were all that were needed to guarantee promotion to the First Division after a two-year hiatus. Sadly, the Division Two championship trophy was ripped from the Hammers' grasp in the cruelest of circumstances, with a 2-1 final day defeat by Notts County seeming meaningless until celebrating fans on the Upton Park pitch heard the news that Oldham had recovered a two-goal deficit against Sheffield Wednesday to win with a last-minute penalty. 'When I heard the truth I broke down in tears,' admitted a devastated Stuart Slater.

There was further reason for a few other players to feel emotional during that summer, with Ray Stewart, Stewart Robson, Iain Dowie and Jimmy Quinn all being shown the exit door. Penalty-king Stewart, who'd recovered from knee ligament damage to play his first league game for two years in April, was allowed to leave on a free transfer to pursue his coaching ambitions. Injury-plagued Robson also departed on a free transfer, joining Coventry City after a short spell on loan. It was the sale of the two strikers that surprised some, however, with Dowie making a £500,000 move to

Southampton after just 12 appearances (and four goals) and Quinn joining Harry Redknapp's Bournemouth for a giveaway £40,000.

To bolster the attack, Mike Small was signed from Brighton for £400,000, while Mitchell Thomas was purchased from Spurs for £500,000 to initially take the left-back slot in the continuing absence of injured Julian Dicks. Kenny Brown – son of former Hammer Ken – was also recruited from Plymouth Argyle (on loan before a tribunal set a fee of £175,000) to fill the other full-back position and the 24-year-old made an inauspicious debut in a 6-1 drubbing by Italian champions Sampdoria in a pre-season tournament. The fun continued with a 2-1 home defeat by Botafogo, memorable for Frank McAvennie and a Brazilian opponent getting sent off for fighting.

Going Down

Having just secured promotion there should have been a mood of buoyancy around Upton Park but an air of gloom soon developed with the Hammers winning just one of their opening eight league games. Prospects improved with surprise wins against Spurs (Thomas scoring the winner in the 2-1 victory against his former club) and Arsenal (Small getting the only goal at Highbury to take his tally to a brilliant 14 in 18 games). A 0-0 draw against Liverpool on 17 November saw the club sitting in 15th position but, instead of grey skies brightening a little, they soon turned ominously black.

In order to comply with the Lord Justice Taylor Report, which demanded all-seater stadia in the wake of the Hillsborough disaster in 1989, West Ham's board of directors announced the advent of the Hammers Bond. This was a fund-raising scheme in which supporters paid between £500 and £975 to secure their rights to a season-ticket, their investment being considered as a 'non-returnable, unsecured loan' to the club. Chairman Martin Cearns insisted that it was the only feasible way of raising the £15 million required to redevelop the Boleyn Ground but, despite a reported £1.5m being spent on the scheme's promotion, fans were enraged. Feeling as if their loyalty was being exploited, they began to voice their disapproval at home games and, with fanzines orchestrating the protest, winds of dissent soon became a furious tornado.

Fans show what they think of the Hammers Bond Scheme.

Following a post-match demonstration at the Wimbledon game in January, fixtures against Everton and Arsenal in the early part of 1992 were disrupted as demonstrators invaded the pitch and the most vivid memory of that period is of a fan sticking a corner flag in the centre-circle before staging a sit-down protest. The item in question was quickly retrieved by Julian Dicks, who'd by now returned from his 14-month injury lay-off and expressed his sympathies with those 'being asked to fork out up to £975 to watch a load of c**p'. 'I never backed the Bond Scheme either,' revealed manager Billy Bonds several years later. 'I thought it was a diabolical liberty.'

The Hammers picked up a measly five points from a possible 24 at Upton Park between November and mid-March to slump to the bottom of the table (although their away form was even worse, losing seven out of eight games in the same period), with relegation soon inevitable. Reflects Bonds, 'We were asking players to perform in an atmosphere that was very hostile. In 25 years at the club I'd never seen anything like it.'

Realising its serious misjudgement, the West Ham board – through new managing director Peter Storrie – ultimately announced that the purchase of a Bond would not be required to buy or renew season tickets, although the few supporters who'd already invested would receive various 'benefits'. The damage was done, however, with the club tumbling out of the top flight as the directors examined other financial initiatives to ensure that the Boleyn Ground would be fully-seated by August 1994.

Much-travelled striker Clive Allen was signed from Chelsea for £250,000 far too late to make a difference, although the final two home games generated joyous scenes. A second-half Kenny Brown goal against Manchester United on 22 April had Alex Ferguson famously complaining of West Ham's 'obscene' level of effort as his team's championship hopes faded, while McAvennie hit his first hat-trick for the club in his farewell game after appearing as a second-half substitute against Nottingham Forest.

The 3-0 win (which also saw Leroy Rosenior make a final appearance) on the season's last day could not prevent the Hammers from finishing bottom for the first time since 1932, but they at least avoided equalling a club record number of league defeats set in that particular relegation season. It was perhaps ironic that as the East Enders dropped, former manager John Lyall was celebrating promotion to the newly-formed Premiership with Ipswich Town. Lyall refused to gloat, offering sympathy towards Billy Bonds for the position he found himself in and bringing his Second Divison champions to Upton Park during the close season of 1992 to play in Ray Stewart's testimonial match (with coach Mick McGiven and players Paul Goddard and Steve Whitton also part of the East Anglian contingent).

An All-Time Low

Hammers MD Peter Storrie had agreed that the club was at 'an all-time low', stressing that salvation would be found in long-term planning rather than any 'quick fix' measures. With that in mind, Harry Redknapp – who'd spent nine years in charge at Bournemouth – was invited to return to Upton Park as assistant manager, while further backroom changes involved Ronnie Boyce moving to chief scout, Paul Hilton relinquishing control of the youth team to oversee the reserves and Tony Carr taking charge of the youngsters. Terence Brown was also elected chairman in succession to Martin Cearns.

'What I first saw at Upton Park shook me to the core – the club was going nowhere,' admitted Redknapp several years later as he recalled how the experience of the Bond Scheme season had left the players' confidence in tatters. With Stuart Slater the only major departure (joining Celtic in an ill-fated £1.5m move), the squad remained largely intact while benefiting from some particularly astute and cost-effective signings. Peter Butler, Mattie Holmes and Mark Robson were recruited from Southend United, Bournemouth and Spurs respectively for a combined initial outlay of just £215,000 and their contributions in midfield and on the flanks proved invaluable as the Hammers recovered from two defeats in their opening three games of the 1992-93 season to manufacture a genuine bid for promotion.

A 5-1 win at Bristol City and a 6-0 demolition of Sunderland in the first two months of the season demonstrated that the spirit had returned. Trevor Morley bounced back from injury to establish a 36-goal strike-pairing with Clive Allen. Defenders Alvin Martin and Tony Gale only managed half a season each but it was the form of their centre half partner Steve Potts which proved vital, the 26-year-old being rewarded with the Hammer of the Year trophy in the spring of 1993.

Potts finished the season wearing the captain's armband after Julian Dicks – who'd initially been awarded it by former boss Lou Macari in the hope that it would help him to mature – had lost it by virtue of missing 13 games due to suspension. The combative

A club mourns its lost hero – floral tributes to Bobby Moore flooded into Upton Park.

left back had won many friends in the crowd with his fight-to-the-finish attitude but too much fight resulted in not enough finishes, with Dicks being sent off three times in less than four months. The manager's main concern was that his wayward star's unruly behaviour – along with that of Martin Allen, who'd accumulated 57 disciplinary points – was going to jeopardise his side's promotion drive but fortunately George Parris, Mitchell Thomas and Kenny Brown provided enough cover to see Hammers through. But thoughts of the present day were dismissed on February 24 when it was announced that cancer had claimed the life of Bobby Moore OBE, the club's most revered player of all-time. With Britain mourning the loss of its former World Cup-winning captain, a minute's silence was held at the following weekend's games and West Ham, with midfielder Ian Bishop wearing Bobby's No. 6 shirt, played out a dull 0-0 draw at Sunderland in a maudlin atmosphere.

The Boleyn Ground, meanwhile, had become the focal point for grieving supporters to express their sorrow and its gates and fences instantly became suffocated by the weight of flowers and Hammers memorabilia donated in loving tribute. The following week's home game against Wolves, on 6 March, saw Ron Greenwood, Geoff Hurst and Martin Peters carry a floral No. 6 shirt onto the pitch prior to kick-off and, on this occasion, Bishop assumed the No. 12 shirt to leave Moore's old number vacant. It was subsequently announced that the new South Stand would carry the legend's name and a special match would be played in his honour to mark its opening the following year. For the record, the Hammers kept their concentration to beat Wolves 3-1 with goals from Morley, Dicks and Holmes.

With the Hammers sitting comfortably in second place, promotion seemed assured until Portsmouth suddenly embarked on an incredible run to go second behind runaway leaders Newcastle. But wins over Brentford, Bristol Rovers and Swindon lifted West Ham back above Pompey on goals scored to take them into a final day shoot-out against Cambridge (who needed victory themselves to avoid relegation). If Portsmouth won their home clash with Grimsby Town, the Hammers had to beat Cambridge and score as many goals in the process. The South Coast side won their fixture 2-1, but West Ham's 2-0 success – with Clive Allen having the final say in the last minute – was enough to ignite sparks of ecstasy among the crowd.

Temperatures had certainly been raised in recent months with Bonds recruiting fiery Scot David Speedie on loan for the final 11 games, with little initial success.Yet the ex-Chelsea striker ignored the hostility of his former Upton Park adversaries to score four crucial goals – including the opener against Cambridge – to become the unlikeliest of Hammers heroes.

Chapter Sixteen: 1993-2000 Premiership Progress

After a yo-yo period of four years (1989-93) in which West Ham endured two relegations and enjoyed two promotions, it's to the club's credit that it has since established itself as a genuine Premiership force. The 1990s saw the face of football completely change, with redeveloped stadia welcoming ever-increasing attendances, Sky Television investing millions of pounds in the coverage and promotion of the sport and the Bosman ruling helping to lift restrictions on the circulation of footballers within Europe (and creating free movement for those out of contract).

The restricted capacity of the Boleyn Ground – just over 26,000 following the £11.5 million construction of the 7,600-seat Bobby Moore Stand (opened in February 1994 to replace the South Bank) and 5,900-seat Centenary Stand (opened in January 1995 to replace the North Bank), plus the installation of seats in the lower East Stand in the summer of 1994 – has not made it easy for the Hammers to compete against the cash-rich likes of Manchester United, Arsenal, Liverpool, Newcastle United and Chelsea. Yet after a turbulent few years in which the focal point was avoiding relegation, the club consolidated to the extent of pushing for a place in European competition at the end of the nineties – ironically a time when funds were diverted away from player purchases and towards the £35m development of a 40,000-capacity Boleyn Ground (scheduled for completion in 2003).

The majority of these years were presided over in management terms by Harry Redknapp, following his displacement of Billy Bonds in the summer of 1994. Bonds had successfully kept the Hammers up in their inaugural Premiership season, despite losing his two major signings in winger Dale Gordon (£750,000 from Glasgow Rangers following the sale of Kevin Keen to Wolves for £600,000) and defender Simon Webster (£500,000 from Charlton) to injury and having to sacrifice his team's major asset, Julian Dicks, in order to instill greater all-round strength.

After just one win in the opening seven games of the 1993-94 campaign, the controversial left back was despatched to Graeme Souness's Liverpool in exchange for direct replacement David Burrows, midfielder Mike Marsh and a cash payment of £250,000 which enabled the purchase of veteran striker Lee Chapman from Portsmouth. The 34-year-old promptly scored as the three new men made their debuts in a shock 2-0 win at Blackburn Rovers in September and any fears of a backlash from unhappy fans were swiftly dispelled as the Hammers lost just two of the next 11 league games to move into the top half of the table. And although a nine-game run without a win between January and March saw the side slip to 15th, relegation was avoided with a 2-1 home win against Ipswich Town and an emphatic 4-1 success at Tottenham (in which Hammer of the Year Trevor Morley scored twice on his way to a 16-goal tally) over the Easter period.

Winds of Change

It was the ideal way of putting a heartbreaking 3-2 FA Cup quarter-final defeat at Luton Town behind them but, if Bonds felt that Premiership survival was going to provide him with a platform to build for future seasons, those hopes were undermined by the winds of change gathering pace on the horizon. After releasing defender 34-year-old Tony Gale and signing Swindon midfielder John Moncur for £1 million in the close season of 1994, the club's purchase of Oxford United's Joey Beauchamp would hardly have fuelled Billy's appetite for the game, with the winger claiming to be 'homesick' just one day after his £1 million move.

But the Hammers boss was further distressed when it was proposed by the club's hierarchy that he accept a new post as a paid director to allow assistant Redknapp to assume direct control of first-team affairs. Harry had been tempted by an offer to return to former club Bournemouth in a senior management role and West Ham – eager to retain the services of somebody they saw as having a growing influence over training and transfer activity – suggested a restructuring to accommodate both men. Bonds, not unnaturally, felt aggrieved to the extent of not only rejecting the motion (accepting a reported £500,000 as his contract was paid up on his departure) but refusing to have any further contact with his former partner. 'I've got no time for the man,' declared Billy to one of this book's authors, feeling that Redknapp had worked events in his own favour, while Harry insisted, 'I'd rather be out of work than have people saying I stitched up my own mate.'

'The situation could have been handled much better,' stated Trevor Brooking (building a career for himself in the media), while managing director Peter Storrie insisted, 'We have nothing to be ashamed of.'

Following Harry's eventual appointment as West Ham's eighth manager (on a five-year contract, with brother-in-law Frank Lampard returning to Upton Park as his assistant), the club's doors became a blur as nearly 100 ins and outs involving around 70 players took place over the next six years. With Redknapp claiming the credit for the Dicks deal, many felt that his gambling instincts in the transfer market were already in evidence and these

50 Greatest Players

LUDEK MIKLOSKO Goalkeeper

Born: Protesov, Czechoslovakia, 9 December 1961

Joined West Ham: 1990 **From:** Banik Ostrava

Debut: v Swindon Town, 18 February 1990

Appearances: 365

Left West Ham: 1998 **For:** Queens Park Rangers

A true gentle giant at 6ft 4in (1.9 m), 'Ludo' was signed by Lou Macari for a bargain £284,000 and found himself making his debut on the day his manager resigned. Quickly establishing himself, the bouncing Czech kept 22 clean sheets in his first full season to equal the record set by Phil Parkes and win the Hammer of the Year award. At international level he amassed a total of 41 caps before announcing his retirement in 1992, while a run of 162 consecutive league appearances for West Ham was only broken following a harsh sending off at Everton in 1995. So dependable during his dominant years, he paid the price for errors during the 1997-98 season and lost his place when Shaka Hislop was signed before the next campaign. At the age of 37, he signed for QPR for a nominal fee, following a three-month loan period.

have since become an established part of the manager's character. Indeed, they've been essential, with Harry often needing to wheel and deal to generate his own funds. With the tearful Joey Beauchamp having been offloaded to Swindon Town in exchange for defender Adrian Whitbread plus £300,000, Harry responded to the team's failure to win (or score in) its opening three games of the 1994-95 campaign by signing Liverpool's attacking midfielder Don Hutchison for a club record £1.5 million and then shrewdly negotiating for the return of two former Upton Park idols in Tony Cottee and, more controversially, Julian Dicks.

Striker Cottee ended his turbulent six-year stay with Everton by taking a pay cut to return to the club in exchange for David Burrows plus cash, while the left-back vacancy was filled by the homecoming of Dicks (for an initial fee of just £100,000, after an injury-riddled spell with Liverpool).

The latter part of 1994 also witnessed the arrivals of Northern Ireland winger Michael Hughes and Danish defender Marc Rieper (on loan from Strasbourg and Brøndby respectively) in the kind of deals that would later become commonplace, while midfielders Peter Butler (£350,000) and Mike Marsh (£400,000) joined Notts County and Coventry respectively. Another departure was that of Lee Chapman, who'd lost his place and never been truly accepted by the fans even when in the side.

The changes in personnel seemed to make little impact, however, with just nine goals being scored in the first 15 league matches of the 1994-95 season. Trevor Morley was sidelined with a cartilage injury, while Cottee – sent off on his debut in the creditable 0-0 draw at Liverpool on September scored just once (on his home debut against Aston Villa) in his first dozen league appearances. A TC hat-trick against Manchester City in December lifted spirits and the team to 17th, but by February it had slipped to 20th, third from bottom with four to go down.

A surprise 1-0 win at Arsenal – courtesy of a Hutchison goal – provided the springboard for recovery, however, and the final 11 games saw just one defeat to secure a final placing of 14th. A 3-0 home win against Liverpool (with Hutch scoring twice against his old side) in the penultimate game guaranteed survival, while a 1-1 draw against Manchester United at Upton Park on the season's final day deprived Alex Ferguson's team (which included Paul Ince) of the Premiership trophy and any chance of a league and cup double. The *Daily Star* mentioned Ludek Miklosko 'looming through the afternoon gloom like Superman without a cape' as he repeatedly defied United to hand the title to Tony Gale Blackburn Rovers.

Redknapp's Goals

Cottee finished the season as 15-goal top scorer (having claimed his 100th league goal for the Hammers) but, with 34-year-old Morley leaving on a free transfer (eventually joining Reading after spending the summer playing for Brann in Norway), the big new signing prior to the 1995-96 'centenary' campaign was that of Marco Boogers. The striker was hailed as being one of Holland's best players after signing from Sparta Rotterdam in a near £1 million deal, but his early days at West Ham degenerated into total farce when, after being sent off during the 2-1 defeat at Manchester United for a wild challenge in just his second game as substitute, the 28-year-old's disillusionment with not starting games resulted in him defecting back home.

As Boogers took his family on holiday and failed to return, claiming to be suffering from stress, headlines suggested that the player was mentally ill and was now living in a caravan! Although Marco would later return to the club before returning to Holland on loan and then being released, Redknapp sought to resolve his striking problem by recruiting former Hammer Iain Dowie from Crystal Palace. The Northern Ireland international returned to Upton Park in a deal that saw Jeroen Boere (another Dutch hitman who'd failed to establish himself following his £165,000 transfer from Go-Ahead

50 Greatest Players

JULIAN DICKS Defender

Born: Bristol, 8 August 1968

Joined West Ham: 1988 **From:** Birmingham City

Debut: v Sheffield Wednesday, 2 April 1988

Appearances: 315 **Goals:** 61

Left West Ham: 1993, 1999 (retired) **For:** Liverpool (returning in 1994)

Nicknamed the 'Terminator' for his tenacity, Dicks was considered a true people's hero, showing total commitment to the cause. The left-back's tackles may have been heavier than a stack of his favoured Metallica albums but insists John Lyall, the man who paid £300,000 for his services, 'He had great touch as well'. Sadly, Julian's poor disciplinary record (being sent off five times during his two periods at Upton Park) undermined any chance of him winning full international recognition (earning just two B caps). 'He's one of the best left backs never to have played for England,' insists Graeme Souness, who took Julian to Liverpool in 1993. He'd already survived one serious knee injury that, according to Billy Bonds, 'would have finished the majority of players' and, despite suffering further damage to the same knee in 1997 (having returned to Upton Park after a problematic year at Anfield), he defied the odds to make a miraculous comeback in September 1998. Harry Redknapp described his return as 'one of the greatest performances I've ever seen' but it wasn't enough to win the defender a permanent place and he announced his retirement the following summer. Four times Hammer of the Year (1990, 1992, 1996 and 1997), Julian bid farewell to the fans with a benefit game against Athletic Bilbao in August, 2000.

Eagles two years earlier) plus £125,000 go to Selhurst Park. Although not the most prolific of marksmen, Dowie showed enough commitment in scoring nine goals in 39 outings during 1995-96 to become runner-up to eventual Hammer of the Year Julian Dicks.

The season could not have got off to a worse start for the defender. On 11 September he was accused of deliberately stamping on the head of grounded opponent John Spencer during the 3-1 home defeat by Chelsea. Sky pundit Andy Gray claimed that Dicks should have been sent off and the left back belatedly got his marching orders five days later when receiving two bookings in the 1-0 loss at Arsenal (during which substitute goalkeeper Les Sealey – who'd arrived as cover for Miklosko the previous season – was forced to make his West Ham debut as an emergency striker!).

50 Greatest Players

STEVE POTTS Defender

Born: Connecticut, USA, 7 May 1967

Joined West Ham: 1983 (as apprentice)

Debut: v QPR, 1 January 1985

Appearances: 480* **Goals:** 1*

* Pre-2000-01

Starting out as a right-back before moving into central defence, Steve Potts has come to personify the ultimate in loyalty, with season 2000-01 representing his 17th year as a professional at the club. Ineligible to play for the United States (where he was born) after appearing for England at schoolboy and youth levels (11 caps), Steve has worn the captain's armband for West Ham's youth, reserve and first teams, generally letting his feet do the talking. His timing in the tackle has always been superb, more than compensating for his lack of height (5ft 7in/1.6 m), with fans recognising his talents by voting him Hammer of the Year in 1993 and 1995. He enjoyed a testimonial in 1997 and, although no longer a first choice, has been as reliable as ever when called into action. Scored his one senior goal in the 7-1 win against Hull City in 1990.

To compound Julian's misery, MP-turned-radio presenter David Mellor described him as 'an animal' on air and further sensationalistic headlines were generated when it emerged that the player's children had received grief at school. Dicks was ultimately banned for three games after being found guilty of bringing the game into disrepute by the Football Association for his altercation with Spencer.

Difficult as it was for some to comprehend, Julian became a model professional as his discipline on the pitch radically improved during the rest of the 1995-96 season, in which the Hammers rebounded from a poor start to record their best placing for 10 years. Marc Rieper's signing was confirmed in a £1.1m deal with Brøndby, Michael Hughes agreed a second loan period as his contract with Strasbourg headed towards expiry (allowing West Ham to take advantage of the Bosman ruling by eventually signing him for no fee), Australian winger Stan Lazaridis arrived in a £300,000 deal after impressing during the Hammers' trip Down Under in summer 1995 and compatriot Robbie Slater arrived in a part-exchange deal that took Mattie Holmes to champions Blackburn. Midfielder Martin Allen, meanwhile, made an emotional departure, deciding to play in a new environment with First Division Portsmouth following the death of his father Dennis.

There were also changes behind the scenes, with Redknapp axeing former Hammers hero Ronnie Boyce from his most recent position of chief scout and replacing reserve-team manager Paul Hilton with former Swansea boss Frank Burrows. Some may have felt concerned at seeing loyal members of the backroom staff being shown the door but Redknapp insisted, 'As manager I have to make decisions. People come and go at every other football club so why shouldn't it happen at West Ham?'

The club had been founded on traditions of stability and loyalty but, if Harry felt that a new philosophy was required to equip Hammers with the best chance of challenging in the Premiership rather than merely making up the numbers, his success in subsequent years would support such a view.

A run of five successive league wins (against Coventry, Nottingham Forest, Spurs, Chelsea and Newcastle) in early 1996 turned a potential relegation fight into a reassuring tenth-place finish, while the youth team (featuring hot prospects Rio Ferdinand and Frank Lampard jnr) enjoyed success under coach Tony Carr, winning the South East Counties championship and reaching the final of the FA Youth Cup.

Harry's Foreign Forays

Much has been said of Redknapp's early forays into the foreign transfer market and it's true that he misjudged certain players – as a lot of managers have done since the Bosman ruling came into effect. 'It's a toss up between Marco Boogers and Florin Raducioiu as my worst ever foreign signing,' declared Harry in his autobiography. Raducioiu, a Romanian international striker, arrived at Upton Park in the summer of 1996 and, as far as some of the fans were concerned, never got a fair crack of the whip. The £2.4m club record signing from Espanyol made just a dozen sporadic appearances as he failed to convince Harry of his worth, despite impressive goals against Manchester United and Sunderland. 'Florin clearly doesn't like the physical side of English football,' complained Redknapp as he refused to bow to pressure from fans as the side struggled during the 1996-97 season.

While opinion remained divided on Raducioiu, who returned to Espanyol for around £1.6m midway through the campaign, fans were unanimous in their disappointment with the other Romanian in the camp, midfielder Ilie Dumitrescu. Following a long saga relating to the renewal of the £1.5m player's work permit, Redknapp invested all the £1.2m received from the sale of out-of-favour Don Hutchison to Sheffield United in Tottenham's East European. There were fleeting glimpses of his talent – most notably in a 2-1 home win against Southampton and, conveniently, in his last game (the 2-2 draw with Manchester United) when seeking to secure his £800,000 move to Mexico in December 1996.

The £1.5 million lost on the two Romanians, however, was easily recouped in one fell swoop with Croatian centre-half Slaven Bilic proving such a success after his £1.65 m arrival from Karlsruhe in February 1996. The trained lawyer was accused of orchestrating his eventual move to Everton in the summer of 1997, with the Goodison Park outfit mysteriously becoming aware of the exact amount to offer (as stated in his contract) that allowed him to talk to other clubs. The £4.5 million fee represented a handsome profit, although fans remained sceptical of Bilic's motives when deferring his move for a few months during the spring of 1997, feeling that a reported £300,000 contractual bonus was more influential than any 'loyalty' to the Hammers' cause.

The 1996-97 campaign was certainly a pivotal one for West Ham United. Veteran defender Alvin Martin had ended a fabulous 22-year association with the club to join neighbours Leyton Orient as player/coach, while 31-year-old Tony Cottee found an £800,000 move to Malaysia's Selangor too lucrative to resist. Legendary Portuguese striker Paolo Futre arrived from AC Milan under the Bosman ruling but the Hammers were wise to show caution, needing to invoke the clause allowing them to terminate the player's contract once his previously injured knee started to cause problems. And injury also ruled out the presence of Richard Hall, a £1.9m signing from Southampton, who sadly had to follow in the boot-prints of fellow defender Simon Webster, eventually having to retire after several years of vain struggle that produced just a handful of appearances.

With Raducioiu out of favour and Iain Dowie in the middle of an incredible 40-game run (eventually spanning 18 months) without a league goal, plus the aforementioned injury problems, the Hammers found themselves near the foot of the table and in a state of crisis. Too much was being asked of the likes of Steve Jones (in his second period at the club following a spell at Bournemouth) and emergency loanee Mike Newell to spearhead the attack and, even though Portuguese attacker Hugo Porfirio – another loan signing – always looked dangerous, it was no surprise that goals were in short supply.

Dowie had scored an embarrassing own goal and then broken an ankle in a 2-1 Coca-Cola Cup defeat at Second Division Stockport in December (a game that a disillusioned Raducioiu decided to miss, preferring to go shopping with his wife – as legend would have us believe), while a humiliating 1-0 home defeat by Wrexham the following month knocked

50 Greatest Players

RIO FERDINAND Defender

Born: Peckham, London, 8 November 1978

Joined West Ham: 1995 (as apprentice)

Debut: v Sheffield Wednesday, 5 May 1996

Appearances: 143* **Goals:** 2*

* Pre-2000-01

A 'Rolls Royce of a player' according to Harry Redknapp, Rio Ferdinand has been tipped by many as an England international for years to come following his emergence from the youth ranks as a 17-year-old in 1996. The south London-born centre half travelled to the World Cup finals in 1998 but, despite having won nine caps, was a surprise casualty when Kevin Keegan named his final squad for Euro 2000, much to the consternation of those at Upton Park. Winner of the Hammer of the Year award in 1998 and 1999, Rio's commanding performances have almost been taken for granted, although he has occasionally been criticised for trying to play his way out of trouble. It's his confidence, composure and class on the ball, however, that catches the eye and has seen him constantly linked with big-money moves to clubs both in England and abroad.

West Ham out of the FA Cup at the third round stage and sparked a post-match pitch invasion. By this point, fans were well aware of the efforts of businessman and former bookmaker Michael Tabor's efforts to win a place on the club's board and, convinced that his £30m offer would provide the funds necessary to purchase the players needed to avoid relegation, they responded to his carefully orchestrated media campaign to win support.

West Ham MD Peter Storrie countered by revealing that there were several conditions attached to Tabor's proposal – one being the removal of chairman Terence Brown (in office since 1992) – and that a large proportion of the money would take the form of interest-bearing loans which would have to be repaid. Whether in response to the fans' fury, pitiful performances or Redknapp's reference to resigning in the wake of the Wrexham disaster, the board succeeded in providing the manager with the financial backing to salvage the situation.

Welsh striker John Hartson arrived from Arsenal for an initial fee of £3.5m (although a club press release indicated that some £5 million might eventually be paid; either way, it smashed the club record) and fellow forward Paul Kitson signed from Newcastle United for £2.3m in February, while midfielder Steve Lomas, a Northern Ireland international, was

Great Players

FRANK LAMPARD JNR Midfielder

Born: Romford, Essex, 20 June 1978

Joined West Ham: 1998 (as apprentice)

Debut: v Coventry, 31 January, 1996

Appearances: 149* **Goals:** 28*

* Pre-2000-01

Son of assistant manager Frank Lampard, 'junior' has fought off early cynicism since making his debut as a 17-year-old to emerge as one of West Ham's major assets. An attacking midfielder with genuine goalscoring instincts, Frank has established himself as captain of the England Under-21 side (winning 19 caps) and can consider himself unfortunate not to have forced his way into Kevin Keegan's full squad for the Euro 2000 championships. Has one full England cap, playing against Belgium in 1999. Like close friend Rio Ferdinand, he has often been the subject of transfer speculation and, although his heart will remain at Upton Park, his ambition to succeed at the very top could well determine where his long-term future lies.

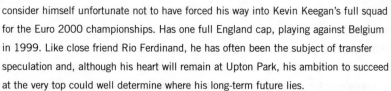

recruited from Manchester City for £1.6m on transfer deadline day. 'That was the big breakthrough,' declared Redknapp on reflection.

Although the Hammers boss has denied that relegation would have prompted his resignation, such investment needed to pay off and Harry's decisions at that time have thankfully proved to be astute ones. Not only was the drop avoided in 1997, thanks mainly to the goals of Kitson and Hartson (a not-so-unlucky 13 between them as one defeat in 10 games lifted the club to 14th), but the upturn in form continued to provide momentum for subsequent seasons.

When it became clear that Porfirio had little intention of signing on a permanent basis, Redknapp swooped in the summer for the £1.75m signature of Israeli international playmaker Eyal Berkovic, who'd impressed during a season at Southampton but had not yet cemented his move from Maccabi Haifa. A further £1.25m was invested in QPR winger Andrew Impey, while midfielder Danny Williamson – a product of the club's youth system who'd impressed before succumbing to injury – was successfully traded for Everton left back David Unsworth and £1m cash.

The full back was an essential acquisition, with resident Hammer of the Year Julian Dicks being ruled out for the entire 1997-98 season after once again requiring major surgery on the left knee that had sidelined him at the beginning of the decade. When Marc Rieper intimated that he may not sign a new contract, just a year from being able to leave for nothing under the Bosman ruling, Redknapp promptly cashed in by selling the big centre half to Celtic for £1.5m and paying £2.3m to Blackburn Rovers for Ian Pearce. It was another good piece of business, with a 29-year-old being replaced by a player six years younger at a net cost of just £800,000.

Looking to the Future with Confidence

The bargain of the 1997-98 season, however, was arguably the acquisition of QPR winger Trevor Sinclair in January, for just £1.6m plus Irishmen Iain Dowie and Keith Rowland, with Michael Hughes having joined Wimbledon for the same amount of cash a few months earlier.

In addition to the new purchases, defender Rio Ferdinand and midfielder Frank Lampard had broken through from the youth scheme (Ferdinand becoming the first Hammer to win a full England cap since Tony Cottee nearly 10 years earlier) and, with such a new-look team in the club's shirts – bearing no sponsor's name for one year after a deal involving a South African airline to succeed long-term backers Dagenham Motors fell through – the Hammers could look towards the future with genuine confidence.

John Hartson smashed his way to 24 goals during his first full season with the club (including an astonishing 17 in 20 games up to 3 December), but the big striker's form deserted him in the early part of 1998 as his size became less of a weapon and more of a handicap. Two red cards in the second half of the campaign deprived the team of his presence for seven games in total and, as the Hammers ultimately fell just one place short of qualifying for Europe (finishing eighth), fans were left wondering what might have been. The Welshman later confessed, 'I got a bit complacent. I honestly felt I'd got my 20 goals and done my bit.'

The striker's former club Arsenal had blocked West Ham's path in all three domestic competitions, knocking them out of both cup tournaments at the quarter-final stage and meekly surrendering the points in their final league game against Aston Villa who claimed the last UEFA Cup spot. The club could take some consolation from the continuing development of the youth system, however, with the youngsters winning the South East Counties championship for the second time in three years. And the loss of coach Frank Burrows, who moved back to Cardiff City, was compensated by the return of Roger Cross, who'd made a few playing appearances in the 1960s.

By the time the 1998-99 season kicked off (with latest Hammer of the Year Rio Ferdinand putting the shame of his recent drink-driving conviction behind him to become West Ham's sole representative at the World Cup finals in France with England), Hartson's former partner, Arsenal's record scorer Ian Wright, had signed for a reported fee of £500,000, but the reaquaintance failed to inspire the anticipated glut of goals. Wright's season was blighted by injury, scoring nine times in 25 appearances.

As the Hammers – now sponsored by Dr Martens – pressed again for a European place and put their traditional cup failings to Northampton Town and Swansea City behind them, Redknapp quickly accepted Wimbledon's shock £7.5m offer for the out-of-touch Hartson. Many attributed the sale to the highly-publicised bust-up between Hartson and Berkovic during training earlier in the season, when cameras recorded the Welshman deliberately kicking the grounded Israeli in the head. An uneasy truce was called but the reality behind the striker's release was that his aim was rarely as accurate when kicking a ball.

Harry had brought goalkeeper Shaka Hislop (as successor to the loyal but fading Ludek Miklosko who eventually joined QPR for a small fee, followed shortly by Tim Breacker), French winger Marc Keller, defenders Neil Ruddock and Javier Margas, plus the controversial Wright to the club for a combined figure of less than £3 million the previous summer (recouped by the sale of the discontent Unsworth to Aston Villa). And now he had the Hartson fee to re-invest – contrary to the *Daily Mail*'s claim that the player had been sacrificed because of a cash crisis. The key to West Ham's potential was how Redknapp spent that money and for many it was incongruous that the £4.5m invested in club record signing Marc-Vivien Foe (a Cameroon international) and £1m in wing back Scott Minto should offer far less in return in playing terms than the £1.75m paid to bring Sheffield Wednesday's Italian outcast, Paolo Di Canio, in from the cold.

Di Canio Arrives

While pundits questioned the controversial forward's temperament – in the wake of his 11-game suspension for pushing over referee Paul Alcock during the Wednesday v Arsenal match the previous September – and punters doubted his goalscoring prowess, Di Canio proved everybody wrong (except Redknapp) by keeping his cool not just in front of goal but officials too. His four goals in 13 appearances towards the end of the 1998-99 season might not have seemed like much on paper but his presence was enough to help inspire West Ham to fifth place – the second best finish in the club's entire history – and a place in the Intertoto Cup.

50 Greatest Players

PAOLO DI CANIO Striker

Born: Rome, Italy, 9 July 1968

Joined West Ham: 1999 **From:** Sheffield Wednesday

Debut: v Wimbledon, 30 January 1999

Appearances: 57* **Goals:** 21*

*Pre-2000-01

Frequently described as a genius by manager Harry Redknapp, the theatrical Italian maverick quickly captured the hearts of the adoring Upton Park faithful – who regaled him with their version of 'La Donna è Mobile' – with a series of polished and passionate displays. Initially considered by some as 'a gamble' because of his temperamental nature – following his push on referee Paul Alcock and subsequent 11-game suspension which signalled the end of his time at Sheffield Wednesday – the former Lazio, Ternana, Juventus, Napoli, AC Milan and Celtic forward soon made his £1.75m transfer fee look an absolute bargain, top-scoring with 17 goals during the 1999-2000 season and winning the Hammer of the Year award. He also won *Match of the Day*'s goal of the season competition for his audacious scissors-kick strike against Wimbledon and assumed the team's captaincy in the absence of Steve Lomas. Incredibly ignored by Italy at full level, he has just nine Under-21 caps to his name.

The irony was not lost on some Hammers fans who recognised that it had hardly been the smoothest of seasons for the club. Aside from the problems relating to Hartson, further disruption was caused by the absence of Javier Margas who spent more time in his Chile homeland than he did in the chilly East End, due to a combination of a persistent knee injury and a homesick wife. The team had scored 10 goals less than the previous campaign but gained one point more, by virtue of the fact that a large proportion of the goals conceded came in a relatively small number of games (the Hammers leaking four or more goals on eight occasions).

A 3-0 home lead against Wimbledon in September had somehow mutated into a 4-3 defeat, while newly-promoted Charlton Athletic had gained an unlikely 4-2 victory at The Valley. That particular match saw Julian Dicks harshly criticised after being exposed in an unfamiliar wing back role, but prior to that he'd made a fantastic comeback when surprisingly recalled for a home Worthington Cup tie against Northampton Town. Sadly, the player's inability to train in an orthodox manner saw him fall out of favour

Great Managers – 1994-Present

HARRY REDKNAPP

Born in Poplar in 1947, Harry spent seven years as a first-teamer at West Ham in the late 60s and early 70s, during which he provided much entertainment with his old-fashioned wing-play. He made his debut against Sunderland on 23 August 1965 and bid farewell in 1972 when transferring to Bournemouth. After a spell with Brentford and in the States with Seattle Sounders, he assisted Bobby Moore at Oxford City and returned to Bournemouth as manager/coach, where he even made a comeback as a player (in a 1982-83 League Cup tie against Manchester United).

Establishing his managerial credentials by taking the Cherries in to the Second Division for the first time in their history in 1987 (winning the championship with a record 97 points), his reputation for using the transfer market efficiently and economically was growing all the time and in 1992 he returned to Upton Park as assistant manager to Billy Bonds. His appointment as manager in 1994 was confirmed in the wake of the controversial departure of Bonds, with Harry pleading his innocence of any wrong doing in an attempt to manoeuvre his colleague out of the Hammers hotseat.

A rollercoaster end to the 90s ensued, with scrapes against relegation in 1995 and 1997 being averted to establish the team as genuine top-half contenders (finishing 8th, 5th and 9th as the new millennium unfolded). The key to recent success lies in Redknapp's success in the transfer market (making huge profits on the likes of Slaven Bilic, John Hartson and Eyal Berkovic as one player is sold to fund the purchase of several others) and the club's aggressive youth scheme, which has produced such talents as Rio Ferdinand, Frank Lampard Jnr, Joe Cole and Michael Carrick.

The question remains as to how much further progress can be made while operating in difficult circumstances.

and, despite making 13 first-team appearances ('not bad for somebody repeatedly told he'd never kick a ball again,' says Dicks), he eventually agreed a retirement package that allowed him to concentrate on his new goal in life – to play golf professionally.

Other Hammers performances that fell well below par that season included a 6-0 spanking at Everton in the penultimate game, which followed a sickening 5-1 home defeat by Leeds United, in which three West Ham players – Wright, Hislop and Lomas – were sent off by card-happy referee Rob Harris to create a piece of unwanted history.

There'd also been a much-publicised mid-term spat between Redknapp and Peter Storrie (whose title had been adapted to Chief Executive/Director of Football) over the sale of Andy Impey to Leicester, with the board insisting that the player be removed from the squad travelling to play at Derby County, despite the £1.5m deal still to be concluded. Storrie would shortly make a controversial departure from Upton Park himself, following nine years of service, when chairman Terence Brown issued a statement announcing a restructuring of responsibilities. Paul Aldridge became managing director and Graham Mackrell left his post at Sheffield Wednesday to become company secretary, although the latter's time in office would end prematurely as a result of the debacle in the middle of the 1999-2000 campaign which saw the Hammers lose their place in the Worthington Cup semi-finals due to the erroneous selection of the cup-tied Manny Omoyinmi.

The Nigerian was immediately loaned out to Scunthorpe and Barnet as his position at Upton Park became untenable and he confessed, 'I've loved West Ham all my life but I accept my career there is definitely over.' He returned to the club towards the end of the season and scored in a reserve outing against Norwich City, but was allowed a free transfer to Oxford United in the summer of 2000. 'It's a decision based purely on football,' insisted Harry Redknapp, who, according to a 'gutted' Omoyinmi, had refused to speak to him.

Ironically, it was the second time that an ineligible player had appeared for West Ham in a cup game that term, with defender Igor Stimac – an early-season signing from Derby County – due to serve a two-game suspension from European action as a legacy of his earlier days with Hadjuk Split. Fortunately, UEFA admitted their negligence in failing to advise the club of Stimac's unavailablity, which was only recognised when the Croat returned to his homeland with the Hammers to play in the UEFA Cup tie against NK Osijek and was booked in the 3-1 win.

Into the New Millennium

Stimac had been one of four new arrivals to support West Ham's 1999-2000 campaign, with fellow Derby man Paulo Wanchope – a Costa Rican striker – having already signed in a £3.5m summer deal, former Ram Gary Charles moving from Benfica for £1 million and veteran defender Stuart Pearce making a free transfer from Newcastle United (all the deals funded by the inevitable £5.75m departure of Eyal Berkovic to Celtic and Stan Lazaridis' £1.5m switch to Birmingham). The 37-year-old England international experienced the most tragic of fortunes, however, breaking his leg twice in a season which also saw similar injuries deprive the Hammers of fellow defender Ian Pearce, goalkeeper Shaka Hislop and 18-year-old playmaker Joe Cole, who'd emerged amid much hype to even become a possible candidate for England's Euro 2000 squad. His injury, incurred in a 2-1 win at Derby in April, ruined such hopes and also did the team little favour towards the end of the season, as a 13-man injury crisis (which even saw fourth-choice goalkeeper Stephen Bywater called into action) wrecked any ambitions of once again claiming a place in European competition.

Some attributed the deteriorating form to the length of the campaign, which had started the previous July with Intertoto Cup games against Finnish part-timers FC Jokerit (beaten 2-1 on aggregate) and Dutch outfit SC Heerenveen (beaten 2-0 on aggregate). A 1-0 home loss to Metz on 10 August in the first leg of the final seemed to signal the end of West Ham's Euro ambitions but a dramatic 3-1 win in France a fortnight later earned the club a place in the UEFA Cup for the very first time in its history.

A 6-1 aggregate saw the Hammers past Osijek in the first round, but a two-goal defeat by Steaua Bucharest in Romania in the first leg of the second round proved too much to overcome as the home tie fizzled out in a 0-0 stalemate. The early start had at least enabled the team to start their Premiership campaign in top gear and four wins from five games saw the club sitting happily in third spot. But indifferent form midway through the season – personified by the erratic performances of the unorthodox Wanchope – undermined the club's efforts as Harry Redknapp struggled to name a consistent line-up, especially in defence.

Options up front were also limited, with the high-earning Ian Wright being allowed to join Celtic on a free transfer following a loan period with Nottingham Forest and injury-plagued Paul Kitson being loaned to Charlton Athletic. For all their idiosyncrasies, however, the Paolo & Paulo striking partnership hit some 32 goals in total for the season, with eventual Hammer of the Year Di Canio winning himself a place in fans' hearts with a string of superbly individualistic performances.

The season ended on a controversial note as midfielders John Moncur and Marc-Vivien Foe were charged with misconduct (and ultimately heavily fined) following angry scenes at the end of the 2-1 defeat at Arsenal, which had seen an heroic performance by a heavily depleted side until referee Paul Durkin inexplicably allowed a blatant handball to go unpunished for the

50 Greatest Players

JOE COLE Midfielder

Born: Islington, London, 8 November 1981

Joined West Ham: 1998 (as apprentice)

Debut: v Swansea City, January 1999

Appearances: 40* **Goals:** 2*

*Pre-2000/01

Widely regarded as the hottest young prospect in the British game, Joe Cole made his debut at the age of 17 years and 55 days to become the second youngest outfield player in West Ham's history. Although carefully nurtured (amid much publicity), the teenage prodigy made 31 appearances during the 1999-2000 season (scoring twice) and, although still adapting to the Premiership, his creativity was such that England manager Kevin Keegan was considering him for his Euro 2000 squad until injury struck. Had made seven appearances for the U-18s and played just once for U-21s at that point. Rated by many as the club's greatest playing asset and, assuming he continues his progress, is a certainty for the full national team.

Gunners to sneak a last-gasp winner. If Redknapp had felt low during the Worthington Cup disaster against Aston Villa earlier in the season, he looked as if his spirits had sunk to new depths at Highbury as he struggled to come to terms with the injustice of it all.

Days later, following the 1-0 defeat at Sunderland that confirmed that Hammers would only finish eighth or ninth, Redknapp was more philosophical. 'It's been a good season again. People don't realise that West Ham have only finished in the top ten 14 times in its entire history and this is only the second time that we've done it three years running,' he said.

At the same time he pointed to the fact that he'd been forced to introduce 18-year-olds such as Bywater, Michael Carrick (voted Young Hammer of the Year), Adam Newton and Shaun Byrne to first-team action, with the club's youth policy (under the aegis of Jimmy Hampson and Jimmy Tindall) now the envy of most of the country. Compensation in excess of £1 million may eventually have to be paid to Charlton for procuring the signature of young striker Jermaine Defoe to professional forms, but such resolution – within league rules – is necessary if the club is not to be left behind. Tony Carr's Under-19s have continued to impress after landing a double in 1999, which saw Coventry thrashed 9-0 over a two-legged final in the FA Youth Cup plus the capture of the FA Premier Academy Under-19 championship in its inaugural year (and again in 1999-2000).

England international Rio Ferdinand, Frank Lampard (who captained the U-21s in the European Championship finals) and Joe Cole would attract astronomical figures if made available for transfer and, while Redknapp finished the 1999-2000 frustrated with the lack of funds available for player purchases – needing to sell Foe to Lyon for £6m before paying £4m for on-loan French striker Frederic Kanoute – the fact remains that the Hammers have invested heavily in securing its top talent to long-term contracts (reflected in their rapidly growing wage bill). This at least leaves the club secure in the knowledge that huge fees can be commanded if and when players seek to pursue their ambitions elsewhere.

The profit on Foe also allowed Redknapp to raid Arsenal for the signatures of veteran left-back Nigel Winterburn and Croatia striker Davor Suker – declaring them 'the best free transfers of the summer' – while Australian centre half Hayden Foxe impressed on trial. At the same time, the wage bill was relieved of the weight of Neil Ruddock, who joined Crystal Palace for an undisclosed figure, while the increased competition for places in attack allowed Paulo Wanchope to make a £3.65m move to newly-promoted Manchester City to become their record signing.

Fans were left hoping the money would not be swallowed up by the redevelopment of the Boleyn Ground, but at least the new stadium – complete with mini-castles which will form the entrance to the West Stand – will finally enable West Ham United to compete more aggressively with the Premiership's super-powers as the new millennium unfolds. Until its completion in 2003, it's likely that the management will have to continue showing prudence and, as the game's elite grow evermore powerful, it can be argued that the Hammers won't always be performing on a level playing field. As the club's history proves, however, it can always be relied upon to produce the unexpected...

THE ESSENTIAL HISTORY OF WEST HAM UNITED

CLUB STATISTICS

The West Ham United Directory

Origins

- Formed by a group of factory workers as Thames Ironworks FC in June 1895, the team entered the London League the following year. In 1898 the club turned professional. They were elected to the Second Division of the Southern League and moved grounds from Hermit Road, Canning Town to the Memorial Grounds, West Ham.
- Promoted to the First Division of the Southern League in 1899, the club stayed there until the outbreak of WWI after changing their name to West Ham United FC and moving to their present Boleyn Ground home in 1904.
- The club were elected to the Second Division of the Football League in 1919.

Honours

FA Cup winners 1964, 1975, 1980; FA Cup finalists 1923; Football League Cup finalists 1966, 1981; European Cup Winners' Cup winners 1964-65; European Cup Winners' Cup finalists 1975-76; Intertoto Cup winners 1999; FA Charity Shield winners (shared) 1965; Division Two (old) Champions 1958, 1981; Division Two (old) runners-up 1922-23, 1990-91, 1992-93; FA Youth Cup winners 1963, 1981, 1999; FA Youth Cup finalists 1957, 1959, 1975, 1996; South East Counties Champions 1984-85, 1995-96, 1997-98; FA Premier Youth Academy Under-19 Champions 1998-99, 1999-2000

League and Premiership Record

Southern League 1898-1915;
Division Two (old) 1919-23, 1932-58, 1978-81, 1989-91; Division One (old) 1923-32, 1958-78, 1981-89, 1991-92; Division One (new) 1992-93; FA Premiership since 1993

Club Information

- Boleyn Ground, Green Street, Upton Park, London E13 9AZ
- Tel: 020 8548 2748 Fax: 020 8548 2758
- Ticket Information: 020 8548 2700
- HammerLine: 09065 861966
- Website: www.westhamunited.co.uk
- Ground capacity: 26,044
- Pitch measurements: 112 x 72 yards
- Chairman: Terence Brown
- Year formed: 1895 as Thames Iron Works FC; 1900 as West Ham United FC
- Turned professional: 1898 as Thames Iron Works FC
- Club nicknames: The Hammers/The Irons
- Previous grounds: 1895-96 Hermit Road Ground; 1896–97 Browning Road; 1897–1904 Memorial Grounds; 1904–present Boleyn Ground
- Colours: Claret and sky blue shirts, white shorts, claret socks with sky blue trim
- Change colours: Navy shirts with light blue trim, navy shorts, navy socks

Managers

West Ham have had only eight managers – a record of the fewest for any British football club – namely: Syd King (1902–32)
Charlie Paynter (1932–50)
Ted Fenton (1950–61)
Ron Greenwood (1961–74)
John Lyall (1974–89)
Lou Macari (1989–90)
Billy Bonds (1990–94)
Harry Redknapp (1994–present)

Records

- Highest attendance: 42,322 v Tottenham Hotspur, Division One, October 17, 1970
- Highest League position: 3rd, Division One, 1985-86
- Record League victory (h): 8-0 v Rotherham United, Division Two, March 8, 1958; 8-0 v Sunderland, Division One, October 19, 1968
- Record League defeat (h): 0-7 v Barnsley, Division Two, September 1, 1919; v Everton, Division One, October 22, 1927; v Sheffield Wednesday, November 28, 1959
- Record Cup victory: 10-0 v Bury, Milk Cup, October 25, 1983
- Record Cup defeat: 0-6 v Oldham Athletic, Littlewoods Cup, February 14, 1990
- Most League points (2 for a win): 66, Division Two, 1980-81
- Most League Points (3 for a win): 88, Division One (new), 1992-93
- Most League goals: 101, Division Two, 1957-58
- Record appearances: Billy Bonds, 793, 1967-88
- Most goals for club: Vic Watson, 326, 1920-35
- Most goals in one season: Vic Watson, 50, 1929-30
- Most goals in one match: Vic Watson, 6 v Leeds United (h), February 9, 1929; Geoff Hurst, 6 v Sunderland (h), October 19, 1968
- Most capped player: Bobby Moore, 108, England
- Record transfer fee paid: £4.5m, Marc-Vivien Foe (Lens), January 1999
- Record transfer fee received: £7.5m, John Hartson (Wimbledon), January 1999

West Ham United celebrate winning the 1940 League War Cup, but they would have to wait until 1964 for their first 'official' FA Cup final victory.

50 Greatest Players

This list was not conceived to be definitive. A list of West Ham's 50 greatest players of all time would be impossible to compile: no two fans would agree on exactly the same list. This one is based on the personal opinions of the authors and contains players that have entertained and enthralled us both over the years, in life and legend. This list will cause discussion and maybe a little argument, but it's good to talk. Some players are old and some are new, but all have earned their place in our list of all-time greats.

No. 1 Bobby Moore (Defender) – 642 games, 28 goals. Simply the greatest West Ham player ever. Bobby also enjoyed a glittering England career (see page 127).

No. 2 Trevor Brooking (Midfielder) – 635 appearances, 102 goals. An England international, Trevor remained loyal to West Ham and was later rewarded with a CBE (see page 170).

No. 3 Geoff Hurst (Striker) – 499 appearances, 252 goals. One of West Ham's greatest goalscorers and one of the 'World Cup trio' (see page 130).

No. 4 Martin Peters (Midfielder/striker) – 364 appearances, 100 goals. The third member of the successful 1960s trio, Martin was 'ten years ahead of his time', according to Sir Alf Ramsey (see page 128).

No. 5 Victor Watson (Striker) – 505 appearances, 326 goals. The holder of all of West Ham's goalscoring records. Hit an incredible 13 hat-tricks in his West Ham career (see page 65).

No. 6 Jimmy Ruffell (Winger) – 548 appearances, 166 goals. The finest winger that has ever played for West Ham, he was also a prolific goalscorer (see page 74).

No. 7 Syd Puddefoot (Forward) – 194 appearances, 107 goals. A prolific goalscorer, made his debut for the Hammers in 1913 before moving to Falkirk for a record fee of £5000. Returned to Upton Park for a second spell in 1932 (see page 48).

No. 8 Billy Bonds (Defender) – 795 appearances, 59 goals. 'Bonzo' played at Upton Park until he was 41, later becoming their seventh manager (see page 193).

No. 9 Frank Lampard (Defender) – 663 appearances, 21 goals. A rugged and determined left back, Frank has enjoyed a West Ham career spanning five decades (see page 172).

No. 10 Alvin Martin (Defender) – 580 appearances, 33 goals. Alvin joined West Ham by signing as a schoolboy in the early 1970s and was a faithful servant of the club until 1996 (see page 194).

No. 11 Phil Parkes (Goalkeeper) – 436 appearances. The safest pair of gloves ever to defend the club's honour, arrived as the world's most expensive goalkeeper (see page 178).

No. 12 Malcolm Allison (Centre half) – 255 appearances, 10 goals. A genuine football visionary, Malcolm was influential in setting up West Ham's famous 'Academy' (see page 87).

No. 13 Phil Woosnam (Inside forward) – 153 appearances, 29 goals. The classy Welsh international brought intelligence, craft and creativity to the side (see page 98).

No. 14 Tony Gale (Defender) – 360 appearances, 7 goals. One of West Ham's best ever defenders, Gale formed a great partnership with Alvin Martin (see page 189).

No. 15 Alan Devonshire (Midfielder) – 446 appearances, 32 goals. The England international and superbly skilful Devonshire teamed up with Trevor Brooking to devastating effect (see page 174).

No. 16 Danny Shea (Inside forward) – 217 appearances, 134 goals. Highly skilful and very fast, Danny was a prolific during his six seasons with the club (see page 42).

No. 17 Pat Holland (Midfielder) – 296 appearances, 32 goals. Pat was an under-rated player and deserves more recognition for the part he played in West Ham's successes of the mid-1970s (see page 156).

No. 18 Frank McAvennie (Striker) – 186 appearances, 57 goals. Frank was a favourite on the terraces during both of his stints with the club. He formed a devastating partnership in front of goal with Tony Cottee (see page 191).

No. 19 Paolo Di Canio (Striker) – 57 appearances, 21 goals. A stroke-of-genius from Harry Redknapp saw the fiery Italian playmaker arrive for a bargain £1.75 million (see page 213).

No. 20 Malcolm Musgrove (Outside left) – 301 appearances, 89 goals. Musgrove was the second-highest Hammers' goalscoring winger of all time (see page 106).

No. 21 Steve Potts (Defender) – 480 appearances, 1 goal. A seventeen-year loyal servant to West Ham United, Steve has captained the side on many occasions (see page 206).

No. 22 Jack Tresadern (Wing half) – 166 appearances, 5 goals. A tenacious, tough tackling left half who won England caps in 1923 (see page 64).

No. 23 Ted Hufton (Goalkeeper) – 402 appearances. Ted was a great keeper and especially famous for his penalty saves (see page 62).

No. 24 Roddy MacEachrane (Half back) – 113 appearances, 6 goals. One of the club's first professionals, Roddy was also the first player to reach 100 appearances for the club (see page 25).

No. 25 Bryan Robson (Striker) – 254 appearances, 104 goals. 'Pop' Robson bounced between the north-east and West Ham for most of his career, enjoying success with all his clubs (see page 140).

No. 26 Noel Cantwell (Defender) – 263 appearances, 11 goals. The roving full back boosted both the Hammers' and the Republic of Ireland's attacking options during his career (see page 96).

No. 27 Frank Lampard, Jnr (Midfielder) – 149 appearances, 28 goals. Following in his West Ham-faithful-father's footsteps, 'Junior' has proved himself time and again at club and Under-21 international level (see page 210).

No. 28 Rio Ferdinand (Defender) – 143 appearances, 2 goals. One of the great future hopes of English football. Has often been the subject of major transfer speculation (see page 209).

No. 29 Tony Cottee (Striker) – 335 appearances, 145 goals. A superbly talented poacher, TC was very popular during both of his terms at Upton Park (see page 181).

No. 30 David Cross (Striker) – 223 appearances, 97 goals. This hardworking journeyman forward found success in East London (see page 161).

No. 31 Alan Sealey (Winger) – 128 appearances, 26 goals. Two goals in the 1965 Cup Winners' Cup final earned Sealey a place in the Hammers hall of fame (see page 120).

No. 32 Ray Stewart (Defender) – 430 appearances, 84 goals. Arrived as Britian's most expensive teenager, Ray became West Ham's record scorer from the penalty spot (see page 186).

No. 33 Ian Bishop (Midfielder) – 293 appearances, 16 goals. This stylish long-haired midfielder was a terrace favourite during his nine years at Upton Park (see page 195).

No. 34 Jim Barrett (Centre half) – 467 appearances, 53 goals. A great character, Jim played in every defensive position and could also score goals (see page 72).

No. 35 Julian Dicks (Defender) – 315 appearances, 61 goals. A genuine cult hero with the fans, he was regularly involved in controversy but still rated as one of the best left backs never to play for England (see page 205).

No. 36 Ludek Miklosko (Goalkeeper) – 365 appearances. A crowd favourite, Ludo was a regular in the side for almost a decade (see page 203).

No. 37 John Dick (Inside left) – 351 appearances, 166 goals. The Hammers' third all-time highest goalscorer (see page 107).

No. 38 Mervyn Day (Goalkeeper) – 233 appearances. Perhaps not the legend he was expected to be, a faithful servant nonetheless (see page 152).

No. 39 Alan Taylor (Striker) – 123 appearances, 36 goals. 'Roy of the Rovers' shot the Hammers all the way to the 1975 FA Cup (see page 148).

No. 40 Ernie Gregory (Goalkeeper) – 406 appearances. One of the longest-serving members of the club, after waiting 10 years for his debut (see page 88).

No. 41 Clyde Best (Striker) – 218 appearances, 58 goals. Clyde was a skilful Bermudan international, famous for his powerful shooting (see page 134).

No. 42 George Hilsdon (Forward) – 92 appearances, 35 goals. One of Syd King's early discoveries, 'Gatling Gun' transferred to Chelsea... luckily he came back (see page 45).

No. 43 Billy Moore (Winger) – 202 appearances, 48 goals. Billy was a fine player who created goals as well as scoring them. After retiring he stayed with the Hammers for another 30 years (see page 57).

No. 44 Dick Walker (Defender) – 311 appearances, 2 goals. A dominant figure at the heart of the West Ham defence, Dick captained West Ham for a five-year period (see page 81).

No. 45 Joe Cole (Midfielder) – 40 appearances, 2 goals. Another of West Ham's (and England's) great hopes for the future, Joe's precocious talents are already evident (see page 217).

No. 46 Len Goulden (Inside forward) – 253 appearances, 55 goals. An Upton Park legend, Len was in the team that won the 1940 Football League War Cup. He was also an England international (see page 76).

No. 47 Tom Bradshaw (Winger) – 12 appearances, 2 goals. One of the earliest Thames Iron Works players, Tom's career was cut tragically short by an early death (see page 24).

No. 48 George Webb (Striker) – 62 appearances, 32 goals. Hammers' first England international, Webb was a fast and lethal forward (see page 36).

No. 49 George Kay (Centre half) – 259 appearances, 17 goals. Captained West Ham to Wembley and promotion in 1923 (see page 58).

No. 50 Robert Stevenson (Full back) – Appearances and goals not known. The Scotsman established a fine reputation as a player and was Irons' first captain (see page 20).

Results and Tables

The following pages include details of every official match played by West Ham United and their predecessors Thames Ironworks. Each season has its own page and is dated at the top. League matches appear first, followed by individual cup competitions. The opponents played at home are written in capital letters and appear in upper and lower case for away games. The date of the match, the score, West Ham United goalscorers and the match attendance are also included. Full League and Cup appearances and the goalscorers are featured separately. The final league table is included at the bottom of each page as well as a Fact File which notes particularly interesting facts and figures for the season as well as any notable transfers etc.

These tables also include the games played by Thames Ironworks and West Ham in the Southern League, local London leagues and various cup competitions before they joined the Football League in season 1919-1920. The results of matches played during the war years, 1914-18 and 1939-45, are not included. During these years the official Football League programme was suspended. There was a huge amount of football played during the wartime years, but teams were greatly disrupted with many players called up to fight and others guesting for various different teams all over the country. For these reasons, wartime football statistics, though interesting, are not regarded as 'official'.

In both the League & Cup Appearances and Goalscorers tables the category 'other' includes matches in the FA Charity Shield and the Intertoto Cup.

Pre-League FA Cup Results 1895-98

1895-96

Friendlies

DATE	OPPONENTS	SCORE
Sep 7	ROYAL ORDNANCE	D 1-1
Sep 14	DARTFORD	W 4-0
Sep 28	Manor Park	W 8-0
Oct 5	Streatham	W 3-0
Oct 16	Old St Stephens	W 4-0
Oct 19	ERITH UNITED	L 1-2
Nov 2	READING	L 2-3
Nov 9	GRENADIER GUARDS	W 4-0
Nov 16	CHARLTON UNITED	W 4-0
Nov 23	WEST CROYDON	W 2-0
Nov 30	COLDSTREAM GUARDS	W 3-1
Dec 7	Dartford	L 0-2
Dec 14	Millwall	L 0-6
Dec 16	OLD ST STEPHENS	W 3-1
Dec 21	GRENADIER GUARDS	L 1-4
Dec 25	SOUTH WEST HAM	W 4-1
Dec 26	WANDSWORTH	W 5-1
Dec 28	LEWISHAM ST MARYS	W 7-1
Jan 4	NOVACASTRIANS	W 6-1

Friendlies

DATE	OPPONENTS	SCORE
Jan 18	UPTON PARK	W 2-1
Jan 20	BARKING WOODVILLE	W 6-2
Jan 25	CIVIL SERVICE	W 5-0
Feb 1	MANOR PARK	W 7-2
Feb 6	ROYAL ORDNANCE	W 2-1
Feb 8	HORNSEY UNITED	W 4-0
Feb 17	VAMPIRES	L 1-3
Feb 22	ST LUKES	W 1-0
Feb 29	Reading	L 2-4
Mar 7	FULHAM	W 5-1
Mar 9	WEST CROYDON	W 5-0
Mar 14	St Lukes	L 1-3
Mar 16	WOOLWICH ARSENAL	L 3-5
Mar 20	WEST BROMWICH ALBION	L 2-4
Mar 28	LEYTON	W 3-0
Mar 30	ROYAL ORDNANCE	L 0-4

DATE	OPPONENTS	SCORE
Apr 3	ST LUKES	D 1-1
Apr 4	LIVERPOOL CASUALS	W 3-1
Apr 6	VAMPIRES	W 6-2
Apr 11	COMMERCIAL ATHLETIC	W 3-1
Apr 18	SOUTH WEST HAM	W 3-0
Apr 25	MILLWALL ATHLETIC	D 1-1

West Ham Charity Cup

Feb 15	Park Grove	W 1-0
	Park Grove protested and forced a replay	
Mar 7	Park Grove	W 3-0
Mar 21	Barking	D 2-2
Mar 28	Barking	D 0-0
Apr 20	Barking	W 1-0

FA CUP

DATE	OPPONENTS	SCORE	ATTENDANCE
Oct 12	Chatham	(QR) L 0-5	3,000

1896-97

London League

DATE	OPPONENTS	SCORE
Sep 19	VAMPIRES	W 3-0
Oct 8	1ST SCOTS GUARDS*	W 2-0
Oct 22	3rd Grenadier Guards	L 1-4
Oct 24	Crouch End	W 1-0
Nov 28	Ilford	D 2-2
Feb 27	Vampires	W 2-1
Mar 6	ILFORD	W 3-2
Mar 13	Barking Woodville	L 0-1
Apr 1	3RD GRENADIER GUARDS	L 0-5
Apr 3	CROUCH END	W 4-1
Apr 8	BARKING WOODVILLE	D 1-1

West Ham Charity Cup

Mar 11	MANOR PARK	W 2-0
Mar 20	West Ham Garfield	L 0-1

London Senior Cup

DATE	OPPONENTS	SCORE
Oct 17	West Norwood	W 2-1
Nov 7	Marcians	W 4-0
Jan 9	WANDSWORTH	W 3-1
Jan 16	BARKING WOODVILLE	W 2-0
Jan 30	BROMLEY	D 3-3
Feb 6	Bromley	D 2-2
Feb 13	Bromley	L 0-2

Essex Senior Cup

Dec 5	Leyton	L 2-3

*The 1st Scots Guards withdrew during the season and their record was deleted. London Welsh were suspended near the end of the season and as a result Thames Ironworks were awarded two wins.

FA CUP

DATE	OPPONENTS	SCORE	ATTENDANCE
Oct 10	Sheppey U	(QR) L 0-8	800

London League

		P	W	D	L	F	A	Pts
1	3rd Grenadier Gds	12	9	1	2	32	13	19
2	Thames Ironworks	12	7	2	3	17	17	16
3	Barking Woodville	12	6	3	3	20	11	15
4	Ilford	12	7	1	4	26	14	15
5	Crouch End	12	4	2	6	14	19	10
6	Vampires	12	3	1	8	10	28	7
7	London Welsh	12	0	2	10	9	26	2

1897-98

London League

DATE	OPPONENTS	SCORE
Sep 11	BRENTFORD	W 1-0
Oct 2	LEYTON	W 4-0
Oct 23	3rd Grenadier Guards	W 1-0
Oct 30	Leyton	W 3-1
Nov 13	BARKING WOODVILLE	W 3-0
Dec 2	2ND GRENADIER GUARDS	W 5-1
Dec 11	Ilford	D 3-3
Jan 1	ILFORD	W 4-0
Jan 8	STANLEY	W 4-2
Jan 15	BROMLEY	W 7-3
Feb 26	Stanley	D 1-1
Mar 12	Barking Woodville	D 0-0
Mar 19	Bromley	W 5-1
Apr 2	3RD GRENADIER GUARDS	W 3-1
Apr 23	Brentford	L 0-1
Apr 30	2nd Grenadier Guards	W 3-1

London Senior Cup

DATE	OPPONENTS	SCORE
Nov 27	Novacastrians	W 1-0
Jan 15	2ND GRENADIER GUARDS	W *
Jan 22	ILFORD	L 1-3

*Walk-over after Guards withdrew

FA Cup

DATE	OPPONENTS	SCORE	GOALSCORERS	ATTENDANCE
Sep 18	REDHILL	W 3-0	Chisholm 2, o.g.	1,000
Sep 25	RE-TRAINING BATTALION	W 2-1	Hatton, Reid	1,000
Oct 16	St Albans	L 0-2		1,000

London League

		P	W	D	L	F	A	Pts
1	Thames Ironworks	16	12	3	1	47	15	27
2	Brent	16	12	2	2	43	17	26
3	Leyton	16	8	4	4	41	33	20
4	3rd Grenadier Gds	16	7	3	6	34	33	17
5	Ilford	16	5	7	4	33	25	17
6	Stanley	16	5	4	7	22	22	14
7	Barking Woodville	16	2	6	8	16	37	10
8	Bromley	16	4	2	10	20	49	10
9	2nd Grenadier Gds	16	0	3	13	17	42	3

Thames Ironworks Season 1898-99

Southern League Division 2

DATE	OPPONENTS	SCORE	GOALSCORERS	ATTENDANCE
Sep 10	Shepherd's Bush	W 3-0	Atkinson 2, Adams	1,500
Sep 24	BRENTFORD	W 3-1	Hay 2, Dove	1,200
Oct 8	Uxbridge	L 1-2	Gresham	2,000
Oct 29	Wycombe	L 1-4	Reid J	1,000
Nov 5	SHEPHERD'S BUSH	W 1-0	Wenham	1,000
Nov 12	St. Albans	W 4-1	Lloyd 3, Reid J	800
Nov 26	Watford	D 0-0		1,000
Dec 3	FULHAM	W 2-1	Reynolds, Gresham	2,000
Dec 17	WATFORD	W 2-1	Lloyd 2	1,500
Dec 24	Chesham	W 3-0	Hird 2, Hounsell	1,000
Dec 31	Maidenhead	W 4-0	McEwan, Hird, Reynolds, Reid J	2,000
Jan 14	WYCOMBE	W 4-1	McEwan, Lloyd 2, o.g.	1,000
Jan 21	Wolverton	W 4-3	Dove, Chisholm, Leonard 2	200
Jan 28	CHESHAM	W 8-1	Lloyd, Reid J, Reynolds 2, Dove, MacEachrane, Gresham 2	2,000
Feb 11	Brentford	W 2-0	Reynolds, Leonard	2,000
Feb 18	UXBRIDGE	W 4-0	Henderson 4	1,500
Mar 4	Southall	W 2-0	Henderson 2	4,000
Mar 9	ST. ALBANS	W 1-0	Reid J	2,000
Mar 18	WOLVERTON	W 2-1	Reid J 2	1,000
Mar 25	SOUTHALL	W 2-0	Reid G, Gilmore	3,000
Apr 8	Fulham	W 1-0	Lloyd	3,000
Apr 15	MAIDENHEAD	W 10-0	Lloyd 3, Leonard 4, Reid J 2, Henderson	3,000

FA Cup

Oct 1	R.E. TRAINING BAT.	(QR 1)	W 2-0	MacEachrane, Gresham	1,000
Oct 15	Brighton United	(QR 2)	D 0-0		2,000
Oct 19	BRIGHTON UNITED	(R)	L 1-4	Hird	2,000

Championship Decider

Apr 22	Cowes	W 3-1*	Hitch, Henderson, Leonard	1,000

*Played at Millwall.

Test Match

Apr 29	Sheppey United	D 1-1*	Hitch	2,000

*Played at Chatham.

League & Cup Appearances

PLAYER	LEAGUE	CUP COMPETITION FA CUP	CH'SHIP/TEST MATCHES	TOTAL
Adams	2	3		5
Atkinson	2			2
Bird	1			1
Brett	1			1
Buller	1			1
Chisholm	15	3	2	20
Cobb	2	3		5
Dove	14	2	1	17
Dunn	11		2	13
Foss	1			1
Gilmore	1			1
Gresham	14	3	1	18
Hay	6	1		7
Henderson	8		2	10
Hird	19	3		22
Hitch	3	2	2	7
Hounsell	2			2
Leonard	10		2	12
Lloyd	11	3		14
MacEachrane	22	3	2	27
Marjeram	8			8
McEwan	8			8
McManus	5		1	6
Moore	21	3	2	26
Niel	2	1		3
Reid G	6			6
Reid J	13		1	14
Reynolds	12		2	14
Tranter	20	3	2	25
Wenham	1			1

Goalscorers

PLAYER	LEAGUE	CUP COMPETITION FA CUP	CH'SHIP/TEST MATCHES	TOTAL
Lloyd	12			12
Reid J	9			9
Henderson	7		1	8
Leonard	7		1	8
Gresham	4	1		5
Reynolds	5			5
Hird	3	1		4
Dove	3			3
MacEachrane	1	1		2
Atkinson	2			2
Hay	2			2
Hitch			2	2
McEwan	2			2
Adams	1			1
Chisholm	1			1
Hounsell	1			1
Gilmore	1			1
Wenham	1			1
Reid G	1			1

Fact File

Thames Ironworks took the field as a professional team for the first ever time.

CLUB SECRETARY: A T Harsent
CAPTAIN: Walter Tranter
TOP SCORER: David Lloyd
BIGGEST WIN: April 15, 1899 10-1 v Maidenhead, Southern League Division 2
HIGHEST ATTENDANCE: March 4, 1899 4,000 v Southall, won 2-0, Southern League Division 2
MAJOR TRANSFERS IN: Tommy Moore from Millwall Athletic, David Lloyd from 3rd Battalion Grenadier Guards

Final Southern League Division 2 Table

	P	W	D	L	F	A	Pts
1 Thames Ironworks	22	19	1	2	64	16	39
2 Wolverton Rly	22	13	4	5	88	43	30
3 Watford	22	14	2	6	62	35	30
4 Brentford	22	11	3	8	59	39	25
5 Wycombe Wanderers	22	10	2	10	55	57	22
6 Southall	22	11	0	11	44	55	22
7 Chesham	22	9	2	11	45	62	20
8 St Albans	22	8	3	11	45	59	19
9 Shepherds Bush	22	7	3	12	37	53	17
10 Fulham	22	6	4	12	36	44	16
11 Uxbridge	22	7	2	13	29	48	16
12 Maidenhead	22	3	2	17	33	86	8

Thames Ironworks Season 1899-1900

Southern League Division 1

DATE	OPPONENTS	SCORE	GOALSCORERS	ATTENDANCE
Sep 16	Reading	L 0-1		3,000
Sep 18	CHATHAM	W 4-0	McKay 2, Carnelly 2	1,000
Oct 7	BEDMINSTER	W 1-0	Joyce	3,000
Nov 4	Tottenham Hotspur	L 0-7		7,000
Nov 11	NEW BROMPTON	D 0-0		2,000
Nov 25	SWINDON TOWN	W 1-0	Adams	2,000
Dec 2	Bristol City	L 0-2		3,000
Dec 16	Southampton	L 1-3	McKay	4,000
Dec 23	MILLWALL ATHLETIC	L 0-2		12,000
Dec 25	Queens Park Rangers	L 0-2		4,000
Dec 30	QUEENS PARK RANGERS	L 1-2	McKay	4,000
Jan 6	Chatham	L 1-3	Carnelly	5,000
Jan 13	READING	L 0-1		4,000
Jan 15	Bristol Rovers	D 1-1	McKay	6,000
Jan 20	Sheppey United	W 3-0	McKay, Carnelly, Joyce	4,000
Jan 24	Gravesend	L 2-1	Carnelly	1,200
Feb 10	Bedminster	L 1-3	Carnelly	2,000
Feb 17	BRISTOL ROVERS	D 0-0		4,000
Feb 24	Portsmouth	L 0-2		2,000
Mar 10	TOTTENHAM HOTSPUR	D 0-0		9,000
Mar 17	New Brompton	L 1-3	o.g.	2,000
Mar 24	GRAVESEND	W 2-1	Carnelly 2	3,500
Mar 31	Swindon Town	L 1-3	o.g.	3,000
Apr 5	PORTSMOUTH	L 2-4	Joyce 2	5,000
Apr 7	BRISTOL CITY	D 0-0		5,000
Apr 9	SOUTHAMPTON	W 4-1	Joyce 3, Allan	4,000
Apr 17	SHEPPEY UNITED	W 4-2	McKay, Joyce, Taylor, o.g.	3,000
Apr 28	Millwall Athletic	W 1-0	McKay	8,000

FA Cup

Sep 23	ROYAL ENGINEERS	(P) W 6-0	Joyce 3, McKay, MacEachrane, Reid	8,000
Sep 30	Grays United	(Q1) W 4-0	Joyce, McKay Carnelly, McManus	750
Oct 14	SHEPPEY UNITED	(Q2) W 4-2	Carnelly 2, Joyce 2	2,000
Oct 28	Dartford	(Q3) W 7-0	Carnelly 2, McKay 2 Joyce, MacEachrane, Bradshaw	1,200
Nov 18	New Brompton	(Q4) D 0-0		3,000
Nov 23	NEW BROMPTON	(R) W 2-0	Carnelly, McKay	3,000
Dec 9	MILLWALL ATHLETIC	(Q5) L 1-2	Bradshaw	13,000

Test Match

Apr 30	Fulham	W 5-1*	Joyce 3, Stewart, o.g.	600

*Played at Tottenham.

League & Cup Appearances

PLAYER	LEAGUE	CUP COMPETITION FA CUP	CH'SHIP/TEST MATCHES	TOTAL
Adams	6	2		8
Allan	21		1	22
Bigden	11	2		13
Bradshaw	5	7		12
Carnelly	27	6	1	34
Corbett	3			3
Craig	17	4	1	22
Dove	15	5	1	21
Dunn	21	7	1	29
Gentle	1	1		2
Gilmore	4			4
Hird	1	3		4
Janes	2			2
Joyce	27	7	1	35
King	16	7		23
MacEachrane	28	7	1	36
MacKay	28	7	1	36
McManus	5	4		9
Moore	27	7	1	35
Reid	1	1		2
Stewart	16		1	17
Sunderland	1			1
Taylor	14		1	15
Turner	4			4
Walker	7			7

Goalscorers

PLAYER	LEAGUE	CUP COMPETITION FA CUP	CH'SHIP/TEST MATCHES	TOTAL
Joyce	8	7	3	18
Carnelly	8	6		14
McKay	8	5		13
MacEachrane		2		2
Bradshaw		2		2
McManus		1		1
Reid		1		1
Adams	1			1
Allan	1			1
Stewart			1	1
Taylor	1			1
Opp o.gs.	3		1	4

Fact File

England international and club captain Tom Bradshaw died on Christmas Day 1899.

CLUB SECRETARY: George Neil
CAPTAIN: Tom Bradshaw
TOP SCORER: Bill Joyce
BIGGEST WIN: October 28, 1899 7-0 v Dartford, FA Cup Qualifying Round 3
HIGHEST ATTENDANCE: December 9, 1899 13,000 v Millwall Athletic, FA Cup Qualifying Round 5
MAJOR TRANSFERS IN: Syd King and Alec Gentle from New Brompton, Tom Bradshaw, Bill Joyce and Kenny McKay from Tottenham Hotspur
MAJOR TRANSFERS OUT: Tom Bradshaw (deceased)

Final Southern League Division 1 Table

		P	W	D	L	F	A	PTS
1	Tottenham Hotspur	28	20	4	4	67	26	44
2	Portsmouth	28	20	1	7	58	27	41
3	Southampton	28	17	1	10	70	33	35
4	Reading	28	15	2	11	41	28	32
5	Swindon Town	28	15	2	11	50	42	32
6	Bedminster	28	13	2	13	44	45	28
7	Millwall Athletic	28	12	3	13	36	37	27
8	Queens Park Rangers	28	12	2	14	49	57	26
9	Bristol City	28	9	7	12	43	47	25
10	Bristol Rovers	28	11	3	14	46	55	25
11	New Brompton	28	9	6	13	39	49	24
12	Gravesend United	28	10	4	14	38	58	24
13	Chatham	28	10	3	15	38	58	23
14	Thames Ironworks	28	8	5	15	30	45	21
15	Sheppey United	28	3	7	18	24	66	13

West Ham United Season 1900-01

Southern League Division 1

DATE	OPPONENTS	SCORE	GOALSCORERS	ATTENDANCE
Sep 1	GRAVESEND	W 7-0	Grassam 4, Reid 2, Hunt	2,000
Sep 8	Millwall	L 1-3	Reid	10,000
Sep 15	SOUTHAMPTON	W 2-0	Reid, Grassam	7,500
Sep 29	BRISTOL CITY	L 1-2	Kaye	5,000
Oct 6	Swindon Town	W 1-0	Corbett	2,000
Oct 13	WATFORD	W 2-0	Corbett, Fenton	4.000
Oct 20	Luton Town	L 0-2		4,000
Oct 27	Tottenham Hotspur	D 0-0		6,000
Nov 10	Portsmouth	L 2-3	Reid, Kaye	5,000
Nov 24	Bristol Rovers	L 0-2		3,000
Dec 1	READING	W 1-0	Ratcliffe	4,000
Dec 15	Gravesend	D 0-0		1,000
Dec 29	Southampton	L 2-3	Fenton, Hunt	4,000
Jan 12	Bristol City	L 0-1		2,500
Jan 19	SWINDON TOWN	W 3-1	Corbett 2, Grassam	4,000
Jan 26	Watford	W 1-0	Grassam	2,000
Feb 9	LUTON TOWN	W 2-0	Taylor, Corbett	1,000
Feb 16	TOTTENHAM HOTSPUR	L 1-4	Grassam	5,500
Feb 23	Queens Park Rangers	W 2-0	Grassam, Taylor	6,000
Mar 2	PORTSMOUTH	D 1-1	MacEachrane	3,000
Mar 9	New Brompton	D 1-1	Hunt	2,000
Mar 16	BRISTOL ROVERS	W 2-0	Corbett, Grassam	4,000
Mar 21	MILLWALL	W 1-0	Corbett	2,500
Mar 23	Kettering Town	W 1-0	Grassam	1,000
Mar 30	KETTERING TOWN	D 1-1	Taylor	1,000
Apr 5	QUEENS PARK RANGERS	W 2-1	Ratcliffe 2	4,000
Apr 10	Reading	L 1-3	Grassam	1,000
Apr 20	NEW BROMPTON	W 2-0	Ratcliffe, Taylor	2,000

FA Cup

Nov 3	OLYMPIC	(3Q Rd)	W 1-0	Fenton	3,000
Nov 17	New Brompton	(4Q Rd)	D 1-1	Corbett	1,200
Nov 21	NEW BROMPTON	(4Q Rd R)	W 4-1	Kaye 2, Corbett, Hunt	4,000
Dec 8	CLAPTON ORIENT	(5Q Rd)	D 1-1	Kaye	10,000
Dec 12	Clapton Orient	(5Q Rd R)	W 3-2	Grassam 3	5,000
Jan 5	LIVERPOOL	(I)	L 0-1		6,000

League & Cup Appearances

PLAYER	LEAGUE	CUP COMPETITION FA CUP	TOTAL
Allan	24	3	27
Corbett	21	2	23
Craig	25	6	31
Dove	13	3	16
Fenton	14	5	19
Grassam	20	3	23
Hunt	27	6	33
Kaye	14	6	20
Kelly	19	3	22
King	22	6	28
MacEachrane	28	6	34
Monteith	24	6	30
Moore	4		4
Neil	1		1
Pinder	1		1
Pudan	2		2
Ratcliffe	17	1	18
Raisbeck	2	2	4
Reid	13	6	19
Taylor	12		12
Tranter	4	2	6
Walker	1		1

Goalscorers

PLAYER	LEAGUE	CUP COMPETITION FA CUP	TOTAL
Grassam	12	3	15
Corbett	7	2	9
Reid	5		5
Kaye	2	3	5
Hunt	3	1	4
Radcliffe	4		4
Taylor	4		4
Fenton	2	1	3
MacEachrane	1		1

Fact File

Billy Grassam scores four goals on his debut against Gravesend in the season's opener.

CLUB SECRETARY: Len Bowen
CAPTAIN: Unknown
TOP SCORER: Billy Grassam
BIGGEST WIN: September 1, 1900 7-0 v Gravesend, Southern League Division 1
HIGHEST ATTENDANCE: September 8, 1900 10,000 v Millwall, lost 1-3, Southern League Division 1; December 8, 1900 10,000 v Clapton Orient, FA Cup Qualifying Round 5

Final Southern League Division 1 Table

		P	W	D	L	F	A	Pts
1	Southampton	28	18	5	5	58	26	41
2	Bristol City	28	17	5	6	54	27	39
3	Portsmouth	28	17	4	7	56	32	38
4	Millwall Athletic	28	17	2	9	55	32	36
5	Tottenham Hotspur	28	16	4	8	55	33	36
6	West Ham United	28	14	5	9	40	28	33
7	Bristol Rovers	28	14	4	10	46	35	32
8	Queens Park Rangers	28	11	4	13	43	48	26
9	Reading	28	8	8	12	24	25	24
10	Luton Town	28	11	2	15	43	49	24
11	Kettering	28	7	9	12	33	46	23
12	New Brompton	28	7	5	16	34	51	19
13	Gravesend United	28	6	7	15	32	85	19
14	Watford	28	6	4	18	24	52	16
15	Swindon Town	28	3	8	17	19	47	14

Season 1901-02

Southern League Division 1

DATE	OPPONENTS	SCORE	GOALSCORERS	ATTENDANCE
Sep 7	Bristol Rovers	W 2-0	Grassam, Corbett	5,000
Sep 14	BRENTFORD	W 2-0	Grassam 2	4,500
Sep 21	New Brompton	D 0-0		4,000
Sep 28	KETTERING TOWN	W 1-0	Grassam	6,000
Sep 30	WELLINGBOROUGH	W 4-2	Corbett 3, Grassam	2,000
Oct 5	Northampton Town	W 4-3	Grassam 2, MacEachrane, o.g.	2,000
Oct 12	LUTON TOWN	W 4-1	Corbett 2, Linward, Ratcliffe	6,000
Oct 19	Watford	D 0-0		4,000
Oct 26	MILLWALL	L 0-2		9,000
Nov 2	TOTTENHAM HOTSPUR	L 0-1		17,000
Nov 9	Queens Park Rangers	L 1-2	Linward	4,000
Nov 23	Reading	L 0-3		5,000
Dec 7	Southampton	L 0-4		4,000
Dec 14	SWINDON TOWN	W 2-1	Linward, MacEachrane	2,000
Dec 21	BRISTOL ROVERS	W 2-0	McDonald 2	2,000
Dec 27	Wellingborough Town	W 2-0	MacEachrane, Allan	2,500
Jan 4	NEW BROMPTON	D 0-0		2,000
Jan 11	Kettering Town	L 0-1		2,000
Jan 18	NORTHAMPTON TOWN	L 0-1		5,000
Jan 25	Luton Town	W 3-0	Hunt 2, Grassam	5,000
Feb 1	WATFORD	W 3-2	Ratcliffe 2, Grassam	2,000
Feb 8	Millwall	D 1-1	Ratcliffe	3,000
Feb 15	Tottenham Hotspur	W 2-1	MacEachrane, Jenkinson	8,000
Feb 22	QUEENS PARK RANGERS	W 4-0	Ratcliffe 2, Hunt 2	4,000
Mar 3	Brentford	W 2-0	Jenkinson, Hunt	500
Mar 8	READING	W 2-1	Ratcliffe, Hunt	6,000
Mar 15	Portsmouth	D 0-0		6,000
Mar 22	SOUTHAMPTON	W 2-1	Grassam, Ratcliffe	7,000
Mar 29	Swindon Town	W 1-0	Ratcliffe	1,000
Apr 12	PORTSMOUTH	D 1-1	Ratcliffe	6,000

FA Cup

Nov 2	Leyton	(3Q Rd) W 1-0	Taylor	2,000
Nov 16	GRAYS	(4Q Rd) L 1-2	Linward	2,000

Fact File

West Ham played Tottenham Hotspur and Leyton on the same day due to an administrative error. A reserve side won at Leyton in an FA Cup match, while the first team went down to Tottenham in the league.

CLUB SECRETARY: Len Bowen
CAPTAIN: Unknown
TOP SCORER: Billy Grassam and George Ratcliffe
BIGGEST WIN: February 22, 1901 4-0 v Queens Park Rangers, Southern League Division 1
HIGHEST ATTENDANCE: November 2, 1901, 17,000 v Tottenham Hotspur, lost 0-1, Southern League Division 1

League & Cup Appearances

PLAYER	LEAGUE	CUP COMPETITION FA CUP	TOTAL
Allan	18	1	19
Ambler	1	1	2
Bigden	28		28
Corbett	12		12
Craig	28	1	29
Fair		1	1
Grassam	29	1	30
Hitchens	1	1	2
Hunt	15		15
Jenkinson	19		19
Jones	15		15
Kelly	12		12
King	28	1	29
Kyle	1	2	3
Linward	30	1	31
MacEachrane	25	1	26
McDonald	4		4
McGeorge		2	2
Monteith	29	1	30
Pinder		1	1
Pudan	5	2	7
Ratcliffe	24	1	25
Taylor		1	1
Wallace	1	1	2
Ward		1	1
Yenson	5	1	6

Goalscorers

PLAYER	LEAGUE	CUP COMPETITION FA CUP	TOTAL
Grassam	10		10
Ratcliffe	10		10
Corbett	6		6
Hunt	6		6
MacEachrane	4		4
Linward	3	1	4
Jenkinson	2		2
McDonald	2		2
Allan	1		1
Taylor		1	1
Opps' o.gs.	1		1

Final Southern League Division 1 Table

		P	W	D	L	F	A	Pts
1	Portsmouth	30	20	7	3	67	24	47
2	Tottenham Hotspur	30	18	6	6	61	22	42
3	Southampton	30	18	6	6	71	28	42
4	West Ham United	30	17	6	7	45	28	40
5	Reading	30	16	7	7	57	24	39
6	Millwall Athletic	30	13	6	11	48	31	32
7	Luton Town	30	11	10	9	31	35	32
8	Kettering Town	30	12	5	13	44	39	29
9	Bristol Rovers	30	12	5	13	43	39	29
10	New Brompton	30	10	7	13	39	38	27
11	Northampton	30	11	5	14	53	64	27
12	Queens Park Rangers	30	8	7	15	34	56	23
13	Watford	30	9	4	17	36	60	22
14	Wellingborough	30	9	4	17	34	72	22
15	Brentford	30	7	6	17	34	61	20
16	Swindon Town	30	2	3	25	17	93	7

Season 1902-03

Southern League Division 1

DATE	OPPONENTS	SCORE	GOALSCORERS	ATTENDANCE
Sep 6	READING	D 1-1	Barnes	7,000
Sep 13	Queens Park Rangers	D 0-0		7,000
Sep 27	Wellingborough Town	L 1-5	Grassam	4,000
Oct 4	BRISTOL ROVERS	W 1-0	Grassam	6,500
Oct 11	Northampton Town	L 0-2		3,000
Oct 18	WATFORD	W 3-1	Grassam 2, Barnes	4,000
Oct 25	Brentford	W 3-0	Grassam 2, Bigden	3,000
Nov 1	Tottenham Hotspur	D 1-1	Grassam	7,000
Nov 8	MILLWALL	L 0-3		10,000
Dec 6	KETTERING TOWN	D 1-1	Grassam	2,500
Dec 20	Reading	L 0-6		4,000
Dec 25	SOUTHAMPTON	L 1-2	Grassam	6,000
Dec 26	Portsmouth	L 0-2		18,000
Dec 27	QUEENS PARK RANGERS	W 2-0	Grassam, Barnes	2,500
Jan 10	WELLINGBOROUGH TOWN	W 3-0	Barnes, Davidson, Grassam	4,000
Jan 17	Bristol Rovers	D 1-1	Wallace	4,000
Jan 24	NORTHAMPTON TOWN	W 3-2	Davidson, Grassam, Wallace	4,000
Jan 31	Watford	L 1-2	Campbell	5,000
Feb 7	BRENTFORD	W 2-0	Grassam 2	3,000
Feb 14	TOTTENHAM HOTSPUR	W 1-0	Wallace	8,000
Mar 7	New Brompton	L 0-2		7,000
Mar 14	SWINDON TOWN	D 1-1	Farrell	4,000
Mar 23	NEW BROMPTON	D 1-1	Farrell	1,000
Mar 28	LUTON TOWN	W 4-1	Grassam 2, Farrell, Bigden	800
Apr 4	Swindon Town	D 1-1	Grassam	2,500
Apr 10	PORTSMOUTH	D 1-1	Grassam	10,000
Apr 13	Southampton	L 0-6		6,000
Apr 15	Kettering Town	D 1-1	Bush	2,000
Apr 18	Luton Town	L 0-4		2,000
Apr 25	Millwall	L 1-2	Grassam	3,000

FA Cup

Dec 1	Lincoln City	(Rd 1) L 0-2		3,000

League & Cup Appearances

PLAYER	LEAGUE	CUP COMPETITION FA CUP	TOTAL
Allan	10	1	11
Barnes	27	1	28
Bigden	30	1	31
Biggar	8		8
Blythe	29	1	30
Bush	2		2
Campbell	18		18
Davidson	9		9
Dow	13	1	14
Eccles	25	1	26
Evans	1		1
Fair	12		12
Farrell	20	1	21
Grassam	29	1	30
Griffiths	22	1	23
Kelly	2	1	3
King	9		9
Linward	10	1	11
McAteer	13		13
Miecznikowski	3		3
Parkinson	2		2
Sugden	1		1
Wallace	16		16
Yenson	19		19

Goalscorers

PLAYER	LEAGUE	CUP COMPETITION FA CUP	TOTAL
Grassam	19		19
Barnes	4		4
Farrell	3		3
Wallace	3		3
Bigden	2		2
Davidson	2		2
Campbell	1		1
Bush	1		1

Fact File

Despite a mediocre season the Hammers were unbeaten at home from Boxing Day until the end of the season.

MANAGER: Syd King
CAPTAIN: Unknown
TOP SCORER: Billy Grassam
BIGGEST WIN: March 28, 1902 4-1 v Luton Town, Southern League Division 1
HIGHEST ATTENDANCE: December 26, 1902 18,000 v Portsmouth, lost 0-2, Division 1
MAJOR TRANSFERS IN: John Campbell from Glasgow Rangers, Joe Blythe from Everton, William Barnes from Sheffield United
MAJOR TRANSFERS OUT: Roddy MacEachrane to Woolwich Arsenal, Charlie Craig to Nottingham Forest, Hugh Monteith to Bury

Final Southern League Division 1 Table

		P	W	D	L	F	A	Pts
1	Southampton	30	20	8	2	83	20	48
2	Reading	30	19	7	4	72	30	45
3	Portsmouth	30	17	7	6	69	32	41
4	Tottenham Hotspur	30	14	7	9	47	31	35
5	Bristol Rovers	30	13	8	9	46	34	34
6	New Brompton	30	11	11	8	37	35	33
7	Millwall Athletic	30	14	3	13	52	37	31
8	Northampton Town	30	12	6	12	39	48	30
9	Queens Park Rangers	30	11	6	13	34	42	28
10	West Ham United	30	9	10	11	35	49	28
11	Luton Town	30	10	7	13	43	44	27
12	Swindon Town	30	10	7	13	38	46	27
13	Kettering	30	8	11	11	33	40	27
14	Wellingborough	30	11	3	16	36	56	25
15	Watford	30	6	4	20	35	87	16
16	Brentford	30	2	1	27	16	84	5

Season 1903-04

Southern League Division 1

DATE	OPPONENTS	SCORE	GOALSCORERS	ATTENDANCE
Sep 5	Millwall	L 2-4	Kirby, Satterthwaite	10,000
Sep 7	KETTERING	W 4-1	Bigden, Lyon 2, Allison	1,000
Sep 12	QUEENS PARK RANGERS	W 1-0	Satterthwaite	6,000
Sep 19	Plymouth Argyle	L 0-2		5,000
Sep 24	LUTON TOWN	D 0-0		3,000
Sep 26	READING	D 1-1	Satterthwaite	10,000
Oct 10	BRISTOL ROVERS	L 1-4	Watts	5,000
Oct 17	Brighton & Hove Albion	L 2-3	Satterthwaite, Fair	4,000
Nov 7	BRENTFORD	L 0-1		2,000
Nov 21	Tottenham Hotspur	L 1-2	Kirby	8,000
Dec 5	New Brompton	D 0-0		4,000
Dec 25	SOUTHAMPTON	W 2-1	Kirby, Satterthwaite	10,000
Dec 26	Portsmouth	L 1-2	Barnes	14,000
Dec 28	FULHAM	W 2-0	Satterthwaite, Kirby	2,000
Jan 2	MILLWALL	L 0-1		10,000
Jan 9	Queens Park Rangers	L 1-2	Kirby	7,000
Jan 16	PLYMOUTH ARGYLE	D 1-1	Kirby	8,000
Jan 30	WELLINGBOROUGH TOWN	W 4-1	Kirby 2, Thompson, Satterthwaite	250
Feb 6	Bristol Rovers	L 0-4		2.000
Feb 13	BRIGHTON & HOVE ALBION	W 5-0	Satterthwaite 4, Lyon	3,000
Feb 27	NORTHAMPTON TOWN	W 2-0	Lyon, Kirby	4,000
Mar 2	Reading	L 0-1		1,000
Mar 5	Brentford	L 0-2		4,000
Mar 12	Swindon Town	L 0-1		3,000
Mar 19	TOTTENHAM HOTSPUR	L 0-2		9,500
Mar 26	Luton Town	L 0-1		5,000
Apr 1	PORTSMOUTH	W 3-0	Satterthwaite 2, Bridgeman	8,000
Apr 2	NEW BROMPTON	D 0-0		5,000
Apr 4	Southampton	D 1-1	Bridgeman	10,000
Apr 7	Northampton Town	W 3-1	Mercer, Allison, Kirby	1,000
Apr 9	Kettering Town	W 1-0	Bridgeman	1,000
Apr 20	Wellingborough Town	L 0-3		3,000
Apr 23	Fulham	D 1-1	Bridgeman	4,000
Apr 30	SWINDON TOWN	L 0-1		4,000

FA Cup

Oct 31	BRIGHTON & HOVE ALBION	(3Q Rd)	W 4-0	Lyon 2, Watts, Satterthwaite	5,000
Nov 14	Clapton Orient	(4Q Rd)	W 3-0	Lyon 2, Satterthwaite	4,500
Nov 28	Chatham	(5Q Rd)	W 5-0	Satterthwaite 3, Kirby, Lyon	5,000
Dec 12	FULHAM	(I)	L 0-1		12,000

League & Cup Appearances

PLAYER	LEAGUE	CUP COMPETITION FA CUP	TOTAL
Allison	28	4	32
Barnes	21	4	25
Bigden	33	4	37
Birnie	1	1	2
Blythe	23	4	27
Bridgeman	18		18
Butchart	3		3
Church	2		2
Cotton	8	1	9
Earl	1		1
Eccles	34	4	38
Fair	7		7
Griffiths	26	3	29
Hilsdon	1		1
Ingham	2		2
Jarvis	2		2
Kirby	33	3	36
Lyon	29	4	33
Mapley	13	4	17
Mercer	8		8
Oakes	14		14
Satterthwaite	32	4	36
Thompson	10		10
Watts	25	4	29

Goalscorers

PLAYER	LEAGUE	CUP COMPETITION FA CUP	TOTAL
Satterthwaite	13	5	18
Kirby	10	1	11
Lyon	4	5	9
Bridgeman	4		4
Watts	1	1	2
Allison	2		2
Bigden	1		1
Barnes	1		1
Fair	1		1
Mercer	1		1
Thompson	1		1

Fact File

Brighton must have been sick of the sight of Charlie Satterthwaite. He scored six times in the three matches West Ham played against them this season.

MANAGER: Syd King
CAPTAIN: Unknown
TOP SCORER: Charlie Satterthwaite
BIGGEST WIN: November 28, 1903 5-0 v Chatham, FA Cup Qualifying Round 5; February 13, 1904 5-0 v Brighton and Hove Albion, Southern League Division 1
HIGHEST ATTENDANCE: December 26, 1903 14,000 v Portsmouth, lost 1-2, Southern League Division 1
MAJOR TRANSFERS IN: Tommy Allison from Reading
MAJOR TRANSFERS OUT: Billy Grassam to Manchester United

Final Southern League Division 1 Table

		P	W	D	L	F	A	Pts
1	Southampton	34	22	6	6	75	30	50
2	Tottenham Hotspur	34	16	11	7	54	37	43
3	Bristol Rovers	34	17	8	9	66	42	42
4	Portsmouth	34	17	8	9	41	38	42
5	Queens Park Rangers	34	15	11	8	53	37	41
6	Reading	34	14	13	7	48	35	41
7	Millwall	34	16	8	10	64	42	40
8	Luton Town	34	14	12	8	38	33	40
9	Plymouth Argyle	34	13	10	11	44	34	36
10	Swindon Town	34	10	11	13	30	42	31
11	Fulham	34	9	12	13	33	34	30
12	West Ham United	34	10	7	17	38	43	27
13	Brentford	34	9	9	16	34	48	27
14	Wellingborough	34	11	5	18	44	63	27
15	Northampton Town	34	10	7	17	36	69	27
16	New Brompton	34	6	13	15	26	43	25
17	Brighton & Hove	34	6	12	16	45	79	24
18	Kettering Town	34	6	7	21	30	78	19

Season 1904-1905

Southern League Division 1

DATE	OPPONENTS	SCORE	GOALSCORERS	ATTENDANCE
Sep 1	MILLWALL	W 3-0	Bridgeman 2, Flynn	10,000
Sep 3	Brentford	D 0-0		7,000
Sep 10	QUEENS PARK RANGERS	L 1-3	Allison	14,000
Sep 17	Millwall	D 1-1	Fletcher	10,000
Sep 24	TOTTENHAM HOTSPUR	D 0-0		16,000
Oct 1	Luton Town	W 2-0	Fletcher, Bridgeman	4,000
Oct 8	SWINDON TOWN	W 2-0	Fletcher, Flynn	6,000
Oct 15	New Brompton	L 0-3		7,000
Oct 22	WELLINGBOROUGH TOWN	W 4-0	Fletcher 3, Flynn	5,000
Oct 29	Southampton	D 2-2	Bridgeman, McCartney	4,000
Nov 5	FULHAM	D 0-0		8,000
Nov 19	PLYMOUTH ARGYLE	W 2-1	Simmons 2	10,000
Nov 26	BRISTOL ROVERS	L 0-2		7,000
Dec 3	Reading	L 0-1		5,000
Dec 17	Northampton Town	L 0-1		4,000
Dec 26	Portsmouth	L 1-4	Blackwood	16,000
Dec 27	BRIGHTON & HOVE ALBION	L 0-1		12,000
Dec 31	BRENTFORD	L 0-1		8,000
Jan 7	Queens Park Rangers	L 0-1		8,000
Jan 21	Tottenham Hotspur	L 0-1		12,000
Jan 28	LUTON TOWN	W 6-2	Carrick 3, Bridgeman 2, Simmons	5,000
Feb 4	Swindon Town	D 3-3	Fletcher, Piercy, Bridgeman	3,000
Feb 11	NEW BROMPTON	W 2-0	Simmons, Hilsdon	6,000
Feb 18	Wellingborough Town	L 0-3		1,500
Feb 25	SOUTHAMPTON	W 2-1	McCartney, Bridgeman	1,500
Mar 11	WATFORD	W 2-0	Carrick, Bridgeman	3,000
Mar 18	Plymouth Argyle	L 0-2		7,000
Mar 25	Brighton & Hove Albion	L 1-3	Bridgeman	5,000
Apr 1	READING	L 0-2		5,000
Apr 8	Bristol Rovers	D 2-2	Carrick, Hilsdon	5,000
Apr 15	NORTHAMPTON TOWN	W 5-1	Carrick, Simmons 2, McCartney, Bridgeman	7,000
Apr 17	Fulham	W 3-0	Allison, Hilsdon, Simmons	1,000
Apr 21	PORTSMOUTH	D 1-1	Bridgeman	6,000
Apr 25	Watford	W 3-0	Simmons, Piercy, Smith	1,000

FA Cup

Dec 10	BRIGHTON & HOVE ALBION (Q 6)	L 1-2	Flynn	6,000

League & Cup Appearances

PLAYER	LEAGUE	CUP COMPETITION FA CUP	TOTAL
Allison	30	1	31
Bamlett	18	1	19
Blackwood	4		4
Bridgeman	27	1	28
Brunton	1		1
Carrick	18		18
Cotton	5		5
Fair	9	1	10
Fletcher	25	1	26
Flynn	20	1	21
Gardner	29		29
Hamilton	5		5
Hammond	10		10
Hilsdon	7		7
Jarvis	22		22
Kingsley	29	1	30
McCartney	28	1	29
Milnes	2		2
Piercy	33	1	34
Russell	16	1	17
Simmons	34	1	35
Smith	2		2

Goalscorers

PLAYER	LEAGUE	CUP COMPETITION FA CUP	TOTAL
Bridgeman	11		11
Simmons	8		8
Fletcher	7		7
Carrick	6		6
Flynn	3	1	4
Hilsdon	4		4
McCartney	3		3
Allison	2		2
Piercy	2		2
Blackwood	1		1
Smith	1		1

Fact File

Bill Bridgeman scored the first ever goal at Upton Park in the opening game of the season against Millwall.

MANAGER: Syd King
CAPTAIN: Dave Gardner
TOP SCORER: Billy Bridgeman
BIGGEST WIN: January 28, 1905 6-2 v Luton Town, Southern League Division 1
HIGHEST ATTENDANCE: September 24, 1904 16,000 v Tottenham Hotspur, drew 0-0, Southern League Division 1
MAJOR TRANSFERS IN: Matt Kingsley and Tommy Bamlett from Newcastle United; Jack Flynn and Jack Fletcher from Reading, William McCartney from Manchester United, 'Chippy' Simmons from West Bromwich Albion

Final Southern League Division 1 Table

		P	W	D	L	F	A	PTS
1	Bristol Rovers	34	20	8	6	74	36	48
2	Reading	34	18	7	9	57	38	43
3	Southampton	34	18	7	9	54	40	43
4	Plymouth Argyle	34	18	5	11	57	39	41
5	Tottenham Hotspur	34	15	8	11	53	34	38
6	Fulham	34	14	10	10	46	34	38
7	Queens Park Rangers	34	14	8	12	51	46	36
8	Portsmouth	34	16	4	14	61	56	36
9	New Brompton	34	11	11	12	40	41	33
10	West Ham United	34	12	8	14	48	42	32
11	Brighton & Hove	34	13	6	15	44	45	32
12	Northampton Town	34	12	8	14	43	54	32
13	Watford	34	14	3	17	41	44	31
14	Brentford	34	10	9	15	33	38	29
15	Millwall	34	11	7	16	38	47	29
16	Swindon Town	34	12	5	17	41	59	29
17	Luton Town	34	12	3	19	45	54	27
18	Wellingborough	34	5	3	26	25	104	13

Season 1905-06

Southern League Division 1

DATE	OPPONENTS	SCORE	GOALSCORERS	ATTENDANCE
Sep 2	SWINDON TOWN	W 1-0	Kitchen	10,000
Sep 9	Millwall	L 0-1		6,500
Sep 16	LUTON TOWN	L 1-2	Blackburn	10,000
Sep 23	Tottenham Hotspur	L 0-2		12,000
Sep 30	BRENTFORD	W 2-0	Blackburn, Wilkinson	8,000
Oct 7	Norwich City	L 0-1		6,000
Oct 14	PLYMOUTH ARGYLE	W 2-1	Blackburn, Mackie	5,000
Oct 21	Southampton	L 0-1		6,000
Oct 28	READING	L 2-3	Ford, Allison	7,000
Nov 4	Watford	L 1-3	Bridgeman	4,000
Nov 11	BRIGHTON & HOVE ALBION	W 2-0	Wilkinson, Mackie	8,000
Nov 18	Northampton Town	L 1-2	Mackie	5,000
Nov 25	Fulham	L 0-1		12,000
Dec 2	QUEENS PARK RANGERS	W 2-0	Hilsdon, Watson	7,500
Dec 9	Bristol Rovers	L 1-2	Hilsdon	5,000
Dec 16	NEW BROMPTON	W 1-0	Jarvis	6,000
Dec 23	PORTSMOUTH	W 1-0	Stapley	8,000
Dec 30	Swindon Town	W 3-2	Watson, Jarvis, Blackburn	4,000
Jan 6	MILLWALL	W 1-0	Watson	15,000
Jan 20	Luton Town	D 1-1	Stapley	5,000
Jan 27	TOTTENHAM HOTSPUR	L 0-1		16,500
Feb 10	NORWICH CITY	W 6-1	Grassam, Watson 2, Stapley 2, Kitchen	6,000
Feb 17	Plymouth Argyle	L 2-4	Kitchen, Grassam	3,000
Feb 26	SOUTHAMPTON	W 3-0	Stapley 2, Bridgeman	5,000
Mar 3	Reading	L 1-6	Watson	5,000
Mar 10	WATFORD	D 0-0		7,000
Mar 17	Brighton & Hove Albion	D 0-0		5,000
Mar 24	NORTHAMPTON TOWN	W 4-1	Stapley 2, Bridgeman 2	4,000
Mar 31	FULHAM	D 0-0		12,000
Apr 7	Queens Park Rangers	W 1-0	Stapley	10,000
Apr 14	BRISTOL ROVERS	W 2-0	Blackburn, Hilsdon	9,000
Apr 21	New Brompton	D 0-0		3,000
Apr 23	Brentford	L 1-3	Grassam	2,000
Apr 28	Portsmouth	L 0-1		5,000

FA Cup

Jan 13	Woolwich Arsenal	(I)	D 1-1	Kitchen	18,000
Jan 18	WOOLWICH ARSENAL	(I R)	L 2-3	Bridgeman, Watson	12,000

League & Cup Appearances

PLAYER	LEAGUE	CUP COMPETITION FA CUP	TOTAL
Allison	28	2	30
Blackburn	30	2	32
Bridgeman	26	2	28
Bush	18	1	19
Cotton	5		5
Featherstone	17		17
Ford	7		7
Gardner	34	2	36
Grassam	14		14
Hammond	4		4
Hilsdon	9	2	11
Hindle	3		3
Jackson	24		24
Jarvis	27	2	29
Kitchen	29	2	31
Mackie	10		10
McCartney	6		6
Milnes		2	2
Piercy	24	2	26
Stapley	13		13
Watson	22	2	24
Wilkinson	14	1	15
Winterhalder H	10		10

Goalscorers

PLAYER	LEAGUE	CUP COMPETITION FA CUP	TOTAL
Stapley	9		9
Watson	6	1	7
Bridgeman	4	1	5
Blackburn	5		5
Kitchen	3	1	4
Mackie	3		3
Hilsdon	3		3
Grassam	3		3
Jarvis	2		2
Wilkinson	2		2
Ford	1		1
Allison	1		1

Fact File

After a 6-1 thrashing at Reading, West Ham let in only one goal in the next seven matches.

MANAGER: Syd King

CAPTAIN: Dave Gardner

TOP SCORER: Harry Stapley

BIGGEST WIN: February 10, 1906 6-1 v Norwich City, Southern League Division 1

HIGHEST ATTENDANCE: January 13, 1906 18,000 v Woolwich Arsenal, drew 1-1, FA Cup Round 1

MAJOR TRANSFERS IN: George Kitchen from Everton, Fred Blackburn from Blackburn Rovers, Billy Grassam from Manchester United

MAJOR TRANSFERS OUT: George Hilsdon to Chelsea

Final Southern League Division 1 Table

		P	W	D	L	F	A	Pts
1	Fulham	34	19	12	3	44	15	50
2	Southampton	34	19	7	8	58	39	45
3	Portsmouth	34	17	9	8	61	35	43
4	Luton Town	34	17	7	10	64	40	41
5	Tottenham Hotspur	34	16	7	11	46	29	39
6	Plymouth Argyle	34	16	7	11	52	33	39
7	Norwich City	34	13	10	11	46	38	36
8	Bristol Rovers	34	15	5	14	56	56	35
9	Brentford	34	14	7	13	43	52	35
10	Reading	34	12	9	13	53	46	33
11	West Ham United	34	14	5	15	42	39	33
12	Millwall	34	11	11	12	38	41	33
13	Queens Park Rangers	34	12	7	15	58	44	31
14	Watford	34	8	10	16	38	57	26
15	Swindon Town	34	8	9	17	31	52	25
16	Brighton & Hove	34	9	7	18	30	55	25
17	New Brompton	34	7	8	19	20	62	22
18	Northampton Town	34	8	5	21	32	79	21

Season 1906-07

Southern League Division 1

DATE	OPPONENTS	SCORE	GOALSCORERS	ATTENDANCE
Sep 1	Tottenham Hotspur	W 2-1	Stapley, Watson	17,000
Sep 8	SWINDON TOWN	W 2-0	Watson, Stapley	10,000
Sep 15	Norwich City	L 2-3	Blackburn, Stapley	10,000
Sep 22	LUTON TOWN	W 5-1	Watson 3, Stapley, Lindsay	13,000
Sep 24	Bristol Rovers	L 0-3		3,000
Sep 29	Crystal Palace	D 1-1	Winterhalder H	10,000
Oct 6	BRENTFORD	W 3-1	Allison, Stapley, Grassam	12,000
Oct 13	Millwall	D 1-1	Stapley	15,000
Oct 15	BRISTOL ROVERS	L 0-1		4,000
Oct 20	LEYTON	W 3-0	Grassam 2, Stapley	12,000
Oct 27	Portsmouth	L 3-4	Grassam 3	12,000
Nov 3	NEW BROMPTON	D 1-1	Stapley	7,000
Nov 10	Plymouth Argyle	D 0-0		10,000
Nov 17	BRIGHTON & HOVE ALBION	D 0-0		5,000
Nov 27	Reading	D 2-2	Grassam, Lindsay	4,000
Dec 1	WATFORD	D 1-1	Stapley	7,000
Dec 8	New Brompton	D 2-2	Stapley, Watson	5,000
Dec 22	Fulham	W 4-1	Watson 3, Blackburn	10,000
Dec 25	SOUTHAMPTON	W 1-0	Stapley	20,000
Dec 29	TOTTENHAM HOTSPUR	W 4-2	Winterhalder A 3, Stapley	14,000
Jan 5	Swindon Town	L 0-2		5,000
Jan 19	NORWICH CITY	W 3-1	Stapley 2, Lindsay	7,000
Jan 26	Luton Town	D 1-1	Stapley	4,000
Feb 9	Brentford	D 0-0		6,000
Feb 16	MILLWALL	L 0-1		16,000
Feb 23	Leyton	D 0-0		10,000
Feb 25	QUEENS PARK RANGERS	W 2-1	Watson, Grassam	4,000
Mar 2	PORTSMOUTH	W 3-0	Stapley 2, Lindsay	11,000
Mar 7	Northampton Town	D 0-0		2,000
Mar 16	PLYMOUTH ARGYLE	D 0-0		6,000
Mar 23	Brighton & Hove Albion	L 0-2		6,000
Mar 25	CRYSTAL PALACE	D 1-1	Winterhalder A	3,000
Mar 30	READING	W 2-0	Blackburn, Allison	6,000
Apr 1	Southampton	W 3-2	Stapley, Watson, Jarvis	8,000
Apr 6	Watford	L 0-2		4,000
Apr 13	NORTHAMPTON TOWN	W 4-0	Stapley 2, Grassam 2	2,500
Apr20	Queens Park Rangers	L 0-2		5,000
Apr 27	FULHAM	W 4-1	Watson, Randall, Winterhalder A, Blackburn	10,000

FA Cup

Jan 12	BLACKPOOL	(Rd 1) W 2-1	Stapley, Winterhalder H	13,000
Feb 2	EVERTON	(Rd 2) L 1-2	Stapley	14,000

League & Cup Appearances

PLAYER	LEAGUE	CUP COMPETITION FA CUP	TOTAL
Allison	36	2	38
Blackburn	29		29
Blythe	3		3
Bourne	1		1
Clarke	1		1
Fair	3		3
Featherstone	2		2
Gardner	14	1	15
Grassam	37	2	39
Hammond	16	1	17
Horn	4		4
Jarvis	30	2	32
Kemp	8		8
Kitchen	37	2	39
Lindsay	37	2	39
Piercy	37	2	39
Randall	1		1
Stapley	35	2	37
Taylor	4		4
Watson	32	2	34
Wildman	37	2	39
Winterhalder A	10		10
Winterhalder H	2	1	3
Woodards	2		2

Goalscorers

PLAYER	LEAGUE	CUP COMPETITION FA CUP	TOTAL
Stapley	20	2	22
Watson	12		12
Grassam	10		10
Winterhalder A	5		5
Lindsay	4		4
Blackburn	4		4
Allison	2		2
Winterhalder H	1	1	2
Jarvis	1		1
Randall	1		1

Fact File

Future skipper Tom Randall scored on his debut in the final match of the season.

MANAGER: Syd King
CAPTAIN: Dave Gardner/Frank Piercy
TOP SCORER: Harry Stapley
BIGGEST WIN: September 22, 1906 5-1 v Luton Town, Southern League Division 1
HIGHEST ATTENDANCE: December 25, 1906 20,000 v Southampton, won 1-0, Southern League Division 1

Final Southern League Division 1 Table

		P	W	D	L	F	A	Pts
1	Fulham	38	20	13	5	58	32	53
2	Portsmouth	38	22	7	9	64	36	51
3	Brighton & Hove	38	18	9	11	53	43	45
4	Luton Town	38	18	9	11	52	52	45
5	West Ham United	38	15	14	9	60	41	44
6	Tottenham Hotspur	38	17	9	12	63	45	43
7	Millwall	38	18	6	14	71	50	42
8	Norwich City	38	15	12	11	57	48	42
9	Watford	38	13	16	9	46	43	42
10	Brentford	38	17	8	13	57	56	42
11	Southampton	38	13	9	16	49	56	35
12	Reading	38	14	6	18	57	47	34
13	Leyton	38	11	12	15	38	60	34
14	Bristol Rovers	38	12	9	17	55	54	33
15	Plymouth Argyle	38	10	13	15	43	50	33
16	New Brompton	38	12	9	17	47	59	33
17	Swindon Town	38	11	11	16	43	54	33
18	Queens Park Rangers	38	11	10	17	47	55	32
19	Crystal Palace	38	8	9	21	46	66	25
20	Northampton Town	38	5	9	24	29	88	19

Season 1907-08

Southern League Division 1

DATE	OPPONENTS	SCORE	GOALSCORERS	ATTENDANCE
Sep 1	SWINDON TOWN	L 1-2	Grassam	8,000
Sep 7	TOTTENHAM HOTSPUR	D 1-1	Blackburn	13,000
Sep 14	Swindon Town	D 1-1	Grassam	5,000
Sep 21	CRYSTAL PALACE	W 1-0	Grassam	8,000
Sep 28	Luton Town	W 3-0	Stapley 2, Grassam	7,000
Oct 5	BRIGHTON & HOVE ALBION	D 0-0		7,000
Oct 12	Portsmouth	W 2-0	Watson, Blackburn	12,000
Oct 19	BRADFORD	D 0-0		12,000
Oct 26	Millwall	L 0-1		13,000
Nov 2	BRENTFORD	W 4-1	Stapley 2, Randall, Grassam	6,000
Nov 9	Bristol Rovers	L 0-1		10,000
Nov 16	LEYTON	L 0-2		8,000
Nov 23	Reading	W 1-0	Watson	6,000
Nov 30	WATFORD	W 2-0	Watson, Stapley	6,000
Dec 7	Norwich City	D 1-1	Grassam	4,500
Dec 14	NORTHAMPTON TOWN	D 1-1	Stapley	4,000
Dec 21	Southampton	D 0-0		6,000
Dec 25	NEW BROMPTON	L 1-2	o.g.	10,000
Dec 26	QUEENS PARK RANGERS	W 3-0	Grassam 2, Featherstone	17,000
Dec 28	PLYMOUTH ARGYLE	D 1-1	Shea	10,000
Jan 4	Tottenham Hotspur	L 2-3	Stapley 2	12,000
Jan 18	Crystal Palace	W 3-1	Watson, Shea, Stapley	8,000
Jan 25	LUTON TOWN	W 1-0	Watson	8,000
Feb 8	PORTSMOUTH	W 2-1	Frost, Watson	10,000
Feb 15	Bradford	W 1-0	Watson	9,000
Feb 22	MILLWALL	L 0-2		12,000
Feb 29	Brentford	L 0-4		4,000
Mar 7	BRISTOL ROVERS	D 0-0		6,000
Mar 14	Leyton	D 2-2	Brown 2	11,000
Mar 21	READING	W 2-1	Grassam, Watson	6,000
Mar 25	Brighton & Hove Albion	L 1-3	Jarvis	1,500
Mar 28	Watford	W 3-2	Jarvis, Stapley, Frost	3,000
Apr 4	NORWICH CITY	W 3-0	Young, Blackburn, Frost	6,000
Apr 11	Northampton Town	L 0-4		6,000
Apr 17	New Brompton	L 0-3		6,000
Apr 18	SOUTHAMPTON	W 4-2	Brown 2, Blackburn, Shea	8,000
Apr 20	Queens Park Rangers	L 0-4		11,000
Apr 25	Plymouth Argyle	L 0-2		4,000

FA Cup

Jan 11	ROTHERHAM CITY	(Rd 1)	W 1-0	Blackburn	9,500
Feb 1	Newcastle United	(Rd 2)	L 0-2		47,000

League & Cup Appearances

PLAYER	LEAGUE	CUP COMPETITION FA CUP	TOTAL
Allison	29		29
Blackburn	36	2	38
Bourne	3		3
Brown	17		17
Clarke	15		15
Featherstone	5	1	6
Frost	13	1	14
Gault	35	2	37
Grassam	32	2	34
Hammond	2	1	3
Harwood	3		3
Horn	4	1	5
Jarvis	29	1	30
Kemp	3		3
Kitchen	23	2	25
Lee	6		6
Lindsay	13		13
Piercy	23	2	25
Randall	7		7
Robertson	1		1
Shea	13	2	15
Stapley	23	2	25
Taylor	25	1	26
Watson	22		22
Wildman	2		2
Woodards	1		1
Young	33	2	35

Goalscorers

PLAYER	LEAGUE	CUP COMPETITION FA CUP	TOTAL
Stapley	10		10
Grassam	9		9
Watson	8		8
Blackburn	4	1	5
Brown	4		4
Shea	3		3
Frost	3		3
Jarvis	2		2
Young	1		1
Randall	1		1
Featherstone	1		1
Opps' o.gs.	1		1

Fact File

Hammers hero-to-be 20-year-old Danny Shea made his debut on 7 December against Norwich City.

MANAGER: Syd King
CAPTAIN: Frank Piercy
TOP SCORER: Harry Stapley
BIGGEST WIN: November 2, 1907 4-1 v Brentford, Southern League Division 1
HIGHEST ATTENDANCE: February 1, 1908 47,000 v Newcastle United, lost 0-2, FA Cup Round 2
MAJOR TRANSFERS IN: Danny Shea from Manor Park Albion

Final Southern League Division 1 Table

		P	W	D	L	F	A	Pts
1	Queens Park Rangers	38	21	9	8	82	57	51
2	Plymouth Argyle	38	19	11	8	50	31	49
3	Millwall	38	19	8	11	49	32	46
4	Crystal Palace	38	17	10	11	54	51	44
5	Swindon Town	38	16	10	12	55	40	42
6	Bristol Rovers	38	16	10	12	59	56	42
7	Tottenham Hotspur	38	17	7	14	59	48	41
8	Northampton Town	38	15	11	12	50	41	41
9	Portsmouth	38	17	6	15	63	52	40
10	West Ham United	38	15	10	13	47	48	40
11	Southampton	38	16	6	16	51	60	38
12	Reading	38	15	6	17	55	50	36
13	Bradford (PA)	38	12	12	14	53	54	36
14	Watford	38	12	10	16	47	59	34
15	Brentford	38	14	5	19	49	52	33
16	Norwich City	38	12	9	17	46	49	33
17	Brighton & Hove	38	12	8	18	46	59	32
18	Luton Town	38	12	6	20	33	56	30
19	Leyton	38	8	11	19	51	73	27
20	New Brompton	38	9	7	22	44	75	25

Season 1908-09

Southern League Division 1

DATE	OPPONENTS	SCORE	GOALSCORERS	ATTENDANCE
Sep 1	QUEENS PARK RANGERS	W 2-0	Foster, Blackburn	7,000
Sep 5	Brighton & Hove Albion	L 2-3	Foster, Burton	6,000
Sep 12	CRYSTAL PALACE	L 0-1		10,000
Sep 19	Brentford	L 0-1		6,000
Sep 26	LUTON TOWN	W 4-0	Foster 2, Piercy, Ashton	3,000
Sep 30	Watford	L 1-2	Shea	3,000
Oct 3	Swindon Town	L 0-3		6,000
Oct 10	PORTSMOUTH	W 3-1	Foster 3	8,000
Oct 17	Queens Park Rangers	L 0-3		6,000
Oct 24	NORTHAMPTON TOWN	W 2-1	Tirrell, Shreeve	9,000
Oct 31	New Brompton	L 1-2	Miller	6,000
Nov 7	MILLWALL	W 1-0	Foster	14,000
Nov 14	Southend United	D 0-0		6,000
Nov 21	COVENTRY CITY	W 2-0	Foster, Randall	6,000
Nov 28	Bristol Rovers	L 0-1		8,000
Dec 5	Plymouth Argyle	L 0-2		7,000
Dec 12	Norwich City	L 3-6	Burton 2, Grassam	4,500
Dec 19	READING	W 2-1	Grassam, Blackburn	5,000
Dec 25	SOUTHAMPTON	W 1-0	Blackburn	15,000
Dec 26	Leyton	L 0-1		20,000
Dec 28	PLYMOUTH ARGYLE	W 4-0	Shea 4	10,000
Jan 2	BRIGHTON & HOVE ALBION	D 1-1	Waggott	5,000
Jan 9	Crystal Palace	D 2-2	Shea 2	5,000
Jan 23	BRENTFORD	W 3-0	Miller, Waggott, Frost	7,000
Jan 30	Luton Town	L 0-1		3,000
Feb 13	Portsmouth	L 1-4	Miller	5,000
Feb 27	Northampton Town	L 0-6		5,000
Mar 6	NEW BROMPTON	L 0-1		3,000
Mar 8	SWINDON TOWN	W 4-2	Shea 3, Costello	4,000
Mar 13	Millwall	L 0-3		9,000
Mar 20	SOUTHEND UNITED	W 4-0	Costello, Piercy, Atkins, Shea	9,000
Mar 27	Coventry City	L 1-3	Shea	7,000
Apr 1	EXETER CITY	W 4-1	Blackburn 2, Miller 2	4,000
Apr 3	BRISTOL ROVERS	L 0-2		7,000
Apr 9	LEYTON	W 1-0	Webb	13,000
Apr 10	WATFORD	W 3-1	Shea 2, Costello	7,000
Apr 12	Southampton	D 2-2	Shea, Webb	7,500
Apr 17	NORWICH CITY	W 2-1	Shea, Blackburn	5,000
Apr 21	Exeter City	L 0-1		7,000
Apr 24	Reading	L 0-1		2,500

FA Cup

Jan 16	Queens Park Rangers	(Rd 1)	D 0-0		17,000
Jan 20	QUEENS PARK RANGERS	(R)	W 1-0	Shea	11,400
Feb 6	Leeds City	(Rd 2)	D 1-1	Miller	31,500
Feb 11	LEEDS CITY	(R)	W 2-1	Shea 2	13,000
Feb 20	NEWCASTLE UNITED	(Rd 3)	D 0-0		17,000
Feb 24	Newcastle United	(R)	L 1-2	Shea	36,500

League & Cup Appearances

PLAYER	LEAGUE	CUP COMPETITION FA CUP	TOTAL
Allison	5		5
Ashton	27	2	29
Atkins	2		2
Blackburn	40	6	46
Bourne	3	2	5
Brown	2		2
Burton	15	4	19
Chalkley	7	4	11
Clarke	1		1
Costello	12		12
Dawson	4		4
Dyer	3		3
Eastwood	6		6
Foster	15		15
Frost	7	4	11
Gault	14		14
Grassam	8	1	9
Harwood	9		9
Jarvis	23	2	25
Kitchen	35	6	41
Miller	11	6	17
Piercy	26		26
Randall	17		17
Shea	35	6	41
Shreeve	19	6	25
Taylor	34	6	40
Tirrell	13	4	17
Waggott	8	1	9
Webb	4		4
Yenson	26	6	32
Young	9		9

Goalscorers

PLAYER	LEAGUE	CUP COMPETITION FA CUP	TOTAL
Shea	16	4	20
Foster	9		9
Blackburn	6		6
Miller	5	1	6
Burton	3		3
Costello	3		3
Piercy	2		2
Waggott	2		2
Grassam	2		2
Webb	2		2
Ashton	1		1
Frost	1		1
Tirrell	1		1
Shreeve	1		1
Randall	1		1
Atkins	1		1

Fact File

3-1 up at half-time against Norwich City in December, West Ham crashed 3-6; they would not win away all season.

MANAGER: Syd King

CAPTAIN: Frank Piercy

TOP SCORER: Danny Shea

BIGGEST WIN: September 26, 1908 4-0 v Luton Town, Southern League Division 1; December 28, 1908 4-0 v Plymouth Argyle, Southern League Division 1; March 20, 1909 4-0 v Southend United, Southern League Division 1

HIGHEST ATTENDANCE: February 24, 1908 36,500 v Newcastle United, lost 1-2, FA Cup Round 3 replay

MAJOR TRANSFERS IN: Jack Foster from Sunderland, Fred Shreeve from Millwall, Bill Yenson from Queens Park Rangers, Herbert Ashton from Accrington

Final Southern League Division 1 Table

		P	W	D	L	F	A	Pts
1	Northampton Town	40	25	5	10	90	45	55
2	Swindon Town	40	22	5	13	96	55	49
3	Southampton	40	19	10	11	67	58	48
4	Portsmouth	40	18	10	12	68	60	46
5	Bristol Rovers	40	17	9	14	60	63	43
6	Exeter City	40	18	6	16	56	65	42
7	New Brompton	40	17	7	16	48	59	41
8	Reading	40	11	18	11	60	57	40
9	Luton Town	40	17	6	17	59	60	40
10	Plymouth Argyle	40	15	10	15	46	47	40
11	Millwall	40	16	6	18	59	61	38
13	Southend United	40	14	10	16	52	54	38
14	Leyton	40	15	8	17	52	55	38
15	Watford	40	14	9	17	51	64	37
16	Queens Park Rangers	40	12	12	16	52	50	36
17	Crystal Palace	40	12	12	16	62	62	36
18	West Ham United	40	16	4	20	56	60	36
19	Brighton & Hove	40	14	7	19	60	61	35
20	Norwich City	40	12	11	17	59	75	35
21	Coventry City	40	15	4	21	64	91	34
22	Brentford	40	13	7	20	59	74	33

Season 1909-10

Southern League Division 1

DATE	OPPONENTS	SCORE	GOALSCORERS	ATTENDANCE
Sep 2	EXETER CITY	W 2-1	Shea 2	5,000
Sep 4	Norwich City	W 3-1	Shea, Blackburn, Haynes	7,000
Sep 11	BRENTFORD	W 3-2	Shea 3	10,000
Sep 13	PORTSMOUTH	L 0-2		6,000
Sep 18	Coventry City	D 2-2	Shea, Haynes	8,000
Sep 25	WATFORD	W 2-0	Shea, Randall	10,000
Sep 29	Portsmouth	D 1-1	Haynes	2,000
Oct 2	Reading	W 3-0	Shea 2, Webb	3.000
Oct 4	BRISTOL ROVERS	W 5-0	Caldwell 3, Shea, Webb	4,000
Oct 9	SOUTHEND UNITED	D 0-0		10,000
Oct 16	Leyton	W 2-1	Caldwell, Webb	13,000
Oct 23	PLYMOUTH ARGYLE	W 4-1	Webb 2, Shea 2	10,000
Oct 25	Bristol Rovers	L 0-1		2,000
Oct 30	Southampton	D 2-2	Shea, Haynes	7,000
Nov 6	CROYDON COM	W 5-1	Shea 2, Ashton, Caldwell, Whiteman	10,000
Nov 13	Millwall	D 0-0		10,000
Nov 20	Plymouth Argyle	D 0-0		8,000
Nov 27	Northampton Town	L 1-3	Webb	7,000
Dec 4	QUEENS PARK RANGERS	L 1-2	Shreeve	12,000
Dec 11	Luton Town	L 2-4	Ashton, Shea	3,000
Dec 18	SWINDON TOWN	D 2-2	Blackburn, Shreeve	10,000
Dec 25	BRIGHTON & HOVE ALBION	D 1-1	Shea	15,000
Dec 27	Brighton & Hove Albion	L 0-3		10,000
Jan 1	NEW BROMPTON	D 2-2	Caldwell, Shea	7,000
Jan 8	NORWICH CITY	W 5-0	Caldwell 2, Shea 2, Cannon	6,000
Jan 22	Brentford	D 0-0		4,000
Jan 29	COVENTRY CITY	W 3-2	Haynes, Ashton, Shea	6,000
Feb 12	READING	D 1-1	Shreeve	8,000
Feb 26	LEYTON	D 0-0		10,000
Mar 2	Watford	L 1-2	Butcher	1,000
Mar 5	Exeter City	L 0-1		6,500
Mar 12	SOUTHAMPTON	D 1-1	Blackburn	4,000
Mar 19	Croydon Com	D 1-1	Webb	6,000
Mar 25	CRYSTAL PALACE	W 3-1	Shea 2, o.g.	15,000
Mar 26	MILLWALL	L 1-2	Shea	12,000
Mar 28	Crystal Palace	W 4-2	Scanes 2, Ashton, Shea	20,000
Mar 29	Southend United	W 1-0	Shea	1,200
Apr 2	New Brompton	L 0-1		5,000
Apr 9	NORTHAMPTON TOWN	W 1-0	Scanes	10,000
Apr 16	Queens Park Rangers	D 3-3	Shea, Waggott, Curtis	7,000
Apr 23	LUTON TOWN	L 1-2	Curtis	4,000
Apr 30	Swindon Town	L 0-5		4,000

FA Cup

Jan 15	CARLISLE UNITED	(Rd 1)	D 1-1	Blackburn	11,000
Jan 20	CARLISLE UNITED	(R)	W 5-0	Blackburn 2, Shea, Webb, Randall	7,000
Feb 5	Wolverhampton W	(Rd 2)	W 5-1	Shea 2, Webb 3	17,000
Feb 19	Queens Park Rangers	(Rd 3)	D 1-1	Webb	31,000
Feb 24	QUEENS PARK RANGERS	(R)	L 0-1		18,000

Fact File

West Ham were knocked out of the FA Cup by a last-gasp Queens Park Rangers goal in extra time.

MANAGER: Syd King

CAPTAIN: Frank Piercy

TOP SCORER: Danny Shea

BIGGEST WIN: October 4, 1909 5-0 v Bristol Rovers, Southern League Division 1; January 8, 1910 5-0 v Norwich City, Southern League Division 1; January 20, 1910 5-0 v Carlisle United, FA Cup Round 1 replay

HIGHEST ATTENDANCE: February 19, 1910 31,000 v Queens Park Rangers, drew 1-1, FA Cup Round 3

MAJOR TRANSFERS IN: Frank Cannon from Queens Park Rangers, Bob Whiteman from Norwich City, Bob Fairman from Birmingham City, George Butcher from St. Albans

League & Cup Appearances

PLAYER	LEAGUE	CUP COMPETITION FA CUP	TOTAL
Ashton	42	5	47
Blackburn	42	5	47
Bourne	4	1	5
Butcher	3		3
Caldwell	35	5	40
Cannon	3.	1	4
Curtis	3		3
Dawson	2		2
Fairman	37	3	40
Geggus	4		4
Haynes	15		15
Kitchen	36	5	41
Lavery	2	2	4
Massey	20	3	23
Piercy	29	5	34
Randall	39	5	44
Scanes	3		3
Shea	38	5	43
Shreeve	41	4	45
Silor	6		6
Waggott	2		2
Wagstaffe	3		3
Webb	18	4	22
Whiteman	33	2	35
Woodards	2		2

Goalscorers

PLAYER	LEAGUE	CUP COMPETITION FA CUP	TOTAL
Shea	28	3	31
Webb	7	5	12
Caldwell	8		8
Blackburn	3	3	6
Haynes	5		5
Ashton	4		4
Shreeve	3		3
Scanes	3		3
Randall	1	1	2
Curtis	2		2
Whiteman	1		1
Cannon	1		1
Butcher	1		1
Waggott	1		1
Opps' o.gs.	1		1

Final Southern League Division 1 Table

		P	W	D	L	F	A	Pts
1	Brighton & Hove	42	23	13	6	69	28	59
2	Swindon Town	42	22	10	10	92	46	54
3	Queens Park Rangers	42	19	13	10	56	47	51
4	Northampton Town	42	22	4	16	90	44	48
5	Southampton	42	16	16	10	64	55	48
6	Portsmouth	42	20	7	15	70	63	47
7	Crystal Palace	42	20	6	16	69	50	46
8	Coventry City	42	19	8	15	71	60	46
9	West Ham United	42	15	15	12	69	56	45
10	Leyton	42	16	11	15	60	46	43
11	Plymouth Argyle	42	16	11	15	60	46	43
12	New Brompton	42	19	5	18	76	74	43
13	Bristol Rovers	42	16	10	16	37	48	42
14	Brentford	42	16	9	17	50	58	41
15	Luton Town	42	15	11	16	72	92	41
16	Millwall	42	15	7	20	45	59	37
17	Norwich City	42	13	9	20	59	78	35
18	Exeter City	42	14	6	22	60	69	34
19	Watford	42	10	13	19	51	76	33
20	Southend United	42	12	9	21	51	90	33
21	Croyden Common	42	13	5	24	52	96	31
22	Reading	42	7	10	25	38	73	24

Season 1910-11

Southern League Division 1

DATE	OPPONENTS	SCORE	GOALSCORERS	ATTENDANCE
Sep 3	SOUTHEND UNITED	D 3-3	Ashton, Webb, Blackburn	15,000
Sep 10	Coventry City	L 0-3		6,000
Sep 12	Queens Park Rangers	W 2-0	Shea 2	7,000
Sep 17	NEW BROMPTON	W 2-0	Shea, Webb	12,000
Sep 24	Millwall	W 2-0	Shea, Blackburn	10,000
Oct 1	QUEENS PARK RANGERS	W 3-0	Shea, Curtis 2	20,000
Oct 8	Norwich City	L 0-2		8,000
Oct 15	Luton Town	D 1-1	Shea	8,000
Oct 22	PORTSMOUTH	W 3-1	Shea, Ashton, Kitchen	10,000
Oct 29	Northampton Town	L 0-2		6,000
Nov 5	BRIGHTON & HOVE ALBION	W 3-1	Shea, Kennedy, Kitchen	14,000
Nov 12	Exeter City	D 0-0		6,000
Nov 19	SWINDON TOWN	W 1-0	Shea	12,000
Nov 26	Bristol Rovers	D 1-1	Shea	6,000
Dec 3	CRYSTAL PALACE	D 1-1	Shea	10,000
Dec 10	Brentford	L 0-3		5,000
Dec 17	LEYTON	W 3-0	Shea, Ashton 2	7,000
Dec 24	Watford	W 3-1	Shea 2, Piercy	2,000
Dec 26	PLYMOUTH ARGYLE	W 4-0	Shea, Webb 2, Rothwell	14,000
Dec 27	Plymouth Argyle	L 0-1		8,000
Dec 31	Southend United	W 6-0	Shea 4, Kennedy, Caldwell	3,000
Jan 7	COVENTRY CITY	D 1-1	Webb	11,000
Jan 21	New Brompton	D 1-1	Ashton	5,000
Jan 28	MILLWALL	D 2-2	Randall, Webb	8,000
Feb 11	NORWICH CITY	W 2-1	Webb, Rothwell	12,000
Feb 18	LUTON TOWN	W 2-0	Kennedy, Piercy	8,000
Mar 4	NORTHAMPTON TOWN	L 1-2	Butcher	10,000
Mar 18	EXETER CITY	W 4-1	Webb 3, Shea	8,000
Mar 25	Swindon Town	L 1-4	Kennedy	6,000
Mar 29	Portsmouth	D 0-0		2,000
Apr 1	BRISTOL ROVERS	D 2-2	Shea, Caldwell	5,000
Apr 8	Crystal Palace	L 1-4	Shea	10,000
Apr 14	SOUTHAMPTON	W 4-1	Shea, Ashton, Harrison, Caldwell	12,000
Apr 15	BRENTFORD	W 2-0	Shea, Butcher	8,000
Apr 17	Southampton	W 1-0	Harrison	8,000
Apr 22	Leyton	L 0-3		10,000
Apr 26	Brighton & Hove Albion	L 0-3		4,000
Apr 29	WATFORD	D 1-1	Shea	5,000

FA Cup

Jan 14	NOTTINGHAM FOREST	(Rd 1)	W 2-1	Shea 2	12,000
Feb 4	PRESTON NORTH END	(Rd 2)	W 3-0	Webb 3	12,000
Feb 25	MANCHESTER UNITED	(Rd 3)	W 2-1	Shea, Caldwell	27,000
Mar 11	BLACKBURN ROVERS	(Rd 4)	L 2-3	Butcher 2	20,000

League & Cup Appearances

PLAYER	LEAGUE	CUP COMPETITION FA CUP	TOTAL
Ashton	37	4	41
Blackburn	16		16
Bourne	1		1
Butcher	26	4	30
Caldwell	38	4	42
Curtis	3		3
Fairman	33	4	37
Frost	2		2
Geggus	14		14
Harrison	5		5
Kennedy	10		10
Kitchen	24	4	28
Lavery	15		15
Massey	13		13
Miellear	1		1
Piercy	32	4	36
Randall	34	4	38
Redwood	1		1
Rothwell	22	4	26
Shea	35	4	39
Shreeve	5		5
Webb	19	4	23
Whiteman	27	4	31
Woodards	5		5

Goalscorers

PLAYER	LEAGUE	CUP COMPETITION FA CUP	TOTAL
Shea	25	3	28
Webb	10	3	13
Ashton	6		6
Caldwell	3	1	4
Butcher	2	2	4
Kennedy	4		4
Kitchen	2		2
Piercy	2		2
Blackburn	2		2
Curtis	2		2
Rothwell	2		2
Harrison	2		2
Randall	1		1

Fact File

West Ham knocked out three Football League Division 1 teams on their way to the quarter-finals of the FA Cup.

MANAGER: Syd King
CAPTAIN: Frank Piercy
TOP SCORER: Danny Shea
BIGGEST WIN: December 31, 1910 6-0 v Southend United, Southern League Division 1
HIGHEST ATTENDANCE: February 25, 1911 27,000 v Manchester United, won 2-1, FA Cup Round 3
MAJOR TRANSFERS IN: Fred Harrison from Fulham

Final Southern League Division 1 Table

		P	W	D	L	F	A	Pts
1	Swindon Town	38	24	5	9	80	31	53
2	Northampton Town	38	18	12	8	54	27	48
3	Brighton & Hove	38	20	8	10	58	35	48
4	Crystal Palace	38	17	13	8	55	48	47
5	West Ham United	38	17	11	10	63	46	45
6	Queens Park Rangers	38	13	14	11	52	41	40
7	Leyton	38	16	8	14	57	52	40
8	Plymouth Argyle	38	15	9	14	54	55	39
9	Luton Town	38	15	8	15	67	63	38
10	Norwich City	38	15	8	15	46	48	38
11	Coventry City	38	16	6	16	65	68	38
12	Brentford	38	14	9	15	41	42	37
13	Exeter City	38	14	9	15	51	53	37
14	Watford	38	13	9	16	49	65	35
15	Millwall	38	11	9	18	42	54	31
16	Bristol Rovers	38	10	10	18	42	55	30
17	Southampton	38	11	8	19	42	67	30
18	New Brompton	38	11	8	19	34	65	30
19	Southend United	38	10	9	19	47	64	29
20	Portsmouth	38	8	11	19	34	53	27

Season 1911-12

Southern League Division 1

DATE	OPPONENTS	SCORE	GOALSCORERS	ATTENDANCE
Sep 2	Crystal Palace	L 0-1		14,000
Sep 9	SOUTHAMPTON	D 2-2	Harrison, Kennedy	8,000
Sep 16	Plymouth Argyle	D 0-0		9,000
Sep 23	READING	W 5-0	Rothwell, Webb, Shea, Whiteman, Piercy	10,000
Sep 30	Watford	L 0-2		6,000
Oct 7	NEW BROMPTON	D 0-0		5,000
Oct 14	Exeter City	D 3-3	Shea 2, Webb	8,000
Oct 21	BRENTFORD	W 7-4	Shea 3, Kennedy 3, Harrison	10,000
Oct 28	Queens Park Rangers	L 1-4	Webb	16,000
Nov 4	MILLWALL	W 2-1	Harrison 2	23,000
Nov 11	LUTON TOWN	W 3-0	Webb, Harrison, Shea	9,000
Nov 18	Bristol Rovers	D 1-1	Shea	7,000
Nov 25	SWINDON TOWN	L 0-2		11,000
Dec 2	Northampton Town	L 2-3	Harrison, Morrison	6,000
Dec 9	BRIGHTON & HOVE ALBION	W 1-0	Shea	7,000
Dec 16	Stoke	L 3-4	Kennedy 2, Randall	8,000
Dec 23	COVENTRY CITY	L 0-1		7,000
Dec 25	LEYTON	W 2-0	Ashton, Butcher	17,000
Dec 30	CRYSTAL PALACE	L 1-6	Shea	8,000
Jan 6	Southampton	W 2-1	Shea 2	3,000
Jan 20	PLYMOUTH ARGYLE	L 0-2		10,000
Jan 27	Reading	L 1-3	Ashton	4,000
Feb 10	New Brompton	W 3-0	Shea 2, Butcher	5,000
Feb 17	EXETER CITY	W 3-2	Shea 2, Harrison	10,000
Mar 2	QUEENS PARK RANGERS	W 3-0	Ashton, Caldwell, Shea	10,000
Mar 9	Millwall	L 1-5	Harrison	28,400
Mar 11	WATFORD	L 1-3	Rothwell	4,000
Mar 16	Luton Town	L 1-2	Harrison	6,000
Mar 23	BRISTOL ROVERS	W 6-2	Shea 2, Harrison 2, Dawson, Woodards	4,000
Mar 27	Brentford	W 2-1	Harrison, o.g.	4,000
Apr 5	NORWICH CITY	W 4-0	Shea 3, Harrison	10,000
Apr 6	NORTHAMPTON TOWN	L 0-2		10,000
Apr 8	Norwich City	D 2-2	Woodards, Shea	12,000
Apr 9	Leyton	L 1-3	Shea	3,000
Apr 13	Brighton & Hove Albion	L 0-2		5,000
Apr 20	STOKE	D 0-0		8,000
Apr 22	Swindon Town	L 1-3	Mackesy	2,000
Apr 27	Coventry City	L 0-2		5,000

FA Cup

Jan 3	GAINSBOROUGH TOWN	Rd 1	W 2-1	Webb, Harrison	14,400
Feb 3	Middlesbrough	(Rd 2)	D 1-1	Harrison	12,300
Feb 8	MIDDLESBROUGH	(R)	W 2-1	Harrison, Ashton	10,000
Feb 24	SWINDON TOWN	(Rd 3)	D 1-1	Butcher	20,000
Feb 28	Swindon Town	(R)	L 0-4		13,328

League & Cup Appearances

PLAYER	LEAGUE	CUP COMPETITION FA CUP	TOTAL
Ashton	23	5	28
Bell	2		2
Blackburn	22	5	27
Bourne	1		1
Bradford	1		1
Burrill	7		7
Butcher	16	3	19
Caldwell	11	3	14
Dawson	10		10
Fairman	20	5	25
Frost	2		2
Geggus	13		13
Glover	29	5	34
Harrison	30	4	34
Hughes	25	5	30
Kennedy	11	2	13
Mackesy	1		1
Massey	5		5
Miellear	2	1	3
Morrison	15		15
Piercy	10	1	11
Randall	23		23
Redwood	9	3	12
Rothwell	24		24
Shea	36	5	41
Walden	2		2
Webb	11	2	13
Whiteman	27	2	29
Woodards	20	4	24

Goalscorers

PLAYER	LEAGUE	CUP COMPETITION FA CUP	TOTAL
Shea	24		24
Harrison	13	3	16
Kennedy	6		6
Webb	4	1	5
Ashton	3	1	4
Butcher	2	1	3
Rothwell	2		2
Woodards	2		2
Whiteman	1		1
Piercy	1		1
Randall	1		1
Caldwell	1		1
Morrison	1		1
Dawson	1		1
Mackesy	1		1
Opps' o.gs.	1		1

Fact File

The 11 goals in the home match with Brentford remains the highest aggregate score for a match involving West Ham.

MANAGER: Syd King
CAPTAIN: Tom Randall
TOP SCORER: Danny Shea
BIGGEST WIN: September 23, 1911 5-0 v Reading, Southern League Division 1
HIGHEST ATTENDANCE: March 5, 1912 28,400 v Millwall, lost 1-5, Southern League Division 1
MAJOR TRANSFERS IN: Horace Glover from Southampton
MAJOR TRANSFERS OUT: George Webb to Manchester City

Final Southern League Division 1 Table

		P	W	D	L	F	A	Pts
1	Queens Park Rangers	38	21	11	6	59	35	53
2	Plymouth Argyle	38	23	6	9	63	31	52
3	Northampton Town	38	22	7	9	82	41	51
4	Swindon Town	38	21	6	11	82	50	48
5	Brighton & Hove	38	19	9	10	73	35	47
6	Coventry City	38	17	8	13	66	54	42
7	Crystal Palace	38	15	10	13	70	46	40
8	Millwall	38	15	10	13	60	57	40
9	Watford	38	13	10	15	56	68	36
10	Stoke	38	13	10	15	51	63	36
11	Reading	38	11	14	13	43	69	36
12	Norwich City	38	10	14	14	40	60	34
13	West Ham United	38	13	7	18	64	69	33
14	Brentford	38	12	9	17	60	65	33
15	Exeter City	38	11	11	16	48	62	33
16	Southampton	38	10	11	17	46	63	31
17	Bristol Rovers	38	9	13	16	41	62	31
18	New Brompton	38	11	9	18	35	72	31
19	Luton Town	38	9	10	19	49	61	28
20	Leyton	38	7	11	20	27	62	25

Season 1912-13

Southern League Division 1

DATE	OPPONENTS	SCORE	GOALSCORERS	ATTENDANCE
Sep 2	EXETER CITY	W 4-0	Shea 2, Harrison, Dawson	9,000
Sep 7	COVENTRY CITY	L 1-2	Ashton	12,000
Sep 14	Watford	W 2-0	Shea, Harrison	5,000
Sep 21	MERTHYR TOWN	D 1-1	Shea	7,000
Sep 28	Crystal Palace	D 1-1	Hilsdon	15,000
Oct 5	PLYMOUTH ARGYLE	W 3-1	Hilsdon, Dawson, Shea	8,000
Oct 12	Southampton	W 3-1	Hilsdon, Shea 2	9,000
Oct 19	READING	L 1-2	Hilsdon	15,000
Oct 26	Norwich City	L 0-2		7,000
Oct 30	Exeter City	D 0-0		2,000
Nov 2	GILLINGHAM	W 4-0	Hilsdon 2, Denyer 2	10,000
Nov 9	Northampton Town	L 3-4	Casey, Burrill, Shea	6,000
Nov 16	QUEENS PARK RANGERS	W 1-0	Denyer	14,000
Nov 23	Brentford	L 1-5	Shea	7,000
Nov 30	MILLWALL	D 1-1	Hilsdon	16,000
Dec 7	Bristol Rovers	L 1-2	Ashton	8,000
Dec 14	SWINDON TOWN	W 4-1	Denyer 2, Hilsdon 2	14,000
Dec 21	Portsmouth	W 2-1	Shea, Ashton	10,000
Dec 25	STOKE	W 5-0	Shea 2, Ashton, Denyer, Askew	8,000
Dec 26	Stoke	W 1-0	Shea	5,000
Dec 28	Coventry City	L 1-4	Shea	7,000
Jan 4	WATFORD	W 2-0	Harrison, Shea	10,000
Jan 18	Merthyr Town	L 2-6	Butcher 2	4,000
Jan 25	CRYSTAL PALACE	D 1-1	Butcher	14,000
Feb 8	Plymouth Argyle	W 2-0	Woodards, Denyer	8,000
Feb 15	SOUTHAMPTON	D 1-1	Harrison	5,000
Mar 1	NORWICH CITY	W 2-1	Hilsdon 2	8,000
Mar 8	Gillingham	D 2-2	Casey 2	5,000
Mar 15	NORTHAMPTON TOWN	D 0-0		9,000
Mar 21	BRIGHTON & HOVE ALBION	D 1-1	Puddefoot	15,000
Mar 22	Queens Park Rangers	W 1-0	Denyer	10,000
Mar 24	Brighton & Hove Albion	D 0-0		11,000
Mar 29	BRENTFORD	W 2-1	Denyer, Hilsdon	7,000
Apr 5	Millwall	W 3-1	Bailey, Ashton, Randall	24,000
Apr 12	BRISTOL ROVERS	W 3-1	Randall, Askew, Hilsdon	8,000
Apr 19	Swindon Town	D 1-1	Denyer	9,000
Apr 23	Reading	D 1-1	Denyer	2,000
Apr 26	PORTSMOUTH	W 2-1	Ashton, Bailey	8,000

FA Cup

Jan 13	West Bromwich Albion	(Rd 1) D 1-1	Harrison	20,000
Jan 16	WEST BROMWICH ALBION	(R) D 2-2	Hilsdon 2	15,000
Jan 22	West Bromwich Albion	(2nd R) W 3-0*	Hilsdon 2, Denyer	27,075
Feb 1	Aston Villa	(Rd 2) L 0-5		50,000

* Played at Stamford Bridge.

League & Cup Appearances

PLAYER	LEAGUE	CUP COMPETITION FA CUP	TOTAL
Ashton	36	4	40
Askew	30	2	32
Bailey	10		10
Blackburn	2		2
Burrill	2		2
Burton	5		5
Butcher	4	2	6
Carter	9		9
Casey	24	4	28
Caton	3		3
Dawson	12		12
Denyer	29	4	33
Forster	25	4	29
Harrison	19	4	23
Hilsdon	32	4	36
Hughes	29	4	33
Irvine	16		16
Mackesy	1		1
Puddefoot	4		4
Randall	35	4	39
Rothwell	32	4	36
Shea	22		22
Whiteman	8		8
Woodards	29	4	33

Goalscorers

PLAYER	LEAGUE	CUP COMPETITION FA CUP	TOTAL
Hilsdon	13	4	17
Shea	15		15
Denyer	11	1	12
Ashton	6		6
Harrison	4	1	5
Casey	3		3
Butcher	3		3
Askew	2		2
Randall	2		2
Dawson	2		2
Bailey	2		2
Puddefoot	1		1
Woodards	1		1
Burrill	1		1

Fact File

West Ham were undefeated in their last 13 games, finishing 3rd in the table – their highest placing since entering the Southern League.

MANAGER: Syd King
CAPTAIN: Tom Randall
TOP SCORER: George Hilsdon
BIGGEST WIN: December 25, 1912 5-0 v Stoke, Southern League Division 1
HIGHEST ATTENDANCE: February 1, 1913 50,000 v Aston Villa, lost 0-5, FA Cup Round 2
MAJOR TRANSFERS IN: George Hilsdon from Chelsea
MAJOR TRANSFERS OUT: Danny Shea to Blackburn Rovers

Final Southern League Division 1 Table

		P	W	D	L	F	A	Pts
1	Plymouth Argyle	38	22	6	10	77	36	50
2	Swindon Town	38	20	8	10	66	41	48
3	West Ham United	38	18	12	8	66	46	48
4	Queens Park Rangers	38	18	10	10	46	35	46
5	Crystal Palace	38	17	11	10	55	36	45
6	Millwall	38	19	7	12	62	43	45
7	Exeter City	38	18	8	12	48	44	44
8	Reading	38	17	8	13	59	55	42
9	Brighton & Hove	38	13	12	13	48	47	38
10	Northampton Town	38	12	12	14	61	48	36
11	Portsmouth	38	14	8	16	41	49	36
12	Merthyr Town	38	12	12	14	42	60	36
13	Coventry City	38	13	8	17	53	59	34
14	Watford	38	12	10	16	43	50	34
15	Gillingham	38	12	10	16	36	53	34
16	Bristol Rovers	38	12	9	17	55	64	33
17	Southampton	38	10	11	17	40	72	31
18	Norwich City	38	10	9	19	39	50	29
19	Brentford	38	11	5	22	42	55	27
20	Stoke	38	10	4	24	39	75	24

Season 1913-14

Southern League Division 1

DATE	OPPONENTS	SCORE	GOALSCORERS	ATTENDANCE
Sep 1	Millwall	D 1-1	Hilsdon	12,000
Sep 6	SWINDON TOWN	L 2-3	Leafe 2	25,000
Sep 13	Bristol Rovers	W 2-1	Denyer A, Leafe	10,000
Sep 20	MERTHYR TOWN	W 3-1	Leafe, Casey, Ashton	15,000
Sep 27	Queens Park Rangers	D 2-2	Leafe, Denyer A	12,000
Oct 4	Plymouth Argyle	L 0-3		10,000
Oct 11	SOUTHAMPTON	W 5-1	Burton, Hilsdon 2, Casey, Ashton	6,000
Oct 18	Reading	L 0-2		8,000
Oct 25	CRYSTAL PALACE	L 1-2	Casey	13,000
Nov 1	Coventry City	W 4-2	Leafe 3, Denyer A	7,000
Nov 8	WATFORD	D 1-1	Denyer A	10,000
Nov 15	Norwich City	L 0-1		7,000
Nov 22	GILLINGHAM	W 3-1	Burrill, Puddefoot, Leafe	10,000
Nov 29	Northampton Town	D 0-0		5,000
Dec 6	SOUTHEND UNITED	L 0-1		10,000
Dec 13	Brighton & Hove Albion	W 1-0	Leafe	6,000
Dec 20	PORTSMOUTH	W 3-2	Puddefoot, Leafe, Denyer A	9,000
Dec 25	EXETER CITY	D 1-1	Puddefoot	18,000
Dec 26	Exeter City	D 1-1	Leafe	7,000
Dec 27	Swindon Town	L 1-4	Puddefoot	8,000
Jan 3	BRISTOL ROVERS	W 6-1	Puddefoot 3, Bailey, Casey, Leafe	14,000
Jan 17	Merthyr Town	W 2-1	Puddefoot, Casey	6,000
Jan 24	QUEENS PARK RANGERS	W 4-1	Leafe, Bailey, Casey 2	11,000
Feb 7	PLYMOUTH ARGYLE	W 2-1	Puddefoot, Leafe	8,000
Feb 14	Southampton	W 3-2	Burton, Bailey, Leafe	7,000
Feb 28	Crystal Palace	W 2-1	Bailey, Ashton	12,000
Mar 7	COVENTRY CITY	W 1-0	Leafe	14,000
Mar 21	NORWICH CITY	D 1-1	Leafe	6,000
Mar 23	READING	D 0-0		5,000
Mar 28	Gillingham	L 1-3	Randall	7,000
Apr 1	Watford	L 0-6		4,000
Apr 4	NORTHAMPTON TOWN	D 1-1	Leafe	10,000
Apr 1	Cardiff City	L 0-2		12,000
Apr 11	Southend United	D 1-1	Bailey	7,000
Apr 13	CARDIFF CITY	D 1-1	Leafe	15,000
Apr 14	MILLWALL	W 3-2	Hilsdon 2, Stallard	15,000
Apr 18	BRIGHTON & HOVE ALBION	D 1-1	Hilsdon	10,000
Apr 25	Portsmouth	L 1-5	Bailey	8,000

FA Cup

Jan 10	CHESTERFIELD	(Rd 1)	W 8-1	Puddefoot 5, Bailey, Leafe, Ashton	16,000
Jan 31	CRYSTAL PALACE	(Rd 2)	W 2-0	Bailey 2	18,000
Feb 21	LIVERPOOL	(Rd 3)	D 1-1	Puddefoot	16,000
Feb 25	Liverpool	(Rd 3 R)	L 1-5	Puddefoot	45,000

League & Cup Appearances

PLAYER	LEAGUE	CUP COMPETITION FA CUP	TOTAL
Ashton	35	4	39
Askew	38	4	42
Bailey	19	4	23
Beal	1		1
Bourne	1		1
Brandon	31	3	34
Burrill	8		8
Burton	19	4	23
Butcher	4		4
Carter	1		1
Casey	24	3	27
Caton	3		3
Denyer A	17		17
Denyer F	2		2
Forster	15		15
Goddard	1		1
Hilsdon	17		17
Hughes	15	4	19
Irvine	5		5
Leafe	33	4	37
Lonsdale	21		21
Mackesy	3		3
Puddefoot	16	4	20
Randall	28	3	31
Rothwell	10	3	13
Stallard	2		2
Tirrell	1		1
Tresardern	4		4
Whiteman	7		7
Woodards	30	4	34

Goalscorers

PLAYER	LEAGUE	CUP COMPETITION FA CUP	TOTAL
Leafe	20	1	21
Puddefoot	9	7	16
Bailey	6	3	9
Casey	7		7
Hilsdon	6		6
Denyer A	5		5
Ashton	3	1	4
Burton	2		2
Randall	1		1
Burrill	1		1
Stallard	1		1

Fact File

New signing Alf Leafe scored in his first four matches.

MANAGER: Syd King

CAPTAIN: Tom Randall

TOP SCORER: Alf Leafe

BIGGEST WIN: January 10, 1914 8-1 v Chesterfield, FA Cup Round 1

HIGHEST ATTENDANCE: February 25, 1914 45,000 v Liverpool, lost 1-5, FA Cup Round 3 replay

MAJOR TRANSFERS IN: Thomas Lonsdale from Grimsby Town, Tom Brandon from Blackburn Rovers, Alf Leafe from Sheffield United

Final Southern League Division 1 Table

		P	W	D	L	F	A	Pts
1	Swindon Town	36	21	8	9	81	41	50
2	Crystal Palace	38	17	16	5	60	32	50
3	Northampton Town	38	14	19	5	50	37	47
4	Reading	38	17	10	11	43	36	44
5	Plymouth Argyle	38	15	13	10	46	42	43
6	West Ham United	38	15	12	11	61	60	42
7	Brighton & Hove	38	15	12	11	43	45	42
8	Queens Park Rangers	38	16	9	13	45	43	41
9	Portsmouth	38	14	12	12	57	48	40
10	Cardiff City	38	13	12	13	46	42	38
11	Southampton	38	15	7	16	55	54	37
12	Exeter City	38	10	16	12	39	38	36
13	Gillingham	38	13	9	16	48	49	35
14	Norwich City	38	9	17	12	49	51	35
15	Millwall	38	11	12	15	51	56	34
16	Southend United	38	10	12	16	41	66	32
17	Bristol Rovers	38	10	11	17	46	67	31
18	Watford	38	10	9	19	50	56	29
19	Merthyr Town	38	9	10	19	38	61	28
20	Coventry City	38	6	14	18	43	68	26

Season 1914-15

Southern League Division 1

DATE	OPPONENTS	SCORE	GOALSCORERS	ATTENDANCE
Sep 1	GILLINGHAM	W 2-1	Puddefoot 2	5,000
Sep 5	Exeter City	L 1-3	Puddefoot	4,000
Sep 9	Gillingham	L 0-4		2,000
Sep 12	LUTON TOWN	W 3-0	Puddefoot 2, Hilsdon	5,000
Sep 19	Portsmouth	L 1-3	Hilsdon	7,000
Sep 26	SWINDON TOWN	D 1-1	Puddefoot	11,000
Oct 3	Southend United	W 1-0	Leafe	5,000
Oct 10	QUEENS PARK RANGERS	D 2-2	Puddefoot, Leafe	12,000
Oct 17	Millwall	L 1-2	Puddefoot	15,000
Oct 24	BRISTOL ROVERS	W 4-1	Bailey, Leafe, Wright, Burton	10,000
Oct 31	Croydon Com	W 2-1	Bailey, Leafe	5,000
Nov 7	READING	W 3-2	Bailey, Leafe, Puddefoot	10,000
Nov 14	Southampton	L 1-3	Leafe	5,000
Nov 21	NORTHAMPTON TOWN	W 1-0	Leafe	8,000
Nov 28	Watford	W 1-0	Bailey	2,000
Dec 5	PLYMOUTH ARGYLE	W 2-0	Butcher, Carr	6,000
Dec 12	CRYSTAL PALACE	L 1-2	Mackesy	5,000
Dec 19	Norwich City	D 0-0		4,000
Dec 25	Brighton & Hove Albion	D 0-0		1,000
Dec 26	BRIGHTON & HOVE ALBION	W 2-1	Puddefoot 2	9,600
Jan 2	EXETER CITY	W 4-1	Puddefoot 3, Fenwick	7,000
Jan 23	PORTSMOUTH	W 4-3	Leafe 2, Burton, Casey	3,000
Jan 30	Swindon Town	D 1-1	Casey	3,000
Feb 6	SOUTHEND UNITED	W 3-1	Puddefoot 2, Leafe	5,000
Feb 13	Queens Park Rangers	D 1-1	Whiteman	5,000
Feb 20	MILLWALL	D 1-1	Puddefoot	17,000
Feb 27	Bristol Rovers	L 0-1		3,000
Mar 6	CROYDON COM	W 1-0	Hilsdon	5,000
Mar 10	Luton Town	W 2-1	Leafe, Bailey	7,000
Mar 13	Reading	L 1-3	Leafe	7,000
Mar 20	SOUTHAMPTON	W 3-0	Leafe, Hilsdon, Stallard	8,000
Mar 27	Northampton Town	D 1-1	Stallard	1,500
Apr 2	CARDIFF CITY	W 2-1	Stallard 2	13,000
Apr 3	WATFORD	W 2-0	Puddefoot, Hilsdon	10,000
Apr 5	Cardiff City	L 1-2	Stallard	10,000
Apr 10	Plymouth Argyle	L 0-1		5,000
Apr 17	Crystal Palace	L 1-2	Stallard	4,000
Apr 24	NORWICH CITY	D 1-1	Stallard	3,000

FA Cup

Jan 9	NEWCASTLE UNITED	(Rd 1) D 2-2	Leafe 2	15,000
Jan 16	Newcastle United	(Rd 1 R) L 2-3	Casey, Leafe	28,130

League & Cup Appearances

PLAYER	LEAGUE	CUP COMPETITION FA CUP	TOTAL
Ashton	14	1	15
Askew	36	2	38
Bailey	20		20
Brandon	2		2
Burton	26	2	28
Butcher	9		9
Carr	5		5
Casey	19	2	21
Caton	8		8
Cope	31	2	33
Fenwick	19	2	21
Hilsdon	20	1	21
Hughes	21	2	23
Leafe	30	2	32
Mackesy	5		5
Puddefoot	35	2	37
Randall	5		5
Speak	13		13
Stallard	11		11
Tirrell	6		6
Tresadern	2		2
Webster	17		17
Whiteman	34	2	36
Woodards	20	2	22
Wright	10		10

Goalscorers

PLAYER	LEAGUE	CUP COMPETITION FA CUP	TOTAL
Puddefoot	18		18
Leafe	13	3	16
Stallard	7		7
Bailey	5		5
Hilsdon	5		5
Casey	2	1	3
Burton	2		2
Fenwick	1		1
Wright	1		1
Whiteman	1		1
Mackesy	1		1
Carr	1		1
Butcher	1		1

Fact File

Syd Puddefoot scored only 2 of his 18 goals this season away from Upton Park.

MANAGER: Syd King
CAPTAIN: Alf Leafe
TOP SCORER: Syd Puddefoot
BIGGEST WIN: October 24, 1914 4-1 v Bristol Rovers, Southern League Division 1; January 2, 1915 4-1 v Exeter City, Southern League Division 1
HIGHEST ATTENDANCE: January 16, 1915 28,130 v Newcastle United, lost 2-3, FA Cup Round 1 replay

Final Southern League Division 1 Table

		P	W	D	L	F	A	PTS
1	Watford	38	22	8	8	68	46	52
2	Reading	38	21	7	10	68	43	49
3	Cardiff City	38	22	4	12	72	38	48
4	West Ham United	38	18	9	11	58	47	45
5	Northampton Town	38	16	11	11	56	51	43
6	Southampton	38	19	5	14	78	74	43
7	Portsmouth	38	16	10	12	54	42	42
8	Millwall	38	16	10	12	50	51	42
9	Swindon Town	38	15	11	12	77	59	41
10	Brighton & Hove	38	16	7	15	46	47	39
11	Exeter City	38	15	8	15	50	41	38
12	Queens Park Rangers	38	13	12	13	55	56	38
13	Norwich City	38	11	14	13	53	56	36
14	Luton Town	38	13	8	17	61	73	34
15	Crystal Palace	38	13	8	17	47	61	34
16	Bristol Rovers	38	14	3	21	53	75	31
17	Plymouth Argyle	38	8	14	16	51	61	30
18	Southend United	38	10	8	20	44	64	28
19	Croyden Common	38	9	9	20	47	63	27
20	Gillingham	38	6	8	24	43	82	20

Season 1919-20

Football League Division 2

DATE	OPPONENTS	SCORE	GOALSCORERS	ATTENDANCE
Aug 30	LINCOLN CITY	D 1-1	Moyes	20,000
Sep 1	Barnsley	L 0-7		6,000
Sep 6	Lincoln City	W 4-1	Puddefoot 2, Burton, Butcher	6,000
Sep 8	BARNSLEY	L 0-2		14,000
Sep 13	Rotherham City	W 1-0	Puddefoot	6,000
Sep 20	ROTHERHAM CITY	W 2-1	Butcher, Puddefoot	20,000
Sep 27	Stoke	L 1-2	Puddefoot	12,000
Oct 4	STOKE	D 1-1	Puddefoot	23,000
Oct 11	Grimsby Town	W 1-0	Turner	6,000
Oct 18	GRIMSBY TOWN	W 1-0	Palmer	20,000
Oct 25	Birmingham	W 1-0	Kay	25,000
Nov 1	BIRMINGHAM	L 1-2	Allen R	20,000
Nov 8	Leicester City	D 0-0		14,000
Nov 15	LEICESTER CITY	W 1-0	Burton	23,000
Nov 22	Fulham	W 2-1	Puddefoot 2	20,000
Nov 29	FULHAM	L 0-1		20,000
Dec 6	Coventry City	D 0-0		15,000
Dec 13	COVENTRY CITY	W 2-0	Bailey, Butcher	15,000
Dec 20	Huddersfield Town	L 0-2		6,000
Dec 25	BRISTOL CITY	W 2-0	Bailey, Butcher	20,000
Dec 26	Bristol City	D 0-0		12,000
Dec 27	HUDDERSFIELD TOWN	D 1-1	Butcher	25,000
Jan 3	Blackpool	D 0-0		7,000
Jan 17	BLACKPOOL	W 1-0	Bailey	26,000
Jan 24	BURY	W 1-0	Kay	20,000
Feb 7	PORT VALE	W 3-1	Puddefoot 3	23,000
Feb 11	Bury	L 0-1		5,000
Feb 14	Port Vale	L 0-1		15,000
Feb 28	Clapton Orient	L 0-1		25,000
Mar 4	CLAPTON ORIENT	L 0-1		15,000
Mar 13	TOTTENHAM HOTSPUR	W 2-1	Puddefoot 2	30,000
Mar 20	South Shields	L 0-3		18,000
Mar 22	Tottenham Hotspur	L 0-2		25,000
Mar 27	SOUTH SHIELDS	W 1-0	Bailey	18,000
Apr 2	NOTTINGHAM FOREST	W 5-1	Puddefoot 4, Bailey	20,000
Apr 3	Wolverhampton W	D 1-1	Bailey	15,000
Apr 5	Nottingham Forest	L 1-2	Bailey	10,000
Apr 10	WOLVERHAMPTON W	W 4-0	Butcher 2, Puddefoot 2	16,000
Apr 17	Hull City	D 1-1	Bailey	8,000
Apr 24	HULL CITY	W 2-1	Bailey, Puddefoot	18,000
Apr 28	Stockport County	L 0-1		5,000
May 1	STOCKPORT COUNTY	W 3-0	Butcher, Kay, Puddefoot	15,000

FA Cup

Jan 10	Southampton	(Rd 1)	D 0-0		12,000
Jan 15	SOUTHAMPTON	(R)	W 3-1	Puddefoot 2, Butcher	25,000
Jan 31	BURY	(Rd 2)	W 6-0	Puddefoot 3, Bailey, Butcher, Smith S	27,000
Feb 21	Tottenham Hotspur	(Rd 3)	L 0-3		47,646

Fact File

Ted Hufton makes his debut against Lincoln City in the opening game of West Ham's first ever Football League season.

MANAGER: Syd King
CAPTAIN: Bill Cope
TOP SCORER: Syd Puddefoot
BIGGEST WIN: January 31, 1920 6-0 v Bury, FA Cup Round 2
HIGHEST ATTENDANCE: February 21, 1920 47,646 v Tottenham Hotspur, lost 0-3, FA Cup Round 3

League & Cup Appearances

PLAYER	LEAGUE	CUP COMPETITION FA CUP	TOTAL
Allen P	4	1	5
Allen R	1		1
Bailey	27	3	30
Biggin	2		2
Birchenough	1		1
Bradshaw	13	1	14
Burton	34	4	38
Butcher	33	4	37
Carter	13	3	16
Cope	29	4	33
Cumming	10		10
Fenwick	2		2
Green	3		3
Hufton	38	4	42
Johnson	2		2
Kay	27	4	31
Lane	9		9
Leafe	15		15
Lee	17		17
Mackesy	5		5
McCrae	35	4	39
Morris	3		3
Moyes	2		2
Murray	2		2
Palmer	12		12
Phipps	1		1
Puddefoot	39	4	43
Roberts	1		1
Smith D	1		1
Smith S	23	4	27
Smithurst	2		2
Stanley	1		1
Tirrell	1		1
Tresadern	35	4	39
Turner	3		3
Webster	2		2
Woodards	9		9
Woodburn	4		4
Young	1		1

Goalscorers

PLAYER	LEAGUE	CUP COMPETITION FA CUP	TOTAL
Puddefoot	21	5	26
Butcher	8	2	10
Bailey	9	1	10
Kay	3		3
Burton	2		2
Moyes	1		1
Palmer	1		1
Turner	1		1
Allen R	1		1
Smith S		1	1

Final Division 2 Table

		P	W	D	L	F	A	Pts
1	Tottenham H	42	32	6	4	102	32	70
2	Huddersfield T	42	28	8	6	97	38	64
3	Birmingham	42	24	8	10	85	34	56
4	Blackpool	42	21	10	11	65	47	52
5	Bury	42	20	8	14	60	44	48
6	Fulham	42	19	9	14	61	50	47
7	West Ham U	42	19	9	14	47	40	47
8	Bristol C	42	13	17	12	46	43	43
9	South Shields	42	15	12	15	58	48	42
10	Stoke	42	18	6	18	60	54	42
11	Hull C	42	18	6	18	78	72	42
12	Barnsley	42	15	10	17	61	55	40
13	Port Vale	42	16	8	18	59	62	40
14	Leicester C	42	15	10	17	41	61	40
15	Clapton Orient	42	16	6	20	51	59	38
16	Stockport Co	42	14	9	19	52	61	37
17	Rotherham Co	42	13	8	21	51	83	34
18	Nottingham F	42	11	9	22	43	73	31
19	Wolverhampton W	42	10	10	22	55	80	30
20	Coventry C	42	9	11	22	35	73	29
21	Lincoln C	42	9	9	24	44	101	27
22	Grimsby T	42	10	5	27	34	75	25

Season 1920-21

Football League Division 2

DATE	OPPONENTS	SCORE	GOALSCORERS	ATTENDANCE
Aug 28	HULL CITY	D 1-1	Puddefoot	28,000
Aug 30	Wolverhampton W	W 2-1	Puddefoot 2	30,000
Sep 4	Hull City	L 1-2	Simmons	12,000
Sep 6	WOLVERHAMPTON W	W 1-0	Puddefoot	15,000
Sep 11	Fulham	D 0-0		30,000
Sep 18	FULHAM	W 2-0	Kay, Puddefoot	20,000
Sep 25	Cardiff City	D 0-0		30,000
Oct 2	CARDIFF CITY	D 1-1	Shea	25,000
Oct 4	Coventry City	W 1-0	Watson	6,000
Oct 9	Leicester City	L 0-1		17,000
Oct 16	LEICESTER CITY	L 0-1		25,000
Oct 23	Blackpool	L 0-1		9,000
Oct 30	BLACKPOOL	D 1-1	Puddefoot	25,000
Nov 6	Sheffield Wednesday	W 1-0	Puddefoot	30,000
Nov 13	SHEFFIELD WEDNESDAY	W 4-0	Puddefoot 4	22,000
Nov 20	Stockport County	L 0-2		9,000
Nov 27	STOCKPORT COUNTY	W 5-0	Leafe 3, Puddefoot 2	20,000
Dec 4	Stoke	L 0-1		10,000
Dec 11	STOKE	W 1-0	Puddefoot	20,000
Dec 25	BIRMINGHAM	D 1-1	Bishop	37,000
Dec 27	Birmingham	L 1-2	Puddefoot	60,000
Jan 1	COVENTRY CITY	W 7-0	Puddefoot 4, Leafe 2, Bishop	8,000
Jan 15	Clapton Orient	W 1-0	Bishop	20,000
Jan 22	CLAPTON ORIENT	W 1-0	James	27,864
Jan 29	Leeds United	W 2-1	Carter, Puddefoot	15,000
Feb 5	LEEDS UNITED	W 3-0	Puddefoot 3	23,000
Feb 12	Bury	L 0-1		10,000
Feb 19	BURY	L 0-1		20,000
Feb 26	Bristol City	L 0-1		20,000
Mar 5	BRISTOL CITY	W 1-0	Puddefoot	25,000
Mar 12	Barnsley	D 1-1	Puddefoot	18,000
Mar 19	BARNSLEY	W 2-1	James, o.g.	20,000
Mar 25	NOTTS COUNTY	L 0-2		25,000
Mar 26	NOTTINGHAM FOREST	W 3-0	Puddefoot 2, Leafe	24,000
Mar 28	Notts County	D 1-1	Puddefoot	22,000
Apr 2	Nottingham Forest	L 0-1		8,000
Apr 9	ROTHERHAM COUNTY	W 1-0	Leafe	20,000
Apr 16	Rotherham County	L 0-2		7,000
Apr 23	PORT VALE	D 1-1	Robinson	15,000
Apr 30	Port Vale	W 2-1	James, Watson	12,000
May 2	SOUTH SHIELDS	W 2-1	Puddefoot, o.g.	15,000
May 7	South Shields	D 0-0		10,000

FA Cup

Jan 8	Sheffield Wednesday	(Rd 1) L 0-1		49,125

League & Cup Appearances

PLAYER	LEAGUE	CUP COMPETITION FA CUP	TOTAL
Allen	28	1	29
Bailey	8		8
Bishop	21	1	22
Bradshaw	1		1
Brown	1		1
Burton	30	1	31
Butcher	1		1
Calladine	1		1
Carter	20	1	21
Cope	36	1	37
Cowell	1		1
Crowther	3		3
Cumming	5		5
Gatland	1		1
Hampson	4		4
Hart	1		1
Hebden	1		1
Hufton	38	1	39
James	18		18
Kay	36	1	37
Lane	10		10
Leafe	13	1	14
Lee	9		9
McCrae	15		15
Palmer	1		1
Puddefoot	38	1	39
Robinson	5		5
Shea	16		16
Simmons	18		18
Smith	1		1
Smithurst	1		1
Tresadern	30	1	31
Watson	9		9
Woodards	7		7
Young	34	1	35

Goalscorers

PLAYER	LEAGUE	CUP COMPETITION FA CUP	TOTAL
Puddefoot	29		29
Leafe	7		7
Bishop	3		3
James	3		3
Watson	2		2
Kay	1		1
Shea	1		1
Simmons	1		1
Carter	1		1
Robinson	1		1
Opps' o.gs.	2		2

Fact File

The Christmas Day tie against Birmingham set a new record attendance at Upton Park of 37,000.

MANAGER: Syd King

CAPTAIN: Bill Cope

TOP SCORER: Syd Puddefoot

BIGGEST WIN: January 1, 1921 7-0 v Coventry City, Division 2

HIGHEST ATTENDANCE: December 27, 1920 60,000 v Birmingham, lost 1-2, Division 2

MAJOR TRANSFERS IN: Jimmy Simmons from Sheffield United, Danny Shea from Blackburn Rovers, Wilf James from Portsmouth, Jack Hebden from Bradford City

MAJOR TRANSFERS OUT: Danny Shea to Fulham, George Butcher to Luton

Final Division 2 Table

		P	W	D	L	F	A	Pts
1	Birmingham	42	24	10	8	79	38	58
2	Cardiff C	42	24	10	8	59	32	58
3	Bristol C	42	19	13	10	49	29	51
4	Blackpool	42	20	10	12	54	42	50
5	West Ham U	42	19	10	13	51	30	48
6	Notts Co	42	18	11	13	55	40	47
7	Clapton Orient	42	16	13	13	43	42	45
8	South Shields	42	17	10	15	61	46	44
9	Fulham	42	16	10	16	43	47	42
10	Sheffield W	42	15	11	16	48	48	41
11	Bury	42	15	10	17	45	49	40
12	Leicester C	42	12	16	14	39	46	40
13	Hull C	42	10	20	12	43	53	40
14	Leeds U	42	14	10	18	40	45	38
15	Wolverhampton W	42	16	6	20	49	66	38
16	Barnsley	42	10	16	16	48	50	36
17	Port Vale	42	11	14	17	43	49	36
18	Nottingham F	42	12	12	18	48	55	36
19	Rotherham Co	42	12	12	18	37	53	36
20	Stoke	42	12	11	19	46	56	35
21	Coventry C	42	12	11	19	39	70	35
22	Stockport Co	42	9	12	21	42	75	30

Season 1921-22

Football League Division 2

DATE	OPPONENTS	SCORE	GOALSCORERS	ATTENDANCE
Aug 27	Stoke	L 0-2		18,000
Aug 29	BRADFORD	W 1-0	o.g.	18,000
Sep 3	STOKE	W 3-0	Allen, Jackson, Puddefoot	20,000
Sep 5	Bradford	L 0-2		8,000
Sep 10	PORT VALE	W 3-0	Puddefoot 2, Watson	15,000
Sep 17	Port Vale	L 1-2	Watson	10,000
Sep 24	SOUTH SHIELDS	D 1-1	Puddefoot	20,000
Oct 1	South Shields	L 0-1		16,000
Oct 3	Coventry City	L 0-2		6,000
Oct 8	BRISTOL CITY	W 3-0	Puddefoot 2, Watson	18,000
Oct 15	Bristol City	W 1-0	Bishop	11,000
Oct 22	NOTTINGHAM FOREST	W 1-0	Watson	20,000
Oct 29	Nottingham Forest	L 0-2		16,000
Nov 5	WOLVERHAMPTON W	W 2-0	Kay, Thirlaway	16,000
Nov 12	Wolverhampton W	W 1-0	Bishop	8,000
Nov 19	BARNSLEY	W 4-0	Puddefoot 2, Bishop, Watson	18,000
Nov 26	Barnsley	D 1-1	Thirlaway	12,000
Dec 10	COVENTRY CITY	W 3-0	Puddefoot 2, Watson	18,000
Dec 17	DERBY COUNTY	W 3-1	Puddefoot 2, James	20,000
Dec 24	Derby County	L 1-3	Kay	5,000
Dec 26	Bury	W 1-0	Allen	20,000
Dec 27	BURY	W 3-2	Puddefoot 2, Bishop	28,785
Dec 31	LEICESTER CITY	W 1-0	Tresadern	20,000
Jan 14	Leicester City	L 1-2	Watson	16,000
Jan 21	Leeds United	D 0-0		7,000
Jan 28	LEEDS UNITED	D 1-1	James	20,000
Feb 4	Hull City	D 0-0		8,000
Feb 11	HULL CITY	D 1-1	Kay	18,000
Feb 25	NOTTS COUNTY	W 2-1	Watson 2	20,000
Mar 4	Crystal Palace	W 2-1	Allen, Watson	8,000
Mar 11	CRYSTAL PALACE	W 2-0	Tresadern, Watson	22,000
Mar 28	ROTHERHAM UNITED	L 1-2	Kay	20,000
Mar 25	Rotherham United	W 1-0	James	10,000
Mar 29	Notts County	D 1-1	Watson	7,000
Apr 1	SHEFFIELD WEDNESDAY	W 2-0	Allen, Kay	20,000
Apr 8	Sheffield Wednesday	L 1-2	Tresadern	4,000
Apr 14	CLAPTON ORIENT	L 1-2	James	30,000
Apr 15	FULHAM	W 1-0	Allen	25,000
Apr 17	Clapton Orient	D 0-0		30,000
Apr 22	Fulham	L 0-2		10,000
Apr 29	BLACKPOOL	L 0-2		18,000
May 6	Blackpool	L 1-3	Williams	12,000

FA Cup

Jan 7	Swansea Town	(Rd 1) D 0-0		26,000
Jan 11	SWANSEA TOWN	(R) D 1-1	Watson	20,000
Jan 16	SWANSEA TOWN	(2nd R) L 0-1*		8,976

* Played at Bristol City.

League & Cup Appearances

PLAYER	LEAGUE	CUP COMPETITION FA CUP	TOTAL
Allen	42	3	45
Bishop	36	3	39
Brown	7		7
Carter	3		3
Cope	41	3	44
Gurkin	1		1
Hampson	9		9
Hebden	19		19
Henderson	12		12
Hodgson	1		1
Hufton	33	3	36
Jackson	3		3
James	36	3	39
Kay	39	3	42
Leafe	3		3
Lee		2	2
Mackesy	1		1
Puddefoot	26	3	29
Robinson	10		10
Ruffell	14	1	15
Simmons	9		9
Smith	3		3
Thirlaway	33	3	36
Tresadern	28	2	30
Turner	4		4
Watson	37	3	40
Waugh	6	1	7
Williams	1		1
Young	5		5

Goalscorers

PLAYER	LEAGUE	CUP COMPETITION FA CUP	TOTAL
Puddefoot	14		14
Watson	12	1	13
Allen	5		5
Kay	5		5
Bishop	4		4
James	4		4
Tresadern	3		3
Thirlaway	2		2
Jackson	1		1
Williams	1		1
Opps' o.gs.	1		1

Fact File

This season saw West Ham remain unbeaten at Upton Park until the visit of Rotherham at the end of March.

MANAGER: Syd King

CAPTAIN: Bill Cope

TOP SCORER: Syd Puddefoot

BIGGEST WIN: November 19, 1921 4-0 v Barnsley, Division 2;

HIGHEST ATTENDANCE: April 14, 1922 30,000 v Clapton Orient (h), lost 1-2, Division 2; April 17, 1922 30,000 v Clapton Orient (a), drew 0-0, Division 2

MAJOR TRANSFERS OUT: Syd Puddefoot to Falkirk, Frank Burton to Charlton Athletic

Final Division 2 Table

		P	W	D	L	F	A	PTS
1	NOTTINGHAM F	42	22	12	8	51	30	56
2	STOKE	42	18	6	8	60	44	52
3	BARNSLEY	42	22	8	12	67	52	52
4	WEST HAM U	42	20	8	14	52	39	48
5	HULL C	42	19	10	13	51	41	48
6	SOUTH SHIELDS	42	17	12	13	43	38	46
7	FULHAM	42	18	9	15	57	38	45
8	LEEDS U	42	16	13	13	48	38	45
9	LEICESTER C	42	14	17	11	39	34	45
10	SHEFFIELD W	42	15	14	13	47	50	44
11	BURY	42	15	10	17	54	55	40
12	DERBY CO	42	15	9	18	60	64	39
13	NOTTS CO	42	12	15	15	47	51	39
14	CRYSTAL PALACE	42	13	13	16	45	51	39
15	CLAPTON ORIENT	42	15	9	18	43	50	39
16	ROTHERHAM CO	42	14	11	17	32	43	39
17	WOLVERHAMPTON W	42	13	11	18	44	49	37
18	PORT VALE	42	14	8	20	43	57	36
19	BLACKPOOL	42	15	5	22	44	57	35
20	COVENTRY C	42	12	10	20	51	60	34
21	BRADFORD PA	42	12	9	21	46	62	33
22	BRISTOL C	42	12	9	21	37	58	33

Season 1922-23

Football League Division 2

DATE	OPPONENTS	SCORE	GOALSCORERS	ATTENDANCE
Aug 26	BRADFORD CITY	L 1-2	Watson	25,000
Aug 28	DERBY COUNTY	D 0-0		16,000
Sep 2	Bradford City	W 1-0	Ruffell	20,000
Sep 4	Derby County	L 1-2	Moore	9,000
Sep 9	ROTHERHAM UNITED	W 4-0	Moore 2, Ruffell, Watson	15,000
Sep 16	Rotherham United	D 2-2	Robinson, Watson	9,000
Sep 23	STOCKPORT COUNTY	L 0-1		18,000
Sep 30	Stockport County	L 1-2	Moore	15,000
Oct 7	SOUTHAMPTON	D 1-1	Crossley	20,000
Oct 14	Southampton	L 0-2		17,000
Oct 21	BLACKPOOL	W 2-0	Watson 2	15,000
Oct 28	Blackpool	L 1-4	Moore	14,000
Nov 4	Leeds United	L 1-3	Moore	12,000
Nov 11	LEEDS UNITED	D 0-0		14,000
Nov 18	CLAPTON ORIENT	W 1-0	Watson	20,000
Nov 25	Clapton Orient	W 2-0	Watson 2	20,000
Dec 2	SOUTH SHIELDS	W 1-0	Moore	14,000
Dec 9	South Shields	D 0-0		7,000
Dec 16	Wolverhampton W	W 4-1	Brown 2, Moore, Watson	13,000
Dec 22	WOLVERHAMPTON W	W 1-0	Watson	15,000
Dec 25	Manchester United	W 2-1	Moore, Brown	17,500
Dec 26	MANCHESTER UNITED	L 0-2		20,000
Dec 30	Coventry City	W 3-1	Watson 3	14,000
Jan 6	COVENTRY CITY	W 1-0	Tresadern	16,000
Jan 20	Port Vale	W 3-1	Bishop, Ruffell, Richards	10,000
Jan 27	PORT VALE	D 0-0		17,000
Feb 10	LEICESTER CITY	D 2-2	Richards, Brown	16,000
Feb 15	Leicester City	W 6-0	Moore 3, Richards, Ruffell, Tresadern	6,000
Feb 17	BARNSLEY	D 0-0		20,000
Mar 3	SHEFFIELD WEDNESDAY	W 2-1	Brown, Moore	16,000
Mar 17	Hull City	D 1-1	Ruffell	10,000
Mar 30	BURY	D 0-0		30,000
Mar 31	Crystal Palace	W 5-1	Watson 4, Brown	14,000
Apr 2	BURY	W 5-2	Watson 2, Richards, Moore, Ruffell	25,000
Apr 7	CRYSTAL PALACE	D 1-1	Watson	25,000
Apr 9	HULL CITY	W 3-0	Brown 2, Richards	10,000
Apr 14	Fulham	W 2-0	Bishop, Moore	33,807
Apr 16	Barnsley	L 0-2		7,000
Apr 18	Notts County	L 0-2		10,000
Apr 21	FULHAM	W 1-0	Watson	20,000
Apr 30	Sheffield Wednesday	W 2-0	Brown, Watson	12,000
May 5	NOTTS COUNTY	L 0-1		26,000

FA Cup

Jan 13	Hull City	(Rd 1)	W 3-2	Watson 2, Moore	14,000
Feb 3	Brighton & Hove Albion	(Rd 2)	D 1-1	Watson	19,531
Feb 7	BRIGHTON & HOVE ALBION	(R)	W 1-0	Moore	20,000
Feb 24	PLYMOUTH ARGYLE	(Rd 3)	W 2-0	Moore, Richards	30,525
Mar 10	Southampton	(Rd 4)	D 1-1	Watson	21,960
Mar 14	SOUTHAMPTON	(R)	D 1-1	Watson	28,000
Mar 19	SOUTHAMPTON	(2nd R)	W 1-0*	Brown	22,184
Mar 24	DERBY COUNTY	(SF)	W 5-2**	Brown 2, Moore 2, Ruffell	50,795
Apr 28	BOLTON WANDERERS	(F)	L 0-2†		126,047

*Played at Villa Park. **Played at Stamford Bridge. †Played at Wembley.

MANAGER: Syd King

CAPTAIN: George Kay

TOP SCORER: Vic Watson

BIGGEST WIN: February 15, 1923 6-0 v Leicester City, Division 2

HIGHEST ATTENDANCE: April 28, 1923 126,047 v Bolton Wanderers, lost 0-2, FA Cup final

MAJOR TRANSFERS IN: Dick Richards from Wolves, Billy Charlton from South Shields, Charlie Crossley from Everton

League & Cup Appearances

PLAYER	LEAGUE	CUP COMPETITION FA CUP	TOTAL
Allen	6	1	7
Bishop	34	8	42
Brown	26	8	34
Burgess	2		2
Carter	10	4	14
Charlton	8		8
Crossley	15	1	16
Edwards	1		1
Fletcher	1		1
Hampson	3		3
Hebden	9		9
Henderson	34	9	43
Hodgson	11		11
Horler	5	2	7
Hufton	39	9	48
Kay	36	5	41
Mackesy	4		4
Moore	42	9	51
Richards	34	9	43
Robinson	3		3
Ruffell	33	9	42
Thirlaway	2		2
Tresadern	37	9	46
Watson	41	9	50
Williams	1		1
Young	25	7	32

Goalscorers

PLAYER	LEAGUE	CUP COMPETITION FA CUP	TOTAL
Watson	22	5	27
Moore	15	5	20
Brown	9	3	12
Ruffell	6	1	7
Richards	5	1	6
Bishop	2		2
Tresadern	2		2
Crossley	1		1
Robinson	1		1

Fact File

West Ham's run from 11 November of 32 league and cup games with only one defeat (against Manchester United on Boxing Day) earned them promotion and a Cup final place.

Final Division 2 Table

		P	W	D	L	F	A	PTS
1	Notts Co	42	23	7	12	46	34	53
2	West Ham U	42	20	11	11	63	38	51
3	Leicester C	42	21	9	12	65	44	51
4	Manchester U	42	17	14	11	51	36	48
5	Blackpool	42	18	11	13	60	43	47
6	Bury	42	18	11	13	55	46	47
7	Leeds U	42	18	11	13	43	36	47
8	Sheffield W	42	17	12	13	54	47	46
9	Barnsley	42	17	11	14	62	51	45
10	Fulham	42	16	12	14	43	32	44
11	Southampton	42	14	14	14	40	40	42
12	Hull C	42	14	14	14	43	45	42
13	South Shields	42	15	10	17	35	44	40
14	Derby Co	42	14	11	17	46	50	39
15	Bradford C	42	12	13	17	41	45	37
16	Crystal Palace	42	13	11	18	54	62	37
17	Port Vale	42	14	9	19	39	51	37
18	Coventry C	42	15	7	20	46	63	37
19	Clapton Orient	42	12	12	18	40	50	36
20	Stockport Co	42	14	8	20	43	58	36
21	Rotherham Co	42	13	9	20	44	63	35
22	Wolverhampton W	42	9	9	24	42	77	27

Season 1923-24

Football League Division 1

DATE	OPPONENTS	SCORE	GOALSCORERS	ATTENDANCE
Aug 25	Sunderland	D 0-0		35,000
Aug 27	ARSENAL	W 1-0	Fletcher	20,000
Sep 1	SUNDERLAND	L 0-1		25,000
Sep 8	CARDIFF CITY	D 0-0		30,000
Sep 10	Arsenal	L 1-4	Hodges	40,000
Sep 15	Cardiff City	L 0-1		33,000
Sep 22	MIDDLESBROUGH	D 1-1	Brown	20,000
Sep 29	Middlesbrough	W 1-0	Yews	22,000
Oct 6	Newcastle United	D 0-0		25,000
Oct 13	NEWCASTLE UNITED	W 1-0	Brown	30,000
Oct 20	Chelsea	D 0-0		51,000
Oct 27	CHELSEA	W 2-0	Kay, Brown	26,000
Nov 3	BIRMINGHAM	W 4-1	Brown, Richardson, Kay, Moore	22,000
Nov 10	Birmingham	L 0-2		22,000
Nov 17	Burnley	L 1-5	Moore	5,000
Nov 24	BURNLEY	D 0-0		20,000
Dec 1	Bolton Wanderers	D 1-1	Brown	20,000
Dec 8	BOLTON WANDERERS	L 0-1		28,000
Dec 15	Nottingham Forest	L 1-2	Edwards	10,000
Dec 22	NOTTINGHAM FOREST	W 3-2	Moore 2, Kay	15,000
Dec 25	Aston Villa	D 1-1	Richardson	40,000
Dec 26	ASTON VILLA	W 1-0	Moore	26,000
Dec 29	Liverpool	L 0-2		24,000
Jan 1	Sheffield United	W 2-0	Gibbins, Brown	30,000
Jan 5	LIVERPOOL	W 1-0	Moore	25,000
Jan 19	Blackburn Rovers	D 0-0		22,000
Jan 26	BLACKBURN ROVERS	L 0-1		20,000
Feb 9	TOTTENHAM HOTSPUR	D 0-0		30,000
Feb 16	Huddersfield Town	D 1-1	Ruffell	10,000
Mar 1	Notts County	D 1-1	Collins	10,000
Mar 8	NOTTS COUNTY	D 1-1	Proctor	20,000
Mar 15	EVERTON	W 2-1	Campbell, Edwards	22,000
Mar 22	Everton	L 1-2	Moore	20,000
Mar 27	HUDDERSFIELD TOWN	L 2-3	Young 2	15,000
Mar 29	WEST BROMWICH ALBION	W 1-0	Ruffell	18,000
Apr 5	West Bromwich Albion	D 0-0		12,000
Apr 12	PRESTON NORTH END	W 3-1	Watson, Moore, Edwards	18,000
Apr 19	Preston North End	L 1-2	Watson	18,000
Apr 21	SHEFFIELD UNITED	D 2-2	Campbell 2	15,000
Apr 22	Tottenham Hotspur	W 1-0	Campbell	20,000
Apr 26	MANCHESTER CITY	L 1-2	Moore	18,000
May 3	Manchester City	L 1-2	Watson	12,000

FA Cup

Jan 12	ABERDARE	(Rd 1) W 5-0	Brown 2, Henderson, Moore, Williams	23,000
Feb 2	LEEDS UNITED	(Rd 2) D 1-1	Kay	30,123
Feb 6	Leeds United	(R) L 0-1		32,000

League & Cup Appearances

PLAYER	LEAGUE	CUP COMPETITION FA CUP	TOTAL
Bishop	31		31
Brown	26	3	29
Cadwell	29	3	32
Campbell	11		11
Carter	16	3	19
Collins	5		5
Edwards	25	2	27
Fletcher	7		7
Gibbins	3		3
Hampson	27	3	30
Hebden	2		2
Henderson	42	3	45
Hodges	2		2
Hodgson	5		5
Hufton	15		15
Kay	40	3	43
Moore	36	3	39
Proctor	7		7
Richards	9	1	10
Richardson	10	1	11
Robinson	1		1
Ruffell	39	3	42
Thirlaway	1		1
Tresadern	10		10
Watson	11		11
Williams	5	2	7
Yews	12		12
Young	35	3	38

Goalscorers

PLAYER	LEAGUE	CUP COMPETITION FA CUP	TOTAL
Moore	9	1	10
Brown	6	2	8
Kay	3	1	4
Campbell	4		4
Watson	3		3
Edwards	3		3
Ruffell	2		2
Young	2		2
Richardson	2		2
Henderson		1	1
Fletcher	1		1
Hodges	1		1
Yews	1		1
Proctor	1		1
Gibbins	1		1
Williams	1		1
Collins	1		1

Fact File

Ted Hufton and Bill Brown both made their debuts for England against Belgium in November. Brown scored in the 2-2 draw but would never win another cap.

MANAGER: Syd King
CAPTAIN: George Kay
TOP SCORER: Billy Moore
BIGGEST WIN: January 12, 1924 4-1 v Aberdare, FA Cup Round 1
HIGHEST ATTENDANCE: October 20, 1923 51,000 v Chelsea, drew 0-0, Division 1
MAJOR TRANSFERS IN: Tommy Yews from Hartlepool United, Norman Proctor from Rotherham County

Final Division 1 Table

		P	W	D	L	F	A	PTS
1	Huddersfield T	42	23	11	8	60	33	57
2	Cardiff C	42	22	13	7	61	34	57
3	Sunderland	42	22	9	11	71	54	53
4	Bolton W	42	18	14	10	68	34	50
5	Sheffield U	42	19	12	11	69	49	50
6	Aston Villa	42	18	13	11	52	37	49
7	Everton	42	18	13	11	62	53	49
8	Blackburn R	42	17	11	14	54	50	45
9	Newcastle U	42	17	10	15	60	54	44
10	Notts Co	42	14	14	14	44	49	42
11	Manchester C	42	15	12	15	54	71	42
12	Liverpool	42	15	11	16	49	48	41
13	West Ham U	42	13	15	14	40	43	41
14	Birmingham	42	13	13	16	41	49	39
15	Tottenham H	42	12	14	16	50	56	38
16	WBA	42	12	14	16	51	62	38
17	Burnley	42	12	12	18	55	60	36
18	Preston NE	42	12	10	20	52	67	34
19	The Arsenal	42	12	9	21	40	63	33
20	Nottingham F	42	10	12	20	42	64	32
21	Chelsea	42	9	14	19	31	53	32
22	Middlesbrough	42	7	8	27	37	60	22

Season 1924-25

Football League Division 1

DATE	OPPONENTS	SCORE	GOALSCORERS	ATTENDANCE
Aug 30	PRESTON NORTH END	W 1-0	Jennings	25,000
Sep 6	Blackburn Rovers	W 1-0	Earle	18,000
Sep 8	NEWCASTLE UNITED	D 0-0		22,000
Sep 13	HUDDERSFIELD TOWN	D 0-0		28,103
Sep 17	Newcastle United	L 1-4	Watson	25,000
Sep 20	Aston Villa	D 1-1	Watson	30,000
Sep 22	Sheffield United	D 1-1	Watson	10,000
Sep 27	ARSENAL	W 1-0	Earle	31,000
Oct 4	Manchester City	L 1-3	o.g.	45,000
Oct 11	BURY	D 1-1	Young	22,000
Oct 18	Nottingham Forest	L 1-2	Jennings	13,000
Oct 25	BURNLEY	W 2-0	Moore, Ruffell	22,000
Nov 1	Leeds United	L 1-2	Watson	17,000
Nov 8	BIRMINGHAM	L 0-1		28,000
Nov 15	West Bromwich Albion	L 1-4	Watson	16,000
Nov 22	TOTTENHAM HOTSPUR	D 1-1	Watson	26,000
Nov 29	Bolton Wanderers	L 0-5		33,000
Dec 6	NOTTS COUNTY	W 3-0	Williams 2, Watson	18,000
Dec 13	Everton	L 0-1		15,000
Dec 20	SUNDERLAND	W 4-1	Watson 2, Moore 2	20,000
Dec 25	CARDIFF CITY	W 3-2	Moore, Watson, Kay	25,000
Dec 26	Cardiff City	L 1-2	Watson	30,000
Dec 27	Preston North End	L 2-3	Watson, Williams	9,000
Jan 3	BLACKBURN ROVERS	W 2-0	Watson, Moore	16,000
Jan 17	Huddersfield Town	W 2-1	Watson, Ruffell	14,000
Jan 24	ASTON VILLA	W 2-0	Watson, Williams	20,000
Feb 7	MANCHESTER CITY	W 4-0	Moore 2, Ruffell, Watson	25,000
Feb 14	Bury	L 2-4	Watson, Yews	15,000
Feb 28	Burnley	L 4-5	Ruffell, Moore, Jennings, Watson	10,000
Mar 7	LEEDS UNITED	D 0-0		15,000
Mar 14	Birmingham	D 1-1	Campbell	20,000
Mar 21	WEST BROMWICH ALBION	W 2-1	Kay, Ruffell	25,000
Mar 23	Arsenal	W 2-1	Ruffell, Campbell	10,000
Mar 28	Tottenham Hotspur	D 1-1	Watson	35,000
Apr 2	NOTTINGHAM FOREST	D 0-0		8,000
Apr 4	BOLTON WANDERERS	D 1-1	Campbell	25,000
Apr 10	Liverpool	L 0-2		30,000
Apr 11	Notts County	L 1-4	Ruffell	10,000
Apr 13	LIVERPOOL	L 0-1		12,000
Apr 14	SHEFFIELD UNITED	W 6-2	Watson 2, Ruffell 2, Earle, Moore	12,000
Apr 18	EVERTON	W 4-1	Earle 2, Moore, Watson	15,000
Apr 25	Sunderland	D 1-1	Earle	10,000

FA Cup

Jan 14	ARSENAL	(Rd 3) D 0-0		26,000
Jan 21	Arsenal	(R) D 2-2	Ruffell 2	34,160
Jan 26	ARSENAL	(2nd R) W 1-0*	Kay	36,955
Jan 31	Nottingham Forest	(Rd 4) W 2-0	Ruffell, Yews	10,955
Feb 21	BLACKPOOL	(Rd 5) D 1-1	Watson	30,000
Feb 25	Blackpool	(R) L 0-3		15,190

*Played at Stamford Bridge.

Fact File

Vic Watson scored 11 goals in ten consecutive matches in the winter of 1924.

MANAGER: Syd King
CAPTAIN: George Kay
TOP SCORER: Vic Watson
BIGGEST WIN: April 14, 1925 6-2 v Sheffield United, Division 1
HIGHEST ATTENDANCE: October 4, 1924 45,000 v Manchester City, lost 1-3, Division 1
MAJOR TRANSFERS IN: Stanley Earle from Arsenal
MAJOR TRANSFERS OUT: Bill Brown to Chelsea, Norman Proctor to Leicester City, Frank Richardson to Swindon Town

League & Cup Appearances

PLAYER	LEAGUE	CUP COMPETITION FA CUP	TOTAL
Barrett	5		5
Bishop	14		14
Cadwell	40	6	46
Campbell	10		10
Carter	19	5	24
Collins	2	1	3
Cowper	2		2
Earle	18		18
Eastman	1		1
Edwards	7		7
Gibbins	1		1
Hampson	27	6	33
Hebden	4	3	7
Henderson	41	6	47
Hodgson	1		1
Horler	15		15
Hufton	8		8
Jennings	9		9
Kaine	7		7
Kay	41	6	47
Moore	32	6	38
Ruffell	42	6	48
Tresadern	4		4
Watson	41	6	47
Williams	15	6	21
Yews	33	6	39
Young	23	3	26

Goalscorers

PLAYER	LEAGUE	CUP COMPETITION FA CUP	TOTAL
Watson	22	1	23
Ruffell	9	3	12
Moore	10		10
Earle	6		6
Williams	4		4
Jennings	3		3
Campbell	3		3
Kay	2	1	3
Yews	1	1	2
Young	1		1
Opps' o.gs.	1		1

Final Division 1 Table

	P	W	D	L	F	A	Pts
1 Huddersfield T	42	21	16	5	69	28	58
2 WBA	42	23	10	9	58	34	56
3 Bolton W	42	22	11	9	76	34	55
4 Liverpool	42	20	10	12	63	55	50
5 Bury	42	17	15	10	54	51	49
6 Newcastle U	42	16	16	10	61	42	48
7 Sunderland	42	19	10	13	64	51	48
8 Birmingham	42	17	12	13	49	53	46
9 Notts Co	42	16	13	13	42	31	45
10 Manchester C	42	17	9	16	76	68	43
11 Cardiff C	42	16	11	15	56	51	43
12 Tottenham H	42	15	12	15	52	43	42
13 West Ham U	42	15	12	15	62	60	42
14 Sheffield U	42	13	13	16	55	63	39
15 Aston Villa	42	13	13	16	58	71	39
16 Blackburn R	42	11	13	18	53	66	35
17 Everton	42	12	11	19	40	60	35
18 Leeds U	42	11	12	19	46	59	34
19 Burnley	42	11	12	19	46	75	34
20 The Arsenal	42	14	5	23	46	58	33
21 Preston NE	42	10	6	26	37	74	26
22 Nottingham F	42	6	12	24	29	65	24

Season 1925-26

Football League Division 1

DATE	OPPONENTS	SCORE	GOALSCORERS	ATTENDANCE
Aug 29	MANCHESTER UNITED	W 1-0	Earle	29,000
Aug 31	CARDIFF CITY	W 3-1	Watson 2, Earle	20,000
Sep 5	Liverpool	D 0-0		30,000
Sep 7	Cardiff City	W 1-0	Watson	25,000
Sep 12	BURNLEY	W 2-0	Ruffell 2	28,000
Sep 19	Leeds United	L 2-5	Watson 2	16,000
Sep 21	Arsenal	L 2-3	Ruffell, Watson	27,000
Sep 26	NEWCASTLE UNITED	W 1-0	Watson	30,000
Oct 3	Bolton Wanderers	L 0-1		18,068
Oct 5	ARSENAL	L 0-4		25,000
Oct 10	NOTTS COUNTY	W 1-0	Williams	29,500
Oct 17	SHEFFIELD UNITED	L 1-3	Earle	22,000
Oct 24	West Bromwich Albion	L 1-7	Ruffell	20,000
Oct 31	MANCHESTER CITY	W 3-1	Ruffell, Bishop, Earle	23,000
Nov 7	Tottenham Hotspur	L 2-4	Yews, Barrett	35,000
Nov 14	BLACKBURN ROVERS	W 2-1	Moore, Watson	25,000
Nov 21	Sunderland	L 1-4	Watson	12,000
Nov 28	HUDDERSFIELD TOWN	L 2-3	Ruffell, Watson	18,000
Dec 5	Everton	L 0-2		25,000
Dec 12	BIRMINGHAM	D 2-2	Watson, Ruffell	18,000
Dec 19	Bury	L 1-4	Watson	12,000
Dec 25	ASTON VILLA	W 5-2	Earle 3, Williams, Watson	27,000
Dec 26	Aston Villa	L 0-2		55,000
Jan 2	Manchester United	L 1-2	Ruffell	28,000
Jan 16	LIVERPOOL	L 1-2	Watson	25,000
Jan 23	Burnley	D 2-2	Barrett, Williams	10,000
Jan 30	LEEDS UNITED	W 4-2	Barrett 3, Moore	22,000
Feb 6	Newcastle United	L 1-4	Barrett	25,000
Feb 13	BOLTON WANDERERS	W 6-0	Gibbins 2, Ruffell 2, Watson 2	30,000
Feb 27	Sheffield United	D 1-1	Moore	25,000
Mar 6	WEST BROMWICH ALBION	W 3-0	Watson 2, Moore	25,000
Mar 13	Manchester City	L 0-2		40,000
Mar 20	TOTTENHAM HOTSPUR	W 3-1	Watson, Ruffell, Kay	35,000
Mar 22	Notts County	D 1-1	Ruffell	9,000
Mar 27	Blackburn Rovers	L 0-1		15,000
Apr 2	LEICESTER CITY	D 1-1	Watson	30,000
Apr 3	SUNDERLAND	W 3-2	Campbell 2, Earle	28,000
Apr 5	Leicester City	D 1-1	Campbell	20,000
Apr 10	Huddersfield Town	L 1-2	Earle	20,000
Apr 17	EVERTON	W 1-0	Campbell	25,000
Apr 24	Birmingham	L 0-1		15,000
May 1	BURY	L 0-2		18,000

FA Cup

Jan 9	Tottenham Hotspur	(Rd 3) L 0-5		49,800

League & Cup Appearances

PLAYER	LEAGUE	CUP COMPETITION FA CUP	TOTAL
Baillie	3		3
Barrett	42	1	43
Bishop	14	1	15
Cadwell	18		18
Campbell	6		6
Carter	29		29
Collins	24	1	25
Earl	8	1	9
Earle	37	1	38
Eastman	1		1
Edwards	4		4
Gibbins	1		1
Hebden	24		24
Henderson	17	1	18
Hodgson	16		16
Horler	5		5
Hufton	38	1	39
Kaine	1		1
Kay	18		18
Moore	30		30
Ruffell	40	1	41
Watson	38	1	39
Weale	3		3
Williams	12	1	13
Yews	32	1	33
Young	1		1

Goalscorers

PLAYER	LEAGUE	CUP COMPETITION FA CUP	TOTAL
Watson	20		20
Ruffell	12		12
Earle	9		9
Barrett	6		6
Moore	4		4
Campbell	4		4
Williams	3		3
Gibbins	2		2
Yews	1		1
Kay	1		1
Bishop	1		1

Fact File

'Big' Jim Barrett, who played in many positions for the club, scored five times in three matches this season when utilised as a forward.

MANAGER: Syd King
CAPTAIN: Billy Moore
TOP SCORER: Vic Watson
BIGGEST WIN: February 13, 1926 6-0 v Bolton Wanderers, Division 1
HIGHEST ATTENDANCE: December 26, 1925 55,000 v Aston Villa, lost 0-2, Division 1

Final Division 1 Table

		P	W	D	L	F	A	PTS
1	Huddersfield T	42	23	11	8	92	60	57
2	The Arsenal	42	22	8	12	87	63	52
3	Sunderland	42	21	6	15	96	80	48
4	Bury	42	20	7	15	85	77	47
5	Sheffield U	42	19	8	15	102	82	46
6	Aston Villa	42	16	12	14	86	76	44
7	Liverpool	42	14	16	12	70	63	44
8	Bolton W	42	17	10	15	75	76	44
9	Manchester U	42	19	6	17	66	73	44
10	Newcastle U	42	16	10	16	84	75	42
11	Everton	42	12	18	12	72	70	42
12	Blackburn R	42	15	11	16	91	80	41
13	WBA	42	16	8	18	79	78	40
14	Birmingham	42	16	8	18	66	81	40
15	Tottenham H	42	15	9	18	66	79	39
16	Cardiff C	42	16	7	19	61	76	39
17	Leicester C	42	14	10	18	70	80	38
18	West Ham U	42	15	7	20	63	76	37
19	Leeds U	42	14	8	20	64	76	36
20	Burnley	42	13	10	19	85	108	36
21	Manchester C	42	12	11	19	89	100	35
22	Notts Co	42	13	7	22	54	74	33

Season 1926-27

Football League Division 1

DATE	OPPONENTS	SCORE	GOALSCORERS	ATTENDANCE
Aug 28	LEICESTER CITY	D 3-3	Earle, Ruffell, Watson	20,000
Sep 4	Everton	W 3-0	Watson 2, Moore	30,000
Sep 6	Sheffield Wednesday	L 0-1		20,000
Sep 11	BLACKBURN ROVERS	L 1-5	Watson	18,000
Sep 18	Huddersfield Town	L 1-2	Watson	16,000
Sep 25	SUNDERLAND	L 1-2	Yews	27,000
Oct 2	West Bromwich Albion	W 3-1	Ruffell, Watson, Earle	18,000
Oct 4	SHEFFIELD WEDNESDAY	D 1-1	Earle	15,000
Oct 9	BURY	L 1-2	Watson	20,000
Oct 16	Arsenal	D 2-2	Gibbins, Watson	40,000
Oct 23	Sheffield United	W 2-0	Ruffell 2	20,000
Oct 30	MANCHESTER UNITED	W 4-0	Gibbins, Watson, Yews, o.g.	20,000
Nov 6	Bolton Wanderers	L 0-2		12,000
Nov 13	ASTON VILLA	W 5-1	Watson 3, Yews, Earle	11,000
Nov 20	Cardiff City	W 2-1	Yews, Watson	11,000
Nov 27	BURNLEY	W 2-1	Watson, Gibbins	20,000
Dec 4	Newcastle United	L 0-2		30,000
Dec 11	LEEDS UNITED	W 3-2	Gibbins, Ruffell, Watson	35,000
Dec 18	Liverpool	D 0-0		25,000
Dec 25	BIRMINGHAM	W 1-0	Earle	30,000
Dec 27	Birmingham	W 2-0	Ruffell, Watson	35,000
Dec 28	Derby County	L 0-3		22,000
Jan 1	DERBY COUNTY	L 1-2	Watson	18,000
Jan 15	Leicester City	L 0-3		20,000
Jan 22	EVERTON	W 2-1	Moore, Watson	12,000
Feb 5	HUDDERSFIELD TOWN	W 3-2	Johnson, Watson, Yews	22,000
Feb 12	Sunderland	W 3-2	Earle, Watson, Yews	10,000
Feb 14	Blackburn Rovers	L 1-4	Yews	10,000
Feb 19	WEST BROMWICH ALBION	L 1-2	Watson	18,000
Feb 26	Bury	W 2-1	Johnson, Yews	15,000
Mar 7	ARSENAL	W 7-0	Watson 3, Johnson, Ruffell, o.g. 2	28,000
Mar 12	SHEFFIELD UNITED	W 3-0	Earle 2, Watson	18,000
Mar 19	Manchester United	W 3-0	Watson 2, Johnson	20,000
Mar 26	BOLTON WANDERERS	D 4-4	Ruffell 2, Watson, Earle	20,000
Apr 2	Aston Villa	W 5-1	Watson 2, Earle, Johnson, Ruffell	20,000
Apr 9	CARDIFF CITY	D 2-2	Earle, Watson	15,000
Apr 15	Tottenham Hotspur	W 3-1	Ruffell 2, Earle	40,000
Apr 16	Burnley	L 1-2	Watson	18,000
Apr 18	TOTTENHAM HOTSPUR	L 1-2	Earle	26,000
Apr 23	NEWCASTLE UNITED	D 1-1	Ruffell	36,000
Apr 30	Leeds United	L 3-6	Watson 2, Johnson	10,000
May 7	LIVERPOOL	D 3-3	Johnson, Collins, Barrett	15,000

FA Cup

Jan 8	TOTTENHAM HOTSPUR	(Rd 3) W 3-2	Watson 3	44,417
Jan 29	BRENTFORD	(Rd 4) D 1-1	Ruffell	40,000
Feb 2	Brentford	(R) L 0-2		25,000

League & Cup Appearances

PLAYER	LEAGUE	CUP COMPETITION FA CUP	TOTAL
Baillie	1		1
Barrett	42	3	45
Bishop	9		9
Cadwell	13		13
Campbell		1	1
Carter	26	3	29
Collins	42	3	45
Dowsey	1		1
Earl	1		1
Earle	42	3	45
Gibbins	22	1	23
Hebden	39	3	42
Hodgson	16		16
Horler	20	3	23
Hufton	40	3	43
Hull	1		1
Johnson	14		14
Kaine	1		1
Moore	12	1	13
Payne	1		1
Ruffell	37	3	40
Watson	42	3	45
Williams	1		1
Yews	39	3	42

Goalscorers

PLAYER	LEAGUE	CUP COMPETITION FA CUP	TOTAL
Watson	34	3	37
Ruffell	13	1	14
Earle	13		13
Yews	8		8
Johnson	7		7
Gibbins	4		4
Moore	2		2
Barrett	1		1
Collins	1		1
Opps' o.gs.	3		3

Fact File

For the first time since the opening of the new West Stand in 1925, the Boleyn Ground record attendance was broken when 44,417 watched the Hammers beat Tottenham in the FA Cup in January.

MANAGER: Syd King
CAPTAIN: Jack Hebden
TOP SCORER: Vic Watson
BIGGEST WIN: March 7, 1927 7-0 v Arsenal, Division 1
HIGHEST ATTENDANCE: January 8, 1927 44,417 v Tottenham Hotspur, won 3-2, FA Cup Round 3

Final Division 1 Table

		P	W	D	L	F	A	Pts
1	Newcastle U	42	25	6	11	96	58	56
2	Huddersfield T	42	17	17	8	76	60	51
3	Sunderland	42	21	7	14	98	70	49
4	Bolton W	42	19	10	13	84	62	48
5	Burnley	42	19	9	14	91	80	47
6	West Ham U	42	19	8	15	86	70	46
7	Leicester C	42	17	12	13	85	70	46
8	Sheffield U	42	17	10	15	74	86	44
9	Liverpool	42	18	7	17	69	61	43
10	Aston Villa	42	18	7	17	81	83	43
11	The Arsenal	42	17	9	16	77	86	43
12	Derby Co	42	17	7	18	86	73	41
13	Tottenham H	42	16	9	17	76	78	41
14	Cardiff C	42	16	9	17	55	65	41
15	Manchester U	42	13	14	15	52	64	40
16	Sheffield W	42	15	9	18	75	92	39
17	Birmingham	42	17	4	21	64	73	38
18	Blackburn R	42	15	8	19	77	96	38
19	Bury	42	12	12	18	68	77	36
20	Everton	42	12	10	20	64	90	34
21	Leeds U	42	11	8	23	69	88	30
22	WBA	42	11	8	23	65	86	30

Season 1927-28

Football League Division 1

DATE	OPPONENTS	SCORE	GOALSCORERS	ATTENDANCE
Aug 27	Derby County	W 3-2	Barrett, Watson, Gibbins	19,000
Sep 1	SUNDERLAND	L 2-4	Ruffell 2	22,000
Sep 3	HUDDERSFIELD TOWN	W 4-2	Earle 2, Yews, Loughlin	28,000
Sep 10	PORTSMOUTH	W 4-2	Loughlin 2, Earle, Ruffell	25,000
Sep 17	Leicester City	W 3-2	Yews, Ruffell, Earle	30,000
Sep 24	LIVERPOOL	W 3-1	Earle, Gibbins, Ruffell	32,000
Oct 1	Arsenal	D 2-2	Gibbins, Earle	40,000
Oct 8	BURNLEY	W 2-0	Gibbins 2	10,000
Oct 15	Bury	L 1-3	Ruffell	18,000
Oct 22	Everton	L 0-7		10,000
Oct 29	MANCHESTER UNITED	L 1-2	Watson	28,000
Nov 5	Tottenham Hotspur	L 3-5	Barrett, Ruffell, Earle	36,000
Nov 12	CARDIFF CITY	W 2-0	Yews, Watson	28,000
Nov 19	Blackburn Rovers	L 0-1		15,000
Nov 26	MIDDLESBROUGH	L 4-5	Yews 2, Gibbins, Watson	15,000
Dec 3	Sheffield Wednesday	L 0-2		25,000
Dec 10	BOLTON WANDERERS	W 2-0	Watson 2	20,000
Dec 17	Birmingham	W 2-1	Yews, Ruffell	30,000
Dec 24	NEWCASTLE UNITED	W 5-2	Ruffell 2, Gibbins 3	25,000
Dec 26	Sheffield United	L 2-6	Yews, Gibbins	25,000
Dec 27	SHEFFIELD UNITED	D 1-1	Yews	20,000
Dec 31	DERBY COUNTY	D 2-2	Watson, Ruffell	22,000
Jan 2	Sunderland	L 2-3	Gibbins 2	23,000
Jan 7	Huddersfield Town	L 2-5	Watson, Yews	8,000
Jan 21	Portsmouth	L 1-2	Gibbins	15,000
Feb 4	Liverpool	W 3-1	Earle, Gibbins, Ruffell	32,000
Feb 11	ARSENAL	D 2-2	Watson 2	35,000
Feb 18	Burnley	D 0-0		12,000
Feb 25	BURY	L 1-2	Ruffell	25,000
Mar 3	EVERTON	D 0-0		32,000
Mar 10	Manchester United	D 1-1	Earle	25,000
Mar 12	LEICESTER CITY	W 4-0	Watson 3, Yews	10,000
Mar 17	TOTTENHAM HOTSPUR	D 1-1	Ruffell	35,000
Mar 24	Cardiff City	W 5-1	Earle 2, Watson 2, Yews	18,000
Mar 31	BLACKBURN ROVERS	W 4-3	Ruffell 2, Moore, Earle	25,000
Apr 6	ASTON VILLA	D 0-0		36,000
Apr 7	Middlesbrough	D 2-2	Moore, Ruffell	25,000
Apr 9	Aston Villa	L 0-1		35,000
Apr 14	SHEFFIELD WEDNESDAY	L 1-2	Barrett	15,000
Apr 21	Bolton Wanderers	L 0-4		10,000
Apr 28	BIRMINGHAM	D 3-3	Barrett 2, Loughlin	16,000
May 5	Newcastle United	L 1-3	Gibbins	20,000

FA Cup

Jan 14	Portsmouth	(Rd 3)	W 2-0	Gibbins, Ruffell	27,692
Jan 28	Huddersfield Town	(Rd 4)	L 1-2	Gibbins	27,000

League & Cup Appearances

PLAYER	LEAGUE	CUP COMPETITION FA CUP	TOTAL
Baillie	10		10
Barrett	34		34
Cadwell	27	2	29
Campbell	1		1
Collins	42	2	44
Cox	26	2	28
Earl	33	2	35
Earle	33	1	34
Gibbins	25	2	27
Hebden	12		12
Henderson	16	2	18
Hodgson	5		5
Horler	2		2
Hufton	23	2	25
Jackson	2		2
Johnson	1		1
Loughlin	10		10
Moore	23	1	24
Norrington	13		13
Robson	1		1
Ruffell	39	2	41
Smith H	1		1
Smith W	1		1
Tate	7		7
Watson	33	2	35
Yews	42	2	44

Goalscorers

PLAYER	LEAGUE	CUP COMPETITION FA CUP	TOTAL
Ruffell	18	1	19
Gibbins	15	2	17
Watson	15		15
Yews	11		11
Earle	11		11
Barrett	5		5
Loughlin	4		4
Moore	2		2

Fact File

Stanley Earle won his only England cap in their 2-0 defeat by Northern Ireland in Belfast.

MANAGER: Syd King
CAPTAIN: Jack Hebden
TOP SCORER: Jimmy Ruffell
BIGGEST WIN: March 24, 1928 5-1 v Cardiff City, Division 1
HIGHEST ATTENDANCE: October 1, 1927 40,000 v Arsenal, drew 2-2, Division 1
MAJOR TRANSFERS IN: James Loughlin from Newcastle United
MAJOR TRANSFERS OUT: Jack Hebden and George Horler to Fulham

Final Division 1 Table

		P	W	D	L	F	A	PTS
1	Everton	42	20	13	9	102	66	53
2	Huddersfield T	42	22	7	13	91	68	51
3	Leicester C	42	18	12	12	96	72	48
4	Derby Co	42	17	10	15	96	83	44
5	Bury	42	20	4	18	80	80	44
6	Cardiff C	42	17	10	15	70	80	44
7	Bolton W	42	16	11	15	81	66	43
8	Aston Villa	42	17	9	16	78	73	43
9	Newcastle U	42	15	13	14	79	81	43
10	Arsenal	42	13	15	14	82	86	41
11	Birmingham	42	13	15	14	70	75	41
12	Blackburn R	42	16	9	17	66	78	41
13	Sheffield U	42	15	10	17	79	86	40
14	Sheffield W	42	13	13	16	81	78	39
15	Sunderland	42	15	9	18	74	76	39
16	Liverpool	42	13	13	16	84	87	39
17	West Ham U	42	14	11	17	81	88	39
18	Manchester U	42	16	7	19	72	80	39
19	Burnley	42	16	7	19	82	98	39
20	Portsmouth	42	16	7	19	66	90	39
21	Tottenham H	42	15	8	19	74	86	38
22	Middlesbrough	42	11	15	16	81	88	37

Season 1928-29

Football Leaague Division 1

DATE	OPPONENTS	SCORE	GOALSCORERS	ATTENDANCE
Aug 25	SHEFFIELD UNITED	W 4-0	Ruffell 2, Barrett, Shone	30,000
Sep 1	Bury	W 3-0	Watson 2, Ruffell	16,000
Sep 3	Burnley	D 3-3	Watson 2, Yews	22,000
Sep 8	ASTON VILLA	W 4-1	Watson 2, Ruffell, Collins	38,000
Sep 10	Cardiff City	L 2-3	Watson, Ruffell	20,000
Sep 15	Leicester City	L 0-5		25,000
Sep 17	CARDIFF CITY	D 1-1	Watson	18,000
Sep 22	MANCHESTER UNITED	W 3-1	Shone 2, Payne	30,000
Sep 29	Leeds United	L 1-4	Watson	30,000
Oct 6	LIVERPOOL	D 1-1	Earle	30,000
Oct 13	Arsenal	W 3-2	Earle, Shone, Ruffell	48,000
Oct 20	EVERTON	L 2-4	Shone, Gibbins	25,000
Oct 29	Blackburn Rovers	L 0-2		20,000
Nov 3	MANCHESTER CITY	W 3-0	Ruffell 2, Yews	26,000
Nov 10	Birmingham	D 2-2	Gibbins, Earle	25,000
Nov 17	PORTSMOUTH	L 0-1		18,000
Nov 24	Bolton Wanderers	L 1-4	Gibbins	10,000
Dec 1	SHEFFIELD WEDNESDAY	W 3-2	Yews 2, Watson	25,000
Dec 8	Derby County	L 0-6		20,000
Dec 15	SUNDERLAND	D 3-3	Ruffell 2, Robson	20,000
Dec 22	Huddersfield Town	L 0-4		12,000
Dec 25	NEWCASTLE UNITED	W 1-0	Gibbins	30,000
Dec 26	Newcastle United	L 0-1		40,000
Dec 29	Sheffield United	D 3-3	Yews, Watson, Ruffell	25,000
Jan 5	BURY	L 2-3	Yews, Watson	15,000
Jan 19	Aston Villa	L 2-5	Watson, Ruffell	30,000
Feb 2	Manchester United	W 3-2	Watson, Gibbins, Ruffell	15,000
Feb 9	LEEDS UNITED	W 8-2	Watson 6, Gibbins, Yews	18,055
Feb 23	ARSENAL	L 3-4	Ruffell 2, Watson	35,000
Mar 4	LEICESTER CITY	W 2-1	Ruffell, Earle	10,000
Mar 9	BLACKBURN ROVERS	D 3-3	Yews 2, Watson	30,000
Mar 12	Liverpool	L 1-2	Watson	12,000
Mar 16	Manchester City	L 2-4	Ruffell, Watson	30,000
Mar 23	BIRMINGHAM	W 2-1	Earle, Watson	20,000
Mar 29	BURNLEY	W 4-0	Ruffell 2, Gibbins, Yews	20,000
Mar 30	Portsmouth	L 0-3		22,000
Apr 6	BOLTON WANDERERS	W 3-0	Watson, Earle, Gibbins	30,000
Apr 10	Everton	W 4-0	Gibbins 3, o.g.	10,000
Apr 13	Sheffield Wednesday	L 0-6		25,000
Apr 20	DERBY COUNTY	D 2-2	Watson 2	20,000
Apr 27	Sunderland	L 1-4	Watson	10,000
May 4	HUDDERSFIELD TOWN	D 1-1	Ruffell	20,000

FA Cup

Jan 12	SUNDERLAND	(Rd 3)	W 1-0	Earle	35,000
Jan 26	CORINTHIANS	(Rd 4)	W 3-0	Earle, Watson, Yews	42,000
Feb 16	Bournemouth	(Rd 5)	D 1-1	Yews	11,346
Feb 20	BOURNEMOUTH	(R)	W 3-1	Barrett, Yews, o.g.	30,217
Mar 2	Portsmouth	(Rd 6)	L 2-3	Barrett 2	39,088

League & Cup Appearances

PLAYER	LEAGUE	CUP COMPETITION FA CUP	TOTAL
Baillie	2	1	3
Barrett	22	2	24
Cadwell	40	5	45
Collins	39	5	44
Coshall	2		2
Cox	20	2	22
Dixon	2		2
Earl	32	5	37
Earle	41	5	46
Gibbins	29	2	31
Hodgson	28	5	33
Hufton	31	4	35
Hull	1		1
Moore	6	1	7
Norrington	14		14
Norris	6		6
Payne	3		3
Robson	5		5
Ruffell	37	5	42
Shone	12		12
Smailes	7	3	10
Smith W	1		1
Tate	7		7
Watson	34	5	39
Yews	41	5	46

Goalscorers

PLAYER	LEAGUE	CUP COMPETITION FA CUP	TOTAL
Watson	29	1	30
Ruffell	20		20
Yews	10	3	13
Gibbins	11		11
Earle	6	2	8
Shone	5		5
Barrett	1	3	4
Collins	1		1
Payne	1		1
Robson	1		1
Opps' o.gs.	1	1	2

Fact File

Two second half goals in the space of 15 minutes brought West Ham back into the FA Cup quarter-final having been 0-3 down at half time. Unfortunately they were not able to grab an equaliser.

MANAGER: Syd King
CAPTAIN: Stanley Earle
TOP SCORER: Vic Watson
BIGGEST WIN: February 9, 1929 8-2 v Leeds United, Division 1
HIGHEST ATTENDANCE: October 13, 1928 48,000 v Arsenal, won 3-2, Division 1
MAJOR TRANSFERS OUT: James Loughlin to Coventry City

Final Division 1 Table

		P	W	D	L	F	A	Pts
1	Sheffield W	42	21	10	11	86	62	52
2	Leicester C	42	21	9	12	96	67	51
3	Aston Villa	42	23	4	15	98	81	50
4	Sunderland	42	20	7	15	93	75	47
5	Liverpool	42	17	12	13	90	64	46
6	Derby Co	42	18	10	14	86	71	46
7	Blackburn R	42	17	11	14	72	63	45
8	Manchester C	42	18	9	15	95	86	45
9	Arsenal	42	16	13	13	77	72	45
10	Newcastle U	42	19	6	17	70	72	44
11	Sheffield U	42	15	11	16	86	85	41
12	Manchester U	42	14	13	15	66	76	41
13	Leeds U	42	16	9	17	71	84	41
14	Bolton W	42	14	12	16	73	80	40
15	Birmingham	42	15	10	17	68	77	40
16	Huddersfield T	42	14	11	17	70	61	39
17	West Ham U	42	15	9	18	86	96	39
18	Everton	42	17	4	21	63	75	38
19	Burnley	42	15	8	19	81	103	38
20	Portsmouth	42	15	6	21	56	80	36
21	Bury	42	12	7	23	62	99	31
22	Cardiff C	42	8	13	21	43	59	29

Season 1929-30

Football League Division 1

DATE	OPPONENTS	SCORE	GOALSCORERS	ATTENDANCE
Aug 31	Blackburn Rovers	D 3-3	Ball, Watson, o.g.	25,000
Sep 4	Birmingham	L 2-4	Watson 2	20,000
Sep 7	MIDDLESBROUGH	W 5-3	Ruffell 2, Ball 2, Watson	35,000
Sep 9	NEWCASTLE UNITED	W 5-1	Yews 2, Ball 2, Watson	25,000
Sep 14	Liverpool	L 1-3	Watson	25,000
Sep 16	BIRMINGHAM	L 0-1		16,000
Sep 21	DERBY COUNTY	W 2-0	Barrett, Ruffell	35,000
Sep 28	MANCHESTER UNITED	W 2-1	Ball, Watson	20,000
Oct 5	Grimsby Town	D 2-2	Watson, Ball	15,000
Oct 12	LEICESTER CITY	L 1-2	Watson	30,000
Oct 19	Manchester City	L 3-4	Yews, Ruffell, Ball	25,000
Oct 26	PORTSMOUTH	L 0-1		25,000
Nov 2	Arsenal	W 1-0	Watson	50,000
Nov 9	EVERTON	W 3-1	Ruffell 2, Watson	30,000
Nov 16	Leeds United	W 3-1	Watson 2, o.g.	15,000
Nov 23	SHEFFIELD WEDNESDAY	D 1-1	Watson	22,000
Nov 30	Burnley	D 1-1	Watson	6,000
Dec 7	SUNDERLAND	D 1-1	Watson	21,000
Dec 14	Bolton Wanderers	L 1-4	Watson	8,000
Dec 21	ASTON VILLA	W 5-2	Watson 3, Gibbins, Ruffell	18,000
Dec 25	HUDDERSFIELD TOWN	L 2-3	Watson, Gibbins	30,000
Dec 26	Huddersfield Town	L 0-3		20,000
Dec 28	BLACKBURN ROVERS	L 2-3	Watson, Ruffell	27,000
Jan 1	Sheffield United	L 2-4	Ball, Ruffell	20,000
Jan 4	Middlesbrough	L 0-2		12,000
Jan 18	LIVERPOOL	W 4-1	Watson, Robson, Barrett, o.g.	25,000
Feb 1	Manchester United	L 2-4	Earle, Watson	20,000
Feb 5	Derby County	L 3-4	Watson 2, o.g.	10,000
Feb 8	GRIMSBY TOWN	W 2-0	Watson, Ruffell	16,500
Feb 20	Leicester City	W 2-1	Watson, Wood	10,000
Feb 22	MANCHESTER CITY	W 3-0	Watson, Barrett, Gibbins	28,000
Mar 8	ARSENAL	W 3-2	Watson 2, Earle	35,000
Mar 12	Portsmouth	L 1-3	Ruffell	10,000
Mar 15	Everton	W 2-1	Watson 2	25,000
Mar 22	LEEDS UNITED	W 3-0	Watson 3	30,000
Mar 29	Sheffield Wednesday	L 1-2	Watson	30,000
Apr 5	BURNLEY	W 1-0	Barrett	15,000
Apr 12	Sunderland	L 2-4	Barrett, Ruffell	20,000
Apr 18	SHEFFIELD UNITED	W 1-0	Watson	30,000
Apr 19	BOLTON WANDERERS	W 5-3	Watson 2, Barrett, Ruffell, Earle	18,000
Apr 26	Aston Villa	W 3-2	Watson 3	22,000
May 3	Newcastle United	L 0-1		48,000

FA Cup

Jan 11	NOTTS COUNTY	(Rd 3)	W 4-0	Watson 2, Barrett, Gibbins	28,384
Jan 25	LEEDS UNITED	(Rd 4)	W 4-1	Watson 4	34,000
Feb 15	MILLWALL	(Rd 5)	W 4-1	Watson 2, Gibbins, Yews	24,000
Mar 1	Arsenal	(R)	L 0-3		40,492

League & Cup Appearances

PLAYER	LEAGUE	CUP COMPETITION FA CUP	TOTAL
Ball	15		15
Barrett	40	4	44
Cadwell	38	4	42
Collins	21	4	25
Cox	32	4	36
Dixon	12		12
Earl	38	4	42
Earle	36	4	40
Gibbins	18	3	21
Hodgson	4		4
Hufton	30	4	34
Norris	19		19
Pollard	7		7
Robson	10	1	11
Ruffell	40	4	44
St Pier	4		4
Wade R	2		2
Wade W	11		11
Watson	40	4	44
Wood	4		4
Yews	41	4	45

Goalscorers

PLAYER	LEAGUE	CUP COMPETITION FA CUP	TOTAL
Watson	42	8	50
Ruffell	13		13
Ball	9		9
Barrett	7	1	8
Gibbins	3	2	5
Yews	3	1	4
Earle	3		3
Wood	1		1
Robson	1		1
Opps' o.gs.	4		4

Fact File

Vic Watson's 42 goals put him at the head of the First Division's marksmen.

MANAGER: Syd King
CAPTAIN: Stanley Earle
TOP SCORER: Vic Watson
BIGGEST WIN: September 9, 1929 5-1 v Newcastle United, Division 1
HIGHEST ATTENDANCE: May 3, 1930 48,000 v Newcastle United, lost 0-1, Division 1

Final Division 1 Table

		P	W	D	L	F	A	Pts
1	Sheffield W	42	26	8	8	105	57	60
2	Derby Co	42	21	8	13	90	82	50
3	Manchester C	42	19	9	14	91	81	47
4	Aston Villa	42	21	5	16	92	83	47
5	Leeds U	42	20	6	16	79	63	46
6	Blackburn R	42	19	7	16	99	93	45
7	West Ham U	42	19	5	18	86	79	43
8	Leicester C	42	17	9	16	86	90	43
9	Sunderland	42	18	7	17	76	80	43
10	Huddersfield T	42	17	9	16	63	69	43
11	Birmingham	42	16	9	17	67	62	41
12	Liverpool	42	16	9	17	63	79	41
13	Portsmouth	42	15	10	17	66	62	40
14	Arsenal	42	14	11	17	78	66	39
15	Bolton W	42	15	9	18	74	74	39
16	Middlesbrough	42	16	6	20	82	84	38
17	Manchester U	42	15	8	19	67	88	38
18	Grimsby T	42	15	7	20	73	89	37
19	Newcastle U	42	15	7	20	71	92	37
20	Sheffield U	42	15	6	21	91	96	36
21	Burnley	42	14	8	20	79	97	36
22	Everton	42	12	11	19	80	92	35

Season 1930-31

Football League Division 1

DATE	OPPONENTS	SCORE	GOALSCORERS	ATTENDANCE
Aug 30	HUDDERSFIELD TOWN	W 2-1	Watson 2	24,000
Sep 1	LIVERPOOL	W 7-0	Watson 4, Earle 2, James	14,000
Sep 6	Aston Villa	L 1-6	Watson	40,000
Sep 8	MIDDLESBROUGH	L 0-3		12,000
Sep 13	CHELSEA	W 4-1	Watson 2, Earle, James	33,201
Sep 17	Middlesbrough	D 2-2	James, Watson	20,000
Sep 20	Newcastle United	L 2-4	Earle, Watson	18,000
Sep 27	SHEFFIELD WEDNESDAY	D 3-3	Gibbins, Ruffell, James	32,000
Oct 4	Grimsby Town	L 0-4		17,000
Oct 11	MANCHESTER UNITED	W 5-1	Gibbins 3, Ruffell, Barrett	26,000
Oct 18	BLACKBURN ROVERS	W 4-3	Yews 2, Gibbins, Ruffell	28,000
Oct 25	Arsenal	D 1-1	Pollard	56,000
Nov 1	SHEFFIELD UNITED	W 4-1	Gibbins 2, Earle, Barrett	25,000
Nov 8	Birmingham	W 2-0	Yews 2	25,000
Nov 15	LEEDS UNITED	D 1-1	Norris	20,000
Nov 22	Derby County	D 1-1	Gibbins	12,324
Nov 29	LEICESTER CITY	W 2-0	Ruffell 2	25,000
Dec 6	Blackpool	W 3-1	Ruffell, Earle, Gibbins	12,000
Dec 13	MANCHESTER CITY	W 2-0	Ruffell 2	22,000
Dec 20	Sunderland	L 1-6	Gibbins	20,000
Dec 25	PORTSMOUTH	W 4-3	Gibbins 2, James, Norris	32,000
Dec 26	Portsmouth	L 0-2		30,000
Dec 27	Huddersfield Town	L 0-2		12,000
Jan 3	ASTON VILLA	D 5-5	Barrett, Yews, Gibbins 2, Harris	25,000
Jan 17	Chelsea	L 1-2	Gibbins	50,000
Jan 26	NEWCASTLE UNITED	W 3-2	Earle, Gibbins, James	10,000
Jan 31	Sheffield Wednesday	L 3-5	Yews, James, Watson	12,000
Feb 7	GRIMSBY TOWN	L 3-4	Ruffell 3	18,000
Feb 14	Manchester United	L 0-1		10,000
Feb 21	Blackburn Rovers	L 0-1		10,000
Feb 28	ARSENAL	L 2-4	Watson, Earle	35,000
Mar 7	Sheffield United	W 2-1	Yews, Ruffell	12,000
Mar 16	BIRMINGHAM	L 1-2	Watson	12,000
Mar 21	Leeds United	L 0-3		10,000
Mar 28	DERBY COUNTY	L 0-1		20,000
Apr 3	BOLTON WANDERERS	L 1-4	Wood	18,000
Apr 4	Leicester City	D 1-1	Gamble	18,000
Apr 6	Bolton Wanderers	L 2-4	Barrett, Gamble	20,000
Apr 11	BLACKPOOL	W 3-2	Musgrave, Gibbins, Ruffell	15,000
Apr 18	Manchester City	D 1-1	Gibbins	15,000
Apr 25	SUNDERLAND	L 0-3		12,000
May 2	Liverpool	L 0-2		25,000

FA Cup

Jan 10	CHELSEA	(Rd 3) L 1-3	Gibbins	21,000

League & Cup Appearances

PLAYER	LEAGUE	CUP COMPETITION FA CUP	TOTAL
Barrett	40	1	41
Cadwell	31	1	32
Collins	38	1	39
Cox	2		2
Dixon	28	1	29
Earl	38	1	39
Earle	36	1	37
England	5		5
Evans	1		1
Fryatt	1		1
Gamble	2		2
Gibbins	21	1	22
Goodacre	6		6
Harris	5		5
Hufton	14		14
James	36	1	37
Musgrave	7		7
Norris	16		16
Pollard	5		5
Robson	1		1
Ruffell	37	1	38
St Pier	6		6
Wade	28	1	29
Watson	18		18
Wood	3		3
Yews	37	1	38

Goalscorers

PLAYER	LEAGUE	CUP COMPETITION FA CUP	TOTAL
Gibbins	18	1	19
Watson	14		14
Ruffell	13		13
Earle	8		8
Yews	7		7
James	7		7
Barrett	4		4
Norris	2		2
Gamble	2		2
Pollard	1		1
Harris	1		1
Musgrave	1		1
Wood	1		1

Final Division 1 Table

		P	W	D	L	F	A	Pts
1	Arsenal	42	28	10	4	127	59	66
2	Aston Villa	42	25	9	8	128	78	59
3	Sheffield W	42	22	8	12	102	75	52
4	Portsmouth	42	18	13	11	84	67	49
5	Huddersfield T	42	18	12	12	81	65	48
6	Derby Co	42	18	10	14	94	79	46
7	Middlesbrough	42	19	8	15	98	90	46
8	Manchester C	42	18	10	14	75	70	46
9	Liverpool	42	15	12	15	86	85	42
10	Blackburn R	42	17	8	17	83	84	42
11	Sunderland	42	16	9	17	89	85	41
12	Chelsea	42	15	10	17	64	67	40
13	Grimsby T	42	17	5	20	82	87	39
14	Bolton W	42	15	9	18	68	81	39
15	Sheffield U	42	14	10	18	78	84	38
16	Leicester C	42	16	6	20	80	95	38
17	Newcastle U	42	15	6	21	78	87	36
18	West Ham U	42	14	8	20	79	94	36
19	Birmingham	42	13	10	19	55	70	36
20	Blackpool	42	11	10	21	71	125	32
21	Leeds U	42	12	7	23	68	81	31
22	Manchester U	42	7	8	27	53	115	22

Fact File

An amazing start to the year saw the Hammers score 15 goals in 5 games, yet win only one of those matches.

MANAGER: Syd King
CAPTAIN: Stanley Earle
TOP SCORER: Vivian Gibbins
BIGGEST WIN: September 1, 1930 7-0 v Liverpool, Division 1
HIGHEST ATTENDANCE: October 25, 1930 56,000 v Arsenal, drew 1-1, Division 1

Season 1931-32

Football League Division 1

DATE	OPPONENTS	SCORE	GOALSCORERS	ATTENDANCE
Aug 29	Bolton Wanderers	W 1-0	Watson	12,000
Aug 31	CHELSEA	W 3-1	Weldon, Watson, Norris	35,000
Sep 5	MIDDLESBROUGH	L 0-2		20,000
Sep 7	Sheffield United	L 0-6		12,000
Sep 12	Huddersfield Town	L 1-3	Watson	12,000
Sep 19	NEWCASTLE UNITED	W 2-1	Watson, Ruffell	28,000
Sep 21	SHEFFIELD UNITED	L 1-2	Ruffell	15,000
Sep 26	Aston Villa	L 2-5	Wood, o.g.	40,000
Oct 3	LEICESTER CITY	L 1-4	Gibbins	25,000
Oct 10	Liverpool	D 2-2	Gibbins, Weldon	25,000
Oct 17	Manchester City	W 1-0	Ruffell	18,000
Oct 24	PORTSMOUTH	W 2-1	Gibbins 2	20,000
Oct 31	Derby County	L 1-5	Watson	10,000
Nov 7	WEST BROMWICH ALBION	L 1-5	Ruffell	20,000
Nov 14	Arsenal	L 1-4	Watson	45,000
Nov 21	BLACKPOOL	D 1-1	Ruffell	16,000
Nov 28	Blackburn Rovers	W 4-2	Barrett, Gibbins, Phillips, Watson	10,000
Dec 5	EVERTON	W 4-2	Ruffell 3, Wood	40,000
Dec 12	Birmingham	L 1-4	Watson	22,000
Dec 19	SUNDERLAND	D 2-2	Watson, Barrett	10,000
Dec 25	Grimsby Town	L 1-2	Watson	14,000
Dec 26	GRIMSBY TOWN	W 3-1	Ruffell 2, Watson	30,000
Jan 2	BOLTON WANDERERS	W 3-1	Watson 2, Ruffell	20,000
Jan 16	Middlesbrough	L 2-3	Watson 2	6,000
Jan 30	Newcastle United	D 2-2	Watson, Cadwell	28,000
Feb 1	HUDDERSFIELD TOWN	D 1-1	Watson	10,000
Feb 6	ASTON VILLA	W 2-1	Phillips, Yews	30,000
Feb 18	Leicester City	L 1-2	Ruffell	12,000
Feb 20	LIVERPOOL	W 1-0	Ruffell	18,000
Mar 2	MANCHESTER CITY	D 1-1	Chalkley	18,000
Mar 5	Portsmouth	L 0-3		15,000
Mar 12	DERBY COUNTY	W 2-1	Ruffell, Watson	24,000
Mar 19	West Bromwich Albion	L 1-3	Phillips	16,000
Mar 25	SHEFFIELD WEDNESDAY	L 1-2	Ruffell	38,000
Mar 26	ARSENAL	D 1-1	Watson	40,000
Mar 28	Sheffield Wednesday	L 1-6	Watson	18,000
Apr 2	Blackpool	L 2-7	Morton, Watson	12,000
Apr 9	BLACKBURN ROVERS	L 1-3	Watson	16,000
Apr 16	Everton	L 1-6	o.g.	35,000
Apr 23	BIRMINGHAM	L 2-4	Wheldon, Watson	12,000
Apr 30	Sunderland	L 0-2		10,000
May 7	Chelsea	L 2-3	Barrett, Yews	30,000

FA Cup

Jan 9	Charlton Athletic	(Rd 3) W 2-1	Watson 2	26,500
Jan 23	Chelsea	(Rd 4) L 1-3	Weldon	36,657

Fact File

March saw Syd Puddefoot, now aged 38, return to the Hammers' team. He was however, unable to help them prevent a drop to Division Two.

MANAGER: Syd King

CAPTAIN: Stanley Earle

TOP SCORER: Vic Watson

BIGGEST WIN: November 28, 1931 4-2 v Blackburn Rovers, Division 1; December 5, 1931 4-2 v Everton, Division 1

HIGHEST ATTENDANCE: November 14, 1931 45,000 v Arsenal, lost 1-4, Division 1

MAJOR TRANSFERS IN: Tony Weldon from Hull City, Syd Puddefoot from Blackburn Rovers, Jackie Morton from Gainsborough Trinity

MAJOR TRANSFERS OUT: Vivian Gibbins to Brentford

League & Cup Appearances

PLAYER	LEAGUE	CUP COMPETITION FA CUP	TOTAL
Barrett	38	2	40
Cadwell	26	2	28
Chalkley	29	2	31
Collins	35	2	37
Cox	9		9
Dixon	20	2	22
Earl	30	2	32
Earle	17		17
Gibbins	9		9
Goodacre	10		10
Harris	2		2
Hufton	22		22
James	4		4
Morton	5		5
Musgrave	3		3
Norris	17		17
Phillips	21	2	23
Pollard	7		7
Puddefoot	7		7
Ruffell	39	2	41
St Pier	7		7
Wade R	2		2
Wade W	5		5
Watson	38	2	40
Weldon	20	2	22
Wood	17		17
Yews	23	2	25

Goalscorers

PLAYER	LEAGUE	CUP COMPETITION FA CUP	TOTAL
Watson	23	2	25
Ruffell	15		15
Gibbins	5		5
Weldon	3	1	4
Barrett	3		3
Phillips	3		3
Yews	2		2
Wood	2		2
Chalkley	1		1
Norris	1		1
Cadwell	1		1
Morton	1		1
Opps' o.gs.	2		2

Final Division 1 Table

		P	W	D	L	F	A	Pts
1	Everton	42	26	4	12	116	64	56
2	Arsenal	42	22	10	10	90	48	54
3	Sheffield W	42	22	6	14	96	82	50
4	Huddersfield T	42	19	10	13	80	63	48
5	Aston Villa	42	19	8	15	104	72	46
6	WBA	42	20	6	16	77	55	46
7	Sheffield U	42	20	6	16	80	75	46
8	Portsmouth	42	19	7	16	62	62	45
9	Birmingham	42	18	8	16	78	67	44
10	Liverpool	42	19	6	17	81	93	44
11	Newcastle U	42	18	6	18	80	87	42
12	Chelsea	42	16	8	18	69	73	40
13	Sunderland	42	15	10	17	67	73	40
14	Manchester C	42	13	12	17	83	73	38
15	Derby Co	42	14	10	18	71	75	38
16	Blackburn R	42	16	6	20	89	95	38
17	Bolton W	42	17	4	21	72	80	38
18	Middlesbrough	42	15	8	19	64	89	38
19	Leicester C	42	15	7	20	74	94	37
20	Blackpool	42	12	9	21	65	102	33
21	Grimsby T	42	13	6	23	67	98	32
22	West Ham U	42	12	7	23	62	107	31

Season 1932-33

Football League Division 2

DATE	OPPONENTS	SCORE	GOALSCORERS	ATTENDANCE
Aug 27	Swansea Town	L 0-1		15,000
Aug 29	BRADFORD CITY	L 2-4	Mills, Pollard	15,000
Sep 3	NOTTS COUNTY	D 1-1	Puddefoot	15,000
Sep 7	Bradford City	L 1-5	Watson V	17,000
Sep 10	Port Vale	L 0-4		8,000
Sep 17	MILLWALL	W 3-0	Watson V 2, Morton	30,000
Sep 24	Southampton	L 3-4	Morton 2, Watson V	10,000
Oct 1	BURY	L 0-1		10,000
Oct 8	Lincoln City	L 0-6		10,000
Oct 15	OLDHAM ATHLETIC	W 5-2	Norris 3, Morton, Watson V	18,000
Oct 22	Preston North End	L 1-4	Mills	8,000
Oct 29	BURNLEY	D 4-4	Watson V 3, Morton	14,000
Nov 5	Bradford	L 0-3		13,000
Nov 12	GRIMSBY TOWN	W 5-2	Wilson 2, Yews, Watson V, o.g.	16,000
Nov 19	Stoke City	D 0-0		10,000
Nov 26	CHARLTON ATHLETIC	W 7-3	Wilson 2, Watson V 2, Barrett, Yews, Morton	23,000
Dec 3	Nottingham Forest	D 2-2	Watson V, Wilson	7,000
Dec 10	MANCHESTER UNITED	W 3-1	Watson V 2, Wilson	15,000
Dec 17	Tottenham Hotspur	D 2-2	Morton, o.g.	46,250
Dec 24	PLYMOUTH ARGYLE	D 2-2	Barrett, Morton	20,000
Dec 26	Fulham	L 2-4	Pollard, Puddefoot	27,861
Dec 27	FULHAM	D 1-1	Watson V	40,000
Dec 31	SWANSEA TOWN	W 3-1	Watson V 2, Barrett	18,000
Jan 7	Notts County	L 0-2		11,000
Jan 21	PORT VALE	W 5-0	Watson V 2, Wilson 2, Barrett	18,000
Jan 30	Millwall	L 0-1		5,000
Feb 4	SOUTHAMPTON	W 3-1	Watson V, Wilson 2	20,000
Feb 11	Bury	L 1-6	Barrett	7,000
Mar 6	PRESTON NORTH END	D 1-1	Puddefoot	12,000
Mar 11	Burnley	L 0-4		10,000
Mar 13	Oldham Athletic	L 2-3	Mills, Wood	6,000
Mar 20	BRADFORD CITY	W 2-1	Watson V 2	12,000
Mar 25	Grimsby Town	L 1-2	Wilson	12,000
Mar 27	LINCOLN CITY	D 0-0		12,000
Apr 1	STOKE CITY	L 1-2	Barrett	23,000
Apr 8	Charlton Athletic	L 1-3	Barrett	30,000
Apr 14	Chesterfield	L 0-1		11,000
Apr 15	NOTTINGHAM FOREST	W 4-3	Barrett, Goulden, Morton, Wood	20,000
Apr 17	CHESTERFIELD	W 3-1	Morton, Pollard, Watson V	21,000
Apr 22	Manchester United	W 2-1	Morton, Wilson	18,000
Apr 29	TOTTENHAM HOTSPUR	W 1-0	Wilson	35,000
May 6	Plymouth Argyle	L 1-4	o.g.	12,000

FA Cup

Jan 14	Corinthians	(Rd 3)	W 2-0	Pollard, Watson V	16,421
Jan 28	WEST BROMWICH ALBION	(Rd 4)	W 2-0	Watson V, Wilson	37,222
Feb 18	Brighton & Hove Albion	(Rd 5)	D 2-2	Musgrave, Watson V	32,310
Feb 22	BRIGHTON & HOVE ALBION	(R)	W 1-0	Morton	36,742
Mar 4	BIRMINGHAM	(Rd 6)	W 4-0	Wilson, Morton, Pollard, o.g.	44,232
Mar 18	EVERTON	(SF)	L 1-2*	Watson V	37,936

*Played at Molineux.

League & Cup Appearances

PLAYER	LEAGUE	CUP COMPETITION FA CUP	TOTAL
Barrett	40	6	46
Cadwell	10	2	12
Chalkley	34	6	40
Cockroft	6		6
Collins	33	6	39
Deacon	3		3
Dixon	3		3
Earl	11		11
Fenton	6		6
Fryatt	2		2
Goodacre	4	6	10
Goulden	7		7
Johnson	5		5
McMahon	13	1	14
Mills	7		7
Morton	36	6	42
Musgrave	23	4	27
Norris	7		7
Pollard	18	6	24
Puddefoot	15		15
Ruffell	8		8
St Pier	7		7
Walker A	33		33
Watson G	26	5	31
Watson V	35	6	41
Wilson	27	6	33
Wood	11	1	12
Yews	32	5	37

Goalscorers

PLAYER	LEAGUE	CUP COMPETITION FA CUP	TOTAL
Watson V	23	4	27
Wilson	13	2	15
Morton	11	2	13
Barrett	8		8
Pollard	3	2	5
Mills	3		3
Norris	3		3
Puddefoot	3		3
Yews	2		2
Goulden	1		1
Musgrave		1	1
Wood	2		1
Opps' o.gs.	3	1	4

Fact File

On 9 November the club's board suspended manager Syd King for three months. By the time two months had elapsed King had committed suicide.

MANAGER: Syd King/Charlie Paynter
CAPTAIN: Jim Barrett
TOP SCORER: Vic Watson
BIGGEST WIN: November 26, 1932 7-3 v Charlton Athletic, Division 1
HIGHEST ATTENDANCE: December 17, 1932 46,250 v Tottenham Hotspur, drew 2-2, Division 1
MAJOR TRANSFERS IN: Arthur Wilson from Southampton, Joe Cockcroft from Gainsborough Trinity

Final Division 2 Table

	P	W	D	L	F	A	Pts
1 Stoke C	42	25	6	11	78	39	56
2 Tottenham H	42	20	15	7	96	51	55
3 Fulham	42	20	10	12	78	65	50
4 Bury	42	20	9	13	84	59	49
5 Nottingham F	42	17	15	10	67	59	49
6 Manchester U	42	15	13	14	71	68	43
7 Millwall	42	16	11	15	59	57	43
8 Bradford PA	42	17	8	17	77	71	42
9 Preston NE	42	16	10	16	74	70	42
10 Swansea T	42	19	4	19	50	54	42
11 Bradford C	42	14	13	15	65	61	41
12 Southampton	42	18	5	19	66	66	41
13 Grimsby T	42	14	13	15	79	84	41
14 Plymouth Arg	42	16	9	17	63	67	41
15 Notts Co	42	15	10	17	67	78	40
16 Oldham Ath	42	15	8	19	67	80	38
17 Port Vale	42	14	10	18	66	79	38
18 Lincoln C	42	12	13	17	72	87	37
19 Burnley	42	11	14	17	67	79	36
20 West Ham U	42	13	9	20	75	93	35
21 Chesterfield	42	12	10	20	61	84	34
22 Charlton Ath	42	12	7	23	60	91	31

Season 1933-34

Football League Division 2

DATE	OPPONENTS	SCORE	GOALSCORERS	ATTENDANCE
Aug 26	BOLTON WANDERERS	W 4-2	Watson V 2, Morton, o.g.	26,000
Aug 30	Plymouth Argyle	D 4-4	Goulden 3, Barrett	25,000
Sep 2	Brentford	L 1-4	Wilson	24,000
Sep 4	PLYMOUTH ARGYLE	W 5-1	Tippett 2, Watson V 2, Landells	20,000
Sep 9	BURNLEY	L 1-2	Tippett	26,000
Sep 16	Oldham Athletic	L 1-4	Tippett	7,000
Sep 23	PRESTON NORTH END	W 6-0	Watson V 3, Goulden, Morton, Tippett	20,000
Sep 20	Bradford	D 0-0		12,000
Oct 7	GRIMSBY TOWN	W 3-1	Morton, Watson V, o.g.	25,000
Oct 14	Nottingham Forest	W 1-0	Wood	10,000
Oct 21	Millwall	D 2-2	Barrett, Watson V	32,000
Oct 28	LINCOLN CITY	W 4-1	Watson V 3, o.g.	23,851
Nov 4	Bury	L 1-2	Watson V	11,000
Nov 11	HULL CITY	W 2-1	Landells, Watson V	23,591
Nov 18	Fulham	L 1-3	Landells	18,000
Nov 25	SOUTHAMPTON	D 0-0		23,160
Dec 2	Blackpool	D 1-1	Ruffell	15,000
Dec 9	BRADFORD CITY	L 1-2	Barrett	20,211
Dec 16	Port Vale	D 0-0		8,000
Dec 23	NOTTS COUNTY	W 5-3	Ruffell 2, Watson V, Morton, Goulden	20,000
Dec 25	SWANSEA TOWN	D 1-1	Watson V	28,000
Dec 26	Swansea Town	D 1-1	Goulden	20,000
Dec 30	Bolton Wanderers	L 1-5	Mills	8,000
Jan 6	BRENTFORD	W 3-2	Watson V 2, Tippett	26,449
Jan 20	Burnley	L 2-4	Barrett, Watson	7,000
Feb 3	Preston North End	L 1-3	Ette	15,000
Feb 7	OLDHAM ATHLETIC	L 1-4	Watson V	10,000
Feb 10	BRADFORD	L 0-1		16,500
Feb 17	Grimsby Town	D 1-1	Morton	10,000
Feb 24	NOTTINGHAM FOREST	W 2-1	Ruffell 2	16,500
Mar 3	MILLWALL	D 1-1	Watson V	26,400
Mar 10	Lincoln City	W 2-0	Ruffell, Wood	6,000
Mar 17	BURY	W 3-1	Fenton 3	17,400
Mar 24	Hull City	L 0-2		7,000
Mar 30	Manchester United	W 1-0	Fenton	32,000
Mar 31	FULHAM	W 5-1	Watson V 3, Goulden, Morton	26,050
Apr 2	MANCHESTER UNITED	W 2-1	Wood 2	18,000
Apr 7	Southampton	L 2-3	Barrett, Watson V	8,000
Apr 14	BLACKPOOL	L 1-2	Watson V	16,600
Apr 21	Bradford City	D 2-2	Fenton, Ruffell	9,000
Apr 28	PORT VALE	W 1-0	Ruffell	12,000
May 5	Notts County	W 2-1	Tippett 2	5,000

FA Cup

Jan 13	BRADFORD CITY	(Rd 3)	W 3-2	Watson V 2, Goulden	28,246
Jan 27	Tottenham Hotspur	(Rd 4)	L 1-4	Watson V	51,747

Fact File

Against Preston North End in September, West Ham found themselves 3-0 up after only 12 minutes.

MANAGER: Charlie Paynter
CAPTAIN: Jim Barrett
TOP SCORER: Vic Watson
BIGGEST WIN: September 23, 1933 6-0 v Preston North End, Division 2
HIGHEST ATTENDANCE: January 27, 1934 51,747 v Tottenham Hotspur, lost 1-4, FA Cup Round 4
MAJOR TRANSFERS IN: Tommy Tippett from Port Vale, Jack Landells from Millwall

League & Cup Appearances

PLAYER	LEAGUE	CUP COMPETITION FA CUP	TOTAL
Anderson	24		24
Barrett	38	2	40
Chalkley	37	2	39
Cockroft	42		42
Collins	17		17
Ette	1		1
Fenton	12		12
Goulden	40	2	42
Inns	4		4
Landells	21	1	22
McMahon	3		3
Mills	4	2	6
Morton	42	2	44
Musgrave	1		1
Robson	3		3
Ruffell	22	2	24
Rutherford	33	2	35
Thorpe	3		3
Tippett	21	1	22
Walker A	37	2	39
Watson G	6		6
Watson V	30	2	32
Wilson	2		2
Wood	16		16
Young	3		3

Goalscorers

PLAYER	LEAGUE	CUP COMPETITION FA CUP	TOTAL
Watson V	26	3	29
Goulden	7	1	8
Ruffell	8		8
Tippett	8		8
Morton	6		6
Barrett	5		5
Fenton	5		5
Wood	4		4
Landells	3		3
Mills	1		1
Wilson	1		1
Ette	1		1
Opps' o.gs.	3		3

Final Division 2 Table

		P	W	D	L	F	A	PTS
1	GRIMSBY T	42	27	5	10	103	59	59
2	PRESTON NE	42	23	6	13	71	52	52
3	BOLTON W	42	21	9	12	79	55	51
4	BRENTFORD	42	22	7	13	85	60	51
5	BRADFORD PA	42	23	3	16	86	67	49
6	BRADFORD C	42	20	6	16	73	67	46
7	WEST HAM U	42	17	11	14	78	70	45
8	PORT VALE	42	19	7	16	60	55	45
9	OLDHAM ATH	42	17	10	15	72	60	44
10	PLYMOUTH ARG	42	15	13	14	69	70	43
11	BLACKPOOL	42	15	13	14	62	64	43
12	BURY	42	17	9	16	70	73	43
13	BURNLEY	42	18	6	18	60	72	42
14	SOUTHAMPTON	42	15	8	19	54	58	38
15	HULL C	42	13	12	17	52	68	38
16	FULHAM	42	15	7	20	48	67	37
17	NOTTINGHAM F	42	13	9	20	73	74	35
18	NOTTS CO	42	12	11	19	53	62	35
19	SWANSEA T	42	10	15	17	51	60	35
20	MANCHESTER U	42	14	6	22	59	85	34
21	MILLWALL	42	11	11	20	39	68	33
22	LINCOLN C	42	9	8	25	44	75	26

Season 1934-35

Football League Division 2

DATE	OPPONENTS	SCORE	GOALSCORERS	ATTENDANCE
Aug 27	BURNLEY	L 1-2	Watson V	20,000
Sep 1	NOTTINGHAM FOREST	W 3-1	Wood 2, Morton	21,000
Sep 3	Burnley	L 2-5	Fenton 2	13,000
Sep 8	Brentford	L 1-4	Fenton	24,000
Sep 15	FULHAM	W 2-1	Morton, Ruffell	20,000
Sep 17	Hull City	L 0-4		5,000
Sep 22	Bradford	W 3-1	Mills 2, Fenton	7,000
Sep 29	PLYMOUTH ARGYLE	W 2-1	Barrett, Mills	22,400
Oct 6	Norwich City	W 2-1	Foreman, Mills	17,000
Oct 13	NEWCASTLE UNITED	W 3-2	Barrett, Mills, Ruffell	29,000
Oct 20	SWANSEA TOWN	W 2-0	Mills, Morton	22,000
Oct 27	Manchester United	L 1-3	Mills	30,000
Nov 3	PORT VALE	W 3-1	Mills 2, Ruffell	22,400
Nov 10	Barnsley	D 1-1	Mills	8,000
Nov 17	SHEFFIELD UNITED	W 2-0	Goulden, Mills	22,500
Nov 24	Bradford City	W 2-0	Foreman, Morton	8,000
Dec 1	NOTTS COUNTY	W 4-0	Watson 3, Ruffell	21,000
Dec 8	Southampton	D 2-2	Ruffell, Watson V	12,000
Dec 15	BOLTON WANDERERS	W 4-1	Ruffell 2, Watson V 2	32,000
Dec 22	Oldham Athletic	W 2-1	Ruffell, Watson V	5,000
Dec 25	Bury	W 4-2	Ruffell 2, Watson V, Wood	15,000
Dec 26	BURY	W 3-0	Ruffell 2, Watson V	40,000
Dec 29	HULL CITY	L 1-2	Ruffell	31,000
Jan 5	Nottingham Forest	L 0-2		16,000
Jan 19	BRENTFORD	W 2-0	Ruffell, Tippett	30,000
Jan 26	Fulham	L 0-3		26,000
Feb 2	BRADFORD	W 2-1	Morton, Ruffell	26,000
Feb 9	Plymouth Argyle	W 1-0	Foreman	11,000
Feb 16	NORWICH CITY	W 1-0	Ruffell	13,700
Feb 23	Newcastle United	L 0-3		25,000
Mar 2	Swansea Town	L 4-5	Foxall 2, Morton, Tippett	10,000
Mar 9	MANCHESTER UNITED	D 0-0		25,000
Mar 16	Port Vale	D 2-2	Mangall, Marshall	10,000
Mar 23	BARNSLEY	W 4-3	Barrett, Goulden, Marshall, Ruffell	25,000
Mar 30	Sheffield United	W 2-1	Mangall 2	17,000
Apr 6	BRADFORD CITY	W 1-0	Mangall	30,000
Apr 13	Notts County	W 2-0	Ruffell, Morton	11,000
Apr 19	Blackpool	L 2-3	Fenton, Barrett	30,000
Apr 20	SOUTHAMPTON	W 2-1	Fenton, Ruffell	31,000
Apr 22	BLACKPOOL	W 2-1	Mangall, Ruffell	38,000
Apr 27	Bolton Wanderers	L 1-3	Goulden	35,000
May 4	OLDHAM ATHLETIC	W 2-0	Barrett, Magnall	25,000

FA Cup

Jan 12	STOCKPORT COUNTY	(Rd 3)	D 1-1	Mills	26,400
Jan 16	Stockport County	(R)	L 0-1		17,911

League & Cup Appearances

PLAYER	LEAGUE	CUP COMPETITION FA CUP	TOTAL
Anderson	2		2
Barrett	41	2	43
Chalkley	42	2	44
Cockroft	42	2	44
Collins	12		12
Conway	41	2	43
Fenton E	32	1	33
Foreman	21	2	23
Foxall	4		4
Gall	1		1
Goulden	40	2	42
Mangall	10		10
Marshall	10		10
Mills	10	2	12
Morton	40	2	42
Ruffell	36	2	38
Tippett	4		4
Walker A	42	2	44
Walker R	3		3
Wallbanks		1	1
Watson G	1		1
Watson V	15		15
Wood	12		12
Young	1		1

Goalscorers

PLAYER	LEAGUE	CUP COMPETITION FA CUP	TOTAL
Ruffell	20		20
Mills	11	1	12
Watson V	10		10
Morton	7		7
Fenton E	6		6
Mangall	6		6
Barrett	5		5
Wood	3		3
Goulden	3		3
Foreman	3		3
Foxall	2		2
Tippett	2		2
Marshall	2		2

Fact File

West Ham missed out on promotion on the last game of the season, but the previous week's defeat at Bolton had put their destiny in the Lancastrians' hands.

MANAGER: Charlie Paynter
CAPTAIN: Jim Barrett
TOP SCORER: Jimmy Ruffell
BIGGEST WIN: December 1, 1934 4-0 v Notts County, Division 2
HIGHEST ATTENDANCE: December 26, 1934 40,000 v Bury, won 3-0, Division 2
MAJOR TRANSFERS IN: Herman Conway from Burnley, Dr James Marshall from Arsenal, Dave Mangall from Birmingham City

Final Division 2 Table

		P	W	D	L	F	A	Pts
1	Brentford	42	26	9	7	93	48	61
2	Bolton W	42	26	4	12	96	48	56
3	West Ham U	42	26	4	12	80	63	56
4	Blackpool	42	21	11	10	79	57	53
5	Manchester U	42	23	4	15	76	55	50
6	Newcastle U	42	22	4	16	89	68	48
7	Fulham	42	17	12	13	76	56	46
8	Plymouth Arg	42	19	8	15	75	64	46
9	Nottingham F	42	17	8	17	76	70	42
10	Bury	42	19	4	19	62	73	42
11	Sheffield U	42	16	9	17	79	70	41
12	Burnley	42	16	9	17	63	73	41
13	Hull C	42	16	8	18	63	74	40
14	Norwich C	42	14	11	17	71	61	39
15	Bradford PA	42	11	16	15	55	63	38
16	Barnsley	42	13	12	17	60	83	38
17	Swansea T	42	14	8	20	56	67	36
18	Port Vale	42	11	12	19	55	74	34
19	Southampton	42	11	12	19	46	75	34
20	Bradford C	42	12	8	22	50	68	32
21	Oldham Ath	42	10	6	26	56	95	26
22	Notts Co	42	9	7	26	46	97	25

Season 1935-36

Football League Division 2

DATE	OPPONENTS	SCORE	GOALSCORERS	ATTENDANCE
Aug 31	Norwich City	L 3-4	Marshall, Morton, Ruffell	29,779
Sep 2	Bradford	L 0-2		16,000
Sep 7	NOTTINGHAM FOREST	W 5-2	Mangall 3, Ruffell 2	30,000
Sep 9	BRADFORD	W 1-0	Goulden	21,000
Sep 14	Blackpool	L 1-4	Marshall	25,000
Sep 16	SHEFFIELD UNITED	W 3-2	Goulden, Mangall, Marshall	30,000
Sep 21	DONCASTER ROVERS	L 1-2	Mangall	30,000
Sep 28	Bury	L 0-3		9,000
Oct 5	BARNSLEY	W 2-0	Mangall 2	25,000
Oct 12	SWANSEA TOWN	W 4-0	Goulden 2, Marshall, o.g.	25,000
Oct 19	Plymouth Argyle	L 1-4	Marshall	19,000
Oct 26	BRADFORD CITY	D 1-1	Mangall	20,000
Nov 2	Newcastle United	D 3-3	Mangall 2, Ruffell	20,000
Nov 9	TOTTENHAM HOTSPUR	D 2-2	Mangall, Ruffell	41,000
Nov 16	Manchester United	W 3-2	Fenton, Foreman, Simpson	25,000
Nov 23	HULL CITY	W 4-1	Ruffell 2, Conwell, Mangall	25,000
Nov 30	Fulham	L 2-4	Mangall, o.g.	27,000
Dec 14	Charlton Athletic	D 2-2	Barrett, Goulden	35,000
Dec 21	PORT VALE	W 4-0	Goulden 2, Foreman, Mangall	18,000
Dec 25	SOUTHAMPTON	D 0-0		30,000
Dec 26	Southampton	W 4-2	Mangall 2, Goulden, o.g.	18,989
Dec 28	NORWICH CITY	W 3-2	Mangall 3	26,000
Jan 4	Nottingham Forest	W 2-0	Goulden, Ruffell	16,000
Jan 18	BLACKPOOL	W 2-1	Foreman, Marshall	15,000
Jan 25	Doncaster Rovers	W 2-0	Lewis, Simpson	12,000
Feb 1	BURY	W 6-0	Lewis 3, Cockroft, Morton, Simpson	27,000
Feb 3	BURNLEY	D 0-0		10,000
Feb 8	Barnsley	W 2-1	Goulden, Morton	12,000
Feb 15	Swansea Town	W 1-0	Mangall	10,000
Feb 22	PLYMOUTH ARGYLE	W 4-2	Barrett, Fenton, Goulden, Morton	20,000
Feb 29	Burnley	L 0-1		6,000
Mar 7	MANCHESTER UNITED	L 1-2	Goulden	31,000
Mar 14	Tottenham Hotspur	W 3-1	Goulden, Marshall, Simpson	58,426
Mar 21	NEWCASTLE UNITED	W 4-1	Marshall 2, Ruffell, Simpson	40,000
Mar 28	Hull City	W 3-2	Goulden. Ruffell, Simpson	5,000
Apr 4	FULHAM	D 0-0		33,000
Apr 10	LEICESTER CITY	W 3-2	Fenton, Goulden, Simpson	39,000
Apr 11	Bradford City	L 1-3	Morton	12,000
Apr 13	Leicester City	D 1-1	Simpson	25,000
Apr 18	CHARLTON ATHLETIC	L 1-3	Simpson	41,500
Apr 25	Port Vale	W 3-2	Mangall 2, Foxall	9,000
May 2	Sheffield United	L 2-4	Foreman, Marshall	24,000

FA Cup

Jan 11	LUTON TOWN	(Rd 3) D 2-2	Mangall, Ruffell	42,000
Jan 15	Luton Town	(R) L 0-4		17,527

Fact File

West Ham scored more goals away from home this season than any other Football League team.

MANAGER: Charlie Paynter
CAPTAIN: Jim Barrett
TOP SCORER: Dave Mangall
BIGGEST WIN: February 1, 1936 6-0 v Bury, Division 2
HIGHEST ATTENDANCE: March 14, 1936 58,426 v Tottenham Hotspur, won 3-1, Division 2
MAJOR TRANSFERS IN: Vincent Blore from Derby County, Peter Simpson from Crystal Palace, Fred Dell from Dartford, Charlie Bicknell from Bradford City

League & Cup Appearances

PLAYER	LEAGUE	CUP COMPETITION FA CUP	TOTAL
Barrett	40	2	42
Bicknell	7		7
Blore	9		9
Chalkley	32	2	34
Cockroft	42	2	44
Collins	1		1
Conway	33	2	35
Conwell	6		6
Dowen	1		1
Fenton E	41	2	43
Foreman	20		20
Foxall	1		1
Goulden	38	2	40
Lewis	4		4
Mangall	25	2	27
Marshall	36		36
Morton	26	2	28
Musgrave	2		2
Parker	2		2
Ruffell	30	2	32
Simpson	20	2	22
Tippett	2		2
Tonner	1		1
Walker A	41	2	43
Walker R	2		2

Goalscorers

PLAYER	LEAGUE	CUP COMPETITION FA CUP	TOTAL
Mangall	22	1	23
Goulden	15		15
Ruffell	10	1	11
Marshall	10		10
Simpson	9		9
Morton	5		5
Foreman	4		4
Lewis	4		4
Fenton	3		3
Barrett	2		2
Cockroft	1		1
Conwell	1		1
Foxall	1		1
Opps' o.gs.	3		3

Final Division 2 Table

		P	W	D	L	F	A	Pts
1	Manchester U	42	22	12	8	85	43	56
2	Charlton Ath	42	22	11	9	85	58	55
3	Sheffield U	42	20	12	10	79	50	52
4	West Ham U	42	22	8	12	90	68	52
5	Tottenham H	42	18	13	11	91	55	49
6	Leicester C	42	19	10	13	79	57	48
7	Plymouth Arg	42	20	8	14	71	57	48
8	Newcastle U	42	20	6	16	88	79	46
9	Fulham	42	15	14	13	76	52	44
10	Blackpool	42	18	7	17	93	72	43
11	Norwich C	42	17	9	16	72	65	43
12	Bradford C	42	15	13	14	55	65	43
13	Swansea T	42	15	9	18	67	76	39
14	Bury	42	13	12	17	66	84	38
15	Burnley	42	12	13	17	50	59	37
16	Bradford PA	42	14	9	19	62	84	37
17	Southampton	42	14	9	19	47	65	37
18	Doncaster R	42	14	9	19	51	71	37
19	Nottingham F	42	12	11	19	69	76	35
20	Barnsley	42	12	9	21	54	80	33
21	Port Vale	42	12	8	22	56	106	32
22	Hull C	42	5	10	27	47	111	20

Season 1936-37

Football League Division 2

DATE	OPPONENTS	SCORE	GOALSCORERS	ATTENDANCE
Aug 29	TOTTENHAM HOTSPUR	W 2-1	Goulden 2	35,000
Aug 31	NEWCASTLE UNITED	L 0-2		23,200
Sep 5	Blackpool	L 0-1		25,000
Sep 9	Newcastle United	L 3-5	Maring 3	22,000
Sep 12	BLACKBURN ROVERS	W 3-1	Goulden, Martin, Morton	28,000
Sep 14	Sheffield United	L 0-2		15,000
Sep 19	Bury	D 1-1	Martin	16,000
Sep 26	LEICESTER CITY	W 4-1	Marshall 2, Goulden, Martin	26,000
Oct 3	Nottingham Forest	L 0-1		20,000
Oct 10	Norwich City	D 3-3	Barrett, Cockroft, Martin	15,000
Oct 17	PLYMOUTH ARGYLE	D 1-1	Morton	28,000
Oct 24	Coventry City	L 0-4		24,000
Oct 31	DONCASTER ROVERS	W 1-0	Guest	15,000
Nov 7	Fulham	L 0-5		20,000
Nov 14	BURNLEY	L 0-2		25,000
Nov 21	Southampton	W 2-0	Adams, Foxall	16,000
Nov 28	SWANSEA TOWN	W 2-0	Foxall, Goulden	19,000
Dec 5	Bradford City	L 1-2	Goulden	7,000
Dec 19	Chesterfield	D 1-1	Morton	10,000
Dec 25	Bradford	L 1-2	Green	17,203
Dec 26	Tottenham Hotspur	W 3-2	Simpson 2, Foxall	34,000
Dec 28	BRADFORD	W 1-0	Morton	16,000
Jan 2	BLACKPOOL	W 3-0	Foxall, Simpson, o.g.	28,000
Jan 9	Blackburn Rovers	W 2-1	Goulden, Morton	8,000
Jan 23	BURY	W 5-1	Small 2, Fenton, Foxall, Goulden	21,000
Feb 4	Leicester City	D 2-2	Goulden, Foxall	7,000
Feb 6	NOTTINGHAM FOREST	D 2-2	Morton 2	20,000
Feb 13	NORWICH CITY	W 4-1	Foxall 2, Morton 2	22,000
Feb 20	Plymouth Argyle	L 0-2		19,000
Feb 27	COVENTRY CITY	W 4-0	Foxall, Green, Morton, Small	15,000
Mar 6	Doncaster Rovers	W 4-1	Foxall, Goulden, Morton, Small	8,000
Mar 13	FULHAM	D 3-3	Goulden, Morton, Small	35,000
Mar 29	Burnley	L 1-2	Small	8,000
Mar 26	BARNSLEY	D 0-0		31,000
Mar 27	SOUTHAMPTON	W 4-0	Goulden 2, Morton, Small	20,000
Mar 29	Barnsley	D 0-0		20,000
Apr 3	Swansea Town	D 0-0		12,000
Apr 10	BRADFORD CITY	W 4-1	Small 2, Foxall, Goulden	18,000
Apr 17	Aston Villa	W 2-0	Kirkcaldie, Small	15,000
Apr 24	CHESTERFIELD	D 1-1	Small	12,000
Apr 26	ASTON VILLA	W 2-1	Goulden, Green	12,000
May 1	SHEFFIELD UNITED	W 1-0	Morton	15,000

FA Cup

Jan 16	BOLTON WANDERERS	(Rd 3)	D 0-0		42,300
Jan 20	Bolton Wanderers	(R)	L 0-1		21,539

League & Cup Appearances

PLAYER	LEAGUE	CUP COMPETITION FA CUP	TOTAL
Adams	3		3
Barrett	11		11
Bicknell	28	2	30
Black	1		1
Chalkley	14		14
Cockroft	42	2	44
Conway	7		7
Conwell	2		2
Corbett D	4		4
Corbett N	1		1
Dell	2		2
Fenton E	28	2	30
Foreman	8		8
Foxall	25	2	27
Goulden	42	2	44
Green	22		22
Guest	3		3
Holmes	2		2
Kirkcaldie	3		3
Marshall	11		11
Martin	11		11
Morton	39	2	41
Ruffell	12		12
Simpson	12	2	14
Small	18	2	20
Walker A	8		8
Walker C	34	2	36
Walker R	27	2	29
Weare	35	2	37
Young	7		7

Goalscorers

PLAYER	LEAGUE	CUP COMPETITION FA CUP	TOTAL
Goulden	15		15
Morton	14		14
Foxall	11		11
Small	11		11
Martin	7		7
Simpson	3		3
Green	3		3
Marshall	2		2
Fenton E	1		1
Barrett	1		1
Cockroft	1		1
Guest	1		1
Adams	1		1
Kirkcaldie	1		1
Opps' o.gs.	1		1

Fact File

In May 1937, Len Goulden scored on his debut for England in a 6-0 victory over Norway in Oslo.

MANAGER: Charlie Paynter
CAPTAIN: Jim Barrett
TOP SCORER: Len Goulden
BIGGEST WIN: January 23, 1937 5-1 v Bury, Division 2
HIGHEST ATTENDANCE: January 16, 1937 42,300 v Bolton Wanderers, drew 0-0, FA Cup Round 3
MAJOR TRANSFERS IN: Tommy Green from West Bromwich Albion
MAJOR TRANSFERS OUT: Dave Mangall to Millwall

Final Division 2 Table

		P	W	D	L	F	A	Pts
1	Leicester C	42	24	8	10	89	57	56
2	Blackpool	42	24	7	11	88	53	55
3	Bury	42	22	8	12	74	55	52
4	Newcastle U	42	22	5	15	80	56	49
5	Plymouth Arg	42	18	13	11	71	53	49
6	West Ham U	42	19	11	12	73	55	49
7	Sheffield U	42	18	10	14	66	54	46
8	Coventry C	42	17	11	14	66	54	45
9	Aston Villa	42	16	12	14	82	70	44
10	Tottenham H	42	17	9	16	88	66	43
11	Fulham	42	15	13	14	71	61	43
12	Blackburn R	42	16	10	16	70	62	42
13	Burnley	42	16	10	16	57	61	42
14	Barnsley	42	16	9	17	50	64	41
15	Chesterfield	42	16	8	18	84	89	40
16	Swansea T	42	15	7	20	50	65	37
17	Norwich C	42	14	8	20	63	71	36
18	Nottingham F	42	12	10	20	68	90	34
19	Southampton	42	11	12	19	53	77	34
20	Bradford PA	42	12	9	21	52	88	33
21	Bradford C	42	9	12	21	54	94	30
22	Doncaster R	42	7	10	25	30	84	24

Season 1937-38

Football League Division 2

DATE	OPPONENTS	SCORE	GOALSCORERS	ATTENDANCE
Aug 28	Aston Villa	L 0-2		45,000
Aug 30	SWANSEA TOWN	W 2-1	Fenton E, Foxall	16,000
Sep 4	BRADFORD	W 3-1	Goulden 2, Macaulay	20,000
Sep 6	Swansea Town	D 0-0		14,000
Sep 11	Stockport County	D 0-0		18,000
Sep 13	CHESTERFIELD	W 5-0	Goulden 2, Small 2, Morton	17,000
Sep 18	Southampton	D 3-3	Small 2, Foxall	20,000
Sep 25	BLACKBURN ROVERS	W 2-0	Foxall, Goulden	30,000
Oct 2	Sheffield Wednesday	L 0-1		20,000
Oct 9	FULHAM	D 0-0		35,000
Oct 16	BARNSLEY	W 4-1	Goulden 2, Foxall, Macaulay	31,000
Oct 23	Luton Town	D 2-2	Small, o.g.	18,000
Oct 30	NEWCASTLE UNITED	W 1-0	Morton	34,000
Nov 6	Nottingham Forest	D 0-0		15,000
Nov 13	COVENTRY CITY	D 0-0		40,000
Nov 20	Tottenham Hotspur	L 0-2		47,691
Nov 27	BURNLEY	W 1-0	Williams	27,000
Dec 4	Bury	L 3-4	Foxall 2, Williams	5,000
Dec 11	SHEFFIELD UNITED	L 0-2		22,000
Dec 27	Norwich City	D 2-2	Williams 2	19,000
Dec 28	NORWICH CITY	D 3-3	Barrett, Green, Williams	27,000
Jan 1	ASTON VILLA	D 1-1	o.g.	32,000
Jan 15	Bradford	L 1-2	Macaulay	6,000
Jan 22	STOCKPORT COUNTY	W 1-0	Macaulay	25,000
Jan 29	SOUTHAMPTON	W 3-1	Foxall, Macaulay, Small	21,000
Feb 5	Blackburn Rovers	L 1-2	Small	13,000
Feb 12	SHEFFIELD WEDNESDAY	W 1-0	Macaulay	19,000
Feb 19	FULHAM	D 1-1	Goulden	23,000
Feb 23	Manchester United	L 0-4		10,000
Feb 26	Barnsley	L 0-1		10,000
Mar 5	LUTON TOWN	D 0-0		20,000
Mar 12	Newcastle United	D 2-2	Foxall 2	20,000
Mar 19	NOTTINGHAM FOREST	W 2-1	Macaulay 2	24,000
Mar 26	Coventry City	D 1-1	o.g.	20,000
Apr 2	TOTTENHAM HOTSPUR	L 1-3	Morton	32,300
Apr 9	Burnley	L 0-2		8,000
Apr 15	PLYMOUTH ARGYLE	L 0-1		23,000
Apr 16	BURY	W 3-1	Fenton E, Green, Macaulay	17,000
Apr 18	Plymouth Argyle	L 1-2	Foxall	22,000
Apr 23	Sheffield United	L 1-3	Fenton E	30,000
Apr 30	MANCHESTER UNITED	W 1-0	Goulden	17,000
May 7	Chesterfield	W 1-0	Macaulay	7,000

FA Cup

Jan 8	Preston North End	(Rd 3) L 0-3		30,198

League & Cup Appearances

PLAYER	LEAGUE	CUP COMPETITION FA CUP	TOTAL
Attwell	1		1
Barrett	8		8
Bicknell	42	1	43
Black	1		1
Cockroft	38	1	39
Conway	19	1	20
Corbett N	6		6
Dell	2		2
Fenton B	3		3
Fenton E	32	1	33
Forde	6		6
Foxall	36		36
Goulden	35	1	36
Green	15	1	16
Kirkcaldie	6	1	7
Macaulay	39		39
Morton	39	1	40
Roberts	1		1
Small	18		18
Turner	6		6
Walker A	1		1
Walker C	35	1	36
Walker R	32	1	33
Weare	23		23
Williams	9	1	10
Wood	8		8
Young	1		1

Goalscorers

PLAYER	LEAGUE	CUP COMPETITION FA CUP	TOTAL
Foxall	10		10
Macaulay	10		10
Goulden	9		9
Small	7		7
Williams	5		5
Fenton E	3		3
Morton	3		3
Green	2		2
Barrett	1		1
Opps' o.gs.	3		3

Fact File

Small, Williams, Fenton, Macaulay and Goulden were all tried at centre forward as West Ham suffered a goalscoring drought.

MANAGER: Charlie Paynter
CAPTAIN: Charlie Bicknell
TOP SCORERS: Stan Foxall and Archie Macaulay
BIGGEST WIN: September 13, 1937 5-0 v Chesterfield, Division 2
HIGHEST ATTENDANCE: November 20, 1937 47,691 v Tottenham Hotspur, lost 0-2, Division 2
MAJOR TRANSFERS IN: Archie Macaulay from Glasgow Rangers, Rod Williams from Reading

Final Division 2 Table

		P	W	D	L	F	A	Pts
1	Aston Villa	42	25	7	10	73	35	57
2	Manchester U	42	22	9	11	82	50	53
3	Sheffield U	42	22	9	11	73	56	53
4	Coventry C	42	20	12	10	66	45	52
5	Tottenham H	42	19	6	17	76	54	44
6	Burnley	42	17	10	15	54	54	44
7	Bradford PA	42	17	9	16	69	56	43
8	Fulham	42	16	11	15	61	57	43
9	West Ham U	42	14	14	14	53	52	42
10	Bury	42	18	5	19	63	60	42
11	Chesterfield	42	16	9	17	63	63	41
12	Luton T	42	15	10	17	89	86	40
13	Plymouth Arg	42	14	12	16	57	65	40
14	Norwich C	42	14	11	17	56	75	39
15	Southampton	42	15	9	18	55	77	39
16	Blackburn R	42	14	10	18	71	80	38
17	Sheffield W	42	14	10	18	49	56	38
18	Swansea T	42	13	12	17	45	73	38
19	Newcastle U	42	14	8	20	51	58	36
20	Nottingham F	42	14	8	20	47	60	36
21	Barnsley	42	11	14	17	50	64	36
22	Stockport Co	42	11	9	22	43	70	31

Season 1938-39

Football League Division 2

DATE	OPPONENTS	SCORE	GOALSCORERS	ATTENDANCE
Aug 27	Fulham	L 2-3	Macaulay 2	25,000
Aug 29	BLACKBURN ROVERS	L 1-2	Macaulay	15,000
Sep 3	SHEFFIELD WEDNESDAY	L 2-3	Fenton B, Morton	23,000
Sep 7	Manchester City	W 4-2	Foxall 2, Fenton B, Morton	18,000
Sep 10	Bury	D 1-1	Small	10,000
Sep 17	COVENTRY CITY	W 4-1	Fenton B 2, Macaulay 2	30,000
Sep 19	Blackburn Rovers	L 1-3	Fenton B	20,000
Sep 24	TRANMERE ROVERS	W 6-1	Macaulay 3, Cockroft, Corbett, Foxall	24,000
Oct 1	Chesterfield	L 0-1		15,000
Oct 8	SWANSEA TOWN	W 5-2	Small 2, Morton 2, Foxall	23,000
Oct 15	Nottingham Forest	D 0-0		17,000
Oct 22	NEWCASTLE UNITED	D 1-1	o.g.	30,200
Oct 29	Tottenham Hotspur	L 1-2	Foxall	52,304
Nov 5	NORWICH CITY	W 2-0	Fenton B, Macaulay	24,600
Nov 12	Luton Town	W 2-1	Macaulay, Small	18,000
Nov 19	PLYMOUTH ARGYLE	W 2-1	Goulden, Macaulay	25,000
Nov 26	Sheffield United	L 1-3	Foxall	18,000
Dec 3	BURNLEY	W 1-0	Morton	22,400
Dec 10	West Bromwich Albion	L 2-3	Macaulay, Small	25,000
Dec 17	SOUTHAMPTON	L 1-2	Small	16,500
Dec 24	FULHAM	W 1-0	Macaulay	8,000
Dec 27	MILLWALL	D 0-0		41,300
Dec 31	Sheffield United	W 4-1	Foxall 2, Morton, Small	30,000
Jan 14	BURY	D 0-0		20,000
Jan 28	Tranmere Rovers	D 2-2	Fenton B, Foxall	10,000
Feb 4	CHESTERFIELD	D 1-1	Macaulay	23,400
Feb 16	Swansea Town	L 2-3	Green, Macaulay	8,000
Feb 18	NOTTINGHAM FOREST	W 5-0	Fenton 2, Foxall, Goulden, Macaulay	16,200
Feb 25	Newcastle United	L 0-2		30,000
Mar 4	TOTTENHAM HOTSPUR	L 0-2		26,400
Mar 11	Norwich City	W 6-2	Small 2, Foxall 2, Morton 2	15,000
Mar 18	LUTON TOWN	L 0-1		23,000
Mar 25	Plymouth Argyle	D 0-0		19,000
Mar 27	Millwall	W 2-0	Foreman, Proudlock	10,000
Apr 1	SHEFFIELD UNITED	D 0-0		21,400
Apr 7	BRADFORD	L 0-2		25,000
Apr 8	Burnley	L 0-1		8,000
Apr 11	Bradford	W 2-1	Gore, Small	8,000
Apr 15	WEST BROMWICH ALBION	W 2-1	Bell, Foxall	16,400
Apr 22	Southampton	W 2-0	Foxall, Goulden	9,931
Apr 24	Coventry City	D 0-0		10,000
May 6	MANCHESTER CITY	W 2-1	Goulden, Hubbard	26,004

FA Cup

Jan 7	Queens Park Rangers	(Rd 3)	W 2-1	Foxall, Morton	22,408
Jan 21	TOTTENHAM HOTSPUR	(Rd 4)	D 3-3	Foxall 2, Macaulay	42,716
Jan 30	Tottenham Hotspur	(R)	D 1-1	Foxall	50,798
Feb 2	TOTTENHAM HOTSPUR	(2nd R)	W 2-1*	Foxall, Macaulay	50,468
Feb 11	Portsmouth	(Rd 5)	L 0-2		47,614

*Played at Highbury.

League & Cup Appearances

PLAYER	LEAGUE	CUP COMPETITION FA CUP	TOTAL
Banner	1		1
Barrett	1		1
Bell	1		1
Bicknell	41	5	46
Burton	1		1
Cockroft	39	3	42
Conway	21		21
Corbett	31	4	35
Fenton B	18	1	19
Fenton E	12	3	15
Forde	1		1
Foreman	6		6
Foxall	40	5	45
Gore	5		5
Goulden	37	5	42
Green	3	1	4
Hubbard	1		1
Kirkcaldie	2		2
Macaulay	36	5	41
Medhurst	21	5	26
Morton	31	4	35
Proudlock	4		4
Small	19	4	23
Turner	5		5
Walker C	41	5	46
Walker R	38	5	43
Wood	2		2
Woodgate	4		4

Goalscorers

PLAYER	LEAGUE	CUP COMPETITION FA CUP	TOTAL
Foxall	14	5	19
Macaulay	16	2	18
Small	11		11
Fenton B	9		9
Morton	7	1	8
Goulden	4		4
Cockroft	1		1
Corbett	1		1
Green	1		1
Foreman	1		1
Proudlock	1		1
Gore	1		1
Bell	1		1
Hubbard	1		1
Opps' o.gs.	1		1

Fact File

The deadlock in the FA Cup tie with Tottenham was finally ended when Archie Macaulay netted an open goal in the second half of extra-time in the second replay.

MANAGER: Charlie Paynter
CAPTAIN: Charlie Bicknell
TOP SCORER: Stan Foxall
BIGGEST WIN: September 24, 1938 6-1 v Tranmere Rovers, Division 2
HIGHEST ATTENDANCE: October 29, 1938 52,304 v Tottenham Hotspur, lost 1-2, Division 2
MAJOR TRANSFERS IN: Cliff Hubbard fron Hull City, Reg Gore from Frickley Colliery

Final Division 2 Table

		P	W	D	L	F	A	PTS
1	BLACKBURN R	42	25	5	12	94	60	55
2	SHEFFIELD U	42	20	14	8	69	41	54
3	SHEFFIELD W	42	21	11	10	88	59	53
4	COVENTRY C	42	21	8	13	62	45	50
5	MANCHESTER C	42	21	7	14	96	72	49
6	CHESTERFIELD	42	20	9	13	69	52	49
7	LUTON T	42	22	5	15	82	66	49
8	TOTTENHAM H	42	19	9	14	67	62	47
9	NEWCASTLE U	42	18	10	14	61	48	46
10	WBA	42	18	9	15	89	72	45
11	WEST HAM U	42	17	10	15	70	52	44
12	FULHAM	42	17	10	15	61	55	44
13	MILLWALL	42	14	14	14	64	53	42
14	BURNLEY	42	15	9	18	50	56	39
15	PLYMOUTH ARG	42	15	8	19	49	55	38
16	BURY	42	12	13	17	65	74	37
17	BRADFORD PA	42	12	11	19	61	82	35
18	SOUTHAMPTON	42	13	9	20	56	82	35
19	SWANSEA T	42	11	12	19	50	83	34
20	NOTTINGHAM F	42	10	11	21	49	82	31
21	NORWICH C	42	13	5	24	50	91	31
22	TRANMERE R	42	6	5	31	39	99	17

Season 1945-46

Division South

DATE	OPPONENTS	SCORE	GOALSCORERS	ATTENDANCE
Aug 25	Birmingham City	W 1-0	Bicknell	30,000
Aug 27	ARSENAL	D 1-1	Whitchurch	25,000
Sep 1	BIRMINGHAM CITY	W 3-2	Foreman 2, Whitchurch	20,000
Sep 8	TOTTENHAM HOTSPUR	D 1-1	Foreman	26,000
Sep 10	ASTON VILLA	L 1-2	Foreman	20,000
Sep 15	Tottenham Hotspur	W 3-2	Hall, Macaulay 2	34,778
Sep 22	Brentford	D 1-1	Hall	19,000
Sep 29	BRENTFORD	L 0-2		23,000
Oct 6	CHELSEA	L 2-4	Foreman, Whitchurch	25,000
Oct 13	Chelsea	W 2-1	Bicknell, Hall	45,000
Oct 20	Millwall	D 0-0		32,000
Oct 27	MILLWALL	W 3-1	Foreman, Hall, Wood	25,000
Nov 3	SOUTHAMPTON	W 3-1	Small 3	20,000
Nov 10	Southampton	D 3-3	Foreman, Woodgate, Wright	17,000
Nov 17	Derby County	L 1-5	Hall	20,000
Nov 24	DERBY COUNTY	L 2-3	Small 2	28,000
Dec 1	LEICESTER CITY	D 2-2	Macaulay, Small	20,000
Dec 8	Leicester City	L 1-4	Woodgate	12,345
Dec 15	Coventry City	W 5-2	Hall 2, Woodgate, Wright 2	11,719
Dec 22	COVENTRY CITY	W 6-3	Foreman 2, Wood, Woodgate, Wright 2	14,000
Dec 25	LUTON TOWN	L 3-4	Fenton, Foreman, Woodgate	10,000
Dec 26	Luton Town	W 4-1	Bicknell, Foreman, Small, Woodgate	14,000
Dec 29	Aston Villa	D 2-2	Bainbridge, o.g.	30,000
Jan 12	Charlton Athletic	L 0-3		45,000
Jan 19	CHARLTON ATHLETIC	W 2-0	Fenton, Foreman	25,000
Feb 2	Fulham	W 1-0	Hall	30,000
Feb 9	Plymouth Argyle	W 2-1	Foreman, Wood	20,000
Feb 16	PLYMOUTH ARGYLE	W 7-0	Travis 4, Woodgate 3	15,000
Feb 23	Portsmouth	W 3-1	Bainbridge, Travis, Woodgate	15,000
Mar 2	PORTSMOUTH	W 3-2	Bainbridge, Bicknell, Woodgate	12,000
Mar 9	Nottingham Forest	D 1-1	Fenton	22,000
Mar 16	NOTTINGHAM FOREST	L 1-3	Small	18,000
Mar 23	NEWPORT COUNTY	W 4-1	Gray, Hall, Macaulay 2	12,000
Mar 30	Newport County	D 2-2	Hall Macaulay	16,000
Apr 6	Wolverhampton W	D 3-3	Macaulay, Wood 2	25,000
Apr 13	WOLVERHAMPTON W	W 2-1	Travis 2	25,000
Apr 19	Swansea Town	W 3-2	Hall 2, Small	25,000
Apr 20	WEST BROMWICH ALBION	D 1-1	Macaulay	24,600
Apr 22	SWANSEA TOWN	W 3-0	Hall 2, Small	14,959
Apr 27	West Bromwich Albion	W 2-1	Macaulay, Small	10,000
Apr 29	FULHAM	L 3-5	Hall 2, Wood	28,000
May 4	Arsenal	L 1-2	Wood	30,000

FA Cup

Jan 5	ARSENAL	(Rd 3 FL)	W 6-0	Hall 2, Wood 2, Bainbridge, Foreman	35,000
Jan 9	Arsenal	(Rd 3 SL)	L 0-1		22,000
Jan 26	Chelsea	(Rd 4 FL)	L 0-2		65,000
Jan 30	CHELSEA	(Rd 4 SL)	W 1-0	Hall	31,000

Fact File

Don Travis scored four goals on his debut for West Ham against Plymouth Argyle in February.

MANAGER: Charlie Paynter
CAPTAIN: Dick Walker
TOP SCORER: George Hall
BIGGEST WIN: Feburary 16, 1946 7-0 v Plymouth Argyle, Division South
HIGHEST ATTENDANCE: January 26, 1946 65,000 v Chelsea, drew 1-1, FA Cup Round 4
MAJOR TRANSFERS IN: George Hall from Bradford
MAJOR TRANSFERS OUT: Len Goulden to Chelsea, Ted Fenton to Colchester United, Charlie Walker to Margate (as manager)

League & Cup Appearances

PLAYER	LEAGUE	CUP COMPETITION FA CUP	TOTAL
Attwell	7		7
Bainbridge	9	3	12
Bicknell	41	4	45
Cater	21	4	25
Corbett N	26		26
Dunn	1		1
Fenton E	37	4	41
Foreman	23	3	26
Forte	1		1
Gray	1		1
Hall	33	4	37
Harris	1		1
Hopkins	1		1
Macaulay	23	2	25
Medhurst	42	4	46
Powell-Besens	1		1
Small	25	4	29
Travis	6		6
Whitchurch	19		19
Wilson	11		11
Wood	30	4	34
Woodgate	39	4	43
Walker C	19		19
Walker R	40	4	44
Wright	5		5

Goalscorers

PLAYER	LEAGUE	CUP COMPETITION FA CUP	TOTAL
Hall	16	3	19
Foreman	13	1	14
Woodgate	12		12
Small	10		10
Macaulay	9		9
Wood	7	2	9
Travis	7		7
Wright	5		5
Bicknell	4		4
Bainbridge	3	1	4
Fenton E	3		3
Whitchurch	3		3
Gray	1		1
Opps' o.gs.	1		1

Final Division South Table

		P	W	D	L	F	A	Pts
1	Birmingham C	42	28	5	9	96	45	61
2	Aston Villa	42	25	11	6	106	58	61
3	Charlton Ath	42	25	10	7	92	45	60
4	Derby Co	42	24	7	11	101	62	55
5	WBA	42	22	8	12	104	69	52
6	Wolverhampton W	42	20	11	11	75	48	51
7	West Ham U	42	20	11	11	94	76	51
8	Fulham	42	20	10	12	93	73	50
9	Tottenham H	42	22	3	17	78	81	47
10	Chelsea	42	19	6	17	92	80	44
11	Arsenal	42	16	11	15	76	73	43
12	Millwall	42	17	8	17	79	105	42
13	Coventry C	42	15	10	17	70	69	40
14	Brentford	42	14	10	18	82	72	38
15	Nottingham F	42	12	13	17	72	73	37
16	Southampton	42	14	9	19	97	105	37
17	Swansea T	42	15	7	20	90	112	37
18	Luton T	42	13	7	22	60	92	33
19	Portsmouth	42	11	6	25	66	87	28
20	Leicester C	42	8	7	27	57	101	23
21	Newport Co	42	9	2	31	52	125	20
22	Plymouth Arg	42	3	8	25	39	120	14

Season 1946-47

Football League Division 2

DATE	OPPONENTS	SCORE	GOALSCORERS	ATTENDANCE
Aug 31	Plymouth Argyle	L 1-3	Wood	26,000
Sep 2	FULHAM	W 3-2	Small, Macaulay 2	28,000
Sep 7	LEICESTER CITY	L 0-2		28,000
Sep 9	Fulham	L 2-3	Wood 2	19,913
Sep 14	Chesterfield	L 1-3	Small	16,000
Sep 21	MILLWALL	W 3-1	Dunn, Small, o.g.	30,400
Sep 28	Bradford	W 1-0	Wood	21,360
Oct 5	MANCHESTER CITY	W 1-0	Macaulay	30,000
Oct 12	Burnley	L 1-2	Small	24,000
Oct 19	TOTTENHAM HOTSPUR	D 2-2	Small, Bainbridge	34,200
Oct 26	Swansea Town	L 1-2	Bainbridge	34,000
Nov 2	NEWCASTLE UNITED	L 0-2		32,000
Nov 9	West Bromwich Albion	W 3-2	Woodgate, Parker, Wood	20,000
Nov 16	BIRMINGHAM CITY	L 0-4		25,000
Nov 23	Coventry City	L 1-2	Wright	12,000
Nov 30	NOTTINGHAM FOREST	D 2-2	Proudlock, Hall	10,000
Dec 7	Southampton	L 2-4	Payne, Bainbridge	17,000
Dec 21	Barnsley	W 2-1	Hall, Payne	10,000
Dec 25	LUTON TOWN	W 2-1	Payne, Woodgate	20,000
Dec 26	Luton Town	L 1-2	Payne	24,000
Dec 28	PLYMOUTH ARGYLE	W 4-1	Bicknell, Small, Payne, Wood	17,000
Jan 1	Sheffield Wednesday	D 1-1	Bainbridge	32,000
Jan 4	Leicester City	L 0-4		25,000
Jan 18	CHESTERFIELD	W 5-0	Wood 2, Hall, Payne, Small	24,000
Jan 25	Millwall	D 0-0		22,000
Feb 1	BRADFORD	D 1-1	Bainbridge	16,845
Feb 8	NEWPORT COUNTY	W 3-0	Neary 2, Woodgate	12,500
Mar 1	SWANSEA TOWN	W 3-0	Neary 2, Hall	21,000
Mar 15	WEST BROMWICH ALBION	W 3-2	Neary 3	24,000
Mar 22	Birmingham City	L 0-3		30,000
Mar 29	COVENTRY CITY	L 1-2	Neary	32,000
Apr 4	Bury	L 0-4		15,000
Apr 5	Nottingham Forest	L 3-4	Neary 2, Parsons	20,000
Apr 7	BURY	D 3-3	Neary 2, Bainbridge	22,400
Apr 12	SOUTHAMPTON	W 4-0	Neary 2, Parsons, Wood	22,000
Apr 19	Newport County	D 1-1	Bainbridge	15,000
Apr 26	BARNSLEY	W 4-0	Parsons 2, Bainbridge, Woodgate	17,000
May 3	SHEFFIELD WEDNESDAY	W 2-1	Neary, Woodgate	25,000
May 17	Tottenham Hotspur	D 0-0		37,500
May 24	Manchester City	L 0-2		28,000
May 26	Newcastle United	W 3-2	Hall, Wood, Bainbridge	35,000
May 31	BURNLEY	L 0-5		30,000

FA Cup

Jan 11	Leicester City	(Rd 3)	L 1-2	Woodgate	26,000

League & Cup Appearances

PLAYER	LEAGUE	CUP COMPETITION FA CUP	TOTAL
Attwell	4		4
Bainbridge	35	1	36
Banner	21		21
Bicknell	19		19
Cater	34	1	35
Corbett N	35	1	36
Devlin	2		2
Dunn	7		7
Forde	24	1	25
Gregory	9		9
Hall	24	1	25
Macaulay	8		8
Medhurst	3		3
Neary	14		14
Parker	10		10
Parsons	12	1	13
Payne	10	1	11
Proudlock	4		4
Sadler	1		1
Small	39	1	40
Taylor	30	1	31
Travis	1		1
Walker R	34	1	35
Wilson	1		1
Wood	33		33
Woodgate	41	1	42
Wright	7		7

Goalscorers

PLAYER	LEAGUE	CUP COMPETITION FA CUP	TOTAL
Neary	15		15
Wood	10		10
Bainbridge	9		9
Small	7		7
Woodgate	5	1	6
Payne	6		6
Hall	5		5
Parsons	4		4
Macaulay	3		3
Bicknell	1		1
Wright	1		1
Dunn	1		1
Proudlock	1		1
Parker	1		1
Opps' o.gs.	1		1

Fact File

New signing Frank Neary scored 15 goals in his 14 games this season.

MANAGER: Charlie Paynter
CAPTAIN: Dick Walker
TOP SCORER: Frank Neary
BIGGEST WIN: January 18, 1947 5-0 v Luton Town, Division 2
HIGHEST ATTENDANCE: May 17, 1947 37,500 v Tottenham Hotspur, drew 0-0, Division 2
MAJOR TRANSFERS IN: Joe Payne from Chelsea, Frank Neary from Queens Park Rangers

Final Division 2 Table

		P	W	D	L	F	A	Pts
1	Manchester C	42	26	10	6	78	35	62
2	Burnley	42	22	14	6	65	29	58
3	Birmingham C	42	25	5	12	74	33	55
4	Chesterfield	42	18	14	10	58	44	50
5	Newcastle U	42	19	10	13	95	62	48
6	Tottenham H	42	17	14	11	65	53	48
7	WBA	42	20	8	14	88	75	48
8	Coventry C	42	16	13	13	66	59	45
9	Leicester C	42	18	7	17	69	64	43
10	Barnsley	42	17	8	17	84	86	42
11	Nottingham F	42	15	10	17	69	74	40
12	West Ham U	42	16	8	18	70	76	40
13	Luton T	42	16	7	19	71	73	39
14	Southampton	42	15	9	18	69	76	39
15	Fulham	42	15	9	18	63	74	39
16	Bradford PA	42	14	11	17	65	77	39
17	Bury	42	12	12	18	80	78	36
18	Millwall	42	14	8	20	56	79	36
19	Plymouth Arg	42	14	5	23	79	96	33
20	Sheffield W	42	12	8	22	67	88	32
21	Swansea T	42	11	7	24	55	83	29
22	Newport Co	42	10	3	29	61	133	23

Season 1947-48

Football League Division 2

DATE	OPPONENTS	SCORE	GOALSCORERS	ATTENDANCE
Aug 23	Bradford	L 1-4	Walker	15,000
Aug 25	MILLWALL	D 1-1	Woodgate	25,000
Aug 30	NOTTINGHAM FOREST	W 2-1	Parsons, o.g.	25,000
Sep 1	Millwall	D 1-1	Small	15,814
Sep 6	Doncaster Rovers	L 0-1		19,953
Sep 8	TOTTENHAM HOTSPUR	D 1-1	Parsons	25,600
Sep 13	SOUTHAMPTON	W 2-0	Hall, Wood	20,400
Sep 15	Tottenham Hotspur	D 2-2	Parsons, Wood	35,000
Sep 20	Bury	W 2-1	Proudlock, Wood	16,498
Sep 27	COVENTRY CITY	W 1-0	Proudlock	25,000
Oct 4	CHESTERFIELD	W 4-0	Tucker 3, Proudlock	26,000
Oct 11	Newcastle United	L 0-1		55,777
Oct 18	BIRMINGHAM CITY	D 0-0		32,000
Oct 25	West Bromwich Albion	W 2-1	Wright 2	40,000
Nov 1	BARNSLEY	W 2-1	Moroney, Small	28,000
Nov 8	Plymouth Argyle	D 1-1	Parsons	29,111
Nov 15	LUTON TOWN	D 0-0		31,000
Nov 22	Brentford	D 1-1	Small	24,161
Nov 29	LEICESTER CITY	D 1-1	Woodgate	23,000
Dec 6	Leeds United	L 1-2	Wright	21,500
Dec 13	FULHAM	W 3-0	Moroney, Parsons, Wright	25,000
Dec 20	BRADFORD	D 0-0		25,000
Dec 26	Sheffield Wednesday	L 3-5	Corbett, Woodgate, Parsons	37,343
Dec 27	SHEFFIELD WEDNESDAY	L 1-4	Stephens	20,000
Jan 3	Nottingham Forest	L 1-2	Woodgate	26,138
Jan 24	DONCASTER ROVERS	W 2-1	Parsons 2	16,000
Jan 31	Southampton	L 1-3	Wright	22,000
Feb 7	BURY	W 2-0	Forde, Woodgate	19,000
Feb 14	Coventry City	W 1-0	Wright	34,000
Feb 28	NEWCASTLE UNITED	L 0-2		30,000
Mar 6	Birmingham City	W 1-0	Dunn	44,000
Mar 13	WEST BROMWICH ALBION	L 0-2		25,000
Mar 20	Barnsley	D 1-1	Parsons	18,000
Mar 26	Cardiff City	W 3-0	Stephens 3	45,000
Mar 27	PLYMOUTH ARGYLE	D 1-1	Stephens	22,000
Mar 29	CARDIFF CITY	W 4-2	Wright 2, Stephens, Parsons	34,000
Apr 3	Luton Town	D 0-0		15,000
Apr 7	Chesterfield	L 0-6		11,554
Apr 10	BRENTFORD	L 0-1		22,000
Apr 17	Leicester City	W 3-1	Woodgate, Hall, Wade	34,856
Apr 24	LEEDS UNITED	W 2-1	Woodgate, Parsons	14,000
May 1	Fulham	D 1-1	Hall	20,000

FA Cup

Jan 10	Blackburn Rovers	(Rd 3)	D 0-0		32,500
Jan 17	BLACKBURN ROVERS	(R)	L 2-4	Parsons, Stephens	30,000

League & Cup Appearances

PLAYER	LEAGUE	CUP COMPETITION FA CUP	TOTAL
Armstrong	1		1
Bainbridge	4		4
Banner	5		5
Cater	7	1	8
Corbett	42	2	44
Devlin	1		1
Dunn	4		4
Forde	42	2	44
Gregory	42	2	44
Hall	9	1	10
Moroney	36	2	38
Neary	3		3
Parker	2		2
Parsons	42	2	44
Proudlock	10		10
Small	14	1	15
Stephens	21	2	23
Travis	4		4
Tucker	5		5
Wade	16	2	18
Walker	39	1	40
Wilson	2		2
Wood	12		12
Woodgate	38	2	40
Wright	21		21
Yeomanson	40	2	42

Goalscorers

PLAYER	LEAGUE	CUP COMPETITION FA CUP	TOTAL
Parsons	11	1	12
Wright	8		8
Woodgate	7		7
Stephens	6	1	7
Wood	3		3
Small	3		3
Hall	3		3
Proudlock	3		3
Tucker	3		3
Moroney	2		2
Forde	1		1
Corbett	1		1
Walker	1		1
Wade	1		1
Dunn	1		1
Opps' o.gs.	1		1

Fact File

West Ham remained unbeaten at home until 27 December, but their home form let them down later in the season.

MANAGER: Charlie Paynter
CAPTAIN: Dick Walker
TOP SCORER: Eric Parsons
BIGGEST WIN: October 4, 1947 4-0 v Chesterfield, Division 2
HIGHEST ATTENDANCE: October 11, 1947 55,777 v Newcastle United, lost 0-1, Division 2
MAJOR TRANSFERS IN: Bill Stephens from Swindon Town, Jack Yeomanson from Margate

Final Division 2 Table

		P	W	D	L	F	A	Pts
1	Birmingham C	42	22	15	5	55	24	59
2	Newcastle U	42	24	8	10	72	41	56
3	Southampton	42	21	10	11	71	53	52
4	Sheffield W	42	20	11	11	66	53	51
5	Cardiff C	42	18	11	13	61	58	47
6	West Ham U	42	16	14	12	55	53	46
7	WBA	42	18	9	15	63	58	45
8	Tottenham H	42	15	14	13	56	43	44
9	Leicester C	42	16	11	15	60	57	43
10	Coventry C	42	14	13	15	59	52	41
11	Fulham	42	15	10	17	47	46	40
12	Barnsley	42	15	10	17	62	64	40
13	Luton T	42	14	12	16	56	59	40
14	Bradford PA	42	16	8	18	68	72	40
15	Brentford	42	13	14	15	44	61	40
16	Chesterfield	42	16	7	19	54	55	39
17	Plymouth Arg	42	9	20	13	40	58	38
18	Leeds U	42	14	8	20	62	72	36
19	Nottingham F	42	12	11	19	54	60	35
20	Bury	42	9	16	17	58	68	34
21	Doncaster R	42	9	11	22	40	66	29
22	Millwall	42	9	11	22	44	74	29

Season 1948-49

Football League Division 2

DATE	OPPONENTS	SCORE	GOALSCORERS	ATTENDANCE
Aug 21	LINCOLN CITY	D 2-2	Wright, McGowan	31,000
Aug 23	Sheffield Wednesday	L 0-3		36,000
Aug 28	Chesterfield	D 0-0		18,000
Aug 30	SHEFFIELD WEDNESDAY	D 2-2	Parsons, Bainbridge	28,000
Sep 4	WEST BROMWICH ALBION	W 1-0	Hall	28,000
Sep 6	Coventry City	L 0-1		16,494
Sep 11	Bury	L 0-2		23,754
Sep 13	COVENTRY CITY	D 2-2	Chapman, o.g.	18,000
Sep 18	PLYMOUTH ARGYLE	W 3-0	Yeomanson, Chapman, Wright	22,000
Sep 25	TOTTENHAM HOTSPUR	W 1-0	Hall	38,400
Oct 2	Brentford	D 0-0		31,400
Oct 9	Blackburn Rovers	D 0-0		23,800
Oct 16	CARDIFF CITY	W 3-1	Parsons, Wright, Chapman	30,000
Oct 23	Queens Park Rangers	L 1-2	Wright	27,500
Oct 30	LUTON TOWN	L 0-1		25,000
Nov 6	Bradford	W 3-2	Parsons, Hall, Woodgate	15,913
Nov 13	SOUTHAMPTON	D 1-1	Woodgate	35,000
Nov 20	Barnsley	W 3-2	Wright, Walker, Woodgate	20,289
Dec 4	Nottingham Forest	L 0-3		23,168
Dec 11	FULHAM	W 1-0	Wright	22,500
Dec 18	Lincoln City	L 3-4	Woodgate 2, Parsons	16,000
Dec 25	LEEDS UNITED	W 3-2	Wright 2, Corbett	21,000
Dec 27	Leeds United	W 3-1	Wright 2, Dick	32,500
Jan 1	CHESTERFIELD	L 1-2	Woodgate	17,000
Jan 15	West Bromwich Albion	L 1-2	Robinson	15,000
Jan 22	BURY	W 2-1	Parsons, Robinson	22,000
Feb 5	Plymouth Argyle	L 0-2		17,000
Feb 12	GRIMSBY TOWN	W 1-0	Robinson	15,000
Feb 19	Tottenham Hotspur	D 1-1	Woodgate	62,980
Mar 5	BLACKBURN ROVERS	W 2-1	Parsons, Wright	18,560
Mar 12	Cardiff City	L 0-4		30,000
Mar 19	QUEENS PARK RANGERS	W 2-0	Woodgate, Robinson	26,000
Mar 26	Luton Town	W 1-0	Robinson	15,587
Apr 2	BRADFORD	W 4-1	Parsons 2, McGowan, o.g.	19,000
Apr 9	Southampton	W 1-0	Robinson	25,000
Apr 15	LEICESTER CITY	W 4-1	Robinson 3, Woodgate	33,000
Apr 16	BARNSLEY	W 2-0	Parsons, McGowan	21,000
Apr 18	Leicester City	D 1-1	Robinson	29,700
Apr 23	Grimsby Town	L 0-3		16,000
Apr 25	BRENTFORD	D 1-1	Bainbridge	15,000
Apr 30	NOTTINGHAM FOREST	L 0-5		15,000
May 7	Fulham	L 0-2		40,000

FA Cup

Jan 8	Luton Town	(Rd 3)	L 1-3	Wade	21,629

League & Cup Appearances

PLAYER	LEAGUE	CUP COMPETITION FA CUP	TOTAL
Bainbridge	16		16
Carroll	5	1	6
Cater	18	1	19
Chapman	7	1	8
Corbett	39	1	40
Devlin	20		20
Dick	14		14
Forde	31		31
Gregory	27	1	28
Hall	17		17
Jackman	1		1
McGowan	15		15
Moroney	36	1	37
Parsons	42	1	43
Robinson	17		17
Stephens	1		1
Taylor	15		15
Tucker	2		2
Wade	8		8
Walker	40	1	41
Wood	3		3
Woodgate	38		38
Wright	21	1	22
Yeomanson	29	1	30

Goalscorers

PLAYER	LEAGUE	CUP COMPETITION FA CUP	TOTAL
Wright	11		11
Robinson	10		10
Parsons	9		9
Woodgate	9		9
McGowan	3		3
Hall	3		3
Chapman	3		3
Bainbridge	2		2
Yeomansin	1		1
Corbett	1		1
Walker	1		1
Dick	1		1
Wade		1	1
Opps' o.gs.	2		2

Final Division 2 Table

		P	W	D	L	F	A	Pts
1	Fulham	42	24	9	9	77	37	57
2	WBA	42	24	8	10	69	39	56
3	Southampton	42	23	9	10	69	36	55
4	Cardiff C	42	19	13	10	62	47	51
5	Tottenham H	42	17	16	9	72	44	50
6	Chesterfield	42	15	17	10	51	45	47
7	West Ham U	42	18	10	14	56	58	46
8	Sheffield W	42	15	13	14	63	56	43
9	Barnsley	42	14	12	16	62	61	40
10	Luton T	42	14	12	16	55	57	40
11	Grimsby T	42	15	10	17	72	76	40
12	Bury	42	17	6	19	67	76	40
13	QPR	42	14	11	17	44	62	39
14	Blackburn R	42	15	8	19	53	63	38
15	Leeds U	42	12	13	17	55	63	37
16	Coventry C	42	15	7	20	55	64	37
17	Bradford PA	42	13	11	18	65	78	37
18	Brentford	42	11	14	17	42	53	36
19	Leicester C	42	10	16	16	62	79	36
20	Plymouth Arg	42	12	12	18	49	64	36
21	Nottingham F	42	14	7	21	50	54	35
22	Lincoln C	42	8	12	22	53	91	28

Fact File

Bill Stephens broke his shin bone in the opening game of the season and would never play for West Ham again.

MANAGER: Charlie Paynter
CAPTAIN: Dick Walker
TOP SCORER: Ken Wright
BIGGEST WIN: April 2, 1949 4-1 v Bradford, Division 2; April 15, 1949 4-1 v Leicester City, Division 2
HIGHEST ATTENDANCE: February 16, 1949 62,980 v Tottenham Hotspur, drew 1-1, Division 2

Season 1949-50

Football League Division 2

DATE	OPPONENTS	SCORE	GOALSCORERS	ATTENDANCE
Aug 20	Luton Town	D 2-2	Robinson, Parsons	17,000
Aug 22	LEEDS UNITED	W 3-1	Robinson 2, McGowan	23,000
Aug 27	BARNSLEY	W 2-1	Gazzard, Bainbridge	28,000
Aug 31	Leeds United	D 2-2	Robinson, Bainbridge	29,500
Sep 3	Plymouth Argyle	W 3-0	Gazzard, Robinson, Parsons	25,521
Sep 6	SOUTHAMPTON	L 1-2	Robinson	25,000
Sep 10	Sheffield United	D 0-0		25,000
Sep 17	GRIMSBY TOWN	W 4-3	Bainbridge 2, Robinson 2	28,000
Sep 24	Queens Park Rangers	W 1-0	Robinson	24,000
Oct 1	PRESTON NORTH END	L 0-3		37,000
Oct 8	CHESTERFIELD	D 1-1	Parsons	26,000
Oct 15	Bradford	L 1-2	Robinson	13,863
Oct 22	LEICESTER CITY	D 2-2	Parsons, Bainbridge	23,000
Oct 29	Bury	L 1-3	Gazzard	16,399
Nov 5	TOTTENHAM HOTSPUR	L 0-1		32,000
Nov 12	Cardiff City	W 1-0	Robinson	17,000
Nov 19	BLACKBURN ROVERS	L 0-2		17,400
Nov 26	Brentford	W 2-0	Robinson 2	21,930
Dec 3	HULL CITY	W 2-1	Robinson, Wade	29,500
Dec 10	Sheffield Wednesday	L 1-2	Wade	24,000
Dec 17	LUTON TOWN	D 0-0		25,000
Dec 24	Barnsley	D 1-1	Parsons	17,295
Dec 26	SWANSEA TOWN	W 3-0	Parsons, Wade, o.g.	24,000
Dec 27	Swansea Town	L 0-1		30,000
Dec 31	PLYMOUTH ARGYLE	D 2-2	Robinson, Wade	19,000
Jan 14	SHEFFIELD UNITED	D 0-0		23,000
Jan 21	Grimsby Town	L 0-2		17,000
Feb 4	QUEENS PARK RANGERS	W 1-0	Robinson	26,000
Feb 18	Preston North End	L 1-2	o.g.	25,000
Feb 25	Chesterfield	L 0-1		3,036
Mar 4	BRADFORD	W 1-0	Parker	17,000
Mar 11	Leicester City	L 1-2	Robinson	28,040
Mar 18	BURY	W 4-0	Parker, Woodgate, Gazzard, Parsons	18,000
Mar 25	Tottenham Hotspur	L 1-4	Robinson	51,124
Apr 1	BRENTFORD	D 2-2	Robinson 2	21,000
Apr 8	Hull City	D 2-2	Robinson, McGowan	27,000
Apr 10	COVENTRY CITY	L 0-1		11,000
Apr 11	Coventry City	L 1-5	Woodgate	26,648
Apr 15	CARDIFF CITY	L 0-1		15,000
Apr 22	Blackburn Rovers	L 0-2		17,400
Apr 29	SHEFFIELD WEDNESDAY	D 2-2	Woodgate 2	10,500
May 6	Southampton	L 2-3	Robinson 2	24,778

FA Cup

Jan 7	IPSWICH TOWN	(Rd 3) W 5-1	Woodgate 2, Gazzard, Wade, Robinson	25,000
Jan 28	EVERTON	(Rd 4) L 1-2	McGowan	26,800

League & Cup Appearances

PLAYER	LEAGUE	CUP COMPETITION FA CUP	TOTAL
Bainbridge	25		25
Barrett	3		3
Cater	4	1	5
Corbett	12		12
Devlin	28	2	30
Forde	27		27
Gazzard	38	2	40
Gregory	42	2	44
Jackman	3		3
Kearns	8		8
McGowan	37	2	39
Moroney	21		21
Parker	32	2	34
Parsons	38	2	40
Robinson	40	2	42
Tucker	2		2
Wade	12	1	13
Walker	39	2	41
Woodgate	29	2	31
Wright	2		2
Yeomanson	20	2	22

Goalscorers

PLAYER	LEAGUE	CUP COMPETITION FA CUP	TOTAL
Robinson	21	1	22
Parsons	7		7
Woodgate	4	2	6
Gazzard	4	1	5
Bainbridge	5		5
Wade	4	1	5
McGowan	2	1	3
Parker	2		2
Opps' o.gs.	2		2

Fact File

Ken Bainbridge scored after only nine seconds of the home game against Barnsley.

MANAGER: Charlie Paynter
CAPTAIN: Dick Walker
TOP SCORER: Bill Robinson
BIGGEST WIN: January 7, 1950 5-1 v Ipswich Town, FA Cup Round 3
HIGHEST ATTENDANCE: March 25, 1950 51,124 v Tottenham Hotspur, lost 1-4, Division 2

Final Division 2 Table

		P	W	D	L	F	A	Pts
1	Tottenham H	42	27	7	8	81	35	61
2	Sheffield W	42	18	16	8	67	48	52
3	Sheffield U	42	19	14	9	68	49	52
4	Southampton	42	19	14	9	64	48	52
5	Leeds U	42	17	13	12	54	45	47
6	Preston NE	42	18	9	15	60	49	45
7	Hull C	42	17	11	14	64	72	45
8	Swansea T	42	17	9	16	53	49	43
9	Brentford	42	15	13	14	44	49	43
10	Cardiff C	42	16	10	16	41	44	42
11	Grimsby T	42	16	8	18	74	73	40
12	Coventry C	42	13	13	16	55	55	39
13	Barnsley	42	13	13	16	64	67	39
14	Chesterfield	42	15	9	18	43	47	39
15	Leicester C	42	12	15	15	55	65	39
16	Blackburn R	42	14	10	18	55	60	38
17	Luton T	42	10	18	14	41	51	38
18	Bury	42	14	9	19	60	65	37
19	West Ham U	42	12	12	18	53	61	36
20	QPR	42	11	12	19	40	57	34
21	Plymouth Arg	42	8	16	18	44	65	32
22	Bradford PA	42	10	11	21	51	77	31

Season 1950-51

Football League Division 2

DATE	OPPONENTS	SCORE	GOALSCORERS	ATTENDANCE
Aug 19	HULL CITY	D 3-3	Gazzard, Robinson, o.g.	30,000
Aug 24	LUTON TOWN	W 2-1	Woodgate, Betts	21,000
Aug 26	Doncaster Rovers	L 0-3		23,678
Aug 28	Luton Town	D 1-1	Gazzard	14,000
Sep 2	BRENTFORD	L 1-2	Parsons	22,000
Sep 4	Cardiff City	L 1-2	Johns	32,000
Sep 9	Blackburn Rovers	W 3-1	Robinson 2, Johns	25,200
Sep 16	SOUTHAMPTON	W 3-0	Gazzard 2, Robinson	22,500
Sep 23	Barnsley	W 2-1	Robinson, Woodgate	25,611
Sep 30	SHEFFIELD UNITED	L 3-5	Robinson 3	25,500
Oct 7	QUEENS PARK RANGERS	W 4-1	Parsons 2, Woodgate, Robinson	26,500
Oct 14	Bury	L 0-3		15,542
Oct 21	LEICESTER CITY	D 0-0		25,000
Oct 28	Chesterfield	W 2-1	Woodgate, Barrett	11,207
Nov 4	COVENTRY CITY	W 3-2	Gazzard 2, Parker	26,000
Nov 11	Manchester City	L 0-2		35,000
Nov 18	PRESTON NORTH END	W 2-0	Robinson, Gazzard	27,000
Nov 25	Notts County	L 1-4	Woodgate	27,078
Dec 2	GRIMSBY TOWN	W 2-1	Barrett, Robinson	18,500
Dec 9	Birmingham City	L 1-3	Robinson	18,000
Dec 16	Hull City	W 2-1	Robinson, Woodgate	20,000
Dec 23	DONCASTER ROVERS	D 0-0		16,000
Dec 25	LEEDS UNITED	W 3-1	Woodgate 3	19,500
Dec 26	Leeds United	L 0-2		32,500
Dec 30	Brentford	D 1-1	Robinson	19,290
Jan 13	BLACKBURN ROVERS	L 2-3	Robinson 2	23,000
Jan 20	Southampton	D 2-2	Robinson, Gazzard	21,000
Feb 3	BARNSLEY	W 4-2	Robinson 2, Gazzard 2	17,000
Feb 17	Sheffield United	D 1-1	Robinson	15,000
Feb 24	Queens Park Rangers	D 3-3	Woodgate 2, McGowan	21,336
Mar 3	BURY	L 2-3	Robinson 2	19,500
Mar 10	Leicester City	L 0-1		23,000
Mar 17	CHESTERFIELD	W 2-0	Robinson, Gazzard	16,000
Mar 23	SWANSEA TOWN	D 1-1	Hooper	25,500
Mar 24	Coventry City	L 0-1		21,881
Mar 26	Swansea Town	L 2-3	Robinson, Hooper	12,000
Mar 31	MANCHESTER CITY	L 2-4	Barrett, Woodgate	22,000
Apr 7	Preston North End	W 1-0	Barrett	30,000
Apr 14	NOTTS COUNTY	W 4-2	Robinson 2, Hooper, Gazzard	26,000
Apr 21	Grimsby Town	W 1-0	Gazzard	13,000
Apr 28	BIRMINGHAM CITY	L 1-2	Kinsell	12,500
May 5	CARDIFF CITY	D 0-0		18,000

FA Cup

Jan 6	CARDIFF CITY	(Rd 3)	W 2-1	Barrett, Gazzard	26,000
Jan 27	Stoke City	(Rd 4)	L 0-1		48,500

League & Cup Appearances

PLAYER	LEAGUE	CUP COMPETITION FA CUP	TOTAL
Allison	10		10
Barrett	22	2	24
Betts	3		3
Devlin	13		13
Foan	5		5
Forde	32	2	34
Gazzard	41	2	43
Gregory	30	2	32
Hooper	11		11
Jackman	4		4
Johns	6		6
Kearns	6	1	7
Kinsell	16	1	17
McGowan	7		7
Moroney	25		25
O'Farrell	18	2	20
Parker	38	2	40
Parsons	11		11
Robinson	40	2	42
Southern	17	2	19
Taylor	12		12
Tucker	3		3
Walker	33	2	35
Woodgate	42	2	44
Yeomanson	17		17

Goalscorers

PLAYER	LEAGUE	CUP COMPETITION FA CUP	TOTAL
Robinson	26		26
Gazzard	13	1	14
Woodgate	12		12
Barrett	4	1	5
Parsons	3		3
Hooper	3		3
Johns	2		2
Parker	1		1
Betts	1		1
Kinsell	1		1
McGowan	1		1
Opps' o.gs.	1		1

Final Division 2 Table

		P	W	D	L	F	A	Pts
1	Preston NE	42	26	5	11	91	49	57
2	Manchester C	42	19	14	9	89	61	52
3	Cardiff C	42	17	16	9	53	45	50
4	Birmingham C	42	20	9	13	64	53	49
5	Leeds U	42	20	8	14	63	55	48
6	Blackburn R	42	19	8	15	65	66	46
7	Coventry C	42	19	7	16	75	59	45
8	Sheffield U	42	16	12	14	72	62	44
9	Brentford	42	18	8	16	75	74	44
10	Hull C	42	16	11	15	74	70	43
11	Doncaster R	42	15	13	14	64	68	43
12	Southampton	42	15	13	14	66	73	43
13	West Ham U	42	16	10	16	68	69	42
14	Leicester C	42	15	11	16	68	58	41
15	Barnsley	42	15	10	17	74	68	40
16	QPR	42	15	10	17	71	82	40
17	Notts Co	42	13	13	16	61	60	39
18	Swansea T	42	16	4	22	54	77	36
19	Luton T	42	9	14	19	57	70	32
20	Bury	42	12	8	22	60	86	32
21	Chesterfield	42	9	12	21	44	69	30
22	Grimsby T	42	8	12	22	61	95	28

Fact File

In September West Ham took the lead three times against Sheffield United, but finished 5-3 losers.

MANAGER: Ted Fenton
CAPTAIN: Dick Walker
TOP SCORER: Bill Robinson
BIGGEST WIN: April 14, 1951 4-0 v Notts County, Division 2
HIGHEST ATTENDANCE: January 27, 1951 48,500 v Stoke City, lost 0-1, FA Cup Round 4
MAJOR TRANSFERS IN: Harry Kinsell from Reading, Frank O'Farrell from Cork United, Malcolm Allison from Charlton Athletic

Season 1951-52

Football League Division 2

DATE	OPPONENTS	SCORE	GOALSCORERS	ATTENDANCE
Aug 18	Queens Park Rangers	L 0-2		19,443
Aug 23	BURY	D 1-1	Robinson	16,000
Aug 25	BLACKBURN ROVERS	W 3-1	Barrett 2, Gazzard	19,500
Aug 29	Bury	L 0-4		10,442
Sep 1	Hull City	D 1-1	Hawkins	35,000
Sep 5	SWANSEA TOWN	D 2-2	Bing, Barrett	15,500
Sep 8	BARNSLEY	W 2-1	Hawkins 2	20,000
Sep 13	Swansea Town	L 1-2	Barrett	16,000
Sep 15	Sheffield United	L 1-6	Bing	30,000
Sep 22	LEEDS UNITED	W 2-0	Hawkins, Woodgate	20,000
Sep 29	COVENTRY CITY	W 3-1	Parker, Hawkins, McGowan	21,000
Oct 6	Rotherham United	L 1-2	Hawkins	20,000
Oct 13	CARDIFF CITY	D 1-1	Hawkins	24,000
Oct 20	Birmingham City	L 1-2	Woodgate	21,000
Oct 27	LEICESTER CITY	L 2-3	Woodgate, Bing	21,000
Nov 3	Nottingham Forest	D 0-0		20,593
Nov 10	BRENTFORD	W 1-0	Hawkins	26,500
Nov 17	Doncaster Rovers	L 1-4	Gregory	20,000
Nov 24	EVERTON	D 3-3	Kinsell, Woodgate, Gazzard	22,500
Dec 1	Southampton	W 2-1	Hawkins, Williams	17,473
Dec 8	SHEFFIELD WEDNESDAY	L 0-6		18,000
Dec 15	QUEENS PARK RANGERS	W 4-2	Hawkins 3, Woodgate	17,500
Dec 22	Blackburn Rovers	L 1-3	O'Farrell	20,000
Dec 25	LUTON TOWN	W 3-0	Hawkins, Gazzard, Gregory	20,000
Dec 26	Luton Town	L 1-6	Gregory	19,654
Dec 29	HULL CITY	W 2-0	Parker Tucker	19,500
Jan 5	Barnsley	D 1-1	Tucker	16,204
Jan 19	SHEFFIELD UNITED	W 5-1	Tucker 3, Gazzard 2	21,000
Jan 26	Leeds United	L 1-3	Gazzard	32,500
Feb 9	Coventry City	W 2-1	Barrett, Hawkins	19,486
Fen 16	ROTHERHAM UNITED	W 2-1	Woodgate, Hawkins	19,000
Mar 1	Cardiff City	D 1-1	o.g.	29,000
Mar 8	BIRMINGHAM CITY	L 0-1		24,000
Mar 15	Leicester City	L 1-3	Andrews	30,038
Mar 22	NOTTINGHAM FOREST	W 3-1	Barrett, Gazzard, O'Farrell	23,500
Apr 5	DONCASTER ROVERS	D 3-3	Gazzard, Barrett, Andrews	18,000
Apr 11	NOTTS COUNTY	W 2-1	Gazzard 2	23,000
Apr 12	Everton	L 0-2		36,428
Apr 14	Notts County	L 0-1		16,306
Apr 19	SOUTHAMPTON	W 4-0	Woodgate 2, Barrett, Kearns	18,500
Apr 21	Brentford	D 1-1	Parker	13,000
Apr 16	Sheffield Wednesday	D 2-2	Barrett, Gazzard	44,011

FA Cup

Jan 12	BLACKPOOL	(Rd 3) W 2-1	Andrews, O'Farrell	38,600
Feb 2	SHEFFIELD UNITED	(Rd 4) D 0-0		35,500
Feb 6	Sheffield United	(R) L 2-4	Woodgate, Gazzard	39,073

Fact File

In the FA Cup West Ham played the part of giant-killers, eliminating a Blackpool team which included Stanley Matthews and Stan Mortensen.

MANAGER: Ted Fenton
CAPTAIN: Malcolm Allison
TOP SCORER: Bert Hawkins
BIGGEST WIN: January 19, 1952 5-1 v Sheffield United, Division 2
HIGHEST ATTENDANCE: April 16, 1952 44,011 v Sheffield Wednesday, drew 2-2, Division 2
MAJOR TRANSFERS IN: George Wright from Margate, Jimmy Andrews from Dundee

League & Cup Appearances

PLAYER	LEAGUE	CUP COMPETITION FA CUP	TOTAL
Allison	38	3	41
Andrews	23	3	26
Barrett	23		23
Bing	10		10
Bond	2		2
Devlin	5		5
Foan	3		3
Forde	7		7
Gazzard	31	3	34
Gregory E	28	3	31
Gregory J	9		9
Hawkins	32	3	35
Hooper	2		2
Kearns	3		3
Kinsell	32	3	35
McGowan	9		9
Moroney	12		12
O'Farrell	41	3	44
Parker	30	3	33
Robinson	4		4
Southern	11		11
Stroud	1		1
Taylor	14		14
Tucker	7	3	10
Walker	4		4
Williams	5		5
Woodgate	38	3	41
Wright	38	3	41

Goalscorers

PLAYER	LEAGUE	CUP COMPETITION FA CUP	TOTAL
Hawkins	15		15
Gazzard	11	1	12
Barrett	9		9
Woodgate	8	1	9
Tucker	5		5
Parker	3		3
O'Farrell	2	1	3
Bing	3		3
Gregory J	3		3
Andrews	2	1	3
Kinsell	1		1
Robinson	1		1
McGowan	1		1
Williams	1		1
Kearns	1		1
Opps' o.gs.	1		1

Final Division 2 Table

	P	W	D	L	F	A	Pts
1 Sheffield W	42	21	11	10	100	66	53
2 Cardiff C	42	20	11	11	72	54	51
3 Birmingham C	42	21	9	12	67	56	51
4 Nottingham F	42	18	13	11	77	62	49
5 Leicester C	42	19	9	14	78	64	47
6 Leeds U	42	18	11	13	59	57	47
7 Everton	42	17	10	15	64	58	44
8 Luton T	42	16	12	14	77	78	44
9 Rotherham U	42	17	8	17	73	71	42
10 Brentford	42	15	12	15	54	55	42
11 Sheffield U	42	18	5	19	90	76	41
12 West Ham U	42	15	11	16	67	77	41
13 Southampton	42	15	11	16	61	73	41
14 Blackburn R	42	17	6	19	54	63	40
15 Notts Co	42	16	7	19	71	68	39
16 Doncaster R	42	13	12	17	55	60	38
17 Bury	42	15	7	20	67	69	37
18 Hull C	42	13	11	18	60	70	37
19 Swansea T	42	12	12	18	72	76	36
20 Barnsley	42	11	14	17	59	72	36
21 Coventry C	42	14	6	22	59	82	34
22 QPR	42	11	12	19	52	81	34

Season 1952-53

Football League Division 2

DATE	OPPONENTS	SCORE	GOALSCORERS	ATTENDANCE
Aug 23	SOUTHAMPTON	W 1-0	Barrett	26,000
Aug 25	Hull City	L 0-1		35,964
Aug 30	Bury	D 1-1	Andrews	14,000
Sep 1	HULL CITY	D 0-0		19,600
Sep 6	BIRMINGHAM CITY	L 1-2	Moroney	25,000
Sep 8	Leicester City	D 0-0		23,382
Sep 13	Luton Town	D 0-0		16,009
Sep 15	LEICESTER CITY	W 4-1	Barrett 2, Woodgate, Kearns	15,500
Sep 20	LEEDS UNITED	D 2-2	Moroney 2	22,500
Sep 27	Plymouth Argyle	D 1-1	Barrett	27,000
Oct 4	ROTHERHAM UNITED	L 2-4	Andrews, o.g.	22,000
Oct 11	Blackburn Rovers	L 0-3		22,400
Oct 18	NOTTINGHAM FOREST	W 3-2	O'Farrell, Southern, Allison	21,500
Oct 25	Everton	L 0-2		38,416
Nov 1	BRENTFORD	W 3-1	Hawkins, McGowan, Tucker	23,500
Nov 8	Doncaster Rovers	D 1-1	Tucker	10,612
Nov 15	SWANSEA TOWN	W 3-0	Kearns, Tucker, Gregory	18,500
Nov 22	Huddersfield Town	W 1-0	Kearns	22,267
Nov 29	SHEFFIELD UNITED	D 1-1	Woodgate	23,000
Dec 6	Barnsley	L 0-2		8,915
Dec 13	LINCOLN CITY	W 5-1	Gregory 2, Foan 2, Kearns	14,500
Dec 20	Southampton	W 2-1	Woodgate, Kearns	12,274
Dec 25	NOTTS COUNTY	D 2-2	Kearns, Foan	24,000
Dec 27	Notts County	D 1-1	Allison	24,189
Jan 3	BURY	W 3-2	Kearns 3	18,000
Jan 17	Birmingham City	L 0-2		22,000
Jan 24	LUTON TOWN	L 0-1		23,500
Feb 7	Leeds United	L 2-3	Kearns, Barrett	17,500
Feb 18	PLYMOUTH ARGYLE	L 0-1		8,000
Feb 21	Rotherham United	D 1-1	Andrews	14,700
Feb 28	BLACKBURN ROVERS	D 0-0		19,500
Mar 7	Nottingham Forest	D 0-0		17,938
Mar 14	EVERTON	W 3-1	Andrews, Hooper, Moroney	19,000
Mar 21	Brentford	W 4-1	Moroney 2, Hooper 2	19,000
Mar 28	DONCASTER ROVERS	L 1-3	Barrett	13,000
Apr 3	FULHAM	L 1-2	Barrett	24,500
Apr 4	Swansea Town	L 1-4	Barrett	20,000
Apr 6	Fulham	W 3-2	Dixon 2, Sexton	22,000
Apr 11	HUDDERSFIELD TOWN	L 0-1		23,000
Apr 18	Sheffield United	L 1-3	Dixon	35,000
Apr 25	BARNSLEY	W 3-1	Dixon, Andrews, Hooper	12,500
May 1	Lincoln City	L 1-3	Barrett	14,235

FA Cup

Jan 10	West Bromwich Albion	(Rd 3) L 1-4	Kearns	35,150

League & Cup Appearances

PLAYER	LEAGUE	CUP COMPETITION FA CUP	TOTAL
Allison	39	1	40
Andrews	23		23
Barrett	26		26
Bing	2		2
Bond	14	1	15
Brown	3		3
Cantwell	4		4
Devlin	1		1
Dixon	6		6
Foan	13	1	14
Gazzard	8		8
Gregory E	42	1	43
Gregory J	15	1	16
Gunning	1		1
Hawkins	2		2
Hooper	12		12
Kearns	21	1	22
Kinsell	25		25
McGowan	5		5
Moroney	18		18
O'Farrell	41	1	42
Parker	39	1	40
Petchey	2		2
Sexton	3		3
Southern	12		12
Tucker	15	1	16
Walker	1		1
Woodgate	29	1	30
Wright	40	1	41

Goalscorers

PLAYER	LEAGUE	CUP COMPETITION FA CUP	TOTAL
Kearns	10	1	11
Barrett	9		9
Moroney	6		6
Andrews	5		5
Hooper	4		4
Dixon	4		4
Woodgate	3		3
Tucker	3		3
Gregory J	3		3
Foan	3		3
Allison	2		2
O'Farrell	1		1
Southern	1		1
McGowan	1		1
Hawkins	1		1
Sexton	1		1
Opps' o.gs.	1		1

Fact File

On 16 April 1953 Upton Park's first match under floodlights took place as West Ham won 3-1 in a friendly match against Tottenham.

MANAGER: Ted Fenton
CAPTAIN: Malcolm Allison
TOP SCORER: Fred Kearns
BIGGEST WIN: December 13, 1952 5-1 v Lincoln City, Division 2
HIGHEST ATTENDANCE: October 25, 1952 38,416 v Everton, lost 0-2, Division 2
MAJOR TRANSFERS IN: Dave Sexton from Luton Town

Final Division 2 Table

	P	W	D	L	F	A	Pts
1 Sheffield U	42	25	10	7	97	55	60
2 Huddersfield T	42	24	10	8	84	33	58
3 Luton T	42	22	8	12	84	49	52
4 Plymouth Arg	42	20	9	13	65	60	49
5 Leicester C	42	18	12	12	89	74	48
6 Birmingham C	42	19	10	13	71	66	48
7 Nottingham F	42	18	8	16	77	67	44
8 Fulham	42	17	10	15	81	71	44
9 Blackburn R	42	18	8	16	68	65	44
10 Leeds U	42	14	15	13	71	63	43
11 Swansea T	42	15	12	15	78	81	42
12 Rotherham U	42	16	9	17	75	74	41
13 Doncaster R	42	12	16	14	58	64	40
14 West Ham U	42	13	13	16	58	60	39
15 Lincoln C	42	11	17	14	64	71	39
16 Everton	42	12	14	16	71	75	38
17 Brentford	42	13	11	18	59	76	37
18 Hull C	42	14	8	20	57	69	36
19 Notts Co	42	14	8	20	60	88	36
20 Bury	42	13	9	20	53	81	35
21 Southampton	42	10	13	19	68	85	33
22 Barnsley	42	5	8	29	47	108	18

Season 1953-54

Football League Division 2

DATE	OPPONENTS	SCORE	GOALSCORERS	ATTENDANCE
Aug 19	LINCOLN CITY	W 5-0	Sexton 2, Parker, Dixon, Andrews	17,000
Aug 22	LEICESTER CITY	W 4-1	Kearns 3, Andrews	22,500
Aug 24	Rotherham United	L 0-5		12,750
Aug 29	Stoke City	D 1-1	Dixon	22,000
Sep 3	ROTHERHAM UNITED	W 3-0	Sexton 3	22,500
Sep 5	FULHAM	W 3-1	Andrews 2, Dixon	30,000
Sep 10	Swansea Town	D 1-1	Southren	20,000
Sep 12	Bristol Rovers	D 2-2	Sexton, Dixon	28,736
Sep 14	SWANSEA TOWN	W 4-1	Dixon 3, Sexton	22,500
Sep 19	Leeds United	W 2-1	Dixon, Hooper	28,000
Sep 26	BIRMINGHAM CITY	L 1-2	o.g.	30,000
Oct 3	Nottingham Forest	L 0-4		22,715
Oct 10	BRENTFORD	L 0-1		25,000
Oct 17	Derby County	L 1-2	Dick	17,689
Oct 24	BLACKBURN ROVERS	W 2-1	Southren, Gazzard	23,000
Oct 31	Doncaster Rovers	L 0-2		15,176
Nov 7	BURY	W 5-0	Dick 3, Sexton, Stroud	19,500
Nov 14	Oldham Athletic	L 1-3	Stroud	12,196
Nov 21	EVERTON	D 1-1	Sexton	25,000
Nov 28	Hull City	L 1-2	Sexton	20,000
Dec 5	NOTTS COUNTY	L 1-2	Dick	16,000
Dec 12	Lincoln City	W 2-1	Dixon, Dick	12,814
Dec 19	Leicester City	L 1-2	Dixon	22,976
Dec 25	LUTON TOWN	W 1-0	Dick	19,500
Dec 27	Luton Town	L 1-3	Dixon	20,133
Jan 16	Fulham	W 4-3	Dick 2, Dixon, Sexton	30,000
Jan 23	BRISTOL ROVERS	D 1-1	Hooper	21,250
Feb 6	LEEDS UNITED	W 5-2	Dixon 2, Hooper, Dick, Andrews	15,500
Feb 13	Birmingham City	L 0-2		22,704
Feb 20	NOTTINGHAM FOREST	D 1-1	Dick	20,000
Feb 27	Brentford	L 1-3	Sexton	15,500
Mar 6	DERBY COUNTY	D 0-0		18,500
Mar 13	Blackburn Rovers	L 1-4	Andrews	25,400
Mar 20	DONCASTER ROVERS	W 2-1	Hooper, Dick	14,500
Mar 27	Everton	W 2-1	Barrett, Dixon	40,718
Apr 3	HULL CITY	W 1-0	Hooper	13,000
Apr 10	Bury	L 0-2		13,370
Apr 12	STOKE CITY	D 2-2	Hooper, Dick	10,500
Apr 16	PLYMOUTH ARGYLE	D 2-2	Arnott 2	16,500
Apr 17	OLDHAM ATHLETIC	L 0-1		13,000
Apr 19	Plymouth Argyle	L 1-2	Dixon	20,938
Apr 24	Notts County	L 1-3	Dixon	10,000

FA Cup

Jan 9	HUDDERSFIELD TOWN	(Rd 3)	W 4-0	Hooper 2, Sexton, Dixon	25,250
Jan 30	BLACKPOOL	(Rd 4)	D 1-1	Dixon	37,000
Feb 3	Blackpool	(R)	L 1-3	Sexton	27,120

League & Cup Appearances

PLAYER	LEAGUE	CUP COMPETITION FA CUP	TOTAL
Allison	42		42
Andrews	31	3	34
Arnott	4		4
Barrett	9		9
Bing	12	3	15
Bond	18	1	19
Cantwell	23	3	26
Chiswick	15	3	18
Dick	39	3	42
Dixon	29	3	32
Foan	4	3	7
Gazzard	1		1
Gregory	27	3	30
Hooper	23		23
Kearns	5	2	7
Kinsell	10		10
Malcolm	14	3	17
McGowan	8		8
Musgrove	4		4
O'Farrell	22	3	25
Parker	28		28
Sexton	31		31
Southern	24		24
Stroud	4		4
Tucker	2		2
Wright	33		33

Goalscorers

PLAYER	LEAGUE	CUP COMPETITION FA CUP	TOTAL
Dixon	17	2	19
Sexton	12	2	14
Dick	13		13
Hooper	6	2	8
Andrews	6		6
Kearns	3		3
Southern	2		2
Stroud	2		2
Arnott	2		2
Parker	1		1
Gazzard	1		1
Barrett	1		1
Opps' o.gs.	1		1

Fact File

West Ham found themselves 3-0 down at Fulham in January, but fought back to win 4-3.

MANAGER: Ted Fenton
CAPTAIN: Malcolm Allison
TOP SCORER: Tommy Dixon
BIGGEST WIN: November 7, 1953 5-0 v Bury, Division 2
HIGHEST ATTENDANCE: March 27, 1954 40,718 v Everton, won 2-1, Division 2
MAJOR TRANSFERS IN: John Dick from Crittall Athletic

Final Division 2 Table

	P	W	D	L	F	A	Pts
1 Leicester C	42	23	10	9	97	60	56
2 Everton	42	20	16	6	92	58	56
3 Blackburn R	42	23	9	10	86	50	55
4 Nottingham F	42	20	12	10	86	59	52
5 Rotherham U	42	21	7	14	80	67	49
6 Luton T	42	18	12	12	64	59	48
7 Birmingham C	42	18	11	13	78	58	47
8 Fulham	42	17	10	15	98	85	44
9 Bristol R	42	14	16	12	64	58	44
10 Leeds U	42	15	13	14	89	81	43
11 Stoke C	42	12	17	13	71	60	41
12 Doncaster R	42	16	9	17	59	63	41
13 West Ham U	42	15	9	18	67	69	39
14 Notts Co	42	13	13	16	54	74	39
15 Hull C	42	16	6	20	64	66	38
16 Lincoln C	42	14	9	19	65	83	37
17 Bury	42	11	14	17	54	72	36
18 Derby Co	42	12	11	19	64	82	35
19 Plymouth Arg	42	9	16	17	65	82	34
20 Swansea T	42	13	8	21	58	82	34
21 Brentford	42	10	11	21	40	78	31
22 Oldham Ath	42	8	9	25	40	89	25

Season 1954-55

Football League Division 2

DATE	OPPONENTS	SCORE	GOALSCORERS	ATTENDANCE
Aug 21	Swansea Town	L 2-5	Dick 2	20,000
Aug 3	Blackburn Rovers	L 2-5	Andrews 2	26,500
Aug 28	NOTTS COUNTY	W 3-0	Andrews, Dick, Hooper	19,000
Aug 30	BLACKBURN ROVERS	L 2-5	Sexton 2	17,500
Sep 4	Liverpool	W 2-1	Sexton, Hooper	37,593
Sep 6	HULL CITY	D 1-1	Hooper	18,500
Sep 11	BRISTOL ROVERS	W 5-2	Sexton, Dick, Andrews, Hooper, O'Farrell	22,500
Sep 13	Hull City	W 1-0	Bond	25,851
Sep 18	Plymouth Argyle	D 1-1	Sexton	18,370
Sep 25	PORT VALE	W 2-0	Sexton, Dick	25,500
Oct 2	Doncaster Rovers	L 1-2	Sexton	13,841
Oct 9	NOTTINGHAM FOREST	W 2-0	Hooper, Foan	25,000
Oct 16	Leeds United	L 1-2	Dick	23,000
Oct 23	STOKE CITY	W 3-0	Dick 2, Sexton	27,200
Oct 30	Middlesbrough	L 0-6		26,000
Nov 6	BIRMINGHAM CITY	D 2-2	Hooper, Dick	25,500
Nov 13	Ipswich Town	W 3-0	Sexton, Dick, Andrews	18,600
Nov 20	LUTON TOWN	W 2-1	Dick, o.g.	23,000
Nov 27	Rotherham United	D 2-2	Dick 2	13,000
Dec 4	BURY	D 3-3	Musgrove 2, Dick	18,100
Dec 11	Lincoln City	L 1-2	Dick	11,056
Dec 18	SWANSEA TOWN	D 3-3	Hooper, Barrett, o.g.	15,000
Dec 25	DERBY COUNTY	W 1-0	Dick	23,500
Dec 27	Derby County	D 0-0		20,473
Jan 1	Notts County	L 1-5	Hooper	21,000
Jan 22	Bristol Rovers	W 4-2	Dick 3, Hooper	27,552
Feb 5	PLYMOUTH ARGYLE	W 6-1	Sexton 3, Dick 2, Bennett	18,200
Feb 12	Port Vale	D 1-1	Hopper	12,620
Feb 24	DONCASTER ROVERS	L 0-1		4,500
Mar 5	LEEDS UNITED	W 2-1	Bennett, Foan	19,500
Mar 12	Stoke City	W 2-0	Musgrove 2	20,498
Mar 19	MIDDLESBROUGH	W 2-1	Dare, Musgrove	22,500
Mar 26	Birmingham City	W 2-1	Dick Musgrove	9,200
Apr 2	IPSWICH TOWN	W 4-0	Dick, Dare, Hooper, Musgrove	23,800
Apr 8	FULHAM	W 2-1	Dick, Musgrove	34,200
Apr 9	Luton Town	L 0-2		25,000
Apr 11	Fulham	D 0-0		22,500
Apr 16	ROTHERHAM UNITED	L 1-2	Dick	24,000
Apr 23	Bury	L 1-4	Dick	9,746
Apr 27	LIVERPOOL	L 0-3		9,000
Apr 30	LINCOLN CITY	L 0-1		10,000
May 2	Nottingham Forest	D 1-1	Andrews	5,675

FA Cup

Jan 8	PORT VALE	(Rd 3) D 2-2	Bennett, Hooper	21,000
Jan 10	Port Vale	(R) L 1-3	Hooper	12,410

League & Cup Appearances

PLAYER	LEAGUE	CUP COMPETITION FA CUP	TOTAL
Allison	25	2	27
Andrews	21	1	22
Arnott	2		2
Barrett	2		2
Bennett	19	2	21
Bing	5	1	6
Blackburn	2	2	4
Bond	25	1	26
Brown	23		23
Cantwell	17	2	19
Chiswick	4		4
Dare	13		13
Dick	39	2	41
Dixon	4		4
Foan	19		19
Hallas	3		3
Hooper	41	2	43
Kinsell	18		18
Malcolm	38	2	40
Moore	1		1
Musgrove	21	1	22
Nelson	2		2
O'Farrell	28	1	29
Parker	7		7
Sexton	25		25
Stroud	1		1
Taylor	38	2	40
Wright	19	1	20

Goalscorers

PLAYER	LEAGUE	CUP COMPETITION FA CUP	TOTAL
Dick	26		26
Hooper	11	2	13
Sexton	12		12
Musgrove	8		8
Andrews	6		6
Bennett	2	1	3
Foan	2		2
Dare	2		2
Bond	1		1
O'Farrell	1		1
Barrett	1		1
Opps' o.gs.	2		2

Fact File

After the victory at Fulham in April, West Ham reached third place in the league, only to fail to win any of their remaining matches.

MANAGER: Ted Fenton

CAPTAIN: Malcolm Allison

TOP SCORER: John Dick

BIGGEST WIN: February 5, 1955 6-1 v Plymouth Argyle, Division 2

HIGHEST ATTENDANCE: September 4, 1954 37,593 v Liverpool, won 2-1, Division 2

MAJOR TRANSFERS IN: Billy Dare from Brentford

Final Division 2 Table

		P	W	D	L	F	A	Pts
1	Birmingham C	42	22	10	10	92	47	54
2	Luton T	42	23	8	11	88	53	54
3	Rotherham U	42	25	4	13	94	64	54
4	Leeds U	42	23	7	12	70	53	53
5	Stoke C	42	21	10	11	69	46	52
6	Blackburn R	42	22	6	14	114	79	50
7	Notts Co	42	21	6	15	74	71	48
8	West Ham U	42	18	10	14	74	70	46
9	Bristol R	42	19	7	16	75	70	45
10	Swansea T	42	17	9	16	86	83	43
11	Liverpool	42	16	10	16	92	96	42
12	Middlesbrough	42	18	6	18	73	82	42
13	Bury	42	15	11	16	77	72	41
14	Fulham	42	14	11	17	76	79	39
15	Nottingham F	42	16	7	19	58	62	39
16	Lincoln C	42	13	10	19	68	79	36
17	Port Vale	42	12	11	19	48	71	35
18	Doncaster R	42	14	7	21	58	95	35
19	Hull C	42	12	10	20	44	69	34
20	Plymouth Arg	42	12	7	23	57	82	31
21	Ipswich T	42	11	6	25	57	92	28
22	Derby Co	42	7	9	26	53	82	23

Season 1955-56

Football League Division 2

DATE	OPPONENTS	SCORE	GOALSCORERS	ATTENDANCE
Aug 20	ROTHERHAM UNITED	D 1-1	Dare	19,000
Aug 22	Port Vale	L 1-2	Allison	19,241
Aug 27	Swansea Town	L 2-4	Bennett, Dare	25,000
Aug 29	PORT VALE	L 0-2		13,000
Sep 3	NOTTS COUNTY	W 6-1	Hooper 2, Dare 2, Dick O'Farrell	17,000
Sep 6	Bristol City	L 1-3	Tucker	25,923
Sep 10	Leeds United	D 3-3	Tucker 2, Dare	21,500
Sep 17	FULHAM	W 2-1	Hooper 2	26,000
Sep 24	Bury	D 1-1	Tucker	10,217
Oct 1	BARNSLEY	W 4-0	Dare 2, Hooper, o.g.	20,500
Oct 8	PLYMOUTH ARGYLE	W 4-0	Tucker 3, Allison	19,750
Oct 15	Liverpool	L 1-3	Hooper	32,187
Oct 22	DONCASTER ROVERS	W 6-1	Hooper 3, Dare, Andrews, Tucker	13,500
Oct 29	Lincoln City	D 1-1	Dare	11,000
Nov 5	BLACKBURN ROVERS	L 2-3	Hooper, Dare	23,000
Nov 12	Hull City	L 1-3	Tucker	24,050
Nov 19	NOTTINGHAM FOREST	L 1-2	Hooper	17,000
Nov 26	Sheffield Wednesday	D 1-1	Tucker	21,670
Dec 3	LEICESTER CITY	L 1-3	Tucker	17,500
Dec 10	Bristol Rovers	D 1-1	Dick	20,728
Dec 17	Rotherham United	L 2-3	Moore, Hooper	10,159
Dec 24	SWANSEA TOWN	W 5-1	Dare, Bond, Dick, Hooper, Tucker	15,000
Dec 26	Middlesbrough	L 0-2		22,000
Dec 27	MIDDLESBROUGH	W 1-0	o.g.	21,500
Dec 31	Notts County	W 1-0	Dare	19,000
Jan 14	LEEDS UNITED	D 1-1	Foan	20,000
Jan 21	Fulham	L 1-3	Dare	25,000
Feb 11	Barnsley	D 1-1	Dare	8,367
Feb 25	LIVERPOOL	W 2-0	o.g. 2	18,840
Mar 10	BRISTOL ROVERS	W 2-1	Hooper, Tucker	20,000
Mar 17	Blackburn Rovers	L 1-4	Matthews	21,600
Mar 19	BURY	W 3-2	Hooper, Dare, Dick	14,300
Mar 24	HULL CITY	D 1-1	Allison	12,750
Mar 26	Doncaster Rovers	L 1-2	Dick	6,272
Mar 30	STOKE CITY	W 2-0	Tucker, Dare	18,000
Mar 31	Plymouth Argyle	W 1-0	Andrews	17,555
Apr 2	Stoke City	L 0-3		17,284
Apr 7	SHEFFIELD WEDNESDAY	D 3-3	Dick 2, Dare	17,750
Apr 14	Leicester City	L 1-2	Blackburn	17,500
Apr 18	Nottingham Forest	D 0-0		15,589
Apr 21	LINCOLN CITY	L 2-4	Dare, Dick	13,500
Apr 28	BRISTOL CITY	W 3-0	Sexton 2, Blackburn	13,000

FA Cup

Jan 7	PRESTON NORTH END	(Rd 3)	W 5-2	Foan 3, Dare 2	29,000
Jan 28	CARDIFF CITY	(Rd 4)	W 2-1	Dare, Dick	35,500
Feb 18	BLACKBURN ROVERS	(Rd 5)	D 0-0		28,000
Feb 28	Blackburn Rovers	(R)	W 3-2	Dick 2, Hooper	29,300
Mar 3	Tottenham Hotspur	(Rd 6)	D 3-3	Dick 3	69,111
Mar 8	TOTTENHAM HOTSPUR	(R)	L 1-2	Dare	36,000

League & Cup Appearances

PLAYER	LEAGUE	CUP COMPETITION FA CUP	TOTAL
Allison	40	6	46
Andrews	16		16
Bennett	7		7
Blackburn	6		6
Bond	34	6	40
Brown	2		2
Cantwell	40	6	46
Dare	40	6	46
Dick	35	6	41
Foan	5	6	11
Gregory	36	6	42
Grice	2		2
Hooper	30	6	36
Lansdowne	2		2
Malcolm	22	6	28
Matthews	9		9
Moore	8		8
Musgrove	8	1	9
O'Farrell	40	6	46
Parker	8		8
Sexton	15		15
Smith	2		2
Stroud	2		2
Taylor	6		6
Tucker	37	5	42
Wright	10		10

Goalscorers

PLAYER	LEAGUE	CUP COMPETITION FA CUP	TOTAL
Dare	18	4	22
Hooper	15	1	16
Dick	8	6	14
Tucker	14		14
Foan	1	3	4
Allison	3		3
Andrews	2		2
Blackburn	2		2
Sexton	2		2
Bennett	1		1
Bond	1		1
O'Farrell	1		1
Moore	1		1
Matthews	1		1
Opps' o.gs.	4		4

Fact File

The West Ham squad this season contained five future top class managers – Malcolm Allison, John Bond, Noel Cantwell, Dave Sexton and Ken Brown.

MANAGER: Ted Fenton
CAPTAIN: Malcolm Allison
TOP SCORER: Billy Dare
BIGGEST WIN: September 3, 1955 6-1 v Notts County, Division 2; October 22, 1955 6-1 v Doncaster Rovers, Division 2
HIGHEST ATTENDANCE: March 3, 1956 69,111 v Tottenham Hotspur, drew 3-3, FA Cup Round 6
MAJOR TRANSFERS IN: Mike Grice from Colchester United
MAJOR TRANSFERS OUT: Harry Hooper to Wolves, Dave Sexton to Leyton Orient

Final Division 2 Table

		P	W	D	L	F	A	Pts
1	Sheffield W	42	21	13	8	101	62	55
2	Leeds U	42	23	6	13	80	60	52
3	Liverpool	42	21	6	15	85	63	48
4	Blackburn R	42	21	6	15	84	65	48
5	Leicester C	42	21	6	15	94	78	48
6	Bristol R	42	21	6	15	84	70	48
7	Nottingham F	42	19	9	14	68	63	47
8	Lincoln C	42	18	10	14	79	65	46
9	Fulham	42	20	6	16	89	79	46
10	Swansea T	42	20	6	16	83	81	46
11	Bristol C	42	19	7	16	80	64	45
12	Port Vale	42	16	13	13	60	58	45
13	Stoke C	42	20	4	18	71	62	44
14	Middlesbrough	42	16	8	18	76	78	40
15	Bury	42	16	8	18	86	90	40
16	West Ham U	42	14	11	17	74	69	39
17	Doncaster R	42	12	11	19	69	96	35
18	Barnsley	42	11	12	19	47	84	34
19	Rotherham U	42	12	9	21	56	75	33
20	Notts Co	42	11	9	22	55	82	31
21	Plymouth Arg	42	10	8	24	54	87	28
22	Hull C	42	10	6	26	53	97	26

Season 1956-57

Football League Division 2

DATE	OPPONENTS	SCORE	GOALSCORERS	ATTENDANCE
Aug 18	Fulham	W 4-1	Dare 2, Grice, Tucker	26,000
Aug 20	BLACKBURN ROVERS	L 1-3	Tucker	19,000
Aug 25	SWANSEA TOWN	L 1-2	Tucker	17,000
Aug 27	Blackburn Rovers	W 2-0	Blackburn, Dick	15,100
Sep 1	Lincoln City	W 2-0	Stroud 2	13,031
Sep 3	LIVERPOOL	D 1-1	O'Farrell	25,000
Sep 8	ROTHERHAM UNITED	D 1-1	Dare	19,200
Sep 15	Port Vale	D 0-0		17,587
Sep 22	BARNSLEY	W 2-0	Dick, Dare	19,500
Sep 29	Sheffield United	L 0-1		24,001
Oct 6	Leyton Orient	W 2-1	Musgrove, o.g.	24,613
Oct 13	HUDDERSFIELD TOWN	L 0-2		22,500
Oct 20	Bristol Rovers	D 1-1	Dick	24,402
Oct 27	GRIMSBY TOWN	L 0-1		17,500
Nov 3	Doncaster Rovers	L 0-3		13,071
Nov 10	STOKE CITY	W 1-0	Tucker	17,500
Nov 17	Middlesbrough	L 1-3	Tucker	32,000
Nov 24	LEICESTER CITY	W 2-1	Lewis, Tucker	20,000
Dec 1	Bury	D 3-3	Dick, Musgrove, Parker	8,757
Dec 8	NOTTS COUNTY	W 2-1	Smith, Dick	15,000
Dec 15	FULHAM	W 2-1	Bond, Musgrove	18,250
Dec 22	Swansea Town	L 1-3	Lewis	18,000
Dec 25	NOTTINGHAM FOREST	W 2-1	Musgrove, Lewis	17,000
Dec 29	LINCOLN CITY	W 2-1	Dare 2	16,100
Jan 12	Rotherham United	W 1-0	Musgrove	10,938
Jan 19	PORT VALE	W 2-1	Smith, Dick	17,250
Feb 2	Barnsley	W 2-1	Dare, Dick	15,861
Feb 9	SHEFFIELD UNITED	W 3-2	Smith, Cantwell, Lewis	22,500
Feb 16	LEYTON ORIENT	W 2-1	Lewis, Lansdowne	36,500
Feb 23	Huddersfield Town	L 2-6	Smith, Lewis	5,878
Mar 2	BRISTOL ROVERS	L 1-2	Lewis	22,500
Mar 9	Grimsby Town	L 1-2	Allison	13,796
Mar 16	DONCASTER ROVERS	D 1-1	Lewis	15,500
Mar 23	Stoke City	W 1-0	Musgrove	19,705
Mar 30	MIDDLESBROUGH	D 1-1	Allison	15,000
Apr 6	Leicester City	L 3-5	Musgrove 2, Allison	33,388
Apr 13	BURY	W 1-0	Dare	9,000
Apr 15	Nottingham Forest	L 0-3		23,107
Apr 19	Bristol City	D 1-1	Allison	24,491
Apr 20	Notts County	L 1-4	Smith	17,803
Apr 22	BRISTOL CITY	W 3-1	Dick, Lewis, Dare	9,500
Apr 27	Liverpool	L 0-1		36,236

FA Cup

DATE	OPPONENTS	SCORE	GOALSCORERS	ATTENDANCE
Jan 5	Grimsby Town	(Rd 3) W 5-3	Lewis, Dick, Smith 2, Musgrove	24,500
Jan 26	Everton	(Rd 4) L 1-2	Dare	55,245

League & Cup Appearances

PLAYER	LEAGUE	CUP COMPETITION FA CUP	TOTAL
Allison	39	2	41
Blackburn	6		6
Bond	30	2	32
Brown	5		5
Cantwell	39	2	41
Cooper	2		2
Dare	30	2	32
Dick	36	2	38
Foan	4		4
Gregory	29		29
Grice	11		11
Johnstone	2		2
Lansdowne	26	2	28
Lewis	24	2	26
Malcolm	37	2	39
Musgrove	39	2	41
Newman	4		4
O'Farrell	7		7
Obeney	1		1
Parker	5		5
Pyke	2		2
Smith J	29	2	31
Smith R	4		4
Stroud	5		5
Tucker	10		10
Wragg	10		10
Wright	13		13
Wyllie	13	2	15

Goalscorers

PLAYER	LEAGUE	CUP COMPETITION FA CUP	TOTAL
Dare	9	1	10
Lewis	9	1	10
Dick	8	1	9
Musgrove	8	1	9
Tucker	6		6
Smith J	4	2	6
Allison	4		4
Stroud	2		2
O'Farrell	1		1
Grice	1		1
Cantwell	1		1
Blackburn	1		1
Smith R	1		1
Lansdowne	1		1
Parker	1		1
Bond	1		1
Opps' o.gs.	1		1

Fact File

Ten wins in twelve games from the end of November took Hammers to fifth spot, but they could not capitalise on their fine form.

MANAGER: Ted Fenton
CAPTAIN: Malcolm Allison
TOP SCORERS: Billy Dare and Eddie Lewis
BIGGEST WIN: August 18, 1956 4-1 v Fulham, Division 2
HIGHEST ATTENDANCE: January 26, 1957 55,245 v Everton, lost 1-2, FA Cup Round 4
MAJOR TRANSFERS IN: Eddie Lewis from Preston
MAJOR TRANSFERS OUT: Frank O'Farrell to Preston

Final Division 2 Table

		P	W	D	L	F	A	Pts
1	Leicester C	42	25	11	6	109	67	61
2	Nottingham F	42	22	10	10	94	55	54
3	Liverpool	42	21	11	10	82	54	53
4	Blackburn R	42	21	10	11	83	75	52
5	Stoke C	42	20	8	14	83	58	48
6	Middlesbrough	42	19	10	13	84	60	48
7	Sheffield U	42	19	8	15	87	76	46
8	West Ham U	42	19	8	15	59	63	46
9	Bristol R	42	18	9	15	81	67	45
10	Swansea T	42	19	7	16	90	90	45
11	Fulham	42	19	4	19	84	76	42
12	Huddersfield T	42	18	6	18	68	74	42
13	Bristol C	42	16	9	17	74	79	41
14	Doncaster R	42	15	10	17	77	77	40
15	Leyton Orient	42	15	10	17	66	84	40
16	Grimsby T	42	17	5	20	61	62	39
17	Rotherham U	42	13	11	18	74	75	37
18	Lincoln C	42	14	6	22	54	80	34
19	Barnsley	42	12	10	20	59	89	34
20	Notts Co	42	9	12	21	58	86	30
21	Bury	42	8	9	25	60	96	25
22	Port Vale	42	8	6	28	57	101	22

Season 1957-58

Football League Division 2

DATE	OPPONENTS	SCORE	GOALSCORERS	ATTENDANCE
Aug 24	LINCOLN CITY	D 2-2	Dare, Allison	19,900
Aug 26	Blackburn Rovers	L 1-2	Dare	18,800
Aug 31	Bristol Rovers	W 3-2	Dare 3	25,910
Sep 2	BLACKBURN ROVERS	D 1-1	Dare	24,000
Sep 7	DERBY COUNTY	W 2-1	Smith, Cantwell	19,000
Sep 9	SHEFFIELD UNITED	L 0-3		22,000
Sep 14	Swansea Town	L 2-3	Dare, Malcolm	25,000
Sep 16	Sheffield United	L 1-2	Dare	7,768
Sep 21	FULHAM	W 3-2	Dare 2, Cantwell	24,000
Sep 28	Barnsley	L 0-1		12,119
Oct 5	LEYTON ORIENT	W 3-2	Smith, Lansdowne, Lewis	26,000
Oct 12	Charlton Athletic	W 3-0	Dare, Smith, Musgrove	30,414
Oct 19	DONCASTER ROVERS	D 1-1	Keeble	20,000
Oct 26	Rotherham United	W 2-1	Bond, Dick	8,781
Nov 2	HUDDERSFIELD TOWN	W 5-2	Musgrove 2, Dick, Keeble, Cantwell	21,500
Nov 9	Grimsby Town	W 2-1	Smith, Dick	11,878
Nov 16	STOKE CITY	W 5-0	Keeble 3, Dick, Dare	23,250
Nov 23	Bristol City	D 1-1	Dick	22,038
Nov 30	CARDIFF CITY	D 1-1	Dick	24,000
Dec 7	Liverpool	D 1-1	Dick	34,030
Dec 14	MIDDLESBROUGH	W 2-1	Musgrove, Bond	21,000
Dec 21	Lincoln City	W 6-1	Dick 2, Keeble 2, Musgrove, Newman	8,375
Dec 25	IPSWICH TOWN	D 1-1	Newman	25,500
Dec 26	Ipswich Town	L 1-2	Bond	21,891
Dec 28	BRISTOL ROVERS	W 6-1	Smith 3, Keeble 2, Dick	28,000
Jan 11	Derby County	W 3-2	Musgrove, Dick, Bond	21,564
Jan 18	SWANSEA TOWN	W 6-2	Keeble 2, Dick, Bond, Cantwell, Lansdowne	27,500
Feb 1	Fulham	D 2-2	Musgrove, Lewis	42,259
Feb 8	BARNSLEY	D 1-1	Lewis	27,000
Feb 20	Leyton Orient	W 4-1	Smith, Dare, Keeble, Dick	25,284
Feb 22	BRISTOL CITY	W 3-2	Malcolm, Dare, Keeble	23,800
Mar 1	Doncaster Rovers	W 2-1	Keeble, Smith	12,401
Mar 8	ROTHERHAM UNITED	W 8-0	Dick 4, Keeble 2, Smith 2	25,000
Mar 15	Huddersfield Town	L 1-3	Grice	19,093
Mar 22	GRIMSBY TOWN	W 2-0	Musgrove, o.g.	25,200
Mar 29	Stoke City	W 4-1	Keeble 2, Grice, Dick	14,514
Apr 4	NOTTS COUNTY	W 3-1	Bond 2, o.g.	30,000
Apr 5	CHARLTON ATHLETIC	D 0-0		30,500
Apr 8	Notts County	L 0-1		18,317
Apr 12	Cardiff City	W 3-0	Dick 2, Malcolm	22,000
Apr 19	LIVERPOOL	D 1-1	Bond	37,750
Apr 26	Middlesbrough	W 3-1	Musgrove, Dick, Keeble	30,000

FA Cup

Jan 4	BLACKPOOL	(Rd 3) W 5-1	Keeble 3, Dick 2	34,000
Jan 25	STOCKPORT COUNTY	(Rd 4) W 3-2	Lewis 2, Keeble	36,000
Feb 15	FULHAM	(Rd 5) L 2-3	Grice, Bond	37,500

Fact File

Malcom Allison was taken ill after the defeat at Sheffield United. He was diagnosed as suffering from tuberculosis. His career was over just as West Ham had reached Division One.

MANAGER: Ted Fenton

CAPTAIN: Noel Cantwell

TOP SCORERS: John Dick and Vic Keeble

BIGGEST WIN: March 8, 1958 8-0 v Rotherham United, Division 2

HIGHEST ATTENDANCE: February 1, 1958 42,259 v Fulham, drew 2-2, Division 2

MAJOR TRANSFERS IN: Vic Keeble from Newcastle United

League & Cup Appearances

PLAYER	LEAGUE	CUP COMPETITION FA CUP	TOTAL
Allison	5		5
Blackburn	1		1
Bond	41	3	44
Brown	41	3	44
Cantwell	33	2	35
Cooper	2		2
Dare	26		26
Dick	41	3	44
Gregory	37	3	40
Grice	29	3	32
Keeble	29	3	32
Lansdowne	17	1	18
Lewis	7	3	10
Malcolm	42	3	45
Musgrove	39	3	42
Nelson	3		3
Neville	3		3
Newman	3		3
Pyke	15	2	17
Rhodes	5		5
Smith	32		32
Wragg	3		3
Wright	8	1	9

Goalscorers

PLAYER	LEAGUE	CUP COMPETITION FA CUP	TOTAL
Dick	21	2	23
Keeble	19	4	23
Dare	14		14
Smith	11		11
Bond	8	1	9
Musgrove	9		9
Lewis	3	2	5
Cantwell	4		4
Malcolm	3		3
Grice	2	1	3
Lansdowne	2		2
Newman	2		2
Allison	1		1
Opps' o.gs.	2		2

Final Division 2 Table

		P	W	D	L	F	A	Pts
1	West Ham U	42	23	11	8	101	54	57
2	Blackburn R	42	22	12	8	93	57	56
3	Charlton Ath	42	24	7	11	107	69	55
4	Liverpool	42	22	10	10	79	54	54
5	Fulham	42	20	12	10	97	59	52
6	Sheffield U	42	21	10	11	75	50	52
7	Middlesbrough	42	19	7	16	83	74	45
8	Ipswich T	42	16	12	14	68	69	44
9	Huddersfield T	42	14	16	12	63	66	44
10	Bristol R	42	17	8	17	85	80	42
11	Stoke C	42	18	6	18	75	73	42
12	Leyton Orient	42	18	5	19	77	79	41
13	Grimsby T	42	17	6	19	86	83	40
14	Barnsley	42	14	12	16	70	74	40
15	Cardiff C	42	14	9	19	63	77	37
16	Derby Co	42	14	8	20	60	81	36
17	Bristol C	42	13	9	20	63	88	35
18	Rotherham U	42	14	5	23	65	101	33
19	Swansea T	42	11	9	22	72	99	31
20	Lincoln C	42	11	9	22	55	82	31
21	Notts Co	42	12	6	24	44	80	30
22	Doncaster R	42	8	11	23	56	88	27

Season 1958-59

Football League Division 1

DATE	OPPONENTS	SCORE	GOALSCORERS	ATTENDANCE
Aug 23	Portsmouth	W 2-1	Dick, Keeble	40,470
Aug 25	WOLVERHAMPTON W	W 2-0	Dick, Smith	37,485
Aug 30	ASTON VILLA	W 7-2	Keeble 2, Dick 2, Musgrove 2, Lansdowne	30,506
Sep 3	Wolverhampton W	D 1-1	Grice	52,317
Sep 6	Luton Town	L 1-4	Keeble	25,715
Sep 8	MANCHESTER UNITED	W 3-2	Dick, Smith, Musgrove	35,672
Sep 13	Nottingham Forest	L 0-4		30,518
Sep 17	Manchester United	L 1-4	Bond	53,276
Sep 20	CHELSEA	W 4-2	Grice, Smith Keeble, Dick	31,127
Sep 27	Blackpool	L 0-2		32,662
Oct 4	BLACKBURN ROVERS	W 6-3	Keeble 4, Cantwell, o.g.	25,280
Oct 11	BIRMINGHAM CITY	L 1-2	Musgrove	29,500
Oct 18	West Bromwich Albion	L 1-2	Keeble	36,991
Oct 25	BURNLEY	W 1-0	Nelson	29,387
Nov 1	Bolton Wanderers	W 2-0	Grice, Dick	31,067
Nov 8	ARSENAL	D 0-0		38,250
Nov 15	Everton	D 2-2	Dick, Bond	40,549
Nov 22	LEICESTER CITY	L 0-3		23,500
Nov 29	Preston North End	L 1-2	Dick	19,436
Dec 6	LEEDS UNITED	L 2-3	Dick, Keeble	22,022
Dec 13	Manchester City	L 1-3	Dick	22,500
Dec 20	PORTSMOUTH	W 6-0	Keeble 2, Woosnam, Dick, Smith, Musgrove	31,500
Dec 25	TOTTENHAM HOTSPUR	W 2-1	Dick, Keeble	26,178
Dec 26	Tottenham Hotspur	W 4-1	Dick, Bond, Keeble, o.g.	43,817
Jan 3	Aston Villa	W 2-1	Cantwell, o.g.	33,360
Jan 31	NOTTINGHAM FOREST	W 5-3	Dick 2, Keeble 2, Woosnam	26,676
Feb 7	Chelsea	L 2-3	Keeble 2	52,968
Feb 16	BLACKPOOL	W 1-0	Dick	28,500
Feb 21	Blackburn Rovers	W 2-1	Keeble, Musgrove	17,163
Feb 28	Birmingham City	L 0-3		21,001
Mar 7	WEST BROMWICH ALBION	W 3-1	Dick 3	30,157
Mar 14	Burnley	L 0-1		17,311
Mar 21	BOLTON WANDERERS	W 4-3	Bond 2, Obeney, Dick	27,722
Mar 27	NEWCASTLE UNITED	W 3-0	Dick, Musgrove, Obeney	35,000
Mar 28	Arsenal	W 2-1	Dick 2	52,452
Mar 30	Newcastle United	L 1-3	Obeney	20,911
Apr 4	EVERTON	W 3-2	Bond, Dick, Grice	28,500
Apr 11	Leicester City	D 1-1	Bond	23,825
Apr 13	LUTON TOWN	D 0-0		27,000
Apr 18	PRESTON NORTH END	D 1-1	Dare	21,500
Apr 20	MANCHESTER CITY	W 5-1	Dick 2, Grice 2, Cantwell	23,500
Apr 25	Leeds United	L 0-1		11,257

FA Cup

Jan 10	Tottenham Hotspur	(Rd 3) L 0-2		56,252

League & Cup Appearances

PLAYER	LEAGUE	CUP COMPETITION FA CUP	TOTAL
Bond	42	1	43
Brown	42	1	43
Cantwell	42	1	43
Dare	2		2
Dick	41	1	42
Dwyer	10		10
Gregory	32	1	33
Grice	42	1	43
Keeble	32	1	33
Kirkup	11		11
Lansdowne	6		6
Malcolm	42	1	43
Moore	5		5
Musgrove	40	1	41
Nelson	12		12
Obeney	6		6
Smillie	4	1	5
Smith	36	1	37
Woosnam	13		13
Wragg	2		2

Goalscorers

PLAYER	LEAGUE	CUP COMPETITION FA CUP	TOTAL
Dick	27		27
Keeble	20		20
Bond	7		7
Musgrove	7		7
Grice	6		6
Smith	4		4
Cantwell	3		3
Obeney	3		3
Woosnam	2		2
Lansdowne	1		1
Nelson	1		1
Dare	1		1
Opps' o.gs.	3		3

Fact File

In April, John Dick played for Scotland in a 1-0 defeat against England at Wembley. It would be his only cap.

MANAGER: Ted Fenton
CAPTAIN: Noel Cantwell
TOP SCORER: John Dick
BIGGEST WIN: December 20, 1958 6-0 v Portsmouth, Division 1
HIGHEST ATTENDANCE: January 10, 1959 56,252 v Tottenham Hotspur, lost 0-2, FA Cup Round 3
MAJOR TRANSFERS IN: Phil Woosnam from Leyton Orient, Noel Dwyer from Wolves

Final Division 1 Table

		P	W	D	L	F	A	Pts
1	Wolverhampton W	42	28	5	9	110	49	61
2	Manchester U	42	24	7	11	103	66	55
3	Arsenal	42	21	8	13	88	68	50
4	Bolton W	42	20	10	12	79	66	50
5	WBA	42	18	13	11	88	68	49
6	West Ham U	42	21	6	15	85	70	48
7	Burnley	42	19	10	13	81	70	48
8	Blackpool	42	18	11	13	66	49	47
9	Birmingham C	42	20	6	16	84	68	46
10	Blackburn R	42	17	10	15	76	70	44
11	Newcastle U	42	17	7	18	80	80	41
12	Preston NE	42	17	7	18	70	77	41
13	Nottingham F	42	17	6	19	71	74	40
14	Chelsea	42	18	4	20	77	98	40
15	Leeds U	42	15	9	18	57	74	39
16	Everton	42	17	4	21	71	87	38
17	Luton T	42	12	13	17	68	71	37
18	Tottenham H	42	13	10	19	85	95	36
19	Leicester C	42	11	10	21	67	98	32
20	Manchester C	42	11	9	22	64	95	31
21	Aston Villa	42	11	8	23	58	87	30
22	Portsmouth	42	6	9	27	64	112	21

Season 1959-60

Football League Division 1

DATE	OPPONENTS	SCORE	GOALSCORERS	ATTENDANCE
Aug 22	LEICESTER CITY	W 3-0	Smith, Keeble, Grice	28,000
Aug 25	Preston North End	D 1-1	Musgrove	29,433
Aug 29	Burnley	W 3-1	Woosnam, Smillie, Grice	26,783
Aug 31	PRESTON NORTH END	W 2-1	Smillie, Keeble	32,000
Sep 5	LEEDS UNITED	L 1-2	Keeble	28,000
Sep 9	Tottenham Hotspur	D 2-2	Keeble, Musgrove	58,909
Sep 12	Bolton Wanderers	L 1-5	Keeble	24,191
Sep 14	TOTTENHAM HOTSPUR	L 1-2	Bond	37,500
Sep 19	Chelsea	W 4-2	Dick 2, Musgrove, Woosnam	54,349
Sep 26	WEST BROMWICH ALBION	W 4-1	Musgrove 2, Woosnam, Grice	30,570
Oct 3	Newcastle United	D 0-0		41,890
Oct 10	LUTON TOWN	W 3-1	Woodley 2, Keeble	23,500
Oct 17	Everton	W 1-0	Musgrove	30,563
Oct 24	BLACKPOOL	W 1-0	Musgrove	32,500
Oct 31	Fulham	L 0-1		44,695
Nov 7	MANCHESTER CITY	W 4-1	Cantwell, Obeney, Musgrove, o.g.	25,500
Nov 14	Arsenal	W 3-1	Dick, Obeney, Musgrove	49,760
Nov 21	WOLVERHAMPTON W	W 3-2	Dick 3	38,000
Nov 28	Sheffield Wednesday	L 0-7		38,367
Dec 5	NOTTINGHAM FOREST	W 4-1	Woosnam 2, Obeney 2	26,000
Dec 12	Blackburn Rovers	L 2-6	Woosnam, Dick	22,400
Dec 19	Leicester City	L 1-2	Obeney	20,000
Dec 26	Birmingham City	L 0-2		29,745
Dec 28	BIRMINGHAM CITY	W 3-1	Musgrove 2, Brett	26,000
Jan 2	BURNLEY	L 2-5	Woosnam, Cantwell	26,000
Jan 16	Leeds United	L 0-3		15,000
Jan 23	BOLTON WANDERERS	L 1-2	Dick	21,600
Feb 6	CHELSEA	W 4-2	Bond 3, Dick	29,500
Feb 20	NEWCASTLE UNITED	L 3-5	Woosnam 2, Dick	25,000
Feb 27	Nottingham Forest	L 1-3	Musgrove	26,317
Mar 5	EVERTON	D 2-2	Bond, Dick	25,000
Mar 9	West Bromwich Albion	L 2-3	Grice, Bond	11,980
Mar 12	Blackpool	L 2-3	Bond, Brett	14,515
Mar 19	BLACKBURN ROVERS	W 2-1	Woosnam, Musgrove	26,000
Mar 30	Manchester City	L 1-3	Musgrove	29,572
Apr 2	ARSENAL	D 0-0		29,000
Apr 11	Wolverhampton W	L 0-5		48,086
Apr 15	MANCHESTER UNITED	W 2-1	Musgrove, Grice	35,000
Apr 16	FULHAM	L 1-2	Smillie	24,085
Apr 18	Manchester United	L 3-5	Dunmore, Cantwell, Scott	34,676
Apr 23	Luton Town	L 1-3	Dunmore	11,404
Apr 30	SHEFFIELD WEDNESDAY	D 1-1	Woosnam	22,000

FA Cup

Jan 9	HUDDERSFIELD TOWN	(Rd 3)	D 1-1	Dick	40,526
Jan 13	HUDDERSFIELD TOWN	(R)	L 1-5	Musgrove	22,605

League & Cup Appearances

PLAYER	LEAGUE	CUP COMPETITION FA CUP	TOTAL
Bond	35	2	37
Bovington	1		1
Brett	7		7
Brown	40	2	42
Cantwell	40	2	42
Cartwright	3		3
Dick	24	1	25
Dunmore	9		9
Dwyer	26	2	28
Gregory	1		1
Grice	34	2	36
Hurst	3		3
Keeble	15		15
Kirkup	16		16
Lansdowne	1		1
Lyall	2		2
Malcolm	40	2	42
Moore	13		13
Musgrove	41	2	43
Obeney	9	2	11
Rhodes	15		15
Scott	4		4
Smillie	13	1	14
Smith	28	2	30
Woodley	3		3
Woosnam	38	2	40
Wragg	1		1

Goalscorers

PLAYER	LEAGUE	CUP COMPETITION FA CUP	TOTAL
Musgrove	15	1	16
Dick	11	1	12
Woosnam	11		11
Bond	7		7
Keeble	6		6
Grice	5		5
Obeney	5		5
Cantwell	3		3
Smillie	3		3
Brett	2		2
Woodley	2		2
Dunmore	2		2
Smith	1		1
Scott	1		1
Opps' o.gs.	1		1

Fact File

After 406 appearances for the club, Ernie Gregory played his final game against Leeds United in September. He would remain at the club in various capacities for another 28 years.

MANAGER: Ted Fenton
CAPTAIN: Noel Cantwell
TOP SCORER: Malcolm Musgrove
BIGGEST WIN: September 26, 1959 4-1 v West Bromwich Albion, Division 1; November 7, 1959 4-1 v Manchester City, Division 1; December 5, 1959 4-1 v Nottingham Forest
HIGHEST ATTENDANCE: September 9, 1959 58,909 v Tottenham Hotspur, drew 2-2, Division 1
MAJOR TRANSFERS IN: Dave Dunmore from Tottenham Hotspur
MAJOR TRANSFERS OUT: Johnny Smith to Tottenham Hotspur

Final Division 1 Table

		P	W	D	L	F	A	PTS
1	Burnley	42	24	7	11	85	61	55
2	Wolverhampton W	42	24	6	12	106	67	54
3	Tottenham H	42	21	11	10	86	50	53
4	WBA	42	19	11	12	83	57	49
5	Sheffield W	42	19	11	12	80	59	49
6	Bolton W	42	20	8	14	59	51	48
7	Manchester U	42	19	7	16	102	80	45
8	Newcastle U	42	18	8	16	82	78	44
9	Preston NE	42	16	12	14	79	76	44
10	Fulham	42	17	10	15	73	80	44
11	Blackpool	42	15	10	17	59	71	40
12	Leicester C	42	13	13	16	66	75	39
13	Arsenal	42	15	9	18	68	80	39
14	West Ham U	42	16	6	20	75	91	38
15	Everton	42	13	11	18	73	78	37
16	Manchester C	42	17	3	22	78	84	37
17	Blackburn R	42	16	5	21	60	70	37
18	Chelsea	42	14	9	19	76	91	37
19	Birmingham C	42	13	10	19	63	80	36
20	Nottingham F	42	13	9	20	50	74	35
21	Leeds U	42	12	10	20	65	92	34
22	Luton T	42	9	12	21	50	73	30

Season 1960-61

Football League Division 1

DATE	OPPONENTS	SCORE	GOALSCORERS	ATTENDANCE
Aug 20	Wolverhampton W	L 2-4	Dick, Woosnam	37,266
Aug 22	ASTON VILLA	W 5-2	Woosnam, Bond, Dick, Dunmore, Musgrove	28,959
Aug 27	BOLTON WANDERERS	W 2-1	Musgrove, Dick	24,283
Aug 29	Aston Villa	L 1-2	Dunmore	30,000
Sep 3	Sheffield Wednesday	L 0-1		28,359
Sep 5	MANCHESTER UNITED	W 2-1	Brett, Musgrove	30,000
Sep 10	Chelsea	L 2-3	Dunmore, Grice	37,870
Sep 14	Manchester United	L 1-6	Brett	33,695
Sep 17	BLACKPOOL	D 3-3	Bond, Musgrove, Woodley	23,521
Sep 24	Everton	L 1-4	Beesley	46,291
Oct 1	BLACKBURN ROVERS	W 3-2	Dick 2, Woosnam	17,519
Oct 8	BIRMINGHAM CITY	W 4-3	Grice 2, Musgrove, Dunmore	16,000
Oct 15	West Bromwich Albion	L 0-1		21,300
Oct 22	PRESTON NORTH END	W 5-2	Musgrove 3, Bond, Dick	16,287
Oct 29	Fulham	D 1-1	Dunmore	20,809
Nov 5	ARSENAL	W 6-0	Dunmore 3, Dick, Woosnam, Malcolm	29,375
Nov 12	Manchester City	W 2-1	Dunmore, Grice	33,721
Nov 19	NOTTINGHAM FOREST	L 2-4	Dunmore, o.g.	21,047
Dec 3	CARDIFF CITY	W 2-0	Musgrove, Dunmore	14,000
Dec 10	Newcastle United	D 5-5	Musgrove, Dick, Bond, Dunmore, o.g.	20,100
Dec 17	WOLVERHAMPTON W	W 5-0	Dunmore 2, Musgrove, Dick, Moore	22,336
Dec 24	Tottenham Hotspur	L 0-2		54,930
Dec 26	TOTTENHAM HOTSPUR	L 0-3		34,481
Dec 31	Bolton Wanderers	L 1-3	Musgrove	15,931
Jan 14	SHEFFIELD WEDNESDAY	D 1-1	Dick	20,620
Jan 21	CHELSEA	W 3-1	Obeney, Woosnam, Dick	21,829
Feb 4	Blackpool	L 0-3		9,947
Feb 11	EVERTON	W 4-0	Obeney 2, Dick, Musgrove	22,322
Feb 25	Birmingham City	L 2-4	Musgrove, Scott	16,850
Mar 4	WEST BROMWICH ALBION	L 1-2	Dick	21,607
Mar 11	Preston North End	L 0-4		12,084
Mar 18	FULHAM	L 1-2	Obeney	18,742
Mar 20	Blackburn Rovers	L 1-4	o.g.	14,000
Mar 25	Arsenal	D 0-0		27,663
Mar 31	LEICESTER CITY	W 1-0	Dick	22,010
Apr 1	NEWCASTLE UNITED	D 1-1	Musgrove	17,103
Apr 3	Leicester City	L 1-5	Kirkup	23,776
Apr 8	Nottingham Forest	D 1-1	Dick	26,081
Apr 15	MANCHESTER CITY	D 1-1	Sealey	17,982
Apr 18	Burnley	D 2-2	Musgrove 2	12,409
Apr 22	Cardiff City	D 1-1	Dick	10,000
Apr 29	BURNLEY	L 1-2	Woosnam	18,761

FA Cup

Jan 7	STOKE CITY	(Rd 3)	D 2-2	Dunmore, Dick	21,545
Jan 11	Stoke City	(R)	L 0-1		28,914

League Cup

Sep 26	CHARLTON ATHLETIC	(Rd 1)	W 3-1	Dick, Musgrove, Moore	12,000
Oct 24	Darlington	(Rd 2)	L 2-3	Dunmore, Dick	16,911

League & Cup Appearances

PLAYER	LEAGUE	CUP COMPETITION FA CUP	LC	TOTAL
Beesley	2			2
Bond	34	1	2	37
Boyce	3			3
Brett	5	1		6
Brown	42	2	2	46
Cantwell	10			10
Cartwright	1		1	2
Dick	34	2	2	38
Dunmore	27	1	2	30
Grice	24	1	1	26
Hurst	6			6
Kirkup	20	1		21
Lyall	21	2	2	25
Malcolm	40	2	2	44
Moore	38	2	2	42
Musgrove	40	2	2	44
Obeney	9			9
Rhodes	36	2	2	40
Scott	12			12
Sealey	6			6
Shearing	6			6
Smillie	3	1		4
Woodley	5		1	6
Woosnam	38	2	1	41

Goalscorers

PLAYER	LEAGUE	CUP COMPETITION FA CUP	LC	TOTAL
Dick	16	1	2	19
Musgrove	17		1	18
Dunmore	14	1	1	16
Woosnam	6			6
Rhodes	4			4
Grice	4			4
Obeney	4			4
Moore	1		1	2
Brett	2			2
Malcolm	1			1
Woodley	1			1
Kirkup	1			1
Beesley	1			1
Scott	1			1
Sealey	1			1
Opps' o.gs.	3			3

Fact File

The 5-2 victory over Preston in October saw the debut of 17-year-old Ronnie Boyce.

MANAGER: Ted Fenton/Ron Greenwood

CAPTAIN: Noel Cantwell/Phil Woosnam

TOP SCORER: John Dick

BIGGEST WIN: November 5, 1960 6-0 v Arsenal, Division 1

HIGHEST ATTENDANCE: December 24, 1960 54,930 v Tottenham Hotspur, lost 0-2, Division 1

MAJOR TRANSFERS OUT: Noel Cantwell to Manchester United

Final Division 1 Table

		P	W	D	L	F	A	Pts
1	Tottenham H	42	31	4	7	115	55	66
2	Sheffield W	42	23	12	7	78	47	58
3	Wolverhampton W	42	25	7	10	103	75	57
4	Burnley	42	22	7	13	102	77	51
5	Everton	42	22	6	14	87	69	50
6	Leicester C	42	18	9	15	87	70	45
7	Manchester U	42	18	9	15	88	76	45
8	Blackburn R	42	15	13	14	77	76	43
9	Aston Villa	42	17	9	16	78	77	43
10	WBA	42	18	5	19	67	71	41
11	Arsenal	42	15	11	16	77	85	41
12	Chelsea	42	15	7	20	98	100	37
13	Manchester C	42	13	11	18	79	90	37
14	Nottingham F	42	14	9	19	62	78	37
15	Cardiff C	42	13	11	18	60	85	37
16	West Ham U	42	13	10	19	77	88	36
17	Fulham	42	14	8	20	72	95	36
18	Bolton W	42	12	11	19	58	73	35
19	Birmingham C	42	14	6	22	62	84	34
20	Blackpool	42	12	9	21	68	73	33
21	Newcastle U	42	11	10	21	86	109	32
22	Preston NE	42	10	10	22	43	71	30

Season 1961-62

Football League Division 1

DATE	OPPONENTS	SCORE	GOALSCORERS	ATTENDANCE
Aug 19	MANCHESTER UNITED	D 1-1	Dick	32,628
Aug 23	Tottenham Hotspur	D 2-2	Woosnam, Musgrove	50,214
Aug 26	Wolverhampton W	L 2-3	Musgrove, Sealey	25,471
Aug 28	TOTTENHAM HOTSPUR	W 2-1	Scott, Sealey	36,348
Sep 2	NOTTINGHAM FOREST	W 3-2	Scott, Sealey, Musgrove	23,000
Sep 4	Blackpool	L 0-2		19,838
Sep 9	Aston Villa	W 4-2	Dick 2, Scott, Sealey	32,000
Sep 16	CHELSEA	W 2-1	Dick, Musgrove	27,000
Sep 18	BLACKPOOL	D 2-2	Musgrove, Boyce	26,000
Sep 23	Sheffield United	W 4-1	Dick 2, Musgrove, Sealey	21,034
Sep 30	LEICESTER CITY	W 4-1	Dick 2, Sealey, Woosnam	26,746
Oct 7	Ipswich Town	L 2-4	Sealey, Musgrove	28,051
Oct 14	BURNLEY	W 2-1	Crawford, Dick	32,234
Oct 21	Fulham	L 0-2		32,275
Oct 28	SHEFFIELD WEDNESDAY	L 2-3	Bond, Dick	26,463
Nov 4	Manchester City	W 5-3	Dick 2, Sealey 2, Musgrove	18,839
Nov 11	WEST BROMWICH ALBION	D 3-3	Musgrove, Sealey, Bond	18,000
Nov 18	Birmingham City	L 0-4		20,645
Nov 25	EVERTON	W 3-1	Dick 2, Crawford	27,100
Dec 2	Arsenal	D 2-2	Tindall 2	47,206
Dec 9	BOLTON WANDERERS	W 1-0	Woosnam	19,472
Dec 17	Manchester United	W 2-1	Dick 2	29,472
Dec 18	WOLVERHAMPTON W	W 4-2	Moore 2, Hurst, Musgrove	21,261
Dec 26	BLACKBURN ROVERS	L 2-3	Tindall, Dick	22,250
Jan 13	Nottingham Forest	L 0-3		20,359
Jan 20	ASTON VILLA	W 2-0	Woosnam, Dick	20,000
Feb 3	Chelsea	W 1-0	Moore	34,258
Feb 10	SHEFFIELD UNITED	L 1-2	Woosnam	21,829
Feb 17	Leicester City	D 2-2	Woosnam, Dick	21,312
Feb 24	IPSWICH TOWN	D 2-2	Dick, Kirkup	27,760
Mar 3	Burnley	L 0-6		24,279
Mar 17	Sheffield Wednesday	D 0-0		31,403
Mar 24	MANCHESTER CITY	L 0-4		25,808
Mar 28	Blackburn Rovers	L 0-1		8,800
Mar 31	West Bromwich Albion	W 1-0	Musgrove	18,000
Apr 6	BIRMINGHAM CITY	D 2-2	Musgrove 2	22,548
Apr 14	Everton	L 0-3		45,171
Apr 20	CARDIFF CITY	W 4-1	Sealey, Crawford, Byrne, o.g.	25,459
Apr 21	ARSENAL	D 3-3	Scott, Dick, Lansdowne	31,912
Apr 23	Cardiff City	L 0-3		11,200
Apr 28	Bolton Wanderers	L 0-1		17,333
Apr 30	FULHAM	W 4-2	Dick 2, Crawford 2	22,000

FA Cup

Jan 6	Plymouth Argyle	(Rd 3) L 0-3		26,915

League Cup

Sep 11	PLYMOUTH ARGYLE	(Rd 1) W 3-2	Crawford 2, Woosnam	12,170
Oct 9	ASTON VILLA	(Rd 2) L 1-3	Musgrove	17,775

Fact File

In the high-scoring match against Manchester City in November, Bobby Moore was sent off in the last minute. It would be the only dismissal of his career.

MANAGER: Ron Greenwood
CAPTAIN: Phil Woosnam
TOP SCORER: John Dick
BIGGEST WIN: November 4, 1961 5-3 v Manchester City, Division 1
HIGHEST ATTENDANCE: August 23, 1961 50,214 v Tottenham Hotspur, drew 2-2, Division 1
MAJOR TRANSFERS IN: Lawrie Leslie from Airdrie, Johnny Byrne from Crystal Palace

League & Cup Appearances

PLAYER	LEAGUE	CUP COMPETITION FA CUP	LC	TOTAL
Bond	37	1	2	40
Bovington	7			7
Boyce	4			4
Brown	38	1	2	41
Burkett	1			1
Byrne	11			11
Crawford	19	1	1	21
Dick	35	1	2	38
Dickie	2			2
Hurst	24	1	2	27
Kirkup	41	1	2	44
Lansdowne	4			4
Leslie	37	1	1	39
Lyall	4			4
Malcolm	8			8
Moore	41	1	2	44
Musgrove	36	1	1	38
Peters	5			5
Rhodes	3		1	4
Scott	22		2	24
Sealey	32		2	34
Tindall	13	1		14
Woodley	4			4
Woosnam	34	1	2	37

Goalscorers

PLAYER	LEAGUE	CUP COMPETITION FA CUP	LC	TOTAL
Dick	23			23
Musgrove	13		1	14
Crawford	5		2	7
Woosnam	6		1	7
Scott	4			4
Moore	3			3
Sealey	3			3
Bond	2			2
Boyce	1			1
Byrne	1			1
Hurst	1			1
Kirkup	1			1
Lansdowne	1			1
Opps' o.gs.	1			1

Final Division 1 Table

		P	W	D	L	F	A	Pts
1	Ipswich T	42	24	8	10	93	67	56
2	Burnley	42	21	11	10	101	67	53
3	Tottenham H	42	21	10	11	88	69	52
4	Everton	42	20	11	11	88	54	51
5	Sheffield U	42	19	9	14	61	69	47
6	Sheffield W	42	20	6	16	72	58	46
7	Aston Villa	42	18	8	16	65	56	44
8	West Ham U	42	17	10	15	76	82	44
9	WBA	42	15	13	14	83	67	43
10	Arsenal	42	16	11	15	71	72	43
11	Bolton W	42	16	10	16	62	66	42
12	Manchester C	42	17	7	18	78	81	41
13	Blackpool	42	15	11	16	70	75	41
14	Leicester C	42	17	6	19	72	71	40
15	Manchester U	42	15	9	18	72	75	39
16	Blackburn R	42	14	11	17	50	58	39
17	Birmingham C	42	14	10	18	65	81	38
18	Wolverhampton W	42	13	10	19	73	86	36
19	Nottingham F	42	13	10	19	63	79	36
20	Fulham	42	13	7	22	66	74	33
21	Cardiff C	42	9	14	19	50	81	32
22	Chelsea	42	9	10	23	63	94	28

Season 1962-63

Football League Division 1

DATE	OPPONENTS	SCORE	GOALSCORERS	ATTENDANCE
Aug 18	Aston Villa	L 1-3	Byrne	37,000
Aug 20	WOLVERHAMPTON W	L 1-4	Musgrove	30,020
Aug 25	TOTTENHAM HOTSPUR	L 1-6	Woosnam	30,000
Aug 29	Wolverhampton W	D 0-0		32,000
Sep 1	Leyton Orient	L 0-2		23,918
Sep 3	LIVERPOOL	W 1-0	Scott	22,262
Sep 8	Manchester City	W 6-1	Musgrove 2, Scott, Byrne, Peters, Hurst	25,000
Sep 12	Liverpool	L 1-2	Byrne	39,261
Sep 14	BLACKPOOL	D 2-2	Musgrove, Scott	24,000
Sep 22	Blackburn Rovers	W 4-0	Hurst, Musgrove, Byrne, Peters	15,400
Sep 29	SHEFFIELD UNITED	D 1-1	Scott	22,707
Oct 6	BIRMINGHAM CITY	W 5-0	Byrne 2, Hurst, Musgrove, Brown	21,039
Oct 13	Arsenal	D 1-1	Scott	49,000
Oct 22	BURNLEY	D 1-1	Hurst	34,612
Oct 27	Manchester United	L 1-3	Musgrove	29,204
Nov 3	BOLTON WANDERERS	L 1-2	Moore	19,866
Nov 10	Leicester City	L 0-2		21,064
Nov 17	FULHAM	D 2-2	Hurst, Peters	17,668
Nov 24	Sheffield Wednesday	W 3-1	Brabrook, Peters, Scott	23,764
Dec 1	WEST BROMWICH ALBION	D 2-2	Moore, Hurst	20,680
Dec 8	Everton	D 1-1	Brabrook	38,701
Dec 15	ASTON VILLA	D 1-1	Peters	21,532
Dec 22	Tottenham Hotspur	D 4-4	Peters, Kirkup, Boyce, Scott	44,106
Dec 29	Nottingham Forest	W 4-3	Brabrook 2, Byrne, o.g.	18,587
Feb 16	Sheffield United	W 2-0	Boyce, Sealey	18,176
Mar 2	ARSENAL	L 0-4		31,967
Mar 9	Burnley	D 1-1	Byrne	17,287
Mar 18	MANCHESTER UNITED	W 3-1	Brown, Sealey, o.g.	28,950
Mar 23	Bolton Wanderers	L 0-3		19,071
Mar 30	SHEFFIELD WEDNESDAY	W 2-0	Hurst, Byrne	22,408
Apr 6	Fulham	L 0-2		26,861
Apr 12	IPSWICH TOWN	L 1-3	Scott	23,170
Apr 13	LEICESTER CITY	W 2-0	Sealey 2	25,689
Apr 15	IPSWICH TOWN	W 3-2	Brabrook, Peters, Hurst	21,971
Apr 20	West Bromwich Albion	L 0-1		11,600
Apr 22	NOTTINGHAM FOREST	W 4-1	Hurst 2, Peters, Moore	18,179
Apr 27	EVERTON	L 1-2	o.g.	28,461
May 1	Birmingham City	L 2-3	Scott, Hurst	14,392
May 4	BLACKBURN ROVERS	L 0-1		18,898
May 11	LEYTON ORIENT	W 2-0	Brabrook, Scott	16,745
May 13	Blackpool	D 0-0		12,434
May 18	MANCHESTER CITY	W 6-1	Hurst 2, Sealey 2, Boyce, Brabrook	16,600

FA Cup

Feb 4	FULHAM	(Rd 3)	D 0-0		21,000
Feb 20	Fulham	(R)	W 2-1	Boyce, Byrne	20,000
Mar 4	SWANSEA TOWN	(Rd 4)	W 1-0	Boyce	25,924
Mar 16	EVERTON	(Rd 5)	W 1-0	Byrne	31,770
Mar 30	Liverpool	(Rd 6)	L 0-1		49,036

League Cup

Sep 26	PLYMOUTH ARGYLE	(Rd 1)	W 6-0	Byrne 3, Peters, Hurst, Musgrove	9,714
Oct 16	Rotherham United	(Rd 2)	L 1-3	Hurst	11,581

MANAGER: Ron Greenwood
CAPTAIN: Bobby Moore
TOP SCORER: Geoff Hurst
BIGGEST WIN: September 26, 1962 6-0 v Plymouth Argyle, League Cup Round 1
HIGHEST ATTENDANCE: March 30, 1963 49,036 v Liverpool, lost 0-1, FA Cup Round 6
MAJOR TRANSFERS IN: Jim Standen from Luton Town, Peter Brabrook from Chelsea
MAJOR TRANSFERS OUT: John Dick to Brentford, Malcom Musgrove to Leyton Orient, Phil Woosnam to Aston Villa

League & Cup Appearances

PLAYER	LEAGUE	CUP COMPETITION FA CUP	LC	TOTAL
Bond	14		2	16
Bovington	10	4	1	15
Boyce	27	5	1	33
Brabrook	29	5		34
Britt	1			1
Brown	40	5	2	47
Burkett	38	5	2	45
Byrne	30	5	2	37
Charles	1			1
Crawford	5			5
Dear	3			3
Dick	2			2
Dickie	2			2
Hurst	27		2	29
Kirkup	27	5		32
Lansdowne	1			1
Leslie	20		2	22
Lyall	4			4
Moore	41	5	1	47
Musgrove	15		2	17
Peters	36	1	2	39
Rhodes	2			2
Scott	27	5	2	34
Sealey	26	5		31
Sissons	1			1
Standen	18	5		23
Woosnam	15		1	16

Goalscorers

PLAYER	LEAGUE	CUP COMPETITION FA CUP	LC	TOTAL
Hurst	13		2	15
Byrne	9	2	3	14
Scott	10			10
Peters	8		1	9
Musgrove	7		1	8
Brabrook	7			7
Sealey	6			6
Boyce	3	2		5
Moore	3			3
Brown	2			2
Kirkup	1			1
Woosnam	1			1
Opps' o.gs.	3			3

Fact File

A West Ham side including Harry Redknapp and Martin Peters won the 1963 FA Youth Cup final beating Liverpool 6-5 on aggregate.

Final Division 1 Table

		P	W	D	L	F	A	Pts
1	Everton	42	25	11	6	84	42	61
2	Tottenham H	42	23	9	10	111	62	55
3	Burnley	42	22	10	10	78	57	54
4	Leicester C	42	20	12	10	79	53	52
5	Wolverhampton W	42	20	10	12	93	65	50
6	Sheffield W	42	19	10	13	77	63	48
7	Arsenal	42	18	10	14	86	77	46
8	Liverpool	42	17	10	15	71	59	44
9	Nottingham F	42	17	10	15	67	69	44
10	Sheffield U	42	16	12	14	58	60	44
11	Blackburn R	42	15	12	15	79	71	42
12	West Ham U	42	14	12	16	73	69	40
13	Blackpool	42	13	14	15	58	64	40
14	WBA	42	16	7	19	71	79	39
15	Aston Villa	42	15	8	19	62	68	38
16	Fulham	42	14	10	18	50	71	38
17	Ipswich T	42	12	11	19	59	78	35
18	Bolton W	42	15	5	22	55	75	35
19	Manchester U	42	12	10	20	67	81	34
20	Birmingham C	42	10	13	19	63	90	33
21	Manchester C	42	10	11	21	58	102	31
22	Leyton Orient	42	6	9	27	37	81	21

Season 1963-64

Football League Division 1

DATE	OPPONENTS	SCORE	GOALSCORERS	ATTENDANCE
Aug 24	Chelsea	D 0-0		46,298
Aug 26	BLACKPOOL	W 3-1	Peters, Boyce, Brabrook	25,533
Aug 30	IPSWICH TOWN	D 2-2	Byrne, Boyce	27,599
Sep 2	Blackpool	W 1-0	Byrne	18,407
Sep 7	SHEFFIELD UNITED	L 2-3	Byrne, Boyce	23,837
Sep 9	Nottingham Forest	L 0-2		26,200
Sep 14	Liverpool	W 2-1	Peters, Hurst	45,495
Sep 17	Nottingham Forest	L 1-3	Byrne	23,369
Sep 21	ASTON VILLA	L 0-1		20,346
Sep 28	Tottenham Hotspur	L 0-3		50,886
Oct 5	WOLVERHAMPTON W	D 1-1	Byrne	21,409
Oct 7	BURNLEY	D 1-1	Sealey	21,372
Oct 12	Sheffield Wednesday	L 0-3		23,503
Oct 19	EVERTON	W 4-2	Brabrook 2, Boyce, Hurst	25,163
Oct 26	Manchester United	W 1-0	Britt	42,120
Nov 2	WEST BROMWICH ALBION	W 4-2	Hurst 2, Brabrook, o.g.	22,888
Nov 9	Arsenal	D 3-3	Byrne 2, Peters	52,742
Nov 16	LEICESTER CITY	D 2-2	Britt, Hurst	23,073
Nov 23	Bolton Wanderers	D 1-1	Hurst	10,864
Nov 30	FULHAM	D 1-1	Moore	23,715
Dec 7	Birmingham City	L 1-2	Britt	15,357
Dec 14	CHELSEA	D 2-2	Byrne 2	21,950
Dec 20	Ipswich Town	L 2-3	Byrne, Brabrook	11,765
Dec 26	BLACKBURN ROVERS	L 2-8	Byrne 2	20,500
Dec 28	Blackburn Rovers	W 3-1	Byrne 2, Hurst	28,990
Jan 11	Sheffield United	L 1-2	Sissons	18,733
Jan 18	LIVERPOOL	W 1-0	Byrne	25,546
Feb 1	Aston Villa	D 2-2	Hurst 2	16,850
Feb 8	TOTTENHAM HOTSPUR	W 4-0	Hurst, Sissons, Boyce, Byrne	36,934
Feb 17	Wolverhampton W	W 2-0	Hurst, Byrne	14,000
Feb 22	SHEFFIELD WEDNESDAY	W 4-3	Byrne 3, Hurst	24,578
Mar 3	Burnley	L 1-3	Byrne	14,328
Mar 7	MANCHESTER UNITED	L 0-2		27,177
Mar 18	Leicester City	D 2-2	Hugo, Burkett	11,980
Mar 21	ARSENAL	D 1-1	Hurst	28,170
Mar 27	STOKE CITY	W 4-1	Moore, Byrne, Boyce, Brabrook	29,484
Mar 28	West Bromwich Albion	W 1-0	Hugo	16,000
Mar 31	Stoke City	L 0-3		24,900
Apr 4	BOLTON WANDERERS	L 2-3	Sealey, Byrne	19,398
Apr 11	Fulham	L 0-2		22,020
Apr 17	BIRMINGHAM CITY	W 5-0	Brabrook 2, Hurst, Sissons, Byrne	22,106
Apr 25	Everton	L 0-2		33,090

FA Cup

Jan 4	CHARLTON ATHLETIC		W 3-0	Hurst, Brabrook, Sissons	34,155
Jan 25	Leyton Orient	(Rd 4)	D 1-1	Brabrook	34,345
Jan 29	LEYTON ORIENT	(R)	W 3-0	Hurst 2, Byrne	35,383
Feb 15	Swindon Town	(Rd 5)	W 3-1	Hurst 2, Byrne	28,582
Feb 29	BURNLEY	(Rd 6)	W 3-2	Byrne 2, Sissons	36,651
Mar 14	MANCHESTER UNITED	(SF)	W 3-1*	Boyce 2, Hurst	65,000
May 2	PRESTON NORTH END	(F)	W 3-2**	Sissons, Hurst, Boyce	100,000

*Played at Hillsborough. **Played at Wembley.

League Cup

Sep 2	LEYTON ORIENT	(Rd 2)	W 2-1	Scott, Byrne	11,800
Oct 16	Aston Villa	(Rd 3)	W 2-0	Bond, Britt	11,194
Nov 19	Swindon Town	(Rd 4)	D 3-3	Hurst, Brabrook, Boyce	12,050
Nov 25	SWINDON TOWN	(R)	W 4-1	Hurst, Brabrook, Byrne, Scott	15,778
Dec 16	WORKINGTON TOWN	(Rd 5)	W 6-0	Byrne 3, Boyce, Hurst, Scott	10,160
Feb 5	Leicester City	(SF FL)	W 3-4	Hurst 2, Sealey	14,087
Mar 23	LEICESTER CITY	(SF SL)	L 0-2		27,393

MANAGER: Ron Greenwood
CAPTAIN: Bobby Moore
TOP SCORER: Johnny Byrne
BIGGEST WIN: December 16, 1963 6-0 v Workington Town, League Cup Round 5
HIGHEST ATTENDANCE: May 2, 1964 100,000 v Preston North End, won 3-2, FA Cup final

League & Cup Appearances

PLAYER	LEAGUE	CUP COMPETITION FA CUP	LC	TOTAL
Bennett	1			1
Bickles	2		1	3
Bond	26	7	6	39
Bovington	22	7	3	32
Boyce	41	7	7	55
Brabrook	38	7	6	51
Britt	9		2	11
Brown	36	7	6	49
Burkett	40	7	7	54
Byrne	33	7	5	45
Charles			2	2
Dear	3			3
Dickie	3			3
Hugo	3			3
Hurst	37	7	6	50
Kirkup	18		1	19
Moore	37	7	6	50
Peters	32		4	36
Scott	10		3	13
Sealey	18		4	22
Sissons	14	7	1	22
Standen	39	7	7	53

Goalscorers

PLAYER	LEAGUE	CUP COMPETITION FA CUP	LC	TOTAL
Byrne	24	4	5	33
Hurst	14	7	5	26
Brabrook	8	2	2	12
Boyce	6	3	2	11
Sissons	3	3		6
Britt	3		1	4
Peters	3			3
Scott			3	3
Sealey	2		1	3
Hugo	2			2
Moore	2			2
Bond			1	1
Burkett	1			1
Opps' o.gs.	1			1

Fact File

1963-64 saw Bobby Moore become the youngest ever England captain and receive the Footballer of the Year award.

Final Division 1 Table

		P	W	D	L	F	A	PTS
1	Liverpool	42	26	5	11	92	45	57
2	Manchester U	42	23	7	12	90	62	53
3	Everton	42	21	10	11	84	64	52
4	Tottenham H	42	22	7	13	97	81	51
5	Chelsea	42	20	10	12	72	56	50
6	Sheffield W	42	19	11	12	84	67	49
7	Blackburn R	42	18	10	14	89	65	46
8	Arsenal	42	17	11	14	90	82	45
9	Burnley	42	17	10	15	71	64	44
10	WBA	42	16	11	15	70	61	43
11	Leicester C	42	16	11	15	61	58	43
12	Sheffield U	42	16	11	15	61	64	43
13	Nottingham F	42	16	9	17	64	68	41
14	West Ham U	42	14	12	16	69	74	40
15	Fulham	42	13	13	16	58	65	39
16	Wolverhampton W	42	12	15	15	70	80	39
17	Stoke C	42	14	10	18	77	78	38
18	Blackpool	42	13	9	20	52	73	35
19	Aston Villa	42	11	12	19	62	71	34
20	Birmingham C	42	11	7	24	54	92	29
21	Bolton W	42	10	8	24	48	80	28
22	Ipswich T	42	9	7	26	56	121	25

Season 1964-65

Football League Division 1

DATE	OPPONENTS	SCORE	GOALSCORERS	ATTENDANCE
Aug 22	Fulham	W 2-1	Byrne, Sissons	31,200
Aug 24	MANCHESTER UNITED	W 3-1	Byrne, Hurst, Sissons	37,070
Aug 28	NOTTINGHAM FOREST	L 2-3	Byrne, Sissons	26,760
Sep 2	Manchester United	L 1-3	o.g.	45,123
Sep 5	Stoke City	L 1-3	Byrne	26,420
Sep 7	Wolverhampton W	W 5-0	Hurst 2, Byrne, Sissons, Moore	26,879
Sep 12	TOTTENHAM HOTSPUR	W 3-2	Byrne 3	36,730
Sep 14	Wolverhampton W	L 3-4	Brabrook, Byrne, o.g.	16,000
Sep 19	Burnley	L 2-3	Byrne, Boyce	13,541
Sep 26	SHEFFIELD UNITED	W 3-1	Byrne 2, Sissons	11,526
Oct 3	Everton	D 1-1	Byrne	45,430
Oct 10	ASTON VILLA	W 3-0	Byrne, Boyce, Peters	20,600
Oct 17	Liverpool	D 2-2	Hurst 2	36,029
Oct 24	SHEFFIELD WEDNESDAY	L 1-2	Brabrook	22,800
Oct 31	Blackpool	W 2-1	Hurst, Brabrook	14,383
Nov 7	BLACKBURN ROVERS	D 1-1	Sissons	22,725
Nov 14	Arsenal	W 3-0	Byrne, Peters Hurst	36,026
Nov 21	LEEDS UNITED	W 3-1	Kirkup, Byrne, Peters	28,150
Nov 28	Chelsea	W 3-0	Sealey, Peters, Hurst	44,204
Dec 5	LEICESTER CITY	D 0-0		20,515
Dec 12	FULHAM	W 2-0	Byrne 2	21,985
Dec 19	Nottingham Forest	L 2-3	Byrne, Hurst	20,009
Dec 26	Birmingham City	L 1-2	Hurst	23,324
Dec 28	BIRMINGHAM CITY	W 2-1	Byrne, Kirkup	23,800
Jan 2	STOKE CITY	L 0-1		23,913
Jan 16	Tottenham Hotspur	L 1-3	Byrne, Sissons	50,000
Jan 23	BURNLEY	W 3-2	Boyce, Bond, Byrne	25,490
Feb 6	Sheffield United	L 1-2	Sealey	16,265
Feb 13	EVERTON	L 0-1		25,163
Feb 20	Sunderland	L 2-3	Byrne, Hurst	32,885
Feb 27	LIVERPOOL	W 2-1	Presland, Hurst	25,750
Mar 6	Sheffield Wednesday	L 0-2		14,931
Mar 13	SUNDERLAND	L 2-3	Dear 2	23,360
Mar 20	Blackburn Rovers	L 0-4		8,990
Mar 27	ARSENAL	W 2-1	Hurst, Byrne	24,000
Mar 31	Aston Villa	W 3-2	Hurst, Byrne, Dear	19,900
Apr 3	Leeds United	L 1-2	Dear	41,918
Apr 12	CHELSEA	W 3-2	Hurst 2, Sissons	33,288
Apr 16	WEST BROMWICH ALBION	W 6-1	Dear 5, Peters	27,706
Apr 17	Leicester City	L 0-1		15,880
Apr 19	West Bromwich Albion	L 2-4	Hurst, Boyce	14,000
Apr 23	BLACKPOOL	W 2-1	Brown, Dear	22,762

FA Cup

Jan 9	BIRMINGHAM CITY	(Rd 3)	W 4-2	Hurst 2, Byrne, Sissons	31,056
Jan 30	CHELSEA	(Rd 4)	L 0-1		37,000

League Cup

Sep 30	Sunderland	(Rd 2)	L 1-4	Brabrook	22,382

European Cup Winners' Cup

Sep 23	La Gantoise	(Rd 1 FL)	W 1-0	Boyce	18,000
Oct 7	LA GANTOISE	(Rd 1 SL)	D 1-1	Byrne	24,000
Nov 25	SPARTA PRAGUE	(Rd 2 FL)	W 2-0	Bond, Sealey	27,590
Dec 9	Sparta Prague	(Rd 2 SL)	L 1-2	Sissons	45,000
Mar 16	Lausanne	(Rd 3 FL)	W 2-1	Dear, Byrne	20,000
Mar 23	LAUSANNE	(Rd 3 SL)	W 4-3	Dear 2, Peters, o.g.	31,780
Apr 7	REAL ZARAGOZA	(SF FL)	W 2-1	Dear, Byrne	35,000
Apr 28	Real Zaragoza	(SF SL)	D 1-1	Sissons	28,000
May 19	TSV München	(F)	W 2-0*	Sealey 2	100,000

*Played at Wembley.

Charity Shield

Aug 16	Liverpool	D 2-2	Hurst, Byrne	38,858

MANAGER: Ron Greenwood

CAPTAIN: Bobby Moore

TOP SCORER: Johnny Byrne

BIGGEST WIN: April 16, 1965 6-1 v West Bromwich Albion, Division 1

HIGHEST ATTENDANCE: May 19, 1965 100,000 v TSV München, won 2-0, European Cup Winners' Cup final

League & Cup Appearances

PLAYER	LEAGUE	CUP COMPETITION				TOTAL
		FA CUP	LC	ECWC	OTHER	
Bennett	1					1
Bickles	2					2
Bond	29	2	1	4	1	37
Bovington	33	2	1	4	1	41
Boyce	41	2	1	9	1	54
Brabrook	22		1	1	1	25
Brown	33	2	1	9	1	46
Burkett	24		1	5	1	31
Byrne	34	2	1	7	1	45
Charles	1					1
Dawkins	1					1
Dear	10			5		15
Dickie				1		1
Hurst	42	1	1	9	1	54
Kirkup	15			5		20
Moore	28			7	1	36
Peters	35	2	1	9		47
Presland	4					4
Scott	6	2				8
Sealey	21	2		7		30
Sissons	38	2	1	9	1	51
Standen	42	2	1	8	1	54

Goalscorers

PLAYER	LEAGUE	CUP COMPETITION				TOTAL
		FA CUP	LC	ECWC	OTHER	
Byrne	25	1		3	1	30
Hurst	17	2			1	20
Dear	10			4		14
Sissons	8	1		2		11
Peters	5			1		6
Boyce	4			1		5
Sealey	2			3		5
Brabrook	3		1			4
Bond	1			1		2
Kirkup	2					2
Brown	1					1
Moore	1					1
Presland	1					1
Opps' o.gs.	2			1		3

Fact File

Brian Dear scored five goals in a 20 minute spell either side of half time against West Bromwich Albion in April.

Final Division 1 Table

		P	W	D	L	F	A	Pts
1	Manchester U	42	26	9	7	89	39	61
2	Leeds U	42	26	9	7	83	52	61
3	Chelsea	42	24	8	10	89	54	56
4	Everton	42	17	15	10	69	60	49
5	Nottingham F	42	17	13	12	71	67	47
6	Tottenham H	42	19	7	16	87	71	45
7	Liverpool	42	17	10	15	67	73	44
8	Sheffield W	42	16	11	15	57	55	43
9	West Ham U	42	19	4	19	82	71	42
10	Blackburn R	42	16	10	16	83	79	42
11	Stoke C	42	16	10	16	67	66	42
12	Burnley	42	16	10	16	70	70	42
13	Arsenal	42	17	7	18	69	75	41
14	WBA	42	13	13	16	70	65	39
15	Sunderland	42	14	9	19	64	74	37
16	Aston Villa	42	16	5	21	57	82	37
17	Blackpool	42	12	11	19	67	78	35
18	Leicester C	42	11	13	18	69	85	35
19	Sheffield U	42	12	11	19	50	64	35
20	Fulham	42	11	12	19	60	78	34
21	Wolverhampton W	42	13	4	25	59	89	30
22	Birmingham C	42	8	11	23	64	96	27

Season 1965-66

Football League Division 1

DATE	OPPONENTS	SCORE	GOALSCORERS	ATTENDANCE
Aug 21	West Bromwich Albion	L 0-3		19,900
Aug 23	SUNDERLAND	D 1-1	Peters	34,700
Aug 28	LEEDS UNITED	W 2-1	Peters, Hurst	27,900
Sep 1	Sunderland	L 1-2	Hurst	48,626
Sep 4	Sheffield United	L 3-5	Byrne, Hurst, Kirkup	15,796
Sep 6	LIVERPOOL	L 1-5	Peters	32,144
Sep 11	LEICESTER CITY	L 2-5	Hurst 2	21,400
Sep 15	Liverpool	D 1-1	Hurst	44,397
Sep 18	Blackburn Rovers	W 2-1	Peters 2	10,178
Sep 25	BLACKPOOL	D 1-1	Hurst	21,000
Oct 2	Fulham	L 0-3		22,310
Oct 9	Nottingham Forest	L 0-5		19,262
Oct 16	SHEFFIELD WEDNESDAY	W 4-2	Britt 2, Sissons, Peters	20,690
Oct 23	Northampton Town	L 1-2	Brown	15,367
Oct 30	STOKE CITY	D 0-0		21,545
Nov 6	Burnley	L 1-3	Britt	16,802
Nov 13	CHELSEA	W 2-1	Brabrook, Peters	31,540
Nov 20	Arsenal	L 2-3	Hurst, Peters	25.855
Nov 27	EVERTON	W 3-0	Sissons 2, Brabrook	21,920
Dec 4	Manchester United	D 0-0		32,924
Dec 11	NEWCASTLE UNITED	W 4-3	Hurst 3, Brabrook	23,758
Dec 18	Sheffield Wednesday	D 0-0		12,996
Jan 1	NOTTINGHAM FOREST	L 0-3		25,131
Jan 8	Newcastle United	L 1-2	Byrne	31,600
Jan 11	Everton	D 2-2	Hurst, Peters	29,915
Jan 15	NORTHAMPTON TOWN	D 1-1	Hurst	21,000
Jan 29	WEST BROMWICH ALBION	W 4-0	Hurst 2, Sissons, Peters	25,500
Feb 5	Leeds United	L 0-5		33,312
Feb 7	Aston Villa	W 2-1	Hurst, Sissons	13,440
Feb 19	SHEFFIELD UNITED	W 4-0	Brabrook, Hurst, Peters, o.g.	21,220
Mar 5	ASTON VILLA	W 4-2	Burkett, Byrne, Brabrook, Hurst	22,058
Mar 12	BLACKBURN ROVERS	W 4-1	Dear, Brabrook, Hurst, Burkett	18,566
Mar 19	Blackpool	L 1-2	Boyce	10,559
Mar 26	FULHAM	L 1-3	Hurst	18,977
Apr 2	BURNLEY	D 1-1	Brabrook	17,635
Apr 8	Tottenham Hotspur	W 4-1	Redknapp, Hurst, Byrne, Boyce	50,188
Apr 9	Chelsea	L 2-6	Bennett, o.g.	35,958
Apr 16	ARSENAL	W 2-1	Byrne, Brabrook	26,022
Apr 25	TOTTENHAM HOTSPUR	W 2-0	Byrne 2	32,231
Apr 30	MANCHESTER UNITED	W 3-2	Hurst 2, Byrne	36,416
May 7	Stoke City	L 0-1		15,670
May 9	Leicester City	L 1-2	Byrne	16,066

FA Cup

Jan 22	Oldham Athletic	(Rd 3)	D 2-2	Burnett, Hurst	25,035
Jan 24	OLDHAM ATHLETIC	(R)	W 2-1	Hurst, Brabrook	35,330
Feb 12	BLACKBURN ROVERS	(Rd 4)	D 3-3	Bloomfield, Hurst, Sissons	32,350
Feb 16	Blackburn Rovers	(R)	L 1-4	Hurst	25,547

League Cup

Sep 21	Bristol Rovers	(Rd 2)	D 3-3	Hurst 2, Byrne	18,354
Sep 29	BRISTOL ROVERS	(R)	W 3-2	Byrne 2, Hurst	13,160
Oct 13	MANSFIELD TOWN	(Rd 3)	W 4-0	Hurst 2, Brabrook, Burnett	11,590
Nov 3	Rotherham United	(Rd 4)	W 2-1	Hurst, Moore	13,902
Nov 17	Grimsby Town	(Rd 5)	D 2-2	Hurst, Charles	16,281
Dec 15	GRIMSBY TOWN	(R)	W 1-0	Hurst	17,500
Dec 20	CARDIFF CITY	(SF FL)	W 5-2	Hurst, Bovington, Sissons Brabrook, Byrne,	19,980
Feb 2	Cardiff City	(SF SL)	W 5-1	Hurst 2, Peters 2, Burnett	14,315
Mar 9	WEST BROMWICH ALBION	(F FL)	W 2-1	Moore, Byrne	28,323
Mar 23	West Bromwich Albion	(F SL)	L 1-4	Peters	31,925

European Cup Winners' Cup

Nov 24	OLYMPIAKOS	(Rd 2 FL)	W 4-0	Hurst 2, Byrne, Brabrook	27,250
Dec 1	Olympiakos	(Rd 2 SL)	D 2-2	Peters 2	40,000
Mar 2	FC MAGDEBURG	(Rd 3 FL)	W 1-0	Byrne	30,620
Mar 16	FC Magdeburg	(Rd 3 SL)	D 1-1	Sissons	35,000
Apr 5	BORUSSIA DORTMUND	(SF FL)	L 1-2	Peters	28,130
Apr 13	Borussia Dortmund	(SF SL)	L 1-3	Byrne	35,000

MANAGER: Ron Greenwood **CAPTAIN:** Bobby Moore
TOP SCORER: Geoff Hurst
BIGGEST WIN: February 2, 1966 5-1 v Cardiff City, League Cup semi-final Second Leg

League & Cup Appearances (substitute)

PLAYER	LEAGUE	CUP COMPETITION FA CUP	LC	ECWC	TOTAL
Bennett	7 (1)		2		9 (1)
Bickles	12 (1)				12 (1)
Bloomfield	9 (1)	2	2		13 (1)
Bovington	31	4	9	4	48
Boyce	16	1	2	4	23
Brabrook	32	4	8	6	50
Britt	10		4		14
Brown	23	3	9	6	41
Burkett	19	4	4	2	29
Burnett	24	4	6	2	36
Byrne	23	3	6	5	37
Charles	25		7	4	36
Dawkins	2				2
Dear	7	1	1	1	10
Dickie	5		2		7
Hurst	39	4	10	6	59
Kirkup	17		4	2	23
Moore	37	4	9	6	56
Peters	40	4	10	6	60
Presland	2				2
Redknapp	7				7
Scott	2				2
Sissons	36	2	9	4	51
Standen	37	4	8	6	55

Goalscorers

PLAYER	LEAGUE	CUP COMPETITION FA CUP	LC	ECWC	TOTAL
Hurst	23	4	11	2	40
Byrne	9		5	3	17
Peters	11		3	3	17
Brabrook	8	1	2	1	12
Sissons	5	1	1	1	8
Britt	3				3
Burnett		1	2		3
Boyce	2				2
Burkett	2				2
Moore			2		2
Bennett	1				1
Bloomfield		1			1
Bovington			1		1
Brown	1				1
Charles			1		1
Dear	1				1
Kirkup	1				1
Redknapp	1				1
Opps' o.gs.	2				2

Fact File

Peter Bennett became the Hammers' first ever substitute in the match against Leeds in April.

Final Division 1 Table

		P	W	D	L	F	A	Pts
1	Liverpool	42	26	9	7	79	34	61
2	Leeds U	42	23	9	10	79	38	55
3	Burnley	42	24	7	11	79	47	55
4	Manchester U	42	18	15	9	84	59	51
5	Chelsea	42	22	7	13	65	53	51
6	WBA	42	19	12	11	91	69	50
7	Leicester C	42	21	7	14	80	65	49
8	Tottenham H	42	16	12	14	75	66	44
9	Sheffield U	42	16	11	15	56	59	43
10	Stoke C	42	15	12	15	65	64	42
11	Everton	42	15	11	16	56	62	41
12	West Ham U	42	15	9	18	70	83	39
13	Blackpool	42	14	9	19	55	65	37
14	Arsenal	42	12	13	17	62	75	37
15	Newcastle U	42	14	9	19	50	63	37
16	Aston Villa	42	15	6	21	69	80	36
17	Sheffield W	42	14	8	20	56	66	36
18	Nottingham F	42	14	8	20	56	72	36
19	Sunderland	42	14	8	20	51	72	36
20	Fulham	42	14	7	21	67	85	35
21	Northampton T	42	10	13	19	55	92	33
22	Blackburn R	42	8	4	30	57	88	20

Season 1966-67

Football League Division 1

DATE	OPPONENTS	SCORE	GOALSCORERS	ATTENDANCE
Aug 20	CHELSEA	L 1-2	Boyce	36,126
Aug 23	Arsenal	L 1-2	Byrne	40,533
Aug 27	Leicester City	L 4-5	Brabrook 2, Hurst 2	26,850
Aug 29	ARSENAL	D 2-2	Moore, Brabrook	34,954
Sep 3	LIVERPOOL	D 1-1	Hurst	33,000
Sep 7	Manchester City	W 4-1	Hurst 2, Boyce, Sissons	31,989
Sep 10	STOKE CITY	D 1-1	Hurst	33,292
Sep 17	Sheffield Wednesday	W 2-0	Boyce, Byrne	29,171
Sep 24	SOUTHAMPTON	D 2-2	Hurst, Peters	32,301
Oct 1	Sunderland	W 4-2	Byrne 2, Hurst, Peters	29,277
Oct 8	EVERTON	L 2-3	Peters, Hurst	32,784
Oct 15	Fulham	L 2-4	Byrne, Hurst	34,826
Oct 26	NOTTINGHAM FOREST	W 3-1	Hurst 2, Bovington	23,000
Oct 29	Sheffield United	L 1-3	Peters	20,579
Nov 5	FULHAM	W 6-1	Hurst 4, Peters 2	22,260
Nov 12	Tottenham Hotspur	W 4-3	Byrne, Brabrook, Sissons, Hurst	29,227
Nov 19	NEWCASTLE UNITED	W 3-0	Peters, Byrne, Hurst	31,285
Nov 26	Leeds United	L 1-2	Hurst	37,382
Dec 3	WEST BROMWICH ALBION	W 3-0	Redknapp, Dear Peters	22,961
Dec 10	Burnley	L 2-4	Hurst 2	19,509
Dec 17	Chelsea	D 5-5	Sissons 2, Brabrook, Peters, Byrne	47,805
Dec 26	Blackpool	W 4-1	Hurst, Dear, Byrne, Sissons	26,901
Dec 27	BLACKPOOL	W 4-0	Byrne, Hurst, Moore, Peters	29,300
Dec 31	LEICESTER CITY	L 0-1		34,168
Jan 7	Liverpool	L 0-2		48,518
Jan 14	Stoke City	D 1-1	Hurst	27,274
Jan 21	SHEFFIELD WEDNESDAY	W 3-0	Dear, Hurst, Sissons	29,220
Feb 4	Southampton	L 2-6	Hurst, Burkett	30,123
Feb 11	SUNDERLAND	D 2-2	Byrne, Hurst	27,965
Feb 25	Everton	L 0-4		42,504
Mar 18	Nottingham Forest	L 0-1		31,426
Mar 24	Aston Villa	W 2-1	Boyce, Peters	28,716
Mar 25	BURNLEY	W 3-2	Peters 2, Sissons	24,428
Mar 28	Aston Villa	W 2-0	Hurst 2	22,033
Apr 1	Manchester United	L 0-3		61,380
Apr 4	SHEFFIELD UNITED	L 0-2		22,006
Apr 22	LEEDS UNITED	L 0-1		25,429
Apr 26	Newcastle United	L 0-1		38,870
Apr 28	West Bromwich Albion	L 1-3	Bennett	23,219
May 6	MANCHESTER UNITED	L 1-6	Charles	38,424
May 9	TOTTENHAM HOTSPUR	L 0-2		35,750
May 13	MANCHESTER UNITED	D 1-1	Peters	17,186

FA Cup

Jan 28	SWINDON TOWN	(Rd 3)	D 3-3	Hurst 3	37,400
Jan 31	Swindon Town	(R)	L 1-3	Sissons	25,789

League Cup

Sep 14	TOTTENHAM HOTSPUR	(Rd 2)	W 1-0	Hurst	34,000
Oct 5	Arsenal	(Rd 3)	W 3-1	Hurst 2, Peters	33,647
Nov 7	LEEDS UNITED	(Rd 4)	W 7-0	Sissons 3, Hurst 3, Peters	27,474
Dec 7	Blackpool	(Rd 5)	W 3-1	Hurst 2, Byrne	15,831
Jan 18	West Bromwich Albion	(SF FL)	L 0-4		29,796
Feb 8	WEST BROMWICH ALBION	(SF SL)	D 2-2	Byrne, Hurst	35,790

Fact File

West Ham scored an amazing 17 goals in one week during November.

MANAGER: Ron Greenwood
CAPTAIN: Bobby Moore
TOP SCORER: Geoff Hurst
BIGGEST WIN: November 7, 1966 7-0 v Leeds United, League Cup Round 4
HIGHEST ATTENDANCE: April 1, 1967 61,380 v Manchester United, lost 0-3, Division 1
MAJOR TRANSFERS OUT: Johnny Byrne to Crystal Palace, Ken Brown to Torquay United

League & Cup Appearances (substitute)

PLAYER	LEAGUE	CUP COMPETITION FA CUP	LC	TOTAL
Andrew	2			2
Bennett	7 (1)		1	8 (1)
Bickles	8	2		10
Bovington	28	2	4	34
Boyce	37	2	5	44
Brabrook	32		5	37
Brown	18		6	24
Burkett	11 (1)	2	2	15 (1)
Burnett	24 (2)		4	28 (2)
Byrne	25	2	5	32
Charles	31		4	35
Dawkins	2 (1)			2 (1)
Dear	4 (1)	2		6 (1)
Eadie	2			2
Hartley	2			2
Heffer	9			9
Howe	0 (1)			0 (1)
Hurst	41	2	6	49
Kitchener	8			8
Mackleworth	3			3
Moore	40	2	6	48
Peters	41	2	6	49
Redknapp	10 (2)			10 (2)
Sealey	4			4
Sissons	34 (1)	2	6	42 (1)
Standen	39	2	6	47

Goalscorers

PLAYER	LEAGUE	CUP COMPETITION FA CUP	LC	TOTAL
Hurst	29	3	9	41
Peters	14		2	16
Byrne	11		2	13
Sissons	7	1	3	11
Brabrook	5			5
Boyce	4			4
Dear	3			3
Moore	2			2
Bennett	1			1
Bovington	1			1
Burkett	1			1
Charles	1			1
Redknapp	1			1

Final Division 1 Table

	P	W	D	L	F	A	PTS
1 Manchester U	42	24	12	6	84	45	60
2 Nottingham F	42	23	10	9	64	41	56
3 Tottenham H	42	24	8	10	71	48	56
4 Leeds U	42	22	11	9	62	42	55
5 Liverpool	42	19	13	10	64	47	51
6 Everton	42	19	10	13	65	46	48
7 Arsenal	42	16	14	12	58	47	46
8 Leicester C	42	18	8	16	78	71	44
9 Chelsea	42	15	14	13	67	62	44
10 Sheffield U	42	16	10	16	52	59	42
11 Sheffield W	42	14	13	15	56	47	41
12 Stoke C	42	17	7	18	63	58	41
13 WBA	42	16	7	19	77	73	39
14 Burnley	42	15	9	18	66	76	39
15 Manchester C	42	12	15	15	43	52	39
16 West Ham U	42	14	8	20	80	84	36
17 Sunderland	42	14	8	20	58	72	36
18 Fulham	42	11	12	19	71	83	34
19 Southampton	42	14	6	22	74	92	34
20 Newcastle U	42	12	9	21	39	81	33
21 Aston Villa	42	11	7	24	54	85	29
22 Blackpool	42	6	9	27	41	76	21

Season 1967-68

Football League Division 1

DATE	OPPONENTS	SCORE	GOALSCORERS	ATTENDANCE
Aug 19	SHEFFIELD WEDNESDAY	L 2-3	Hurst, Peters	29,603
Aug 21	BURNLEY	W 4-2	Hurst 2, Peters, Redknapp	30,420
Aug 26	Tottenham Hotspur	L 1-5	Sissons	55,831
Aug 29	Burnley	D 3-3	Hurst, Moore, Peters	16,620
Sep 2	MANCHESTER UNITED	L 1-3	Peters	36,562
Sep 5	Everton	L 0-2		46,762
Sep 9	Sunderland	W 5-1	Hurst 2, Redknapp, Moore, Peters	39,772
Sep 16	WOLVERHAMPTON W	L 1-2	Hurst	30,780
Sep 23	Fulham	W 3-0	Hurst, Moore, Sissons	29,234
Sep 30	LEEDS UNITED	D 0-0		29,740
Oct 7	STOKE CITY	L 3-4	Hurst 2, Peters	24,471
Oct 14	Liverpool	L 1-3	Peters	46,951
Oct 23	SOUTHAMPTON	L 0-1		32,550
Oct 30	Chelsea	W 3-1	Dear, Hurst, Peters	40,303
Nov 11	Newcastle United	L 0-1		32,850
Nov 18	MANCHESTER CITY	L 2-3	Hurst, Peters	25,425
Nov 25	Arsenal	D 0-0		42,029
Dec 2	SHEFFIELD UNITED	W 3-0	Sisson 2, Brabrook	22,510
Dec 8	Coventry City	D 1-1	Hurst	28,393
Dec 11	WEST BROMWICH ALBION	L 2-3	Brabrook, Hurst	18,340
Dec 16	Sheffield Wednesday	L 1-4	Dear	24,003
Dec 23	TOTTENHAM HOTSPUR	W 2-1	Bonds, Dear	32,116
Dec 26	LEICESTER CITY	W 4-2	Dear 3, Brooking	26,520
Dec 30	Leicester City	W 4-2	Dear 2, Brooking, Sissons	24,589
Jan 6	Manchester United	L 1-3	Brooking	58,498
Jan 20	Wolverhampton W	W 2-1	Dear, Hurst	32,273
Feb 3	FULHAM	W 7-2	Brooking 2, Hurst 2, Dear, Moore, Peters	31,248
Feb 10	Leeds United	L 1-2	Dear	41,814
Feb 26	Stoke City	L 0-2		16,092
Mar 16	Southampton	D 0-0		27,734
Mar 23	CHELSEA	L 0-1		36,301
Mar 29	ARSENAL	D 1-1	Brooking	33,942
Apr 6	NEWCASTLE UNITED	W 5-0	Brooking 3, Sissons 2	27,780
Apr 12	NOTTINGHAM FOREST	W 3-0	Dear 2, Sissons	36,589
Apr 13	Manchester City	L 0-3		38,754
Apr 16	Nottingham Forest	D 1-1	Peters	22,198
Apr 20	LIVERPOOL	W 1-0	Peters	33,060
Apr24	SUNDERLAND	D 1-1	Dear	29,153
Apr 27	Sheffield United	W 2-1	Hurst 2	19,530
May 1	West Bromwich Albion	L 1-3	Peters	25,009
May 4	COVENTRY CITY	D 0-0		30,180
May 11	EVERTON	D 1-1	Peters	28,880

FA Cup

Jan 27	Burnley	(Rd 3) W 3-1	Peters 2, Dear	23,452
Feb 17	Stoke City	(Rd 4) W 3-0	Sissons 2, Hurst	36,704
Mar 9	SHEFFIELD UNITED	(Rd 5) L 1-2	Dear	38,440

League Cup

Sep 13	Walsall	(Rd 2) W 5-1	Peters 2, Brabrook, Hurst, o.g.	17,752
Oct 11	BOLTON WANDERERS	(Rd 3) W 4-1	Hurst 4	20,510
Nov 1	Huddersfield Town	(Rd 4) L 0-2		17,729

Fact File

Trevor Brooking made his Hammers debut in the 3-3 draw with Burnley at Turf Moor.

MANAGER: Ron Greenwood
CAPTAIN: Bobby Moore
TOP SCORER: Geoff Hurst
BIGGEST WIN: February 3, 1968 7-2 v Fulham, Division 1
HIGHEST ATTENDANCE: January 6, 1968 58,498 v Manchester United, lost 1-3, Division 1
MAJOR TRANSFERS IN: Billy Bonds from Charlton Athletic, John Cushley from Celtic, Bobby Ferguson from Kilmarnock, Alan Stephenson from Crystal Palace
MAJOR TRANSFERS OUT: Dennis Burnett to Millwall, Alan Sealey to Plymouth Argyle

League & Cup Appearances (substitute)

PLAYER	LEAGUE	CUP COMPETITION FA CUP	LC	TOTAL
Bennett	2 (1)	2		4 (1)
Bonds	37	3	2	42
Bovington	6			6
Boyce	38	1	3	42
Brabrook	14		3	17
Brooking	24 (1)	3		27 (1)
Burkett	8		1	9
Charles	19 (1)		3	22 (1)
Cushley	27	3	3	33
Dear	25 (1)	3	1	29 (1)
Ferguson	39	3	2	44
Heffer	1			1
Howe	2			2
Hurst	38	3	3	44
Kitchener	3		1	4
Lampard	19	3		22
Moore	40	3	3	46
Peters	40	3	3	46
Redknapp	28		2 (1)	30 (1)
Sissons	37	3	2	42
Standen	3		1	4
Stephenson	12			12

Goalscorers

PLAYER	LEAGUE	CUP COMPETITION FA CUP	LC	TOTAL
Hurst	19	1	5	25
Peters	14	2	2	18
Dear	14	2		16
Sissons	8	2		10
Brooking	9			9
Moore	4			4
Brabrook	2		1	3
Redknapp	2			2
Bonds	1			1
Opps' o.gs.			1	1

Final Division 1 Table

		P	W	D	L	F	A	Pts
1	Manchester C	42	26	6	10	86	43	58
2	Manchester U	42	24	8	10	89	55	56
3	Liverpool	42	22	11	9	71	40	55
4	Leeds U	42	22	9	11	71	41	53
5	Everton	42	23	6	13	67	40	52
6	Chelsea	42	18	12	12	62	68	48
7	Tottenham H	42	19	9	14	70	59	47
8	WBA	42	17	12	13	75	62	46
9	Arsenal	42	17	10	15	60	56	44
10	Newcastle U	42	13	15	14	54	67	41
11	Nottingham F	42	14	11	17	52	64	39
12	West Ham U	42	14	10	18	73	69	38
13	Leicester C	42	13	12	17	64	69	38
14	Burnley	42	14	10	18	64	71	38
15	Sunderland	42	13	11	18	51	61	37
16	Southampton	42	13	11	18	66	83	37
17	Wolverhampton W	42	14	8	20	66	75	36
18	Stoke C	42	14	7	21	50	73	35
19	Sheffield W	42	11	12	19	51	63	34
20	Coventry C	42	9	15	18	51	71	33
21	Sheffield U	42	11	10	21	49	70	32
22	Fulham	42	10	7	25	56	98	27

Season 1968-69

Football League Division 1

DATE	OPPONENTS	SCORE	GOALSCORERS	ATTENDANCE
Aug 10	Newcastle United	D 1-1	Dear	36,830
Aug 14	Stoke City	W 2-0	Peters, Sissons	22,131
Aug 17	NOTTINGHAM FOREST	W 1-0	Hurst	31,114
Aug 19	EVERTON	L 1-4	Peters	34,895
Aug 24	Coventry City	W 2-1	Peters, Brooking	33,716
Aug 26	BURNLEY	W 5-0	Hurst 2, Brooking 2, Peters	28,430
Aug 31	WEST BROMWICH ALBION	W 4-0	Peters 3, Redknapp	29,908
Sep 7	Manchester United	D 1-1	Hurst	63,274
Sep 14	TOTTENHAM HOTSPUR	D 2-2	Peters, Hurst	35,802
Sep 21	Chelsea	D 1-1	Peters	58,062
Sep 28	SHEFFIELD WEDNESDAY	D 1-1	Hurst	31,182
Oct 5	SOUTHAMPTON	D 0-0		29,558
Oct 8	Burnley	L 1-3	Brooking	13,869
Oct 12	Leeds United	L 0-2		40,786
Oct 19	SUNDERLAND	W 8-0	Hurst 6, Moore, Brooking	24,718
Oct 26	Arsenal	D 0-0		59,533
Nov 2	QUEENS PARK RANGERS	W 4-3	Moore, Peters, Hurst, Redknapp	36,008
Nov 9	Wolverhampton W	L 0-2		29,704
Nov 16	LEICESTER CITY	W 4-0	Dear 2, Peters, o.g.	26,328
Nov 23	Ipswich Town	D 2-2	Hurst 2	28,964
Nov 30	MANCHESTER CITY	W 2-1	Hurst, Peters	33,082
Dec 7	Liverpool	L 0-2		48,632
Dec 14	LEEDS UNITED	D 1-1	Peters	24,718
Dec 21	Sunderland	L 1-2	Hurst	23,094
Dec 26	Southampton	D 2-2	Hurst 2	27,465
Jan 11	Queens Park Rangers	D 1-1	Dear	28,645
Feb 1	Leicester City	D 1-1	Dear	31,002
Feb 22	LIVERPOOL	D 1-1	Sissons	36,498
Mar 1	NEWCASTLE UNITED	W 3-1	Brooking, Peters, Hurst	26,336
Mar 8	Nottingham Forest	W 1-0	Hurst	24,303
Mar 14	COVENTRY CITY	W 5-2	Hurst 2, Sissons, Peters, Bonds	29,053
Mar 21	IPSWICH TOWN	L 1-3	Hurst	32,574
Mar 24	WOLVERHAMPTON W	W 3-1	Peters 2, Brooking	25,221
Mar 29	MANCHESTER UNITED	D 0-0		41,546
Apr 1	Everton	L 0-1		37,212
Apr 5	Sheffield Wednesday	D 1-1	Hurst	24,268
Apr 8	STOKE CITY	D 0-0		26,577
Apr 12	CHELSEA	D 0-0		32,332
Apr 14	West Bromwich Albion	L 1-3	Peters	20,092
Apr 19	Tottenham Hotspur	L 0-1		50,970
Apr 21	ARSENAL	L 1-2	Sissons	34,941
Apr 30	Manchester City	D 1-1	Peters	31,846

FA Cup

Jan 4	BRISTOL CITY	(Rd 3)	W 3-2	Peters 2, Hurst	32,526
Jan 25	Huddersfield Town	(Rd 4)	W 2-0	Peters, Hurst	30,992
Jan 26	Mansfield Town	(Rd 5)	L 0-3		21,117

League Cup

Sep 4	BOLTON WANDERERS	(Rd 2)	W 7-2	Hurst 3, Peters, Sissons, Brooking, Redknapp	24,937
Sep 25	COVENTRY CITY	(Rd 3)	D 0-0		27,594
Oct 1	Coventry City	(R)	L 2-3	Hurst, Peters	25,988

League & Cup Appearances (substitute)

PLAYER	LEAGUE	CUP COMPETITION FA CUP	LC	TOTAL
Bennett	1			1
Bonds	42	3	2	47
Boyce	37 (2)	2 (1)	3	42 (3)
Brooking	29 (3)	2	3	34 (3)
Charles	35	1	3	39
Cross	0 (1)			0 (1)
Cushley	9	1	1	11
Dear	11		1	12
Death	1			1
Ferguson	39	3	3	45
Grotier	2			2
Hartley	2 (1)			2 (1)
Heffer		1		1
Holland	1			1
Howe	13	1	1	15
Hurst	42	3	3	48
Lampard	1			1
Lindsay	5 (1)	3		8 (1)
Miller	0 (1)			0 (1)
Moore	41	3	3	47
Peters	42	3	3	48
Redknapp	36	3	3	42
Sissons	31 (1)	1	2	34 (1)
Stephenson	42	3	2	47

Goalscorers

PLAYER	LEAGUE	CUP COMPETITION FA CUP	LC	TOTAL
Hurst	25	2	4	31
Peters	19	3	2	24
Brooking	7		1	8
Dear	5			5
Sissons	4		1	5
Redknapp	2		1	3
Moore	2			2
Bonds	1			1
Opps' o.gs.	1			1

Fact File

Geoff Hurst scored four penalties in two days in March. Two for England in a 5-2 win over France and two for West Ham in an identical victory against Coventry City.

MANAGER: Ron Greenwood
CAPTAIN: Bobby Moore
TOP SCORER: Geoff Hurst
BIGGEST WIN: October 19, 1968 8-0 v Sunderland, Division 1
HIGHEST ATTENDANCE: September 7, 1968 63,274 v Manchester United, drew 1-1, Division 1

Final Division 1 Table

		P	W	D	L	F	A	Pts
1	Leeds U	42	27	13	2	66	26	67
2	Liverpool	42	25	11	6	63	24	61
3	Everton	42	21	15	6	77	36	57
4	Arsenal	42	22	12	8	56	27	56
5	Chelsea	42	20	10	12	73	53	50
6	Tottenham H	42	14	17	11	61	51	45
7	Southampton	42	16	13	13	57	48	45
8	West Ham U	42	13	18	11	66	50	44
9	Newcastle U	42	15	14	13	61	55	44
10	WBA	42	16	11	15	64	67	43
11	Manchester U	42	15	12	15	57	53	42
12	Ipswich T	42	15	11	16	59	60	41
13	Manchester C	42	15	10	17	64	55	40
14	Burnley	42	15	9	18	55	82	39
15	Sheffield W	42	10	16	16	41	54	36
16	Wolverhampton W	42	10	15	17	41	58	35
17	Sunderland	42	11	12	19	43	67	34
18	Nottingham F	42	10	13	19	45	57	33
19	Stoke C	42	9	15	18	40	63	33
20	Coventry C	42	10	11	21	46	64	31
21	Leicester C	42	9	12	21	39	68	30
22	QPR	42	4	10	28	39	95	18

Season 1969-70

Football League Division 1

DATE	OPPONENTS	SCORE	GOALSCORERS	ATTENDANCE
Aug 9	NEWCASTLE UNITED	W 1-0	Hurst	33,323
Aug 11	CHELSEA	W 2-0	Hurst, Peters	39,003
Aug 16	Stoke City	L 1-2	Lindsay	23,361
Aug 20	Chelsea	D 0-0		43,347
Aug 23	WEST BROMWICH ALBION	L 1-3	Peters	32,867
Aug 25	ARSENAL	D 1-1	Cross	39,590
Aug 30	Nottingham Forest	L 0-1		29,097
Sep 6	Tottenham Hotspur	L 0-1		40,561
Sep 13	Everton	L 0-2		49,052
Sep 20	SHEFFIELD WEDNESDAY	W 3-0	Hurst, Redknapp, o.g.	23,487
Sep 27	Manchester United	L 2-5	Hurst 2	58,579
Oct 4	BURNLEY	W 3-1	Best 2, Brooking	26,445
Oct 6	STOKE CITY	D 3-3	Best, Brooking, Sissons	26,860
Oct 11	Coventry City	D 2-2	Brooking, Sissons	34,277
Oct 18	Wolverhampton W	L 0-1		28,762
Oct 25	SUNDERLAND	D 1-1	Peters	29,171
Nov 1	Southampton	D 1-1	Brooking	26,894
Nov 8	CRYSTAL PALACE	W 2-1	Best, Hurst	31,515
Nov 15	Liverpool	L 0-2		39,668
Nov 22	DERBY COUNTY	W 3-0	Hurst 2, Peters	32,485
Nov 29	Ipswich Town	L 0-1		17,456
Dec 6	MANCHESTER CITY	L 0-4		27,491
Dec 13	EVERTON	L 0-1		26,689
Dec 17	Leeds United	L 1-4	Hurst	30,659
Dec 20	Tottenham Hotspur	W 2-0	Hurst, Peters	23,375
Dec 26	West Bromwich Albion	L 1-3	Peters	32,867
Dec 27	NOTTINGHAM FOREST	D 1-1	Bonds	31,829
Jan 10	Sheffield Wednesday	W 3-2	Peters 2, Hurst	28,135
Jan 17	MANCHESTER UNITED	D 0-0		41,643
Jan 31	Burnley	L 2-3	Eustace, Lindsay	14,454
Feb 11	COVENTRY CITY	L 1-2	Hurst	22,723
Feb 21	Sunderland	W 1-0	Hurst	16,900
Feb 28	SOUTHAMPTON	D 0-0		27,088
Mar 2	Newcastle United	L 1-4	Eustace	27,500
Mar 7	Derby County	L 0-3		35,615
Mar 14	IPSWICH TOWN	D 0-0		20,934
Mar 21	Manchester City	W 5-1	Hurst 2, Greaves 2, Boyce	28,353
Mar 24	Crystal Palace	D 0-0		34,801
Mar 28	LIVERPOOL	W 1-0	Holland	38,239
Mar 31	WOLVERHAMPTON W	W 3-0	Greaves, Bonds, Howe	26,386
Apr 2	LEEDS UNITED	D 2-2	Best, Bonds	26,140
Apr 4	Arsenal	L 1-2	Greaves	36,218

FA Cup

Jan 3	Middlesbrough	(Rd 3)	L 1-2	Stephenson	31,295

League Cup

Sep 3	HALIFAX TOWN	(Rd 2)	W 4-2	Hurst 2, Best, Lampard	20,717
Sep 23	Nottingham Forest	(Rd 3)	L 0-1		20,939

League & Cup Appearances (substitute)

PLAYER	LEAGUE	CUP COMPETITION FA CUP	LC	TOTAL
Bennett	11 (1)			11 (1)
Best	24	1	1	26
Bonds	42	1	2	45
Boyce	18 (2)	1	1	20 (2)
Brooking	20 (1)		2	22 (1)
Charles	5			5
Cross	5 (1)		1	6 (1)
Cushley	2			2
Eustace	14			14
Ferguson	30	1	2	33
Greaves	6			6
Grotier	12			12
Heffer	0 (1)			0 (1)
Holland	8			8
Howe	32 (1)	1		33 (1)
Hurst	38 (1)	1	2	41 (1)
Lampard	30	1	2	33
Lindsay	17		1	18
Llewellyn	0 (2)			0 (2)
Miller	1 (1)			1 (1)
Moore	40	1	2	43
Peters	31	1	2	34
Redknapp	23	0 (1)	2	25 (1)
Sissons	19 (1)	1		20 (1)
Stephenson	34	1	2	37

Goalscorers

PLAYER	LEAGUE	CUP COMPETITION FA CUP	LC	TOTAL
Hurst	16		2	18
Peters	7			7
Best	5		1	6
Brooking	4			4
Greaves	4			4
Bonds	3			3
Eustace	2			2
Lindsay	2			2
Sissons	2			2
Boyce	1			1
Cross	1			1
Holland	1			1
Howe	1			1
Lampard			1	1
Redknapp	1			1
Stephenson		1		1
Opps' o.gs.	1			1

Fact File

Jimmy Greaves scored within ten minutes of his debut against Manchester City in March.

MANAGER: Ron Greenwood

CAPTAIN: Bobby Moore

TOP SCORER: Geoff Hurst

BIGGEST WIN: March 21, 1970 5-1 v Manchester City, Division 1

HIGHEST ATTENDANCE: September 27, 1969 58,579 v Manchester United, lost 2-5, Division 1

MAJOR TRANSFERS IN: Peter Eustace from Sheffield Wednesday, Jimmy Greaves from Tottenham Hotspur

MAJOR TRANSFERS OUT: Martin Peters to Tottenham Hotspur

Final Division 1 Table

		P	W	D	L	F	A	Pts
1	Everton	42	29	8	5	72	34	66
2	Leeds U	42	21	15	6	84	49	57
3	Chelsea	42	21	13	8	70	50	55
4	Derby Co	42	22	9	11	64	37	53
5	Liverpool	42	20	11	11	65	42	51
6	Coventry C	42	19	11	12	58	48	49
7	Newcastle U	42	17	13	12	57	35	47
8	Manchester U	42	14	17	11	66	61	45
9	Stoke C	42	15	15	12	56	52	45
10	Manchester C	42	16	11	15	55	48	43
11	Tottenham H	42	17	9	16	54	55	43
12	Arsenal	42	12	18	12	51	49	42
13	Wolverhampton W	42	12	16	14	55	57	40
14	Burnley	42	12	15	15	56	61	39
15	Nottingham F	42	10	18	14	50	71	38
16	WBA	42	14	9	19	58	66	37
17	West Ham U	42	12	12	18	51	60	36
18	Ipswich T	42	10	11	21	40	63	31
19	Southampton	42	6	17	19	46	67	29
20	Crystal Palace	42	6	15	21	34	68	27
21	Sunderland	42	6	14	22	30	68	26
22	Sheffield W	42	8	9	25	40	71	25

Season 1970-71

Football League Division 1

DATE	OPPONENTS	SCORE	GOALSCORERS	ATTENDANCE
Aug 15	Tottenham Hotspur	D 2-2	Greaves, Bennett	53,640
Aug 17	ARSENAL	D 0-0		39,004
Aug 22	CHELSEA	D 2-2	Howe, Hurst	39,240
Aug 26	Leeds United	L 0-3		42,677
Aug 29	Manchester United	D 1-1	Hurst	50,643
Aug 31	SOUTHAMPTON	D 1-1	Hurst (pen)	26,213
Sep 5	EVERTON	L 1-2	Moore	29,171
Sep 12	West Bromwich Albion	L 1-2	Howe	24,913
Sep 19	NEWCASTLE UNITED	L 0-2		25,841
Sep 26	Huddersfield Town	D 1-1	Hurst (pen)	20,887
Oct 3	BURNLEY	W 3-1	Hurst 3	23,295
Oct 10	Stoke City	L 1-2	Greaves	23,035
Oct 17	TOTTENHAM HOTSPUR	D 2-2	Eustace, Hurst	42,322
Oct 24	Crystal Palace	D 1-1	Howe	41,486
Oct 31	BLACKPOOL	W 2-1	Greaves, Eustace	26,239
Nov 7	Ipswich Town	L 1-2	Hurst	22,990
Nov 14	WOLVERHAMPTON W	D 3-3	Best 2, Moore	23,978
Nov 21	Manchester City	L 0-2		28,485
Nov 28	COVENTRY CITY	L 1-2	Best	22,800
Dec 5	Derby County	W 4-2	Greaves, Brooking, Best 2	30,806
Dec 12	LIVERPOOL	L 1-2	Greaves	27,459
Dec 19	Chelsea	L 1-2	Lampard	42,075
Jan 9	Arsenal	L 0-2		49,007
Jan 16	LEEDS UNITED	L 2-3	Eustace, Brooking	34,396
Feb 6	DERBY COUNTY	L 1-4	Eustace	26,606
Feb 9	Coventry City	W 1-0	Greaves	25,083
Feb 16	Liverpool	L 0-1		38,082
Feb 20	MANCHESTER CITY	D 0-0		30,168
Feb 24	NOTTINGHAM FOREST	W 2-0	Hurst, Robson	35,601
Feb 27	Blackpool	D 1-1	Hurst (pen)	15,639
Mar 6	CRYSTAL PALACE	D 0-0		26,157
Mar 13	Wolverhampton W	L 0-2		25,066
Mar 20	IPSWICH TOWN	D 2-2	Greaves 2	25,957
Mar 30	Everton	W 1-0	o.g.	28,794
Apr 3	MANCHESTER UNITED	W 2-1	Hurst, Robson	38,507
Apr 9	WEST BROMWICH ALBION	W 2-1	Robson, Greaves	34,981
Apr 10	Nottingham Forest	L 0-1		23,032
Apr 13	Burnley	L 0-1		15,822
Apr 17	STOKE CITY	W 1-0	Hurst	26,269
Apr 24	Newcastle United	D 1-1	Hurst	22,720
Apr 27	Southampton	W 2-1	Taylor, Hurst	19,395
May 1	HUDDERSFIELD TOWN	L 0-1		24,983

FA Cup

Jan 2	Blackpool	(Rd 3)	L 0-4		21,814

League Cup

Sep 9	HULL CITY	(Rd 2)	W 1-0	Eustace	19,116
Oct 6	Coventry City	(Rd 3)	L 1-3	Hurst	19,362

League & Cup Appearances (substitute)

PLAYER	LEAGUE	CUP COMPETITION		TOTAL
		FA CUP	LC	
Ayris	6 (1)	1	1	8 (1)
Bennett	8			8
Best	20 (2)	1	2	23 (2)
Bonds	37	1	2	40
Boyce	13			13
Brooking	17 (2)		1	18 (2)
Dear	4	0 (1)		4 (1)
Eustace	25 (2)	1	2	28 (2)
Ferguson	23	1		24
Greaves	30 (2)	1	1	32 (2)
Grotier	19		2	21
Heffer	1 (2)			1 (2)
Holland	2 (1)			2 (1)
Howe	20 (1)	1	1	22 (1)
Hurst	39		2	41
Lampard	41	1	2	44
Lindsay	14 (2)	1	1	16 (2)
Llewellyn	1 (1)			1 (1)
McDowell	25			2
Moore	38 (1)	1	2	41 (1)
Redknapp	20 (1)		1	21 (1)
Robson	14			14
Stephenson	15 (1)		2	17 (1)
Taylor	30	1		31

Goalscorers

PLAYER	LEAGUE	CUP COMPETITION		TOTAL
		FA CUP	LC	
Hurst	14		1	15
Greaves	9			9
Best	5			5
Eustace	4		1	5
Howe	3			3
Robson	3			3
Brooking	2			2
Moore	2			2
Bennett	1			1
Lampard	1			1
Taylor	1			1
Opps' o.gs.	1			1

Fact File

Bobby Moore and Jimmy Greaves were suspended by West Ham for attending a night club before the defeat at Blackpool in the FA Cup. They returned to the side in February.

MANAGER: Ron Greenwood
CAPTAIN: Bobby Moore
TOP SCORER: Geoff Hurst
BIGGEST WIN: December 5, 1970 4-2 v Derby County, Division 1
HIGHEST ATTENDANCE: August 15, 1970 53,640 v Tottenham Hotspur, drew 2-2, Division 1
MAJOR TRANSFERS IN: Tommy Taylor from Orient, Bryan Robson from Newcastle United
MAJOR TRANSFERS OUT: John Sissons to Sheffield Wednesday, Jimmy Greaves (retired)

Final Division 1 Table

		P	W	D	L	F	A	PTS
1	Arsenal	42	29	7	6	71	29	65
2	Leeds U	42	27	10	5	72	30	64
3	Tottenham H	42	19	14	9	54	33	52
4	Wolverhampton W	42	22	8	12	64	54	52
5	Liverpool	42	17	17	8	42	24	51
6	Chelsea	42	18	15	9	52	42	51
7	Southampton	42	17	12	13	56	44	46
8	Manchester U	42	16	11	15	65	66	43
9	Derby Co	42	16	10	16	56	54	42
10	Coventry C	42	16	10	16	37	38	42
11	Manchester C	42	12	17	13	47	42	41
12	Newcastle U	42	14	13	15	44	46	41
13	Stoke C	42	12	13	17	44	48	37
14	Everton	42	12	13	17	54	60	37
15	Huddersfield T	42	11	14	17	40	49	36
16	Nottingham F	42	14	8	20	42	61	36
17	WBA	42	10	15	17	58	75	35
18	Crystal Palace	42	12	11	19	39	57	35
19	Ipswich T	42	12	10	20	42	48	34
20	West Ham U	42	10	14	18	47	60	34
21	Burnley	42	7	13	22	29	63	27
22	Blackpool	42	4	15	23	34	66	23

Season 1971-72

Football League Division 1

DATE	OPPONENTS	SCORE	GOALSCORERS	ATTENDANCE
Aug 14	WEST BROMWICH ALBION	L 0-1		27,420
Aug 18	Derby County	L 0-2		30,583
Aug 21	Nottingham Forest	L 0-1		17,185
Aug 23	IPSWICH TOWN	D 0-0		25,714
Aug 28	EVERTON	W 1-0	Best	26,878
Aug 30	COVENTRY CITY	W 4-0	Best 2, Hurst, Robson	28,176
Sep 4	Newcastle United	D 2-2	Hurst, Robson	31,910
Sep 11	CHELSEA	W 2-1	Best 2	36,866
Sep 18	Manchester United	L 2-4	Best, Brooking	53,334
Sep 25	STOKE CITY	W 2-1	Best, Moore	29,193
Oct 2	Leeds United	D 0-0		30,942
Oct 9	LEICESTER CITY	D 1-1	Hurst	31,060
Oct 16	West Bromwich Albion	D 0-0		20,740
Oct 23	WOLVERHAMPTON W	W 1-0	Best	33,883
Oct 30	Crystal Palace	W 3-0	Coker, Bonds, Best	41,540
Nov 6	SHEFFIELD UNITED	L 1-2	Robson	36,595
Nov 13	Huddersfield Town	L 0-1		14,177
Nov 20	MANCHESTER CITY	L 0-2		33,694
Nov 27	Liverpool	L 0-1		43,399
Dec 4	ARSENAL	D 0-0		35,155
Dec 11	Southampton	D 3-3	Bonds, Best, Brooking	20,506
Dec 18	NEWCASTLE UNITED	L 0-1		21,991
Dec 27	Tottenham Hotspur	W 1-0	Best	53,888
Jan 1	MANCHESTER UNITED	W 3-0	Robson, Best, Hurst	41,892
Jan 8	Everton	L 1-2	Hurst (pen)	38,482
Jan 22	DERBY COUNTY	D 3-3	Lampard, Robson, Brooking	31,045
Jan 29	Ipswich Town	L 0-1		22,766
Feb 12	Wolverhampton W	L 0-1		26,852
Feb 19	CRYSTAL PALACE	D 1-1	Best	28,209
Feb 29	Sheffield United	L 0-3		24,034
Mar 4	HUDDERSFIELD TOWN	W 3-0	Best 2, Robson	18,521
Mar 11	Leicester City	L 0-2		23,345
Mar 18	NOTTINGHAM FOREST	W 4-2	Robson 2, Hurst, Brooking	20,960
Mar 21	Coventry City	D 1-1	Best	18,640
Mar 25	Chelsea	L 1-3	Best	45,137
Mar 31	LEEDS UNITED	D 2-2	Bonds, Hurst	41,003
Apr 1	TOTTENHAM HOTSPUR	W 2-0	Brooking, Coker	30,763
Apr 4	Stoke City	D 0-0		24,688
Apr 8	Manchester City	L 1-3	Hurst	38,491
Apr 15	LIVERPOOL	L 0-2		32,660
Apr 22	Arsenal	L 1-2	Brooking	42,251
May 1	SOUTHAMPTON	W 1-0	Robson	18,479

FA Cup

Jan 15	LUTON TOWN	(Rd 3)	W 2-1	Hurst, Best	32,099
Feb 9	Hereford United	(Rd 4)	D 0-0		15,000
Feb 14	HEREFORD UNITED	(R)	W 3-1	Hurst 3	42,271
Feb 26	Huddersfield Town	(Rd 5)	L 2-4	Robson, Best	27,080

League Cup

Sep 8	CARDIFF CITY	(Rd 2)	D 1-1	Bonds	24,432
Sep 22	Cardiff City	(R)	W 2-1	Hurst 2	30,100
Oct 6	LEEDS UNITED	(Rd 3)	D 0-0		35,890
Oct 20	Leeds United	(R)	W 1-0†	Best	26,504
Oct 27	LIVERPOOL	(Rd 4)	W 2-1	Hurst, Robson	40,878
Nov 17	SHEFFIELD UNITED	(QF)	W 5-0	Robson 3, Best 2	36,834
Dec 8	Stoke City	(SF FL)	W 2-1	Hurst (pen), Best	36,400
Dec 15	STOKE CITY	(SF SL)	L 0-1†		38,771
Jan 5	STOKE CITY	(R)	D 0-0*		46,916
Jan 26	STOKE CITY	(2nd R)	L 2-3**	Bonds, Brooking	49,247

†After extra time. *Played at Old Trafford. **Played at Hillsborough.

MANAGER: Ron Greenwood
CAPTAIN: Bobby Moore
TOP SCORER: Clyde Best
BIGGEST WIN: November 17, 1971 5-0 v Sheffield United, League Cup quarter-final
HIGHEST ATTENDANCE: December 27, 1971 53,888 v Tottenham Hotspur, won 1-0, Division 1

League & Cup Appearances (substitute)

PLAYER	LEAGUE	CUP COMPETITION		TOTAL
		FA CUP	LC	
Ayris	11 (1)		1	12 (1)
Best	42	4	10	56
Bonds	42	4	10	56
Boyce	0 (1)			0 (1)
Brooking	40	4	10	54
Charles	4			4
Coker	5			5
Durrell	5 (1)			5 (1)
Eustace	2	0 (1)	0 (1)	2 (2)
Ferguson	36	4	10	50
Grotier	6			6
Heffer	0 (1)	0 (1)		0 (2)
Holland	4			4
Howe	1 (4)		0 (2)	1 (6)
Hurst	34	4	10	48
Lampard	39	4	10	53
Llewellyn	1 (1)			1 (1)
Lock	1 (2)			1 (2)
McDowell	40	4	10	54
Moore	40	4	10	54
Redknapp	22	4	9	35
Robson	42	4	10	56
Stephenson	3 (1)			3 (1)
Taylor	42	4	10	56

Goalscorers

PLAYER	LEAGUE	CUP COMPETITION		TOTAL
		FA CUP	LC	
Best	17	2	4	23
Hurst	8	4	4	16
Robson	9	1	4	14
Brooking	6		1	7
Bonds	3		2	5
Coker	2			2
Lampard	1			1
Moore	1			1

Fact File

The League Cup semi-final second replay against Stoke City saw Bobby Moore take over in goal when Bobby Ferguson was concussed after 13 minutes.

Final Division 1 Table

		P	W	D	L	F	A	PTS
1	Derby Co	42	24	10	8	69	33	58
2	Leeds U	42	24	9	9	73	31	57
3	Liverpool	42	24	9	9	64	30	57
4	Manchester C	42	23	11	8	77	45	57
5	Arsenal	42	22	8	12	58	40	52
6	Tottenham H	42	19	13	10	63	42	51
7	Chelsea	42	18	12	12	58	49	48
8	Manchester U	42	19	10	13	69	61	48
9	Wolverhampton W	42	18	11	13	65	57	47
10	Sheffield U	42	17	12	13	61	60	46
11	Newcastle U	42	15	11	16	49	52	41
12	Leicester C	42	13	13	16	41	46	39
13	Ipswich T	42	11	16	15	39	53	38
14	West Ham U	42	12	12	18	47	51	36
15	Everton	42	9	18	15	37	48	36
16	WBA	42	12	11	19	42	54	35
17	Stoke C	42	10	15	17	39	56	35
18	Coventry C	42	9	15	18	44	67	33
19	Southampton	42	12	7	23	52	80	31
20	Crystal Palace	42	8	13	21	39	65	29
21	Nottingham F	42	8	9	25	47	81	25
22	Huddersfield T	42	6	13	23	27	59	25

Season 1972-73

Football League Division 1

DATE	OPPONENTS	SCORE	GOALSCORERS	ATTENDANCE
Aug 12	West Bromwich Albion	D 0-0		21,509
Aug 14	COVENTRY CITY	W 1-0	Best	27,498
Aug 19	LEICESTER CITY	W 5-2	Moore, Coker, Robson 2, Tyler	25,414
Aug 22	Wolverhampton W	L 0-3		21,958
Aug 26	Liverpool	L 2-3	Robson 2	50,491
Aug 29	Arsenal	L 0-1		43,802
Sep 2	MANCHESTER UNITED	D 2-2	Robson 2	31,939
Sep 9	Chelsea	W 3-1	Taylor, Moore, Bonds	34,392
Sep 16	NORWICH CITY	W 4-0	Brooking, Robson 2, Taylor	27,780
Sep 23	Tottenham Hotspur	L 0-1		51,700
Sep 30	BIRMINGHAM CITY	W 2-0	Bonds, Best	26,482
Oct 7	Ipswich Town	D 1-1	Best	22,377
Oct 14	SHEFFIELD UNITED	W 3-1	Brooking, Robson 2	25,379
Oct 21	Manchester City	L 3-4	Best, Ayris, Moore	30,890
Oct 28	CRYSTAL PALACE	W 4-0	Brooking 2, McDowell, Robson	28,894
Nov 4	WOLVERHAMPTON W	D 2-2	Robson, Brooking	29,524
Nov 11	Coventry City	L 1-3	McDowell	27,189
Nov 18	DERBY COUNTY	L 1-2	Robson	28,154
Nov 25	Everton	W 2-1	Brooking, Best	27,558
Dec 2	NEWCASTLE UNITED	D 1-1	Brooking	23,785
Dec 9	Leeds United	L 0-1		30,270
Dec 16	STOKE CITY	W 3-2	Robson 2, Best	23,269
Dec 23	Southampton	D 0-0		19,429
Dec 26	TOTTENHAM HOTSPUR	D 2-2	Robson 2 (1 pen)	37,397
Dec 30	Leicester City	L 1-2	Brooking	19,341
Jan 6	LIVERPOOL	L 0-1		34,480
Jan 20	Manchester United	D 2-2	Robson, Best	50,878
Jan 27	CHELSEA	W 3-1	Taylor, Robson 2	33,336
Feb 10	Norwich City	W 1-0	Robson	32,597
Feb 17	WEST BROMWICH ALBION	W 2-1	Bonds, Robson	26,071
Feb 24	Stoke City	L 0-2		21,855
Mar 2	IPSWICH TOWN	L 0-1		37,004
Mar 10	Sheffield United	D 0-0		24,024
Mar 17	MANCHESTER CITY	W 2-1	MacDougall, Robson	29,370
Mar 24	Crystal Palace	W 3-1	Robson, Brooking, MacDougall	36,915
Mar 31	EVERTON	W 2-0	Robson, Lock	25,531
Apr 7	Newcastle United	W 2-1	MacDougall 2	24,030
Apr 14	LEEDS UNITED	D 1-1	Holland	38,804
Apr 20	SOUTHAMPTON	W 4-3	Robson 3, Brooking	33,039
Apr 21	Derby County	D 1-1	Lutton	28,727
Apr 23	Birmingham City	D 0-0		36,942
Apr 28	ARSENAL	L 1-2	o.g.	37,366

FA Cup

Jan 13	Port Vale	(Rd 3)	W 1-0	Holland	20,619
Feb 3	Hull City	(Rd 4)	L 0-1		32,390

League Cup

Sep 6	BRISTOL CITY	(Rd 2)	W 2-1	McDowell, Hurst	17,688
Oct 4	Stockport County	(Rd 3)	L 1-2	Best	13,410

League & Cup Appearances (substitute)

PLAYER	LEAGUE	CUP COMPETITION FA CUP	LC	TOTAL
Ayris	13 (2)			13 (2)
Best	41 (1)	2	2	45 (1)
Bonds	39	2	2	43
Boyce	0 (2)			0 (2)
Brooking	40	2	2	44
Charles	7 (2)	0 (1)		7 (3)
Coker	4			4
Ferguson	31	2		33
Grotier	11		2	13
Holland	30 (2)	2	2	34 (2)
Lampard	38	2	2	42
Lock	14 (4)	0 (1)		14 (5)
Lutton	4 (2)			4 (2)
MacDougall	10			10
McDowell	38	2	2	42
Moore	42	2	2	46
Robson	42	2	2	46
Taylor	37	2	2	41
Tyler	21	2	2	25

Goalscorers

PLAYER	LEAGUE	CUP COMPETITION FA CUP	LC	TOTAL
Robson	28			28
Brooking	11			11
Best	7		2	9
MacDougall	4			4
Bonds	3			3
McDowell	2		1	3
Moore	3			3
Taylor	3			3
Holland	1	1		2
Ayris	1			1
Coker	1			1
Lock	1			1
Lutton	1			1
Tyler	1			1
Opps' o.gs.	1			1

Fact File

In February, Bobby Moore won his 100th England cap against Scotland in the Scottish FA Centenary match.

MANAGER: Ron Greenwood

CAPTAIN: Bobby Moore

TOP SCORER: Bryan Robson

BIGGEST WIN: September 16, 1972 4-0 v Norwich City, Division 1; October 28, 1972 4-0 v Crystal Palace, Division 1

HIGHEST ATTENDANCE: September 23, 1972 51,700 v Tottenham Hotspur, lost 0-1, Division 1

MAJOR TRANSFERS IN: Dudley Tyler from Hereford United, Ted MacDougall from Manchester United

MAJOR TRANSFERS OUT: Harry Redknapp to Bournemouth, Geoff Hurst to Stoke City, Peter Eustace to Sheffield Wednesday

Final Division 1 Table

	P	W	D	L	F	A	Pts
1 Liverpool	42	25	10	7	72	42	60
2 Arsenal	42	23	11	8	57	43	57
3 Leeds U	42	21	11	10	71	45	53
4 Ipswich T	42	17	14	11	55	45	48
5 Wolverhampton W	42	18	11	13	66	54	47
6 West Ham U	42	17	12	13	67	53	46
7 Derby Co	42	19	8	15	56	54	46
8 Tottenham H	42	16	13	13	58	48	45
9 Newcastle U	42	16	13	13	60	51	45
10 Birmingham C	42	15	12	15	53	54	42
11 Manchester C	42	15	11	16	57	60	41
12 Chelsea	42	13	14	15	49	51	40
13 Southampton	42	11	18	13	47	52	40
14 Sheffield U	42	15	10	17	51	59	40
15 Stoke C	42	14	10	18	61	56	38
16 Leicester C	42	10	17	15	40	46	37
17 Everton	42	13	11	18	41	49	37
18 Manchester U	42	12	13	17	44	60	37
19 Coventry C	42	13	9	20	40	55	35
20 Norwich C	42	11	10	21	36	63	32
21 Crystal Palace	42	9	12	21	41	58	30
22 WBA	42	9	10	23	38	62	28

Season 1973-74

Football League Division 1

DATE	OPPONENTS	SCORE	GOALSCORERS	ATTENDANCE
Aug 25	NEWCASTLE UNITED	L 1-2	Robson	28,169
Aug 27	IPSWICH TOWN	D 3-3	Bonds, Brooking, Best	23,335
Sep 1	Norwich City	D 2-2	Best, Robson	25,706
Sep 4	Queens Park Rangers	D 0-0		28,360
Sep 8	TOTTENHAM HOTSPUR	L 0-1		30,888
Sep 10	QUEENS PARK RANGERS	L 2-3	Robson, Bonds (pen)	26,042
Sep 15	Manchester United	L 1-3	Bonds (pen)	44,757
Sep 22	LEICESTER CITY	D 1-1	Robson	23,567
Sep 29	Stoke City	L 0-2		16,395
Oct 6	BURNLEY	L 0-1		23,604
Oct 13	Everton	L 0-1		34,708
Oct 20	Coventry City	W 1-0	McDowell	21,097
Oct 27	DERBY COUNTY	D 0-0		31,237
Nov 3	Leeds United	L 1-4	MacDougall	36,869
Nov 10	SHEFFIELD UNITED	D 2-2	Bonds, Brooking	21,243
Nov 17	Wolverhampton W	D 0-0		19,587
Nov 24	ARSENAL	L 1-3	Bonds	28,287
Dec 1	Liverpool	L 0-1		34,857
Dec 8	MANCHESTER CITY	W 2-1	Brooking, o.g.	20,790
Dec 15	Birmingham City	L 1-3	Gould	23,787
Dec 22	STOKE CITY	L 0-2		16,513
Dec 26	Chelsea	W 4-2	Lampard, Gould, Best 2	26,982
Dec 29	Tottenham Hotspur	L 0-2		33,172
Jan 1	NORWICH CITY	W 4-2	Gould, Paddon 2, Brooking	32,259
Jan 12	MANCHESTER UNITED	W 2-1	Bonds, Holland	34,147
Jan 19	Newcastle United	D 1-1	Holland	27,216
Feb 2	BIRMINGHAM CITY	D 0-0		27,948
Feb 5	Ipswich Town	W 3-1	o.g., McDowell, Best	25,747
Feb 9	Leicester City	W 1-0	Best	27,032
Feb 16	EVERTON	W 4-3	Paddon, Best 2, Bonds	29,347
Feb 23	Burnley	D 1-1	Paddon	18,216
Mar 2	CHELSEA	W 3-0	Bonds 3	34,043
Mar 9	Derby County	D 1-1	Bonds	24,684
Mar 16	COVENTRY CITY	L 2-3	Bonds 2 (1 pen)	25,502
Mar 23	Sheffield United	L 0-1		19,467
Mar 30	LEEDS UNITED	W 3-1	Best, Robson, Brooking	38,416
Apr 6	Arsenal	D 0-0		37,868
Apr 12	SOUTHAMPTON	W 4-1	Robson 2, Best 2	34,163
Apr 13	WOLVERHAMPTON W	D 0-0		29,488
Apr 15	Southampton	D 1-1	Best	26,515
Apr 20	Manchester City	L 1-2	Gould	29,700
Apr 27	LIVERPOOL	D 2-2	Lampard, Brooking	36,160

FA Cup

Jan 5	HEREFORD UNITED	(Rd 3) D 1-1	Holland	23,087
Jan 8	Hereford United	(R) L 1-2	Best	17,423

League Cup

Oct 8	LIVERPOOL	(Rd 2) D 2-2	McDougall, Robson	25,840
Oct 29	Liverpool	(R) L 0-1		26,002

League & Cup Appearances (substitute)

PLAYER	LEAGUE	CUP COMPETITION FA CUP	LC	TOTAL
Ayris	5		1	6
Best	34	2	2	38
Bonds	40	2	1	43
Brooking	38		2	40
Charles	1			1
Coker	0 (1)	1		1 (1)
Coleman	31 (2)	1	2	34 (2)
Day	33	2	2	37
Ferguson	9			9
Gould	11 (1)	1		12 (1)
Holland	20 (3)	1 (1)	0 (2)	21 (6)
Lampard	42	2	2	46
Lock	9 (2)		2	11 (2)
Lutton	4 (2)	1		5 (2)
MacDougall	14		1	15
McDowell	33	1	2	36
McGiven	21	2		23
Moore	22	1	1	24
Paddon	24	2		26
Robson	22		1	23
Taylor	40	2	2	44
Tyler	8		1	9
Wooler	1 (1)	1		2 (1)

Goalscorers

PLAYER	LEAGUE	CUP COMPETITION FA CUP	LC	TOTAL
Best	12	1		13
Bonds	13			13
Robson	7		1	8
Brooking	6			6
Gould	4			4
Paddon	4			4
Holland	2	1		3
Lampard	2			2
MacDougall	1		1	2
McDowell	2			2
Opps' o.gs.	2			2

Fact File

In April, Trevor Brooking won his first England cap in a 0-0 draw with Portugal.

MANAGER: Ron Greenwood

CAPTAIN: Bobby Moore/Billy Bonds

TOP SCORERS: Clyde Best and Billy Bonds

BIGGEST WIN: April 12, 1974 4-1 v Southampton, Division 1

HIGHEST ATTENDANCE: September 15, 1973 44,757 v Manchester United, lost 1-3, Division 1

MAJOR TRANSFERS IN: Keith Coleman and Mick McGiven from Sunderland, Bobby Gould from Bristol City, Graham Paddon from Norwich City

MAJOR TRANSFERS OUT: Ted MacDougall to Norwich City, Bobby Moore to Fulham

Final Division 1 Table

		P	W	D	L	F	A	Pts
1	Leeds U	42	24	14	4	66	31	62
2	Liverpool	42	22	13	7	52	31	57
3	Derby Co	42	17	14	11	52	42	48
4	Ipswich T	42	18	11	13	67	58	47
5	Stoke C	42	15	16	11	54	42	46
6	Burnley	42	16	14	12	56	53	46
7	Everton	42	16	12	14	50	48	44
8	QPR	42	13	17	12	56	52	43
9	Leicester C	42	13	16	13	51	41	42
10	Arsenal	42	14	14	14	49	51	42
11	Tottenham H	42	14	14	14	45	50	42
12	Wolverhampton W	42	13	15	14	49	49	41
13	Sheffield U	42	14	12	16	44	49	40
14	Manchester C	42	14	12	16	39	46	40
15	Newcastle U	42	13	12	17	49	48	38
16	Coventry C	42	14	10	18	43	54	38
17	Chelsea	42	12	13	17	56	60	37
18	West Ham U	42	11	15	16	55	60	37
19	Birmingham C	42	12	13	17	52	64	37
20	Southampton	42	11	14	17	47	68	36
21	Manchester U	42	10	12	20	38	48	32
22	Norwich C	42	7	15	20	37	62	29

Season 1974-1975

Football League Division 1

DATE	OPPONENTS	SCORE	GOALSCORERS	ATTENDANCE
Aug 17	Manchester City	L 0-4		30,240
Aug 19	LUTON TOWN	W 2-0	Lampard, Bonds	23,182
Aug 24	EVERTON	L 2-3	Bonds (pen), McDowell	22,486
Aug 28	Luton Town	D 0-0		16,931
Aug 31	Newcastle United	L 0-2		30,780
Sep 7	SHEFFIELD UNITED	L 1-2	Jennings	20,977
Sep 14	Tottenham Hotspur	L 1-2	Lampard	27,959
Sep 21	LEICESTER CITY	W 6-2	Jennings 2, Bonds, Gould 2, Robson	21,377
Sep 25	BIRMINGHAM CITY	W 3-0	Paddon, Jennings, Robson	29,495
Sep 28	Burnley	W 5-3	Robson 2, Brooking, Jennings, Bonds	17,613
Oct 5	DERBY COUNTY	D 2-2	Robson, Bonds	32,900
Oct 12	Coventry City	D 1-1	Gould	22,519
Oct 15	Everton	D 1-1	Gould	31,855
Oct 19	IPSWICH TOWN	W 1-0	Jennings	33,543
Oct 26	Arsenal	L 0-3		41,004
Nov 2	MIDDLESBROUGH	W 3-0	Robson, o.g., Paddon	28,915
Nov 9	Carlisle United	W 1-0	Lampard	14,141
Nov 16	WOLVERHAMPTON W	W 5-2	Bonds (pen), Brooking, Lampard, Jennings, Gould	31,708
Nov 23	Liverpool	D 1-1	Robson	46,346
Nov 30	Queens Park Rangers	W 2-0	Jennings, Paddon	28,356
Dec 7	LEEDS UNITED	W 2-1	Gould, Jennings	39,562
Dec 14	MANCHESTER CITY	D 0-0		33,908
Dec 21	Chelsea	D 1-1	Gould	34,969
Dec 26	TOTTENHAM HOTSPUR	D 1-1	Robson	37,682
Dec 28	Stoke City	L 1-2	Holland	33,498
Jan 11	Leeds United	L 1-2	Robson	40,099
Jan 18	QUEENS PARK RANGERS	D 2-2	Jennings, Bonds (pen)	28,772
Feb 1	CARLISLE UNITED	W 2-0	Jennings, Holland	26,805
Feb 8	Middlesbrough	D 0-0		29,179
Feb 19	LIVERPOOL	D 0-0		40,256
Feb 22	Wolverhampton W	L 1-3	Gould	24,791
Feb 28	NEWCASTLE UNITED	L 0-1		32,753
Mar 15	BURNLEY	W 2-1	Robson, Taylor A	28,830
Mar 18	Birmingham City	D 1-1	Taylor A	34,000
Mar 22	Sheffield United	L 2-3	Gould, Jennings	25,527
Mar 28	STOKE CITY	D 2-2	Brooking, Jennings	29,811
Mar 29	CHELSEA	L 0-1		31,025
Apr 1	Leicester City	L 0-3		30,408
Apr 12	Derby County	L 0-1		31,336
Apr 19	COVENTRY CITY	L 1-2	Holland	27,431
Apr 26	Ipswich Town	L 1-4	Holland	31,592
Apr 28	ARSENAL	W 1-0	Paddon	30,195

FA Cup

Jan 4	Southampton	(Rd 3)	W 2-1	Lampard, Gould	24,615
Jan 25	SWINDON TOWN	(Rd 4)	D 1-1	Jennings	35,679
Jan 28	Swindon Town	(R)	W 2-1	Brooking, Holland	27,749
Feb 15	QUEENS PARK RANGERS	(Rd 5)	W 2-1	Holland, Robson	39,193
Mar 8	Arsenal	(QF)	W 2-0	Taylor A 2	56,742
Apr 5	Ipswich Town	(SF)	D 0-0*		58,000
Apr 9	Ipswich Town	(R)	2-1**	Taylor A 2	45,344
May 3	Fulham	(F)	W 2-0 †	Taylor A 2	100,000

*Played at Villa Park. **Played at Stamford Bridge. †Played at Wembley.

League Cup

Sep 11	Tranmere Rovers	(Rd 2)	D 0-0		8,638
Sep 18	TRANMERE ROVERS	(R)	W 6-0	Bonds 2 (1 pen), Ayris, Gould 3 (1 pen)	15,854
Oct 8	Fulham	(Rd 3)	L 1-2	Brooking	29,611

MANAGER: John Lyall
CAPTAIN: Billy Bonds
TOP SCORER: Billy Jennings
BIGGEST WIN: September 18, 1974 6-0 v Tranmere Rovers, League Cup Round 2 replay
HIGHEST ATTENDANCE: May 3, 1975 100,000 v Fulham, won 2-0, FA Cup final
MAJOR TRANSFERS IN: Billy Jennings from Watford, Keith Robson from Newcastle United, Alan Taylor from Rochdale
MAJOR TRANSFERS OUT: Bryan Robson to Sunderland

League & Cup Appearances (substitute)

PLAYER	LEAGUE	CUP COMPETITION FA CUP	LC	TOTAL
Ayris	2 (4)		3	5 (4)
Best	12 (3)	2	1	15 (3)
Bonds	31	8	3	42
Brooking	36	8	3	47
Coleman	27 (2)	1	1	29 (2)
Curbishley	1 (1)			1 (1)
Day	42	8	3	53
Gould	31 (3)	3	2	36 (3)
Holland	18 (4)	4 (3)	1 (1)	23 (8)
Jennings	32	8		40
Lampard	40	8	3	51
Lock	41 (1)	8	3	52 (1)
McDowell	33 (1)	8	2	43 (1)
Paddon	40	8	3	51
Robson	25	3	2	30
Taylor	11 (3)	4		15 (3)
Wooler	1			1

Goalscorers

PLAYER	LEAGUE	CUP COMPETITION FA CUP	LC	TOTAL
Jennings	13	1		14
Gould	9	1	3	13
Robson	10	1		11
Bonds	7		2	9
Taylor	2	6		8
Holland	4	2		6
Brooking	3	1	1	5
Lampard	4	1		5
Paddon	4			4
Ayris			1	1
McDowell	1			1
Opps' o.gs.	1			1

Fact File

Mervyn Day was named as this season's PFA Young Player of the Year.

Final Division 1 Table

	P	W	D	L	F	A	Pts
1 Derby Co	42	21	11	10	67	49	53
2 Liverpool	42	20	11	11	60	39	51
3 Ipswich T	42	23	5	14	66	44	51
4 Everton	42	16	18	8	56	42	50
5 Stoke C	42	17	15	10	64	48	49
6 Sheffield U	42	18	13	11	58	51	49
7 Middlesbrough	42	18	12	12	54	40	48
8 Manchester C	42	18	10	14	54	54	46
9 Leeds U	42	16	13	13	57	49	45
10 Burnley	42	17	11	14	68	67	45
11 QPR	42	16	10	16	54	54	42
12 Wolverhampton W	42	14	11	17	57	54	39
13 West Ham U	42	13	13	16	58	59	39
14 Coventry C	42	12	15	15	51	62	39
15 Newcastle U	42	15	9	18	59	72	39
16 Arsenal	42	13	11	18	47	49	37
17 Birmingham C	42	14	9	19	53	61	37
18 Leicester C	42	12	12	18	46	60	36
19 Tottenham H	42	13	8	21	52	63	34
20 Luton T	42	11	11	20	47	65	33
21 Chelsea	42	9	15	18	42	72	33
22 Carlisle U	42	12	5	25	43	59	29

Season 1975-76

Football League Division 1

DATE	OPPONENTS	SCORE	GOALSCORERS	ATTENDANCE
Aug 16	Stoke City	W 2-1	Gould, Taylor A	23,744
Aug 19	Liverpool	D 2-2	Taylor A 2	40,564
Aug 23	BURNLEY	W 3-2	Taylor A 2, Paddon	28,048
Aug 25	TOTTENHAM HOTSPUR	W 1-0	Robson	36,567
Aug 30	Queens Park Rangers	D 1-1	Jennings	28,408
Sep 6	MANCHESTER CITY	W 1-0	Lampard	29,752
Sep 13	Leicester City	D 3-3	Bonds, Lampard, Holland	21,413
Sep 20	SHEFFIELD UNITED	W 2-0	T Taylor, Best	28,744
Sep 27	Wolverhampton W	W 1-0	Paddon	18,455
Oct 4	EVERTON	L 0-1		31,005
Oct 11	NEWCASTLE UNITED	W 2-1	Curbishley, A Taylor	30,400
Oct 18	Middlesbrough	L 0-3		25,831
Oct 25	MANCHESTER UNITED	W 2-1	A Taylor, Gould	38,528
Nov 1	Birmingham City	W 5-1	Brooking, o.g., Lampard, Taylor A 2	28,474
Nov 11	COVENTRY CITY	D 1-1	Robson	29,501
Nov 15	Derby County	L 1-2	Brooking	31,172
Nov 22	MIDDLESBROUGH	W 2-1	Jennings, Holland	26,914
Nov 29	ARSENAL	W 1-0	Taylor A	31,012
Dec 6	Norwich City	L 0-1		27,020
Dec 13	Burnley	L 0-2		14,907
Dec 20	STOKE CITY	W 3-1	Jennings 3	21,135
Dec 26	Aston Villa	L 1-4	Jennings	51,300
Dec 12	IPSWICH TOWN	L 1-2	Taylor T (pen)	32,741
Jan 10	LEICESTER CITY	D 1-1	Taylor A	24,615
Jan 17	Manchester City	L 0-3		32,147
Jan 24	QUEENS PARK RANGERS	W 1-0	Taylor A	26,677
Jan 31	LIVERPOOL	L 0-4		26,741
Feb 7	Tottenham Hotspur	D 1-1	Brooking	32,832
Feb 14	Coventry City	L 0-2		16,173
Feb 21	DERBY COUNTY	L 1-2	Brooking	24,941
Feb 23	LEEDS UNITED	D 1-1	Taylor A	28,025
Feb 28	Manchester United	L 0-4		57,240
Mar 6	BIRMINGHAM CITY	L 1-2	Curbishley	19,868
Mar 9	Leeds United	D 1-1	Jennings	28,453
Mar 13	Newcastle United	L 1-2	Jennings	32,842
Mar 20	Arsenal	L 1-6	Jennings	34,011
Mar 27	NORWICH CITY	L 0-1		20,628
Apr 3	WOLVERHAMPTON W	D 0-0		16,769
Apr 10	Sheffield United	L 2-3	Jennings 2	18,797
Apr 17	ASTON VILLA	D 2-2	Robson, Brooking	21,642
Apr 19	Ipswich Town	L 0-4		28,217
Apr 24	Everton	L 0-2		26,101

FA Cup

Jan 3	LIVERPOOL	(Rd 3)	L 0-2		32,363

League Cup

Sep 9	BRISTOL CITY	(Rd 2)	D 0-0		19,837
Sep 24	Bristol City	(R)	W 3-1	Brooking, Best, Taylor A	19,643
Oct 8	DARLINGTON	(Rd 3)	W 3-0	Paddon, Robson, Bonds (pen)	19,844
Nov 12	Tottenham Hotspur	(Rd 4)	D 0-0		49,125
Nov 24	TOTTENHAM HOTSPUR	(R)	L 0-2		38,443

European Cup Winners' Cup

Sep 17	Lahden Reipas	(Rd 1 FL)	D 2-2	Brooking, Bonds	4,587
Oct 1	LAHDEN REIPAS	(Rd 1 SL)	W 3-0	Robson, Holland, Jennings	24,131
Oct 22	Ararat Erevan	(Rd 2 FL)	D 1-1	Taylor A	66,662
Nov 5	ARARAT EREVAN	(Rd 2 SL)	W 3-1	Paddon, Robson, Taylor A	30,399
Mar 3	Den Haag	(QF) (1L)	L 2-4	Jennings 2	26,000
Mar 17	DEN HAAG	(QF) (2L)	W 3-1	Taylor A , Lampard, Bonds	29,829
Mar 31	Eintracht Frankfurt	(SF FL)	L 1-2	Paddon	45,000
Apr 14	EINTRACHT FRANKFURT	(SF SL)	W 3-1	Brooking 2, Robson	39,202
May 5	Anderlecht	(F)	L 2-4*	Holland, Robson	58,000

*Played at Heysel Stadium, Brussels.

Charity Shield

Aug 9	Derby County	L 0-2†	59,000

†Played at Wembley.

MANAGER: John Lyall
CAPTAIN: Billy Bonds
TOP SCORER: Alan Taylor
BIGGEST WIN: November 1, 1975 5-1 v Birmingham City, Division 1
HIGHEST ATTENDANCE: October 22, 1975 66,662 v Ararat Erevan, drew 1-1, European Cup Winners' Cup, Round 2 Second Leg
MAJOR TRANSFERS OUT: Clyde Best to Tampa Bay Rowdies

League & Cup Appearances (substitute)

PLAYER	LEAGUE	CUP COMPETITION				TOTAL
		FA CUP	LC	ECWC	OTHER	
Ayris	3 (6)		0 (1)			3 (7)
Best	5 (2)		2			7 (2)
Bonds	17 (1)		5	9		31 (1)
Brooking	34	1	4	7	1	47
Coleman	26	1	1	6	0 (1)	34 (1)
Curbishley	12 (2)	1		1 (1)		14 (3)
Day	41	1	5	9	1	57
Ferguson	1					1
Gould	4 (1)			1	1	6 (1)
Holland	35	1	5	7	1	49
Jennings	26 (4)	1	1 (2)	5	1	34 (6)
Lampard	37	1	4	9	1	52
Lock	26	1	5	4	1	37
McDowell	36 (1)		5	7	1	49 (1)
McGiven	6 (1)	1		1 (1)		8 (2)
Orhan	5					5
Paddon	39	1	5	9	1	55
Pike	0 (3)					0 (3)
Robson	33 (1)		4	9	0 (1)	46 (2)
Taylor A	33 (2)	1	4	6	1	45 (2)
Taylor T	42		5	9	1	57
Wooler	1					1

Goalscorers

PLAYER	LEAGUE	CUP COMPETITION				TOTAL
		FA CUP	LC	ECWC	OTHER	
Taylor A	13		1	3		17
Jennings	11			3		14
Brooking	5		1	3		9
Robson	3		1	4		8
Paddon	2		1	2		5
Bonds	1		1	2		4
Holland	2			2		4
Lampard	3			1		4
Best	1		1			2
Gould	2					2
Taylor T	2					2
Curbishley	1					1
Opps' o.gs.	1					1

Fact File

West Ham had a fine start to the season remaining unbeaten in their first nine games, however they failed to win any of their last 16 league matches.

Final Division 1 Table

		P	W	D	L	F	A	Pts
1	Liverpool	42	23	14	5	66	31	60
2	QPR	42	24	11	7	67	33	59
3	Manchester U	42	23	10	10	68	42	56
4	Derby Co	42	21	11	10	75	58	53
5	Leeds U	42	21	9	12	65	46	51
6	Ipswich T	42	16	14	12	54	48	46
7	Leicester C	42	13	19	10	48	51	45
8	Manchester C	42	16	12	15	64	46	43
9	Tottenham H	42	14	15	13	63	63	43
10	Norwich C	42	16	10	16	58	58	42
11	Everton	42	15	12	15	60	66	42
12	Stoke C	42	15	11	16	48	50	41
13	Middlesbrough	42	15	10	17	46	45	40
14	Coventry C	42	13	14	15	47	57	40
15	Newcastle U	42	15	9	18	71	62	39
16	Aston Villa	42	11	17	14	51	59	39
17	Arsenal	42	13	10	19	47	53	36
18	West Ham U	42	13	10	19	48	71	36
19	Birmingham C	42	13	7	22	57	75	33
20	Wolverhampton W	42	10	10	22	51	68	30
21	Burnley	42	9	10	23	43	66	28
22	Sheffield U	42	6	10	26	33	82	22

Season 1976-77

Football League Division 1

DATE	OPPONENTS	SCORE	GOALSCORERS	ATTENDANCE
Aug 21	Aston Villa	L 0-4		39,102
Aug 23	QUEENS PARK RANGERS	W 1-0	Paddon	31,668
Aug 28	LEICESTER CITY	D 0-0		24,960
Sep 4	Stoke City	L 1-2	Taylor A	19,131
Sep 11	ARSENAL	L 0-2		31,965
Sep 18	Bristol City	D 1-1	Taylor A	28,932
Sep 25	SUNDERLAND	D 1-1	Jennings	24,319
Oct 2	Manchester City	L 0-1		37,795
Oct 6	LEEDS UNITED	L 1-3	Jennings	21,909
Oct 16	IPSWICH TOWN	L 0-2		24,534
Oct 23	Everton	L 2-3	o.g., Bonds	23,163
Oct 30	West Bromwich Albion	L 0-3		19,856
Nov 6	TOTTENHAM HOTSPUR	W 5-3	Robson B, Bonds, Jennings, Brooking, Curbishley	28,997
Nov 10	Norwich City	L 0-1		24,762
Nov 20	NEWCASTLE UNITED	L 1-2	Robson B	21,324
Nov 27	Manchester United	W 2-0	Brooking, Jennings	55,366
Dec 4	MIDDLESBROUGH	L 0-1		20,184
Dec 18	LIVERPOOL	W 2-0	Brooking, Jennings	24,175
Dec 27	Birmingham City	D 0-0		39,978
Jan 1	Tottenham Hotspur	L 1-2	Brooking	44,972
Jan 3	WEST BROMWICH ALBION	D 0-0		25,236
Jan 22	ASTON VILLA	L 0-1		27,577
Feb 5	Leicester City	L 0-2		16,201
Feb 12	STOKE CITY	W 1-0	Robson B	20,160
Feb 19	Arsenal	W 3-2	Taylor A 2, Jennings	38,221
Feb 26	BRISTOL CITY	W 2-0	Bonds (pen), Jennings	29,713
Mar 5	Sunderland	L 0-6		35,357
Mar 12	MANCHESTER CITY	W 1-0	Robson B	24,974
Mar 22	Ipswich Town	L 1-4	Robson B (pen)	27,315
Apr 2	EVERTON	D 2-2	Robson 2 (pen)	22,518
Apr 4	Queens Park Rangers	D 1-1	Robson B	24,930
Apr 8	BIRMINGHAM CITY	D 2-2	Jennings, Pike	28,167
Apr 9	Coventry City	D 1-1	Robson B	15,816
Apr 11	NORWICH CITY	W 1-0	Pike	27,084
Apr 16	Newcastle United	L 0-3		30,967
Apr 20	Derby County	D 1-1	Pike (pen)	21,380
Apr 26	Leeds United	D 1-1	Robson B	16,891
Apr 29	Middlesbrough	D 1-1	Robson B	16,500
May 4	COVENTRY CITY	W 2-0	Robson B, Pike (pen)	25,461
May 7	DERBY COUNTY	D 2-2	Pike, Jennings	32,079
May 14	Liverpool	D 0-0		55,675
May 16	MANCHESTER UNITED	W 4-2	Lampard, Robson B 2, Pike	29,311

FA Cup

Jan 8	BOLTON WANDERERS	(Rd 3)	W 2-1	Jennings, Pike	24,147
Jan 29	Aston Villa	(Rd 4)	L 0-3		46,954

League Cup

Sep 1	BARNSLEY	(Rd 2)	W 3-0	Holland 2, Paddon	17,889
Sep 21	Charlton Athletic	(Rd 3)	W 1-0	Taylor A	32,898
Oct 27	QUEENS PARK RANGERS	(Rd 4)	L 0-2		24,565

League & Cup Appearances (substitute)

PLAYER	LEAGUE	CUP COMPETITION FA CUP	LC	TOTAL
Ayris	1 (2)			1 (2)
Bonds	41	2	3	46
Brooking	42	2	3	47
Coleman	12 (1)		2	14 (1)
Curbishley	8 (2)	1	1	10 (2)
Day	42	2	3	47
Devonshire	27 (1)		1	28 (1)
Green	22	2	2	26
Holland	6		1	7
Jennings	27 (4)	2	2	31 (4)
Lampard	36	2	1	39
Lock	25 (1)	2	2	29 (1)
McGiven	15 (1)		2	17 (1)
Orhan	1 (2)		1	2 (2)
Otulakowski	10 (2)			10 (2)
Paddon	12		3	15
Pike	20	1		21
Radford	18	1		19
Robson B	30	2		32
Robson K	7 (2)		1	8 (2)
Taylor A	24 (1)	1	2	27 (1)
Taylor T	36	2	3	41

Goalscorers

PLAYER	LEAGUE	CUP COMPETITION FA CUP	LC	TOTAL
Robson B	14			14
Jennings	8	1		9
Pike	6	1		7
Taylor A	5		1	6
Brooking	4			4
Bonds	3			3
Holland			2	2
Paddon	1		1	2
Curbishley	1			1
Lampard	1			1
Opps' o.gs.	1			1

Fact File

After the 6-0 defeat at the hands of Sunderland, West Ham lost only two matches in their next 15 games.

MANAGER: John Lyall
CAPTAIN: Billy Bonds
TOP SCORER: Bryan Robson
BIGGEST WIN: November 6, 1976 5-3 v Tottenham Hotspur, Division 1
HIGHEST ATTENDANCE: May 14, 1977 55,675 v Liverpool, drew 0-0, Division 1
MAJOR TRANSFERS IN: Bill Green from Carlisle, Bryan Robson from Sunderland, Alan Devonshire from Southall, John Radford from Arsenal
MAJOR TRANSFERS OUT: Graham Paddon to Norwich City

Final Division 1 Table

		P	W	D	L	F	A	Pts
1	Liverpool	42	23	11	8	62	33	57
2	Manchester C	42	21	14	7	60	34	56
3	Ipswich T	42	22	8	12	66	39	56
4	Aston Villa	42	22	7	13	76	50	51
5	Newcastle U	42	18	13	11	64	49	49
6	Manchester U	42	18	11	13	71	62	47
7	WBA	42	16	13	13	62	56	45
8	Arsenal	42	16	11	15	64	59	43
9	Everton	42	14	14	14	62	64	42
10	Leeds U	42	15	12	15	48	51	42
11	Leicester C	42	12	18	12	47	60	42
12	Middlesbrough	42	14	13	15	40	45	41
13	Birmingham C	42	13	12	17	63	61	38
14	QPR	42	13	12	17	47	52	38
15	Derby Co	42	9	19	14	50	55	37
16	Norwich C	42	14	9	19	47	64	37
17	West Ham U	42	11	14	17	46	65	36
18	Bristol C	42	11	13	18	38	48	35
19	Coventry C	42	10	15	17	48	59	35
20	Sunderland	42	11	12	19	46	54	34
21	Stoke C	42	10	14	18	28	51	34
22	Tottenham H	42	12	9	21	48	72	33

Season 1977-78

Football League Division 1

DATE	OPPONENTS	SCORE	GOALSCORERS	ATTENDANCE
Aug 20	NORWICH CITY	L 1-3	Robson (pen)	28,178
Aug 24	Leicester City	L 0-1		18,310
Aug 28	MANCHESTER CITY	L 0-1		25,278
Sep 3	Newcastle United	W 3-2	Jennings, Taylor, Robson	26,983
Sep 10	QUEENS PARK RANGERS	D 2-2	Holland, Lock	26,922
Sep 17	Bristol City	L 2-3	Robson, Pike	21,180
Sep 24	EVERTON	D 1-1	o.g.	25,296
Oct 1	Arsenal	L 0-3		41,245
Oct 3	MIDDLESBROUGH	L 0-2		26,508
Oct 8	NOTTINGHAM FOREST	D 0-0		26,126
Oct 15	Wolverhampton W	D 2-2	Pike, Robson	19,366
Oct 22	ASTON VILLA	D 2-2	Taylor T, Hales	26,599
Oct 29	Ipswich Town	W 2-0	Hales 2	27,308
Nov 5	Coventry City	L 0-1		23,276
Nov 11	WEST BROMWICH ALBION	D 3-3	Robson (pen), Devonshire 2	23,601
Nov 19	Derby County	L 1-2	Bonds	23,273
Nov 26	LEEDS UNITED	L 0-1		26,883
Dec 3	Liverpool	L 0-2		39,659
Dec 10	MANCHESTER UNITED	W 2-1	Hales, Brooking	20,759
Dec 17	West Bromwich Albion	L 0-1		18,868
Dec 26	BIRMINGHAM CITY	W 1-0	Curbishley	25,572
Dec 27	Chelsea	L 1-2	Robson	44,093
Dec 31	LEICESTER CITY	W 3-2	McDowell, Hales, Cross	25,455
Jan 2	Norwich City	D 2-2	Devonshire, Hales	29,480
Jan 14	Manchester City	L 2-3	Brooking, Cross	43,627
Jan 21	NEWCASTLE UNITED	W 1-0	Hales	25,461
Feb 11	BRISTOL CITY	L 1-2	Robson	19,934
Feb 18	Everton	L 1-2	Hales	33,862
Feb 25	ARSENAL	D 2-2	Taylor A, Cross	31,675
Mar 4	Nottingham Forest	L 0-2		33,924
Mar 11	WOLVERHAMTON W	L 1-2	Hales	23,525
Mar 14	Queens Park Rangers	L 0-1		20,394
Mar 18	Aston Villa	L 1-4	Brooking	28,275
Mar 24	IPSWICH TOWN	W 3-0	Cross 3	23,867
Mar 25	CHELSEA	W 3-1	Brooking, Green, Holland	24,987
Mar 28	Birmingham City	L 0-3		23,554
Apr 1	COVENTRY CITY	W 2-1	Taylor T, Holland	19,260
Apr 8	Leeds United	W 2-1	Martin, Hales	22,953
Apr 15	DERBY COUNTY	W 3-0	Robson 2, Cross	25,424
Apr 22	Manchester United	L 0-3		54,089
Apr 25	Middlesbrough	W 2-1	Cross 2	13,247
Apr 29	LIVERPOOL	L 0-2		28,903

FA Cup

Jan 7	WATFORD	(Rd 3)	W 1-0	Robson	36,745
Jan 28	QUEENS PARK RANGERS	(Rd 4)	D 1-1	Bonds	35,566
Jan 31	Queens Park Rangers	(R)	L 1-6	Robson	24,057

League Cup

Aug 30	Nottingham Forest	(Rd 2)	L 0-5		18,224

League & Cup Appearances (substitute)

PLAYER	LEAGUE	CUP COMPETITION FA CUP	LC	TOTAL
Bonds	29	3		32
Brooking	37	2		39
Brush	23 (1)		1	24 (1)
Cross	21	3		24
Curbishley	31 (1)	3	1	35 (1)
Day	23		1	24
Devonshire	32 (2)	3	1	36 (2)
Ferguson	19	3		22
Green	13		1	14
Hales	23 (1)	3		26 (1)
Holland	18 (3)	1		19 (3)
Jennings	2			2
Lampard	40	3	1	44
Lock	6		1	7
Martin	5 (2)			5 (2)
McDowell	12 (2)	3		15 (2)
McGiven	4			4
Otulakowski	0 (5)			0 (5)
Pike	25 (3)	0 (1)	1	26 (4)
Radford	10		1	11
Robson	37	3	1	41
Taylor A	10 (1)	0 (1)	1	11 (2)
Taylor T	42	3		45

Goalscorers

PLAYER	LEAGUE	CUP COMPETITION FA CUP	LC	TOTAL
Robson	9	2		11
Hales	10			10
Cross	9			9
Brooking	4			4
Devonshire	3			3
Holland	3			3
Bonds	1	1		2
Pike	2			2
Taylor A	2			2
Taylor T	2			2
Curbishley	1			1
Green	1			1
Jennings	1			1
Lock	1			1
Martin	1			1
McDowell	1			1
Opps' o.gs.	1			1

Fact File

To avoid relegation, West Ham required a point from their final game of the season against Liverpool at Upton Park. The Hammers lost 2-0.

MANAGER: John Lyall
CAPTAIN: Billy Bonds
TOP SCORER: Bryan Robson
BIGGEST WIN: March 24, 1978 3-0 v Ipswich Town, Division 1; April 15, 1978 3-0 v Derby County, Division 1
HIGHEST ATTENDANCE: December 27, 1978 44,093 v Chelsea, lost 1-2, Division 1
MAJOR TRANSFERS IN: Derek Hales from Derby County, David Cross from West Bromwich Albion
MAJOR TRANSFERS OUT: Keith Robson to Cardiff City, John Radford to Blackburn Rovers

Final Division 1 Table

		P	W	D	L	F	A	Pts
1	Nottingham F	42	25	14	3	69	24	64
2	Liverpool	42	24	9	9	65	34	57
3	Everton	42	22	11	9	76	45	55
4	Manchester C	42	20	12	10	74	51	52
5	Arsenal	42	21	10	11	60	37	52
6	WBA	42	18	14	10	62	53	50
7	Coventry C	42	18	12	12	75	62	48
8	Aston Villa	42	18	10	14	57	42	46
9	Leeds U	42	18	10	14	63	53	46
10	Manchester U	42	16	10	16	67	63	42
11	Birmingham C	42	16	9	17	55	60	41
12	Derby Co	42	14	13	15	54	59	41
13	Norwich C	42	11	18	13	52	66	40
14	Middlesbrough	42	12	15	15	42	54	39
15	Wolverhampton W	42	12	12	18	51	64	36
16	Chelsea	42	11	14	17	46	69	36
17	Bristol C	42	11	13	18	49	53	35
18	Ipswich T	42	11	13	18	47	61	35
19	QPR	42	9	15	18	47	64	33
20	West Ham U	42	12	8	22	52	69	32
21	Newcastle U	42	6	10	26	42	78	22
22	Leicester C	42	5	12	25	26	70	22

Season 1978-79

Football League Division 2

DATE	OPPONENTS	SCORE	GOALSCORERS	ATTENDANCE
Aug 19	NOTTS COUNTY	W 5-2	Cross 3, o.g., Devonshire	25,387
Aug 23	Newcastle United	W 3-0	Devonshire, Cross, Robson	27,233
Aug 26	Crystal Palace	D 1-1	Taylor A	32,611
Sep 2	FULHAM	L 0-1		25,778
Sep 9	Burnley	L 2-3	Cross 2	12,303
Sep 16	BRISTOL ROVERS	W 2-0	Robson, Brooking	22,189
Sep 23	SHEFFIELD UNITED	W 2-0	Robson 2 (2 pen)	24,361
Sep 30	Sunderland	L 1-2	Cross	23,676
Oct 7	MILLWALL	W 3-0	Robson 3 (1 pen)	22,000
Oct 14	Oldham Athletic	D 2-2	Robson 2	10,143
Oct 21	STOKE CITY	D 1-1	Brooking	27,859
Oct 28	Brighton & Hove Albion	W 2-1	Robson 2	32,634
Nov 4	PRESTON NORTH END	W 3-1	Lampard, Devonshire, Cross	23,579
Nov 11	Notts County	L 0-1		11,002
Nov 18	CRYSTAL PALACE	D 1-1	Bonds	31,245
Nov 21	Fulham	D 0-0		26,556
Nov 25	Leicester City	W 2-1	Cross 2	16,149
Dec 2	CAMBRIDGE UNITED	W 5-0	Taylor A, Robson 2, Bonds, Curbishley	21,379
Dec 9	Wrexham	L 3-4	Cross, Lampard, Robson	15,787
Dec 16	CHARLTON ATHLETIC	W 2-0	Robson, Cross	23,833
Dec 26	ORIENT	L 0-2		29,220
Dec 30	BLACKBURN ROVERS	W 4-0	Robson, Taylor, Cross, o.g.	21,269
Jan 20	Bristol Rovers	W 1-0	Robson	12,418
Feb 10	SUNDERLAND	D 3-3	Cross 2, Robson	24,998
Feb 24	OLDHAM ATHLETIC	W 3-0	Holland, Martin, Robson	26,052
Feb 26	Luton Town	W 4-1	Cross 2, Devonshire, Robson	14,205
Mar 3	Stoke City	L 0-2		24,912
Mar 10	BRIGHTON & HOVE ALBION	D 0-0		35,802
Mar 17	Preston North End	D 0-0		15,376
Mar 24	NEWCASTLE UNITED	W 5-0	Devonshire, Robson, Lampard, McDowell 2	24,650
Mar 31	LEICESTER CITY	D 1-1	Robson	23,992
Apr 2	Sheffield United	L 0-3		17,720
Apr 7	Cambridge United	D 0-0		11,406
Apr 9	LUTON TOWN	W 1-0	o.g.	25,498
Apr 14	Orient	W 2-0	Holland, Pike	17,517
Apr 16	CARDIFF CITY	D 1-1	Holland	29,058
Apr 21	Charlton Athletic	D 0-0		22,816
Apr 24	BURNLEY	W 3-1	Bonds, Pike, Robson	24,139
Apr 28	WREXHAM	D 1-1	Bonds	28,865
May 5	Blackburn Rovers	L 0-1		7,585
May 11	Cardiff City	D 0-0		13,140
May 14	Millwall	L 1-2	Robson	11,917

FA Cup

Jan 9	Newport County	(Rd 3) L 1-2	Robson	14,124

League Cup

Aug 30	SWINDON TOWN	(Rd 2) L 1-2	Robson	19,672

Fact File

Despite suffering only two defeats at home all season, West Ham failed to sustain the form that took them into the top two in October.

MANAGER: John Lyall

CAPTAIN: Billy Bonds

TOP SCORER: Bryan Robson

BIGGEST WIN: December 2, 1978 5-0 v Cambridge United, Division 2; March 24, 1979 5-0 v Newcastle United, Division 2

HIGHEST ATTENDANCE: March 10, 1979 35,802 v Brighton & Hove Albion, drew 0-0, Division 2

MAJOR TRANSFERS IN: Phil Parkes from Queens Park Rangers

MAJOR TRANSFERS OUT: Bill Green to Peterborough, Derek Hales to Charlton Athletic, Kevin Lock to Fulham

League & Cup Appearances (substitute)

PLAYER	LEAGUE	CUP COMPETITION		TOTAL
		FA CUP	LC	
Bonds	39	1	1	41
Brignull	0 (1)			0 (1)
Brooking	21	1		22
Brush	42	1	1	44
Cross	40	1	1	42
Curbishley	26 (1)		1	27 (1)
Day	13	1		14
Devonshire	41	1	1	43
Ferguson	11		1	12
Holland	39		1	40
Jennings	2 (2)			2 (2)
Lampard	28 (1)	1	1	30 (1)
Lansdowne	0 (1)			0 (1)
Martin	22	1		23
McDowell	26 (2)	1		27 (2)
Morgan	2			2
Parkes	18			18
Pike	10 (4)		0 (1)	10 (5)
Robson	40	1	1	42
Taylor A	10 (3)	1	1	12 (3)
Taylor T	32		1	33

Goalscorers

PLAYER	LEAGUE	CUP COMPETITION		TOTAL
		FA CUP	LC	
Robson	24	1	1	26
Cross	17			17
Devonshire	5			5
Bonds	4			4
Holland	3			3
Lampard	3			3
Taylor A	3			3
Brooking	2			2
McDowell	2			2
Curbishley	1			1
Martin	1			1
Pike	1			1
Opps' o.gs.	3			3

Final Division 2 Table

		P	W	D	L	F	A	PTS
1	Crystal Palace	42	19	19	4	51	24	57
2	Brighton & HA	42	23	10	9	72	39	56
3	Stoke C	42	20	16	6	58	31	56
4	Sunderland	42	22	11	9	70	44	55
5	West Ham U	42	18	14	10	70	39	50
6	Notts Co	42	14	16	12	48	60	44
7	Preston NE	42	12	18	12	59	57	42
8	Newcastle U	42	17	8	17	51	55	42
9	Cardiff C	42	16	10	16	56	70	42
10	Fulham	42	13	15	14	50	47	41
11	Orient	42	15	10	17	51	51	40
12	Cambridge U	42	12	16	14	44	52	40
13	Burnley	42	14	12	16	51	62	40
14	Oldham Ath	42	13	13	16	52	61	39
15	Wrexham	42	12	14	16	45	42	38
16	Bristol R	42	14	10	18	48	60	38
17	Leicester C	42	10	17	15	43	52	37
18	Luton T	42	13	10	19	60	57	36
19	Charlton Ath	42	11	13	18	60	69	35
20	Sheffield U	42	11	12	19	52	69	34
21	Millwall	42	11	10	21	42	61	32
22	Blackburn R	42	10	10	22	41	72	30

Season 1979-80

Football League Division 2

DATE	OPPONENTS	SCORE	GOALSCORERS	ATTENDANCE
Aug 18	Wrexham	L 0-1		13,036
Aug 20	CHELSEA	L 0-1		21,627
Aug 25	OLDHAM ATHLETIC	W 1-0	Holland	18,319
Sep 1	Watford	L 0-2		23,329
Sep 8	Preston North End	D 1-1	Cross	10,460
Sep 15	SUNDERLAND	W 2-0	Cross, Pearson	24,021
Sep 22	Queens Park Rangers	L 0-3		24,692
Sep 29	BURNLEY	W 2-1	Stewart (pen), Lansdowne	18,327
Oct 6	NEWCASTLE UNITED	D 1-1	Cross	23,206
Oct 13	Leicester City	W 2-1	Martin, Cross	22,472
Oct 20	LUTON TOWN	L 1-2	Allen	25,049
Oct 27	Notts County	W 1-0	Holland	12,256
Nov 3	WREXHAM	W 1-0	Pike	20,595
Nov 10	Fulham	W 2-1	Stewart (pen), Cross	16,476
Nov 14	Chelsea	L 1-2	Holland	30,859
Nov 17	SWANSEA CITY	W 2-0	Brooking, Cross	21,210
Nov 24	CARDIFF CITY	W 3-0	Cross, Stewart 2 (2 pens)	20,242
Dec 1	Charlton Athletic	L 0-1		19,021
Dec 8	BRISTOL ROVERS	W 2-1	Cross 2	17,763
Dec 15	Shrewsbury Town	L 0-3		8,513
Dec 21	CAMBRIDGE UNITED	W 3-1	Stewart, Pearson, Neighbour	11,721
Jan 1	Orient	W 4-0	Pearson 2, Devonshire, Pike	23,885
Jan 12	WATFORD	D 1-1	Bonds	23,553
Jan 19	PRESTON NORTH END	W 2-0	Stewart (pen), Allen	17,603
Feb 9	QUEENS PARK RANGERS	W 2-1	Pearson, o.g.	26,037
Feb 19	Burnley	W 1-0	Devonshire	10,610
Feb 23	LEICESTER CITY	W 3-1	Pike, Cross, Holland	27,762
Mar 1	Luton Town	D 1-1	Stewart	20,040
Mar 11	NOTTS COUNTY	L 1-2	Pike	24,844
Mar 15	Newcastle United	D 0-0		25,431
Mar 22	FULHAM	L 2-3	Devonshire, Stewart (pen)	30,030
Mar 29	Swansea City	L 1-2	Devonshire	13,275
Apr 1	Cambridge United	L 0-2		8,863
Apr 5	ORIENT	W 2-0	o.g., Brooking	22,066
Apr 7	Birmingham City	D 0-0		28,377
Apr 19	Cardiff City	W 1-0	Stewart	12,076
Apr 22	BIRMINGHAM CITY	L 1-2	Martin	37,167
Apr 26	SHREWSBURY TOWN	L 1-3	Brooking	19,765
Apr 29	Oldham Athletic	D 0-0		8,214
May 3	Bristol Rovers	W 2-0	Devonshire, Cross	9,824
May 5	CHARLTON ATHLETIC	W 4-1	Pike, Morgan, Cross, Stewart (pen)	19,314
May 12	Sunderland	L 0-2		47,000

FA Cup

Jan 5	West Bromwich Albion	(Rd 3)	D 1-1	Pearson	20,572
Jan 8	WEST BROMWICH ALBION	(R)	W 2-1	Pike, Brooking	30,689
Jan 26	Orient	(Rd 4)	W 3-2	o.g., Stewart 2(1 pen)	21,521
Feb 16	SWANSEA CITY	(Rd 5)	W 2-0	Allen, Cross	30,497
Mar 8	ASTON VILLA	(QF)	W 1-0	Stewart (pen)	36,393
Apr 12	Everton	(SF)	D 1-1*	Pearson	47,685
Apr 16	Everton	(R)	W 2-1**	Devonshire, Lampard	40,720
May 10	Arsenal	(F)	W 1-0†	Brooking	100,000

*Played at Villa Park. **Played at Elland Road. †Played at Wembley.

League Cup

Aug 28	BARNSLEY	(Rd 2 FL)	W 3-1	Brooking, Pearson, Cross	12,320
Sep 4	Barnsley	(Rd 2 SL)	W 2-0	Cross 2	15,898
Sep 25	SOUTHEND UNITED	(Rd 3)	D 1-1	Cross	19,658
Oct 1	Southend United	(R)	D 0-0*		22,497
Oct 8	SOUTHEND UNITED	(2nd R)	W 5-1	Lansdowne 3, Holland, Stewart (pen)	19,718
Oct 31	Sunderland	(Rd 4)	D 1-1	Pike	30.302
Nov 5	SUNDERLAND	(R)	W 2-1	Martin, Cross	24,454
Dec 4	NOTTINGHAM FOREST	(QF)	D 0-0		35,856
Dec 12	Nottingham Forest	(R)	L 0-3		25,462

*After extra time.

MANAGER: John Lyall **CAPTAIN:** Billy Bonds
TOP SCORER: David Cross **BIGGEST WIN:** October 8, 1979 5-1 v Southend United, League Cup Round 3, second replay
HIGHEST ATTENDANCE: May 10, 1980 100,000 v Arsenal, won 1-0, FA Cup final
MAJOR TRANSFERS IN: Stuart Pearson from Manchester United
MAJOR TRANSFERS OUT: John McDowell and Alan Taylor to Norwich City, Bryan Robson to Sunderland, Tommy Taylor, Mervyn Day and Billy Jennings to Orient

League & Cup Appearances (substitute)

PLAYER	LEAGUE	CUP COMPETITION FA CUP	LC	TOTAL
Allen	31	7 (1)	7	45 (1)
Banton	2 (2)		1	3 (2)
Bonds	34	5	9	48
Brooking	37	7	8	52
Brush	27	6	4	37
Cross	38 (1)	5	9	52 (1)
Devonshire	34	8	7	49
Ferguson	2		1	3
Holland	21 (5)	1	8	30 (5)
Lampard	35 (1)	7	6	48 (1)
Lansdowne	5 (3)		4 (1)	9 (4)
Martin	40	7	8	55
Morgan	4 (2)		1	5 (2)
Neighbour	22 (1)	4		26 (1)
Parkes	40	8	8	56
Pearson	24 (1)	8	3	35 (1)
Pike	27 (4)	7 (1)	6	40 (5)
Smith	1		1	2
Stewart	38	8	8	54

Goalscorers

PLAYER	LEAGUE	CUP COMPETITION FA CUP	LC	TOTAL
Cross	12	1	5	18
Stewart	10	3	1	14
Pearson	5	2	1	8
Pike	5	1	1	7
Brooking	3	2	1	6
Devonshire	5	1		6
Holland	4		1	5
Lansdowne	1		3	4
Allen	2	1		3
Martin	2		1	3
Bonds	1			1
Lampard		1		1
Morgan	1			1
Neighbour	1			1
Opps' o.gs.	2	1		3

Fact File

Paul Allen had only just celebrated his seventeenth birthday when he made his debut against Burnley in September.

Final Division 2 Table

		P	W	D	L	F	A	Pts
1	Leicester C	42	21	13	8	58	38	55
2	Sunderland	42	21	12	9	69	42	54
3	Birmingham C	42	21	11	10	58	38	53
4	Chelsea	42	23	7	12	66	52	53
5	QPR	42	18	13	11	75	53	49
6	Luton T	42	16	17	9	66	45	49
7	West Ham U	42	20	7	15	54	43	47
8	Cambridge U	42	14	16	12	61	53	44
9	Newcastle U	42	15	14	13	53	49	44
10	Preston NE	42	12	19	11	56	52	43
11	Oldham Ath	42	16	11	15	49	53	43
12	Swansea C	42	17	9	16	48	53	43
13	Shrewsbury T	42	18	5	19	60	53	41
14	Orient	42	12	17	13	48	54	41
15	Cardiff C	42	16	8	18	41	48	40
16	Wrexham	42	16	6	20	40	49	38
17	Notts Co	42	11	15	16	51	52	37
18	Watford	42	12	13	17	39	46	37
19	Bristol R	42	11	13	18	50	64	35
20	Fulham	42	11	7	24	42	74	29
21	Burnley	42	6	15	21	39	73	27
22	Charlton Ath	42	6	10	26	39	78	22

Season 1980-81

Football League Division 2

DATE	OPPONENTS	SCORE	GOALSCORERS	ATTENDANCE
Aug 16	LUTON TOWN	L 1-2	Stewart Goddard	27,933
Aug 19	Bristol City	D 1-1	Cross	13,554
Aug 23	Preston North End	D 0-0		9,063
Aug 30	NOTTS COUNTY	W 4-0	Cross, Goddard 2, Stewart (pen)	21,769
Sep 6	Chelsea	W 1-0	o.g.	32,669
Sep 13	SHREWSBURY TOWN	W 3-0	o.g., Goddard, Cross	22,339
Sep 20	WATFORD	W 3-2	Cross, Barnes, Brooking	24,288
Sep 27	Cambridge United	W 2-1	Goddard, Cross	8,591
Oct 4	Newcastle United	D 0-0		24,848
Oct 7	CARDIFF CITY	W 1-0	Neighbour	20,402
Oct 11	BLACKBURN ROVERS	W 2-0	Cross 2	32,402
Oct 18	Oldham Athletic	D 0-0		8,344
Oct 25	BOLTON WANDERERS	W 2-1	o.g., Pike	25,257
Nov 1	Bristol Rovers	W 1-0	Goddard	6,328
Nov 8	GRIMSBY TOWN	W 2-1	Cross 2	25,468
Nov 11	BRISTOL CITY	W 5-0	Goddard 2, Martin, Brooking, Cross	25,210
Nov 15	Luton Town	L 2-3	Brooking 2	17,031
Nov 22	SWANSEA CITY	W 2-0	Cross, Goddard	27,376
Nov 26	Derby County	L 0-2		18,446
Nov 29	Wrexham	D 2-2	Devonshire, Goddard	8,941
Dec 6	SHEFFIELD WEDNESDAY	W 2-1	Brooking, Holland	30,746
Dec 13	Blackburn Rovers	D 0-0		13,279
Dec 20	DERBY COUNTY	W 3-1	Cross, Goddard, Brooking	24,071
Dec 26	Queens Park Rangers	L 0-3		23,811
Dec 27	ORIENT	W 2-1	Holland, Allen	34,408
Jan 10	Swansea City	W 3-1	Brooking, Pike, Cross	22,110
Jan 17	Notts County	D 1-1	Holland	13,718
Jan 31	PRESTON NORTH END	W 5-0	Goddard, Pike, Lampard, Devonshire 2	26,413
Feb 7	Shrewsbury Town	W 2-0	Devonshire, Cross	9,201
Feb 14	CHELSEA	W 4-0	Brooking 2, Cross, Devonshire	35,164
Feb 21	CAMBRIDGE UNITED	W 4-2	Devonshire, Goddard, Stewart 2 (1 pen)	36,002
Feb 28	Watford	W 2-1	Cross 2	20,786
Mar 7	NEWCASTLE UNITED	W 1-0	Cross	26,274
Mar 21	OLDHAM ATHLETIC	D 1-1	Goddard	24,394
Mar 28	Bolton Wanderers	D 1-1	Brooking	13,271
Apr 4	BRISTOL ROVERS	W 2-0	Pike, Goddard	23,544
Apr 11	Grimsby Town	W 5-1	Cross 4, Pike	17,924
Apr 18	Orient	W 2-0	Neighbour, Pike	14,592
Apr 21	QUEENS PARK RANGERS	W 3-0	Goddard 3	24,599
May 2	WREXHAM	W 1-0	Stewart (pen)	30,515
May 6	Cardiff City	D 0-0		10,558
May 8	Sheffield Wednesday	W 1-0	Morgan	21,087

FA Cup

Jan 3	WREXHAM	(Rd 3) D 1-1	Stewart (pen)	30,137
Jan 6	Wrexham	(R) D 0-0**		13,643
Jan 19	Wrexham	(2nd R) L 0-1**		14,615

**After extra time.

League Cup

Aug 26	Burnley	(Rd 2 FL) W 2-0	Goddard, Cross	6,818
Sep 2	BURNLEY	(Rd 2 SL) 4-0	Stewart (pen), Goddard, o.g., Pike	15,216
Sep 23	Charlton Athletic	(Rd 3) W 2-1	Cross 2	17,884
Oct 28	BARNSLEY	(Rd 4) W 2-1	Martin, Cross	21,548
Dec 2	TOTTENHAM HOTSPUR	(QF) W 1-0	Cross	36,003
Jan 27	Coventry City	(SF FL) L 2-3	Bonds, o.g.	35,468
Feb 10	COVENTRY CITY	(SF SL) W 2-0	Goddard, Neighbour	36,551
Mar 14	Liverpool	(F) D 1-1†	Stewart (pen)	100,000
Apr 1	Liverpool	(R) L 1-2††	Goddard	36,693

†Played at Wembley. ††Played at Villa Park.

European Cup Winners' Cup

Sep 17	Castilla	(Rd 1 FL) L 1-3	Cross	40,000
Oct 1	CASTILLA	(Rd 1 SL) 5-1*	Pike, Cross 3, Goddard	262
Oct 22	POLI TIMISOARA	(Rd 2 FL) W 4-0	Bonds, Goddard, Stewart (pen), Cross	27,257
Nov 5	Poli Timisoara	(Rd 2 SL) L 0-1		25,000
Mar 4	DYNAMO TBILISI	(Rd 3 FL) L 1-4	Cross	34,957
Mar 18	Dynamo Tbilisi	(Rd 3 SL) W 1-0	Pearson	80,000

*Behind closed doors.

Charity Shield

Aug 9	Liverpool	L 0-1*		90,000

*Played at Wembley.

League & Cup Appearances (substitute)

PLAYER	LEAGUE	CUP COMPETITION				TOTAL
		FA CUP	LC	ECWC	OTHER	
Allen	1 (2)	1	1 (2)	1 (1)	1	5 (5)
Barnes	1 (5)		1	0 (1)		2 (6)
Bonds	41	3	8	6	1	59
Brooking	36	3	7	4	1 (1)	51
Brush	8 (3)	1	3	1 (3)	1	14 (6)
Cross	41	3	9	6	1	60
Devonshire	39	3	9	4	1	56
Goddard	37	3	9	6		55
Holland	25	2	4	3	1	35
Lampard	38 (1)	2	8	6		54 (1)
Martin	41	3	9	6	1	60
Morgan	5 (1)			1 (2)	0 (1)	6 (4)
Neighbour	22 (2)	0 (1)	4	4		30 (3)
Parkes	42	3	9	6	1	61
Pearson	2 (3)		0 (2)	0 (1)		2 (6)
Pike	42	3	9	6	1	61
Stewart	41	3	9	6	1	60

Goalscorers

PLAYER	LEAGUE	CUP COMPETITION				TOTAL
		FA CUP	LC	ECWC	OTHER	
Cross	22		5	6		33
Goddard	17		4	2		23
Brooking	10					10
Stewart	5	1	2	1		9
Pike	6		1	1		8
Devonshire	6					6
Holland	3					3
Neighbour	2		1			3
Allen	1					1
Barnes	1					1
Bonds			1	1		2
Martin	1		1			2
Lampard	1					1
Morgan	1					1
Pearson				1		1
Opps' o.g.s.	3		2			5

Fact File

West Ham became champions on 11 April after beating Grimsby 5-1. The youth team (including Alan Dickens and Tony Cottee) added to the celebrations by winning the FA Youth Cup.

Final Division 2 Table

	P	W	D	L	F	A	Pts
1 West Ham U	42	28	10	4	79	29	66
2 Notts Co	42	18	17	7	49	38	53
3 Swansea C	42	18	14	10	64	44	50
4 Blackburn R	42	16	18	8	42	29	50
5 Luton T	42	18	12	12	61	46	48
6 Derby Co	42	15	15	12	57	52	45
7 Grimsby T	42	15	15	12	44	42	45
8 QPR	42	15	13	14	56	46	43
9 Watford	42	16	11	15	50	45	43
10 Sheffield W	42	17	8	17	53	51	42
11 Newcastle U	42	14	14	14	30	45	42
12 Chelsea	42	14	12	16	46	41	40
13 Cambridge U	42	17	6	17	53	65	40
14 Shrewsbury T	42	11	17	14	46	47	39
15 Oldham Ath	42	12	15	15	39	48	39
16 Wrexham	42	12	14	16	43	45	38
17 Orient	42	13	12	17	52	56	38
18 Bolton W	42	14	10	18	61	66	38
19 Cardiff C	42	12	12	18	44	60	36
20 Preston NE	42	11	14	17	41	62	36
21 Bristol C	42	7	16	19	29	51	30
22 Bristol R	42	5	13	24	34	65	23

Season 1981-82

Football League Division 1

DATE	OPPONENTS	SCORE	GOALSCORERS	ATTENDANCE
Aug 29	BRIGHTON & HOVE ALBION	D 1-1	Stewart (pen)	30,468
Sep 2	Tottenham Hotspur	W 4-0	Cross 4	41,200
Sep 5	Sunderland	W 2-0	Goddard, Cross	28,347
Sep 12	STOKE CITY	W 3-2	Goddard 2, Stewart (pen)	28,774
Sep 19	West Bromwich Albion	D 0-0		19,516
Sep 22	SOUTHAMPTON	W 4-2	Goddard 3, Pike	34,026
Sep 26	LIVERPOOL	D 1-1	Pike	30,802
Oct 3	Birmingham City	D 2-2	Cross 2	22,290
Oct 10	EVERTON	D 1-1	Martin	31,608
Oct 17	Aston Villa	L 2-3	Brooking, Cross	32,064
Oct 24	Notts County	D 1-1	Brooking	12,505
Oct 31	MIDDLESBROUGH	W 3-2	Neighbour, Goddard, Stewart (pen)	27,604
Nov 7	Nottingham Forest	D 0-0		26,327
Nov 21	COVENTRY CITY	W 5-2	Brooking, Neighbour, Martin 2, Stewart (pen)	26,065
Nov 28	Leeds United	D 3-3	Brooking 2, Cross	25,637
Dec 5	ARSENAL	L 1-2	Pearson	33,833
Jan 5	Liverpool	L 0-3		28,427
Jan 16	Brighton & Hove Albion	L 0-1		22,620
Jan 27	Manchester United	L 0-1		41,291
Jan 30	WEST BROMWICH ALBION	W 3-1	Goddard, Cross 2	24,423
Feb 2	MANCHESTER CITY	D 1-1	Bonds	26,552
Feb 6	Stoke City	L 1-2	Van der Elst	11,987
Feb 13	BIRMINGHAM CITY	D 2-2	Orr, Stewart (pen)	22,512
Feb 20	Southampton	L 1-2	Stewart (pen)	24,026
Feb 27	Everton	D 0-0		28,618
Mar 2	IPSWICH TOWN	W 2-0	Devonshire, Van der Elst	24,846
Mar 6	ASTON VILLA	D 2-2	Stewart (pen), Van der Elst	26,894
Mar 13	NOTTS COUNTY	W 1-0	Stewart (pen)	22,145
Mar 20	Middlesbrough	W 3-2	Van der Elst, Goddard 2	12,134
Mar 27	NOTTINGHAM FOREST	L 0-1		24,633
Mar 30	Swansea City	W 1-0	Van der Elst	20,272
Apr 3	Manchester City	W 1-0	Goddard	30,875
Apr 6	WOLVERHAMPTON W	W 3-1	Martin, Goddard 2	20,651
Apr 10	SWANSEA CITY	D 1-1	Goddard	25,566
Apr 13	Ipswich Town	L 2-3	Cross 2	28,767
Apr 17	Coventry City	L 0-1		13,398
Apr 24	LEEDS UNITED	W 4-3	Cross, Brooking 2, Stewart Goddard 2	24,748
May 1	Arsenal	L 0-2		34,977
May 4	SUNDERLAND	D 1-1	Stewart Goddard 2	17,130
May 8	MANCHESTER UNITED	D 1-1	Cross	26,337
May 10	TOTTENHAM HOTSPUR	D 2-2	Brooking, Goddard	27,667
May 15	Wolverhampton W	L 1-2	Cross	13,283

FA Cup

Jan 2	EVERTON	(Rd 3)	W 2-1	Bonds, Cross	24,431
Jan 23	Watford	(Rd 4)	L 0-2		27,004

League Cup

Oct 7	Derby County	(Rd 2 FL)	W 3-2	Cross, Brooking, Stewart (pen)	13,764
Oct 27	DERBY COUNTY	(Rd 2 SL)	W 2-0	Goddard 2	21,043
Nov 10	WEST BROMWICH ALBION	(Rd 3)	D 2-2	Stewart (pen), Cross	24,168
Nov 24	West Bromwich Albion	(R)	D 1-1*	Stewart (pen)	15,869
Dec 1	WEST BROMWICH ALBION	(2nd R)	L 0-1		24,760

*After extra time.

League & Cup Appearances (substitute)

PLAYER	LEAGUE	CUP COMPETITION FA CUP	LC	TOTAL
Allen	27 (1)		0 (2)	27 (3)
Banton	0 (1)			0 (1)
Barnes	1 (2)			1 (2)
Bonds	29	2	4	35
Brooking	34	2	5	41
Brush	10 (3)		1	11 (3)
Cowie	5 (1)			5 (1)
Cross	38	2	5	45
Devonshire	35	1	5	41
Goddard	38 (1)	2	5	45 (1)
Houghton	0 (1)			0 (1)
La Ronde	6 (1)			6 (1)
Lampard	27 (1)	2	5	34 (1)
Martin	28	2	5	35
McAlister	3		1	4
Neighbour	19 (4)	2	5	26 (4)
Orr	24			24
Parkes	39	2	4	45
Pearson	2 (2)	0 (2)		2 (4)
Pike	34	2	5	41
Stewart	42	2	5	49
Van der Elst	21 (1)	1		22 (1)

Goalscorers

PLAYER	LEAGUE	CUP COMPETITION FA CUP	LC	TOTAL
Cross	16	1	2	19
Goddard	15		2	17
Stewart	10		3	13
Brooking	8		1	9
Van der Elst	5			5
Martin	4			4
Bonds	1	1		2
Neighbour	2			2
Pike	2			2
Devonshire	1			1
Orr	1			1
Pearson	1			1

Fact File

Unbeaten at the end of September, West Ham found themselves sitting on top of the league.

MANAGER: John Lyall
CAPTAIN: Billy Bonds
TOP SCORER: David Cross
BIGGEST WIN: September 2, 1981 4-0 v Tottenham Hotspur, Division 1
HIGHEST ATTENDANCE: January 27, 1982 41,291 v Manchester United, lost 0-1, Division 1
MAJOR TRANSFERS IN: Tom McAlister from Swindon Town, Francois Van Der Elst from New York Cosmos, Neil Orr from Morton

Final Division 1 Table

		P	W	D	L	F	A	Pts
1	Liverpool	42	26	9	7	80	32	87
2	Ipswich T	42	26	5	11	75	53	83
3	Manchester U	42	22	12	8	59	29	78
4	Tottenham H	42	20	11	11	67	48	71
5	Arsenal	42	20	11	11	48	37	71
6	Swansea C	42	21	6	15	58	51	69
7	Southampton	42	19	9	14	72	67	66
8	Everton	42	17	13	12	56	50	64
9	West Ham U	42	14	16	12	66	57	58
10	Manchester C	42	15	13	14	49	50	58
11	Aston Villa	42	15	12	15	55	53	57
12	Nottingham F	42	15	12	15	42	48	57
13	Brighton & HA	42	13	13	16	43	52	52
14	Coventry C	42	13	11	18	56	62	50
15	Notts Co	42	13	8	21	61	69	47
16	Birmingham C	42	10	14	18	53	61	44
17	WBA	42	11	11	20	46	57	44
18	Stoke C	42	12	8	22	44	63	44
19	Sunderland	42	11	11	20	38	58	44
20	Leeds U	42	10	12	20	39	61	42
21	Wolverhampton W	42	10	10	22	32	63	40
22	Middlesbrough	42	8	15	19	34	52	39

Season 1982-83

Football League Division 1

DATE	OPPONENTS	SCORE	GOALSCORERS	ATTENDANCE
Aug 28	NOTTINGHAM FOREST	L 1-2	Stewart (pen)	23,796
Aug 31	Luton Town	W 2-0	Goddard, Bonds	13,402
Sep 4	Sunderland	L 0-1		19,239
Sep 7	IPSWICH TOWN	D 1-1	Lampard	21,963
Sep 11	BIRMINGHAM CITY	W 5-0	Van der Elst, Goddard, Stewart (pen), Martin, Clark	18,754
Sep 18	West Bromwich Albion	W 2-1	Clark, Van der Elst	15,321
Sep 25	MANCHESTER CITY	W 4-1	Clark 2, Goddard, Van der Elst	23,883
Oct 2	Arsenal	W 3-2	Van der Elst, Goddard, Martin	30,484
Oct 9	LIVERPOOL	W 3-1	Martin, Pike, Clark	32,500
Oct 16	Southampton	L 0-3		19,840
Oct 23	Brighton & Hove Albion	L 1-3	Devonshire	20,490
Oct 30	MANCHESTER UNITED	W 3-1	Goddard, Stewart (pen), Pike	31,684
Nov 6	Stoke City	L 2-5	Stewart (pen), Pike	17,589
Nov 13	NORWICH CITY	W 1-0	Clark	22,463
Nov 20	Tottenham Hotspur	L 1-2	Van der Elst	41,960
Nov 27	EVERTON	W 2-0	o.g., Bonds	21,424
Dec 4	Aston Villa	L 0-1		24,658
Dec 11	COVENTRY CITY	L 0-3		19,321
Dec 18	Notts County	W 2-1	Dickens, o.g.	8,457
Dec 27	SWANSEA CITY	W 3-2	Stewart (pen), Van der Elst, Goddard	23,843
Dec 29	Watford	L 1-2	Stewart (pen)	24,870
Jan 1	TOTTENHAM HOTSPUR	W 3-0	Cottee, Stewart (pen), Pike	33,383
Jan 4	LUTON TOWN	L 2-3	Cottee, Clark	21,435
Jan 15	Nottingham Forest	L 0-1		17,031
Jan 22	WEST BROMWICH ALBION	L 0-1		19,887
Feb 5	Birmingham City	L 0-3		12,539
Feb 26	SOUTHAMPTON	D 1-1	Lampard	19,626
Mar 5	BRIGHTON & HOVE ALBION	W 2-1	Dickens, Cottee	16,850
Mar 12	Liverpool	L 0-3		28,511
Mar 19	STOKE CITY	D 1-1	o.g.	16,466
Mar 22	Manchester United	L 1-2	Devonshire	30,227
Mar 26	Norwich City	D 1-1	Dickens	18,582
Apr 2	WATFORD	W 2-1	Van der Elst, Swindlehurst	22,647
Apr 5	Swansea City	W 5-1	Pike 2, Devonshire, Dickens 2	13,303
Apr 9	SUNDERLAND	W 2-1	Dickens, Goddard	20,053
Apr 16	Manchester City	L 0-2		23,015
Apr 23	ASTON VILLA	W 2-0	Swindlehurst, Bonds	21,822
Apr 30	Everton	L 0-2		16,355
May 3	Ipswich Town	W 2-1	Goddard, Stewart (pen)	18,690
May 7	NOTTS COUNTY	W 2-0	Van der Elst, Goddard	17,534
May 10	ARSENAL	L 1-3	Van der Elst	28,930
May 14	Coventry City	W 4-2	Goddard, Cottee 2, Swindlehurst	10,919

FA Cup

Jan 8	Manchester United	(Rd 3) L 0-2		44,143

Milk Cup

Oct 6	Stoke City	(Rd 2 FL) D 1-1	Stewart (pen)	18,079
Oct 26	STOKE CITY	(Rd 2 SL) W 2-1	Goddard, Clark	18,270
Nov 10	Lincoln City	(Rd 3) D 1-1	Goddard	13,899
Nov 29	LINCOLN CITY	(R) W 2-1	Stewart, Clark	13,686
Dec 7	Notts County	(Rd 4) D 3-3	Van der Elst 3	7,525
Dec 21	NOTTS COUNTY	(R) W 3-0	Stewart (pen), Clark, Allen	13,140
Jan 18	Liverpool	(QF) L 1-2	Allen	23,953

MANAGER: John Lyall
CAPTAIN: Billy Bonds
TOP SCORERS: Paul Goddard and Francois Van Der Elst
BIGGEST WIN: September 11, 1982 5-0 v Birmingham City, Division 1
HIGHEST ATTENDANCE: November 20, 1982 41,960 v Tottenham Hotspur, lost 1-2, Division 1
MAJOR TRANSFERS IN: Sandy Clark from Airdrie, David Swindlehurst from Derby County
MAJOR TRANSFERS OUT: David Cross to Manchester City, Sandy Clark to Glasgow Rangers

League & Cup Appearances (substitute)

PLAYER	LEAGUE	CUP COMPETITION FA CUP	MILK	TOTAL
Allen	33	1	7	41
Barnes	0		0 (1)	0 (1)
Bonds	34	1	4	39
Brooking	1			1
Brush	6		2 (1)	8 (1)
Clark	26	1	7	34
Cottee	3 (5)	1		4 (5)
Cowie	1 (1)		1	2 (1)
Devonshire	39	1	6	46
Dickens	12 (3)			12 (3)
Gallagher	8 (1)	1	1	10 (1)
Goddard	39		7	46
Lampard	37	1	4	42
Martin	38		7	45
Morgan	3 (4)			3 (4)
Neighbour	3		2 (1)	5 (1)
Orr	9 (5)		4	13 (5)
Parkes	42	1	7	50
Pike	40	1	7	48
Stewart	39	1	6	46
Swindlehurst	9			9
Van der Elst	40	1	5 (1)	46 (1)

Goalscorers

PLAYER	LEAGUE	CUP COMPETITION FA CUP	MILK	TOTAL
Goddard	10		2	12
Van der Elst	9		3	12
Stewart	8		3	11
Clark	7		3	10
Dickens	6			6
Pike	6			6
Cottee	5			5
Bonds	3			3
Devonshire	3			3
Martin	3			3
Swindlehurst	3			3
Allen			2	2
Lampard	2			2
Opps' o.gs.	3			3

Fact File

Tony Cottee scored a goal on his debut against Tottenham Hotspur on New Year's Day.

Final Division 1 Table

		P	W	D	L	F	A	Pts
1	Liverpool	42	24	10	8	87	37	82
2	Watford	42	22	5	15	74	57	71
3	Manchester U	42	19	13	8	56	38	70
4	Tottenham H	42	20	9	13	65	50	69
5	Nottingham F	42	20	9	13	62	50	69
6	Aston Villa	42	21	5	16	62	50	68
7	Everton	42	18	10	14	66	48	64
8	West Ham U	42	20	4	18	68	62	64
9	Ipswich T	42	15	13	14	64	50	58
10	Arsenal	42	16	10	16	58	56	58
11	WBA	42	15	12	15	51	49	57
12	Southampton	42	15	12	15	54	58	57
13	Stoke C	42	16	9	17	53	64	57
14	Norwich C	42	14	12	16	52	58	54
15	Notts Co	42	15	7	20	55	71	52
16	Sunderland	42	12	14	16	48	61	50
17	Birmingham C	42	12	15	16	40	55	50
18	Luton T	42	12	13	17	65	84	49
19	Coventry C	42	13	9	20	48	59	48
20	Manchester C	42	13	8	21	47	70	47
21	Swansea C	42	10	11	21	51	69	41
22	Brighton & HA	42	9	13	20	38	68	40

Season 1983-84

Football League Division 1

DATE	OPPONENTS	SCORE	GOALSCORERS	ATTENDANCE
Aug 27	BIRMINGHAM CITY	W 4-0	Cottee 2, Martin, Swindlehurst	19,729
Aug 29	Everton	W 1-0	Walford	20,375
Sep 3	Tottenham Hotspur	W 2-0	Whitton, Swindlehurst	38,042
Sep 6	LEICESTER CITY	W 3-1	Walford, Swindlehurst, Cottee	22,131
Sep 10	COVENTRY CITY	W 5-2	Swindlehurst 3, Whitton 2	22,195
Sep 17	West Bromwich Albion	L 0-1		15,161
Sep 24	NOTTS COUNTY	W 3-0	Brooking, Goddard, Stewart (pen)	20,613
Oct 1	Stoke City	L 1-3	Stewart (pen)	13,852
Oct 15	LIVERPOOL	L 1-3	Devonshire	32,555
Oct 22	NORWICH CITY	D 0-0		18,958
Oct 28	Watford	D 0-0		14,559
Nov 5	IPSWICH TOWN	W 2-1	Swindlehurst 2	20,682
Nov 12	Wolverhampton W	W 3-0	Brooking, Swindlehurst, Cottee	12,062
Nov 19	Sunderland	W 1-0	Swindlehurst	19,921
Nov 27	MANCHESTER UNITED	D 1-1	Swindlhurst	23,355
Dec 3	Aston Villa	L 0-1		21,297
Dec 10	ARSENAL	W 3-1	Brooking, o.g., Pike	25,118
Dec 17	Nottingham Forest	L 0-3		14,544
Dec 26	SOUTHAMPTON	L 0-1		22,221
Dec 27	Luton Town	W 1-0	Cottee	16,343
Dec 31	TOTTENHAM HOTSPUR	W 4-1	Cottee, Martin, Stewart, Brooking	30,939
Jan 2	Notts County	D 2-2	Stewart (pen), Swindlehurst	8,667
Jan 14	Birmingham City	L 0-3		10,334
Jan 21	WEST BROMWICH ALBION	W 1-0	Cottee	17,213
Feb 4	STOKE CITY	W 3-0	Barnes, Cottee, Stewart (pen)	18,775
Feb 7	Queens Park Rangers	D 1-1	Cottee	20,102
Feb 11	Coventry City	W 2-1	o.g., Cottee	13,271
Feb 21	WATFORD	L 2-4	Swindlehurst, Barnes	19,241
Feb 25	Norwich City	L 0-1		16,294
Mar 3	Ipswich Town	W 3-0	Hilton, o.g., Cottee	17,297
Mar 10	WOLVERHAMPTON W	D 1-1	Cottee	18,111
Mar 17	Leicester City	L 1-4	Stewart (pen)	13,533
Mar 31	QUEENS PARK RANGERS	D 2-2	Pike, Cottee	21,099
Apr 7	Liverpool	L 0-6		38,359
Apr 14	SUNDERLAND	L 0-1		16,558
Apr 17	LUTON TOWN	W 3-1	Cottee 2, Martin	15,430
Apr 21	Southampton	L 0-2		20,846
Apr 28	Manchester United	D 0-0		44,124
May 5	ASTON VILLA	L 0-1		17,930
May 7	Arsenal	D 3-3	Whitton 2, Hilton	33,347
May 12	NOTTINGHAM FOREST	L 1-2	Stewart (pen)	18,468
May 14	EVERTON	L 0-1		25,452

FA Cup

Jan 7	WIGAN ATHLETIC	(Rd 3)	W 1-0	Stewart (pen)	16,000
Jan 28	Crystal Palace	(Rd 4)	D 1-1	Swindlehurst	27,590
Jan 31	CRYSTAL PALACE	(R)	W 2-0	Pike, Barnes	27,127
Feb 18	Birmingham City	(Rd 5)	L 0-3		29,570

Milk Cup

Oct 4	Bury	(Rd 2 FL)	W 2-1	Goddard, Orr	8,050
Oct 25	BURY	(Rd 2 SL)	W 10-0	Cottee 4, Martin, Brooking 2, Devonshire 2, Stewart (pen)	10,896
Nov 8	BRIGHTON & HOVE ALBION	(Rd 3)	W 1-0	Swindlehurst	17,082
Nov 30	EVERTON	(Rd 4)	D 2-2	o.g., Pike	19,702
Dec 6	Everton	(R)	L 0-2		21,609

MANAGER: John Lyall **CAPTAIN:** Billy Bonds
TOP SCORER: Tony Cottee
BIGGEST WIN: October 25, 1983 10-0 v Bury, Milk Cup, Round 2 Second Leg
HIGHEST ATTENDANCE: April 28, 1984 44,124 v Manchester United, drew 0-0, Division 1
MAJOR TRANSFERS IN: Steve Walford from Norwich City, Steve Whitton from Coventry, Paul Hilton from Bury
MAJOR TRANSFERS OUT: Francois Van Der Elst to Lokeren, Trevor Brooking (retired)

League & Cup Appearances (substitute)

PLAYER	LEAGUE	CUP COMPETITION		TOTAL
		FA CUP	MILK	
Allen	19	1 (2)	1	21 (2)
Barnes	11 (2)	3 (1)		14 (3)
Bonds	27	0 (1)	2	29 (1)
Brooking	35	3	5	43
Brush	10	4		14
Cottee	37 (2)	4	4	45 (2)
Devonshire	22	1	4	27
Dickens	7 (3)	1	0 (1)	8 (4)
Donald	1 (1)			1 (1)
Goddard	3 (2)		1	4 (2)
Hilton	7 (1)			7 (1)
Lampard	17 (1)	3	3	23 (1)
Martin	29	1	5	35
Orr	28 (1)	4	2 (2)	34 (3)
Parkes	42	4	5	51
Pike	27 (1)	2	5	34 (1)
Stewart	42	4	5	51
Swindlehurst	35 (1)	4	5	44 (1)
Walford	41	4	5	50
Whitton	22	1	3	26

Goalscorers

PLAYER	LEAGUE	CUP COMPETITION		TOTAL
		FA CUP	MILK	
Cottee	15		4	19
Swindlehurst	13	1	1	15
Stewart	7	1	1	9
Brooking	4		2	6
Whitton	5			5
Martin	3		1	4
Pike	2	1	1	4
Barnes	2	1		3
Devonshire	1		2	3
Goddard	1		1	2
Hilton	2			2
Walford	2			2
Orr			1	1
Opps' o.gs.	3		1	4

Fact File

West Ham's 10-0 destruction of Bury in the League Cup is the club's record victory.

Final Division 1 Table

		P	W	D	L	F	A	Pts
1	Liverpool	42	22	14	6	73	32	80
2	Southampton	42	22	11	9	66	38	77
3	Nottingham F	42	22	8	12	76	45	74
4	Manchester U	42	20	14	8	71	41	74
5	QPR	42	22	7	13	67	37	73
6	Arsenal	42	19	9	15	74	60	63
7	Everton	42	16	14	12	44	42	62
8	Tottenham H	42	17	10	15	64	65	61
9	West Ham U	42	17	9	16	60	55	60
10	Aston Villa	42	17	9	16	59	61	60
11	Watford	42	16	9	17	68	77	57
12	Ipswich T	42	15	8	19	55	57	53
13	Sunderland	42	13	13	16	42	53	52
14	Norwich C	42	12	15	15	48	49	51
15	Leicester C	42	13	12	17	65	68	51
16	Luton T	42	14	9	19	53	66	51
17	WBA	42	14	9	19	48	62	51
18	Stoke C	42	13	11	18	44	63	50
19	Coventry C	42	13	11	18	57	77	50
20	Birmingham C	42	12	12	18	39	50	48
21	Notts Co	42	10	11	21	50	72	41
22	Wolverhampton W	42	6	11	25	27	80	29

Season 1984-85

Football League Division 1

DATE	OPPONENTS	SCORE	GOALSCORERS	ATTENDANCE
Aug 25	IPSWICH TOWN	D 0-0		19,032
Aug 27	Liverpool	L 0-3		32,633
Sep 1	Southampton	W 3-2	Goddard 2, Dickens	18,488
Sep 4	COVENTRY CITY	W 3-1	Stewart 2 (2 pen), Cottee	14,949
Sep 8	WATFORD	W 2-0	o.g., Barnes	20,377
Sep 15	Chelsea	L 0-3		32,411
Sep 22	Nottingham Forest	D 0-0		17,434
Sep 29	Newcastle United	D 1-1	Allen	29,452
Oct 6	LEICESTER CITY	W 3-1	Stewart (pen), Bonds, Cottee	15,306
Oct 13	Manchester United	L 1-5	Goddard	44,559
Oct 20	Stoke City	W 4-2	o.g., Cottee, Goddard, Allen	9,945
Oct 27	ARSENAL	W 3-1	Cottee, Goddard, Pike	33,218
Nov 3	Aston Villa	D 0-0		15,709
Nov 10	EVERTON	L 0-1		24,089
Nov 17	SUNDERLAND	W 1-0	Cottee	15,204
Nov 24	Luton Town	D 2-2	Whitton, Martin	10,789
Dec 1	WEST BROMWICH ALBION	L 0-2		15,572
Dec 8	Norwich City	L 0-1		13,908
Dec 15	SHEFFIELD WEDNESDAY	D 0-0		14,896
Dec 22	SOUTHAMPTON	L 2-3	Cottee 2	14,221
Dec 26	Tottenham Hotspur	D 2-2	Cottee, Goddard	37,198
Dec 29	Coventry City	W 2-1	Cottee 2	10,775
Jan 1	QUEENS PARK RANGERS	L 1-3	Brush	20,857
Feb 2	NEWCASTLE UNITED	D 1-1	Allen	17,723
Feb 23	ASTON VILLA	L 1-2	Goddard	14,845
Mar 2	Arsenal	L 1-2	Cottee	25,818
Mar 15	MANCHESTER UNITED	D 2-2	Stewart (pen), o.g.	16,674
Mar 23	Leicester City	L 0-1		11,375
Mar 30	Nottingham Forest	W 2-1	Cottee, Goddard	13,560
Apr 2	Watford	L 0-5		17,884
Apr 6	TOTTENHAM HOTSPUR	D 1-1	Dickens	24,435
Apr 8	Queens Park Rangers	L 2-4	Cottee 2	16,085
Apr 13	CHELSEA	D 1-1	Cottee	19,003
Apr 20	Sunderland	W 1-0	Goddard	15,622
Apr 27	LUTON TOWN	D 0-0		17,303
May 4	West Bromwich Albion	L 1-5	Stewart (pen)	8,878
May 6	NORWICH CITY	W 1-0	Barnes	16,233
May 8	Everton	L 0-3		32,657
May 11	Sheffield Wednesday	L 1-2	Cottee	24,314
May 14	STOKE CITY	W 5-1	Bonds 2, Pike, Hilton Stewart (pen)	13,362
May 17	Ipswich Town	W 1-0	Cottee	19,326
May 20	LIVERPOOL	L 0-3		22,408

FA Cup

Jan 5	PORT VALE	(Rd 3) W 4-1	Dickens, Goddard 3	11,452
Feb 4	NORWICH CITY	(Rd 4) W 2-1	Pike, Stewart (pen)	20,098
Mar 4	Wimbledon	(Rd 5) D 1-1	Cottee	13,500
Mar 6	WIMBLEDON	(R) W 5-1	Cottee 3, Dickens, Allen	20,258
Mar 9	Manchester United	(QF) L 2-4	o.g., Allen	46,769

Milk Cup

Sep 25	Bristol City	(Rd 2 FL) D 2-2	Cottee, Walford	15,894
Oct 9	BRISTOL CITY	(Rd 2 SL) W 6-1	Cottee 2, Goddard 2, Whitton, Walford	11,376
Oct 31	Manchester City	(Rd 3) D 0-0		20,510
Nov 6	MANCHESTER CITY	(R) L 1-2	Whitton	17,461

Fact File

Frank Lampard made his last Hammers appearance in the final game of the season against Liverpool.

MANAGER: John Lyall **CAPTAIN:** Alvin Martin
TOP SCORER: Tony Cottee
BIGGEST WIN: October 9, 1984 6-1 v Bristol City, Milk Cup, Round 2 Second Leg
HIGHEST ATTENDANCE: March 9, 1985 46,769 v Manchester United, lost 2-4, FA Cup quarter-final
MAJOR TRANSFERS IN: Tony Gale from Fulham
MAJOR TRANSFERS OUT: Frank Lampard (retired)

League & Cup Appearances (substitute)

PLAYER	LEAGUE	CUP COMPETITION FA CUP	MILK	TOTAL
Allen	38	5	4	47
Barnes	18 (2)	2	1 (1)	21 (3)
Bonds	19 (3)		4	23 (3)
Brush	18	5		23
Campbell	2			2
Cottee	40 (1)	5	4	49 (1)
Devonshire		2		2
Dickens	24 (1)	4	1 (1)	29 (2)
Gale	36 (1)	1	3	40 (1)
Goddard	38 (2)	5	3	46 (2)
Hilton	5 (4)	1 (1)		6 (5)
Lampard	1			1
Martin	40	5	4	49
McAlister	32	5	4	41
McPherson	1			1
Orr	17 (3)	4	1 (1)	22 (4)
Parkes	10			10
Parris	1			1
Pike	30	4	4	38
Potts	1			1
Stewart	37	4	4	45
Swindlehurst	8 (8)	0 (1)		8 (9)
Walford	33	3	4	40
Whitton	13 (4)		3	16 (4)

Goalscorers

PLAYER	LEAGUE	CUP COMPETITION FA CUP	MILK	TOTAL
Cottee	17	4	3	24
Goddard	9	3	2	14
Stewart	6	1		7
Allen	3	2		5
Dickens	2	2		4
Bonds	3			3
Pike	2	1		3
Whitton	1		2	3
Barnes	2			2
Walford			2	2
Brush	1			1
Hilton	1			1
Martin	1			1
Opps' o.gs.	3	1		4

Final Division 1 Table

		P	W	D	L	F	A	Pts
1	Everton	42	28	6	8	88	43	90
2	Liverpool	42	22	11	9	68	35	77
3	Tottenham H	42	23	8	11	78	51	77
4	Manchester U	42	22	10	10	77	47	76
5	Southampton	42	19	11	12	56	47	68
6	Chelsea	42	18	12	12	63	48	66
7	Arsenal	42	19	9	14	61	49	66
8	Sheffield W	42	17	14	11	58	45	65
9	Nottingham F	42	19	7	16	56	48	64
10	Aston Villa	42	15	11	16	60	60	56
11	Watford	42	14	13	15	81	71	55
12	WBA	42	16	7	19	58	62	55
13	Luton T	42	15	9	18	57	61	54
14	Newcastle U	42	13	13	16	55	70	52
15	Leicester C	42	15	6	21	65	73	51
16	West Ham U	42	13	12	17	51	68	51
17	Ipswich T	42	13	11	18	46	57	50
18	Coventry C	42	15	5	22	47	64	50
19	QPR	42	13	11	18	53	72	50
20	Norwich C	42	13	10	19	46	64	49
21	Sunderland	42	10	10	22	40	62	40
22	Stoke C	42	3	8	31	24	91	17

Season 1985-86

Football League Division 1

DATE	OPPONENTS	SCORE	GOALSCORERS	ATTENDANCE
Aug 17	Birmingham City	L 0-1		11,164
Aug 20	QUEENS PARK RANGERS	W 3-1	McAvennie 2, Dickens	15,530
Aug 24	LUTON TOWN	L 0-1		14,104
Aug 26	Manchester United	L 0-2		50,773
Aug 31	LIVERPOOL	D 2-2	McAvennie 2	19,762
Sep 3	Southampton	D 1-1	McAvennie	14,477
Sep 7	Sheffield Wednesday	D 2-2	McAvennie, Cottee	19,287
Sep 14	LEICESTER CITY	W 3-0	McAvennie, Devonshire, Cottee	12,125
Sep 21	Manchester City	D 2-2	Cottee, o.g.	22,001
Sep 28	NOTTINGHAM FOREST	W 4-2	Cottee, McAvennie 2, Dickens	14,540
Oct 5	Newcastle United	W 2-1	McAvennie, Cottee	26,709
Oct 12	ARSENAL	D 0-0		24,057
Oct 19	ASTON VILLA	W 4-1	McAvennie 2, Cottee 2	15,034
Oct 26	Ipswich Town	W 1-0	Cottee	16,849
Nov 2	EVERTON	W 2-1	McAvennie 2	23,844
Nov 9	Oxford United	W 2-1	Cottee, Ward	13,140
Nov 16	WATFORD	W 2-1	McAvennie, Ward	21,490
Nov 23	Coventry City	W 1-0	McAvennie	11,042
Nov 30	WEST BROMWICH ALBION	W 4-0	Cottee, Parris, Devonshire, Orr	16,325
Dec 7	Queens Park Rangers	W 1-0	McAvennie	23,836
Dec 14	BIRMINGHAM CITY	W 2-0	McAvennie, Stewart (pen)	17,481
Dec 21	Luton Town	D 0-0		14,599
Dec 26	Tottenham Hotspur	L 0-1		33,835
Jan 11	Leicester City	W 1-0	McAvennie	11,359
Jan 18	Liverpool	L 1-3	Dickens	41,056
Feb 2	MANCHESTER UNITED	W 2-1	Ward, Cottee	22,642
Mar 15	Arsenal	L 0-1		31,240
Mar 19	Aston Villa	L 1-2	o.g.	11,579
Mar 22	SHEFFIELD WEDNESDAY	W 1-0	McAvennie	16,604
Mar 29	Chelsea	W 4-0	Devonshire, Cottee 2, McAvennie	29,955
Mar 31	TOTTENHAM HOTSPUR	W 2-1	Cottee, McAvennie	27,497
Apr 2	Nottingham Forest	L 1-2	Cottee	17,498
Apr 8	SOUTHAMPTON	W 1-0	Martin	22,459
Apr 12	OXFORD UNITED	W 3-1	o.g., McAvennie, Stewart (pen)	23,956
Apr 15	CHELSEA	L 1-2	Cottee	29,361
Apr 19	Watford	W 2-0	Cottee, McAvennie	16,651
Apr 21	NEWCASTLE UNITED	W 8-1	Martin 3 (1 pen), Stewart, Orr, o.g., Goddard	24,735
Apr 26	COVENTRY CITY	W 1-0	Cottee	27,251
Apr 28	MANCHESTER CITY	W 1-0	Stewart (pen)	27,153
Apr 30	IPSWICH TOWN	W 2-1	Dickens, Stewart (pen)	31,121
May 3	West Bromwich Albion	W 3-2	McAvennie, Cottee, Stewart (pen)	17,651
May 5	Everton	L 1-3	Cottee	40,073

FA Cup

Jan 5	Charlton Athletic	(Rd 3)	W 1-0	Cottee	13,037
Jan 25	IPSWICH TOWN	(Rd 4)	D 0-0		25,035
Feb 4	Ipswich Town	(R)	D 1-1*	Cottee	25,384
Feb 6	Ipswich Town	(2nd R)	W 1-0*	Cottee	14,515
Mar 5	MANCHESTER UNITED	(R5)	D 1-1	McAvennie	26,441
Mar 9	Manchester United	(R)	W 2-0	Pike, Stewart (pen)	30,441
Mar 12	Sheffield Wednesday	(QF)	L 1-2	Cottee	35,522

*After extra time.

Milk Cup

Sep 24	SWANSEA CITY	(Rd 2 FL)	W 3-0	Cottee, McAvennie, Stewart (pen)	9,282
Oct 8	Swansea City	(Rd 2 SL)	W 3-2	Stewart 2 (2 pen), Cottee	3,584
Oct 29	Manchester United	(Rd 3)	L 0-1		32,057

MANAGER: John Lyall
CAPTAIN: Alvin Martin
TOP SCORER: Frank McAvennie
BIGGEST WIN: April 21, 1986 8-1 v Newcastle United, Division 1
HIGHEST ATTENDANCE: August 26, 1985 50,773 v Manchester United, lost 0-2, Division 1
MAJOR TRANSFERS IN: Mark Ward from Oldham Athletic, Frank McAvennie from St Mirren

League & Cup Appearances (substitute)

PLAYER	LEAGUE	CUP COMPETITION FA CUP	MILK	TOTAL
Barnes	0 (1)			0 (1)
Campbell	1 (2)			1 (2)
Cottee	41 (1)	7	3	51 (1)
Devonshire	38	6	3	47
Dickens	40 (1)	7	3	50 (1)
Gale	42	7	3	52
Goddard	1 (5)	0 (1)		1 (6)
Hilton	2			2
Martin	40	7	3	50
McAvennie	41	7	3	51
Orr	33 (3)	1 (1)	3	37 (4)
Parkes	42	7	3	52
Parris	23 (3)	7	0 (2)	30 (5)
Pike	10	5		15
Potts	0 (1)			0 (1)
Stewart	39	6	3	48
Walford	27	3	3	33
Ward	42	7	3	52

Goalscorers

PLAYER	LEAGUE	CUP COMPETITION FA CUP	MILK	TOTAL
McAvennie	26	1	1	28
Cottee	20	4	2	26
Stewart	6	1	3	10
Dickens	4			4
Martin	4			4
Devonshire	3			3
Ward	3			3
Orr	2			2
Goddard	1			1
Parris	1			1
Pike		1		1
Opps' o.gs.	4			4

Fact File

West Ham finished in third position, their best ever Division One placing and Tony Cottee was named as the 1986 PFA Young Player of the Year.

Final Division 1 Table

		P	W	D	L	F	A	Pts
1	Liverpool	42	26	10	6	89	37	88
2	Everton	42	26	8	8	87	41	86
3	West Ham U	42	26	6	10	74	40	84
4	Manchester U	42	22	10	10	70	36	76
5	Sheffield W	42	21	10	11	63	54	73
6	Chelsea	42	20	11	11	57	56	71
7	Arsenal	42	20	9	13	49	47	69
8	Nottingham F	42	19	11	12	69	53	68
9	Luton T	42	18	12	12	61	44	66
10	Tottenham H	42	19	8	15	74	52	65
11	Newcastle U	42	17	12	13	67	72	63
12	Watford	42	16	11	15	69	62	59
13	QPR	42	15	7	20	53	64	52
14	Southampton	42	12	10	20	51	62	46
15	Manchester C	42	11	12	19	43	57	45
16	Aston Villa	42	10	14	18	51	67	44
17	Coventry C	42	11	10	21	48	71	43
18	Oxford U	42	10	12	20	62	80	42
19	Leicester C	42	10	12	20	54	76	42
20	Ipswich T	42	11	8	23	32	55	41
21	Birmingham C	42	8	5	29	30	73	29
22	WBA	42	4	12	26	35	89	24

Season 1986-87

Football League Division 1

DATE	OPPONENTS	SCORE	GOALSCORERS	ATTENDANCE
Aug 23	COVENTRY CITY	W 1-0	Gale	21,368
Aug 25	Manchester United	W 3-2	McAvennie 2, Devonshire	43,306
Aug 30	Oxford United	D 0-0		11,684
Sep 2	NOTTINGHAM FOREST	L 1-2	McAvennie	21,305
Sep 6	LIVERPOOL	L 2-5	Stewart (pen), Cottee	29,807
Sep 13	Queens Park Rangers	W 3-2	Cottee 3	19,257
Sep 20	LUTON TOWN	W 2-0	Parris, Gale	19,133
Sep 27	Sheffield Wednesday	D 2-2	Martin, Orr	25,715
Oct 4	Watford	D 2-2	Dickens, McAvennie	17,120
Oct 11	CHELSEA	W 5-3	McAvennie, Cottee 2, Stewart 2 (2 pen)	26,859
Oct 18	Norwich City	D 1-1	Goddard	22,884
Oct 25	CHARLTON ATHLETIC	L 1-3	Cottee	24,141
Nov 2	EVERTON	W 1-0	Dickens	19,094
Nov 8	Arsenal	D 0-0		36,084
Nov 15	Wimbledon	W 1-0	Cottee	10,342
Nov 22	ASTON VILLA	D 1-1	Cottee	21,959
Nov 30	Newcastle United	L 0-4		22,077
Dec 6	SOUTHAMPTON	W 3-1	Ince, Devonshire, Cottee (pen)	18,111
Dec 13	Manchester City	L 1-3	Martin	19,067
Dec 20	QUEENS PARK RANGERS	D 1-1	Cottee (pen)	17,290
Dec 26	Tottenham Hotspur	L 0-4		39,019
Dec 27	WIMBLEDON	L 2-3	Cottee, Hilton	19,122
Jan 1	LEICESTER CITY	W 4-1	Cottee 2, Dickens, McAvennie	16,625
Jan 3	Liverpool	L 0-1		41,286
Jan 24	Coventry City	W 3-1	Cottee 3	14,191
Feb 7	OXFORD UNITED	L 0-1		15,220
Feb 14	Nottingham Forest	D 1-1	Stewart (pen)	19,373
Feb 28	Luton Town	L 1-2	Cottee	11,101
Mar 7	Charlton Athletic	L 1-2	Robson	10,100
Mar 14	NORWICH CITY	L 0-2		21,531
Mar 21	Chelsea	L 0-1		25,386
Mar 24	SHEFFIELD WEDNESDAY	L 0-2		13,514
Mar 28	WATFORD	W 1-0	Parris	16,485
Apr 8	ARSENAL	W 3-1	Cottee 2 (1 pen), Brady	26,174
Apr 11	Everton	L 0-4		35,731
Apr 14	MANCHESTER UNITED	D 0-0		23,486
Apr 18	Leicester City	L 0-2		10,434
Apr 20	TOTTENHAM HOTSPUR	W 2-1	McAvennie, Cottee (pen)	23,972
Apr 25	Aston Villa	L 0-4		13,584
May 2	NEWCASTLE UNITED	D 1-1	Ward	17,844
May 4	Southampton	L 0-1		16,810
May 9	MANCHESTER CITY	W 2-0	Cottee, Brady	18,413

FA Cup

Jan 10	Orient	(Rd 3)	D 1-1	Hilton	19,225
Jan 31	ORIENT	(R)	W 4-1	Parris, Keen, McAvennie, Cottee	19,424
Feb 9	SHEFFIELD UNITED	(Rd 4)	W 4-0	McAvennie 2, Robson, Gale	17,194
Feb 21	Sheffield Wednesday	(Rd 5)	W 1-1	McAvennie	30,257
Feb 25	SHEFFIELD WEDNESDAY	(R)	L 0-2		30,257

Littlewoods Cup

Sep 23	Preston North End	(Rd 2 FL)	D 1-1	Ward	13,153
Oct 7	PRESTON NORTH END	(Rd 2 SL)	W 4-1	Cottee 3, Dickens	12,742
Oct 29	Watford	(Rd 3)	W 3-2	Goddard, Dickens, Ward	17,523
Nov 18	OXFORD UNITED	(Rd 4)	W 1-0	Cottee (pen)	20,530
Jan 27	TOTTENHAM HOTSPUR	(QF)	D 1-1	Cottee	29,477
Feb 2	Tottenham Hotspur	(R)	L 0-5		41,995

MANAGER: John Lyall
CAPTAIN: Alvin Martin
TOP SCORER: Tony Cottee
BIGGEST WIN: February 9, 1987 4-0 v Sheffield United, FA Cup Round 4
HIGHEST ATTENDANCE: August 25, 1986 43,306 v Manchester United, won 3-2, Division 1
MAJOR TRANSFERS IN: Stewart Robson from Arsenal, Liam Brady from Ascoli, Gary Strodder from Lincoln City, Tommy McQueen from Aberdeen
MAJOR TRANSFERS OUT: Paul Goddard to Newcastle United

League & Cup Appearances (substitute)

PLAYER	LEAGUE	CUP COMPETITION		TOTAL
		FA CUP	LITTLEWOODS	
Bonds	13 (4)	3 (1)	1 (2)	17 (7)
Brady	12			12
Cottee	42	5	6	53
Devonshire	20	3	4	27
Dickens	31 (5)	2 (1)	4	37 (6)
Dolan	0 (1)			0 (1)
Gale	32	4	4	40
Goddard	3 (1)		1	4 (1)
Hilton	15 (1)	2	4 (1)	21 (2)
Ince	7 (3)	1		8 (3)
Keen	7 (6)	1 (1)	2	10 (7)
Martin	16	1	3	20
McAlister	9			9
McAvennie	36	4	5	45
McQueen	9			9
Orr	21 (1)	1	4	26 (1)
Parkes	33	5	6	44
Parris	35 (1)	5	6	46 (1)
Pike	10 (1)	4	1	15 (1)
Potts	8			8
Robson	18	3	2	23
Stewart	23	3	3	29
Strodder	12			12
Walford	13 (1)	3	4 (1)	20 (2)
Ward	37	5	6	48

Goalscorers

PLAYER	LEAGUE	CUP COMPETITION		TOTAL
		FA CUP	LITTLEWOODS	
Cottee	22	1	5	28
McAvennie	7	4		11
Dickens	3		2	5
Stewart	4			4
Gale	2	1		3
Robson	2	1		3
Ward	1		2	3
Brady	2			2
Devonshire	2			2
Goddard	1		1	2
Hilton	1	1		2
Martin	2			2
Parris	1	1		2
Ince	1			1
Keen		1		1
Orr	1			1

Fact File

Nineteen year-old Paul Ince scored on his home debut against Southampton.

Final Division 1 Table

		P	W	D	L	F	A	Pts
1	Everton	42	26	8	8	76	31	86
2	Liverpool	42	23	8	11	72	42	77
3	Tottenham H	42	21	8	13	68	43	71
4	Arsenal	42	20	10	12	58	35	70
5	Norwich C	42	17	17	8	53	51	68
6	Wimbledon	42	19	9	14	57	50	66
7	Luton T	42	18	12	12	47	45	66
8	Nottingham F	42	18	11	13	64	51	65
9	Watford	42	18	9	15	67	54	63
10	Coventry C	42	17	12	13	50	45	63
11	Manchester U	42	14	14	14	52	45	56
12	Southampton	42	14	10	18	69	68	52
13	Sheffield W	42	13	13	16	58	59	52
14	Chelsea	42	13	13	16	53	64	52
15	West Ham U	42	14	10	18	52	67	52
16	QPR	42	13	11	18	48	64	50
17	Newcastle U	42	12	11	19	47	65	47
18	Oxford U	42	11	13	18	44	69	46
19	Charlton Ath	42	11	11	20	45	55	44
20	Leicester C	42	11	9	22	54	76	42
21	Manchester C	42	8	15	19	36	57	39
22	Aston Villa	42	8	12	22	45	79	36

Season 1987-88

Barclays League Division 1

DATE	OPPONENTS	SCORE	GOALSCORERS	ATTENDANCE
Aug 15	QUEENS PARK RANGERS	L 0-3		22,881
Aug 22	Luton Town	D 2-2	Brady, Stewart (pen)	18,073
Aug 29	NORWICH CITY	W 2-0	Cottee 2	16,394
Aug 31	Portsmouth	L 1-2	Strodder	16,104
Sep 5	LIVERPOOL	D 1-1	Cottee	29,865
Sep 12	Wimbledon	D 1-1	Cottee	8,507
Sep 19	TOTTENHAM HOTSPUR	L 0-1		27,750
Sep 26	Arsenal	L 0-1		40,127
Oct 3	DERBY COUNTY	D 1-1	Brady	17,226
Oct 10	CHARLTON ATHLETIC	D 1-1	Ince	15,757
Oct 17	Oxford United	W 2-1	o.g., Cottee	9,092
Oct 25	MANCHESTER UNITED	D 1-1	Stewart (pen)	19,863
Oct 31	Watford	W 2-1	Dickens, Cottee	14,427
Nov 7	SHEFFIELD WEDNESDAY	L 0-1		16,277
Nov 14	Everton	L 1-3	Hilton	29,405
Nov 21	NOTTINGHAM FOREST	W 3-2	Cottee 2, Stewart (pen)	17,216
Nov 28	Coventry City	D 0-0		16,740
Dec 5	SOUTHAMPTON	W 2-1	Keen, Dickens	14,975
Dec 12	Chelsea	D 1-1	Parris	22,850
Dec 19	NEWCASTLE UNITED	W 2-1	Robson, Ince	18,679
Dec 26	WIMBLEDON	L 1-2	Stewart (pen)	18,605
Dec 28	Tottenham Hotspur	L 1-2	Hilton	39,456
Jan 1	Norwich City	L 1-4	Cottee	20,069
Jan 2	LUTON TOWN	D 1-1	Ince	16,716
Jan 16	Queens Park Rangers	W 1-0	Dickens	14,509
Feb 6	Liverpool	D 0-0		42,049
Feb 13	PORTSMOUTH	D 1-1	Cottee	18,639
Feb 27	Derby County	L 0-1		16,301
Mar 5	OXFORD UNITED	D 1-1	Ward	14,980
Mar 12	Charlton Athletic	L 0-3		8,118
Mar 19	WATFORD	W 1-0	Rosenior	16,051
Mar 26	Manchester United	L 1-3	Rosenior	37,269
Apr 2	Sheffield Wednesday	L 1-2	Rosenior	18,435
Apr 4	EVERTON	D 0-0		21,195
Apr 12	ARSENAL	L 0-1		26,746
Apr 20	Nottingham Forest	D 0-0		15,775
Apr 23	COVENTRY CITY	D 1-1	Cottee	17,733
Apr 30	Southampton	L 1-2	Cottee	15,652
May 2	CHELSEA	W 4-1	Rosenior 2, Hilton, Cottee	28,521
May 7	Newcastle United	L 1-2	Robson	23,731

FA Cup

Jan 9	CHARLTON ATHLETIC	(Rd 3) W 2-0	Brady, Cottee	22,043
Jan 30	Queens Park Rangers	(Rd 4) L 1-3	Cottee	23,651

Littlewoods Cup

Sep 22	Barnsley	(Rd 2 FL) D 0-0		10,330
Oct 6	BARNSLEY	(Rd 2 SL) L 2-5*	Keen, Robson	12,403

*After extra time.

League & Cup Appearances (substitute)

PLAYER	LEAGUE	CUP COMPETITION FA CUP	LITTLEWOODS	TOTAL
Bonds	22	2		24
Brady	21 (1)	2	2	25 (1)
Cottee	40	2	2	44
Devonshire	1			1
Dickens	25 (3)	1	0 (1)	26 (4)
Dicks	8			8
Dolan	1 (3)			1 (3)
Gale	17 (1)	2		19 (1)
Hilton	9 (5)	1 (1)	0 (1)	10 (7)
Ince	26 (2)	0 (1)	2	28 (3)
Keen	19 (4)		1	20 (4)
Martin	15		2	17
McAlister	39	2	2	43
McAvennie	8		1	9
McQueen	10 (2)	1	1 (1)	12 (3)
Orr	1			1
Parkes	1			1
Parris	27 (3)		2	29 (3)
Potts	7 (1)	1	1	9 (1)
Robson	37	2	2	41
Rosenior	9			9
Slater	0 (2)			0 (2)
Stewart	33	2		35
Strodder	27 (3)	2	2	31 (3)
Ward	37	2	2	41

Goalscorers

PLAYER	LEAGUE	CUP COMPETITION FA CUP	LITTLEWOODS	TOTAL
Cottee	13	2		15
Rosenior	5			5
Stewart	4			4
Brady	2	1		3
Dickens	3			3
Hilton	3			3
Ince	3			3
Robson	2		1	3
Keen	1		1	2
Parris	1			1
Strodder	1			1
Ward	1			1
Opps' o.gs.	1			1

Fact File

Billy Bonds was 41 years old when he played the final game of his career against Southampton in April.

MANAGER: John Lyall
CAPTAIN: Alvin Martin
TOP SCORER: Tony Cottee
BIGGEST WIN: May 2, 1988 4-1 v Chelsea, Division 1
HIGHEST ATTENDANCE: February 6, 1988 42,049 v Liverpool, drew 0-0, Division 1
MAJOR TRANSFERS IN: Leroy Ronsenior from Fulham, Julian Dicks from Birmingham City
MAJOR TRANSFERS OUT: Geoff Pike to Notts County, Neil Orr to Hibernian, Frank McAvennie to Celtic

Final Division 1 Table

	P	W	D	L	F	A	Pts
1 Liverpool	40	26	12	2	87	24	90
2 Manchester U	40	23	12	5	71	38	81
3 Nottingham F	40	20	13	7	67	39	73
4 Everton	40	19	13	8	53	27	70
5 QPR	40	19	10	11	48	38	67
6 Arsenal	40	18	12	10	58	39	66
7 Wimbledon	40	14	15	11	58	47	57
8 Newcastle U	40	14	14	12	55	53	56
9 Luton T	40	14	11	15	57	58	53
10 Coventry C	40	13	14	13	46	53	53
11 Sheffield W	40	15	8	17	52	66	53
12 Southampton	40	12	14	14	49	53	50
13 Tottenham H	40	12	11	17	38	48	47
14 Norwich C	40	12	9	19	40	52	45
15 Derby Co	40	10	13	17	35	45	43
16 West Ham U	40	9	15	16	40	52	42
17 Charlton Ath	40	9	15	16	38	52	42
18 Chelsea	40	9	15	16	50	68	42
19 Portsmouth	40	7	14	19	36	66	35
20 Watford	40	7	11	22	27	51	32
21 Oxford U	40	6	13	21	44	80	31

Season 1988-89

Barclays League Division 1

DATE	OPPONENTS	SCORE	GOALSCORERS	ATTENDANCE
Aug 27	Southampton	L 0-4		18,407
Sep 3	CHARLTON	L 1-3	Keen (pen)	19,566
Sep 10	Wimbledon	W 1-0	Ward	7,730
Sep 17	ASTON VILLA	D 2-2	o.g., Kelly	19,186
Sep 24	Manchester United	L 0-2		39,941
Oct 1	ARSENAL	L 1-4	Dickens	27,658
Oct 8	Middlesbrough	L 0-1		19,608
Oct 15	Queens Park Rangers	L 1-2	Kelly	14,566
Oct 22	NEWCASTLE UNITED	W 2-0	Dickens, Stewart (pen)	17,765
Oct 29	LIVERPOOL	L 0-2		30,188
Nov 5	Coventry City	D 1-1	Kelly	14,651
Nov 12	NOTTINGHAM FOREST	D 3-3	Kelly 2, Rosenior	21,583
Nov 19	Luton Town	L 1-4	Martin	9,308
Nov 26	EVERTON	L 0-1		22,176
Dec 3	Millwall	W 1-0	Ince	20,105
Dec 10	SHEFFIELD WEDNESDAY	D 0-0		16,676
Dec 17	TOTTENHAM HOTSPUR	L 0-2		28,365
Dec 27	Norwich City	L 1-2	Stewart (pen)	17,491
Dec 31	Charlton Athletic	D 0-0		11,084
Jan 2	WIMBLEDON	L 1-2	Rosenior	18,346
Jan 14	Derby County	W 2-1	Kelly, Brady	16,796
Jan 21	MANCHESTER UNITED	L 1-3	Brady (pen)	29,822
Feb 4	Arsenal	L 1-2	Dicks	40,139
Feb 25	QUEENS PARK RANGERS	D 0-0		17,371
Mar 11	COVENTRY CITY	D 1-1	Ince	15,205
Mar 25	Aston Villa	W 1-0	Ince	22,471
Mar 27	NORWICH CITY	L 0-2		27,265
Apr 1	Tottenham Hotspur	L 0-3		28,376
Apr 8	DERBY COUNTY	D 1-1	Rosenior	16,560
Apr 11	MIDDLESBROUGH	L 1-2	Keen	16,217
Apr 15	SOUTHAMPTON	L 1-2	Brady (pen)	14,766
Apr 22	MILLWALL	W 3-0	Dicks, Dickens, Parris	16,603
May 3	Newcastle United	W 2-1	Keen, Ward	14,202
May 6	LUTON TOWN	W 1-0	Dickens	18,606
May 9	Sheffield Wednesday	W 2-0	Dickens, Rosenior	19,905
May 13	Everton	L 1-3	Slater	21,964
May 18	Nottingham Forest	W 2-1	Rosenior 2	20,943
May 23	Liverpool	L 1-5	Rosenior	41,855

FA Cup

Jan 8	ARSENAL	(Rd 3) D	2-2	Dickens, o.g.	22,017
Jan 11	Arsenal	(R) W	1-0	Rosenior	44,124
Jan 28	Swindon Town	(Rd 4) D	0-0		18,627
Feb 1	SWINDON TOWN	(R) W	1-0	Rosenior	24,723
Feb 18	Charlton Athletic	(Rd 5) W	1-0	Slater	18,785
Mar 18	NORWICH CITY	(QF) D	0-0		29,119
Mar 22	Norwich City	(QF) L	1-3	Ince	25,785

Littlewoods Cup

Sep 27	Sunderland	(Rd 2 FL) W	3-0	Kelly 2, Rosenior	13,691
Oct 12	SUNDERLAND	(Rd 2 SL) W	2-1	Kelly, Dickens	10,558
Nov 1	DERBY COUNTY	(Rd 3) W	5-0	Martin 2, Stewart (pen), Rosenior, Keen	14,226
Nov 30	LIVERPOOL	(Rd 4) W	4-1	Ince 2, o.g., Gale	26,971
Jan 18	ASTON VILLA	(QF) W	2-1	Ince, Kelly	30,110
Feb 12	LUTON TOWN	(SF FL) L	0-3		24,602
Mar 1	Luton Town	(SF SL) L	0-2		12,020

League & Cup Appearances (substitute)

PLAYER	LEAGUE	CUP COMPETITION		TOTAL
		FA CUP	LITTLEWOODS	
Brady	21 (1)	7	4 (1)	32 (2)
Devonshire	14 (6)	7	4	25 (6)
Dickens	34 (3)	5 (2)	6	45 (5)
Dicks	34	6	7	47
Gale	31	5	6	42
Hilton	9 (2)	0 (1)	2	11 (3)
Ince	32 (1)	7	7	46 (1)
Keen	16 (8)	0 (5)	1 (1)	17 (9)
Kelly	21 (4)	6	6 (1)	33 (5)
Martin	27	5	5	37
McAlister	2			2
McAvennie	8 (1)			8 (1)
McKnight	23	4	6	33
McQueen	0 (2)			0 (2)
Parkes	13	3	1	17
Parris	23 (4)	1	3	27 (4)
Potts	23 (5)	7	5 (1)	35 (6)
Robson	6		1	7
Rosenior	26 (2)	4	5	35 (2)
Slater	16 (2)	3	1	20 (2)
Stewart	5 (1)	2	1	8 (1)
Strodder	4 (3)	2 (2)	1	7 (5)
Ward	30	3	5 (1)	38 (1)

Goalscorers

PLAYER	LEAGUE	CUP COMPETITION		TOTAL
		FA CUP	LITTLEWOODS	
Rosenior	7	2	2	11
Kelly	6		4	10
Dickens	5	1	1	7
Ince	3	1	3	7
Keen	3		1	4
Brady	3			3
Martin	1		2	3
Stewart	2		1	3
Dicks	2			2
Slater	1	1		2
Ward	2			2
Gale			1	1
Parris	1			1
Opps' o.gs.	1	1	1	3

Fact File

Tony Cottee was signed by Everton for a then British record of £2,200,000.

MANAGER: John Lyall
CAPTAIN: Alvin Martin
TOP SCORER: Leroy Ronsenior
BIGGEST WIN: November 1, 1988 5-0 v Derby County, Littlewoods Cup Round 3
HIGHEST ATTENDANCE: January 11, 1989 44,124 v Arsenal, won 1-0, FA Cup Round 3
MAJOR TRANSFERS IN: Allen McKnight and Frank McAvennie from Celtic, David Kelly from Walsall
MAJOR TRANSFERS OUT: Tony Cottee to Everton

Final Division 1 Table

		P	W	D	L	F	A	Pts
1	Arsenal	38	22	10	6	73	36	76
2	Liverpool	38	22	10	6	65	28	76
3	Nottingham F	38	17	13	8	64	43	64
4	Norwich C	38	17	11	10	48	45	62
5	Derby Co	38	17	7	14	40	38	58
6	Tottenham H	38	15	12	11	60	46	57
7	Coventry C	38	14	13	11	47	42	55
8	Everton	38	14	12	12	50	45	54
9	QPR	38	14	11	13	43	37	53
10	Millwall	38	14	11	13	47	52	53
11	Manchester U	38	13	12	13	45	35	51
12	Wimbledon	38	14	9	15	50	46	51
13	Southampton	38	10	15	13	52	66	45
14	Charlton Ath	38	10	12	16	44	58	42
15	Sheffield W	38	10	12	16	34	51	42
16	Luton T	38	10	11	17	42	52	41
17	Aston Villa	38	9	13	16	45	56	40
18	Middlesbrough	38	9	12	17	44	61	39
19	West Ham U	38	10	8	20	37	62	38
20	Newcastle U	38	7	10	21	32	63	31

Season 1989-90

Barclays League Division 2

DATE	OPPONENTS	SCORE	GOALSCORERS	ATTENDANCE
Aug 19	Stoke City	D 1-1	Keen	16,058
Aug 23	BRADFORD CITY	W 2-0	Slater 2	19,914
Aug 26	PLYMOUTH ARGYLE	W 3-2	Kelly, Allen, Keen	20,231
Sep 2	Hull City	D 1-1	Ward	9,235
Sep 9	SWINDON TOWN	D 1-1	Allen	21,469
Sep 16	Brighton & Hove Albion	L 0-3		12,689
Sep 23	WATFORD	W 1-0	Dicks (pen)	20,728
Sep 26	Portsmouth	W 1-0	Rosenior	12,632
Sep 30	WEST BROMWICH ALBION	L 2-3	Dolan, Parris	19,842
Oct 7	LEEDS UNITED	L 0-1		23,539
Oct 14	Sheffield United	W 2-0	Ward 2 (1 pen)	20,822
Oct 18	SUNDERLAND	W 5-0	Allen, Slater, Keen, Dolan 2	20,901
Oct 21	Port Vale	D 2-2	Keen, Slater	8,899
Oct 28	OXFORD UNITED	W 3-2	Parris, Slater, Dicks	19,177
Nov 1	Bournemouth	D 1-1	Strodder	9,979
Nov 4	Wolverhampton W	L 0-1		22,231
Nov 11	NEWCASTLE UNITED	D 0-0		25,892
Nov 18	MIDDLESBROUGH	W 2-0	Slater, Dicks (pen)	18,720
Nov 25	Blackburn Rovers	L 4-5	Brady, Dicks (pen), Ward, Slater	10,215
Dec 2	STOKE CITY	D 0-0		17,704
Dec 9	Bradford City	L 1-2	Ward	9,257
Dec 16	OLDHAM ATHLETIC	L 0-2		14,960
Dec 26	Ipswich Town	L 0-1		24,365
Dec 30	Leicester City	L 0-1		16,925
Jan 1	BARNSLEY	W 4-2	Allen, Keen 2, Dicks (pen)	18,391
Jan 13	Plymouth Argyle	D 1-1	Quinn	11,671
Jan 20	HULL CITY	L 1-2	Morley	16,847
Feb 10	BRIGHTON & HOVE ALBION	W 3-1	Quinn 2, Dicks	19,101
Feb 18	Swindon Town	D 2-2	Quinn 2	16,105
Feb 24	BLACKBURN ROVERS	D 1-1	Quinn	20,054
Mar 3	Middlesbrough	W 1-0	Allen	23,617
Mar 10	PORTSMOUTH	W 2-1	Allen, Dicks (pen)	20,961
Mar 13	Watford	W 1-0	Morley	15,683
Mar 17	Leeds United	L 2-3	Morley, o.g.	32,536
Mar 21	SHEFFIELD UNITED	W 5-0	Morley, Quinn 3 (1 pen), Allen	21,629
Mar 24	Sunderland	L 3-4	Quinn 2, Morley	13,896
Mar 31	PORT VALE	D 2-2	Morley, Gale	20,507
Apr 4	West Bromwich Albion	W 3-1	Quinn, Bishop, Keen	11,556
Apr 7	Oxford United	W 2-0	Morley, Quinn	8,371
Apr 11	BOURNEMOUTH	W 4-1	o.g., Bishop, Dicks (pen)	20,202
Apr 14	Barnsley	D 1-1	Morley	10,344
Apr 17	IPSWICH TOWN	W 2-0	Allen, Keen	25,178
Apr 21	Oldham Athletic	L 0-3		12,190
Apr 28	Newcastle United	L 1-2	Dicks (pen)	31,496
May 2	LEICESTER CITY	W 3-1	Rosenior, Keen, Morley	17,939
May 5	WOLVERHAMPTON W	W 4-0	Keen, Morley, Robson, Brady	22,509

FA Cup

Jan 6	Torquay United	(Rd 3)	L 0-1		5,342

Littlewoods Cup

Sep 19	Birmingham City	(Rd 2 FL)	W 2-1	Allen, Slater	10,987
Oct 4	BIRMINGHAM CITY	(Rd 2 SL)	D 1-1	Dicks	12,187
Oct 25	Aston Villa	(Rd 3)	D 0-0		20,989
Nov 8	ASTON VILLA	(R)	W 1-0	Dicks	23,833
Nov 22	WIMBLEDON	(Rd 4)	W 1-0	Allen	24,746
Jan 17	DERBY COUNTY	(QF)	D 1-1	Dicks	25,035
Jan 24	Derby County	(R)	D 0-0*		22,510
Jan 31	DERBY COUNTY	(2nd R)	W 2-1	Slater, Keen	25,166
Feb 14	Oldham Athletic	(SF FL)	L 0-6		19,263
Mar 7	OLDHAM ATHLETIC	(SF SL)	W 3-0	Martin, Dicks (pen), Kelly	15,431

*After extra time.

Fact File

Martin Allen made a goalscoring start to his West Ham career against Plymouth Argyle.

MANAGER: Lou Macari/Billy Bonds **CAPTAIN:** Julian Dicks

TOP SCORERS: Julian Dicks and Jimmy Quinn

BIGGEST WIN: March 21, 1990 5-0 v Sheffield United, Division 2

HIGHEST ATTENDANCE: March 17, 1990 32,536 v Leeds United, lost 2-3, Division 2

League & Cup Appearances (substitute)

PLAYER	LEAGUE	CUP COMPETITION		TOTAL
		FA CUP	LITTLEWOODS	
Allen	39	1	6	46
Bishop	13 (4)	1		14 (4)
Brady	25 (8)		8 (2)	33 (10)
Devonshire	3 (4)		0 (3)	3 (7)
Dicks	40	1	9	50
Dolan	8 (2)		4	12 (2)
Fashnau	2		0 (1)	2 (1)
Foster	20 (2)			20 (2)
Gale	36	1	7	44
Ince	1			1
Keen	43 (1)	1	10	54 (1)
Kelly D	8 (8)		5 (2)	13 (10)
Kelly P	0 (1)			0 (1)
Martin	31	1	10	42
McAvennie	1 (4)			1 (4)
McQueen	5 (2)		1 (2)	6 (4)
Miklosko	18		1	19
Milne			0 (1)	0 (1)
Morley	18 (1)	1		19 (1)
Parkes	22	1	9	32
Parris	35 (3)	1	9	45 (3)
Potts	30 (2)	1	8	39 (2)
Quinn	18 (3)	1		19 (3)
Robson	7		3	10
Rosenior	4 (1)	0 (1)	2	6 (2)
Slater	40		9 (1)	49 (1)
Strodder	16		5	21
Suckling	6			6
Ward	17 (2)		4	21 (2)

Goalscorers

PLAYER	LEAGUE	CUP COMPETITION		TOTAL
		FA CUP	LITTLEWOODS	
Dicks	9		4	13
Quinn	13			13
Allen	9		2	11
Keen	10		1	11
Morley	10			10
Slater	7		2	9
Ward	5			5
Dolan	3			3
Bishop	2			2
Brady	2			2
Kelly D	1		1	2
Parris	2			2
Rosenior	2			2
Gale	1			1
Martin			1	1
Robson	1			1
Strodder	1			1
Opps' o.gs.	2			2

Final Division 2 Table

		P	W	D	L	F	A	Pts
1	Leeds U	46	24	13	9	79	52	85
2	Sheffield U	46	24	13	9	78	58	85
3	Newcastle U	46	22	14	10	80	55	80
4	Swindon T	46	20	14	12	79	59	74
5	Blackburn R	46	19	17	10	74	59	74
6	Sunderland	46	20	14	12	70	64	74
7	West Ham U	46	20	12	14	80	57	72
8	Oldham Ath	46	19	14	13	70	57	71
9	Ipswich T	46	19	12	15	67	66	69
10	Wolverhampton W	46	18	13	15	67	60	67
11	Port Vale	46	15	16	15	62	57	61
12	Portsmouth	46	15	16	15	62	65	61
13	Leicester C	46	15	14	17	67	79	59
14	Hull C	46	14	16	16	58	65	58
15	Watford	46	14	15	17	58	60	57
16	Plymouth Arg	46	14	13	19	58	63	55
17	Oxford U	46	15	9	22	57	66	54
18	Brighton & HA	46	15	9	22	56	72	54
19	Barnsley	46	13	15	18	49	71	54
20	WBA	46	12	15	19	67	71	51
21	Middlesbrough	46	13	11	22	52	63	50
22	Bournemouth	46	12	12	22	57	76	48
23	Bradford C	46	9	14	23	44	68	41
24	Stoke C	46	6	19	21	35	63	37

Season 1990-91

Barclays League Division 2

DATE	OPPONENTS	SCORE	GOALSCORERS	ATTENDANCE
Aug 25	Middlesbrough	D 0-0		20,680
Aug 29	PORTSMOUTH	D 1-1	McAvennie	20,835
Sep 1	WATFORD	W 1-0	Dicks (pen)	19,872
Sep 8	Leicester City	W 2-1	o.g., Morley	14,605
Sep 15	WOLVERHAMPTON W	D 1-1	Martin	23,241
Sep 19	IPSWICH TOWN	W 3-1	Bishop, Quinn, Morley	18,764
Sep 22	Newcastle United	D 1-1	Morley	25,462
Sep 29	Sheffield Wednesday	D 1-1	Dicks	28,786
Oct 3	OXFORD UNITED	W 2-0	Foster, Morley	18,125
Oct 6	HULL CITY	W 7-1	Quinn 2, Potts, Morley Dicks 2 (1 pen), Parris,	19,472
Oct 13	Bristol City	D 1-1	McAvennie	16,838
Oct 20	Swindon Town	W 1-0	McAvennie	13,658
Oct 24	BLACKBURN ROVERS	W 1-0	Bishop	20,003
Oct 27	CHARLTON ATHLETIC	W 2-1	Allen 2	24,019
Nov 3	Notts County	W 1-0	Morley	10,871
Nov 10	Millwall	D 1-1	McAvennie	20,591
Nov 17	BRIGHTON & HOVE ALBION	W 2-1	Slater, Foster	23,082
Nov 24	Plymouth Argyle	W 1-0	McAvennie	11,490
Dec 1	WEST BROMWICH ALBION	W 3-1	Parris, Morley, McAvennie	24,753
Dec 8	Portsmouth	W 1-0	Morley	12,045
Dec 15	MIDDLESBROUGH	D 0-0		23,705
Dec 22	Barnsley	L 0-1		10,348
Dec 26	OLDHAM ATHLETIC	W 2-0	Morley, Slater	24,950
Dec 29	PORT VALE	D 0-0		23,603
Jan 1	Bristol Rovers	W 1-0	Quinn	7,932
Jan 12	Watford	W 1-0	Morley	17,172
Jan 19	LEICESTER CITY	W 1-0	Parris	21,652
Feb 2	Wolverhampton W	L 1-2	McAvennie	19,454
Feb 24	MILLWALL	W 3-1	McAvennie 2, Morley	20,503
Mar 2	West Bromwich Albion	D 0-0		16,089
Mar 5	PLYMOUTH ARGYLE	D 2-2	o.g., Breacker	18,933
Mar 13	Oxford United	L 1-2	Quinn	8,225
Mar 16	SHEFFIELD WEDNESDAY	L 1-3	Quinn	26,182
Mar 20	BRISTOL CITY	W 1-0	Gale	22,951
Mar 23	Hull City	D 0-0		9,558
Mar 29	Oldham Athletic	D 1-1	Bishop (pen)	16,932
Apr 1	BARNSLEY	W 3-2	McAvennie, Dowie, Foster	24,607
Apr 6	Port Vale	W 1-0	Bishop	9,658
Apr 10	Brighton & Hove Albion	L 0-1		11,904
Apr 17	Ipswich Town	W 1-0	Morley	20,290
Apr 20	SWINDON TOWN	W 2-0	Parris, Dowie	25,944
Apr 24	NEWCASTLE UNITED	D 1-1	Dowie	24,195
Apr 27	Blackburn Rovers	L 1-3	Dowie	10,808
May 4	Charlton Athletic	D 1-1	Allen	16,137
May 8	BRISTOL ROVERS	W 1-0	Slater	23,054
May 11	NOTTS COUNTY	L 1-2	Parris	26,551

FA Cup

Jan 5	Aldershot	(Rd 3) D 0-0*		22,929
Jan 16	ALDERSHOT	(R) W 6-1	Morley 2, Slater, Parris, Bishop, Quinn	21,484
Jan 26	Luton Town	(Rd 4) D 1-1	Parris	12,087
Jan 30	LUTON TOWN	(R) W 5-0	Parris, Bishop, McAvennie, Morley 2	25,659
Feb 16	CREWE ALEXANDRA	(Rd 5) W 1-0	Quinn	25,298
Mar 11	EVERTON	(QF) W 2-1	Foster, Slater	28,161
Apr 14	Nottingham Forest	(SF) L 0-4**		40,041

*Played at Upton Park. **Played at Villa Park.

Rumbelows Cup

Sep 26	STOKE CITY	(Rd 2 FL) W 3-0	Dicks (pen), Keen, Quinn	15,870
Oct 10	Stoke City	(Rd 2 SL) W 2-1	Allen 2	8,411
Oct 31	Oxford United	(Rd 3) L 1-2	Morley	7,528

MANAGER: Billy Bonds

CAPTAIN: Julian Dicks/Ian Bishop

TOP SCORER: Trevor Morley

BIGGEST WIN: October 6, 1990 7-1 v Hull City, Division 2

HIGHEST ATTENDANCE: April 14, 1991 40,041 v Nottingham Forest, lost 0-4, FA Cup semi-final

MAJOR TRANSFERS IN: Chris Hughton from Tottenham Hotspur, Tim Breacker and Iain Dowie from Luton Town

MAJOR TRANSFERS OUT: Gary Strodder to West Bromwich Albion, Stewart Robson to Coventry City

League & Cup Appearances (substitute)

PLAYER	LEAGUE	CUP COMPETITION FA CUP	RUMBELOWS	TOTAL
Allen	28 (12)	2	3	33 (12)
Bishop	40	5 (1)	3	48 (1)
Breacker	23 (1)	6		29 (1)
Carr	1 (2)			1 (2)
Clarke	0 (1)			0 (1)
Dicks	13		2	15
Dowie	12			12
Foster	36	3	3	42
Gale	23 (1)	7	0 (1)	30 (2)
Hughton	32	7		39
Kevin	36 (4)	6 (1)	3	45 (5)
Livett	1	0 (1)		1 (1)
Martin	20		3	23
McAvennie	24 (10)	3 (1)	0 (1)	27 (12)
Miklosko	46	7	3	56
Morley	38	6	3	47
Parris	37 (7)	7	2 (1)	46 (8)
Potts	36 (1)	7	2	45 (1)
Quinn	16 (10)	3 (2)	3	22 (12)
Robson	0 (1)	1		1 (1)
Rosenior	0 (2)			0 (2)
Rush	2 (3)		1	3 (3)
Slater	37 (3)	7	2	46 (3)
Stewart	5			5

Goalscorers

PLAYER	LEAGUE	CUP COMPETITION FA CUP	RUMBELOWS	TOTAL
Morley	12	4	1	17
McAvennie	10	1		11
Quinn	6	2	1	9
Parris	5	3		8
Bishop	4	2		6
Allan	3		2	5
Dicks	4		1	5
Slater	3	2		5
Dowie	4			4
Foster	3	1		4
Breacker	1			1
Gale	1			1
Kevin			1	1
Potts	1			1
Martin	1			1
Opps' o.gs.	2			2

Fact File

West Ham were denied the championship by an injury-time penalty winner for Oldham against Sheffield Wednesday in the last game of the season.

Final Division 2 Table

	P	W	D	L	F	A	PTS
1 Oldham Ath	46	25	13	8	83	53	88
2 West Ham U	46	24	15	7	60	34	87
3 Sheffield W	46	22	16	7	80	51	82
4 Notts Co	46	23	11	12	76	55	80
5 Millwall	46	20	13	13	70	51	73
6 Brighton & HA	46	21	7	18	63	69	70
7 Middlesbrough	46	20	9	17	66	47	69
8 Barnsley	46	19	12	15	63	48	69
9 Bristol C	46	20	7	19	68	71	67
10 Oxford U	46	14	19	13	69	66	61
11 Newcastle U	46	14	17	15	49	56	59
12 Wolverhampton W	46	13	19	14	63	63	58
13 Bristol R	46	15	13	18	56	59	58
14 Ipswich T	46	13	18	15	60	68	57
15 Port Vale	46	15	12	19	56	64	57
16 Charlton Ath	46	13	17	16	57	61	56
17 Portsmouth	46	14	11	21	58	70	53
18 Plymouth Arg	46	12	17	17	54	68	53
19 Blackburn R	46	14	10	22	51	66	52
20 Watford	46	12	15	19	45	59	51
21 Swindon T	46	12	14	20	65	73	50
22 Leicester C	46	14	8	24	60	83	50
23 WBA	46	10	18	18	52	61	48
24 Hull C	46	10	15	21	57	85	45

Season 1991-92

Barclays League Division 1

DATE	OPPONENTS	SCORE	GOALSCORERS	ATTENDANCE
Aug 17	LUTON TOWN	D 0-0		25,079
Aug 20	Sheffield United	D 1-1	Small	21,463
Aug 24	Wimbledon	L 0-2		10,801
Aug 28	ASTON VILLA	W 3-1	Small, Rosenior, Brown	23,644
Aug 31	NOTTS COUNTY	L 0-2		20,093
Sep 4	Queens Park Rangers	D 0-0		16,616
Sep 7	CHELSEA	D 1-1	Small	18,875
Sep 14	Norwich City	L 1-2	Small	15,348
Sep 17	Crystal Palace	W 3-2	Thomas, Morley, Small	21,363
Sep 21	MANCHESTER CITY	L 1-2	Brown	25,558
Sep 28	Nottingham Forest	D 2-2	Small 2	25,613
Oct 5	COVENTRY CITY	L 0-1		21,817
Oct 19	Oldham Athletic	D 2-2	Small, McAvennie	14,365
Oct 26	TOTTENHAM HOTSPUR	W 2-1	Small, Thomas	23,946
Nov 2	Arsenal	W 1-0	Small	33,539
Nov 17	LIVERPOOL	D 0-0		23,569
Nov 23	Manchester United	L 1-2	McAvennie	47,185
Nov 31	SHEFFIELD WEDNESDAY	L 1-2	Breacker	24,116
Dec 7	Everton	L 0-4		21,563
Dec 21	SHEFFIELD UNITED	D 1-1	Dicks (pen)	19,287
Dec 26	Aston Villa	L 1-3	McAvennie	31,959
Dec 28	Notts County	L 0-3		11,163
Jan 1	LEEDS UNITED	L 1-3	Dicks (pen)	21,766
Jan 11	WIMBLEDON	D 1-1	Morley	18,485
Jan 18	Luton Town	W 1-0	Small	11,088
Feb 1	OLDHAM ATHLETIC	W 1-0	Thomas	19,012
Feb 22	Sheffield Wednesday	L 1-2	Small	24,150
Feb 29	EVERTON	L 0-2		20,976
Mar 3	Southampton	L 0-1		14,548
Mar 11	Liverpool	L 0-1		30,821
Mar 14	ARSENAL	L 0-2		22,640
Mar 21	QUEENS PARK RANGERS	D 2-2	Small, Breacker	20,401
Mar 28	Leeds United	D 0-0		31,101
Apr 1	Tottenham Hotspur	L 0-3		31,809
Apr 4	Chelsea	L 1-2	Allen C	20,684
Apr 11	NORWICH CITY	W 4-0	Rush 2, Dicks (pen), Bishop	16,896
Apr 14	SOUTHAMPTON	L 0-1		18,298
Apr 18	Manchester City	L 0-2		25,601
Apr 20	CRYSTAL PALACE	L 0-2		17,710
Apr 22	MANCHESTER UNITED	W 1-0	Brown	24,197
Apr 25	Coventry City	L 0-1		15,398
May 2	NOTTINGHAM FOREST	W 3-0	McAvennie 3	20,629

FA Cup

Jan 4	Farnborough	(Rd 3) D 1-1*	Dicks	23,449
Jan 14	FARNBOROUGH	(R) W 1-0	Morley	23,869
Jan 25	WREXHAM	(Rd 4) D 2-2	Dicks, Morley	24,712
Feb 4	Wrexham	(R) W 1-0	Foster	17,995
Feb 15	Sunderland	(Rd 5) D 1-1	Small	25,475
Feb 26	SUNDERLAND	(R) L 2-3	Allen M 2	25,830

Rumbelows Cup

Sep 24	Bradford City	(Rd 2 FL) D 1-1	Small	7,034
Oct 9	BRADFORD CITY	(Rd 2 SL) W 4-0	Keen, Morley, Parris, Small	17,232
Oct 29	Sheffield United	(Rd 3) W 2-0	McAvennie, Small (pen)	11,144
Dec 4	Norwich City	(Rd 4) L 1-2	Small	16,325

*Played at Upton Park.

MANAGER: Billy Bonds

CAPTAIN: Ian Bishop/Julian Dicks

TOP SCORER: Mike Small

BIGGEST WIN: April 11, 1992 4-0 v Norwich City, Division 1; October 9, 1991 4-0 v Bradford City, Rumbelows Cup, Round 2 Second Leg

HIGHEST ATTENDANCE: November 23, 1991 47,185 v Manchester United, lost 1-2, Division 1

MAJOR TRANSFERS IN: Mitchell Thomas from Tottenham Hotspur, Mike Small from Brighton, Kenny Brown from Plymouth Argyle, Clive Allen from Chelsea

MAJOR TRANSFERS OUT: Jimmy Quinn to Bournemouth, Iain Dowie to Southampton

League & Cup Appearances (substitute)

PLAYER	LEAGUE	CUP COMPETITION		TOTAL
		FA CUP	RUMBELOWS	
Allen C	4			4
Allen M	14 (5)	2	1 (1)	17 (6)
Atteveld	1	2		3
Bishop	41	3	4	48
Breacker	33 (1)	6	4	43 (1)
Brown	25 (2)	4	1	30 (2)
Clarke	0 (1)			0 (1)
Dicks	23	6		29
Foster	24	5	2	31
Gale	24 (1)	2	3 (1)	29 (2)
Hughton	0 (1)			0 (1)
Keen	20 (9)	5	2	27 (9)
Martin A	7			7
Martin D	1 (1)	0 (1)		1 (2)
McAvennie	16 (4)	4	2 (1)	22 (5)
Miklosko	36	3	4	43
Morley	13 (11)	2 (3)	2	17 (14)
Parks	6			39
Parris	20 (1)		4	24 (1)
Potts	34	5	3	42
Rosenior	5 (4)			5 (4)
Rush	3 (7)			3 (7)
Slater	41	6	4	51
Small	37 (3)	4 (1)	4	45 (4)
Thomas	34 (1)	4	4	42 (1)

Goalscorers

PLAYER	LEAGUE	CUP COMPETITION		TOTAL
		FA CUP	RUMBELOWS	
Small	13	1	4	18
McAvennie	6		1	7
Dicks	3	2		5
Morley	2	2	1	5
Brown	3			3
Thomas	3			3
Breacker	2			2
Rush	2			2
Allen M		2		2
Allen C	1			1
Bishop	1			1
Foster		1		1
Keen			1	1
Parks			1	1
Rosenior	1			1

Fact File

Defeat at Crystal Palace in April sent West Ham down to the new Division One.

Final Division 1 Table

		P	W	D	L	F	A	Pts
1	Leeds U	42	22	16	4	74	37	82
2	Manchester U	42	21	15	6	63	33	78
3	Sheffield W	42	21	12	9	62	49	75
4	Arsenal	42	19	15	8	81	46	72
5	Manchester C	42	20	10	12	61	48	70
6	Liverpool	42	16	16	10	47	40	64
7	Aston Villa	42	17	9	16	48	44	60
8	Nottingham F	42	16	11	15	60	58	59
9	Sheffield U	42	16	9	17	65	63	57
10	Crystal Palace	42	14	15	13	53	61	57
11	QPR	42	12	18	12	48	47	54
12	Everton	42	13	14	15	52	51	53
13	Wimbledon	42	13	14	15	53	53	53
14	Chelsea	42	13	14	15	50	60	53
15	Tottenham H	42	15	7	20	58	63	52
16	Southampton	42	14	10	18	39	55	52
17	Oldham Ath	42	14	9	19	63	67	51
18	Norwich C	42	11	12	19	47	63	45
19	Coventry C	42	11	11	20	35	44	44
20	Luton T	42	10	12	20	38	71	42
21	Notts Co	42	10	10	22	40	62	40
22	West Ham U	42	9	11	22	37	59	38

Season 1992-93

Football League Division 1 (New)

DATE	OPPONENTS	SCORE	GOALSCORERS	ATTENDANCE
Aug 16	Barnsley	W 1-0	Allen C	6,761
Aug 22	CHARLTON ATHLETIC	L 0-1		17,054
Aug 29	Newcastle United	L 0-2		29,855
Sep 5	WATFORD	W 2-1	Allen M, Allen C	11,921
Sep 12	Peterborough	W 3-1	Morley, Allen M, Keen	10,657
Sep 15	Bristol City	W 5-1	Robson, Allen C 2, Morley 2	14,130
Sep 20	DERBY COUNTY	D 1-1	Morley	11,493
Sep 27	Portsmouth	W 1-0	Allen C	12,158
Oct 4	Wolverhampton W	D 0-0		14,391
Oct 11	SUNDERLAND	W 6-0	Keen, Morley, Allen M, Martin, Robson 2	10,326
Oct 17	Bristol Rovers	W 4-0	Morley, Dicks (pen), Keen, Allen C	6,189
Oct 24	SWINDON TOWN	L 0-1		17,842
Oct 31	Cambridge United	L 1-2	Morley	7,214
Nov 3	Grimsby Town	D 1-1	Morley	9,119
Nov 7	NOTTS COUNTY	W 2-0	Allen C, Morley	12,345
Nov 15	Millwall	L 1-2	Robson	12,445
Nov 21	OXFORD UNITED	W 5-3	Allen C, Breacker, Morley, Dicks 2	11,842
Nov 28	BIRMINGHAM CITY	W 3-1	C Allen 2, Morley	15,004
Dec 4	Tranmere Rovers	L 2-5	Morley, Allen C	11,782
Dec 12	SOUTHEND UNITED	W 2-0	Morley, Allen C	15,739
Dec 20	Brentford	D 0-0		11,912
Dec 26	Charlton Athletic	D 1-1	Dicks	8,337
Dec 28	LUTON TOWN	D 2-2	Dicks (pen), Breacker	18,786
Jan 10	Derby County	W 2-0	Robson, Morley	13,737
Jan 16	PORTSMOUTH	W 2-0	Morley, Foster	18,127
Jan 27	BRISTOL CITY	W 2-0	Morley, Robson	12,118
Jan 30	Leicester City	W 2-1	Robson, Gale	18,838
Feb 6	BARNSLEY	D 1-1	Jones	14,101
Frb 9	PETERBOROUGH	W 2-1	Butler, Jones	12,537
Feb 13	Watford	W 2-1	Robson, Keen	13,115
Feb 21	NEWCASTLE UNITED	D 0-0		24,159
Feb 27	Sunderland	D 0-0		19,068
Mar 6	WOLVERHAMPTON W	W 3-1	Morley, Dicks (pen), Holmes	24,679
Mar 9	GRIMSBY TOWN	W 2-1	Dicks 2	13,170
Mar 13	Notts County	L 0-1		10,272
Mar 20	TRANMERE ROVERS	W 2-0	Dicks 2 (2 pen)	16,369
Mar 23	Oxford United	L 0-1		9,506
Mar 28	MILLWALL	D 2-2	Keen, Morley	15,723
Apr 3	Birmingham City	W 2-1	Brown, Bishop	19,053
Apr 7	Southend United	L 0-1		12,813
Apr 11	LEICESTER CITY	W 3-0	Speedie 2, Keen	13,951
Apr 13	Luton Town	L 0-2		10,959
Apr 17	BRENTFORD	W 4-0	Butler, Keen, Morley, M Allen	16,522
Apr 24	BRISTOL ROVERS	W 2-1	Dicks (pen), Speedie	16,682
May 2	Swindon Town	W 3-1	Morley, Allen C, Brown	17,004
May 8	CAMBRIDGE UNITED	W 2-0	Speedie, Allen C	27,399

FA Cup

Jan 2	West Bromwich Albion	(Rd 3	W 2-0	Allen C, Robson	25,896
Jan 24	Barnsley	(Rd 4)	L 1-4	Morley (pen)	13,716

Coca-Cola Cup

Sep 23	CREWE ALEXANDRA	(Rd 2 FL)	D 0-0		6,981
Oct 7	Crewe Alexandra	(Rd 2 SL)	L 0-2		5,427

MANAGER: Billy Bonds

CAPTAIN: Julian Dicks

TOP SCORER: Trevor Morley

BIGGEST WIN: October 11, 1992 6-0 v Sunderland, Division 1

HIGHEST ATTENDANCE: August 29, 1992 29,855 v Newcastle United, lost 0-2, Division 1

MAJOR TRANSFERS IN: Mark Robson from Tottenham Hotspur, Peter Butler from Southend United, Matty Holmes from Bournemouth, Steve Jones from Billericay Town

MAJOR TRANSFERS OUT: Stuart Slater to Celtic, George Parris to Birmingham City

League & Cup Appearances (substitute)

PLAYER	LEAGUE	CUP COMPETITION		TOTAL
		FA CUP	COCA-COLA	
Allen C	25 (2)	1	2	28 (2)
Allen M	33 (1)	2	2	37 (1)
Bishop	15 (7)			15 (7)
Breacker	39	2	2	43
Brown	13 (2)	1		14 (2)
Bunbury	2 (2)			2 (2)
Butler	39	2	2	43
Clarke	0 (1)			0 (1)
Dicks	34	1	1	36
Foster	3 (3)	1		4 (3)
Gale	21 (2)			21 (2)
Holmes	6 (12)	1		7 (12)
Jones	4 (2)			4 (2)
Keen	46	2	2	50
Martin	23	1	2	26
Miklosko	46	2	2	50
Morley	41	2	2	45
Parris	10 (6)			10 (6)
Potts	46	2	2	50
Robson	41 (3)	2	2	45 (3)
Small	5 (4)		0 (1)	5 (5)
Speedie	11			11
Thomas	3		1	4

Goalscorers

PLAYER	LEAGUE	CUP COMPETITION		TOTAL
		FA CUP	COCA-COLA	
Morley	20	1		21
Allen C	14	1		15
Dicks	11			11
Robson	8	1		9
Keen	7			7
Allen M	4			4
Speedie	4			4
Breacker	2			2
Brown	2			2
Butler	2			2
Jones	2			2
Bishop	1			1
Foster	1			1
Gale	1			1
Martin	1			1

Fact File

Julian Dicks was sent off three times this season at Newcastle, Wolves and Derby.

Final Division 1 Table (New)

		P	W	D	L	F	A	PTS
1	NEWCASTLE U	46	29	9	8	92	38	96
2	WEST HAM U	46	26	10	10	81	41	88
3	PORTSMOUTH	46	26	10	10	80	46	88
4	TRANMERE R	46	23	10	13	72	56	79
5	SWINDON T	46	21	13	12	74	59	76
6	LEICESTER C	46	22	10	14	71	64	76
7	MILLWALL	46	18	16	12	65	53	70
8	DERBY CO	46	19	9	18	68	57	66
9	GRIMSBY T	46	19	7	20	58	57	64
10	PETERBOROUGH U	46	16	14	16	55	63	62
11	WOLVERHAMPTON W	46	16	13	17	57	56	61
12	CHARLTON ATH	46	16	13	17	49	46	61
13	BARNSLEY	46	17	9	20	56	60	60
14	OXFORD U	46	14	14	18	53	56	56
15	BRISTOL C	46	14	14	18	49	67	56
16	WATFORD	46	14	13	19	57	71	55
17	NOTTS CO	46	12	16	18	55	70	52
18	SOUTHEND U	46	13	13	20	54	64	52
19	BIRMINGHAM C	46	13	12	21	50	72	51
20	LUTON T	46	10	21	15	48	62	51
21	SUNDERLAND	46	13	11	22	50	64	50
22	BRENTFORD	46	13	10	23	52	71	49
23	CAMBRIDGE U	46	11	16	19	48	69	49
24	BRISTOL R	46	10	11	25	55	87	41

Season 1993-94

Premier League

DATE	OPPONENTS	SCORE	GOALSCORERS	ATTENDANCE
Aug 14	WIMBLEDON	L 0-2		20,369
Aug 17	Leeds United	L 0-1		34,588
Aug 21	Coventry City	D 1-1	Gordon	12,864
Aug 25	SHEFFIELD WEDNESDAY	W 2-0	Allen C 2	19,441
Aug 28	QUEENS PARK RANGERS	L 0-4		18,084
Sep 1	Manchester United	L 0-3		44,613
Sep 11	SWINDON TOWN	D 0-0		15,777
Sep 18	Blackburn Rovers	W 2-0	Chapman, Morley	14,437
Sep 25	Newcastle United	L 0-2		34,179
Oct 2	CHELSEA	W 1-0	Morley	18,917
Oct 16	ASTON VILLA	D 0-0		20,416
Oct 23	Norwich City	D 0-0		20,175
Nov 1	MANCHESTER CITY	W 3-1	Burrows, Chapman, Holmes	16,605
Nov 6	Liverpool	L 0-2		42,254
Nov 20	OLDHAM ATHLETIC	W 2-0	Martin, Morley	17,211
Nov 24	ARSENAL	D 0-0		20,279
Nov 29	Southampton	W 2-0	Morley, Chapman	13,258
Dec 4	Wimbledon	W 2-1	Chapman 2	10,903
Dec 8	LEEDS UNITED	L 0-1		20,468
Dec 11	COVENTRY CITY	W 3-2	Breacker, Butler, Morley (pen)	17,243
Dec 18	Sheffield Wednesday	L 0-5		26,350
Dec 27	Ipswich Town	D 1-1	Chapman	20,988
Dec 28	TOTTENHAM HOTSPUR	L 1-3	Holmes	20,787
Jan 1	Everton	W 1-0	Breacker	19,602
Jan 3	SHEFFIELD UNITED	D 0-0		20,365
Jan 15	Aston Villa	L 1-3	Allen M	28,869
Jan 24	NORWICH CITY	D 3-3	o.g., Jones, Morley	20,738
Feb 12	Manchester City	D 0-0		29,118
Feb 26	MANCHESTER UNITED	D 2-2	Chapman, Morley	28,832
Mar 5	Swindon Town	D 1-1	Morley	15,929
Mar 19	NEWCASTLE UNITED	L 2-4	Breacker, Martin	23,132
Mar 26	Chelsea	L 0-2		19,545
Mar 28	Sheffield United	L 2-3	Bishop, Holmes	13,646
Apr 2	IPSWICH TOWN	W 2-1	Rush, Morley	18,307
Apr 4	Tottenham Hotspur	W 4-1	Jones, Morley 2 (1 pen), Marsh	31,502
Apr 9	EVERTON	L 0-1		20,243
Apr 16	Oldham Athletic	W 2-1	Allen M, Morley	11,669
Apr 23	LIVERPOOL	L 1-2	Allen M	26,106
Apr 27	BLACKBURN ROVERS	L 1-2	Allen M	22,186
Apr 30	Arsenal	W 2-0	Morley, Allen M	33,700
May 3	Queens Park Rangers	D 0-0		10,850
May 7	SOUTHAMPTON	D 3-3	Williamson, Allen M, o.g.	26,952

FA Cup

Jan 8	WATFORD	(Rd 3)	W 2-1	Allen M, Marsh	19,802
Jan 29	Notts County	(Rd 4)	D 1-1	Jones	14,952
Feb 9	NOTTS COUNTY	(R)	W 1-0*	Chapman	23,373
Feb 19	Kidderminster	(Rd 5)	W 1-0	Chapman	8,000
Mar 14	LUTON TOWN	(QF)	D 0-0		27,331
Mar 23	Luton Town	(R)	L 2-3	Allen M, Bishop	13,166

*After extra time.

Coca-Cola Cup

Sep 22	CHESTERFIELD	(Rd 2 FL)	W 5-1	Morley 2 (1 pen), Chapman 2, Burrows	12,1823
Oct 5	Chesterfield	(Rd 2 SL)	W 2-0	Allen M, Boere	4,890
Oct 27	Nottingham Forest	(Rd 3)	L 1-2	Morley	17,857

MANAGER: Billy Bonds

CAPTAIN: Julian Dicks/Steve Potts

TOP SCORER: Trevor Morley

BIGGEST WIN: September 22, 1993 5-1 v Chesterfield, Coca-Cola Cup, Round 2 First Leg

HIGHEST ATTENDANCE: September 1, 1993 44,613 v Manchester United, lost 0-3, Premier League

MAJOR TRANSFERS IN: Dale Gordon from Rangers, Keith Rowland from Bournemouth, Simon Webster from Charlton Athletic, Mike Marsh and David Burrows from Liverpool, Lee Chapman from Portsmouth

MAJOR TRANSFERS OUT: Kevin Keen to Wolves, Julian Dicks to Liverpool, Clive Allen to Millwall, Mitchell Thomas to Luton Town, Colin Foster to Watford

League & Cup Appearances (substitute)

PLAYER	LEAGUE	CUP COMPETITION		TOTAL
		FA CUP	COCA-COLA	
Allen C	7	1 (2)		8 (2)
Allen M	20 (6)	6	0 (2)	26 (8)
Bishop	36	6	3	45
Boere	0 (4)		0 (1)	0 (5)
Breacker	40	6	2	48
Brown	6 (3)	2 (1)		8 (4)
Burrows	25	3	3	31
Butler	26	1	2	29
Chapman	26 (4)	6	3	35 (4)
Dicks	7			7
Foster	5			5
Gale	31 (1)	1	2	34 (1)
Gordon	8		1	9
Holmes	33 (1)	4	3	40 (1)
Jones	3 (5)	2 (2)		5 (7)
Marquis	(1)			0 (1)
Marsh	33	6	3	42
Martin	6 (1)	3	1	10 (1)
Miklosko	42	6	3	51
Mitchell	(1)			0 (1)
Morley	39 (3)	3 (1)	3	45 (4)
Potts	41	6	3	50
Robson	1 (2)			1 (2)
Rowland	16 (7)	4	1	21 (7)
Rush	9 (1)			9 (1)
Williamson	2 (1)			2 (1)

Goalscorers

PLAYER	LEAGUE	CUP COMPETITION		TOTAL
		FA CUP	COCA-COLA	
Morley	13		3	16
Chapman	7	2	2	11
Allen M	6	2	1	9
Breacker	3			3
Holmes	3			3
Jones	2	1		3
Allen C	2			2
Bishop	1	1		2
Burrows	1		1	2
Marsh	1	1		2
Martin	2			2
Boere			1	1
Butler	1			1
Gordon	1			1
Rush	1			1
Williamson	1			1
Opps' o.gs.	2			2

Fact File

In March the new Bobby Moore Stand was officially opened at a memorial match for Hammers' hero.

Final Premier League Table

		P	W	D	L	F	A	Pts
1	Manchester U	42	27	11	4	80	38	92
2	Blackburn R	42	25	9	8	63	36	84
3	Newcastle U	42	23	8	11	82	41	77
4	Arsenal	42	18	17	7	53	28	71
5	Leeds U	42	18	16	8	65	39	70
6	Wimbledon	42	18	11	13	56	53	65
7	Sheffield W	42	16	16	10	76	54	64
8	Liverpool	42	17	9	16	59	55	60
9	QPR	42	16	12	14	62	61	60
10	Aston Villa	42	15	12	15	46	50	57
11	Coventry C	42	14	14	14	43	45	56
12	Norwich C	42	12	17	13	65	61	53
13	West Ham U	42	13	13	16	47	58	52
14	Chelsea	42	13	12	17	49	53	51
15	Tottenham H	42	11	12	19	54	59	45
16	Manchester C	42	9	18	15	38	49	45
17	Everton	42	12	8	22	42	63	44
18	Southampton	42	12	7	23	49	66	43
19	Ipswich T	42	9	16	17	35	58	43
20	Sheffield U	42	8	18	16	42	60	42
21	Oldham Ath	42	9	13	20	42	68	40
22	Swindon T	42	5	15	22	47	100	30

Season 1994-95

Premier League

DATE	OPPONENTS	SCORE	GOALSCORERS	ATTENDANCE
Aug 20	LEEDS UNITED	D 0-0		18,610
Aug 24	Manchester City	L 0-3		19,150
Aug 27	Norwich City	L 0-1		19,110
Aug 31	NEWCASTLE UNITED	L 1-3	Hutchison (pen)	18,580
Sep 10	Liverpool	D 0-0		30,907
Sep 17	ASTON VILLA	W 1-0	Cottee	18,326
Sep 25	ARSENAL	L 0-2		18,498
Oct 2	Chelsea	W 2-1	Allen, Moncur	18,696
Oct 8	CRYSTAL PALACE	W 1-0	Hutchison	16,959
Oct 15	Manchester United	L 0-1		43,795
Oct 22	SOUTHAMPTON	W 2-0	Allen, Rush	18,853
Oct 29	Tottenham Hotspur	L 1-3	Rush	24,271
Nov 1	Everton	L 0-1		28,338
Nov 5	LEICESTER CITY	W 1-0	Dicks (pen)	18,780
Nov 19	Sheffield Wednesday	L 0-1		25,300
Nov 26	COVENTRY CITY	L 0-1		17,251
Dec 4	Queens Park Rangers	L 1-2	Boere	12,780
Dec 10	Leeds United	D 2-2	Boere 2	28,987
Dec 17	MANCHESTER CITY	W 3-0	Cottee 3	17,286
Dec 26	IPSWICH TOWN	D 1-1	Cottee	20,562
Dec 28	Wimbledon	L 0-1		11,212
Dec 31	NOTTINGHAM FOREST	W 3-1	Cottee, Bishop, Hughes	20,644
Jan 2	Blackburn Rovers	L 2-4	Cottee, Dicks	25,503
Jan 14	TOTTENHAM HOTSPUR	L 1-2	Boere	24,573
Jan 23	SHEFFIELD WEDNESDAY	L 0-2		14,554
Feb 4	Leicester City	W 2-1	Cottee, Dicks (pen)	20,375
Feb 13	EVERTON	D 2-2	Cottee 2	21,081
Feb 18	Coventry	L 0-2		17,554
Feb 25	CHELSEA	L 1-2	Hutchison	21,500
Mar 5	Arsenal	W 1-0	Hutchison	34,295
Mar 8	Newcastle United	L 0-2		34,595
Mar 11	NORWICH CITY	D 2-2	Cottee 2	21,464
Mar 15	Southampton	D 1-1	Hutchison	15,178
Mar 18	Aston Villa	W 2-0	Moncur, Hutchison	28,682
Apr 8	Nottingham Forest	D 1-1	Dicks	28,361
Apr 13	WIMBLEDON	W 3-0	Dicks (pen), Boere, Cottee	21,084
Apr 17	Ipswich Town	D 1-1	Boere	19,099
Apr 30	BLACKBURN ROVERS	W 2-0	Rieper, Hutchison	24,202
May 3	QUEENS PARK RANGERS	D 0-0		22,923
May 6	Crystal Palace	L 0-1		18,224
May 10	LIVERPOOL	W 3-0	Holmes, Hutchison 2	22,446
May 14	MANCHESTER UNITED	D 1-1	Hughes	24,783

FA Cup

Jan 7	Wycombe Wanderers	(Rd 3)	W 2-0	Cottee, Brown	9,007
Jan 28	Queens Park Rangers	(Rd 4)	L 0-1		17,694

Coca-Cola Cup

Sep 20	Walsall	(Rd 2 FL)	L 1-2	o.g.	5,994
Oct 5	WALSALL	(Rd 2 SL)	W 2-0*	Hutchison, Moncur	13,553
Oct 26	CHELSEA	(Rd 3)	W 1-0	Hutchison	18,815
Nov 30	BOLTON WANDERERS	(Rd 4)	L 1-3	Cottee	18,190

*After extra time.

MANAGER: Harry Redknapp

CAPTAIN: Steve Potts

TOP SCORER: Tony Cottee

BIGGEST WIN: December 17, 1994 3-0 v Manchester City, Premier League; April 13, 1995 3-0 v Wimbledon, Premier League; May 10, 1995 3-0 v Liverpool, Premier League;

HIGHEST ATTENDANCE: October 15, 1994 43,795 v Manchester United, lost 0-1, Premier League

MAJOR TRANSFERS IN: John Moncur from Swindon, Don Hutchison from Liverpool, Tony Cottee from Everton, Julian Dicks from Liverpool, Les Sealey from Blackpool, Marc Rieper from Brondby

MAJOR TRANSFERS OUT: David Burrows to Everton, Peter Butler to Notts County, Lee Chapman to Ipswich Town

League & Cup Appearances (substitute)

PLAYER	LEAGUE	CUP COMPETITION		TOTAL
		FA CUP	COCA-COLA	
Allen	26 (3)	1	3	30 (3)
Bishop	31	2	3	36
Boere	15 (5)	2	1	18 (5)
Breacker	33	2	3	38
Brown	8 (1)	0 (1)	1 (1)	9 (3)
Burrows	4			4
Butler	5			5
Chapman	7 (3)		1 (1)	8 (4)
Cottee	31	2	3	36
Dicks	29	2	2	33
Holmes	24	1	1	26
Hughes	15 (2)	2		17 (2)
Hutchison	22 (1)	0 (1)	3	25 (2)
Jones	1 (1)			1 (1)
Marsh	13 (3)		3	16 (3)
Martin	24	2	2	28
Miklosko	42	2	4	48
Moncur	30	2	3	35
Morley	10 (4)	0 (1)	0 (1)	10 (6)
Potts	42	2	4	48
Rieper	17 (4)			17 (4)
Rowland	11 (1)		2	13 (1)
Rush	15 (8)		3	18 (8)
Webster	0 (5)			0 (5)
Whitbread	3 (5)		2 (1)	5 (6)
Williamson	4			4

Goalscorers

PLAYER	LEAGUE	CUP COMPETITION		TOTAL
		FA CUP	COCA-COLA	
Cottee	13	1	1	15
Hutchison	9		2	11
Boere	6			6
Dicks	5			5
Moncur	2		1	3
Allen	2			2
Hughes	2			2
Rush	2			2
Bishop	1			1
Brown		1		1
Holmes	1			1
Rieper	1			1
Opps' o.gs.			1	1

Fact File

Only one defeat in their last 11 matches enabled West Ham to escape the relegation zone and finish in mid-table safety.

Final Premier League Table

		P	W	D	L	F	A	Pts
1	Blackburn R	42	27	8	7	80	39	89
2	Manchester U	42	26	10	6	77	28	88
3	Nottingham F	42	22	11	9	72	43	77
4	Liverpool	42	21	11	10	65	37	74
5	Leeds U	42	20	13	9	59	38	73
6	Newcastle U	42	20	12	10	67	47	72
7	Tottenham H	42	16	14	12	66	58	62
8	QPR	42	17	9	16	61	59	60
9	Wimbledon	42	15	11	16	48	65	56
10	Southampton	42	12	18	12	61	63	54
11	Chelsea	42	13	15	14	50	55	54
12	Arsenal	42	13	12	17	52	49	51
13	Sheffield W	42	13	12	17	49	57	51
14	West Ham U	42	13	11	18	44	48	50
15	Everton	42	11	17	14	44	51	50
16	Coventry C	42	12	14	16	44	62	50
17	Manchester C	42	12	13	17	53	64	49
18	Aston Villa	42	11	15	16	51	56	48
19	Crystal Palace	42	11	12	19	34	49	45
20	Norwich C	42	10	13	19	37	54	43
21	Leicester C	42	6	11	25	45	80	29
22	Ipswich T	42	7	6	29	36	93	27

Season 1995-96

Premier League

DATE	OPPONENTS	SCORE	GOALSCORERS	ATTENDANCE
Aug 19	LEEDS UNITED	L 1-2	Williamson	22,901
Aug 23	Manchester United	L 1-2	o.g.	31,966
Aug 26	Nottingham Forest	D 1-1	Allen	26,645
Aug 30	TOTTENHAM HOTSPUR	D 1-1	Hutchison	23,516
Sep 11	CHELSEA	L 1-3	Hutchison	19,228
Sep 16	Arsenal	L 0-1		38,065
Sep 23	EVERTON	W 2-1	Dicks 2 (2 pen)	21,085
Oct 2	Southampton	D 0-0		13,568
Oct 16	Wimbledon	W 1-0	Cottee	9,411
Oct 21	BLACKBURN ROVERS	D 1-1	Dowie	21,776
Oct 28	Sheffield Wednesday	W 1-0	Dowie	23,917
Nov 4	ASTON VILLA	L 1-4	Dicks (pen)	23,.637
Nov 18	Bolton Wanderers	W 3-0	Bishop, Cottee, Williamson	19,047
Nov 22	LIVERPOOL	D 0-0		24,324
Nov 25	QUEENS PARK RANGERS	W 1-0	Cottee	21,504
Dec 2	Blackburn Rovers	L 2-4	Dicks (pen), Slater	26,638
Dec 11	Everton	L 0-3		31,778
Dec 16	SOUTHAMPTON	W 2-1	Cottee, Dowie	18,501
Dec 23	Middlesbrough	L 2-4	Cottee, Dicks	28,640
Jan 1	Manchester City	L 1-2	Dowie	26,024
Jan 13	Leeds United	L 0-2		30,472
Jan 22	MANCHESTER UNITED	L 0-1		24,197
Jan 31	COVENTRY CITY	W 3-2	Rieper, Cottee, Dowie	18,884
Feb 3	NOTTINGHAM FOREST	W 1-0	Slater	21,651
Feb 12	Tottenham Hotspur	W 1-0	Dani	29,781
Feb 17	Chelsea	W 2-1	Dicks, Williamson	25,252
Feb 21	NEWCASTLE UNITED	W 2-0	Williamson, Cottee	23,843
Feb 24	ARSENAL	L 0-1		24,217
Mar 2	Coventry City	D 2-2	Cottee, Rieper	17,448
Mar 9	MIDDLESBROUGH	W 2-0	Dowie, Dicks (pen)	23,850
Mar 18	Newcastle United	L 0-3		36,331
Mar 23	MANCHESTER CITY	W 4-2	Dowie 2, Dicks, Dani	24,017
Apr 6	WIMBLEDON	D 1-1	Dicks	20,462
Apr 8	Liverpool	L 0-2		40,326
Apr 13	BOLTON WANDERERS	W 1-0	Cottee	23,086
Apr 17	Aston Villa	D 1-1	Cottee	26,768
Apr 27	Queens Park Rangers	L 0-3		18,828
May 5	SHEFFIELD WEDNESDAY	D 1-1	Dicks	23,790

FA Cup

Jan 6	SOUTHEND UNITED	(Rd 3) W 2-0	Moncur, Hughes	23,284
Feb 7	GRIMSBY TOWN	(Rd 4) D 1-1	Dowie	22,030
Feb 14	Grimsby Town	(R) L 0-3		8,382

Coca-Cola Cup

Sep 20	Bristol Rovers	(Rd 2 FL) W 1-0	Moncur	7,103
Oct 4	BRISTOL ROVERS	(Rd 2 SL) W 3-0	Dicks (pen), Bishop, Cottee	15,375
Oct 25	Southampton	(Rd 3) L 1-2	Cottee	11,059

League & Cup Appearances (substitute)

PLAYER	LEAGUE	CUP COMPETITION FA CUP	COCA-COLA	TOTAL
Allen	3			3
Bilic	13			13
Bishop	35	3	3	41
Boere	0 (1)			0 (1)
Boogers	0 (4)			0 (4)
Breacker	19 (3)		2	21 (3)
Brown	3			3
Cottee	3 (3)	3	3	9 (3)
Dani	3 (6)			3 (6)
Dicks	34	3	3	40
Dowie	33	3	3	39
Dumitrescu	2 (1)			2 (1)
Ferdinand	0 (1)			0 (1)
Finn	1			1
Gordon	0 (1)			0 (1)
Harkes	6 (5)	1 (1)		7 (6)
Hughes	28	3	2	33
Hutchison	8 (4)			8 (4)
Lampard	0 (2)			0 (2)
Lazaridis	2 (2)	0 (1)	1	3 (3)
Martin	1 (4)	1	2	4 (4)
Miklosko	36	3	3	42
Moncur	19 (1)	1	3	23 (1)
Potts	34	3	3	40
Rieper	35 (1)	3	2 (1)	40 (2)
Rowland	19 (4)	1 (1)		20 (5)
Sealey	1 (1)			1 (1)
Slater	16 (6)	1	3	20 (6)
Watson	0 (1)			0 (1)
Whitbread	0 (2)			0 (2)
Williamson	28 (1)	3	0 (1)	31 (2)

Goalscorers

PLAYER	LEAGUE	CUP COMPETITION FA CUP	COCA-COLA	TOTAL
Cottee	10		2	12
Dicks	10		1	11
Dowie	8	1		9
Williamson	4			4
Bishop	1		1	2
Dani	2			2
Hutchison	2			2
Moncur		1	1	2
Rieper	2			2
Slater	2			2
Allen	1			1
Hughes		1		1
Opps' o.gs.	1			1

Fact File

Neil Finn became the Premiership's youngest-ever player when a goalkeeping crisis saw him thrown into the side against Manchester City on New Year's Day.

MANAGER: Harry Redknapp **CAPTAIN:** Julian Dicks
TOP SCORER: Tony Cottee
BIGGEST WIN: November 18, 1995 3-0 v Bolton, Premier League
HIGHEST ATTENDANCE: April 8, 1996 40,326 v Liverpool, lost 0-2, Premier Division
MAJOR TRANSFERS IN: Stan Lazaridis from Western Australia, Marco Boogers from Sparta Rotterdam, Robbie Slater from Blackburn Rovers, Iain Dowie from Crystal Palace, Slaven Bilic from Karlsruhe, Illie Dumitrescu from Tottenham Hotspur, Michael Hughes from Strasbourg
MAJOR TRANSFERS OUT: Mattie Holmes to Blackburn Rovers, Matthew Rush to Norwich City, Martin Allen to Portsmouth, Don Hutchison to Sheffield United

Final Premier League Table

		P	W	D	L	F	A	Pts
1	Manchester U	38	25	7	6	73	35	82
2	Newcastle U	38	24	6	8	66	37	78
3	Liverpool	38	20	11	7	70	34	71
4	Aston Villa	38	18	9	11	52	35	63
5	Arsenal	38	17	12	9	49	32	63
6	Everton	38	17	10	11	64	44	61
7	Blackburn R	38	18	7	13	61	47	61
8	Tottenham H	38	16	13	9	50	38	61
9	Nottingham F	38	15	13	10	50	54	58
10	West Ham U	38	14	9	15	43	52	51
11	Chelsea	38	12	14	12	46	44	50
12	Middlesbrough	38	11	10	17	35	50	43
13	Leeds U	38	12	7	19	40	57	43
14	Wimbledon	38	10	11	17	55	70	41
15	Sheffield W	38	10	10	18	48	61	40
16	Coventry C	38	8	14	16	42	60	38
17	Southampton	38	9	11	18	34	52	38
18	Manchester C	38	9	11	18	33	58	38
19	QPR	38	9	6	23	38	57	33
20	Bolton W	38	8	5	25	39	71	29

Season 1996-97

Premier League

DATE	OPPONENTS	SCORE	GOALSCORERS	ATTENDANCE
Aug 17	Arsenal	L 0-2		38,056
Aug 21	COVENTRY CITY	D 1-1	Rieper	21,680
Aug 24	SOUTHAMPTON	W 2-1	Hughes, Dicks (pen)	21,227
Sep 4	Middlesbrough	L 1-4	Hughes	30,060
Sep 8	Sunderland	D 0-0		18,642
Sep 14	WIMBLEDON	L 0-2		1,294
Sep 21	Nottingham Forest	W 2-0	Bowen, Hughes	23,352
Sep 29	LIVERPOOL	L 1-2	Bilic	25,064
Oct 12	Everton	L 1-2	Dicks (pen)	36,571
Oct 19	LEICESTER CITY	W 1-0	Moncur	22,285
Oct 26	BLACKBURN ROVERS	W 2-1	Porfirio, o.g.	23,947
Nov 2	Tottenham Hotspur	L 0-1		32,999
Nov 16	Newcastle United	D 1-1	Rowland	36,552
Nov 23	DERBY COUNTY	D 1-1	Bishop	24,576
Nov 30	Sheffield Wednesday	D 0-0		22,321
Dec 4	ASTON VILLA	L 0-2		19,105
Dec 8	MANCHESTER UNITED	D 2-2	Raducioiu, Dicks (pen)	25,045
Dec 21	Chelsea	L 1-3	Porfirio	28,315
Dec 28	SUNDERLAND	W 2-0	Bilic, Raducioiu	24,077
Jan 1	NOTTINGHAM FOREST	L 0-1		22,358
Jan 11	Liverpool	D 0-0		40,102
Jan 20	LEEDS UNITED	L 0-2		19,441
Jan 29	ARSENAL	L 1-2	o.g.	24,382
Feb 1	Blackburn Rovers	L 1-2	Ferdinand	21,994
Feb 15	Derby County	L 0-1		18,057
Feb 24	TOTTENHAM HOTSPUR	W 4-3	Dicks 2 (1 pen), Kitson, Hartson	23,998
Mar 1	Leeds United	L 0-1		30,575
Mar 12	CHELSEA	W 3-2	Dicks (pen), Kitson 2	24,502
Mar 15	Aston Villa	D 0-0		35,992
Mar 18	Wimbledon	D 1-1	Lazaridis	15,771
Mar 22	Coventry City	W 3-1	Hartson 2, Ferdinand	22,291
Apr 9	MIDDLESBROUGH	D 0-0		23,988
Apr 12	Southampton	L 0-2		15,244
Apr 19	EVERTON	D 2-2	Kitson 2	24,525
Apr 23	Leicester City	W 1-0	Moncur	20,327
May 3	Sheffield Wednesday	W 5-1	Kitson 3, Hartson 2	24,960
May 6	NEWCASTLE UNITED	D 0-0		24,617
May 11	Manchester United	L 0-2		55,249

FA Cup

Jan 4	Wrexham	(Rd 3)	D 1-1	Porfirio	9,747
Jan 25	WREXHAM	(R)	L 0-1		16,763

Coca-Cola Cup

Sep 18	Barnet	(R2 FL)	D 1-1	Cottee	3,849
Sep 25	BARNET	(R2 SL)	W 1-0	Bilic	15,264
Oct 23	NOTTINGHAM FOREST	(Rd 3)	W 4-1	Dowie 2, Porfirio, Dicks (pen)	19,402
Nov 27	STOCKPORT COUNTY	(Rd 4)	D 1-1	Raducioiu	20,061
Dec 18	Stockport County	(R)	L 1-2	Dicks	9,834

League & Cup Appearances (substitute)

PLAYER	LEAGUE	CUP COMPETITION		TOTAL
		FA CUP	COCA-COLA	
Bilic	35	1	5	41
Bishop	26 (3)	2	5	33 (3)
Bowen	15 (2)		3	18 (2)
Boylan	0 (1)			0 (1)
Breacker	22 (4)	2	3	27 (4)
Cottee	2 (1)		2	4 (1)
Dicks	31	2	5	38
Dowie	18 (5)		5	23 (5)
Dumitrescu	3 (4)		2 (1)	5 (5)
Ferdinand	11 (4)	1	0 (1)	12 (5)
Futre	4 (5)			4 (5)
Hall	7			7
Hartson	11			11
Hughes	31 (2)	2	4	37 (2)
Jones	5 (3)	2	0 (1)	7 (4)
Kitson	14			14
Lampard	3 (10)	1	1 (1)	5 (11)
Lazaridis	13 (9)	1	3 (1)	17 (10)
Lomas	7			7
Mautone	1		2	3
Miklosko	36	2	3	41
Moncur	26 (1)	1	4	31 (1)
Newell	6 (1)			6 (1)
Omoyinni	0 (1)			0 (1)
Porfirio	15 (8)	1 (1)	2	18 (9)
Potts	17 (3)	1	1	19 (3)
Raducioiu	6 (5)		1	7 (5)
Rieper	26 (2)	1	4	31 (2)
Rowland	11 (4)			11 (4)
Sealey	1 (1)			1 (1)
Slater	2 (1)			2 (1)
Williamson	13 (2)	2	0 (1)	15 (3)

Goalscorers

PLAYER	LEAGUE	CUP COMPETITION		TOTAL
		FA CUP	COCA-COLA	
Dicks	6		2	8
Kitson	8			8
Hartson	5			5
Porfirio	2	1	1	4
Bilic	2		1	3
Hughes	3			3
Radicioiu	2		1	3
Dowie			2	2
Ferdinand	2			2
Moncur	2			2
Bishop	1			1
Bowen	1			1
Cottee			1	1
Lazaridis	1			1
Rieper	1			1
Rowland	1			1
Opps' o.gs.	2			2

Fact File

West Ham provided the backbone of Northern Ireland's team this season in the shape of Lomas, Dowie, Rowland and Hughes.

MANAGER: Harry Redknapp **CAPTAIN:** Julian Dicks/Steve Potts
TOP SCORERS: Julian Dicks and Paul Kitson
BIGGEST WIN: May 3, 1997 5-1 v Sheffield Wednesday, Premier League
HIGHEST ATTENDANCE: May 11, 1997 55,249 v Manchester United, lost 0-2, Premier League
MAJOR TRANSFERS IN: Paulo Futre from AC Milan, Richard Hall from Southampton, Florin Raducioiu from Espanol, Mark Bowen from Norwich City, Hugo Porfirio from Sporting Lisbon, Paul Kitson from Newcastle United, John Hartson from Arsenal, Steve Lomas from Manchester City
MAJOR TRANSFERS OUT: Robbie Slater to Southampton, Tony Cottee to Selangor, Florin Raducioiu to Espanol, Illie Dumitrescu to Futball America, Kenny Brown to Birmingham City, Slaven Bilic to Everton

Final Premier League Table

		P	W	D	L	F	A	PTS
1	MANCHESTER U	38	21	12	5	76	44	75
2	NEWCASTLE U	38	19	11	8	73	40	68
3	ARSENAL	38	19	11	8	62	32	68
4	LIVERPOOL	38	19	11	8	62	37	68
5	ASTON VILLA	38	17	10	11	47	34	61
6	CHELSEA	38	16	11	11	58	55	59
7	SHEFFIELD W	38	14	15	9	50	51	57
8	WIMBLEDON	38	15	11	12	49	46	56
9	LEICESTER C	38	12	11	15	46	54	47
10	TOTTENHAM H	38	13	7	18	44	51	46
11	LEEDS U	38	11	13	14	28	38	46
12	DERBY CO	38	11	13	14	45	58	46
13	BLACKBURN R	38	9	15	14	42	43	42
14	WEST HAM U	38	10	12	16	39	48	42
15	EVERTON	38	10	12	16	44	57	42
16	SOUTHAMPTON	38	10	11	17	50	56	41
17	COVENTRY C	38	9	14	15	38	54	41
18	SUNDERLAND	38	10	10	18	35	53	40
19	MIDDLESBROUGH	38	10	12	16	51	60	39
20	NOTTINGHAM F	38	6	16	16	31	59	34

MIDDLESBROUGH DEDUCTED THREE POINTS FOR FAILURE TO FULFIL A FIXTURE ON A GIVEN DATE.

Season 1997-98

Premier League

DATE	OPPONENTS	SCORE	GOALSCORERS	ATTENDANCE
Aug 9	Barnsley	W 2-1	Hartson, Lampard	18,666
Aug 13	TOTTENHAM HOTSPUR	W 2-1	Hartson, Berkovic	25,354
Aug 23	Everton	L 1-2	o.g.	34,356
Aug 27	Coventry City	D 1-1	Kitson	18,289
Aug 30	WIMBLEDON	W 3-1	Hartson, Rieper, Berkovic	24,516
Sep 12	Manchester United	L 1-2	Hartson	55,068
Sep 20	NEWCASTLE UNITED	L 0-1		25,884
Sep 24	Arsenal	L 0-4		38,012
Sep 27	LIVERPOOL	W 2-1	Hartson, Berkovic	25,908
Oct 4	Southampton	L 0-3		15,212
Oct 18	BOLTON WANDERERS	W 3-0	Hartson 2, Berkovic	24,864
Oct 27	Leicester City	L 1-2	Berkovic	20,201
Nov 3	CRYSTAL PALACE	D 2-2*	Hartson, Lampard	23,728
Nov 9	Chelsea	L 1-2	Hartson (pen)	34,382
Nov 23	Leeds United	L 1-3	Lampard	30,031
Nov 29	ASTON VILLA	W 2-1	Hartson 2	24,976
Dec 3	CRYSTAL PALACE	W 4-1	Hartson, Berkovic, Unsworth, Lomas	23,335
Dec 6	Derby County	L 0-2		29,300
Dec 13	SHEFFIELD WEDNESDAY	W 1-0	Kitson	24,344
Dec 20	Blackburn Rovers	L 0-3		21,653
Dec 26	COVENTRY CITY	W 1-0	Kitson	24,532
Dec 28	Wimbledon	W 2-1	o.g., Kitson	22,087
Jan 10	BARNSLEY	W 6-0	Lampard, Abou 2, Moncur, Hartson, Lazaridis	23,714
Jan 17	Tottenham Hotspur	L 0-1		30,284
Jan 31	EVERTON	D 2-2	Sinclair 2	25,905
Feb 7	Newcastle United	W 1-0	Lazaridis	36,736
Feb 21	Bolton Wanderers	D 1-1	Sinclair	25,000
Mar 2	ARSENAL	D 0-0		25,717
Mar 11	MANCHESTER UNITED	D 1-1	Sinclair	25,892
Mar 14	CHELSEA	W 2-1	Sinclair, Unsworth	25,829
Mar 30	LEEDS UNITED	W 3-0	Hartson, Abou, Pearce	24,107
Apr 4	Aston Villa	L 0-2		39,372
Apr 11	DERBY COUNTY	D 0-0		25,155
Apr 13	Sheffield Wednesday	D 1-1	Berkovic	28,036
Apr 18	BLACKBURN ROVERS	W 2-1	Hartson 2	24,733
Apr 25	SOUTHAMPTON	L 2-4	Sinclair, Lomas	25,878
May 2	Liverpool	L 0-5		44,414
May 5	Crystal Palace	D 3-3	Lampard, Omoyinmi 2	19,129
May 10	LEICESTER CITY	W 4-3	Abou 2, Lampard, Sinclair	25,781

* Game abandoned, result void.

FA Cup

Jan 3	EMLEY	(Rd 3)	W 2-1	Lampard, Hartson	18,629
Jan 25	Manchester City	(Rd 4)	W 2-1	Berkovic, Lomas	26,495
Feb 14	BLACKBURN ROVERS	(Rd 5)	D 2-2	Kitson, Berkovic	25,729
Feb 25	Blackburn Rovers	(R)	D 1-1**	Hartson	21,972
Mar 8	Arsenal	(QF)	D 1-1	Pearce	38,077
Mar 17	ARSENAL	(R)	D 1-1†	Hartson	25,859

**Won 5-4 on penalties. †Lost 4-3 on penalties.

Coca-Cola Cup

Sep 16	Huddersfield Town	(Rd 2 FL)	L 0-1		8,525
Sep 29	HUDDERSFIELD TOWN	(Rd 2 SL)	W 3-0	Hartson 3	16,137
Oct 15	ASTON VILLA	(Rd 3)	W 3-0	Hartson 2, Lampard	20,360
Nov 19	WALSALL	(Rd 4)	W 4-1	Lampard 3, Hartson	17,463
Jan 6	ARSENAL	(QF)	L 1-2	Abou	24,770

MANAGER: Harry Redknapp
CAPTAIN: Steve Lomas
TOP SCORER: John Hartson
BIGGEST WIN: January 10, 1998 6-0 v Barnsley, Premier League
HIGHEST ATTENDANCE: September 12, 1997 55,068 v Manchester United, lost 1-2, Premier League
MAJOR TRANSFERS IN: Eyal Berkovic from Maccabi Haifa, Craig Forrest from Ipswich Town, David Unsworth from Everton, Ian Pearce from Blackburn Rovers, Andy Impey and Trevor Sinclair from Queens Park Rangers, Samassi Abou from Cannes
MAJOR TRANSFERS OUT: Danny Williamson to Everton, Marc Rieper to Celtic, Michael Hughes to Wimbledon, Ludek Miklosko, Iain Dowie and Keith Rowland to Queens Park Rangers

League & Cup Appearances (substitute)

PLAYER	LEAGUE	CUP COMPETITION		TOTAL
		FA CUP	COCA-COLA	
Abou	12 (7)	3 (2)	1 (1)	16 (10)
Alves	0 (4)			(4)
Berkovic	34 (1)	6	5	45 (1)
Bishop	3	0 (1)		3 (1)
Breacker	18 (1)	2 (1)	4	24 (2)
Dowie	7 (5)	0 (1)	2 (1)	9 (7)
Ferdinand	35	6	5	46
Forrest	13	4	3	20
Hartson	32	5	5	42
Hodges	0 (2)		0 (3)	0 (5)
Hughes	2 (3)		1	3 (3)
Impey	19	3	3	25
Kitson	12 (1)	2	2	16 (1)
Lama	12	2		14
Lampard	27 (4)	6	5	38 (4)
Lazaridis	27 (1)	6	1	34 (1)
Lomas	33	5	4	42
Mean	0 (3)			0 (3)
Miklosko	13		2	15
Moore	0 (1)	0 (1)		0 (2)
Moncur	17 (3)	2 (1)	1	20 (4)
Omoyinmi	1 (4)			1 (4)
Pearce	30	6	3	39
Potts	14 (9)	4 (1)	3 (1)	21 (11)
Rieper	5			5
Rowland	6 (1)		0 (2)	6 (3)
Sinclair	14			14
Terrier	0 (1)			0 (1)
Unsworth	32	4	5	41

Goalscorers

PLAYER	LEAGUE	CUP COMPETITION		TOTAL
		FA CUP	COCA-COLA	
Hartson	15	3	6	24
Lampard	5	1	4	10
Berkovic	7	2		9
Sinclair	7			7
Abou	5		1	6
Kitson	4	1		5
Lomas	2	1		3
Lazaridis	2			2
Omoyinmi	2			2
Pearce	1	1		2
Unsworth	2			2
Moncur	1			1
Rieper	1			1
Opps' o.gs.	2			2

Fact File

West Ham were eliminated from the FA Cup quarter-finals when Samassi Abou hit the post in a penalty shoot-out against Arsenal.

Final Premier League Table

		P	W	D	L	F	A	Pts
1	Arsenal	38	23	9	6	68	33	78
2	Manchester U	38	23	8	7	73	26	77
3	Liverpool	38	18	11	9	68	42	65
4	Chelsea	38	20	3	15	71	43	63
5	Leeds U	38	17	8	13	57	46	59
6	Blackburn R	38	16	10	12	57	52	58
7	Aston Villa	38	17	6	15	49	48	57
8	West Ham U	38	16	8	14	56	57	56
9	Derby Co	38	16	7	15	52	49	55
10	Leicester C	38	13	14	11	51	41	53
11	Coventry C	38	12	16	10	46	44	52
12	Southampton	38	14	6	18	50	55	48
13	Newcastle U	38	11	11	16	35	44	44
14	Tottenham H	38	11	11	16	44	56	44
15	Wimbledon	38	10	14	14	34	46	44
16	Sheffield W	38	12	8	18	52	67	44
17	Everton	38	9	13	16	41	56	40
18	Bolton W	38	9	13	16	41	61	40
19	Barnsley	38	10	5	23	37	82	35
20	Crystal Palace	38	8	9	21	37	71	33

Season 1998-99

Premier League

DATE	OPPONENTS	SCORE	GOALSCORERS	ATTENDANCE
Aug 15	Sheffield Wednesday	W 1-0	Wright	30,236
Aug 22	MANCHESTER UNITED	D 0-0		26,039
Aug 29	Coventry City	D 0-0		20,818
Sep 9	WIMBLEDON	L 3-4	Wright 2, Hartson	25,311
Sep 12	LIVERPOOL	W 2-1	Hartson, Berkovic	26,029
Sep 19	Nottingham Forest	D 0-0		26,463
Sep 28	SOUTHAMPTON	W 1-0	Wright	23,153
Oct 3	Blackburn Rovers	L 0-3		25,213
Oct 17	ASTON VILLA	D 0-0		26,002
Oct 24	Charlton Athletic	L 2-4	o.g., Berkovic	20,043
Oct 31	Newcastle United	W 3-0	Wright 2, Sinclair	36,744
Nov 8	CHELSEA	D 1-1	Ruddock	26,023
Nov 14	LEICESTER CITY	W 3-2	Kitson, Lomas, Lampard	25,652
Nov 22	Derby County	W 2-0	Hartson, Keller	31,366
Nov 28	TOTTENHAM HOTSPUR	W 2-1	Sinclair 2	26,044
Dec 4	Leeds United	L 0-4		36,320
Dec 11	Middlesbrough	L 0-1		34,623
Dec 19	EVERTON	W 2-1	Keller, Sinclair	25,998
Dec 26	Arsenal	L 0-1		38,098
Dec 28	COVENTRY CITY	W 2-0	Wright, Hartson	25,662
Jan 10	Manchester United	L 1-4	Lampard	55,180
Jan 16	SHEFFIELD WEDNESDAY	L 0-4		25,642
Jan 30	Wimbledon	D 0-0		23,035
Feb 6	ARSENAL	L 0-4		26,042
Feb 13	NOTTINGHAM FOREST	W 2-1	Pearce, Lampard	25,458
Feb 20	Liverpool	D 2-2	Lampard, Keller	44,511
Feb 27	BLACKBURN ROVERS	W 2-0	Pearce, Di Canio	25,529
Mar 6	Southampton	L 0-1		15,240
Mar 13	Chelsea	W 1-0	Kitson	34,765
Mar 20	NEWCASTLE UNITED	W 2-0	Di Canio, Kitson	25,997
Apr 2	Aston Villa	D 0-0		36,813
Apr 5	CHARLTON ATHLETIC	L 0-1		26,041
Apr 10	Leicester City	D 0-0		20,402
Apr 17	DERBY COUNTY	W 5-1	Di Canio, Berkovic, Wright, Ruddock, Sinclair	25,485
Apr 24	Tottenham Hotspur	W 2-1	Wright, Keller	36,089
May 1	LEEDS UNITED	L 1-5	Di Canio	25,997
May 8	Everton	L 0-6		40,049
May 16	MIDDLESBROUGH	W 4-0	Sinclair 2, Keller, Lampard	25,902

FA Cup

Jan 2	SWANSEA CITY	(Rd 3)	D 1-1	Dicks	26,039
Jan 12	Swansea City	(R)	L 0-1		10,116

Worthington Cup

Sep 15	Northampton Town	(Rd 2 FL)	L 0-2		7,254
Sep 22	NORTHAMPTON TOWN	(Rd 2 SL)	W 1-0	Lampard	25,435

Fact File

West Ham qualified for European competition (the Intertoto Cup) via the league for the very first time.

MANAGER: Harry Redknapp **CAPTAIN:** Steve Lomas

TOP SCORER: Ian Wright

BIGGEST WIN: April 17, 1999 5-1 v Derby County, Premier League

HIGHEST ATTENDANCE: January 10, 1999 55,180 v Manchester United, lost 1-4, Premier League

MAJOR TRANSFERS IN: Marc Keller from Karlsruhe, Ian Wright from Arsenal, Neil Ruddock from Liverpool, Scott Minto from Benfica, Paolo Di Canio from Sheffield Wednesday, Javier Margas from Deportivo Universidad Catolica de Chile, Shaka Hislop from Newcastle United Marc-Vivien Foe from Lens

MAJOR TRANSFERS OUT: Ian Bishop to Manchester City, Andy Impey to Leicester City

League & Cup Appearances (substitute)

PLAYER	LEAGUE	CUP COMPETITION		TOTAL
		FA CUP	WORTHINGTON	
Abou	2 (1)	0 (1)	0	2 (2)
Berkovic	28 (2)	1 (1)	1	30 (3)
Breacker	2 (1)	1	0 (1)	3 (2)
Cole	2 (6)	0 (1)		2 (7)
Coyne	0 (1)			0 (1)
Di Canio	12 (1)			12 (1)
Dicks	9	2	1	12
Ferdinand	31	1	1	33
Foe	13			13
Forrest	1 (1)			1 (1)
Hall		0 (1)		0 (1)
Hartson	16 (1)	2	1	19 (1)
Hislop	37	2	2	41
Hodges	0 (1)			0 (1)
Holligan	0 (1)			0 (1)
Impey	6 (2)		1	7 (2)
Keller	17 (4)		1	18 (4)
Kitson	13 (4)			13 (4)
Lampard	38	1	2	41
Lazaridis	11 (4)	2	1	14 (4)
Lomas	30		2	32
Margas	3			3
Minto	13 (1)			13 (1)
Moncur	6 (8)		1	7 (8)
Omoyinmi	0 (3)	1 (1)	0 (1)	1 (5)
Pearce	33	1	2	36
Potts	11 (8)	1	2	14 (8)
Ruddock	27	2	1	30
Sinclair	36	2	2	40
Wright	20 (2)	1	2	23 (2)

Goalscorers

PLAYER	LEAGUE	CUP COMPETITION		TOTAL
		FA CUP	WORTHINGTON	
Wright	9			9
Sinclair	7			7
Lampard	5		1	6
Keller	5			5
Di Canio	4			4
Hartson	4			4
Berkovic	3			3
Kitson	3			3
Pearce	2			2
Ruddock	2			2
Dicks		1		1
Lomas	1			1
Opps' o.gs.	1			1

Final Premier League Table

		P	W	D	L	F	A	PTS
1	Manchester United	38	22	13	3	80	37	79
2	Arsenal	38	22	12	4	59	17	78
3	Chelsea	38	20	15	3	57	30	67
4	Leeds United	38	18	13	7	62	34	67
5	West Ham United	38	16	9	13	46	53	57
6	Aston Villa	38	15	10	13	51	46	55
7	Liverpool	38	15	9	14	68	49	54
8	Derby County	38	13	13	12	40	45	52
9	Middlesbrough	38	12	15	11	48	54	51
10	Leicester City	38	12	13	13	40	46	49
11	Tottenham Hotspur	38	11	14	13	47	50	47
12	Sheffield Wednesday	38	13	7	18	41	42	46
13	Newcastle United	38	11	13	14	48	54	46
14	Everton	38	11	10	17	42	47	43
15	Coventry City	38	11	9	18	39	51	42
16	Wimbledon	38	10	12	16	40	63	42
17	Southampton	38	11	8	19	37	64	41
18	Charlton Athletic	38	8	12	18	41	56	36
19	Blackburn Rovers	38	7	14	17	38	52	35
20	Nottingham Forest	38	7	9	22	35	69	30

Season 1999-2000

Premier League

DATE	OPPONENTS	SCORE	GOALSCORERS	ATTENDANCE
Aug 7	TOTTENHAM HOTSPUR	W 1-0	Lampard	26,010
Aug 16	Aston Villa	D 2-2	o.g., Sinclair	26,250
Aug 21	LEICESTER CITY	W 2-1	Wanchope, Di Canio	23,631
Aug 28	Bradford City	W 3-0	Di Canio, Sinclair, Wanchope	17,926
Sep 11	WATFORD	W 1-0	Di Canio	25,310
Sep 19	Everton	L 0-1		35,154
Sep 25	Coventry City	L 0-1		19,993
Oct 3	ARSENAL	W 2-1	Di Canio 2	26,009
Oct 17	Middlesbrough	L 0-2		31,862
Oct 24	SUNDERLAND	D 1-1	Sinclair	26,022
Oct 27	Liverpool	L 0-1		44,012
Oct 30	Leeds United	L 0-1		40,190
Nov 7	Chelsea	D 0-0		34,935
Nov 21	SHEFFIELD WEDNESDAY	W 4-3	Wanchope, Di Canio (pen), Foe, Lampard	23,015
Nov 27	LIVERPOOL	W 1-0	Sinclair	26,043
Dec 6	Tottenham Hotspur	D 0-0		36,233
Dec 18	MANCHESTER UNITED	L 2-4	Di Canio 2	26,037
Dec 26	Wimbledon	D 2-2	Sinclair, Lampard	21,180
Dec 28	DERBY COUNTY	D 1-1	Di Canio	24,998
Jan 3	Newcastle United	D 2-2	Lampard, Stimac	36,314
Jan 15	ASTON VILLA	D 1-1	Di Canio	24,237
Jan 22	Leicester City	W 3-1	Wanchope 2, Di Canio	19,019
Feb 5	Southampton	L 1-2	Lampard	15,257
Feb 12	BRADFORD CITY	W 5-4	Sinclair, Moncur, Cole, Di Canio (pen), Lampard	25,417
Feb 26	EVERTON	L 0-4		26,025
Mar 4	Watford	W 2-1	Lomas, Wanchope	18,619
Mar 8	SOUTHAMPTON	W 2-0	Sinclair, Wanchope	23,484
Mar 11	Sheffield Wednesday	L 1-3	Lampard	21,147
Mar 18	CHELSEA	D 0-0		26,041
Mar 26	WIMBLEDON	W 2-1	Di Canio, Kanoute	22,438
Apr 1	Manchester United	L 1-7	Wanchope	61,611
Apr 12	NEWCASTLE UNITED	W 2-1	Wanchope 2	25,817
Apr 15	Derby County	W 2-1	Wanchope 2	31,202
Apr 22	COVENTRY CITY	W 5-0	Carrick, Margas, Di Canio 2, Kanoute	24,719
Apr 29	MIDDLESBROUGH	L 0-1		25,472
May 2	Arsenal	L 1-2	Di Canio	38,093
May 6	Sunderland	L 0-1		41,684
May 14	LEEDS UNITED	D 0-0		26,044

FA Cup

Dec 11	Tranmere Rovers	(Rd 3) L 0-1			13,629

Worthington Cup

Oct 13	BOURNEMOUTH	(Rd 3) W	2-0	Lampard, Keller	22,067
Nov 30	Birmingham City	(Rd 4) W	3-2	Lomas, Kitson, Cole	17,728
Dec 15	ASTON VILLA	(QF) D	2-2*	Lampard, Di Canio	23,974
Jan 11	ASTON VILLA	(R) L	1-3	Lampard	25,592

*Won 5-4 on penalties. Result void due to ineligible player.

UEFA Cup

Sep 16	NK OSIJEK	(Rd 1 FL) W	3-0	Wanchope, Di Canio, Lampard	25,331
Sep 30	NK Osijek	(Rd 1 SL) W	3-1	Kitson, Ruddock, Foe	15,000
Oct 21	Steaua Bucharest	(Rd 2 FL) L	0-2		12,500
Nov 4	STEAUA BUCHAREST	(Rd 2 SL) D	0-0		24,514

Intertoto Cup

Jul 17	JOKERIT	(Rd 3 FL) W	1-0	Kitson	11,908
Jul24	Jokerit	(Rd 3 SL) D	1-1	Lampard	7,667
Jul 28	HEERENVEEN	(SF FL) W	1-0	Lampard	7,485
Aug 4	Heerenveen	(SF SL) W	1-0	Wanchope	13,500
Aug 10	METZ	(F FL) L	0-1		25,372
Aug 24	Metz	(F SL) W	3-1	Sinclair, Lampard, Wanchope	19,599

MANAGER: Harry Redknapp **CAPTAIN:** Steve Lomas **TOP SCORER:** Paolo Di Canio **BIGGEST WIN:** April 22, 2000 5-0 v Coventry City, Premier League **HIGHEST ATTENDANCE:** April 1, 2000 61,611 v Manchester United, lost 1-7, Premier League **MAJOR TRANSFERS IN:** Paolo Wanchope and Igor Stimac from Derby County, Stuart Pearce from Newcastle United, Nigel Winterburn and Davor Suker from Arsenal **MAJOR TRANSFERS OUT:** Ian Wright and Eyal Berkovic to Celtic, Paolo Wanchope to Manchester City, Neil Ruddock to Crystal Palace, Marc-Vivien Foe to Lyon

League & Cup Appearances (substitute)

PLAYER	LEAGUE	CUP COMPETITION				TOTAL
		FA CUP	WC	UEFA	OTHER	
Byrne	0 (1)					0 (1)
Bywater	3 (1)					3 (1)
Carrick	4 (4)				0 (1)	4 (5)
Charles	2 (2)		1			3 (1)
Cole	17 (5)	1	2 (1)	1 (1)	1 (2)	22 (9)
Di Canio	29 (1)	1	3	4	6	43 (1)
Ferdinand	33	1	3	3	6	46
Feuer	3					3
Foe	25	1	3	2 (1)	3	34 (1)
Forrest	9 (2)				1	10 (2)
Hislop	22	1	3	4	5	35
Ilic	1					1
Kanoute	8					8
Keller	19 (4)		2 (1)	3	3 (1)	27 (6)
Kitson	4 (6)	0 (1)	0 (2)	1 (2)	2 (3)	7 (14)
Lampard	34	1	3	4	6	48
Lomas	25	1	2	4	6	38
Margas	15 (3)		1	2 (1)		18 (4)
Minto	15 (3)	1	1		5	22 (3)
Moncur	20 (2)			2	3 (1)	25 (3)
Newton	0 (2)	0 (1)				0 (3)
Pearce I	1				1 (1)	2 (1)
Pearce S	8					8
Potts	16 (1)	1	1	3	4 (1)	24 (2)
Ruddock	12 (3)	1	2 (1)	2 (1)	3	20 (5)
Sinclair	36	1	2 (1)	4	6	49 (1)
Stimac	24		2	2		28
Wanchope	33 (2)	0 (1)	2	3 (1)	4	42 (4)
Wright					0 (1)	0 (1)

Goalscorers

PLAYER	LEAGUE	CUP COMPETITION				TOTAL
		FA CUP	WC	UEFA	OTHER	
Di Canio	16			1		16
Wanchope	12			1	2	15
Lampard	7		2	1	3	13
Sinclair	7				1	8
Kitson			1	1	1	3
Cole	1		1			2
Foe	1			1		2
Kanoute	2					2
Lomas	1		1			2
Carrick	1					1
Keller			1			1
Margas	1					1
Moncur	1					1
Ruddock				1		1
Stimac	1					1
Opps' o.gs.	1					1

Fact File

A total of five goalkeepers appeared for the West Ham first team this season.

Final Premier League Table

		P	W	D	L	F	A	PTS
1	MANCHESTER UNITED	38	28	7	3	97	45	91
2	ARSENAL	38	22	7	9	73	43	73
3	LEEDS UNITED	38	21	6	11	58	43	69
4	LIVERPOOL	38	19	10	9	51	30	67
5	CHELSEA	38	18	11	9	53	34	65
6	ASTON VILLA	38	15	13	10	46	35	58
7	SUNDERLAND	38	16	10	12	57	56	58
8	LEICESTER CITY	38	16	7	15	55	55	55
9	WEST HAM UNITED	38	15	10	13	52	53	55
10	TOTTENHAM HOTSPUR	38	15	8	15	57	49	53
11	NEWCASTLE UNITED	38	14	10	14	63	54	52
12	MIDDLESBROUGH	38	14	10	14	46	52	52
13	EVERTON	38	12	14	12	59	49	50
14	COVENTRY CITY	38	12	8	18	47	54	44
15	SOUTHAMPTON	38	12	8	18	45	62	44
16	DERBY COUNTY	38	9	11	18	44	57	38
17	BRADFORD CITY	38	9	9	20	38	68	36
18	WIMBLEDON	38	7	12	19	46	74	33
19	SHEFFIELD WEDNESDAY	38	8	7	23	38	70	31
20	WATFORD	38	6	6	26	35	77	24

Career Records (Players with over 200 Appearances*)

These records cover the complete listing of West Ham United from 1895-2000, including the years 1898 to 1915 when they played in the Southern League.

PLAYER	JOINED/LEFT	LEAGUE	FA CUP	LEAGUE CUP	EUROPE	TOTAL
Allen Martin	1989-1996	163 (27)	14	15 (4)		192 (31)
Allison Malcolm	1950-1958	238	17			255
Ashton Herbert	1908-1915	224	25			249
Barrett Jim G.	1924-1939	442	25			467
Best Clyde	1969-1976	178 (8)	12	20		210 (8)
Bishop Ian	1989-1998	240 (14)	16 (2)	21		277 (16)
Blackburn Fred	1905-1913	217	20			237
Bond John	1951-1965	381	30	13	4	428
Bonds Billy	1967-1988	655 (8)	46 (2)	65 (2)	15	781 (12)
Boyce Ron	1960-1973	275 (7)	20 (1)	23	13	331 (8)
Brabrook Peter	1962-1968	167	17	23	7	214
Breacker Tim	1990-1999	229 (11)	27 (1)	20 (1)		276 (14)
Brooking Trevor	1976-1984	521 (7)	40	55	11 (1)	627 (8)
Brown Ken	1952-1967	386	26	28	15	455
Byrne Johnny	1961-1967	156	18	19	12	205
Cadwell Albert	1923-1933	272	25			297
Cantwell Noel	1952-1961	248	15			263
Chalkley Alf	1931-1937	188	14			202
Cockroft Joe	1932-1939	251	12			263
Collins Jimmy	1923-1936	311	25			336
Cottee Tony	1983-1996	266 (13)	29	27		322 (13)
Cross David	1977-1982	178 (1)	14	24	6	222 (1)
Day Mervyn	1973-1979	194	14	14	9	233
Devonshire Alan	1976-1990	345 (13)	36	45 (3)	4	430 (16)
Dick John	1953-1963	326	21	4		351
Dickens Alan	1982-1989	173 (19)	19 (3)	14 (3)		206 (25)
Dicks Julian	1988-1999	262	23	30		315
Earl Alfred	1925-1933	191	15			206
Earle Stan	1924-1932	258	15			273
Ferguson Bobby	1967-1980	240	17	19		276
Gale Tony	1984-1994	293 (7)	29 (1)	28 (2)		350 (10)
Goddard Paul	1980-1987	159 (11)	10 (1)	26	6	201 (12)
Goulden Len	1932-1945	239	14			253
Gregory Ernie	1946-1960	382	24			406
Holland Pat	1968-1981	227 (18)	12 (4)	22 (3)	10	271 (25)

***Totals include substitute appearances**

PLAYER	JOINED/LEFT	LEAGUE	FA CUP	LEAGUE CUP	EUROPE	TOTAL
Hufton Ted	1919-1932	371	31			402
Hurst Geoff	1959-1972	410 (1)	26	47	15	498 (1)
Kay George	1919-1926	237	22			259
Keen Kevin	1986-1993	187 (32)	15 (7)	21 (1)		223 (40)
Kitchen George	1905-1911	184	21			205
Lampard Frank	1967-1985	546 (5)	43	54	15	658 (5)
McDowell John	1970-1979	243 (6)	19	21	7	290 (6)
Malcolm Andy	1953-1962	283	21	2		306
Martin Alvin	1974-1996	462 (7)	40	71	6	573 (7)
Miklosko Ludek	1989-1998	315	25	25		365
Moore Bobby	1958-1974	543 (1)	36	49	13	641 (1)
Moore William	1922-1929	181	21			202
Morley Trevor	1989-1995	158 (20)	14 (6)	10 (1)		174 (27)
Morton John	1931-1939	258	17			275
Musgrove Malcolm	1953-1963	283	13	5		301
O'Farrell Frank	1950-1957	197	13			210
Parker Derek	1946-1957	199	8			207
Parkes Phil	1979-1990	344	34	52		436
Parris George	1984-1993	211 (28)	21	27 (3)		259 (31)
Peters Martin	1961-1970	302	16	31	15	364
Piercy Frank	1902-1912	214	17			231
Pike Geoff	1975-1987	275 (16)	29 (2)	38 (1)	6	348 (19)
Potts Steve	1984-	360 (31)	41 (1)	37 (2)	7 (1)	445 (35)
Randall Tom	1906-1915	189	16			205
Robson Bryan	1970-1979	227	12	15		254
Ruffell Jimmy	1921-1937	505	43			548
Shea Daniel	1907-1913	179	22			201
Sissons John	1962-1970	210 (3)	18	21	13	262 (3)
Standen Jim	1962-1968	178	20	23	14	235
Stewart Ray	1979-1991	344 (1)	35 (1)	44	6	429 (1)
Taylor Tommy	1970-1979	340	21	26	9	396
Walker Richard	1934-1953	292	19			311
Watson Victor	1920-1935	462	43			505
Woodgate Terry	1938-1953	259	16			275
Yews Tommy	1923-1933	346	5			361

Hammer of the Year (since 1970)

1970-71	Billy Bonds
1971-72	Trevor Brooking
1972-73	Bryan Robson
1973-74	Billy Bonds
1974-75	Billy Bonds
1975-76	Trevor Brooking
1976-77	Trevor Brooking
1977-78	Trevor Brooking
1978-79	Alan Devonshire
1979-80	Alvin Martin
1980-81	Phil Parkes
1981-82	Alvin Martin
1982-83	Alvin Martin
1983-84	Trevor Brooking
1984-85	Paul Allen
1985-86	Tony Cottee
1986-87	Billy Bonds
1987-88	Stewart Robson
1988-89	Paul Ince
1989-90	Julian Dicks
1990-91	Ludek Miklosko
1991-92	Julian Dicks
1992-93	Steve Potts
1993-94	Trevor Morley
1994-95	Steve Potts
1995-96	Julian Dicks
1996-97	Julian Dicks
1997-98	Rio Ferdinand
1998-99	Rio Ferdinand
1999-2000	Paolo Di Canio

Paolo Di Canio was Hammer of the Year 2000.